REAL TEXTS
READING AND WRITING ACROSS THE DISCIPLINES

Dean Ward

Calvin College

Elizabeth Vander Lei

Calvin College

With contributions by
William J. Vande Kopple

PEARSON
Longman

New York   San Francisco   Boston
London   Toronto   Sydney   Tokyo   Singapore   Madrid
Mexico City   Munich   Paris   Cape Town   Hong Kong   Montreal

Executive Editor: Lynn M. Huddon
Senior Marketing Manager: Sandra McGuire
Senior Supplement Editor: Donna Campion
Production Manager: Denise Phillip
Project Coordination, Text Design, and Electronic Page Makeup: Electronic Publishing Services
    Inc., NYC
Senior Cover Design Manager: Nancy Danahy
Cover Designer: Nancy Sacks
Cover Images: © Getty Images, Inc.
Photo Researcher: Toby Zausner
Manufacturing Buyer: Roy Pickering
Printer and Binder: R.R. Donnelley & Sons/Crawfordville
Cover Printer: R.R. Donnelley & Sons/Crawfordville

For permission to use copyrighted material, grateful acknowledgement is made to the copyright
holders on pp. 504–506, which are hereby made part of this copyright page.

Library of Congress Cataloging-in-Publication Data

Ward, Dean.
    Real texts : reading and writing across the disciplines / Dean Ward, Elizabeth Vander Lei.
        p. cm.
    Includes index.
    ISBN-13: 978-0-321-31743-8
    ISBN-10:   0-321-31743-2
    1. English language—Rhetoric—Problems, exercises, etc. 2. Report writing—Problems, exercises, etc.
3. Interdisciplinary approach in education. I. Vander Lei, Elizabeth. II. Title.

    PE1408.W3213 2008
    808'.0427—dc22

                                        2007045610

Please visit us at www.ablongman.com

ISBN 13: 978-0-321-31743-8

ISBN 10:   0-321-31743-2

1 2 3 4 5 6 7 8 9 10—DOC—10 09 08 07

CONTENTS

9 SOCIOLOGY: SEARCHING FOR CAUSES OF SOCIAL PROBLEMS 264

ALTERNATE CONTENTS—BY DISCIPLINARY GROUPS

READING AND WRITING IN THE PROFESSIONS

PREFACE

PRINCIPLES

Real Texts. This book contains real academic, professional, and public texts—what professors, students, and professionals write every day. Reading these selections, students learn how writers from a variety of disciplines and professions use writing effectively.

Best Practices. This book affirms that good writing happens in all academic disciplines, and that the "best practices" of these disciplines provide important rhetorical lessons for all writers. As students observe these best practices, they expand their ability to read effectively. When students enact these practices in their own writing, they follow the Aristotelian advice to seek "*all* available means of persuasion."

Writing Creates Change. This book points out how writing can change readers and the world. Often, professionals write because their expertise helps them understand real-world problems and potential solutions. By writing, they help others recognize and solve problems. Unfortunately, students rarely write with the hope that their writing somehow matters outside the classroom. Without that belief, students are not motivated to improve their writing. These real-world readings encourage students to develop their own rhetorical skills by persuading them that writing makes a difference.

Rhetoric as Course Content. These readings showcase particular rhetorical lessons from the academic disciplines that students are likely to encounter as undergraduates. The rhetoric of the expert writers in these disciplines is the content of this book.

REALITIES

This book asks its readers to acknowledge several realities:

- **Students' daily rhetorical experience is broader than that of their instructors.** Regardless of their major, college students read and write in a variety of academic disciplines. While professors typically engage a small set of closely-related issues and write in a few familiar genres, students must learn to read and write about a variety of academic topics in many genres.
- **College-level reading and writing is difficult.** It is difficult because professors do most of their thinking and writing within disciplinary boundaries and because professors and students concentrate on complex real-world problems and solutions. It is effective because different disciplines have developed distinct strategies to meet their particular rhetorical challenges.
- **To write efficiently and effectively, students must learn how to transfer rhetorical strategies into new writing situations.** To do so, students need to be (1) aware of the rhetorical strategies they already possess, (2) trained to analyze new rhetorical strategies they encounter as they read in the disciplines, and (3) able to adapt and apply the rhetorical strategies they learn to fit the rhetorical challenges they will face. When we use the phrase *portable rhetorical lesson*, we are advocating the practice of adapting, not merely imitating, rhetorical strategies from one situation to meet the needs of another.
- **Reading and writing are collaborative activities.** English teachers are well-prepared to help students learn how to read and write better, but they cannot possibly know "best practices" from all academic disciplines. For this information, teachers can rely on experts and students who have contributed to this book; students can contribute what they've learned when writing in other disciplines.

FEATURES

Four Main Parts of the Book

Part One: Reading, Writing, and Rhetorical Choice includes two introductory chapters that discuss types of rhetorical choices that writers in all disciplines and professions make. These chapters help students better understand the rhetorical lessons in later chapters and make better rhetorical choices when they are writing. Chapter 1 considers rhetorical choices about topic, purpose, and point; Chapter 2 considers rhetorical choices about audience, evidence, methods, organization, style, and visual design.

The remaining parts are organized by the various ways writing creates change.

Part Two: Analyzing People and Culture. Writers use analysis to change readers' understanding of a subject, reshaping readers' assumptions and the actions that follow from assumptions.

Part Three: Reporting Knowledge. Writers can use knowledge, developed through research and analysis, to give readers the means and materials for creating change.

Part Four: Recommending Action. Writers use analysis and knowledge to advocate that readers act in a specific way.

The Parts of Each Chapter

Each chapter in Parts Two through Four contains the following:

Chapter Introduction	• An overview of the discipline's rhetorical practices and the chapter's portable rhetorical lesson.* which is marked by an ➤ in each chapter. A "To Think About" activity that introduces students to these practices and lessons.
Writing in the Discipline	• Published writing in the discipline, selected, introduced, and annotated by an expert in the discipline. "Reading Tips" on how to read in the genre. An essay on "Notes on Grammar, Style, and Rhetoric" that focuses on a distinctive linguistic feature of the reading.
Student Writing	• A sample of student writing in the discipline, introduced and annotated by the student.
Public Writing	• Published writing by an expert in the discipline for a general audience.
More Disciplinary Writing	• Additional writing in the discipline. In chapters with a difficult first reading, this fourth reading is more accessible.
Assignments	• Reading response questions after each reading. A set of longer writing assignments at the end of each chapter asking students to apply the portable rhetorical lesson, make connections across disciplines, or conduct research.

---

*The team that assembled the readings and emphases for this book shortened "portable rhetorical lesson" to PRL, pronouncing it *pearl*. You and your class can decide if the acronym is convenient or corny.

Flexibility in Assigning Readings.   The thorough introductions to each chapter and each reading allow an instructor to use the readings in any order. Furthermore, teachers can combine readings from a variety of chapters to offer lessons that apply directly to a particular writing assignment. Consider, for example, readings that would help students who are writing a research paper. When writing about research, students must summarize published research; summary is the focus of Chapter 5: Chemistry. They must decide whether it is appropriate to include personal observation; Chapter 12: Nursing, teaches that lesson. And they must cite and document sources effectively, a lesson that Chapter 7: Political Science, teaches well. Similar lessons are available for any writing assignment.

A Note on Titles and Citation Styles

You will see that the titles in this book vary in punctuation and that the citations and lists of references appear in various styles. Our guiding principle was to retain the style of the original publications and student papers. Honoring the originals in this way provides another lesson in the reality of rich disciplinary variety.

For Instructors

The Instructor's Manual offers practical—and sometimes playful—advice on using *Real Texts* in a composition course. The Manual begins with a chapter on ways to apply the "Principles" section of this preface to create coherence and unity in a course. The Manual's chapters then parallel those of the book, discussing main opportunities and challenges, portable rhetorical lessons, preparations for reading, exercises, reading response questions, in-class activities, and major assignments.

My Comp Lab   MyCompLab is a Web application that offers comprehensive and integrated resources for every writer. With MyCompLab, students can learn from interactive tutorials and instruction; practice and develop their skills with grammar, writing, and research exercises; share their writing and collaborate with peers; and receive comments on their writing from instructors and tutors. Go to http://www.mycomplab.com to register for these premiere resources and much more.

Pearson Longman offers a wide array of other supplementary materials perfect for use in first-year composition courses as well as more advanced settings, some available at no additional cost when packaged with a Pearson text, and some available at a deep discount. Please contact your local Pearson Arts and Sciences sales consultant to find out more.

ACKNOWLEDGMENTS

The editorial team: From our earliest conversations about this book, we realized that we would depend on the help of a cross-disciplinary team of faculty members, professionals, and students. The faculty and professionals developed the principles and assembled and introduced most of the readings for the book. They patiently explained their disciplinary rhetorical traditions to us, to the students on the team, and to students who will read the book. We are deeply grateful for all they gave to this book and all they have taught us. It is their expertise and passion for student writing that invigorates every page of this book. So we extend thanks to Cheryl Brandsen, sociology; Robert Eames, marketing; Mary Flikkema, nursing; Simona Goi, political science; Kathi Groenendyk, speech communication; Elizabeth Howell, biology; David Koetje, biotechnology; Henry Luttikhuizen, art history; Darla McCarthy, chemistry; Richard Plantinga, religion; Mary VanderGoot, psychology; and William J. Vande Kopple, English.

Student partners collaborated with each member of the faculty and professional team. In our early meetings, the student authors sat elbow-to-elbow with professors around the conference table. They contributed ideas, challenged our assumptions, and taught us much about what motivates student writers. And, of course, their own writing and ideas about learning shape every chapter. Most of these students have graduated now; they continue to improve the world through their words, and we thank them: Janette Curtis and Ben Fiet, psychology; Cherilyn Dudley, English; Arianne Folkema, chemistry; Curt Gritters and Megan Nyenhuis, nursing; J. Robin King, political science; Stephanie McElroy, biology; Laura McGiness, speech communications; Rebecca Merz, art history; Philip Park, religion; Meghan Sheehan, biotechnology; Sarah Steen, marketing; Joy Van Marion, sociology.

An individual who played a critical role in this book is William J. Vande Kopple. He authored the "Notes on Grammar, Style, and Rhetoric." His ability to discern telling linguistic habits in the disciplines allowed us to link large-scale and sentence-level rhetorical practices. His essays also show great respect for each disciplinary tradition. The "Notes" thereby model a positive attitude toward learning about writing from all writing traditions—a lesson that sits at the heart of this book.

Special thanks go to Mandy Suhr-Systema, who, as an undergraduate McGregor Fellow, quickly grasped complex ideas and brought both insight and passion to the project. She helped us shape the idea of a "portable rhetorical lesson" into something that we could hope to be able to teach to others, and she was instrumental in refining the portable rhetorical lesson in each chapter.

The students who have populated our classes also deserve our thanks. They suffered through rough drafts with kindness and equanimity, and they offered many suggestions that have greatly improved this textbook.

We relied heavily on the competence and good will of the administrative staff in the Provost's office and the Department of English at Calvin College: Caroline Chadderdon, Heidi Rienstra, Melissa Van Til, and Becky Moon. Without their help, we would not have completed this project. The work-study students in the English Department (notably, Kris Nevin and Ryan Stegink) photocopied, scanned readings, and ran errands. Kris Nevin offered excellent help with the index. Bob Alderink rescued our graphics more than once. We are grateful for their assistance.

Our initial research was supported by a grant from the Calvin Center for Christian Scholarship, and we are grateful for their generous support of cross-disciplinary collaboration. The McGregor Fellows program supported the development of this textbook by funding our collaboration with Mandy Suhr-Systema, and Calvin College provided support in the form of a sabbatical release for Elizabeth Vander Lei. Throughout the project we have been ably assisted by the professors who make up the advisory board for Calvin College's Academic Writing Program, in particular, co-directors Karen Saupe and Kathi Groenendyk.

Of course, many of our colleagues, at Calvin College and across the country, deserve special recognition. Colleagues in the English Department tested chapters for us and provided helpful feedback: Megan Berglund, Chad Engbers, and Karen Saupe. Many in the department have contributed ideas, scholarly references, or pedagogical strategies. We thank the many people who have advised and encouraged us throughout; David Rosenwasser and Jill Stephen have been friends to us and our work, and we pay special homage to E. Shelley Reid who has been a good friend and a wise advisor throughout this project.

And, of course, the folks at Longman have been terrific. Doug Day and Susan Kunchandy nudged us toward the idea for this textbook in the first place, and Joe Opiela and Ginny Blanford helped us bring it to completion. Nicole Solano and Jessica Riu were welcome and able hands in the Longman office. The production team was efficient and humane; we thank them all, especially those with whom we had frequent contact: Scott Hitchcock, Jenny Bevington, Tobi Zausner, and Teresa Ward. The readers who carefully reviewed drafts of this book, offering encouragement, ideas, strategies, and even language, helped in innumerable ways: Valerie K. Anderson, York College of the City University of New York; Jacob Agatucci, Central Oregon Community College; Larry Beason, University of South Alabama; Glenn Blalock, Texas A & M University; James Countryman, University of Minnesota; Christine Caver, University of Texas at San Antonio; Ana Douglass, Truckee Meadows Community College; Hank Galmish, Green River Community College; Peggy E. Gipson, Oklahoma Christian University; John Hagaman, Western Kentucky University; K. Elaine Hays, Saint Joseph College; Joe Lostracco, Austin Community College; Crystal McCage, Central Oregon Community College; Debbie Olson, Central Washington University; Risë A. Quay, Central Oregon Community College; Robert A. Schwegler, University of Rhode Island; Roy T. Stamper, North Carolina State University; and Joseph Sullivan, Marietta College.

Lynn Huddon at Longman deserves our deep and abiding gratitude for taking on this project. As our primary editor, Lynn asked the right questions and pressed us, Thoreau-like, to simplify, simplify, simplify. She helped us develop our ideas into a textbook that teachers and students can use.

To our families, we owe a debt of gratitude that stretches the capacity of words. Thank you.

Dean Ward
Elizabeth Vander Lei

PART ONE

READING, WRITING, AND RHETORICAL CHOICE

Each of the readings in this book will teach you new rhetorical options, strategic choices that writers use in different disciplines and genres. We contend that many rhetorical strategies common in a particular discipline can be useful in other situations as well. So we call them "portable rhetorical lessons." We believe that they will increase the rhetorical means available to you and will help you to be more agile in adapting to unique rhetorical tasks.

But before we send you into the whirl of new and different kinds of writing and the rhetorical lessons you will find in this book, we offer you some grounding—a way of managing all that complexity. We focus first on "common rhetorical choices," the general types of choices available to and necessary for writers in every discipline and in every type of writing.

COMMON RHETORICAL CHOICES

All writers share common needs: to find a purpose, to express a point, to organize parts, to establish a relationship with an audience, and so on. We suggest nine categories of choices that all writers have in common. These categories form the content of Chapters 1 and 2, and we introduce them here in a shorthand version.

We admit that categories will break down if you push hard on them; all categories imposed on writing do. In practice, a writer's choices are infinitely complex: endless in number and always dependent on the context surrounding an individual writing task.

It is also the case that in any particular writing task some choices will demand less work on your part than other choices. Some choices will be made for you; for example, the *organization* of a lab report (introduction, methods, results, and discussion) will be given in a lab manual. In other cases a type of choice could be relatively unimportant: you won't worry too much about the visual design of an in-class, handwritten response to a teacher's question.

Overall, though, the categories of common choices will ensure that you cover all the basics. You will know that you haven't skipped anything major as you analyze the rhetoric of something you read or plan the strategy for something you write. We hope that using the device of these common choices will help you to manage reading and writing purposefully while making you more self-conscious and wise about your individual choices. For your convenience, the following table lists the nine choices in terms of questions—and sub-questions—that writers ask themselves as they make choices.

Table 1   Categories of Common Rhetorical Choices

Main Questions	Sub-Questions
The "What" Questions (These focus your attention on the content of your writing.)	
1. What is my *purpose?*	• What are the effects—the changes in readers—that I hope to create? • How do I discover my purpose? • Do I announce the purpose explicitly or convey the purpose gradually or implicitly?
2. What is my *topic?*	• What do experts in my field already know about the topic I have chosen? • What topics do experts in a field consider worth knowing? • What topics do experts in a field believe are possible to know?
3. What is my *point?*	• In what form do I express my main point—theses, hypotheses, or recommendations? • Is my main point a single point (such as a thesis statement) or a set of closely related points (such as a pair of interrelated hypotheses or a set of recommendations to accomplish a particular goal)? • What need does my point meet for my reader?
The "How" Questions (These focus your attention on strategies for effective writing.)	
4. How can I establish an effective *relationship* between me and my audience?	• What aspects of myself do I want to convey to the reader? • How can I convince my audience that I am aware of them and addressing their needs, assumptions, and expectations? • How can I establish a relationship of trust and respect with my audience?
5. How should I use *evidence* to clarify and support my points?	• What kinds of evidence will persuade my audience—statistical data, facts, quotations, personal observations, images? • How much evidence is necessary? • How should I present the evidence—summary, paraphrase, synthesis, graphic representation (tables, charts, diagrams)? • How do I give credit to the sources of my evidence? What citation style should I use?

(continued)

6. How should I use *research methods* to discover reliable evidence for my points?	• What is my central research question? What methods will produce the most convincing evidence for an answer? • What are the accepted research methods of the discipline I'm writing in? • How should I communicate my methods to my audience—in a separate "Methods" section or in the way I present my evidence throughout?
7. How should I *organize* my writing?	• How many main parts will I divide my writing into? • How will I arrange the parts—in what order and in how many levels and sub-levels of importance? • How can I create patterns to write more effectively? • How can I connect the parts (transitions, headings)?
8. How do I make *stylistic* choices that will help me to achieve my goals?	• What kind of style does my audience expect? • How can I use style to emphasize my individuality and yet respect the traditions that other writers have established? • What particular choices will create the stylistic effects I want?
9. How should I construct an effective *visual design*?	• How can I use visual features such as headings, headers, and white space to sharpen focus and clarify organization? • How can I use visual features such as italics, boldface, and bullet points to enhance individual words and sentences? • How should I choose among, construct, and incorporate graphic aids (tables, graphs, diagrams, and so forth)? • If an image is responsible for conveying important meaning, how can I emphasize it and connect it to the text?

UNDERSTANDING WHAT A WRITER SAYS

RHETORIC: WHAT READERS AND WRITERS DO

Chapter 1 and Chapter 2 describe nine choices that all writers make when they compose. We cast these choices as responses to questions that you ask yourself when reading or writing. If you read with an eye for the choices that the writer has made, you will better understand what you read, and you will discover strategies to use in your own writing.

Learning how to make effective choices about what you want to say and how to say it—rhetorical choices—has drawn students to study rhetoric for thousands of years. Outside of colleges and universities people sometimes use the term *rhetoric* to describe an unethical use of language, such as "empty rhetoric." But you will find us and your instructor talking about rhetoric in positive terms, as strategies that make it possible to read and write effectively. In fact, Aristotle describes rhetoric as the process of discovering "all available means of persuasion." If you learn to think about reading and writing as processes of discovering different strategies, you should become more aware of the various choices, or "means," available to you.

As you learn to pay attention to rhetorical questions and choices, it may also help to think about some broadly defined categories of purposes for writing: analyzing, reporting, and recommending (the categories that organize Parts Two, Three, and Four). These categories correspond to key activities in classical rhetoric: searching for relationships among ideas in a piece of writing, finding the central question that a writer attempts to answer, and understanding the context (for example, the relationship between the author and audience).

4

Analysis requires breaking a whole into its constituent parts and clarifying the relationships between those parts. We do this kind of work regularly when we compare, define, categorize, and assess strengths and weaknesses. In your reading, if you determine the main ideas and how those ideas relate to each other, you'll have a richer understanding of the writer's meaning. In your writing, when you analyze a complex issue by exploring the relationships between its parts, you understand your subject more completely. When you emphasize the parts and their relationships to each other, you help your reader understand.

Reporting knowledge requires gathering and then formulating information and ideas so that they are clear, accessible, and useful for readers. In order to read and process knowledge efficiently, you should determine the author's main point: the central, most pressing question that the author is answering. Similarly, if you want your readers to process what you report, you must determine and focus attention on your own central point—your research question. You can then zero in on what you and your readers most care about, and you can assemble reasoning and evidence that will help you accomplish your goal.

When recommending change, you must pay close attention to the rhetorical context to determine what evidence and logic will persuade readers to act on recommendations. When reading, you will be persuaded to act if the writer convinces you that he or she understands your needs and that the recommendations will meet those needs. A persuasive writer will also acknowledge the contexts that affect your desire and ability to act, and provide the specific information that will make it possible for you to act on the recommendations. Likewise, when you recommend change, you will need to understand the context of your readers' needs, desires, and abilities to act, thus persuading them that the changes and actions you advocate are both manageable and desirable.

Finally, it's worth noting that since classical times, writers have looked to the ideas and strategies of others to help them improve their own writing. That is the assumption with which we began this chapter and which drives this whole book. However, to analyze the writing of others, you need to know something about yourself as a reader and a writer. So we begin: with you. In the following section we discuss ways that you can monitor, evaluate, and improve your reading and writing habits.

Rhetorical Reading

When reading is most pleasurable for me, it is like a fishing trip to a large and complex lake, a lake with numerous bays and inlets, seemingly endless islands and channels, and creek channels braiding their way from the main lake through thick marshes to ponds where great blue herons hold one-legged poses among the reeds. I always fish such lakes with a deep, almost clenching, excitement, the excitement of being on water that might yield to me creatures more wondrous than any I have ever wrested from the dark before. But I never go without some apprehension, too, for on such lakes it is possible to become disoriented, even lost for a time. I like the excitement and apprehension: the emotions of a quest.

William J. Vande Kopple

Many of us read fiction like this, for the enjoyment of the quest. But we rarely approach the reading required of us in school or on the job in the same way. How can you find the kind of engagement and satisfaction that Vande Kopple describes when you're reading (and writing) required texts? A couple of hints come directly from Vande Kopple's metaphor: When fishing, he focuses on a particular variety of fish. From experience and research, he knows its habits and its preferred environment; he alters his gear, his technique, and his choice of fishing location in response to that knowledge. People read for a variety of purposes: curiosity, amusement, the need for information. Sometimes they're just curious, so they search for information from websites like Answers.com and Wikipedia. But usually people seek information and ideas that they need to use. They might read up on a scientific method so that they can replicate it and thereby confirm or contradict the results of another scientist (Chapter 8). They might consider different perspectives on the purpose of education so they can create effective teaching plans (Chapter 11). When you read, you, too, are fishing for something: information, evidence for your own writing, or rhetorical strategies that you can use yourself. Some of the readings in this book will be outside of your usual range of interest or experience. While we provide some help in the form of marginal explanations, we have not simplified the vocabulary, the sentence structures, or the concepts. To get the most out of these readings you will need to read like Vande Kopple fishes— intending to make the most of it. To help you do so, we offer the following advice:

- Skim the reading before you set your homework schedule so you can assess how long the reading will take you. Readings that are longer generally take longer to read as do readings from fields unfamiliar to you or with unfamiliar vocabulary. You can expect that reading for both "*what*" and "*how*" will take longer than reading for "*what*" alone.

- If the reading appears to be difficult, read when you are able to give it your best attention. The exercise at the end of this section can help you with this.

- Break up your reading to keep your mind fresh. Divide your reading into either chunks of time or chunks of text and then give yourself a break.

- Read in a team. Readers in professional settings often read as part of a group. Team members use different parts of information for different aspects of a project. If your instructor allows it, read like professionals do. Because your instructor will hold you responsible for the entire reading, though, be sure that you organize your team so that everyone understands the reading completely.

- Consider your instructor as a model reader. Listen carefully to how she talks about texts, what she focuses on, the other texts she refers to, and how she applies the text to course material. Are you focusing on what she values?

Here are some ways to put these ideas to work:

- Inventory your biorhythms and study habits. When are you most able to concentrate on what you're reading? What environment helps you concentrate—for example, do you need silence or music? Do you need to be around other people or alone? Before you start inventorying, commit to being honest with yourself: what works for one person may not for the next.
- Ask around. Observe (or ask about!) the reading habits of successful students. What strategies might work for you?
- Try something new. Make a list of study habits that would improve your ability to concentrate on your reading. Try them out, one at a time.

Rhetorical Writing

> Writing is like being flogged in a dungeon. It is like this because we're being held prisoner here at school, and we are tortured with writing assignments. Writing is like being flogged because it is a painful process that can go on for hours, and you just wish that you would die. It is also like being flogged because weeks later you get your grade, and seeing it, like seeing scars on your body, reminds you of a past painful experience.
>
> *Marty, first-year student*

Thinking about the writing assignments you've faced in college, you may find yourself agreeing with Marty: as a student you have little control over your writing. You hope that you'll endure the pain with dignity and that the subsequent scars won't be too disfiguring. And, to Marty's credit, it's true that academic writing offers you less freedom than writing a blog or even a letter to the editor of the local newspaper. When writing in college, if you want to earn academic credit, you have to complete the task the teacher assigns; sometimes you won't be allowed to pick the topic or even the methods. Although students don't like to hear it, the writing of professionals is often constrained in exactly these ways. And while writing in professional settings sometimes feels like the grand adventure that Vande Kopple describes at the beginning of this chapter, sometimes it feels like a flogging, too.

Writing most often feels like a flogging when the writing task is either too simple or too complex. Simplistic tasks bore writers, and when writers are bored, bad things happen: writers put off the work because they find it purposeless. Because they are not engaged in the intricacies of the task, they make sloppy errors in grammar and thinking. Complex tasks overwhelm students by requiring them to try too many new things, to write about topics that are vitally important, or to write to audiences they find intimidating. When writers feel over-challenged, bad things happen, too: writers become anxious, so they write hurriedly, or they procrastinate, or they get a bad case of writer's block and don't write at all. Pretty much, students have the same response to both overly simplistic and overly complex tasks: they avoid writing. We call this response "doing a Bartleby," after the title character in a Herman Melville short story who politely refuses to work, using the phrase "I would prefer not to." All writers feel the pull of the Bartleby response; effective writers have developed strategies for countering that feeling. Here are some of the more commonly used strategies:

- *Develop a professional view of writing.* Students often think of "writing" as putting words on the page. But most professional writers take into account all stages of a project, from when they realize that a problem exists, through their research on that problem, to the final negotiations with the publisher. Record your ideas, your developing sense of purpose, and your struggles to locate the central question you're answering. These notes will give you words and ideas to work from when you put words on the page.

- *Accept recursivity.* While many students think of writing as a linear process— choosing a topic, researching, outlining, drafting, and editing—professional writers see it differently. They're not surprised when the act of putting words on the page gives them new insight into the topic, their main point, or new directions for research. And they take advantage of those insights to improve their text.

- *Seek out new strategies for writing.* While students may have been told that there is one "right" way to write, professional writers know two things: that people compose in a variety of ways and that the strategies writers use change over their lifetimes.

- *Get moving and stay moving.* It's common to hear students talk about writing as an activity that requires inspiration: they refer to writing as "flowing" out of them, they talk about their "muse," and they complain of writer's block. Yet few professional writers talk this way. For them, writing is their day-job; they cannot rely on the whims of a muse or the happy arrival of an inspired idea. If you think of writing as something more than drafting, you realize that you can work on other aspects of a writing project when the words aren't coming. If you think of writing as a non-linear process, you recognize that writer's block may be a sign that you need to rethink what you're writing about. If you think of writing in more than one way, you can try a different composing strategy when you feel uninspired. You can freewrite or outline, talk with a friend, or take a walk—try out strategies that others use to find what they want to say and how they want to say it.

Here are some ways to put these ideas to work:

- *Create a short history of yourself as a writer.* Where and when did you write when you were in high school? What tools did you use? Who helped you as you wrote? Contrasting your writing then and now, you may discover that you've left behind some good habits and a supportive environment for writing. How could you replicate the good features of your high school writing in your college environment?

- *Attend to your ability to pay attention.* How long can you concentrate on your writing before your interest starts to fade? What indicates that you have lost your ability to concentrate? What activities refresh your mind, body, and spirit?

READING AND WRITING FOR THE "WHAT" QUESTIONS: PURPOSE, TOPIC, AND POINT

Readers and writers "meet" because they share common needs. A nurse has an idea that she believes will improve health care for children, and she shares it by writing a paper; other nurses want to offer better health care, so they need to read about new ideas. In the content of written documents—the "what" of reading and writing—writers and readers make connections that help them change their world.

Question 1: What is my purpose?

To make effective rhetorical choices—in college, on the job, or in a public role—you need to clarify why you are writing. *You* need to know your purpose in order to choose the strategies that will achieve your aim. You need to make your *readers* aware of your purpose so you can keep their attention focused and avoid misleading them.

Sub-questions:

- What are the effects—the changes in readers—that I hope to create? Is the reader supposed to understand my subject differently, possess new knowledge, take some specific action?
- How do I discover my purpose? When does a situation (such as an assignment given by a teacher or employer) dictate the purpose, and when does a situation (such as a decision to write a letter to the editor) require that I find my own purpose?
- Do I announce the purpose explicitly or convey the purpose gradually or implicitly? When is it to my advantage to say exactly what change I hope to create in this audience, and when is it better to let the purpose emerge slowly and subtly?

Reading for Purpose.   Before you begin reading, determine your reasons for reading—and let that purpose shape how you read. For example, if you are looking for particular information—such as evidence to support a claim or details about a research method—you'll probably skim texts, searching for the particulars you want; if you are reading to gain a more complete understanding of a complex issue, however, you'll read more slowly, connecting ideas and judging whether the evidence supports the claims. Notably, your purposes for reading do not always match an author's purpose for writing; you are, finally, the one in control. Generally speaking, however, if you stay aware of an author's purpose, you'll be a more efficient reader and will probably be more successful in accomplishing your purpose as a reader.

Consider this example from Chapter 5, Chemistry. On first look, if you are not into chemistry, Martin Alexander's essay "Aging, Bioavailability, and Overestimation of Risk from Environmental Pollutants" looks like a hard read. Yet if you understand Alexander's purpose, you'll slice through the technicalities that might otherwise trip you up. Alexander argues that scientists mistakenly estimate the risks of environmental pollutants because they use poor methods for measuring pollutants. His purpose is to change those methods. As you read, ask, "How does this part help him persuade his readers that the current methods are faulty and that we need better ones?" Asking that question allows you to manage the complexity of Alexander's essay. Remember that all writers have a particular reason for writing—they want to persuade readers to examine their assumptions, learn some new information, or act in a specific way.

Writing for Purpose.   To determine your own purpose for writing, consider the effect you hope to have on yourself, your reader, or the world. Why are you writing? To understand something or someone else better? To find and organize information about a topic? To report new knowledge? To persuade your reader to believe a certain way? Once you know why you're writing, you can check yourself by asking, "How does what I'm writing—every section, paragraph, sentence—help me accomplish my purpose?" If you can't answer that question, it's time to revise.

Taking the time to figure out your purpose for writing is the most important way to "avoid the Bartleby." Everyone hates to write if they write without a goal or without believing they can accomplish that goal.

You may recall that Parts Two, Three, and Four of this book are organized by common *purposes* for writing. Purposes in Part Four are easiest to recognize; the readings aim to persuade readers to act on recommendations—to try different methods of caring for patients or to buy a chair. Readings in Part Three share the purpose of reporting useful knowledge—how to minimize injuries when training athletes or how to provide enough food without hurting the environment. Part Two includes examples of analytical writing—interpreting an ancient culture through its art or analyzing how a political speech influences its audience. Writers analyze for the purpose of understanding, and understanding is obviously foundational for all writing.

Question 2: What is my topic?

Remember the times that you have had the freedom to choose your topic; sometimes doing that is very hard. What's the range of your options? What do you care about that an audience will also care about? To further complicate things, each discipline imposes its own expectations about what are and are not appropriate topics. A literary critic might find it worthwhile to research a culture's courting traditions through its poetry; a biologist would consider courting impossible to test scientifically and instead focus on the function of pheromones in sexual attraction.

Biologists like topics that involve classifying and discovering causes. Literary critics like topics that investigate paradox and the ways reality can hide behind surface appearance. Your teachers in introductory courses in the disciplines often choose your paper topics for you: you do not yet know what they consider knowable and worth knowing, so they have to tell you.

Sub-questions:

- What do experts in my field already know about the topic I have chosen? (New research is always grounded in existing research.)
- What topics do experts in a field consider worth knowing? Given all the research questions that could drive a study, which questions lead to useful answers?
- What topics do experts in a field believe are knowable? Are there some topics about which the field simply believes it is impossible to learn anything useful?

Reading for the Topic.   Research on reading suggests that people understand what they read and remember it better when they connect it to what they already know. But readers come to a text with a wide range of background knowledge and experiences: what is news to one may be old hat to another. When reading, you can save time and still read effectively if you take a moment to reflect on what you already know about the topic. Then, as you read, focus your attention on what is new to you. You can test your understanding of what you've read in one of the following three ways: explain what you read to a child, give an example that demonstrates the main idea, or translate the information into a new context. If you can do any one of these three tasks, you likely understand the information thoroughly.

   If the topic is entirely new to you, learn a little bit about it before you begin reading. Research on college students' reading abilities suggests that when students have a general understanding of a topic they are able to determine which are the most important points in a reading and better able to understand those points. To improve your understanding of a topic, consider these strategies:

- If you know only a little or nothing about the topic, search out general information from websites like Answers.com or Wikipedia before you start reading.
- Note important information in the text by highlighting or underlining it. This will help you find that information later when you need to use it.
- Define unfamiliar terms. If you need to understand a concept thoroughly, look up definitions of terms, re-write them in your own words, and create web diagrams of related terms to help you understand relationships among ideas.

Writing about a Topic.   Common sense tells you that to write meaningfully about a topic, you have to know something about it, but college lore abounds with stories of students who "BS'd" their way to good grades on term papers or successfully fudged lab results. While occasionally you may be able to get a good grade for writing about what you do not know or understand, professors and other professionals—those who have reason to read carefully what you've written or those who are enacting changes that you recommend—are likely to respond to such writing with frustration or even anger. It's a good way to get expelled or to lose your job!

Furthermore, you have an ethical responsibility to learn all you can about your topic. Imagine that you are a drug company representative, trying to convince a psychiatrist to consider prescribing a new antidepressant. If you persuade her to prescribe the drug without exploring and reporting on harmful side-effects, you have violated the trust that readers put in writers, and you have put the psychiatrist's clients at risk.

To select a topic, consider these questions:

- What's the range of your options? How much freedom has your teacher given you, and how familiar are you with the possibilities within that range?
- What do you care about that an audience will also care about?
- What topics does the discipline that you are writing in consider worth knowing and possible to know?

To learn about a topic, you should develop a general understanding of its history, relationships, and internal organization in the following ways:

- Trace the history of scholarly or professional conversation about your topic. Who has cared about this topic? Who has been affected by scholarly or professional research on this topic? When did professionals first research this topic? What problem or question compelled them to do so? What scholarly disciplines research this topic?
- Learn about the relationship between your topic and topics associated with it. Did this topic grow out of another one? What is its current relationship to that topic? Who were the prominent professional or scholarly voices in the research? What methods have professionals used to research this topic?

Question 3: What is my point?

When a writer has a concrete sense of purpose, he or she will want to express the point clearly. Without making a point, you cannot accomplish your purpose (unless your purpose, as in some propaganda, is to confuse your readers). A writer may delay stating the point in order to build up some suspense or anticipation, but the reader cannot finish reading without knowing the point. Writing teachers get troubled by a lot of problems in students' writing, but there is nothing more frustrating than coming to the end of a paper and wondering, "What is the *point?*"

Sub-questions:

- In what form do I express my main point—theses, hypotheses, or recommendations (three common methods of expressing the point)?
- Is my main point a single point (such as a thesis statement) or a set of closely related points (such as a pair of interrelated hypotheses or a set of recommendations)?
- What need does my point meet for my reader?

Reading for the Point.   While a purpose motivates an author to write about a topic, the author's *point* is the main thing she has to say about the topic. The author may state her point most succinctly in a thesis, a hypothesis, or a set of recommendations. The author then focuses attention on the main point in the introduction and develops the reader's understanding of the complexities of that point throughout the essay. To develop a thorough understanding of an author's point, try some of the following strategies:

- Look for a study guide or a set of review questions to accompany an assigned reading. Often textbooks or instructors provide these to indicate significant aspects of the author's point. When you do not have such guidance, compare the ideas and information in each section to the most succinct statement of the author's point.
- Summarize the reading in three to five sentences, emphasizing connections among the ideas that make up the author's main point.
- Jot down the point of each paragraph in the margin of the text. This will help you create an outline (which will be invaluable when you review the reading as you're writing). To determine the point of each paragraph, look at the first sentence in the paragraph—the topic sentence. Contrast that to the content of the rest of the paragraph to determine if it offers the main idea of the paragraph. To determine the main point of a table or graph, look at its title. Then look for the connections between the main point of the paragraph or graphic and the main point of the whole document.
- Outline the reading on a separate piece of paper to track the flow of ideas throughout a reading. To do this you have to think hard about hierarchical relationships within the text, asking yourself questions like "Why did the author create a new paragraph at this point?" "Is this a new point?" "Is this a sub-point?" "An example?"

Writing for the Point.   Remember that your readers enter your writing without knowing what your point is, and you must somehow focus their attention on that point. You might do that, for example, by stating a thesis at the end of an introduction. As you focus readers' attention, you also focus your attention; and self-confidence emerges. Being confident about your point allows you to assess the value of the new ideas, information, and arguments that you discover as you complete the work. Questions like the following can guide you as you develop your point:

- How does your point answer your research question? One of the best ways to focus your writing on a point is to craft a specific research question. The concept of a research question comes from scientific inquiry; in that context the research question outlines the problem that the hypothesis proposes to answer. But research questions work well in other settings, too. You can use a research question to establish the problem that your work will eventually answer with a thesis, a hypothesis, or a set of recommendations. Writers in many disciplines find it helpful to include a final version of the research question as part of the introduction to an academic essay. Use the research questions you discover in the readings in this textbook as models for your own.

- What does your reader think of your point? When you write for a course, and the teacher is your reader, the teacher will tell you if the point is worthwhile. So you should confirm your planned point with your instructor. As you work, your initial ideas and your knowledge will change. These changes may lead to changes in your point, so check in regularly with your instructor as your writing evolves and your point sharpens. The lesson of writing about topics that your reader considers worthwhile will be essential for writing outside of college.

CONCLUSION

Reading in order to locate a writer's purpose, topic, and point will make you a more confident and effective reader. Making careful rhetorical choices about your purpose, topic, and point will make you a more confident and effective writer. You will develop more understanding of your habits, exercise and improve your habits, and dramatically improve your chances of enjoying reading and writing. You may even learn to feel less like you are being flogged when you write. So you can, instead of "doing a Bartleby," enjoy the challenge and adventure of reading and writing.

UNDERSTANDING HOW A WRITER PERSUADES READERS

HOW WRITERS AND READERS RELATE TO ONE ANOTHER

In Chapter 1, we considered what writers and readers need to know if they want to write or to read well—a clear understanding of purpose, topic, and point. In this chapter, we consider how readers experience a text as they read it and how writers can shape the reader's experience. When you read strategically—that is, read to discover the rhetorical strategies an author has used—you can better understand why you respond as you do to a text, and you can read more intentionally. When you write strategically—that is, pay attention to how readers will experience your text—you increase the chances that readers will respond to your text as you want them to.

Reading texts analytically reveals authors' choices for these strategic—or "how"—questions. You will find the author answering these "how" questions with choices about words and sentences, evidence, or visual design. For example, as you read an advertisement for a gaming system, you should pay attention to how the author uses evidence, sentence style, and visual design to persuade you to spend your hard-earned cash. Your experience as a strategic reader of texts will teach you strategies for your writing.

In addition to discovering authors' answers to the "how" questions, you must consider the text in the context of its "rhetorical situation," or the situation that brings together an author, a reader, and a text. These elements exert influence on each other. So, for example, a writer will choose a different tactic for a hostile audience than for a friendly one, and a reader will invest trust in an author who appears believable but will be skeptical about an authors who seems biased or ignorant.

In this textbook, we pay special attention to how disciplinary context has shaped the rhetorical choices that writers make. Looking at the rhetorical choices that authors make in Parts Two, Three, and Four can help you think about how to answer the following "how" questions in your own rhetorical situations.

READING AND WRITING FOR THE "HOW" QUESTIONS: AUDIENCE, EVIDENCE, METHOD, ORGANIZATION, STYLE, AND VISUAL DESIGN

Question 4: How can I establish an effective relationship with my audience?

How you write tells readers a lot about the relationship you want to have with them. Readers quickly pick up tones of defensiveness or arrogance; they pick up tones of humility and sincerity. And the judgments that you make about the authors you read should remind you that others will make judgments about you as an author.

Sub-Questions:

- How can I convey a sense of my character, creating a personality in my writing?
- How can I convince my audience that I am aware of them and addressing their needs, assumptions, and expectations?
- How can I establish a relationship of trust and respect with my audience?

Reading to Discover How Authors Build Relationships with Their Audiences.   To understand the relationship between yourself and an author, you must first analyze the author's competence and values—and the strategies the author uses to persuade the reader to accept those values. Writers are sometimes incompetent or unethical. While in general you can presume that something published by an academic journal or press has been reviewed by experts, inaccuracies, sloppy methods, and bad logic still sneak into print. This is, of course, even more true of texts that have not been reviewed by experts. Furthermore, what an author values about the world—the assumptions he makes about how the world works and what is important—will profoundly shape his purpose for writing and his point. You should analyze not only what the author values but also how he seeks your assent to those values: Does he presume you'll agree? Demand that you agree? Explain why you should agree?

Secondly, you must consider how the author interacts with you, the reader. Does the author seem to care whether or not you understand him? Some authors, perhaps trying to prove something about themselves, the topic, or their field, seem to complicate things as much as possible. Others write to themselves: readers may have trouble understanding because the writer isn't intending to communicate with others; he focuses on making meaning for himself.

To evaluate the author's competence and what the author values, ask questions like these as you read:

- How does the author's writing compare to the way other writers describe or explain the same subject? That is, does any other reading make you suspicious about this author? Are the author's methods consistent with those used by other scholars in the field? Does the author show command of the full range of knowledge in the field? Do other scholars in the field value this author's work? Do they refer to it in their own research?

- What values and assumptions does the author rely on to make his point? Do you share those values and assumptions? Is the author aware of and forthright about his values and assumptions, comparing them openly to those that differ?

To evaluate how the author interacts with the reader, ask these kinds of questions as you read:

- Who is the author's intended reader? What evidence shows the extent to which the author understands the intended audience's needs, knowledge, experiences, values, and assumptions?

- How carefully does the author provide context for his points? How much background information does the author provide and in what form does he provide that information? How do these contexts meet audience needs?

Writing to Establish a Relationship with an Audience.   When you write, you present yourself to the reader, and you do so in the hopes of having a positive effect on your audience. Of course you stand a better chance of influencing your audience if you create a good relationship with them.

To earn your audience's trust, consider the following strategies:

- Develop your own expertise. Read widely in the field and refer to your reading in your text.
- Rely on the expertise of others. At critical spots in your writing—places where it is crucial that the reader believe you—depend on the information, ideas, or recommendations of researchers who are recognized as experts in the field.
- Consider whether your own experience is somehow relevant to your subject. If it is, how might it enhance your credibility with your audience?
- Make good use of any specialized knowledge you have. How can you use the expertise that you've developed in your academic major, in a job, or doing public service?

- Explore the assumptions you share with the experts writing about this topic. What assumptions do you share with your reader? If your assumptions do not match those of the experts and your reader, you can choose either to de-emphasize the difference or to emphasize the difference and attempt to persuade the reader to think differently.

When you write, you must take into account not only your own expertise but also the situation of your reader. Try practicing the following:

- Pay attention to what your reader knows. Be quite sure that your reader knows information before you refer to it. If you are unsure about your reader's level of knowledge, direct the reader to sources of additional information.

- Accommodate your reader's assumptions. You can assume that your reader shares assumptions about how the physical world works; you can be less sure that your reader shares your assumptions about politics, religion, social policy, and the nature or purpose of human life. On issues like these you can accommodate your reader's assumptions without compromising your own by adopting the rhetorical practice of sociologists and creating a theoretical framework that lays out the assumptions that will guide your work.

- Recognize your reader's experience. Even if you and your reader grew up in the same culture, because of differences in age, gender, race, economic class, or geography, your reader will have experienced that culture differently. Make allusions to shared experiences only when you are fairly certain that your reader will recognize them.

- Respect your reader's needs and expectations. Readers read because they hope to use what they've read, and they read with expectations about format, genre, and context. Unless you have good reason to do otherwise, write so that readers can find information quickly and understand it thoroughly—so that they can put your text to good use.

- Respond to your reader's abilities. Readers do not all read with the same skill, ease, or pleasure. Accommodate your reader by using simpler sentence structures and repeating information at complex or crucial parts of your writing.

Question 5: How should I use evidence to clarify and support my points?

Writing tasks can require vastly different kinds and amounts of evidence. A single eyewitness account might be enough to convince an audience of jurors in a court case, and a well-conducted study of an exemplary case will persuade some political scientists, but a natural scientist might have to repeat an experiment thousands of times to gather enough detail to prove a hypothesis. Whatever the situation, however, you cannot write effectively unless you provide your audience with the evidence they require to be convinced—presented in an accessible form.

Sub-questions:

- What kinds of evidence will persuade audiences—statistical data (presented in tables and graphs), quotations, personal observations, images?
- How much evidence is necessary in different kinds of writing?
- How should I present the evidence—summary, paraphrase, synthesis, graphic representation (tables, charts, diagrams)?
- How do I give credit to the sources of my evidence? What citation style should I use?

Reading to Discover an Author's Use of Evidence.   What counts as evidence, how much evidence an author provides, and the form in which the author provides the evidence give clues about the author's purpose and point. A statistic about the number of people who suffer chronic pain, for example, can provide a good overview, but it gives no insight into the nature of their suffering. A verbal description of an art object cannot include the amount of information that a photograph can, but a photograph cannot focus the reader's attention on specific details the way verbal description can. In addition to thinking about the kinds of evidence a writer uses, you will want to ask questions like the following:

- How much evidence does the author provide? Does the author, for example, rely on a small number of compelling pieces of evidence (such as a lawyer uses a few reliable eyewitnesses in a court case) or on many small details (in the way a lawyer would gather a large number of circumstantial details)?
- How does the author present the evidence? How much has the author shaped the evidence through summary and paraphrase? How accurately has the author presented the information? How completely has the author represented the available research?
- What are the sources of the author's evidence (scientific research, scholarly analysis, personal testimony) and how are the sources cited?

Writing with Evidence.   You will have to determine what kinds of and how much evidence to use in your writing. And if an assignment does not guide you in making those decisions, you will have to look at models and consider options. Kinds of evidence include: statistics, facts, experimental data, examples, anecdotes, quotations, expert opinions, and personal experience.

Finding enough evidence also causes writers big headaches. Most student writers underestimate the amount of time it will take them to track down all the information they need to understand a topic thoroughly enough to write effectively. And few students know how to use information databases well enough to access the full range of information on their topic. The best strategy is to consult the experts: research librarians. Working with a research librarian will not only teach you how to use specific research databases but also how to conduct research in general.

To use evidence effectively in your writing, you must account for the sources and nature of the evidence:

- What is the source of the evidence? How reliable is this source for this type of evidence?

- Who "owns" the information? Someone—either a person or group—claims intellectual property rights to most valuable information. If you fail to acknowledge the words, data, or ideas of others, either mistakenly or intentionally, you risk being accused of intellectual dishonesty—plagiarism.

- How relevant is the evidence to your time and place? Evidence originates in a particular time and place and, consequently, it reflects the knowledge and ways of thinking of that time period. Writers must carefully assess the relevance of the evidence to the current state of knowledge and ways of thinking about a topic.

- What acknowledgement for intellectual property should you provide? What writers acknowledge and how they acknowledge it varies across rhetorical situations, disciplines, and professions. Therefore, it's wise to consult with others about what to acknowledge and the citation style you should use.

Once you have found evidence, you should consider carefully how the evidence expands, alters, or contradicts your initial ideas about your topic, and you should adjust your thinking, your research question, and your claims accordingly.

When you consider how to use the evidence in your writing, you will need to decide how to present it. The basic forms for presenting evidence are the following:

- *Citation.* When you cite other research (in parentheses, footnotes, or endnotes) without including additional information, you demonstrate that you researched thoroughly, yet you also keep your readers focused on what you have to say about your research question.

- *Quotation.* When you quote evidence, you invite the original author—his words, sentence structures, and ideas—into your writing. Because you do not control the focus of the quoted author's words and ideas, readers may be inclined to trust quotations more than summary or paraphrase, so quotations work well for evidence that is cutting-edge, surprising, or controversial. Refer to the style manual that writers in your discipline use to determine the form of your quotation.

- *Paraphrase.* When you paraphrase, you manipulate your source less than when you summarize because your paraphrase roughly matches the length of the original. Paraphrase when you want to fit the tone or sentence structure of evidence to your own writing. Also paraphrase to better fit evidence into your own focus without misrepresenting the intent of the original author.

- *Summary.* Effective summaries balance between focusing on the particular evidence most relevant to your point and accurately portraying the point of the source that you are summarizing. You can choose to summarize evidence visually (in tables or graphs) or verbally.

- *Synthesis.* When you synthesize, you help the reader understand the topical and logical connections among pieces of evidence. Synthesize to blend evidence from a variety of sources to support your own idea and to demonstrate that many scholars agree with your way of thinking. Also synthesize to represent the history of thinking about a topic in a "research review" or "literature review" section of an academic essay.

How much evidence you should provide depends on such complex factors as the audience's openness to the argument and the type of evidence you're using. So answering questions about evidence will press you to reconsider—and maybe revise—your ideas about how to address your audience, how to organize your argument, and how to make best use of the visual design of your writing project.

Question 6: How should I use research methods to discover reliable evidence for my points?

Effective methods provide evidence that reliably tests your conclusions—your point or points. Imagine that you want to learn how an audience of potential customers for a business you have started will respond to a new advertising campaign. You decide to gather data to test your campaign by showing the ads to people at a shopping mall and getting their responses. After you gather your data, you learn that the mall had been running a senior citizen's event that day. The average age of your test market was over fifty—while your product is aimed at people in their twenties. Your *method* has resulted in useless evidence.

Whether or not writers state their methods explicitly, every credible writer will use reliable research methods to uncover—and test—their ideas and information. Even if you are writing to a general audience, you will want your readers to believe that you did something more intentional than stumble across ideas and information. If you are writing to a specialized audience (including college teachers), that audience will expect that the content of your writing has grown out of accepted research methods.

Sub-questions:

- What is my central research question? What methods will produce the most convincing evidence for an answer?
- What are the accepted research methods of the discipline I'm writing in?
- How should I communicate my methods to my audience—in a separate "Methods" section or in the way I present my evidence throughout?

Reading to Discover an Author's Methods.   Good readers analyze writers' research methods. Readers want to know that what they are reading is trustworthy; it can't be based on bad evidence.

Writing in the natural and social sciences, in which authors must persuade readers that the evidence is objective and reliable, traditionally includes a "Methods" section (see, for example, the "Methods" section in the first reading in Chapters 8, Biology; 9, Sociology; and 12, Nursing). Readers scrutinize scientific methods in the following ways:

- Assessing how authors follow and adapt the protocols of well-established methods: Has this method proven trustworthy in previous research? How has the researcher adjusted the method to fit her particular topic? Has the author provided enough information so that another set of researchers could replicate the method?

- Assessing the data that the method produces: Does the method provide data that prove or disprove the hypothesis? Are the data statistically significant? In the "Results" section, where the data are presented, authors will include the statistical information that indicates exactly how reliable the data are. Respectable journals will publish papers only if the data reach a certain standard of reliability (for example, results that have at least a 90 percent chance of being accurate); good readers will pay attention to what that standard is.

In both the social sciences and the humanities, writers often use what is called a "case study" method. For example, in the political science chapter, author Christopher Layne bases his argument on four cases in which powerful democratic countries almost went to war. Literary critics also use methods that are similar to case studies. They start with a theory and test it against the evidence—selected poems, novels, etc.

Generally, in the humanities the research methods can be inferred from the kinds of evidence included and how the author cites the evidence. If a writer includes extensive citations (footnotes, endnotes, parenthetical citations in the text), you know that he has searched library databases and read all of the published research on the topic. If a writer includes details from personal observation, personal observation is probably among the research methods accepted in that field. To discover methods in non-scientific writing:

- Find the author's research question. What question drives the research, and what method will yield a reliable answer to that question?

- Question the author's research method. How thoroughly did the author research? What types of sources did the author review? Are the sources respected by other experts? Do they represent a balance of perspectives on the topic? (Your research librarian can help you to answer these questions.)

Writing with Methods.   A good rule-of-thumb in science writing is that you should include only the information that may have affected your results. So, for example, you need not record the size of the beaker, but you should include the strength of the chlorine solution you added to the beaker. You should list the materials and equipment you used as well as the processes you followed and the precautions you took. If you have important reasons for doing something as you did, include that reasoning in explaining your methods. In non-scientific texts, where traces of your method are diffused throughout your writing, be sure to conduct thorough and balanced research (using only random websites or Wikipedia will encourage readers to doubt your evidence). Furthermore:

- Cite your sources (using the documentation style that is accepted in a particular discipline). Make absolutely sure that you give credit to authors from whom you gathered the ideas and information. Failure to do this is plagiarism.

- If you use evidence that you have summarized or paraphrased, provide a citation.

- Use a combination of primary and secondary evidence that is appropriate to your topic and discipline. Primary evidence is the raw content of what researchers study. For example, in literary research primary evidence is the literary texts; in history it is the old newspapers, diaries, or archeological artifacts; in sociology it is the actual social interactions. Secondary evidence includes what other researchers have written about the primary evidence.

Question 7: How should I organize my writing?

Purposeful organization is essential to readers. It gives readers a sense of where they are in a piece of writing so they don't feel lost. And organizational patterns can create almost subconscious rhythms that shape a reader's perception of the direction a text is taking. Organizational patterns can play with a reader by creating suspense and surprise, or they can recreate the familiarity of walking a well-known path.

Sub-questions:

- How many main parts will I divide my writing into?
- How will I arrange the parts—in what order and in how many levels and sub-levels of importance?
- How can I create patterns or repetitions to write more effectively?
- How can I connect the parts? Does the paper I'm writing call for transitions to create a sense of logical connectedness, or should I use headings that will allow my readers to find the main parts and read them in the order they prefer?

Reading to Discover an Author's Organization.   The way an author organizes a text depends heavily on the reader's expectations and on requirements of the genre and discipline. In general, authors begin by giving the reader a reason to read and enough background information to read well. They also establish their topic and point. Look for these features in an abstract and introduction. Authors typically end a text by telling the reader what to do with what they've just read. It is therefore helpful to check whether the introduction and conclusion match and clarify the author's purpose and point.

You can begin to make connections between organization and an author's goals by asking:

- How is the author's organization typical of writing in this discipline? Why do writers in this discipline organize texts in this way? What kind of reading does this type of organization encourage—skimming, reading only some parts, reading straight from start to finish?

- What does the author's organization emphasize? What parts does it de-emphasize? How does the author show relationships among the parts of the text? Are all parts of the text well-connected? Do some seem tangential? Are some parts more fully developed (with more evidence, more discussion) than others?

- What kind of experience does the author provide for the reader through the organization of the text? Are there surprises that heighten the impact of the conclusion? Are the parts predictably arranged so readers always know where they are? What expectations does the author have for the reader at the outset? What does the author direct the reader to do at the conclusion?

Writing for Organization.   Sometimes the organization of your text will be determined for you. For example, most scientific reports follow a commonly used format: Introduction, Methods and Materials, Results, Discussion. Many business reports start with an executive summary and then move into an analysis of a business problem, a description of a way to solve that problem including associated costs, and a list of recommendations—specific actions that the business should take to enact the solution. When you have to develop your own organizational plan, remember these guidelines: readers expect to understand a problem before they are interested in the solution to that problem; they expect to learn about older research before newer research; and they expect to understand general concepts before they learn about specific ones. When you organize your text, consider the following:

- What are the common organizational patterns used by other writers in this context?

- How can you craft an organizational pattern that will best convey and emphasize your main point?

- How do you want the reader to experience the text? What will capture her interest? What knowledge does she already have? What information does she need to learn before she can understand your argument?

Question 8: How do I make stylistic choices that will help me to achieve my goals?

When we ask students to define style, they tend to talk about either being *in* style (doing, saying, wearing the things that the larger culture has decided are *in* style) or *having* style (doing, saying, wearing things that are unique, individualistic). Style in writing is a matter of balancing the conventional (being *in* style) and the unique (*having* style). You cannot be so individualistic that you confuse your audience, nor can you be so conventional that you sound like a robot. While a lot of robotic writers, in fact, do quite well for themselves, we hope you'll make better choices.

Sub-questions:

- What kind of style does the audience for a particular piece of writing expect—formal, informal, jargon-dependent, reasonable, passionate?
- How can I use style to emphasize my individuality and yet respect the traditions that other writers have established?
- What particular choices will create the stylistic effects I want? Should I emphasize verbs, adjectives, concrete nouns, contractions, slang, sentence patterns?

Reading to Discover an Author's Style.   When most people think of an author's "style," they think of the author's distinctive "voice" or presence in a text, and certainly this is one aspect of style. Sometimes people describe style as if it is a separate, added feature of writing—as frosting is to a cake, and sometimes this is the case. But style is more than either of these. As you will learn in the "Notes on Grammar, Style, and Rhetoric" in each following chapter, an author's stylistic choices profoundly affect the reader's experience. As you read to analyze an author's style, begin with the following general questions:

- Why does the author use this style? Does it seem that the author's style results from habit, a wish to be consistent with the style of others in the field, a desire to present a certain personality to the reader, an attempt to appeal to the reader's emotions?
- What effect does the author's style have on the readability of the text? Does the author's style enhance the reader's ability to understand and agree with the author's point?
- How do relatively small deviations from formal, conventional style (contractions, slang, sentence fragments) shape readers' responses to a text and its author?
- How does the author's style focus the reader's attention in the text? What does the author's style emphasize? What does it de-emphasize?

Writing for Style.   Although some writers think of style as an unchangeable feature of a writer—like the size of his feet—we prefer to think about style as the culmination of rhetorical choices that the author has made. Different situations call for different stylistic choices. Many writers, especially student writers, find it helpful to think about style throughout the composing process:

- *Developing ideas:* As you explore the research of others to develop and refine your own ideas, keep track of the metaphors, visual images, sentences, and chunks of text that you find especially effective. Analyze them to determine why they are so effective and to discover styles of presenting ideas that can help you develop your own ideas.

- *Composing:* When you find yourself struggling to write, take a break from drafting and play with your words. For example, list the five people or things that are the "doers" within your topic. List the main actions of these doers and the people or things altered by that action. Now, put these in relationship to each other. Start with a simple sentence structure: Put one of the doers in the subject position of your sentence, one of the actions in the verb position, and someone or something that gets altered in the object position. Does this help you think about the relationships among people or ideas? After you create a few simple sentences, try joining them together with the words "because," "if," "although," and "therefore." The resulting complex sentence structures may help you better understand the complex relationships within your topic.

- *Editing:* When you are revising your writing, concentrate on how your style shapes the reader's experience of your text. Normally, you should write as succinctly as possible, using active-voice verbs, choosing sentence structures that create rhythms, and employing metaphors or similes to help the reader conceptualize a complex idea.

Question 9: How should I construct an effective visual design?

If we were to show you a few pages from published papers in several different disciplines—even if we held them far enough away so you could not read the words, you would probably be able to (1) notice different visual features and (2) make pretty accurate guesses about what disciplines the papers came from. Randomly flip to different readings in this book, and you'll see what we mean. Disciplines have strong traditions for how visual design is or is not employed.

In fields such as English and philosophy the implicit message is that visuals are a bit unfair or at least beside the point. Your logic should move elegantly from one point to the next; your words should be deft enough describe any mental pictures you wish to create, so why would you need visual aids?

In business, on the other hand, writers know that images are efficient—and powerful. People who use mostly words think of images as ways to illustrate what they write verbally, but those who work with images know that images communicate on their own, differently from words. If they had to choose one or the other, they might sooner give up words than pictures. Fortunately, they don't have to choose. Computerized graphics technology allows anyone to create sophisticated visual designs and merge images and words; images have become simple to cut and paste, and writing textbooks typically include sections about visual design. Visual design and graphic elements that complement and extend the meaning of written texts are expected. So keep your eyes open, and model the effective designs that you see.

Sub-questions:

- How can I use visual features such as headings, headers, and white space to sharpen focus and clarify organization?
- How can I use visual features such as italics, boldface, and bullet points to emphasize individual words and sentences?
- How should I choose among, construct, and incorporate graphics (tables, graphs, diagrams, and so forth)?
- If an image is responsible for conveying important meaning, how can I emphasize it and connect it to the text?

Reading to Discover an Author's Visual Design.   When you read something that has both words and pictures, what do you look at first? The pictures, of course—unless the words (a title, for example) have been blown up to a huge, bizarre font; then the words might catch your eye. In either case the visual design commands your attention. Remember that everything about writing, even the simplest text, is printed in visual form, so choices of fonts, margin size, boldface, extra spaces before a heading, even whether or not to use headings, are all visual design choices.

To understand the meaning conveyed by visual design as you are reading, you will first want to scan the visual character of a document; then, study individual design features. Ask questions like these:

- Does the visual design seem minimal? Some writers pay no attention to visual design; the design choices might have been made by the writer's word-processing program. In such cases you might not want to read meaning into the visual design.
- If there are obvious visual choices that a writer has made, what purpose did the author have in mind? If you see headings, for example (as you will in most of the readings in this book), do the headings identify parts of a text that you would expect to find (such as a "Methods" or "Results" section in a scientific paper)? If headings identify familiar parts, they may also indicate a writer who wants the reader to find the parts and be able to jump around rather than reading the parts in order. If headings identify a series of related ideas, the author may be using them to help readers comprehend the logical sequence of parts. Using headings in that way encourages reading a text from start to

finish. If there are no headings, the author may want to reveal the structure of the document gradually, bringing an element of surprise to your reading.

- If tables, graphs, and photographs are identified (for example, "Table 1" or "Figure 1"), does the text refer to those visual elements? If a writer explains a table, for example, and refers you to the table, you know that the words and graphics are working together and that you will have to read them together to comprehend them.
- If an author uses decorative visuals (double lines around textboxes; three-dimensional, colored bar charts), can you discern whether the author intended the visual elements to help set the tone for the text? (Sometimes visual design is just a result of someone enjoying their graphics software too much and not caring about meaning.)

Writing for Visual Design.   The contemporary writer has to be a visual designer. You can leave your design choices up to your software program, but if the program creates a poor design, you—not Bill Gates—will take the blame. You will therefore need to ask yourself the following design questions:

- *For visually simple texts:* What font or fonts do you want? (There is rarely a reason to use more than two different fonts.) Do you want to use signposts? (Headers and headings, for example, can reinforce the organizational pattern and serve as a map of the text.) How much white space do you want per page?
- *For more visually complex texts:* If you use tables, graphs, illustrations, or photographs, how should you identify them and anchor them to your words by referring to them in your text?
- *For visually rich texts:* If you are creating a text that looks something like the "Leap Productivity and Health Impact Study," (Chapter 14, pages 495–501), you will want to plan the full layout. Gather all the visual and verbal elements and "storyboard" them into a coherent whole in which all the pieces contribute to the purpose and point of your document. If you are not experienced in visual design, experiment and get feedback from others to help you understand what design choices do and do not work.

CONCLUSION

As you read examples of writing from many disciplines, we hope you will discover a richly realistic panorama of different kinds of writing. We also hope that the first two chapters of this book have prepared you to analyze the rhetorical choices of the authors you read—and to apply the lessons of the readings in your own rhetorical choices. Finally, we hope that all of this work will develop in you a more self-conscious, more self-confident reader and writer—prepared for and committed to creating change through your reading and writing.

PART TWO

ANALYZING PEOPLE AND CULTURE

This book claims that people write to create change. Part Two includes examples of analysis, which breaks complex ideas into understandable parts. And that understanding reveals and challenges people's assumptions, what people believe to be true. In the short term, it is often hard to see the real-world effects of this work—our understanding and assumptions can change slowly and subtly. In the long term, however, changing what readers assume—what they believe—will change how they think and act.

A speech printed in Chapter 3 illustrates the point. At the National Prayer Breakfast in 1998 President Bill Clinton read a speech he had written—to apologize for a sexual affair he had with White House intern Monica Lewinsky. The purpose of that speech was to convince the public that President Clinton was not wicked, heartless, or self-serving, and to convince them that he was genuinely sorry. He was trying, in other words, to change people's assumptions by admitting to his faults and noting the mitigating circumstances.

In Chapter 4 (on the role of religion in public life) Hanna Rosin's analysis argues that the "religion card" was used effectively in recent elections but that it may backfire on politicians in upcoming elections. Rosin hopes that her essay will change our understanding of and assumptions about religious rhetoric enough that we will recognize politicians' tactics and respond to them wisely.

A powerful example of change through analysis appears in Chapter 5. In *Silent Spring*, published in 1962, Rachel Carson wrote about the environment to change the American assumptions about pollution. As a result *Silent Spring* is often cited as the book that ignited the environmental movement.

The changes that result from reading about art history (Chapter 6) can be very subtle, but when we analyze other cultures through their art, we gain new knowledge that challenges our assumptions about those cultures. In that way it changes our understanding and attitudes, it opens our minds, and it makes us more likely to think, learn, and act differently.

A NOTE ON PORTABLE RHETORICAL LESSONS

In each chapter in Parts Two through Four we ask you to pay special attention to one example of a rhetorical strategy practiced in the discipline of the chapter. We believe that unique rhetorical strategies have evolved in each academic discipline. Once you learn these strategies you can use them to help you write well in a variety of settings.

Consider a few examples: As a writer you will need to analyze audiences, so you will best learn to do that from writers of speeches and marketing campaigns—experts at *audience analysis*. You will probably need to make complicated information accessible and meaningful to non-experts, so you will learn to do that from natural and social scientists—experts at *analyzing and presenting data*. You may need to compose position papers on extremely complex topics where there is no right answer, so learn to do that from biotechnologists—experts at *compromise and balanced persuasion*. Every chapter offers discussion and demonstration of that discipline's gifts of special rhetorical expertise.

The twelve portable rhetorical lessons do not, however, add up to "twelve most important lessons about writing." They are only examples; dozens more could have come to hand, and we hope you will discover—and use—dozens more on your own as you read throughout your life.

3

SPEECH COMMUNICATION: ANALYZING AUDIENCE

Each of the readings in this chapter shares a common focus—the speeches that presidents make as they try to save themselves from political catastrophe. The readings include two presidential speeches and two essays that analyze the rhetoric of presidential speeches. Giving a speech, communicating face-to-face, evokes a feeling of intimacy and immediacy. But a politician savvy enough to make it to the White House knows that altering the opinions of the audience in front of him is only a small part of the job. Most presidential speeches appear on television and the Internet. They reach many audiences—supporters, opponents, professionals who analyze speeches, and the general public. Persuading audiences as broad and varied as these is very tricky business.

Presidents use the speeches in this chapter to change public opinion. They interpret their own or their administration's actions in ways that offer their listeners a new way of interpreting facts and new reasons for believing in the speaker. President Clinton, apologizing for the Monica Lewinsky affair, tried to reverse the effects of his public denial of the affair by facing what he called the "rock-bottom truth." These tactics of re-interpreting facts and events explain why this chapter is in Part Two, in which we focus on writing that relies on analysis and interpretation, writing that creates change by changing an audience's thinking.

A Portable Rhetorical Lesson:

Writing for Audiences

To change peoples' minds, and to do so in the high-stakes situation of restoring the public faith, a speaker must carefully analyze the many audiences he hopes to persuade. Granted, speeches differ in many important ways from writing. When you give a speech, you can see at least some members of your audience, and adjust as you receive feedback from them. But these presidential speeches are similar to written texts because the speakers generally get one shot, in front of a camera, to read a text that they (usually with the help of a team of speech writers) have revised and rehearsed. In this way they rely on analyzing their audience in much the same way as someone composing a written text.

So imagine yourself in the position of one of these presidents. What do you do first? President Clinton was well-known for using focus groups (small groups of people who represent a larger population). Political insiders reported that when a persuasive theme emerged from a focus group, the Clinton administration would change its messages within hours, making use of that new theme to persuade people. If a focus group responded well to the theme "It takes a village," that is what the public would hear—until a different focus group responded well to a new theme.

You might dislike the focus-group method of doing politics; you might choose instead to say that you will simply speak the truth and not pander to the whims of public opinion. But how do you "speak the truth" to millions of people? Different areas of the country, different political factions, and different individuals will understand your words differently. How can you possibly speak "truth" to all of them when they hear a variety of truths from the same words?

Analyzing an audience and writing to their needs tests the rhetorical muscle of speech writers. That is why we hope this chapter, with its examples of presidents fitting their words to their audiences, will help you to see and begin to practice this difficult—and absolutely critical—rhetorical task.

Chapter Topics: The practice of responding to controversy is the general topic, but the political situations that give rise to high-stakes communication form the more particular topics.

To Think About. . .

In *Anne of Green Gables*, author Lucy Maude Montgomery tells the tale of Anne Shirley, a high-spirited girl who was adopted by an elderly brother and sister, Matthew and Marilla Cuthbert. Early in her stay with the Cuthberts, Anne responded in anger to a neighbor who criticized her appearance. Facing an ultimatum from Marilla that she must either apologize or return to the orphanage, Anne decided to apologize. This is what she said to the offended neighbor:

"Oh, Mrs. Lynde, I am so extremely sorry," she said with a quiver in her voice. "I could never express all my sorrow, no, not if I used up a whole dictionary. You must just imagine it. I behaved terribly to you—and I've disgraced the dear friends, Matthew and Marilla, who have let me stay at Green Gables although I'm not a boy. I'm a dreadfully wicked and ungrateful girl, and I deserve to be punished and cast out by respectable people forever. It was very wicked of me to fly into a temper because you told me the truth. It *was* the truth; every word you said was true. My hair is red and I'm freckled and skinny and ugly. What I said to you was true, too, but I shouldn't have said it. Oh, Mrs. Lynde, please, please, forgive me. If you refuse it will be a lifelong sorrow to me. You wouldn't like to inflict a lifelong sorrow on a poor little orphan girl would you, even if she had a dreadful temper? Oh, I am sure you wouldn't. Please say you forgive me, Mrs. Lynde."

Afterward, Anne reflected on her speech: "'I apologized pretty well, didn't I?' she said proudly as they went down the lane. 'I thought since I had to do it I might as well do it thoroughly.'"
Read the apology again.

- Anne has two audiences for this speech: Mrs. Lynde and Marilla Cuthbert. Which parts of the apology does Anne direct to Mrs. Lynde? Which parts does she direct to Marilla?
- Not everything in this speech expresses regret (presumably the function of an apology). List the parts of the apology that do something else. Speculate about the function of these parts to the success of the overall apology. What do these parts accomplish?

WRITING IN SPEECH COMMUNICATION

Introduction by Kathi Groenendyk, Professor of Rhetoric

Scholars studying communication and rhetoric examine a range of communication texts—presidential speeches, popular television shows, newspapers, and propaganda posters, to name a few. What's in common? Communication scholars try to understand how the person creating the message (the rhetor) communicates certain meanings to an audience in a particular situation. Some of the most interesting studies examine the multiple audiences a rhetor may face.

In 1998, the evening news often looked like a soap opera. Did he have an affair with a younger woman? How could he cheat on his wife? Who knew about this affair? Were his enemies trying to blackmail him?

The main character in this melodrama was President William Jefferson Clinton, described as the "Comeback Kid" after earlier allegations of adultery failed to diminish his political success. But Clinton's sexual relationship with White House intern Monica Lewinsky ignited a political storm of special councils, investigations, and impeachment hearings. In January, 1998, Clinton publicly denied having an affair with Lewinsky, saying on television, "I did not have sexual relations with that woman, Miss Lewinsky."

Yet in August, Clinton admitted to the affair and apologized for both the affair and his earlier misstatements. Presidential critics and the public, however, were unmoved. A string of apologies followed, culminating in Clinton's speech at the Prayer Breakfast in September. Although many in the media praised the speech, many critics and members of the public continued to question Clinton's sincerity and morality. The following December, the House of Representatives voted to impeach President Clinton on charges of perjury and obstruction of justice. The Senate failed to vote for impeachment, however.

Clinton faced a significant challenge: to whom was he speaking? What did they believe about him? What moral and political perspectives influenced those beliefs? Clinton's first audience was the clergy present at the Prayer Breakfast, many of whom regularly attended that White House function. These ministers likely wanted sincere moral reflection, perhaps an acknowledgement of his sin, and a plea for forgiveness—a reflection of his professed religious faith. Yet Clinton's speech was reprinted and replayed in the national and international media, broadening his audience significantly. How could he make generalizations about what this large audience knew and believed? Critics of Clinton's administration, primarily Republicans, wanted an apology and an acknowledgement that Clinton had tarnished the presidential office—a statement Clinton refused to make. Supporters of Clinton, however, wished Clinton to remain strong, to concede nothing to his opponents. Many foreign observers, especially in Europe, were not at all troubled by Clinton's affair. Clinton's situation and the response to it serves as a helpful example of how to assess audience and situation, usually the topic of one of the first classes a speech major takes. Adapting messages to different audiences and situations is central to their studies and careers.

Certain themes or strategies are often common in certain types, or genres, of communication. For example, an after-dinner speech given at a high-school sports award banquet will resemble the qualities of an after-dinner speech given at a local ladies' literary club; the genre is chosen to suit the audience and situation. We can better evaluate presidential addresses, then, if we examine the requirements of particular kinds of speech genres. Analyzing a speech by its genre helps a researcher notice the most important elements of a particular type of speech.

In the situation that President Clinton faced, he had two avenues of self-defense open to him: forensic defense (which focuses on Constitutional law) or personal apologia (which focuses on the character of the person defending himself). He chose a personal apologia for his Prayer Breakfast speech.

By analyzing the means of persuasion available to other speech writers, readers can learn how to improve their own speeches. Genre criticism prompts the reader and future speaker to ask, "What does an audience usually hear in this situation? What does the audience expect to hear? How can I best respond to this situation? What has worked well or poorly in similar situations?"

Communication scholars, then, enable us to be better communicators with the variety of audiences we may face and be better critics of the speeches we encounter.

✓ READING TIPS

Read President Clinton's address as you would listen to a speech—straight through, at a normal speaking pace. Pay attention to the main ideas and language choices. Try to imagine how President Clinton would have delivered the speech: where would he pause, when would his voice get softer or stronger? Track your emotions and thoughts as you read: when is the speech more or less persuasive?

Speech to the Annual White House Prayer Breakfast, September 11, 1998

President Bill Clinton

Clinton begins his speech by identifying with the audience directly before him. He's seems less a host and more a participant.

Clinton describes his uncertainty, violating a basic rule in speech communication classes. In this case, however, Clinton's uncertainty attests to the sincerity of his words.

With this gesture Clinton indicates this speech is his own composition.

Clinton reaches out to another of his audiences—his critics— by acknowledging the failure of his earlier apologies.

Clinton uses the language of the clergy in his audience, building his credibility with them.

Clinton inserts some forensic self-defense in this personal apologia.

Thank you very much, ladies and gentlemen. Welcome to the White House and to this day to which Hillary and the Vice President and I look forward so much every year.

This is always an important day for our country, for the reasons that the Vice President said. It is an unusual and, I think, unusually important day today. I may not be quite as easy with my words today as I have been in years past, and I was up rather late last night thinking about and praying about what I ought to say today. And rather unusually for me, I actually tried to write it down. So if you will forgive me, I will do my best to say what it is I want to say to you, and I may have to take my glasses out to read my own writing. [Clinton puts on bifocals and pulls out hand-written notes.]

First, I want to say to all of you that, as you might imagine, I have been on quite a journey these last few weeks to get to the end of this, to the rock-bottom truth of where I am and where we all are.

I agree with those who have said that in my first statement after I testified I was not contrite enough. I don't think there is a fancy way to say that I have sinned.

It is important to me that everybody who has been hurt know that the sorrow I feel is genuine: first and most important, my family; also my friends, my staff, my Cabinet, Monica Lewinsky and her family, and the American people. I have asked all for their forgiveness.

But I believe that to be forgiven, more than sorrow is required—at least two more things: first, genuine repentance, a determination to change and to repair breaches of my own making. I have repented. Second, what my Bible calls a "broken spirit"; an understanding that I must have God's help to be the person that I want to be, a willingness to give the very forgiveness I seek, a renunciation of the pride and the anger which cloud judgment, lead people to excuse and compare and to blame and complain.

Now, what does all this mean for me and for us? First, I will instruct my lawyers to mount a vigorous defense, using all available appropriate arguments. But legal language must not obscure the fact that I have done wrong.

Second, I will continue on the path of repentance, seeking pastoral support and that of other caring people so that they can hold me accountable for my own commitment.

Third, I will intensify my efforts to lead our country and the world toward peace and freedom, prosperity and harmony, in the hope that with a broken spirit and a still strong heart I can be used for greater good, for we have many blessings and many challenges and so much work to do.

In this, I ask for your prayers and for your help in healing our Nation. And though I cannot move beyond or forget this— indeed, I must always keep it as a caution light in my life—it is very important that our Nation move forward.

I am very grateful for the many, many people, clergy and ordinary citizens alike, who have written me with wise counsel. I am profoundly grateful for the support of so many Americans who somehow, through it all, seem to still know that I care about them a great deal, that I care about their problems and their dreams. I am grateful for those who have stood by me and who say that in this case and many others, the bounds of privacy have been excessively and unwisely invaded. That may be. Nevertheless, in this case, it may be a blessing, because I still sinned. And if my repentance is genuine and sustained, and if I can maintain both a broken spirit and a strong heart, then good can come of this for our country as well as for me and my family.

> Clinton shows humility, which would appeal to the clergy gathered at the White House and to the general American public, too.

The children of this country can learn in a profound way that integrity is important and selfishness is wrong, but God can change us and make us strong at the broken places. I want to embody those lessons for the children of this country—for that little boy in Florida who came up to me and said that he wanted to grow up and be President and to be just like me. I want the parents of all the children in America to be able to say that to their children.

> Clinton indicates that his actions have not irreparably compromised the honor or authority of the president's office.

A couple of days ago when I was in Florida a Jewish friend of mine gave me this liturgy book called *Gates of Repentance*. And there was this incredible passage from the Yom Kippur liturgy. I would like to read it to you:

> By citing a Jewish text, Clinton appeals to the Jewish clergy members in his audience.

Now is the time for turning. The leaves are beginning to turn from green to red to orange. The birds are beginning to turn and are heading once more toward the south. The animals are beginning to turn to storing their food for the winter. For leaves, birds, and animals, turning comes instinctively. But for us, turning does not come so easily. It takes an act of will for us to make a turn. It means breaking old habits. It means admitting that we have been wrong, and this is never easy. It means losing face. It means starting all over again. And this is always painful. It means saying I am sorry. It means recognizing that we have the ability to change. These things are terribly hard to do. But unless we turn, we will be trapped forever in yesterday's ways. Lord help us to turn, from callousness to sensitivity, from hostility to love, from pettiness to purpose, from envy to contentment, from carelessness to discipline, from fear to faith. Turn us around, O Lord, and bring us back toward you. Revive our lives as at the beginning, and turn us toward each other, Lord, for in isolation there is no life.

> By joining his friend and his audience in his thanks, Clinton encourages his audience to think of him as a friend—someone who can be forgiven.

I thank my friend for that. I thank you for being here. I ask you to share my prayer that God will search me and know my heart, try me and know my anxious thoughts, see if there is any hurtfulness in me, and lead me toward the life everlasting. I ask that God give me a clean heart, let me walk by faith and not sight.

> Clinton invokes the words of a religious benediction to end his speech. Since the situation is a prayer breakfast and the audience clergy members, such a conclusion seems fitting. Once again, he adopts a humble stance—asking for forgiveness from his audience.

I ask once again to be able to love my neighbor—all my neighbors—as myself, to be an instrument of God's peace; to let the words of my mouth and the meditations of my heart and, in the end, the work of my hands, be pleasing.

This is what I wanted to say to you today.

Thank you. God bless you.

READING RESPONSES

1. President Clinton begins his speech by recognizing the immediate audience for his comments—those who have been invited to the White House Prayer Breakfast. A few paragraphs later, he lists "everybody who has been hurt" as audiences for this apology. To whom is Clinton referring? Why do you believe so? Imagining (or remembering) yourself at the time the speech was given, do you find yourself persuaded? Inclined to forgive?

2. Write out a definition of "apology," including all the features that an apology must have. Does President Clinton's speech fit your definition of an apology? What features of an apology does it contain? What features are missing?

3. Toward the end of his speech, President Clinton quotes from a Yom Kippur liturgy that uses first-person-plural pronouns—"we," "us," "our." Who does Clinton include with these pronouns? What is his message to those who he has included in his apology?

NOTES ON GRAMMAR, STYLE, AND RHETORIC: SENTENCE SUBJECTS

In "Rhetoric to Forestall Impeachment," (reprinted at the end of this chapter) Karlyn Kohrs Campbell and Kathleen Hall Jamieson write that personal apologias "shift the focus from the attacker(s) to the defender and present the character of the accused in ways that are appealing to the audience" (page 55). In his address, Clinton works hard to focus on himself and to present himself in a favorable light. And he accomplishes much of this work by using particular kinds of sentence subjects.

Most traditional definitions of the subject of a sentence describe it as what the sentence is about. But subjects can also be described in terms of the roles that the person or thing named by the subject usually play. The subject usually names who or what acts, experiences something, is described, is identified further, or is acted upon.

Examining the sentence subjects in a speech or written text can reveal much about what the speaker or writer is most serious about focusing on and even about how he or she organizes the presentation. What is most striking is how President Clinton uses subjects to focus attention on himself. Not including the introductory and concluding *thank you's*, there are 70 independent clauses in the speech. Of these, 27 have the personal pronoun *I* as the grammatical subject. In almost 40 percent of the independent clauses, then, Clinton focuses solely on himself. Adding the dependent clauses in the speech (such as "because I still sinned"), we find 22 more clauses with *I* as the subject. President Clinton is not the only entity focused on in the subjects of this speech, but he is clearly the dominant focal point.

Clinton also uses sentence subjects to present himself and his case in a favorable light, and he does so in several interesting ways. First, when he is not using subjects to focus on himself, he often uses them to focus on entities or ideas that his hearers almost certainly would view with favor. For example, consider the quoted liturgy that he received from a friend. This liturgy deals with the theme of change. First it describes turnings in the natural world (for example, the turning of leaves from green to orange). Then it takes up the matter of turnings in human beings. When it does so, the liturgy is concerned with, among other things, "breaking old habits," admitting wrong, "losing face," and "starting all over again." These concepts would cast Clinton in a favorable light, especially at a breakfast for members of the clergy. Probably sensing this, for a significant portion of the speech Clinton keeps the focus on these concepts by means of sentence subjects. In 8 sentences out of 12 consecutive ones, he uses as the subject either the word *turning* or the pronoun *it* as a substitute for *turning*. And the subject of one other of these 12 sentences is the closely related "for us to make a turn." Thus, it would probably be nearly impossible to hear this speech and not associate President Clinton with some admirable "turning."

A second way in which Clinton uses sentence subjects to present himself in a favorable light appears in the following sentence near the beginning of the speech: "It is important to me that everybody who has been hurt know that the sorrow I feel is genuine—first and most important, my family, also my friends, my staff, my Cabinet, Monica Lewinsky and her family, and the American people."

What is the subject of this rather long sentence? You might be inclined to say that the subject is *It*, but that would be incorrect. Used in this way, the word *it* is an expletive, a word that holds the place ordinarily occupied by the subject. The actual complete subject begins with "that everybody" and includes everything after it up to the period.

If Clinton had expressed all this material before "is important to me," the sentence would have moved from a very long subject to a relatively short predicate, usually an awkward order in English. In choosing a short-to-long order, he produces a more smoothly flowing sentence. And his long sentence subject allows him to keep his hearers focusing on two important agenda items—stressing that he is truly sorry for his sin, and naming all those to whom he is apologizing. It is a very long sentence subject, but it is meant to do a great deal of work.

Finally, we should look at some constructions that appear here as sentence fragments but that one might expect to see serving as sentence subjects. Just after the sentence quoted immediately above, Clinton goes on to say that "to be forgiven, more than sorrow is required." He adds that at least two other things are needed. After mentioning the first of these, genuine repentance, he stresses that he has repented. Then, as he comes to the second thing needed for forgiveness, he starts to punctuate noun phrases as sentences: "Second, what my Bible calls a broken spirit. An understanding that I must have God's help to be the person that I want to be. A willingness to give the very forgiveness I seek."

Hearers could well have expected each of these phrases to serve as the subject of a sentence moving into a predicate like *is required to be forgiven*. But Clinton omits any possible predicate. In this context, doing so has two effects. First, it presents the ideas in these phrases as beyond debate. Readers and hearers do not tend to argue with listed possible subjects. If you were to come up to someone and say, "A broken spirit," that person would be likely to ask you, "What about it?" However, readers and hearers react differently to a statement produced by combining a subject and a predicate. A statement is something that can be debated. If you were to come up to someone and say, "A broken spirit is necessary to be forgiven," that person might disagree and argue with your claim. By not connecting some phrases to a predicate, Clinton works to move his hearers to accept his view of forgiveness without debate.

But secondly and similarly, he never explicitly states that he himself has a broken spirit, understands that he needs God's help, or that he is willing to extend forgiveness to others. His listing of these possible subjects implies all that.

In Your Own Writing . . .

- Decide what you want your audience to focus on and put that in the subject position of your sentences.
- Choose your verbs with care so that they shape the reader's attitude toward what you've chosen for the subject of your sentences.
- Consider if a listing of subjects can help you present information without sparking opposition from the reader.

STUDENT WRITING IN SPEECH COMMUNICATION

Introduction by Laura McGiness, communication arts and sciences major

The Assignment. In a class called "American Voices," we devoted the entire semester to studying and discussing speeches throughout American history. The final assignment asked us to critically interpret an American rhetorical text by using analytical tools we had learned in class. We had to identify a significant issue or set of issues related to the text's rhetoric that we would like to explore, develop a central claim for our papers about these issues, and support our theses with a logical and clear argument. We could focus on a variety of issues, such as these: What is the meaning of the text, and how is it revealed? How does the structure of the text relate to its message? What narratives or myths are developed in the speech, and how do they relate to cultural ideals?

The Content. Since understanding the audience is an integral part of effective public speaking, my analysis focused on strategies that President Bill Clinton used to reach a diverse audience in his public address at the Presidential Prayer Breakfast in September of 1998. Particularly, I explored how Clinton fit the content of his speech within the genre of a personal apologia and how this allowed him to present a likeable persona that could appeal to both his immediate audience of clergymen and his broader audience of the American public. I also wrote about the way that the historical context and audience's values affected Clinton's potential for rhetorical success in this speech.

Learning to Write in Speech Communication. Oratory is only considered effective communication when the speaker, audience, and text interact; therefore, communications students must also appreciate these important relationships. Speakers must suit both the content and style of the speech with their audience in mind in order to successfully communicate. They must speak about a pertinent topic that the audience can understand and deliver the speech in such a way that makes the audience willing to listen. Likewise, if the content and style of the speech are appropriate but speakers damage their credibility (either before or during the speech), they are not likely to persuade the audience.

Therefore, good public speakers intentionally choose various rhetorical strategies to persuade their audiences, and writers in the communications discipline must be able to identify these strategies. But analyzing oratory goes beyond simple identification. When I analyzed Clinton's speech, I had to explain how and why his rhetorical strategies either worked or didn't work; I also had to speculate about why Clinton may have chosen particular strategies in his speech. I considered a variety of issues related to my speech text before deciding on my central claim. I asked myself some questions: What is the purpose of the speech and how is that revealed? What is the structure of the text and how does that relate to its message? How does the speaker relate to his audience? I then had to decide which topics would most effectively support my main point and how I could best explain these ideas in my paper. After that analysis, I was able to develop a clear central claim and support that thesis with logical evidence.

Creating Change through Writing in Communication Studies. The essence of rhetoric is persuasion, and when we persuade effectively, we affect how an audience thinks and acts. Clinton tried to persuade his audience through his speech, and I tried to persuade my audience to accept my thesis and logical analysis. Clearly what was at stake for me was much less dramatic than for President Clinton. However, I also faced ethical complications: I thought Clinton did a good job with this speech, but I personally opposed his moral decisions regarding the scandal. Recognizing that I would have to defend the content of my paper, I wanted to analyze his speech as fairly as possible without compromising my personal beliefs. Persuasion involves more than our ability to create a convincing argument. Since it has the potential to influence many people, we must be sure that we use rhetoric to argue for justifiable topics. Of course we write speeches to persuade, to change, but that does not mean that we can use rhetoric irresponsibly.

Apologizing to Friends, Enemies, and Everyone In Between: Analyzing Clinton's Rhetoric

Laura McGiness

I intentionally began with an anecdote that my readers could relate to, but I tried to present it in such a way that focused readers on the nature of an audience.

We all get plenty of practice apologizing for our mistakes. And the more we apologize, the more we appreciate how our audience influences the way we ask for forgiveness. For instance, an apology for being late would sound different if I were speaking to my boss as opposed to one of my friends. When we know what our audience expects to hear, we can adjust our apology accordingly. However, apologizing to a group of people rather than an individual suddenly makes the task much more challenging. When President Bill Clinton spoke at the Presidential Prayer Breakfast in September of 1998, at the height of the Monica Lewinsky sex scandal, he faced the daunting task of crafting an apology that would be appropriate and meaningful to multiple audiences: the clergymen in attendance at the prayer breakfast, who heard it live, and the American public, who would hear it broadcasted later. In an attempt to influence his immediate and wide-ranging audiences, Clinton suited both his content and style to the genre of a personal apologia, which offered him the greatest potential for rhetorical success.

The thesis must focus on one or several specific aspects of the speech. I decided to explore the genre of a personal apologia because I believe it enabled Clinton to meet certain rhetorical goals that he otherwise would not have been able to accomplish.

In this "Prayer Breakfast Speech" Clinton appears to have learned from his previous failed apology only a few weeks earlier in August of 1998. That nationally-televised speech, nicknamed the "Map Room Speech," took the form of forensic self-defense, which argues that (1) the president had kept the oath of office, (2) the accusers had undermined the Constitution, and (3) the president is responsible to the people and the Constitution, not to the Congressional accusers. As a forensic self-defense, his August apology sounded insincere. Many Americans found the formal language and distant style inconsistent with the highly personal nature of his situation. Moreover, the fact that Clinton spoke into a television camera rather than directly addressing a live audience contributed to the impersonal tone of this speech. His decision to begin a speech about such a delicate moral decision with information about his grand jury indictment seemed devoid of true emotion. He focused a large part of his content on legal issues related to the investigation, which further degraded the personal manner of this speech. Clinton ended by actually

The element of surprise, whether or not it helps a speaker, always gains audience attention. Therefore, it is worth exploring how this surprising element of Clinton's speech ultimately worked against him in this situation.

rebuking his audience, a tactic that many Americans would not have expected. In fact, Clinton even portrayed himself as the victim of ruthless privacy invasion, a rhetorical move that did not help him establish a desirable ethos throughout the speech. By the end of the speech, Clinton seemed to be saying that his audience should apologize to him, an understandably awkward situation considering the fact that this speech was supposed to be Clinton's apology to them. Self-defense, at this point, was futile. His supporters did not need to hear an apology because they already approved of his leadership despite his moral weaknesses. His enemies used the speech to further accuse Clinton of placing blame on external factors outside his control rather than taking personal responsibility for the situation. The nature of his speech as a self-defense rather than an apology likely left many moderate Americans still wondering about the authenticity of Clinton's remorse. His personal apologia at the Prayer Breakfast, on the other hand, provided him with the tools necessary to develop a persona that proved more rhetorically effective for his diverse audiences.

Since we know that Clinton was trying to appeal to a very broad audience, it helps to examine particular parts of that audience. Knowing how specific groups of Americans might have reacted to this speech furthers our understanding of the speech's purpose and overall effect.

Campbell and Jamieson point out the various factors that comprise a personal apologia: (1) a shift in focus from the accuser to the defender, (2) a favorable presentation of the defender's personal character, (3) a personal tone, (4) an argument that the actions do not merit impeachment, and (5) an argument that the actions do not call executive leadership into question. Given that Clinton delivered this speech at a prayer breakfast, his decision to share a personal apologia was an appropriate strategy. The apology's personal nature and emphasis allow Clinton to display a greater degree of sincerity and humility, values that the clergymen in his audience would have anticipated and appreciated. These qualities also enable Clinton to discuss his personal journey of repentance—again, another ideal highly esteemed among his audience members. Furthermore, the very fact that a live audience is listening to his address strengthens the personal nature of his speech. The personal apologia also proves effective for Clinton's broader audience of the American people. Clinton often referred to religious themes in his speech, a tactic that could have alienated some members of his more broad audience. However, once again, the personal nature of the apology, and the humble persona that it allowed Clinton to embody, enabled his message to resonate with many Americans. Most people appreciate a humble and repentant spirit in a sincere apology.

Here I refer directly to a text we read in class so that my professor can see that I am fulfilling the requirement to analyze a speech using the knowledge I gained in the class.

Contrasting the defiant nature of his Map Room Speech, Clinton focuses attention away from his accusers and instead directs it toward himself: "First, I want to say to all of you that, as you might imagine, I have been on quite a journey these last few weeks." When he does address his enemies, he approaches their accusations in a gracious and humble manner by paradoxically noting that the invasion of his privacy, although a painful experience, may ultimately produce a stronger man and country. Therefore, instead of attacking his opponents, he smartly uses their accusations to further strengthen his personal appeal. He employs a classic and effective rhetorical strategy by establishing common ground with and goodwill towards his critics: he mentions near the beginning that he agrees with their criticisms of his past apologies. Furthermore, he fashions various aspects of his content in such a way that could particularly resonate with his immediate audience. When he states, ". . . hope that with a broken spirit and a still strong heart I can be used for greater good," he suggests the principles of grace and mercy. The clergymen in attendance would have predominantly valued these ideals and appreciated Clinton's intention to use the lessons learned through this ordeal for "greater good" in the future.

Since Clinton's moral failures had resulted in legal action against him, he naturally needed to address this issue in his speech. However, his previous speech met with disastrous results when he focused too heavily on this particular aspect. In his Prayer Breakfast speech, however, Clinton wisely establishes the point that his actions did not merit impeachment, "I will instruct my lawyers to mount a vigorous defense, using all available appropriate arguments," and then he quickly moves on to the spiritual implications of his actions. Obviously, his immediate audience would find this emphasis appropriate, and it also helps further establish his ethos among his audience of the American public. Additionally, Clinton suggests that his mistakes have not permanently damaged his leadership abilities by noting his continuing goals for leading America ("I will intensify my efforts to lead our country and the world toward peace and freedom"). He builds on this idea with a touching story about the little Florida boy. By mentioning that children can still look up to him as a role model, not necessarily because of his moral actions but because of his repentance and ability to learn from mistakes, Clinton effectively points out, albeit indirectly, that he is still a legitimate leader. Granted, some members of his audience would disagree with this point; nevertheless, Clinton includes this argument to strengthen his credibility among audience members who are willing to support his leadership.

> With background established, here's where I begin my analysis of the speech.

> This is an example of when I speculate about why Clinton crafted his speech as he did.

> Clinton indirectly suggests rather than explicitly states his legal innocence. Depending on how one views Clinton's personal character and intentions, it could either help or hinder his credibility at this point in the speech.

> It is very important that Clinton makes this distinction about his position as a role model, considering that his immediate audience valued moral uprightness. If he had simply said that children should grow up to be like him, without distinguishing which aspects of his character were worth imitating, his audience could have been offended by the suggestion that their children should grow up to make impure moral choices.

Since a personal apologia, by its very nature, must be sincere, Clinton's stylistic choices prove equally as important as his content. Mending broken trust is a nearly impossible task. We often find it difficult to forgive others based solely on their words. While the apology may sound good, how can we be sure that this individual isn't still lying to us? Therefore, however convincing the content of Clinton's personal apologia, it would have been a complete loss without a convincing presentation of the content. In other words, Clinton's language delivery was necessary to the effectiveness of his message. His style both reiterated and enabled his content. Primarily, his decision to write the speech himself signified the profound personal nature of this speech. His continual use of the personal pronoun *I* emphasizes this point. Clinton's admission of uncertainty regarding his personal message, while violating a basic guideline of public speaking, works in this situation to further demonstrate the authenticity of his apology and develop his humble persona.

Sensitive to his immediate audience, Clinton often speaks in religious terms. Toward the beginning of his address, he invokes clerical vocabulary by using phrases such as "repentance," "a broken spirit," and "forgiveness." All of these phrases helped him build his credibility with his immediate audience. Acknowledging the fact that repentance takes time, Clinton asks for prayer in helping him and the country move forward; naturally, the religious leaders in his audience would have appreciated his request for God's help in healing the emotional scars of this experience. Clinton further reaches out to his immediate audience by quoting a passage from the Yom Kippur liturgy, appealing to the Jewish members of his audience. Finally, Clinton ends his speech by combining phrases from the Prayer of Saint Francis and the Bible, leaving his religiously-minded immediate audience with spiritual themes.

On a more general level, the speech's simple and direct style helps Clinton's overall message. Whereas a more formal and polished speaking style normally befits a president, the highly personal nature of this speech demanded that Clinton present himself in the most genuine way possible. Therefore, he strategically avoids using complicated words or phrases and instead delivers his speech in a way that emphasizes his humanity—it sounds like a heartfelt apology. He accentuates this point early on by admitting that he might not deliver this speech with his normal charisma because he had struggled to find the right words to share.

Rhetoric never occurs in a vacuum; the historical, social, and political context in which a speech is delivered always affects the speech itself and the audience's response in some way. This speech is a somewhat extreme example of the context's effect upon an audience.

At this point, an important rhetorical situation appears. Although the speech itself displays many rhetorical strengths, the context in which Clinton delivered it also proves

As Clinton spoke to multiple audiences, I wrote this paper for multiple audiences: my professor and students who would read this textbook. Knowing that some students may read this paper with little to no understanding of communication theory, I explained this idea in a more detailed manner than I may have if I was only writing for my professor.

Since we can't get inside the head of each audience member, it is ultimately impossible to finally assess the overall "effectiveness" of the speech, because individuals interpreted its message differently. Therefore, the concluding paragraph provides me with a place to merely speculate why Clinton chose certain rhetorical strategies and how those choices most likely affected his audience members.

fundamentally significant. His humility and remorse appear genuine in this speech, which strengthens his credibility with the audience; however, one cannot forget that he had already severely damaged his credibility before the speech took place. By the time he delivered this address, his audience had been following this sad saga for nearly nine months and had likely already judged his behavior and personal character. Naturally, some members of both audiences were hesitant to forgive Clinton or were downright opposed to accepting his apology from the onset. No matter how effectively he presented his personal character in this speech, his audience's diversity made it nearly impossible for him to completely repair his reputation and trustworthiness in a single rhetorical act. This demonstrates the important rhetorical phenomenon of the audience: speakers do not simply act upon passive audience members nor persuade by injecting them with information or arguments. Audience members use their own perceptions and beliefs to critically interpret all speeches within their contexts. Clinton's personal apologia is an extreme example of the context retaining just as much rhetorical influence as the speech itself.

Given the context, the speech itself contained appropriate content and a meaningful delivery style that allowed Clinton to develop the most appealing persona possible. Though we cannot measure the overall effect of this speech, his intentional rhetorical choices strengthened the impact of his personal apologia. Where this speech lacked the formality and finesse of typical presidential addresses, it contained vulnerable and humble pleas for forgiveness. In so doing, Clinton made the most of a challenging rhetorical situation.

Work Cited

Campbell, Karlyn Kohrs and Kathleen Hall Jamieson. *Deeds Done in Words: Presidential Rhetoric and the Genres of Governance.* Chicago: The University of Chicago Press, 1994. 127–43.

READING RESPONSES

1. Which two parts of McGiness's analysis do you find most persuasive? For each part, list the features that McGiness uses to persuade you.
2. In her introduction, McGiness describes how her own feelings about Clinton's actions shaped her analysis of his speech and her claim about that

speech. Note places in her essay that seem affected by McGiness's feelings. For each place, describe how you see her feelings shaping the essay.

3. When she presents her analysis of Clinton's speech, McGiness focuses first on the content of the speech and then on the style. Analyze the style of McGiness's essay, paying special attention to her word choice, her sentence structures, and her sentence subjects. What changes would you recommend if she were delivering the paper as an oral presentation?

PUBLIC WRITING IN COMMUNICATION STUDIES

Introduction

Place yourself in President Bush's position soon after Hurricane Katrina devastated New Orleans and other parts of the Gulf Coast: a growing number of citizens angrily accuse the administration of incompetence in providing relief to the disaster area and injustice towards New Orleans' poor black population. The number of critical voices grows. President Bush and his administration decide that he must speak to the nation, but should he apologize for the poor disaster preparation and relief? How does a speaker face a skeptical—maybe even hostile—audience?

In this speech, President Bush tries to gain the audience's trust, acknowledging the victims' desperation ("grieving for the dead, and looking for meaning in a tragedy that seems so blind and random") and their bravery ("a powerful American determination to clear the ruins and build better than before"). He also appeals to a "united country," which both names his ideal audience and challenges his audience to become united. In his seventh paragraph, Bush also lists the recovery that has happened (electric power and river shipments restored, levee breaks repaired, among others), and then outlines his plan for further action.

Bush does not acknowledge responsibility for the poor response until much later in the speech, yet he does not apologize. He states, "I, as President, am responsible for the problem, and for the solution." He does not let the audience doubt his position of authority, nor does he cast himself as weak. But he does not apologize until he has fully described the action that federal agencies are currently planning, and then only implicitly.

Did President Bush make the right choices when he addressed an upset nation? The day after his speech, the *New York Times* reported that evacuees, Governor Kathleen Babineaux Blanco (Democrat), and Senator Mary L. Landrieu (Democrat) responded positively, with Landrieu claiming that the ideas were "innovative and bold." As time passes, historians and other critics will question further Bush's ability to reframe his work after this natural disaster.

Post-Katrina Speech from Jackson Square, New Orleans, September 15, 2005
President George W. Bush

Good evening. I'm speaking to you from the city of New Orleans—nearly empty, still partly under water, and waiting for life and hope to return. Eastward from Lake Pontchartrain, across the Mississippi coast, to Alabama into Florida, millions of lives were changed in a day by a cruel and wasteful storm.

In the aftermath, we have seen fellow citizens left stunned and uprooted, searching for loved ones, and grieving for the dead, and looking for meaning in a tragedy that seems so blind and random. We've also witnessed the kind of desperation no citizen of this great and generous nation should ever have to know—fellow Americans calling out for food and water, vulnerable people left at the mercy of criminals who had no mercy, and the bodies of the dead lying uncovered and untended in the street.

These days of sorrow and outrage have also been marked by acts of courage and kindness that make all Americans proud. Coast Guard and other personnel rescued tens of thousands of people from flooded neighborhoods. Religious congregations and families have welcomed strangers as brothers and sisters and neighbors. In the community of Chalmette, when two men tried to break into a home, the owner invited them to stay—and took in 15 other people who had no place to go. At Tulane Hospital for Children, doctors and nurses did not eat for days so patients could have food, and eventually carried the patients on their backs up eight flights of stairs to helicopters.

Many first responders were victims themselves, wounded healers, with a sense of duty greater than their own suffering. When I met Steve Scott of the Biloxi Fire Department, he and his colleagues were conducting a house-to-house search for survivors. Steve told me this: "I lost my house and I lost my cars, but I still got my family . . . and I still got my spirit."

Across the Gulf Coast, among people who have lost much, and suffered much, and given to the limit of their power, we are seeing that same spirit—a core of strength that survives all hurt, a faith in God no storm can take away, and a powerful American determination to clear the ruins and build better than before.

Tonight so many victims of the hurricane and the flood are far from home and friends and familiar things. You need to know that our whole nation cares about you, and in the journey ahead you're not alone. To all who carry a burden of loss, I extend the deepest sympathy of our country. To every person who has served and sacrificed in this emergency, I offer the gratitude of our country. And tonight I also offer this pledge of the American people: Throughout the area hit by the hurricane, we will do what it takes, we will stay as long as it takes, to help citizens rebuild their communities and their lives. And all who question the future of the Crescent City need to know there is no way to imagine America without New Orleans, and this great city will rise again.

The work of rescue is largely finished; the work of recovery is moving forward. In nearly all of Mississippi, electric power has been restored. Trade is starting to return to the Port of New Orleans, and agricultural shipments are moving down the Mississippi River. All major gasoline pipelines are now in operation, preventing the supply disruptions that many feared. The breaks in the levees have been closed, the pumps are running, and the water here in New Orleans is receding by the hour. Environmental officials are on the ground, taking water samples, identifying and dealing with hazardous debris, and working to get drinking water and waste water treatment systems operating again. And some very sad duties are being carried out by professionals who gather the dead, treat them with respect, and prepare them for their rest.

In the task of recovery and rebuilding, some of the hardest work is still ahead, and it will require the creative skill and generosity of a united country.

Our first commitment is to meet the immediate needs of those who had to flee their homes and leave all their possessions behind. For these Americans, every night brings uncertainty, every day requires new courage, and in the months to come will bring more than their fair share of struggles.

The Department of Homeland Security is registering evacuees who are now in shelters and churches, or private homes, whether in the Gulf region or far away. I have signed an order providing immediate assistance to people from the disaster area. As of today, more than 500,000 evacuee families have gotten emergency help to pay for food, clothing, and other essentials. Evacuees who have not yet registered should contact FEMA or the Red Cross. We need to know who you are, because many of you will be eligible for broader assistance in the future. Many families were separated during the evacuation, and we are working to help you reunite. Please call this number: 1–877–568–3317—that's 1–877–568–3317—and we will work to bring your family back together, and pay for your travel to reach them.

In addition, we're taking steps to ensure that evacuees do not have to travel great distances or navigate bureaucracies to get the benefits that are there for them. The Department of Health and Human Services has sent more than 1,500 health professionals, along with over 50 tons of medical supplies—including vaccines and antibiotics and medicines for people with chronic conditions such as diabetes. The Social Security Administration is delivering checks. The Department of Labor is helping displaced persons apply for temporary jobs and unemployment benefits. And the Postal Service is registering new addresses so that people can get their mail.

To carry out the first stages of the relief effort and begin rebuilding at once, I have asked for, and the Congress has provided, more than $60 billion. This is an unprecedented response to an unprecedented crisis, which demonstrates the compassion and resolve of our nation.

Our second commitment is to help the citizens of the Gulf Coast to overcome this disaster, put their lives back together, and rebuild their communities. Along this coast, for mile after mile, the wind and water swept the land clean. In Mississippi, many thousands of houses were damaged or destroyed. In New Orleans and surrounding parishes, more than a quarter-million houses are no longer safe to live in. Hundreds of thousands of people from across this region will need to find longer-term housing.

Our goal is to get people out of the shelters by the middle of October. So we're providing direct assistance to evacuees that allows them to rent apartments, and many already are moving into places of their own. A number of states have taken in evacuees and shown them great compassion—admitting children to school, and providing health care. So I will work with the Congress to ensure that states are reimbursed for these extra expenses.

In the disaster area, and in cities that have received huge numbers of displaced people, we're beginning to bring in mobile homes and trailers for temporary use. To relieve the burden on local health care facilities in the region, we're sending extra doctors and nurses to these areas. We're also providing money that can be used to cover overtime pay for police and fire departments while the cities and towns rebuild.

Near New Orleans, and Biloxi, and other cities, housing is urgently needed for police and firefighters, other service providers, and the many workers who are going to rebuild these cities. Right now, many are sleeping on ships we have brought to the Port of New Orleans—and more ships are on their way to the region. And we'll provide mobile homes, and supply them with basic services, as close to construction areas as possible, so the rebuilding process can go forward as quickly as possible.

And the federal government will undertake a close partnership with the states of Louisiana and Mississippi, the city of New Orleans, and other Gulf Coast cities, so they can rebuild in a sensible, well-planned way. Federal funds will cover the great majority of the costs of repairing public infrastructure in the disaster zone, from roads and bridges to schools and water systems. Our goal is to get the work done quickly. And taxpayers expect this work to be done honestly and wisely—so we'll have a team of inspectors general reviewing all expenditures.

In the rebuilding process, there will be many important decisions and many details to resolve, yet we're moving forward according to some clear principles. The federal government will be fully engaged in the mission, but Governor Barbour, Governor Blanco, Mayor Nagin, and other state and local leaders will have the primary role in planning for their own future. Clearly, communities will need to move decisively to change zoning laws and building codes, in order to avoid a repeat of what we've seen. And in the work of rebuilding, as many jobs as possible should go to the men and women who live in Louisiana, Mississippi, and Alabama.

Our third commitment is this: When communities are rebuilt, they must be even better and stronger than before the storm. Within the Gulf region are some of the most beautiful and historic places in America. As all of us saw on television, there's also some deep, persistent poverty in this region, as well. That poverty has roots in a history of racial discrimination, which cut off generations from the opportunity of America. We have a duty to confront this poverty with bold action. So let us restore all that we have cherished from yesterday, and let us rise above the legacy of inequality. When the streets are rebuilt, there should be many new businesses, including minority-owned businesses, along those streets. When the houses are rebuilt, more families should own, not rent, those houses. When the regional economy revives, local people should be prepared for the jobs being created.

Americans want the Gulf Coast not just to survive, but to thrive; not just to cope, but to overcome. We want evacuees to come home, for the best of reasons—because they have a real chance at a better life in a place they love.

When one resident of this city who lost his home was asked by a reporter if he would relocate, he said, "Naw, I will rebuild—but I will build higher." That is our vision for the future, in this city and beyond: We'll not just rebuild, we'll build higher and better. To meet this goal, I will listen to good ideas from Congress, and state and local officials, and the private sector. I believe we should start with three initiatives that the Congress should pass.

Tonight I propose the creation of a Gulf Opportunity Zone, encompassing the region of the disaster in Louisiana and Mississippi and Alabama. Within this zone, we should provide immediate incentives for job-creating investment, tax relief for small businesses, incentives to companies that create jobs, and loans and loan guarantees for small businesses, including minority-owned enterprises, to get them up and running again. It is entrepreneurship that creates jobs and opportunity; it is entrepreneurship that helps break the cycle of poverty; and we will take the side of entrepreneurs as they lead the economic revival of the Gulf region.

I propose the creation of Worker Recovery Accounts to help those evacuees who need extra help finding work. Under this plan, the federal government would provide accounts of up to $5,000, which these evacuees could draw upon for job training and education to help them get a good job, and for child care expenses during their job search.

And to help lower-income citizens in the hurricane region build new and better lives, I also propose that Congress pass an Urban Homesteading Act. Under this approach, we will identify property in the region owned by the federal government, and provide building sites to low-income citizens free of charge, through a lottery. In return, they would pledge to build on the lot, with either a mortgage or help from a charitable organization like Habitat for Humanity. Home ownership is one of the great strengths of any community, and it must be a central part of our vision for the revival of this region.

In the long run, the New Orleans area has a particular challenge, because much of the city lies below sea level. The people who call it home need to have reassurance that their lives will be safer in the years to come. Protecting a city that sits lower than the water around it is not easy, but it can, and has been done. City and parish officials in New Orleans, and state officials in Louisiana will have a large part in the engineering decisions to come. And the Army Corps of Engineers will work at their side to make the flood protection system stronger than it has ever been.

The work that has begun in the Gulf Coast region will be one of the largest reconstruction efforts the world has ever seen. When that job is done, all Americans will have something to be very proud of—and all Americans are needed in this common effort. It is the armies of compassion—charities and houses of worship, and idealistic men and women—that give our reconstruction effort its humanity. They offer to those who hurt a friendly face, an arm around the shoulder, and the reassurance that in hard times, they can count on someone who cares. By land, by sea, and by air, good people wanting to make a difference deployed to the Gulf Coast, and they've been working around the clock ever since.

The cash needed to support the armies of compassion is great, and Americans have given generously. For example, the private fundraising effort led by former Presidents Bush and Clinton has already received pledges of more than $100 million. Some of that money is going to the Governors to be used for immediate needs within their states. A portion will also be sent to local houses of worship to help reimburse them for the expense of helping others. This evening the need is still urgent, and I ask the American people to continue donating to the Salvation Army, the Red Cross, other good charities, and religious congregations in the region.

It's also essential for the many organizations of our country to reach out to your fellow citizens in the Gulf area. So I've asked USA Freedom Corps to create an information clearinghouse, available at usafreedomcorps.gov, so that families anywhere in the country can find opportunities to help families in the region, or a school can support a school. And I challenge existing organizations—churches, and Scout troops, or labor union locals to get in touch with their counterparts in Mississippi, Louisiana, or Alabama, and learn what they can do to help. In this great national enterprise, important work can be done by everyone, and everyone should find their role and do their part.

The government of this nation will do its part, as well. Our cities must have clear and up-to-date plans for responding to natural disasters, and disease outbreaks, or a terrorist attack, for evacuating large numbers of people in an emergency, and for providing the food and water and security they would need. In a time of terror threats and weapons of mass destruction, the danger to our citizens reaches much wider than a fault line or a flood plain. I consider detailed emergency planning to be a national security priority, and therefore, I've ordered the Department of Homeland Security to undertake an immediate review, in cooperation with local counterparts, of emergency plans in every major city in America.

I also want to know all the facts about the government response to Hurricane Katrina. The storm involved a massive flood, a major supply and security operation, and an evacuation order affecting more than a million people. It was not a normal hurricane—and the normal disaster relief system was not equal to it. Many of the men and women of the Coast Guard, the Federal Emergency Management Agency, the United States military, the National Guard, Homeland Security, and state and local governments performed skillfully under the worst conditions. Yet the system, at every level of government, was not well-coordinated, and was overwhelmed in the first few days. It is now clear that a challenge on this scale requires greater federal authority and a broader role for the armed forces—the institution of our government most capable of massive logistical operations on a moment's notice.

Four years after the frightening experience of September the 11th, Americans have every right to expect a more effective response in a time of emergency. When the federal government fails to meet such an obligation, I, as President, am responsible for the problem, and for the solution. So I've ordered every Cabinet Secretary to participate in a comprehensive review of the government response to the hurricane. This government will learn the lessons of Hurricane Katrina. We're going to review every action and make necessary changes, so that we are better prepared for any challenge of nature, or act of evil men, that could threaten our people.

The United States Congress also has an important oversight function to perform. Congress is preparing an investigation, and I will work with members of both parties to make sure this effort is thorough.

In the life of this nation, we have often been reminded that nature is an awesome force, and that all life is fragile. We're the heirs of men and women who lived through those first terrible winters at Jamestown and Plymouth, who rebuilt Chicago after a great fire, and San Francisco after a great earthquake, who reclaimed the prairie from the Dust Bowl of the 1930s. Every time, the people of this land have come back from fire, flood, and storm to build anew—and to build better than what we had before. Americans have never left our destiny to the whims of nature—and we will not start now.

These trials have also reminded us that we are often stronger than we know—with the help of grace and one another. They remind us of a hope beyond all pain and death, a God who welcomes the lost to a house not made with hands. And they remind us that we're tied together in this life, in this nation—and that the despair of any touches us all.

I know that when you sit on the steps of a porch where a home once stood, or sleep on a cot in a crowded shelter, it is hard to imagine a bright future. But that future will come. The streets of Biloxi and Gulfport will again be filled with lovely homes and the sound of children playing. The churches of Alabama will have their broken steeples mended and their congregations whole. And here in New Orleans, the street cars will once again rumble down St. Charles, and the passionate soul of a great city will return.

In this place, there's a custom for the funerals of jazz musicians. The funeral procession parades slowly through the streets, followed by a band playing a mournful dirge as it moves to the cemetery. Once the casket has been laid in place, the band breaks into a joyful "second line"—symbolizing the triumph of the spirit over death. Tonight the Gulf Coast is still coming through the dirge—yet we will live to see the second line.

Thank you, and may God bless America.

READING RESPONSES

1. President Bush ends his speech with an image of New Orleans funeral bands playing first sad music and then joyful. List the "sad" sections of this speech and then the "joyful" ones. How do they relate to each other?
2. Prior to this speech, many had criticized the federal government for responding too slowly to the needs of the victims of Hurricane Katrina. Note the places where President Bush responds to those criticisms. How would you describe his responses? How are they like/unlike an apology?

> **3.** President Bush devotes much of his speech to listing the actions of specific federal agencies. How do you think employees of those agencies responded? How did those who were affected by the hurricane respond? How do you think President Bush hoped Americans in general would respond?

MORE WRITING IN SPEECH COMMUNICATION

Introduction

When a president of the United States speaks, people—lots of people—listen. One group—scholars of speech communication—analyze the speech, noting how the particular features of the speech fit the audience(s) of the speech and the situation in which it was given. But how do these scholars know what to look for?

Professors of speech communication—all professors, actually—regularly debate what matters in their academic field—which topics are the most important to research and what are the best ways to understand those topics. Most professors engage in this debate by publishing scholarly articles and books. While the professors' immediate audience is professors in their field, these texts are used by many others such as journalists and business executives.

In this chapter on presidential apologies, in a reading from their book *Deeds Done in Words: Presidential Rhetoric and the Genres of Governance*, Professors Karlyn Kohrs Campbell and Kathleen Hall Jamieson analyze the speeches that six presidents have made when they have faced serious political challenges to their presidencies. The authors identify the two main strategies available to presidents in this kind of trouble: a forensic defense and a personal apologia. Research like this can significantly affect public apologies in the United States. First, it can help people analyze the strategies that speakers use when they apologize. As a result, professors, students, journalists and the general public can better understand apologies and judge whether to accept them. Second, this research can help those who need to make apologies.

Rhetoric to Forestall Impeachment

Karlyn Kohrs Campbell and Kathleen Hall Jamieson

Chapter 7, *Deeds Done in Words: Presidential Rhetoric and the Genres of Governance*

. . . In this and the following chapter, we discuss the issue of the rhetorical advantage that presidents have in interbranch and public discourse, an issue we believe to be essential if one is to understand the rhetorical and, hence, the political power presidents wield. Whatever their constitutional status, the three branches of government are not equal rhetorically. Once invested in office, presidents ordinarily are at a significant rhetorical advantage because they speak with a single voice, whereas Congress and the Supreme Court rarely do. Dissenting opinions are a routine part of most Supreme Court decisions. Congressional action follows debate that includes conflicting views of legislative intent, and, as a practical matter, legislation must speak for itself to the courts and to those who must implement its provisions.[1] Presidents can speak whenever, wherever, and on whatever topic they choose, whereas Congress and the court cannot speak without following established procedures and securing a majority vote of their members. For these reasons, among others, the constitutionally co-equal branches of government are not rhetorical peers.

The significance of rhetorical inequality is most sharply illustrated in the presidential rhetoric responding to charges of misconduct. There is an enormous difference between the rhetorical status of presidents so charged, but not yet formally accused, and that of presidents against whom formal charges have been made in impeachment proceedings. Further, two strikingly different defenses, one personal, the other presidential, are available, depending on the nature of the accusations made. Until Congress is able to formulate accusations of potentially impeachable offenses or to initiate formal impeachment proceedings, presidents are in a rhetorically superior position from which they can act to forestall the emergence of a congressional majority.

Once a formal process has begun, however, that relationship shifts dramatically. The president then confronts as accuser a constitutionally designated co-equal branch of government. The president no longer controls the terms of the debate but must respond to specific charges. Moreover, because of the nature of the charges, one important option, the personal apologia described below, ordinarily is foreclosed, thus diminishing the persuasive powers of the president. Once impeachment proceedings begin, there is an immediate jury—a House committee, the House as a whole, or the Senate—that judges the charges and reaches a verdict while the citizenry watches and judges the proceedings.[2] Finally, the president's absence from these rhetorical settings diminishes the opportunity to use the symbolic power of the presidency in defense. . . .

Although few presidents have escaped charges of misconduct or corruption,[4] there have been six instances in which some sort of formal charge of violating the oath of office has elicited a rhetorical response. Presidents Jackson, Tyler, and Buchanan responded to formal actions by the Congress, such as a committee report or a censure resolution; Presidents Andrew Johnson and Nixon responded to formal impeachment proceedings. Lincoln's statement of self-defense, by contrast, was made in response to resolutions passed by a convention of New York Democrats who condemned him for suspending habeas corpus and for placing the antiwar agitator Clement L. Vallandigham under military arrest.[5] In this chapter we examine those responses in some detail and contrast them to another, more recent instance of presidential self-defense, that made by Ronald Reagan in his speech of March 4, 1987. Although no formal charges had been leveled, we have included an analysis of Reagan's speech here because it illustrates a particular strategy, the personal apologia, that is available as a form of presidential self-defense only under some circumstances.[6] By its very existence, Reagan's speech responding to the conclusions of the Tower Commission, a group appointed by Reagan himself, indicates the importance of the commission report. In this chapter, then, we look at all responses presidents have made to formal charges of violating the oath of office, short of impeachment, whether by Congress or a citizens' group, and a speech by Reagan that clearly illustrates the apologia as a strategy in presidential self-defense.

There are two kinds of defense a president can offer to charges of misconduct, a forensic response or a personal apologia, and it is these two defenses that we examine in the rest of this chapter. The personal apologia is a strategic response to an accusation. Effective apologias are single, unified responses to a series of charges that shift the focus from the attacker(s) to the defender and present the character of the accused in ways that are appealing to the audience. When this address is delivered by a president, it will suggest that the charges, if proved, would not constitute impeachable offenses and that they do not call executive leadership into question.

The substance of some apologias is autobiographical material that makes the original charges appear implausible or irrelevant.[7] Famous examples of this strategy include Cardinal Newman's *Apologia pro Vita Sua*,[8] Socrates's responses to Miletus in Plato's *Apology*, and Richard Nixon's response to charges of a secret campaign fund in the "Checkers" speech, the most famous and successful personal apologia in U.S. political history.

When evidence for the argument it contains is drawn from the intimate details of the rhetor's life, the apologia is a peculiarly personal rhetorical document. This particular form of self-defense both opens rhetorical possibilities and imposes limitations on the president who chooses to exercise it. The audience, as citizens, knows that the president is a fallible human being. Consequently, personal peccadilloes are not treated as impeachable offenses, although they may create a climate more conducive to impeachment, as occurred in the case of Andrew Johnson. On the other hand, instances of presidential misconduct, that is, violating the oath of office, are not likely to be transcended by the kind of defense that is the core of the personal apologia. As Lincoln argued in the example analyzed below, the attack of the New York Democrats was not on him as a person but for actions he had taken in his role as the president. A personal attack might have been ignored; an attack on the presidency had to be defended on constitutional grounds. . . .

Ronald Reagan's speech of March 4, 1987, responding to the Tower Commission report is . . . a personal apologia by a president. The Tower Commission report constituted a series of accusations against the president, suggesting mismanagement of his subordinates such that foreign policy initiatives were carried out in undesirable, potentially illegal ways, contrary to congressional enactment. Whether the charges made in the report might become the bases for articles of impeachment lay in the future—at issue in the Iran-Contra hearings being held by a joint congressional committee during the summer of 1987. As a result, in March of 1987, Reagan was responding to charges, but he was not yet in a situation that threatened him with removal; consequently, the personal apologia was an available option.

A personal apologia admits that the charges made warrant a response; in some instances, there is an admission of error, for example, there was an appearance of evil, mistakes were made, subordinates acted improperly, but errors are blamed on qualities of character that are presented as admirable. Reagan's speech followed this pattern.

Reagan admitted that errors had occurred. He said: "I've studied the board's report. Its findings are honest, convincing, and highly critical, and I accept them."[11] Speaking of the policy that traded arms to Iran for hostages in Lebanon, he said: "It was a mistake" (220). However, he never suggested that he, as the president, had committed errors, and he remained in his presidential role only to a limited extent. He said: "I take full responsibility for my own actions and for those of my administration. . . . It happened on my watch" (220). Later, he added, "I didn't know about any diversion of funds to the Contras. But as President, I cannot escape responsibility" (221).

The crux of Reagan's response was a presentation of his own character. He defended his delay in speaking to the American public by saying that he was waiting for the complete story, a defense that suggested that he was ignorant of what was going on, a recurring theme in the speech. That defense was supported by an appeal to character: "I'm often accused of being an optimist, and it's true I had to hunt pretty hard to find good news in the board's report, . . . but I was very relieved to read this sentence, '. . . the board is convinced that the president does indeed want the full story to be told'" (220). Listeners were told about the feelings of the president: "As angry as I may be about activities undertaken without my knowledge. . . . And as personally distasteful as I find secret bank accounts. . . . My heart and my best intentions still tell me. . . ," and, most important, "I let my personal concern for the hostages spill over into the geopolitical strategy of reaching out to Iran" (220).

Finally, at the end of the speech, listeners were offered a moral lesson, directly related to Reagan's character:

> Now what should happen when you make a mistake is this: You take your knocks, you learn your lessons, and then you move on. That's the healthiest way to deal with a problem. . . . You know, by the time you reach my age, you've made plenty of mistakes if you've lived your life properly. So you learn. You put things in perspective. You pull your energies together. You change. You go forward. (222)

These last statements were canny choices in a personal apologia, simultaneously revealing Reagan's character and rehearsing the way the audience was to respond to the speech. These comments may not be eloquent pleas, they may not ring through the ages as rhetorical master touches, but, coupled with Reagan's personal popularity, they were effective. They presented Reagan as a man who acted and, hence, erred; as a man who learned from his errors; as a man who was mentally healthy; and as a man who was not destroyed by facing evidence of his own fallibility. Hearers also discovered, or rediscovered, what would be appropriate behavior on their part—to learn the lesson and move on, to put mistakes into perspective (and proceed with the business of the country, not congressional investigations), to change, and to move forward. Those comments also framed audience interpretation of what Reagan did in the speech, suggesting he had admitted mistakes (he had not), learned from them, and was acting decisively to change the situation, actions detailed in the second half of the speech.

The speech did not respond to charges that might lead to impeachment. He skirted such issues by saying of the transfer of funds to the Nicaraguan Contras: "The Tower board was not able to find out what happened to this money, so the facts here will be left to the continuing investigations of the court-appointed independent counsel and the two congressional investigating committees. . . . As I told the Tower board, I didn't know about any diversion of funds to the Contras" (221). Because the legal situation was ambiguous, and because details were not known, Reagan had the rhetorical option of the personal apologia available to him. However, that option is not ordinarily available to presidents when charged with violations of their oath of office. As Reagan framed the issue, he had been charged with poor foreign policy and a poor management style. These he explained in terms of admirable qualities of character that were fully intelligible to listeners. But anger, distaste, disappointment, "heart," and personal concern for individuals are not adequate responses to charges that the president has failed "to preserve, protect, and defend the Constitution" or "to see that the laws are faithfully executed."[12] That is why Richard Nixon could successfully employ the apologia as a vice-presidential candidate in 1952 but could not use it when charged with the impeachable offenses that were part of Watergate. . . .

When a president has been formally charged with misconduct, the rhetorical picture changes. When the charges are ill-founded and largely political, as they were in the case of Andrew Johnson, a personal apologia may still be possible as part of an overall defense, but in the face of such serious charges, a forensic defense is also required. Instances of presidential self-defense before formal impeachment proceedings reveal the arguments typically developed in such rhetoric, and they are found in the case of Abraham Lincoln, who defended actions taken in wartime in response to accusations originating outside Congress, and as well as in the responses of Jackson, Tyler, and Buchanan to charges brought by members of Congress.

Lincoln's statement of self-defense is significant not only because it was a response to the accusations of ordinary citizens, albeit gathered at a state Democratic convention—Lincoln used these resolutions as the occasion to respond to the general case against him—but also because it was a defense of extraordinary actions taken in wartime. Because of these special circumstances, Lincoln's response is a test case for disclosing typical lines of argument that presidents use in defending themselves against charges of misconduct. In addition, this special case illustrates the importance of public opinion in the presidential rhetoric of self-defense.[14]

Ordinarily, formal objections to the behavior of a president originate in Congress, but in one significant instance, charges of misconduct came from a convention of Democrats meeting in Albany, New York. The resolutions passed there were sent to Lincoln in May of 1863; he responded to them in a letter dated almost a month later. The issue involved Clement L. Vallandigham of Ohio, who lost his congressional seat in the 1862 elections and whose crime was making speeches exhorting soldiers to desert and urging others not to support the Union's military efforts. Lincoln had suspended *habeas corpus* throughout the Union on September 24, 1862, an act that left Vallandigham without legal recourse when he was placed under military arrest.

The resolution to which Lincoln responded was "a declaration of censure upon the administration for supposed unconstitutional action, such as making military arrests" (311). Like the congressional actions to which other presidents responded, the declaration of censure challenged his conduct of the presidency. Lincoln explained that he would not have responded to the charge "if there were no apprehension that more injurious consequences than any merely personal to myself might follow" (312). In other words, he was responding in his role as president and in defense of his behavior in that role.

Lincoln's letter was a closely argued brief that addressed each of the charges made in the resolutions. In refutation, Lincoln argued that (1) his actions in suspending *habeas corpus* were constitutional, (2) his duties as commander in chief required that in Vallandigham's case he act in a manner consistent with the actions he took toward deserters, and (3) his actions resembled those of Andrew Jackson in the battle of New Orleans.[15] In addition, Lincoln reaffirmed his role as president of all the people by arguing that there was no partisanship involved in the arrest of this Democratic politician from Ohio, that he had been slow—some might argue too slow—to take such measures, and that ordering the arrest, however justified it may have been, was painful to him.

Lincoln responded with great care to the charge that his actions were unconstitutional. The resolutions of accusation showed particular concern for constitutional protections for the citizen on trial for treason, and his accusers argued, as he quoted, "'that these safe-guards of the rights of the citizen against the pretensions of arbitrary power were intended more especially for his [*sic*] protection in times of civil commotion'" (312). In response, he produced two arguments. First, he wrote:

> Ours is a case of rebellion—so called by the resolutions before me—in fact, a clear, flagrant, and gigantic case of rebellion and the provision of the Constitution that "the privilege of the writ of *habeas corpus* shall not be suspended unless when, in cases of rebellion or invasion, the public safety may require it," is the provision which specially applies to our present case. This provision plainly attests the understanding of those who made the Constitution that ordinary courts of justice are inadequate to "cases of rebellion"—attests their purpose that, in such cases, men [*sic*] may be held in custody whom the courts, acting on ordinary rules, would discharge. . . . and its suspension is allowed by the Constitution on purpose that men may be arrested and held who cannot be proved to be guilty of a defined crime, "when in cases of rebellion or invasion, the public safety may require it." (316)

Similarly, he rejected the distinction made in the third resolution "that military arrests may be constitutional in localities where rebellion actually exists, but that such arrests are unconstitutional in localities where rebellion or insurrection does not actually exist." He responded: "Inasmuch, however, as the Constitution itself makes no such distinction, I am unable to believe that there is any such constitutional distinction" (318). He strengthened the claim that his action was constitutional through a pair of analogies:

> I can no more be persuaded that the government can constitutionally take no strong measures in time of rebellion, because it can be shown that the same could not be lawfully taken in time of peace, than I can be persuaded that a particular drug is not good medicine for a sick man because it can be shown to not be good for a well one. Nor am I able to appreciate the danger apprehended by the meeting, that the American people will by means of military arrests during the rebellion lose the right of public discussion, the liberty of speech and the press, the law of evidence, trial by jury, and *habeas corpus* throughout the indefinite peaceful future which I trust lies before them, any more than I am able to believe that a man could contract so strong an appetite for emetics during temporary illness as to persist in feeding upon them during the remainder of his healthy life. (320–21)

Lincoln's claim that his behavior was constitutional also was grounded in his view of his duty as commander in chief. Lincoln described the events that led to his action this way:

> Mr. Vallandigham avows his hostility to the war on the part of the Union; and his arrest was made because he was laboring, with some effect, to prevent the raising of troops, to encourage desertions from the army, and to leave the rebellion without an adequate military force to suppress it. . . . He was warring upon the military, and this gave the military constitutional jurisdiction to lay hands upon him. (319)

Because the resolutions "support the administration in every constitutional and lawful measure to suppress the rebellion" (311), Lincoln was able to use his accusers' agreement that the rebellion must be suppressed by military force as the basis for an impassioned comparison justifying his action in this case:

> Long experience has shown that armies cannot be maintained unless desertion shall be punished by the severe penalty of death. The case requires, and the law and the Constitution sanction, this punishment. Must I shoot a simple-minded soldier boy who deserts, while I must not touch a hair of a wily agitator who induces him to desert? (319–20)

A third justification of his action was drawn from the behavior of Andrew Jackson, who became president after the events described. As Lincoln told the story, after the peace treaty had been concluded following the battle of New Orleans but before it was announced officially, a man published a newspaper article denouncing the martial law then in effect. Jackson arrested him. When a lawyer procured a writ of *habeas corpus* from a federal judge, Jackson arrested the lawyer and the judge. After the treaty was announced, the judge called General Jackson into court and fined him $1,000 for having arrested him and the others.

Jackson paid the fine, but thirty years afterward, Congress refunded principal and interest. Lincoln commented:

> It may be remarked—first, that we had the same Constitution then as now; secondly, that we then had a case of invasion, and now we have a case of rebellion; and, thirdly, that the permanent right of the people to public discussion, the liberty of speech and of the press, the trial by jury, the law of evidence, and the *habeas corpus*, suffered no detriment whatever by that conduct of General Jackson, or its subsequent approval by the American Congress. (323)

Lincoln used Jackson's action and subsequent congressional approval of it as precedents justifying his decision.

These arguments directly refuted the charges made in the resolutions, and they illustrate typical ways of defending the constitutionality of presidential action. Moreover, like other presidents charged with misconduct, Lincoln also asserted that the actions of his accusers undermined the Constitution and threatened its survival. . . .

Although he made explicit efforts to praise the New York Democrats as patriots and to acknowledge beliefs that he and they shared, Lincoln not only implied that his accusers were aiding the rebels but also condemned their partisanship. Those who voted the resolutions identified themselves as Democrats. Lincoln responded:

> In this time of national peril I would have preferred to meet you upon a level one step higher than any party platform, because I am sure that from such more elevated position we could do better battle for the country we all love than we possibly can from those lower ones. . . . But since you have denied me this I will yet be thankful for the country's sake that not all Democrats have done so. He on whose discretionary judgment Mr. Vallandigham was arrested and tried is a Democrat, having no old party affinity with me, and the judge who rejected the constitutional view expressed in these resolutions, by refusing to discharge Mr. Vallandigham on *habeas corpus* is a Democrat of better days than these, having received his judicial mantle at the hands of President Jackson. And still more: of all those Democrats who are nobly exposing their lives and shedding their blood on the battle-field, I have learned that many approve the course taken with Mr. Vallandigham, while I have not heard of a single one condemning it. (321–22)

In other words, Democrats who were true patriots supported the president's actions and recognized them as part of his effort to preserve the Union. . . .

Although generated under unusual circumstances, Lincoln's letter made the basic arguments found in other presidential statements of self-defense. Whether questioned by a group of citizens, as Lincoln was, or formally upbraided or censured by Congress, presidents who responded chose three basic lines of argument: (1) they had kept their oath of office to preserve, protect, and defend the Constitution; (2) the actions of their accusers undermined the Constitution; and (3) the president is responsible ultimately to the people and to the Constitution, not to congressional accusers.

This focus on the presidential oath, on the Constitution, and on the people is a direct by-product of the compact ratified in the inauguration. There, except under the most unusual circumstances, the country, the Congress, and the court witness presidents swearing that they will preserve, protect, and defend the Constitution. If they fail to do so, they not only have violated the oath but also have broken the compact made with the people and with history. A central argument of the inaugural address is that just as a president inherits the Constitution intact from those who preceded, so it will be transmitted intact to those who succeed. . . .

Finally, there are the cases of presidents' arguing that their responsibility is to the people and to the Constitution, not to the attackers from Congress: Buchanan, for example, said that the president "is the only direct representative on earth of the people of all and each of the sovereign States. To them, and to them alone, is he [*sic*] responsible whilst acting within the sphere of his constitutional duty, and not in any manner to the House of Representatives."[35] Tyler affirmed that it was to the people, Providence, and the law of the land "that I hold myself answerable as a moral agent for a free and conscientious discharge of the duties which they have imposed upon me." He protested against House actions,

> in the name of the people, by whose will I stand where I do, by whose authority I exercised the power which I am charged with having usurped, and to whom I am responsible for a fair and faithful discharge according to my own convictions of duty of the high stewardship confided to me by them.[36]

Jackson said all branches of the government are "servants of the American people, without power or right to control or censure each other in the service of their common superior, save only in the manner and to the degree which that superior has prescribed," adding that the president is accountable "at the bar of public opinion for every act of his [*sic*] Administration."[37]

Making the people the ultimate jury is a reminder that the president has been invested with office by the people: they have witnessed the oath, they were constituted as the audience in the inaugural, and they remain the audience as performance in office is attacked. The view embodied in the president's message is that what the people give, only the people can take away. If Congress is to remove the president from office, the people must acquiesce. This is a rhetorical, not a constitutional requirement, but it looms large in impeachment debates.[38]

These lines of argument typify presidential defenses against charges of misconduct. Each is grounded in the special role of the president in our system of government and in the president's unique relationship to the citizenry. When these lines of argument fail to forestall the process of impeachment, the rhetoric of the president changes.

Conclusion

When faced with accusations short of formal charges of impeachment, presidents remain in a powerful, persuasive position *vis-à-vis* their accusers. They are able to respond to the charges forensically or through an apologia, and they have the freedom to define the grounds for debate, to attack their accusers as threatening the system of government itself, and to appeal for final vindication to the people. . . .

Notes

1. Courts also examine the legislative history of any act.
2. For a discussion of this kind of rhetorical situation, see S. Michael Halloran, "Doing Public Business in Public," in *Form and Genre: Shaping Rhetorical Action*, ed. Karlyn Kohrs Campbell and Kathleen Hall Jamieson (Falls Church, Va.: Speech Communication Association, 1978), ll8–38.
4. C. Vann Woodward, ed., Introduction to *Responses of the Presidents to Charges of Misconduct* (New York: Delacorte, 1974), xii.
5. That conflict eventually was part of two Supreme Court decisions. However, as Edward Keynes points out, "With the exception of Chief Justice Roger Taney's opinion in *Ex parte Merryman*, 17 F. Cas. 144 (C.C.D. Md. 1861) (No. 9,487), the Federal courts sustained President Lincoln's exercise of extraconstitutional power. Indeed in *Ex parte Vallandigham*, 68 U.S. (1 Wall.) 243 (1864), the Court avoided a confrontation with the president by denying its jurisdiction to review or reverse the findings of a military commission. Only after the Civil War had ended, in *Ex parte Milligan*, 71 U.S. (4 Wall.) 2 (1866), did the Supreme Court challenge the president's authority to suspend the privilege to the writ of habeas corpus and to substitute a military commission for a civilian court outside the actual theater of military operations" (*Undeclared War: Twilight Zone of Constitutional Power* [University Park: Pennsylvania State University Press, 1982], 173).
6. The most obvious difference among these seven instances of self-defense is that six of them are responses by the president speaking as the president and one, that of Reagan, is by the president speaking as a person. They share a concern to forestall impeachment; in Reagan's case, the Tower Commission's findings were an implicit accusation of presidential mismanagement and suggested the possibility that its findings might lead to charges of impeachable offenses.
7. A discussion of the nature of the apologia and its rhetorical advantages may be found in Edwin Black, *Rhetorical Criticism; A Study in Method* (1965; reprint Madison: University of Wisconsin Press, 1978), 151–61.
8. John Henry Cardinal Newman, *Apologia pro Vita Sua*, ed. Charles Frederick Harold (New York: Longmans, Green, 1947).
11. *Weekly Compilation of Presidential Documents* 23 (9):220. Subsequent page citations are in parentheses in the text.
12. Note that Reagan's apologia is paradoxical, asking us to forgive him for acts committed in his administration of which he was ignorant.
14. Abraham Lincoln, "To Erastus Corning and Others, June 12, 1863," in *The Writings of Abraham Lincoln*, 8 vols., ed. Arthur Brooks Lapley (New York: G. P. Putnam's Sons, 1906), 6:3ll-25. Subsequent page references will be in parentheses in the text.
15. This is an intriguing comparison, as Jackson was not president at the time of the actions in question.
35. James D. Richardson, ed., *A Compilation of the Messages and Papers of The Presidents*, 1789–1908, 11 vols. (Washington, D.C.: Bureau of National Literature and Art, 1909), 5:615.
36. Richardson, 4:193.
37. Richardson, 3:71–72. Although Nixon failed to forestall the impeachment process, he also made the arguments described in this chapter. For example, Nixon labeled the charges "wild accusations," "rumor, gossip, innuendo," and "third-hand hearsay charges" (*Public Papers*, 1974, 391, and *Public Papers*, 1973, 547). Nixon's brief to the Supreme Court invoked the threat of judicial encroachment on the executive by arguing that the very principle of separation of powers meant that the lower court lacked the power it had claimed ("The President's Main Brief in United States v. Nixon," *United States v. Nixon*, ed. Leon Friedman [New York: Chelsea House, 1974], 337–47), and predicted that if the arguments of the special prosecutor prevail, "that decision will alter the nature of the American Presidency profoundly and irreparably. If sustained, it will alter, equally irreparably, the delicate balance that has existed between three heretofore separate and coequal branches of government" (403). Nixon's Supreme Court brief also argued that his

actions were consistent with those of seventeen past presidents, from 1796 to the present (354–561) and charged: "The characterization of the President of the United States as an un-indicted co-conspirator, is nothing less than an attempt to nullify the presumption of innocence by a secret, non-adversary proceeding. The presumption of innocence is a fundamental of American justice; the grand jury's procedure is an implication of guilt which corrupts the idea" (390). Similarly, in producing some of the White House tapes, Nixon said: "In giving you these records—blemishes and all—I am placing my trust in the basic fairness of the American people (*Public Papers*, 1974, 396).

38. Because members of the House are elected every two years, this argument is an indirect appeal to vote out of office those who are endangering the presidency. Because most congressional efforts to charge a president with misconduct require long gestation, it is likely that the people will have an opportunity to act on this appeal. The president can also claim that in the next election, members of the House and Senate will be repudiated by the people should they act unfairly. The potential force of this view is demonstrated by a comparison of the membership of the Congress elected in 1974, following the resignation of Richard Nixon, with that of the Congress elected in 1972.

READING RESPONSES

1. Reread the quotes from Lincoln's speech. Which ones seem to be personal apology? Which ones seem to be forensic apology?
2. Try to determine the features of personal apology and forensic apology. Create a list of characteristics of each and then, from that list, create a definition of each.
3. Professors Campbell and Jamieson provide extensive historical detail and cite long passages from the speeches they're analyzing. How do those writerly strategies shape their relationships with different readers? Consider at least two of their audiences in your response: other professors, students, journalists, those making apologies, or the American public.

WRITING ASSIGNMENTS

ASSIGNMENT 1:
APPLYING THE PORTABLE RHETORICAL LESSON

Background: In 1987, Senator Joseph Biden sought the Democratic nomination for the 1988 presidential election. And then disaster struck. The press learned that Biden had borrowed parts of a campaign speech from Neil Kinnock, a British politician. Biden dismissed the criticism, noting that he had credited Kinnock on other occasions and that politicians commonly borrow from one another's speeches. Then the press reported that Biden had failed a law school class because he had plagiarized, using a single footnote to cite a five-page chunk of borrowed text. Biden argued that his plagiarism was unintentional—he had been unaware of the citation practices expected of him. Finally, amid accusations that he had over-stated his academic achievements and that other speeches also contained borrowed material, Biden quit the race. If Senator Biden were to run for the Democratic presidential nomination at some point in the future, he would first have to put to rest the lingering questions about his past plagiarism.

Your task for this assignment is to write a speech for Senator Biden that closes the door on the past and opens it to future possibility. Your speech will have at least two audiences: Democrats who are voting in the primaries, as well as all those who will vote in the general election.

As you begin drafting, decide whether to apologize, defend Biden's actions, or combine apology with defense. Determine how specific you will be about Biden's previous actions and what kind of context will you provide for those acts. Choose language that will be effective with Democrats while not alienating the general population. Be sure to fit your speech to Senator Biden's tone and verbal mannerisms. You may need to read some of his previous speeches to do this effectively.

ASSIGNMENT 2: MAKING CONNECTIONS

Background: While few of us will ever apologize before an international audience as President Clinton did, academics regularly defend their ideas from the critique. They do so in "exchange" sections of major research journals, before governmental bodies, and in subsequent articles that they publish. An example of this kind of critique and response to it occurs in the readings in Chapter 10: Biotechnology.

Your task for this assignment is to analyze how academics in biotechnology (or, if your instructor allows it, academics in your own discipline) respond to the critique of others. Analyze one of the readings from the biotechnology chapter to determine how the authors describe not only the critique that they're responding to but also those who do the critiquing; what they focus the readers' attention on as well as the strategies they use to do so; and how they persuade the reader to focus on the future.

As you begin drafting, consider who would be interested in your findings and what they could do with the information that you provide. How comfortable are you with the uses to which others might put your research? What uses would you like to encourage, and how can you encourage readers to do those? What uses would you like to discourage, and how can you discourage readers from doing those?

ASSIGNMENT 3: DOING THE RESEARCH

Background: Nearly every college and university has a policy on plagiarism. In fact, the National Council of Writing Program Administrators has drafted a position statement on plagiarism found online at http://wpacouncil.org/node/9. These policies usually include a description of plagiarism and the consequences that result when students plagiarize.

Your task for this assignment is to collect data and write a report that either justifies your school's plagiarism policy or suggests future revisions to the policy. To begin, determine the kind of information you want to gather about plagiarism at your institution and how you will gather that information. Are you interested in how students think about plagiarism? How much and what kinds of plagiarism occur? How teachers detect plagiarism? How they train students to avoid plagiarism? How attitudes about plagiarism at your school fit with those nationwide?

As you begin drafting, consider the audiences of your report carefully. If you justify the policy, your primary audience will be students. But others will be interested, too: teachers and administrators rely on documents such as yours as they talk about plagiarism with students. If you recommend revisions to the plagiarism policy, your primary audience will be school administrators who must approve such changes, but you can expect that teachers and students will read the document carefully, too. Decide on the central message of the report, its organization, and its tone. Determine the type and amount of evidence you will include in the report and how you will present that evidence.

4

RELIGION AND SOCIETY: ANALYZING CULTURAL ASSUMPTIONS

The thesis-based writing in this chapter characterizes writing in the humanities. If you compared this chapter's readings to those in Part Four of this book, readings that recommend action, you might be inclined to think, "*That's* the kind of writing that affects how people act. Writing in the humanities just has to be interesting; it doesn't have to do anything." But writing in the humanities does in fact *do* something. It enriches our understanding of human culture, and it challenges us to rethink what we assume about how the human world operates. By enriching and challenging us, humanities writing changes what we believe—and therefore how we act. Each of us acts based on what we believe, on the assumptions we hold. If you assume, for example, that your first responsibility is to support your family, you might try to make as much money as possible to protect against unforeseen events, selecting investments only by their rate of return. If, on the other hand, you assume that you are responsible for supporting human rights efforts in developing countries, you might invest your money differently. Actions grow from assumptions, and if someone persuades you to rethink your assumptions, your actions will change as well.

A Portable Rhetorical Lesson:
Writing Thesis-Driven Arguments

You will probably recognize the form of the readings in this chapter. Most high-school and college writing classes emphasize thesis-based writing. The thesis statement is the rhetorical lesson for this chapter.

Not surprisingly, the success of a thesis-driven paper depends on the quality of the thesis. So, to clarify what a good thesis is, let's think for a minute about what a thesis is not. First, it is not a statement of fact. The statement, "Gas prices have risen 20 percent in the past five months" is not a thesis statement. There is no arguing with it, and a key feature of a thesis is that a reasonable person can argue about it. Second, a thesis is not a statement of personal belief, such as a religious belief; again, there's nothing in such a statement about which readers could argue. Third, a thesis is not a hypothesis. In later chapters you will read more about hypotheses, but for now it is enough to know that a hypothesis is a testable solution to a problem or research question. A hypothesis, tested by accepted scientific methods, can be proven true or false; it is set up to be testable, not arguable.

A thesis, on the other hand, says to a reader: "I think X; let me explain why you should agree that this is a reasonable thing to think." Consider this example: a student wishes to talk with his or her teacher about a draft of a thesis-based paper. The conversation might well begin with the teacher asking the student to point out the thesis. The student responds by pointing to the last sentence in her first paragraph. The teacher presses the student, saying, "OK, that's your thesis. Do you really believe it?" If the student says, "Yes, I believe my thesis," the teacher could counter with "Why?" The teacher asks why to get the student to think about what evidence and reasoning convinced her to believe in her thesis—and how she can use that evidence and reasoning to convince the reader to believe the thesis, too. But the teacher probably has a second reason for asking why. The teacher is trying to help the student pin-point the *assumptions* that lie behind the student's belief in the thesis.

It is important for writers to recognize the assumptions they are making because unexamined assumptions can derail a thesis-driven essay. Philip Park's essay (the student writing in this chapter), for example, argues against the assumptions that scholars make about (1) what is possible to know about religion and (2) what research methods reveal useful knowledge about religion. Park also assumes the following (from his introduction, page 84), "I also claim that theological speculation like Berger's can provide important knowledge about religion." Robert Bellah's essay, the first reading of this chapter, was published in 1967, and it employs the unstated assumption that it is worthwhile to learn from history (a common assumption in the humanities). You may also detect some unspoken assumptions that were safe enough for Bellah to hold in 1967 but that now invite more disagreement.

Here is a key point about thesis statements. When writers are fully aware of and honest about their assumptions, when they root a thesis in research and thinking and experience, then writers enjoy confidence in their theses—and enthusiasm about the prospect of convincing readers. The introduction to Phil Park's essay is a good example of this process. Phil kept working at his thesis until he convinced himself that his idea was reasonable. He then reproduced for his readers the process that led him to be convinced, working in that way to convince his readers.

As far as "portability" goes, there are few rhetorical tools more broadly applicable than the thesis statement. You have written them for many classes—in the humanities and other disciplines. You have possibly written them in messages to friends (for example: "I think you should drive to Jack's tonight. I've been feeling sick, and I've driven the last two times." This is an argument based on assumptions about what is fair and on knowl-edge of past experiences.). You'll use theses throughout your life—because they can be so effective. A good thesis creates results.

Chapter Topics: Although the main topic is approached from a variety of angles in the readings of this chapter, each reading is about the role of religion in public life, which also brings politics and sociology into the topics of the chapter.

To Think About. . .

Americans have recited the Pledge of Allegiance since 1892; in 1942, Congress formally adopted a version of the pledge that read: "I pledge allegiance to the flag of the United States of America and to the Republic for which it stands, one Nation indivisible, with liberty and justice for all." That's right, no "under God." Congress added those two words in 1954. In 2004, Michael Newdow argued to the Supreme Court that the words "under God" are unconstitutional because they discriminate against people who do not believe in a god. According to Linda Greenhouse of the Associated Press, Newdow claimed, "Government is doing this to my child: they're putting her in a milieu where she says, 'Hey, the government is saying that there is a god and my dad says no.'"[*]

- Do you agree with Newdow?
- Do these words in the Pledge of Allegiance assume the existence of God? What else might those words indicate?
- What grounds might some people use to oppose Newdow's argument?

Newdow concluded, "There's a principle here, and I'm hoping the court will uphold this principle so that we can finally go back and have every American want to stand up, face the flag, place their hand over their heart and pledge to one nation, indivisible, not divided by religion, with liberty and justice for all."

Newdow argues for a version of the Pledge of Allegiance that all people, regard-less of their religious beliefs, can recite with enthusiasm. He emphasizes the value of national unity.

- What does he assume about social unity? What good does social unity produce?
- Why do you think he doesn't emphasize citizens' rights instead?

[*]Linda Greenhouse, "Atheist Presents Case for Taking God from Pledge," *New York Times On the Web,* March 25, 2004.

WRITING IN RELIGION AND SOCIETY

Introduction by Richard Plantinga,
Professor of Religion

To understand the place of religion in American life and society, we must bear in mind that the founders of the United States envisioned it as a new, better world. Many of them believed that the young republic was chosen by God to be a blessing to the world (analogous to Israel as depicted in the Hebrew Bible). Despite this belief, the founders wanted to avoid the problems that national religions had caused in Europe. As America's founders looked across the Atlantic Ocean to the countries from which they originally hailed, they were negatively impressed by Europe's national churches (the Anglican Church in England, the Presbyterian Church in Scotland, etc.). They were also unhappily aware of the restrictions on religious freedom that nations imposed on citizens who professed a faith different from the one sanctioned by the state. As a result, when they crafted the Constitution of the United States (1787), they disallowed a national religion. The First Amendment of the Constitution declares: "Congress shall make no law respecting an establishment of religion, or prohibiting the free exercise thereof."

Even though the United States has never had a national religion, religion has always played an important role in national life. Describing how religion functions in American society has been an ongoing interest of Robert Bellah (born in 1927), retired professor of sociology at the University of California at Berkeley. His well-known and much-cited essay on the subject, "Civil Religion in America," was first published in 1967. To fully appreciate Bellah's argument, you must remember the time in which he wrote. In 1960, the country had elected a young, charismatic, Catholic president, who articulated a vision embraced by many, especially the young. On November 22, 1963, a shocked nation learned that President John Fitzgerald Kennedy had been assassinated in Dallas, Texas. He left to his successor, President Lyndon Baines Johnson, an escalating conflict in Vietnam as well as an unfinished agenda for addressing social inequalities like poverty and racism. As Johnson sought to win the war in Vietnam, he simultaneously attempted to build a "Great Society" at home. In this "Great Society," civil rights would flourish and poverty would be eradicated. In this tumultuous decade Robert Bellah wrote his essay.

In "Civil Religion in America," Bellah tries to accomplish three things. First, he catalogs the features of civil religion by analyzing how government officials use religion in speeches and documents. Second, he looks for historical reasons for the nature of civil religion in the United States—the historical events or philosophies that shaped it. Finally, Bellah speculates how civil religion might change in the future and what future influences it might have.

The structure of "Civil Religion in America" is typical for a thesis-based essay except for the opening abstract. Bellah begins the body of the essay by using an example—President Kennedy's inaugural address—to pose questions about the generic references to "God" in presidential addresses and government documents like the Declaration of Independence. The rest of the essay answers the questions he poses. At the end of his introduction, Bellah explains the importance of the topic: "These questions are worth pursuing because they raise the issue of how civil religion relates to the political society on the one hand and to private religious organization on the other" (page 72). Following this justification, Bellah states his thesis: "there actually exists alongside of and rather clearly differentiated from the churches an elaborate and well-institutionalized civil religion in America" (70–71). He provides specifics about his thesis by noting that "[t]his public religious dimension is expressed in a set of beliefs, symbols, and rituals that I am calling the American civil religion" (73).

In this provocative and still relevant essay, Bellah makes some key assumptions about religion—and assumptions are always debatable. His definition of religion—"a collection of beliefs, symbols, and rituals with respect to sacred things and institutionalized in a collectivity" (76)—is very close to the famous definition offered by Émile Durkheim, the father of sociology. Like Durkheim, Bellah holds that religion is more than just private beliefs. Rather, Bellah and Durkheim argued that religion is public, too; and they believed that a "civil" religion expresses the key beliefs and practices that bind a society together.

✓READING TIPS

You cannot scan this type of writing; you need to read it from start to finish. But you can read efficiently. First, read the abstract carefully. You can judge Bellah's success by deciding whether or not he persuades you of his thesis, which he states in the abstract. Second, pay attention to the structure that the section headings reveal. Each heading points to a period of American history, and if you discover the pattern, you will better understand Bellah's argument and purposes.

Civil Religion in America
Robert N. Bellah

Daedalus, Journal of the American Academy of Arts and Sciences, Winter 1967.

[Abstract]

While some have argued that Christianity is the national faith, and others that church and synagogue celebrate only the generalized religion of "the American Way of Life," few have realized that there actually exists alongside of and rather clearly differentiated

An abstract is only occasionally used in essays in the humanities. This opening paragraph differs from a scientific abstract in that it does not summarize the essay. Rather, it states the essay's thesis.

By starting with Kennedy, just four years after his assassination and when Americans cherished his memory, Bellah puts himself at an immediate advantage with his readers.

Bellah presents himself as reasonable, open to different opinions—a good strategy to use at the beginning of a very opinionated essay.

from the churches an elaborate and well-institutionalized civil religion in America. This article argues not only that there is such a thing, but also that this religion—or perhaps better, this religious dimension—has its own seriousness and integrity and requires the same care in understanding that any other religion does.[1]

The Kennedy Inaugural

Kennedy's inaugural address of 20 January 1961 serves as an example and a clue with which to introduce this complex subject. That address began:

We observe today not a victory of party but a celebration of freedom—symbolizing an end as well as a beginning—signifying renewal as well as change. For I have sworn before you and Almighty God the same solemn oath our forebears prescribed nearly a century and three quarters ago.

The world is very different now. For man holds in his mortal hands the power to abolish all forms of human poverty and to abolish all forms of human life. And yet the same revolutionary beliefs for which our forebears fought are still at issue around the globe— the belief that the rights of man come not from the generosity of the state but from the hand of God.

And it concluded:

Finally, whether you are citizens of America or of the world, ask of us the same high standards of strength and sacrifice that we shall ask of you. With a good conscience our only sure reward, with history the final judge of our deeds, let us go forth to lead the land we love, asking His blessing and His help, but knowing that here on earth God's work must truly be our own.

These are the three places in this brief address in which Kennedy mentioned the name of God. If we could understand why he mentioned God, the way in which he did it, and what he meant to say in those three references, we would understand much about American civil religion. But this is not a simple or obvious task, and American students of religion would probably differ widely in their interpretation of these passages.

Let us consider first the placing of the three references. They occur in the two opening paragraphs and in the closing paragraph, thus providing a sort of frame for more concrete remarks that form the middle part of the speech. Looking beyond this particular speech, we would find that similar references to God are almost invariably to be found in the pronouncements of American presidents on solemn occasions, though usually not in the working messages that the president

In the 1960s, many scholars assumed that the nation was becoming increasingly secular. Many now disagree with that assumption. America seems to be diversely religiously engaged.

In this paragraph Bellah justifies what he has presented and pauses for reflection. The pause helps the reader move from focusing on the past to the present, and then from the present to the future.

Bellah makes a key point here with respect to his argument. In civil religion, references are not to specific religions (e.g., Methodism) but to a general idea of "God."

sends to Congress on various concrete issues. How, then, are we to interpret this placing of references to God?

It might be argued that the passages quoted reveal the essentially irrelevant role of religion in the very secular society that is America. The placing of the references in this speech as well as in public life generally indicates that religion has "only a ceremonial significance"; it gets only a sentimental nod that serves largely to placate the more unenlightened members of the community before a discussion of the really serious business with which religion has nothing whatever to do. A cynical observer might even say that an American president has to mention God or risk losing votes. A semblance of piety is merely one of the unwritten qualifications for the office, a bit more traditional than but not essentially different from the present-day requirement of a pleasing television personality.

But we know enough about the function of ceremonial and ritual in various societies to make us suspicious of dismissing something as unimportant because it is "only a ritual." What people say on solemn occasions need not be taken at face value, but it is often indicative of deep-seated values and commitments that are not made explicit in the course of everyday life. Following this line of argument, it is worth considering whether the very special placing of the references to God in Kennedy's address may not reveal something rather important and serious about religion in American life.

It might be countered that the very way in which Kennedy made his references reveals the essentially vestigial place of religion today. He did not refer to any religion in particular. He did not refer to Jesus Christ, or to Moses, or to the Christian church; certainly he did not refer to the Catholic Church. In fact, his only reference was to the concept of God, a word that almost all Americans can accept but that means so many different things to so many different people that it is almost an empty sign. Is this not just another indication that in America religion is considered vaguely to be a good thing, but that people care so little about it that it has lost any content whatever? Isn't Eisenhower reported to have said "Our government makes no sense unless it is founded in a deeply felt religious faith—and I don't care what it is,"[2] and isn't that a complete negation of any real religion?

These questions are worth pursuing because they raise the issue of how civil religion relates to the political society, on the one hand, and to private religious organization, on the other. President Kennedy was a Christian, more specifically a Catholic

This is a key issue, namely, the relation between the private and public dimensions in religion. Civil religion is public. Toward the end of the paragraph, Bellah indicates why the private-public matter is so important: The United States was founded on the principle of the separation of church (private) and state (public), as indicated in the First Amendment to the Constitution, but civil religion extends beyond the private sphere.

Christian. Thus his general references to God do not mean that he lacked a specific religious commitment. But why, then, did he not include some remark to the effect that Christ is the Lord of the world or some indication of respect for the Catholic Church? He did not because these are matters of his own private religious belief and of his own particular church; they are not matters relevant in any direct way to the conduct of his public office. Others with different religious views and commitments to different churches or denominations are equally qualified participants in the political process. The principle of separation of church and state guarantees the freedom of religious belief and association, but at the same time clearly segregates the religious sphere, which is considered to be essentially private, from the political one.

Considering the separation of church and state, how is a president justified in using the word *God* at all? The answer is that the separation of church and state has not denied the political realm a religious dimension. Although matters of personal religious belief, worship, and association are considered to be strictly private affairs, there are, at the same time, certain common elements of religious orientation that the great majority of Americans share. These have played a crucial role in the development of American institutions and still provide a religious dimension for the whole fabric of American life, including the political sphere. This public religious dimension is expressed in a set of beliefs, symbols, and rituals that I am calling the American civil religion. The inauguration of a president is an important ceremonial event in this religion. It reaffirms, among other things, the religious legitimation of the highest political authority.

Through most of this paragraph Bellah is restating his thesis and then listing the features of civil religion. In a long essay, it usually helps to remind your readers of your thesis to keep their attention focused on it.

Let us look more closely at what Kennedy actually said. First, he said, "I have sworn before you and Almighty God the same solemn oath our forebears prescribed nearly a century and three quarters ago." The oath is the oath of office, including the acceptance of the obligation to uphold the Constitution. He swears it before the people (you) and God. Beyond the Constitution, then, the president's obligation extends not only to the people but to God. In American political theory, sovereignty rests, of course, with the people, but implicitly, and often explicitly, the ultimate sovereignty has been attributed to God. This is the meaning of the motto, "In God we trust," as well as the inclusion of the phrase "under God" in the pledge to the flag. What difference does it make that sovereignty belongs to God? Though the will of the people as expressed in the

self-governing, or having the right to self-government

majority vote is carefully institutionalized as the operative source of political authority, it is deprived of an ultimate significance. The will of the people is not itself the criterion of right and wrong. There is a higher criterion in terms of which this will can be judged; it is possible that the people may be wrong. The president's obligation extends to the higher criterion.

When Kennedy says that "the rights of man come not from the generosity of the state but from the hand of God," he is stressing this point again. It does not matter whether the state is the expression of the will of an autocratic monarch or of the "people"; the rights of man are more basic than any political structure and provide a point of revolutionary leverage from which any state structure may be radically altered. That is the basis for his reassertion of the revolutionary significance of America.

> "Absolutism" is a conception of government that democracy rejects. It refers to the idea that kings have absolute rule over their subjects. Their power to rule in this fashion they understood to come from God, whom they represent.

But the religious dimension of political life as recognized by Kennedy not only provides a grounding for the rights of man that makes any form of political absolutism illegitimate, it also provides a transcendent goal for the political process. This is implied in his final words that "here on earth God's work must truly be our own." What he means here is, I think, more clearly spelled out in a previous paragraph, the wording of which, incidentally, has a distinctly Biblical ring:

Now the trumpet summons us again—not as a call to bear arms, though arms we need—not as a call to battle, though embattled we are—but a call to bear the burden of a long twilight struggle, year in and year out, "rejoicing in hope, patient in tribulation"—a struggle against the common enemies of man: tyranny, poverty, disease and war itself.

The whole address can be understood as only the most recent statement of a theme that lies very deep in the American tradition, namely the obligation, both collective and individual, to carry out God's will on earth. This was the motivating spirit of those who founded America, and it has been present in every generation since. Just below the surface throughout Kennedy's inaugural address, it becomes explicit in the closing statement that God's work must be our own. That this very activist and noncontemplative conception of the fundamental religious obligation, which has been historically associated with the Protestant position, should be enunciated so clearly in the first major statement of the first Catholic president seems to underline how deeply established it is in the American outlook. Let us now consider the form and history of the civil religious tradition in which Kennedy was speaking.

The Idea of a Civil Religion

The phrase *civil religion* is, of course, Rousseau's. In Chapter 8, Book 4 of *The Social Contract*, he outlines the simple dogmas of the civil religion: the existence of God, the life to come, the reward of virtue and the punishment of vice, and the exclusion of religious intolerance. All other religious opinions are outside the cognizance of the state and may be freely held by citizens. While the phrase *civil religion* was not used, to the best of my knowledge, by the founding fathers, and I am certainly not arguing for the particular influence of Rousseau, it is clear that similar ideas, as part of the cultural climate of the late eighteenth century, were to be found among the Americans. . . .

Kennedy's inaugural pointed to the religious aspect of the Declaration of Independence, and it might be well to look at that document a bit more closely. There are four references to God. The first speaks of the "Laws of Nature and of Nature's God," which entitle any people to be independent. The second is the famous statement that all men "are endowed by their Creator with certain inalienable Rights." Here Jefferson is locating the fundamental legitimacy of the new nation in a conception of "higher law" that is itself based on both classical natural law and Biblical religion. The third is an appeal to "the Supreme Judge of the world for the rectitude of our intentions," and the last indicates "a firm reliance on the protection of divine Providence." In these last two references, a Biblical God of history who stands in judgment over the world is indicated. . . .

The words and acts of the founding fathers, especially the first few presidents, shaped the form and tone of the civil religion as it has been maintained ever since. Though much is selectively derived from Christianity, this religion is clearly not itself Christianity. For one thing, neither Washington nor Adams nor Jefferson mentions Christ in his inaugural address; nor do any of the subsequent presidents, although not one of them fails to mention God.[3] The God of the civil religion is not only rather "unitarian," he is also on the austere side, much more related to order, law, and right than to salvation and love. Even though he is somewhat deist in cast, he is by no means simply a watchmaker God. He is actively interested and involved in history, with a special concern for America. Here the analogy has much less to do with natural law than with ancient Israel; the equation of America with Israel in the idea of the "American Israel" is not infrequent. . . .[4]

After the first section, which introduces the idea of civil religion by analyzing the Kennedy inaugural, Bellah in this section seeks to provide historical background and the basic point of his argument.

Jean-Jacques Rousseau was a Swiss thinker who lived 1712–1778. Writers in the humanities often ground their claims in particular philosophical theories.

"Unitarian" is a reference to a concept of God as simply one, not the Trinitarian God of traditional Christianity.

Deism (from the Latin term for God, "*deus*") is a seventeenth and eighteenth century position that declares general belief in God and an afterlife. The beliefs in deism fit the beliefs in civil religion quite closely.

This conception of religion is adapted from the French sociologist Émile Durkheim (1858–1917). See Bellah's first endnote where he shows his dependence on this early twentieth century source.

What we have, then, from the earliest years of the republic is a collection of beliefs, symbols, and rituals with respect to sacred things and institutionalized in a collectivity. This religion—there seems no other word for it—while not antithetical to and indeed sharing much in common with Christianity, was neither sectarian nor in any specific sense Christian. At a time when the society was overwhelmingly Christian, it seems unlikely that this lack of Christian reference was meant to spare the feelings of the tiny non-Christian minority. Rather, the civil religion expressed what those who set the precedents felt was appropriate under the circumstances. It reflected their private as well as public views. Nor was the civil religion simply "religion in general." While generality was undoubtedly seen as a virtue by some, . . . the civil religion was specific enough when it came to the topic of America. Precisely because of this specificity, the civil religion was saved from empty formalism and served as a genuine vehicle of national religious self-understanding.

"Sectarian" is the adjectival form of the word sect, meaning party, group, or faction.

But the civil religion was not, in the minds of Franklin, Washington, Jefferson, or other leaders, with the exception of a few radicals like Tom Paine, ever felt to be a substitute for Christianity. There was an implicit but quite clear division of function between the civil religion and Christianity. Under the doctrine of religious liberty, an exceptionally wide sphere of personal piety and voluntary social action was left to the churches. But the churches were neither to control the state nor to be controlled by it. The national magistrate, whatever his private religious views, operates under the rubrics of the civil religion as long as he is in his official capacity, as we have already seen in the case of Kennedy. This accommodation was undoubtedly the product of a particular historical moment and of a cultural background dominated by Protestantism of several varieties and by the Enlightenment, but it has survived despite subsequent changes in the cultural and religious climate.

A magistrate is a government representative empowered to administer the law, such as a judge or a president.

Civil War and Civil Religion

In this next section, Bellah demonstrates the origins and development of the American civil religion in the Revolutionary War against Britain and in the American Civil War.

Until the Civil War, the American civil religion focused above all on the event of the Revolution, which was seen as the final act of the Exodus from the old lands across the waters. The Declaration of Independence and the Constitution were the sacred scriptures and Washington the divinely appointed Moses who led his people out of the hands of tyranny. The Civil War, which Sidney Mead calls "the center of American history,"[5] was the second great event that involved the national self-understanding so deeply as to require expression in civil religion. . . .

The Civil War raised the deepest questions of national meaning. The man who not only formulated but in his own person embodied its meaning for Americans was Abraham Lincoln. For him the issue was not in the first instance slavery but "whether that nation, or any nation so conceived, and so dedicated, can long endure.". . .

The phrases of Jefferson constantly echo in Lincoln's speeches. His task was, first of all, to save the Union—not for America alone but for the meaning of America to the whole world so unforgettably etched in the last phrase of the Gettysburg Address.

But inevitably the issue of slavery as the deeper cause of the conflict had to be faced. In the second inaugural, Lincoln related slavery and the war in an ultimate perspective:

If we shall suppose that American slavery is one of those offenses which, in the providence of God, must needs come, but which, having continued through His appointed time, He now wills to remove, and that He gives to both North and South this terrible war as the woe due to those by whom the offense came, shall we discern therein any departure from those divine attributes which the believers in a living God always ascribe to Him? Fondly do we hope, fervently do we pray, that this mighty scourge of war may speedily pass away. Yet, if God wills that it continue until all the wealth piled by the bondsman's two hundred and fifty years of unrequited toil shall be sunk, and until every drop of blood drawn with the lash shall be paid by another drawn with the sword, as was said three thousand years ago, so still it must be said "the judgements of the Lord are true and righteous altogether."

But he closes on a note if not of redemption then of reconciliation—"With malice toward none, with charity for all."

With the Civil War, a new theme of death, sacrifice, and rebirth enters the new civil religion. It is symbolized in the life and death of Lincoln. Nowhere is it stated more vividly than in the Gettysburg Address, itself part of the Lincolnian "New Testament" among the civil scriptures. Robert Lowell has recently pointed out the "insistent use of birth images" in this speech explicitly devoted to "these honored dead": "brought forth," "conceived," "created," "a new birth of freedom." He goes on to say:

The Gettysburg Address is a symbolic and sacramental act. Its verbal quality is resonance combined with a logical, matter of fact, prosaic brevity. . . . In his words, Lincoln symbolically died, just as the Union soldiers really died—and as he himself was soon really to die. By his words, he gave the field of battle a symbolic significance that it has lacked. For us and our country, he left Jefferson's ideals of freedom and equality joined to the Christian sacrificial act of death and rebirth. I believe this is the meaning that goes beyond sect or religion and beyond peace and war, and is now part of our lives as a challenge, obstacle and hope.[6]

Lowell is certainly right in pointing out the Christian quality of the symbolism here, but he is also right in quickly disavowing any sectarian implication. The earlier symbolism of the civil religion had been Hebraic without being in any specific sense Jewish. The Gettysburg symbolism (". . . those who here gave their lives, that that nation might live") is Christian without having anything to do with the Christian church. . . .

The Civil Religion Today

In reifying and giving a name to something that, though pervasive enough when you look at it, has gone on only semi-consciously, there is risk of severely distorting the data. But the reification and the naming have already begun. The religious critics of "religion in general," or of the "religion of the 'American Way of Life,'" or of "American Shinto" have really been talking about the civil religion. As usual in religious polemic, they take as criteria the best in their own religious tradition and as typical the worst in the tradition of the civil religion. Against these critics, I would argue that the civil religion at its best is a genuine apprehension of universal and transcendent religious reality as seen in or, one could almost say, as revealed through the experience of the American people. Like all religions, it has suffered various deformations and demonic distortions. At its best, it has neither been so general that it has lacked incisive relevance to the American scene nor so particular that it has placed American society above universal human values. . . .

With respect to America's role in the world, the dangers of distortion are greater and the built-in safeguards of the tradition weaker. The theme of the American Israel was used, almost from the beginning, as a justification for the shameful treatment of the Indians so characteristic of our history. It can be overtly or implicitly linked to the ideal of manifest destiny that has been used to legitimate several adventures in imperialism since the early nineteenth century. Never has the danger been greater than today. The issue is not so much one of imperial expansion, of which we are accused, as of the tendency to assimilate all governments or parties in the world that support our immediate policies or call upon our help by invoking the notion of free institutions and democratic values. Those nations that are for the

The term *reification* comes from the Latin term for "thing" (*res*). To reify, therefore, is to bring something into being through speaking.

A key equation in the civil religion is the identification of the ancient nation of Israel with the United States. Just as Israel was to bring goodness and hope to the ancient world, so America saw itself as being charged with bringing virtues to the new world.

"Manifest destiny" is the idea that America was destined to possess much of the continent of North America, "from sea to shining sea."

moment "on our side" become "the free world." A repressive and unstable military dictatorship in South Vietnam becomes "the free people of South Vietnam and their government." It is then part of the role of America as the New Jerusalem and "the last hope of earth" to defend such governments with treasure and eventually with blood. When our soldiers are actually dying, it becomes possible to consecrate the struggle further by invoking the great theme of sacrifice. For the majority of the American people who are unable to judge whether the people in South Vietnam (or wherever) are "free like us," such arguments are convincing. Fortunately President Johnson has been less ready to assert that "God has favored our undertaking" in the case of Vietnam than with respect to civil rights. But others are not so hesitant. The civil religion has exercised long-term pressure for the humane solution of our greatest domestic problem, the treatment of the Negro American. It remains to be seen how relevant it can become for our role in the world at large, and whether we can effectually stand for "the revolutionary beliefs for which our forebears fought," in John F. Kennedy's words.

The civil religion is obviously involved in the most pressing moral and political issues of the day. But it is also caught in another kind of crisis, theoretical and theological, of which it is at the moment largely unaware. "God" has clearly been a central symbol in the civil religion from the beginning and remains so today. This symbol is just as central to the civil religion as it is to Judaism or Christianity. In the late eighteenth century this posed no problem; even Tom Paine, contrary to his detractors, was not an atheist. From left to right and regardless of church or sect, all could accept the idea of God. But today, as even *Time* has recognized, the meaning of the word *God* is by no means so clear or so obvious. There is no formal creed in the civil religion. We have had a Catholic President; it is conceivable that we could have a Jewish one. But could we have an agnostic president? Could a man with conscientious scruples about using the word *God* the way Kennedy and Johnson have used it be elected chief magistrate of our country? If the whole God symbolism requires reformulation, there will be obvious consequences for the civil religion, consequences perhaps of liberal alienation and of fundamentalist ossification that have not so far been prominent in this realm. The civil religion has been a point of articulation between the profoundest commitments of Western religious and philosophical tradition and the common beliefs of ordinary Americans. It is not too soon to consider how the deepening theological crisis may affect the future of this articulation. . . .

By mentioning "liberal alienation" and "fundamentalist ossification" in the same sentence with "God symbolism," Bellah seems to have in mind two opposite tendencies of religious groups. Liberals, he suggests, find the traditional idea of God troubling; fundamentalists define God in particular ways that suit their group's religious beliefs.

Behind the civil religion at every point lie Biblical archetypes: Exodus, Chosen People, Promised Land, New Jerusalem,
Sacrificial Death and Rebirth. But it is also genuinely American
and genuinely new. It has its own prophets and its own martyrs,
its own sacred events and sacred places, its own solemn rituals
and symbols. It is concerned that America be a society as per-
fectly in accord with the will of God as men can make it, and a
light to all nations.

It has often been used and is being used today as a cloak for
petty interests and ugly passions. It is in need—as any living
faith—of continual reformation, of being measured by universal
standards. But it is not evident that it is incapable of growth and
new insight.

> Bellah ends the piece by reiterating his point about the ongoing relevance of civil religion. In a "post-9/11" world his point is indeed suggestive.

It does not make any decisions for us. It does not remove
us from moral ambiguity, from being, in Lincoln's fine phrase,
an "almost chosen people." But it is a heritage of moral and religious experience from which we still have much to learn as we
formulate the decisions that lie ahead.

References

1. Why something so obvious should have escaped serious analytical attention is itself an interesting problem. Part of the reason is probably the controversial nature of the subject. From the earliest years of the nineteenth century, conservative religious and political groups have argued that Christianity is, in fact, the national religion. Some of them from time to time and as recently as the 1950s proposed constitutional amendments that would explicitly recognize the sovereignty of Christ. In defending the doctrine of separation of church and state, opponents of such groups have denied that the national polity has, intrinsically, anything to do with religion at all. The moderates on this issue have insisted that the American state has taken a permissive and indeed supportive attitude toward religious groups (tax exemptions, et cetera), thus favoring religion but still missing the positive institutionalization with which I am concerned. But part of the reason this issue has been left in obscurity is certainly due to the peculiarly Western concept of "religion" as denoting a single type of collectivity of which an individual can be a member of one and only one at a time. The Durkheimian notion that every group has a religious dimension, which would be seen as obvious in southern or eastern Asia, is foreign to us. This obscures the recognition of such dimensions in our society.
2. Dwight D. Eisenhower, in Will Herberg, *Protestant-Catholic-Jew* (Garden City, N.Y.: Doubleday & Co., 1955), 97.
3. God is mentioned or referred to in all inaugural addresses but Washington's second, which is a very brief (two paragraphs) and perfunctory acknowledgement. It is not without interest that the actual word "God" does not appear until Monroe's second inaugural, March 5, 1821. In his first inaugural, Washington refers to God as "that Almighty Being who rules the universe," "Great Author of every public and private good," "Invisible Hand," and "benign Parent of the Human Race." John Adams refers to God as "Providence," "Being who is supreme over all," "Patron of Order," "Fountain of Justice," and "Protector in all ages of the world of virtuous liberty." Jefferson speaks of "that Infinite Power which rules the destinies of

the universe," and "that Being in whose hands we are." Madison speaks of "that Almighty Being whose power regulates the destiny of nations," and "Heaven." Monroe uses "Providence" and "the Almighty" in his first inaugural and finally "Almighty God" in his second. See *Inaugural Addresses of the Presidents of the United States from George Washington 1789 to Harry S. Truman 1949*, 82d Congress, 2d Session, House Document No. 540, 1952.

4. For example, Abiel Abbot, pastor of the First Church in Haverhill, Massachusetts, delivered a Thanksgiving sermon in 1799, *Traits of Resemblance in the People of the United States of America to Ancient Israel*, in which he said, "It has been often remarked that the people of the United States come nearer to a parallel with Ancient Israel, than any other nation upon the globe. Hence 'Our American Israel' is a term frequently used; and common consent allows it apt and proper." In Hans Kohn, *The Idea of Nationalism* (New York: Macmillan Co., 1961), 665.

5. Sidney E. Mead, *The Lively Experiment* (New York: Harper & Row, 1963), 12.

6. Robert Lowell, "On the Gettysburg Address" in Allan Nevins, ed., *Lincoln and the Gettysburg Address* (Urbana, Ill.: Univ. of Ill. Press, 1964), 88–89.

READING RESPONSES

1. Many scholars in religious studies still use Bellah's essay in their research. List the claims that Bellah makes that you believe are still true about America. List Bellah's claims that you find outdated or untrue about America.

2. In his article, Bellah justifies the kind of evidence he uses to support his theory by claiming that "what people say on solemn occasions need not be taken at face value, but it is often indicative of deep-seated values and commitments that are not made explicit in everyday life." Do you agree with Bellah? Has Bellah provided enough evidence to persuade you? List three other kinds of evidence that you would find equally or even more persuasive.

3. Bellah calls the religious dimension of Americans' public discourse a "civic religion." Some might see these terms to be mutually exclusive. Do you? In your answer, provide definitions and examples of what is "civic" and "religious" to support your claim.

NOTES ON GRAMMAR, STYLE, AND RHETORIC:
FIRST-PERSON PRONOUNS

Nearly every time students receive a writing assignment, one or two will linger after class to ask questions. And it seems that one question is always something like this: "In this next essay, may I use the word *I*? All of my high-school teachers told me not to, but I'm the one doing the writing, so why shouldn't I be up front about that fact and use *I* when it feels natural?"

Robert N. Bellah uses first-person pronouns in "Civil Religion in America," and his essay can help us answer that question. Even though his essay is an extended piece of formal academic prose, he often uses the pronoun *I*. For example, he uses this pronoun when he clarifies his use of terms: "This public religious dimension is expressed in a set of beliefs, symbols, and rituals that I am calling American civil religion" (page 73). Further, he uses *I* to indicate how he personally reacts to others' claims that bear on his case: "Against these critics, I would argue that the civil religion at its best is a genuine apprehension of universal and transcendant religious reality..."(78).

But Bellah's pronouns get even more intriguing when he shifts from the first-person singular *I* to the first-person plurals *we* and *us*. With these plural pronouns, he invites readers to take on a certain role. But soon after that, he proceeds as if he can assume that they have accepted his invitation.

What role does he initially invite readers to accept? He uses *we* to invite readers to become co-explorers with him of the phenomenon he calls American civil religion: "If we could understand why he [President Kennedy] mentioned God, the way in which he did, and what he meant to say in those three references [to God], we would understand much about American civil religion" (71).

Soon after he issues this invitation, however, it becomes clear that Bellah assumes that readers have accepted the role of co-explorers since at several points where he uses some kind of transition marker, he refers both to his readers and to himself. In the paragraph immediately following his opening invitation, he announces his opening exploratory move: "Let us consider first the placing of the three references [to God]" (71). After he examines the issue of Kennedy's referring to God, he pauses and directs his readers: "Let us look more closely at what Kennedy actually said" (73). And when he thinks that readers need a reminder about the ground that they and he have already covered, he again uses a first-person plural pronoun: "The national magistrate...operates under the rubrics of the civil religion..., as we have already seen in the case of Kennedy." (76).

As Bellah moves along, he shows with his use of *we* and *us* that he is making other striking assumptions. For example, he writes as if he can assume what his readers know: "But we know enough about the function of ceremonial and ritual in various societies to make us suspicious of dismissing something as unimportant because it is 'only a ritual'" (72).

Furthermore, toward the end of his essay Bellah's use of *we* and *us* leads to something even more striking: He assumes that his readers not only are exploring American's civil religion but also are participating in it. He is, one suspects, trying to clinch his case for the existence of an American civil religion by leading his readers to admit that they see the civil religion in themselves. This may be the best explanation of Bellah's use of sentences such as his concluding one: "But it [the civil religion] is a heritage of moral and religious experience from which we still have much to learn as we formulate the decisions that lie ahead" (80).

With all these uses of *we* and *us*, then, Bellah is attempting something extraordinary. These pronouns reflect his attempt to unite readers with him in what he presents as a clear and companionable exploration of a significant subject. Beyond that, what better way is there to persuade readers that a social movement exists than to have them recognize that they themselves already believe in it and contribute to it?

If in your own writing you could use *we* and *us* in ways that move readers to accept the roles you are suggesting for them, you would experience a remarkable degree of rhetorical power. But before imitating Bellah's use of first-person pronouns, you must remember several things. First, when Bellah wrote this essay, he already had more impressive credentials as an author than many of us might ever have. Second, he had a long essay with which to build a relationship with his readers. And third, most of his original readers probably had some connection to the United States and the civil religion he sees there.

In this light, consider what would happen if his readers do not share the assumptions signaled by Bellah's uses of *we* and *us*. That, of course, is not likely to happen as he marks the way for his readers, using expressions such as "Let us consider first." But it could very well happen as he signals assumptions about what readers know. And it could happen even more easily with his assumption that readers represent and enact America's civil religion. Just imagine how non-U. S. citizens who despise aspects of U.S. culture and foreign policy would react to the assumption that they have much to learn from American civil religion in order "to formulate the decisions that lie ahead" (80). With such readers, Bellah's use of *we* and *us* would fail: They would probably deny all of his claims and be angry that he had ever made them. The tactic of using *we* and *us*, therefore, is one that in some situations can have great rhetorical power and in others can lead to rhetorical ruin.

In Your Own Writing . . .

Before using any first-person singular or plural pronouns in one of your own essays, you must be able to answer "yes" to both of these questions:

- First, will it likely seem logical and natural to your readers for you to signal your personal role in carrying out various tasks associated with the essay (such as providing guideposts to the essay's structure and detailing what you mean by certain phrases)?
- Second, will the roles that you suggest for your readers be roles that they could conceivably agree to take on?

STUDENT WRITING IN RELIGION AND SOCIETY

Introduction by Philip Park, religious studies major

The Assignment. I was told to write a thesis-driven term paper, about 6,000 words long. The assignment required that "the paper must argue a thesis clearly and consistently, based on the research done and the evidence presented."

The Content. Peter Berger was a sociologist who studied religion. I read two books by him and realized that between writing the first and the second he'd changed his ideas about research methods. The first book argued that only observable evidence could be used to explain religion. In the second book Berger speculates that observable characteristics in human beings may tell us about a supernatural reality that lies beyond our physical one. I wondered why Berger would abandon his previous commitment to observable evidence and how he could use observable evidence to talk about what we cannot observe. Answering these questions became the purpose of my paper.

Learning to Write in the Humanities. I first discovered that researchers in the humanities argue about scholarly assumptions when I was assigned to read Charlotte Allen's article "Is Nothing Sacred?" Allen notes that most scholars of religious studies attempt to conduct their research without assuming that a sacred or transcendent aspect of reality actually exists; if scholars assumed the existence of a sacred element, readers would dismiss their research as non-academic. Because they assume that any transcendent aspect of reality is off-limits for researchers, scholars use only objective evidence to support their claims.

For that same class, I read Berger's "classic," *The Sacred Canopy: Elements of a Sociological Theory of Religion.* In it, he theorizes that religion is constructed largely by society; in his appendix he emphasizes that his sociological theories are based exclusively on observable evidence and that, consequently, he is making no claims regarding theological truth. Berger reasons that he is committed to studying only that which is observable because he is engaged in "an enterprise of sociological theorizing." In this way I learned that the assumptions a humanities writer chooses affects the type of evidence he uses.

While reading books by Berger and scholarship about him, I began to form an opinion about Berger's mixture of theology and sociology and its relation to the controversy over acceptable methods of research. This opinion gradually became my thesis statement, the main argument of my paper. I say "gradually" because it was only through researching primary sources (works by Berger) and secondary sources (works about Berger) that I developed a specific thesis. First, I carefully examined the evidence that supported as well as contradicted my thesis. For instance, if someone disagreed about what I had to say about Berger, could I make a counterargument? What evidence could I use?

Once I gathered what I thought was a sufficient amount of evidence, I began writing the paper. I first introduced the reader to the context and the problem that my thesis responded to. In this case, I introduce religious studies by briefly describing its beginnings. Then, of course, I describe the problem: how two groups argue about the method for studying religion. After the introduction, I present evidence and argumentation that I hope will convince my reader.

Because I argue in my thesis for the value of a non-scientific approach, I begin by describing Berger's two books to show the weaknesses of an exclusively scientific approach. I also claim that theological speculation like Berger's can provide important knowledge about religion. In my presentation and analysis of the scholarly criticism of Berger's non-scientific method, I expand this idea that theological speculation can bring a different kind of understanding of religion. I then question the assumptions underlying the preference for the scientific approach to the study of religion, asserting that Berger's method of study is an equally valid way of understanding the phenomenon.

I conclude by noting the general lessons that all thinkers and researchers can learn from Berger's example. In my conclusion, I remind the reader of the importance of the problem I tackled in my thesis, and I address the "so what?" question that the reader will ask after finishing my paper. In this case, I discuss the role of assumptions in our search for and interpretation of evidence.

Creating Change Through Writing in Religious Studies. Even though it may seem that students write term papers just to get a grade in a class, I think that writing term papers helps students change the world around them in a few important ways. First, when writing term papers, students practice a method for figuring out what they believe in general about a topic and, specifically, what they want to claim about a topic. People have to know what they believe and why before they can set out to make change. Second, students analyze the assumptions authors use and decide whether or not they agree with those assumptions. Doing this helps students figure out what others believe and why. Knowing that, they are better prepared to create arguments that will convince people to think in a new or different way about a topic.

Peter Berger and the Study of Religion: An Examination of Sociological Method

Philip Park

Introduction: Religion and the Study of Religion

The quest to understand the human experience is not a new one. For millennia, people have questioned the nature of humanity. These questions of human identity have led to speculation regarding the possibility that we exist in some kind of relation to a being or a reality beyond the physical, observable reality. Eventually, such theological speculation has led to groups holding particular beliefs and attitudes about the sacred, giving birth to what we today would name "religion."

Religion (I mean to include all of the world's major religions) has influenced much of human history throughout the world. Clearly, then, studying religion can provide unique insight into how human beings, alone or in groups, make sense of reality. Since the late nineteenth century, religion has become a topic of academic research for scholars from a variety of academic disciplines. And recently the study of religion has become more controversial. At the center of much of this controversy is the method that scholars in academic settings should use to study religion.[1] Some scholars believe that religion should be approached scientifically by examining only what is observable. These scholars are called the functionalists. The substantivists, on the other hand, believe that such a method ignores the "element of the sacred" and the study of religion should acknowledge the unobservable reality at the center of religious thought.[2]

> From the beginning, I wanted to make it clear that I was making an argument about the assumptions that sociologists of religion hold.

This disagreement raises a critical question regarding the very assumptions that underlie religious studies: Can and should theological speculation (speculation about the unobservable) be part of the academic study of religion, where scholars disagree not only about theological matters but also about what counts as academically respectable scholarship?

> Here is the question that the paper will answer.

Thinking about this disagreement, one does well to consider the thought of American sociologist Peter L. Berger. The number of works he has published on religion is impressive, and the importance of his role in popular and academic thinking on religion cannot be ignored. Berger writes with a mixture of sociological and theological insight. It is this mixture, however, that has attracted criticism from scholars who believe that the study of religion should be limited solely to that which is clearly observable. After discussing two of his earlier books on religion, *The Sacred Canopy* (1967) and *A Rumor of Angels* (1969), I will argue that Berger's method, though exceeding the bounds of scientific study, provides a much needed non-scientific approach to the study of religion, a field typically marked by an exclusive adherence to scientific modes of investigation that can easily preclude a holistic understanding of religion.

> This thesis statement is my answer to the question I pose at the end of the preceding paragraph.

The Sacred Canopy and *A Rumor of Angels:* The Limits of Scientific Study

Berger described his personal theological convictions in his earlier *The Precarious Vision* (1961);[3] in *The Sacred Canopy* he states that he aims to "move strictly within the frame of reference of sociological theory." As a result, he acts as a "methodological atheist" and "view religion as a human projection."[4] Using the functionalist approach to the study of religion, he attempts to remain "value-free" and commits to studying only that which is observable in order so his work can be considered sociology, which is, after all, a social *science*.[5]

Berger begins *The Sacred Canopy* with an analysis of society: "Society is a dialectic phenomenon in that it is a human product, and nothing but a human product, that yet continuously acts back upon its producer."[6] We have created society, and, in turn, society has created us. Berger applies this theory of society as a human-made product to the phenomenon of religion; he theorizes that the creation and maintenance of religion are human efforts as well.[7]

Berger's scientific method here is obvious: he is intent on two things: engaging in "an enterprise of sociological theorizing," one that "bracket[s] the ultimate status of religious definitions of reality,"[8] and avoiding any theological statements or statements based on that which cannot be observed. In so doing, Berger separates observable reality and ultimate reality—that is, a transcendent reality that is beyond human interpretation. He limits the scope of his research to observable reality. Consequently, he admits that he does not, and cannot, assume that there actually exists a being or reality beyond what we can clearly see, as doing so would cause him to cross the boundaries of sociological science.[9]

It is within these boundaries that Berger concludes that all of one's beliefs are dependent on one's social environment. In *A Rumor of Angels*, he argues that sociology allows people to see that society and all that is found within it are constructions made by members of that particular society, a society located in a specific time and geographical location. Everything, from a sociological perspective, seems to be relative to one's society.

If sociology's conclusion that our beliefs are relative to our time and place is indeed true, adherents of religion are bound to be disappointed. Religions claim that their theology tells the one, true story of humanity, a story that lies beyond physical, observable reality. For believers, theology holds the truth about ultimate reality. An exclusively sociological approach, on the other hand, seems to focus solely on the observable reality and also seems to render futile any attempt to speculate about this ultimate reality. After all, how is the one, true story about ultimate reality, if it exists at all, to be known by us if all our ideas are relative to our specific contexts?

Berger answers this question raised by relativity's challenge: ". . . [R]elativizing analysis, in being pushed to its final consequence, bends back upon itself. The relativizers are relativized."[10] What he means is that those who wish to relativize a particular belief because it is contingent upon a society have to realize that their own view that "all is relative" is also a "product. . . of human history, [a] social construction. . . undertaken by human beings."[11] Relativizers, too, cannot claim to know that their view that all our beliefs are relative and that objective truth is unattainable or inexistent is absolutely and irrefutably true. Their claims about relativizing analysis are also influenced by their particular history and geography, and they, too, cannot claim to access truth.

> In this paragraph I was trying to focus attention on the clash of assumptions of the two methods of studying religion. Researchers' assumptions determine their methods.

If Berger remains committed to an exclusively scientific approach based solely on observable evidence, he cannot, as we have seen, make statements about what is theologically true about ultimate reality, an activity outside the boundaries of the scientific method. It is this attempt to understand ultimate reality, however, that fills the very substance of religion, and ignoring this quest leads only to a superficial understanding of a phenomenon based largely on that which is unobservable. As someone engaged in the holistic study of religion, Berger embarks on his own exploratory journey into the territory of theology.[12] In *The Sacred Canopy* Berger engages in what he calls "a conversation between sociology and theology," aiming to continue basing his conclusions on observable data. After examining some of his observations of universal human characteristics, he explores the possibility that these observations imply something about a transcendent reality. In the same way that the mathematical mind produces content that corresponds to a mathematical reality outside the mind, Berger suggests that the "religious projections of man. . . [could correspond] to a reality that is superhuman and supernatural."[13] Berger believes that a study of humanity and its religious projections may lead to knowledge of the ultimate reality that may exist beyond the observable reality to which we have access.

> This sentence summarizes Berger's claim.

Berger suggests that "signals of transcendence" can be found in all human beings, specifically in their desire for order, playfulness, hope, justice, and humor. We have a "propensity for order" and a trust in the order of the universe. We are playful creatures, and, in play, we step out of the "'serious' world in which people suffer and die" and into a world of "beatific immunity." We are hopeful creatures, and our hope often lies in the future. We have a sense of justice, demanding at least that those who deserve damnation receive damnation. Lastly, we have a sense of humor that "reflects the imprisonment of the human spirit in the world" and "recognizes and relativizes the "comic discrepancy in the human condition."[14] These phenomena of the human experience, although found within "'natural' reality. . . appear to point beyond that reality," according to Berger.[15]

Criticism and Analysis

> It helps my credibility to describe how others have critiqued Berger's method before I make my own assessment.

Although he bases his conclusions about the supernatural on what he can observe in human experiences, Berger is no longer working from "within the frame of reference of sociological theory." His modest conclusions about the supernatural, including his assumption that such a supernatural reality exists, cannot be verified through observation and thus cannot be called "scientific." Annette Ahern suggests that he wears two hats in this discussion: As a theologian, he holds that "rumors of angels" permeate our reality as "signals of transcendence," while, as a sociologist, he simply describes these phenomena as universal characteristics found in human beings.[16] Regarding his theological speculations, S.D. Gaede states that Berger writes "from the perspective not of scientific disinterest but of one who is religiously curious."[17] Not only do critics note his lack of testable hypotheses and his lack of more observable research, but they also accuse him of imposing his Christian biases on criteria for what constitutes observable data.[18] Consequently, his work has been used more often to build appreciation for religion than to study it.[19]

We must, however, carefully evaluate the criticism Berger's approach has received. Religious studies, which was first named *Religionswissenschaft*, or "science of religion," first presented a more "scientific" approach to religion and a branch of study intentionally differentiated from theology and philosophy of religion,[20] but we must now ask whether such a scientific approach is an adequate way to study religion. Should theology and philosophy of religion continue to be excluded from religious studies? Clearly, both are unique ways to gain a deeper understanding of either religion in general or a specific religion. Even if one does not believe in the validity of Berger's theological position, one walks away from Berger's book more educated on the thought-process affirmed by many religions. Exploring the theological framework of religion results in an understanding of religion that cannot be gained from a scholar's scientific observations.

As Hunter P. Mabry reminds us, "we need. . . a healthy respect for the autonomy of each discipline as a mode of apprehension, and a capacity to recognize the insights provided by each as fragmentary, partial illuminations of areas of reality which cannot be fully comprehended by any single mode of investigation."[21] Each discipline has unique tools for gathering, analyzing, and interpreting data on religion and religious experiences. Scholars from each discipline can bring unique insights into the phenomenon of religion, and through each discipline, our understanding of religion gains depth as well as breadth.[22]

The emphasis on a scientific, mono-disciplinary method, on the other hand, holds the danger of concluding that "religious experience is nothing more than those aspects accessible to and comprehensible through his or her particular discipline," which would "contravene. . . the norms of scientific study."[23] As Berger demonstrates in *A Rumor of Angels*, a strict attempt to investigate only the observable can blind one to other observable data, such as what he sees as signals of transcendence. A so-called observable account of human existence that does not include humanity's "consciousness of something beyond itself" is, according to Berger, simply not faithful to the spirit of a science based on observation.[24] After all, this human consciousness is an observable human impulse even if the "something" is not observable. Berger's approach questions the commonly accepted idea that a scientific account of religion should cancel out human theological speculation.

It does not need to be said that the study of religion as Berger proposes it invites controversy. Although this study can provide insight into human religious impulses, Berger's method sets theological truth as a goal, a goal that is rejected by most mainstream academic researchers. Most scholars agree that speculation about ultimate reality cannot rightfully be called an "academic" study of religion.

Here I turn to my evaluation of Berger's method. Given my evaluation of Berger's critics above, the reader shouldn't be surprised that I agree with Berger.

This widely accepted view of what can and cannot be studied in the academic setting provides insight into a variety of assumptions held in academia. For instance, many scholars affirm the separation of theology from religious studies based on their theological beliefs. Some hold that a transcendent, unobservable reality does not exist. Consequently no such thing as theology or an objective theological truth exists, either. Others argue that if such a reality does indeed exist, we cannot perceive or understand it. Some scholars believe that theological truth does exist and is accessible to us but that the academic setting is not the proper place for study of it. Berger, clearly, does not share these assumptions. He assumes that there is such an ultimate, theological reality and that it is the task of academic study to pursue it.

Once we realize that this controversy revolves around a set of differing assumptions, we will see that the idea that the scientific mode of investigation is the only or the better way of acquiring knowledge is based on similar assumptions. We must realize that Berger's method not only provides an alternative approach to religious studies but that it, as a means to acquiring knowledge, is not secondary to the scientific approach simply because it is based on a different set of assumptions.

> Once again I want to remind readers of my focus on scholars' assumptions.

Conclusion

In a culture in which scholars highly value the scientific method, Berger provides a refreshing perspective. His non-scientific approach to the "science of religion" demonstrates that it is possible to learn about religion in other ways, ways that account for a fuller range of human experience. If accounts of religion do not address the human impulses that shape religion, they will offer only a partial understanding of the phenomenon. Berger, realizing the limitations of the scientific approach, explores theological ground in his sociological work and offers a unique and much needed approach to knowledge in religious studies. Though his insights may very well hold theological truth, one does not need to subscribe to Berger's theology to appreciate the benefits of his multidisciplinary approach. His exploration of theology in religious studies, at the very least, reminds us that we are creatures who often describe human experience in a spiritual way. And, if academic research in the humanities has left us with anything, it might be the simple truth that in understanding the experiences of others, we come to a better understanding of our own.

> In my conclusion I want to extend my thesis to address the larger topic of the purpose of research in the humanities.

Though some scholars may consider Berger's research as non-academic, his scholarship has furthered the perennial quest to understand the human experience. He has been able to provide these new insights only because he was willing to challenge the generally held assumptions in academia. Berger's challenge provides a valuable reminder to anyone who attempts to understand human experience: All of us work within a framework of assumptions that shapes the way we interpret human experiences. And, if we are honest in our desire to understand, we will discover that our intellectual search will often require us to examine not only the assumptions that underlie ideas of others but also those that underlie our own.

> In the end, I want to add a subtle reminder that I'm not just trying to assess scholars' assumptions, but possibly to change my readers' assumptions.

Notes

1. Charlotte Allen, "Is Nothing Sacred? Casting out the Gods from Religious Studies," *Lingua Franca* (November 1996): 32.
2. Annette Ahern, "Re-enchanting the World: Berger's Sacramental Approach to Religion," *Toronto Journal of Theology* vol. 11, no. 1 (Spring 1995): 24.
3. Peter L. Berger, *The Precarious Vision: A Sociologist Looks at Social Fictions and Christian Faith* (1961; reprint. Westport, CT: Greenwood, 1976), 166.
4. Peter L. Berger, *The Sacred Canopy: Elements of Sociological Theory of Religion* (New York: Doubleday, 1967), 180.
5. Berger, *The Sacred Canopy*, 180.
6. Berger, *The Sacred Canopy*, 3.
7. Paul R. Johnson, "Society, Knowledge, and Religion: The Perspective of Peter Berger," *Perspectives in Religious Studies* 3 (Fall 1976): 299.
8. Berger, *The Sacred Canopy*, 180.
9. Berger, *The Sacred Canopy*, 180.
10. Berger, *A Rumor of Angels*, 47.
11. Berger, *A Rumor of Angels*, 52.
12. Berger, *The Sacred Canopy*, 185.
13. Berger, *A Rumor of Angels*, 53.
14. Berger, *A Rumor of Angels*, 60–79.
15. Berger, *A Rumor of Angels*, 59.
16. Ahern, "Re-enchanting the World," 26.
17. S.D. Gaede, "Excursus: The Problem of Truth," in *Making Sense of Modern Times: Peter L. Berger and the Vision of Interpretive Sociology*, ed. James Davidson Hunter and Stephen C. Ainlay (New York: Routledge and Kegan Paul, 1986): 162.
18. Robert C. Fuller, "Religion and Empiricism in the Works of Peter Berger," *Zygon* vol. 22, no. 4 (December 1987), 507. Robert Wuthnow, "Religion as Sacred Canopy," in *Making Sense of Modern Times: Peter L. Berger and the Vision of Interpretive Sociology*, ed. James Davidson Hunter and Stephen C. Ainlay (New York: Routledge and Kegal Paul, 1986): 139.
19. Wuthnow, "Religion as Sacred Canopy," 139.
20. Annette Ahern, "Towards an Academic Praxis in Religious Studies: Berger's Dual-Citizenship Approach," *Studies in Religion/Sciences Religieuses* vol. 20, no. 3 (Summer 1991): 334.
21. Hunter P. Mabry, "Sociology and Theological Research: Some Assumptions and Issues," *Bangalore Theological Forum* vol. 16 (Sept.–Dec. 1984), 160–1.
22. Mabry, "Sociology and Theological Research," 161.
23. Mabry, "Sociology and Theological Research," 161.
24. Fuller, "Religion and Empiricism," 504.

READING RESPONSES

1. Respond to Philip Park's thesis. Did Park convince you? If so, describe the part of his argument that persuaded you. Or, after reading Park's essay, do you disagree with his thesis? On what grounds do you disagree with him?

2. Philip Park focuses on the assumptions that Berger relies on in *The Sacred Canopy* and *The Rumor of Angels* to explain how Berger's research changed. What assumptions does Park rely on in his essay? Which of those assumptions do you agree with? Which do you reject?

3. Park concludes his essay with the claim that "if we are honest in our desire to understand, we will discover that our intellectual search will often require us to examine not only the assumptions that underlie ideas of others but also those that underlie our own." What possible dangers are associated with this kind of intellectual search? Are these dangers worth risking?

PUBLIC WRITING IN RELIGION AND SOCIETY

Introduction

During the 2004 presidential campaign, all the candidates discussed the ongoing war in Iraq. In the following letter to the editor, published in the *New York Times* a few days before the election, 34 professors of religious studies criticize the incumbent, President George W. Bush, for describing the Iraq War in religious terms. The authors state a thesis (the first paragraph) and then use the thesis to call readers to act: "We call for the repudiation of Mr. Bush's war and his misuse of religion to defend or sanctify it." Since they sent the letter to a newspaper on the eve of the presidential election, it is likely that they were hoping that people would act by voting for someone other than President Bush.

This is a very short letter, but it is packed with assumptions that affect whether or not readers will be persuaded. First, the authors claim that President Bush used religion to gain political advantage. If President Bush was trying to use religion for political reasons, he must have assumed two things: first, that most Americans would support a war that was part of "God's plan for humanity" and, second, that describing the war in this way would win political support for the war (specifically) and for his re-election campaign (generally). Interestingly, it seems clear that the authors of the letter also assumed these two things. If they didn't, they wouldn't claim that President Bush's use of religious terms gives him a political advantage.

The authors also assume several things that affect the evidence they provide to support their claim. For example, in the first sentence, the authors presume that the original reasons for the war in Iraq have "proved false" without presenting evidence that this is so. It may be that they expect that their reference to "original arguments" would remind readers that U.S. soldiers found no weapons of mass destruction. Later in the letter, the authors presume that the Iraq War is part of the Bush administration's "failed policies" without noting which policies they are referring to or providing evidence that these policies have "failed." Finally, the authors presume that religion should not be used for political purposes, an assumption that relies on the idea of a "wall of separation" between church and state. This is an assumption that most Americans accept, but it competes with assumptions based on civil religion—the assumptions that the authors of the letter believe President Bush used when justifying the war in Iraq. The authors are challenging President Bush's use of civil religion by challenging the assumptions he uses to establish his thesis.

Letter to the Editor: Religion and War

New York Times, Nov. 2, 2004, p. A26

To the Editor:

As each of the administration's original arguments for war has proved false, the claim that we serve God's plan for humanity by advancing freedom in Iraq has become President Bush's chief rationale.

We are persuaded that motives for the war are more varied and more questionable than the president acknowledges. Geopolitical calculations, desires for vengeance, military opportunism and corporate interest—most notably, greed for oil—all accompanied, and at times overshadowed, the religious and moral considerations.

To package this motley collection under the heading of "freedom" is not only deliberately misleading as well as an offense to language and reason, but also a familiar political strategy. To misrepresent such policies as God's will, however, seems little short of sacrilege. We deplore this attempt to wrap failed policies in religious rhetoric. We call for the repudiation of Mr. Bush's war and his misuse of religion to defend or sanctify it.

Bruce Lincoln

Chicago, Oct. 28, 2004

[The writer is a professor of history of religions at the University of Chicago Divinity School. The letter was also signed by 33 other faculty members.]

READING RESPONSES

1. List the possible reasons the authors might have had for writing this letter. What do you think was their primary reason for writing?
2. List the parts of the letter that you find most persuasive and those that you find least persuasive.
3. The authors claim that President Bush misused religion to justify the war in Iraq. What do you believe to be the proper role of religion in U.S. politics?

MORE WRITING IN RELIGION AND SOCIETY

Introduction

Hanna Rosin covered religion for the *Washington Post* from 1998 to 2001. The essay reprinted here appeared in the *Atlantic Monthly* soon after the 2004 presidential election. It is one of a cluster of articles that speculate about how the election outcome reflects changes in American society. Rosin suggests that relationships among religious Americans are changing and that the new relationships significantly affect American politics, just as America's civil religion does. Rosin claims that it isn't particularly useful to compare Americans who hold some kind of spiritual belief with those who don't because 95 percent of Americans claim to believe in a god or some kind of higher power. In the past, Americans identified themselves according to their religious affiliation—the religious group that they belonged to. Now, Rosin argues, religious Americans feel less allegiance to their particular religious group and a stronger connection with those who share their views on religious issues such as the nature of sacred documents like the Bible or the Koran and social issues such as abortion, gay marriage, and euthanasia.

Rosin challenges two long-held assumptions about religion in American life. First is the assumption that a "culture war" exists between those who are religious and those who are not. Rosin confirms the presence, indeed the deepening, of a culture war, but she claims that it is occurring within religious circles. The second assumption is that people who belong to the same religious organization believe the same things. Rosin argues that this is not true; instead, she claims, within particular religious organizations "modernists" take a more progressive view on theological and social issues, and "traditionalists" take a more conservative view.

Because Rosin believes that her readers hold both of these assumptions, she uses a great deal of evidence in her essay. The variety of evidence (statistical data, interview data, historical research) helps Rosin to convince readers that these two assumptions are false. If readers agree that the evidence invalidates these assumptions, readers are open to agreeing with the thesis, which is starkly printed and highlighted on a separate line at the beginning of the essay, a journalist's trick for getting right to the point.

Beyond Belief

Hanna Rosin

Atlantic Monthly, Jan–Feb. 2005

The real religious divide in the United States isn't between the churched and the unchurched. It's between different kinds of believers.

Richard Land is gloating, and who can blame him? When I called him a few weeks after the 2004 election, he said he'd been driving around his home town of Nashville with his cell phone ringing constantly, CNN on one line, *Time* magazine on the other—everyone wanting to ask the prominent Southern Baptist how his people had managed to win the election for George W. Bush. Yes, he told me, "we white evangelicals were the driving engine" of the president's victory. But then he veered into the kind of interview a quarterback gives in the locker room, in which he thanks the offensive line and the tight end and the coach and, well, really the whole team for bringing it home. "You'd be shocked," Land said, "at the number of Catholics who voted for this president. You'd be shocked at the number of Orthodox Jews, even observant Jews. This was a victory for all people of traditional moral values."

"Moral values." The phrase has turned into the hanging chad of the 2004 election, the cliché no one takes seriously. Do the debates over Iraq and the economy not involve moral values? Is everyone in the exit polls who didn't check that box a secular hedonist? As a way of explaining the outcome of the election, the "morality issue" has been amply debunked as all but meaningless.

But when Land uses the phrase to express his feeling of oneness with his Catholic (not to mention Jewish) brethren, it counts as a momentous development. Land does not, after all, come from some Quaker meetinghouse where all religious viewpoints are equally welcome. Rather, as the president of the Southern Baptists' Ethics and Religious Liberty Commission, he comes out of a tradition that has called the papacy the "mark of the beast." (It's no coincidence that in the Left Behind series so beloved by evangelicals, a former American cardinal serves as lackey to the Antichrist.) Yet Land is not shy about announcing now, "I've got more in common with Pope John Paul II than I do with Jimmy Carter or Bill Clinton." Of course, he still has theological differences with Catholics, but "these differences are *in addition to* the basics," he says. "Together we believe in the virgin-born son, who died on the cross and was resurrected on Easter Sunday—really resurrected, like *The Washington Post* could have reported it. We both say all human life is sacred, that marriage is between a man and a woman, that homosexual behavior is contrary to God's will." All this is just "more relevant," he says, "than whether I'm Catholic or Protestant."

Much of the post-election commentary about the "God gap" followed the old culture-war lines drawn by Pat Buchanan at the 1992 Republican National Convention, describing this presidential race as pitting the people of God against the godless. But although that has an epic sound to it, it's wrong—if only because there are far too few godless in the country to bring John Kerry to near parity. (Gallup polls show that only five percent of Americans don't believe in God or a higher power.) Rather, the election results confirmed an idea that sociologists have been dancing around for the past decade: that the more fundamental divide is *within* religious America, between different kinds of believers. Gradually the nation's spiritual map is being redrawn into two large blocs called traditionalist and modern—or orthodox and progressive, or rejectionist and accommodationist, or some other pair of labels that academics have yet to dream up.

For most of American history, of course, the important religious divides were between denominations—not just between Protestants and Catholics and Jews but between Lutherans and Episcopalians and Southern Baptists and the other endlessly fine-tuned sects. But since the 1970s fundamental disagreements have emerged within virtually all these denominations—over abortion, over gay rights, over modernity and religion's role in it. "There's a fault line running through American religions," Land says. "And that fault line is running not between denominations but through them."

Evidence for Land's claim pops up in newspapers every year starting around springtime, when many denominations hold their biennial or quadrennial meetings. In the past the subject of contention was typically abortion; of late it's more likely to have been homosexuality. The story line is remarkably consistent. A gay minister has been ordained, or a group of bishops have blessed a gay union. An internal trial is held, and sanctions are handed out. At the denomination meeting liberal protesters wearing rainbow stoles light candles; a conservative group called Solid Rock or First Principles threatens to break away and start a splinter faction unless the denomination holds fast to tradition. A vote is taken, and the denomination barely avoids schism. Last year the Episcopal Church got the most-dramatic headlines, after an openly gay bishop was ordained in New Hampshire and a coalition of congregations broke off from the American church. But similar rifts have appeared in the past few years within the United Methodists, the Presbyterians, the Lutherans—almost any denomination one can name. Nor is it just the mainline Protestant churches. At their June meeting the American Catholic bishops split over how strictly to hold politicians accountable for their positions on abortion. When Reform rabbis sanctioned gay unions, in 2000, Conservative and Orthodox rabbis issued statements objecting. And last year the Southern Baptists voted to pull out of the Baptist World Alliance, citing a move toward liberalism that includes tolerance of homosexuality and women clergy. The proximate cause was the acceptance into the alliance of a more liberal evangelical group, the Cooperative Baptists.

Every four years since 1992 a group of political scientists sponsored by the Pew Forum on Religion and Public Life has attempted to track these shifting loyalties; with each survey, says John C. Green, a professor of political science at the University of Akron and a member of the group, "the argument for the culture war in religion gets more convincing." The survey subdivides the three largest religious groups—evangelicals, mainstream Protestants, and Catholics—into "traditionalists," "centrists," and "modernists." Traditionalists are defined as having a "high view of the authority of the Bible" and worshiping regularly; they say they want to preserve "traditional beliefs and practices in a changing world." Centrists are defined as wanting to adapt beliefs to new times, while modernists have unabashedly heterodox beliefs, worship infrequently, and support upending traditional doctrines to reflect a modern view. The three categories are similar in size (centrists are a little larger and modernists a little smaller) and have remained about the same size over the dozen years of the survey.

On a wide range of issues, traditionalists agree with one another across denominations while strongly disagreeing with modernists in their own religion. For example, 32 percent of traditionalist evangelicals and 26 percent of traditionalist Catholics say abortion should always be illegal, compared with only seven percent of modernist evangelicals and three percent of modernist Catholics.

The divide between traditionalists and modernists is likely to widen in the coming years. In a recent study of twenty- to thirty-four-year-olds Robert Wuthnow, the head of the Center for the Study of Religion at Princeton University, found that ideological splits were much more pronounced than they had been in a similar study he conducted in the mid-1970s. In particular he found that political and religious views were tracking more closely, with the most religious more avidly pro-life, and the spiritual but less traditionally religious more avidly pro-choice.

Even some who are skeptical of an American "culture war" concede that religious traditionalists are gelling into a united force. According to Alan Wolfe, the author of *One Nation, After All* (1998), "The theological differences between conservative Catholics and Protestants that created five hundred years of conflict and violence have been superseded by political agreement. They are simply not interested in citing theology so long as they agree on abortion. People like Wuthnow are saying this has been going on for fifteen, twenty years. But there's an intensity this time around, much more so than most of us were prepared for."

What does the country's religious divide mean for the future? Much depends on how modernists respond to the surge of activism on the traditionalist side. If religious America is truly undergoing a culture war, it is at the moment a lopsided one. "There's a sense of complete reversal from the late fifties and early sixties," says James Davison Hunter, the author of *Culture Wars: The Struggle to Define America* (1991). "Conservatives within denominations are so well mobilized, while progressives within Protestantism and Catholicism find themselves flat-footed, without any coherent course of action or any way to make sense of what's going on." Typically, Hunter says, evangelicals are wary of mainstream society, and prone to doomsday predictions. But he found them brimming with a "stunning sense of optimism" when he recently visited an evangelical church in Houston. "Their understanding of their own hopes and dreams about the culture were entirely linked to getting out the vote for Bush. They seemed very pragmatic, very pleased."

For the moment, at least. It's an open question whether religious traditionalists will maintain the level of political engagement they showed in the 2004 election. The greatest obstacle here may be not a modernist backlash but the burden of high expectations. Already there are signs that evangelicals may be headed for a crushing disappointment. Following Bush's victory, James Dobson, of the evangelical group Focus on the Family, declared that if the Republicans don't deliver on issues such as abortion and gay marriage, "I believe they'll pay a price in the next election." Similarly, Bob Jones III, the president of Bob Jones University, read an open letter to Bush in chapel: "In your re-election, God has graciously granted America—though she doesn't deserve it—a reprieve from the agenda of paganism. You have been given a mandate. . . . Don't equivocate. Put your agenda on the front burner and let it boil. . . . Honor the Lord, and He will honor you."

It's not hard to imagine that perhaps six months, or a year, or three years down the road, religious traditionalists will face frustration and a sense of betrayal by the political system with which they are now engaging so enthusiastically. It wouldn't be the first time. After the election the conservative luminary Paul Weyrich issued a letter to evangelicals exulting, "God is indeed a Republican. He must be. His hand helped re-elect a president, with a popular mandate." And yet only five years ago Weyrich, who in the 1970s helped found the Heritage Foundation and coined the phrase "Moral Majority," was disillusioned about conservative Christians' ability to influence the national agenda on abortion and other issues. "Politics has failed," he wrote then. His prescription at the time: "Drop out of this culture" and find places "where we can live godly, righteous and sober lives." In 2008 we'll see if Weyrich and other religious conservatives remain engaged or start dropping out again.

READING RESPONSES

1. Rosin states her thesis at the beginning of the essay and reinforces it with evidence throughout. But her last paragraph moves beyond the thesis, asking readers to "imagine" the not-too-distant future. What does Rosin gain by asking readers to speculate with her?

2. Write out the two assumptions that Rosin challenges. List the evidence and summarize the reasoning she uses to prove that each one is outdated. For each assumption, note whether or not she convinced you.

3. In her thesis, Rosin argues that political analysts have misunderstood how religious belief divides Americans. How does religious belief unify Americans? What good can result from that unity? What harm?

WRITING ASSIGNMENTS

ASSIGNMENT 1: APPLYING THE PORTABLE RHETORICAL LESSON

Background: Since Bellah wrote his article in 1967, some things have changed and some have remained the same about how Americans invoke civic religion.

Your task for this assignment is to select a recent speech given by an American politician on an important occasion—an inauguration, for example, a State of the

Union speech, a televised address to the nation, or a eulogy at the funeral for a well-known public official. You can find the text for speeches like these on the Internet. For example, the White House provides transcripts of major presidential speeches at www.whitehouse.gov.

Read the speech carefully, noting each instance in which the speaker invokes civic religion. Then analyze the speaker's use of civic religion, noting how it is similar to the uses that Bellah describes. Describe carefully the ways in which you see the speaker using civic religion differently. Does the speaker invoke civic religion often or infrequently? If the speaker doesn't seem to refer to civic religion much, analyze the rest of the speech carefully. What does the speaker use in place of civic religion? Critique the speaker's alternative to civic religion. Do you think it is as effective? More effective? Support your critique with sound reasoning.

ASSIGNMENT 2: MAKING CONNECTIONS

Background: Chapter 8 (Biology) contains an article written by Marguerite Holloway entitled "The Female Hurt" (pp. 250–257). In that article Holloway details the kinds of sports injuries most common in female athletes and speculates about the reasons that female athletes are more susceptible than male athletes to certain kinds of injuries. Holloway puts some of the blame for these injuries on the assumptions that coaches, doctors, and female athletes make regarding the female body. But Holloway herself bases her claim on assumptions about the nature of athletic training and the importance of athletics, to name just two.

Your task for this assignment is to critique the role of assumptions in Marguerite Holloway's article, paying attention both to the assumptions of female athletes and those who support them and to the assumptions that Holloway makes in her article.

- Read Holloway's article carefully, noting the assumptions that people make regarding the female body and the effect of these assumptions on the rate of injury and type of injury to female athletes.
- Re-read Holloway's article again, looking carefully for the assumptions that support Holloway's claim. You might find it helpful to first write out what you believe to be the most important claims in her article. Then, look at the evidence she uses to support each claim. What assumptions connect the evidence to the claim? Do you agree with these assumptions? Take another look at Holloway's word choice. Where do her words indicate her assumptions?

ASSIGNMENT 3: DOING THE RESEARCH

Background: Because letters to the editor are short, they often contain strong claims that rely heavily on assumptions that the author hopes the reader will share. In the letter to the editor that serves as the public reading for this chapter, Bruce Lincoln and 33 other faculty members claim that President George W. Bush represents his political decisions about the war in Iraq as "God's will." To agree with Lincoln, readers have to agree with two assumptions: that President Bush does what they say he does and (if he does so) that he does so as a "political strategy." Fortunately, the first of these assumptions can be investigated and the product of that investigation can help you assess the second assumption.

Your task is to respond to Lincoln's letter, extending the argument that he and his fellow signers make about President Bush's justification for the Iraq War or rebutting their claims. To do so you must investigate the assumptions that Lincoln and his fellow signers make in their letter to the editor. Have they accurately characterized President Bush's evolving justifications for going to war with Iraq? To answer that question, research President Bush's public comments regarding the Iraq War during the six months preceding Lincoln's letter to the *New York Times*: May–October, 2004. You may find it helpful to consult with a reference librarian to locate President Bush's major policy speeches about the Iraq War during this time. Analyze the reasons that President Bush provides, comparing them to Lincoln's description.

As you begin drafting, consider carefully how your own assumptions about the reasons that nations should go to war affect your analysis of President Bush's reasoning. Consider, too, what assumptions your audience holds about the function of civil religion in contemporary American politics, the role of the U.S. president, and the presidency of George W. Bush specifically. Be sure to craft a thesis that is arguable and reasonable. Use examples from the speeches you analyzed to bolster your arguments.

CHEMISTRY: SUMMARIZING RESEARCH

When students think of writing in the natural sciences, they typically envision reports of scientific research (you will find samples of those in Chapter 8, Biology and Chapter 12, Nursing). Such publications report the news from the front lines of scientific study, and they sometimes make world-changing headlines. But scientists also commonly read and write review essays. Next to the breaking news of reported discoveries, review essays appear to be the shy, quiet characters of scientific writing, but they are powerful tools for change.

Scientists use review essays to summarize a body of published research on a particular subject. When they summarize, scientists include some but not all of the facts; they choose what is or is not important to include, thereby interpreting the shape of a field and selecting its most important features.

Martin Alexander's review, for example, summarizes the established scientific evidence on the effects of toxic pollutants in the soil. Alexander undertakes that rather routine-sounding exercise with the purpose of changing the way that the government measures the biological danger of toxic sites. In other words, Alexander's work had the potential of changing the ways that the U.S. government spends money on measuring toxins *and* of changing which sites we declare to be unsafe—a change with potential multi-billion-dollar consequences.

A Portable Rhetorical Lesson:
Summarizing to Shape the Future

It is hard to think of a writing activity more widely practiced, more powerful, or more underappreciated than a summary. In this chapter we hope that you will learn the art and power of purposeful summary from those who wield it regularly and effectively—natural scientists. Each of the writing samples is a type of review essay. Each essay conveys a sense that the author has researched thoroughly and has summarized fairly.

Imagine that the history of a particular area of science is like a jigsaw puzzle. But all the pieces do not come in one box; they have to be discovered. At any point in time some pieces have been discovered and some have not. A reviewer implicitly says, "Here are the puzzle pieces that we have discovered so far, this is the picture they seem to be forming, so these are the pieces we need to look for next."

Of course, no one knows what the "real" picture is. Two different reviewers, summarizing the same set of puzzle pieces, might argue in favor of two very different emerging pictures and call for a search for two very different sets of missing pieces. The reviewer whose argument "wins" (the one that has the greater influence in the scientific community) exercises great influence over the course of future research—and thus changes future science-news headlines.

The abstract of the first reading, Alexander's review essay, offers another way to see how the chapter's portable rhetorical lesson operates. The three-sentence abstract forms a three-part thesis statement: (1) toxic compounds left in the soil become less harmful to living organisms over time, (2) current methods of measuring toxins do not account for this drop in harmfulness, (3) therefore, we need to do new research to find more useful methods. Points 1 and 2 summarize the pieces of the puzzle that have been found, but they do so with the purpose of setting up point 3, where science needs to look in the future.

You use a similar rhetorical strategy when you write an introduction to a research paper (in fact, the student-written piece in this chapter is just such an introduction). You summarize what researchers already know about your topic so you can justify your own research. You show that there are missing pieces of a picture puzzle so that the pieces that your research adds appear as part of a larger, more significant picture.

Chapter Topics: The common topic of the chapter readings is pollution—whether caused by careless waste or terrorist attack. The various readings discuss methods that we use to measure pollution and its effects, practices for cleaning the environment, attempts to heal those who have been harmed by pollutants, and options for preventing pollution.

To Think About. . .

The U.S. Environmental Protection Agency is watching the San Fernando Valley closely because the water in its aquifers is contaminated by industrial waste that soaked through the ground and into the aquifers. Before the EPA ordered restrictions, the watershed was the chief water source for 800,000 people. The EPA required the cities of Los Angeles and Burbank to close wells in the San Fernando watershed and to provide clean water from other, more expensive sources. But over three million people live over those polluted aquifers.

Should Los Angeleans be afraid? More to the point—should you be afraid? You may drink bottled water, but the water you use to brush your teeth, take a shower, and wash your dishes probably comes from the tap—and that probably comes from a ground source of water like an aquifer. Are you in danger? One of the chief sources of public information about water quality is the EPA website (www.epa.gov). Search the site for information regarding water pollution in your area, keeping careful notes on the steps you take and the information you find. Now, review your experience and answer the following questions:

- List the help that the site offered you.
- List the obstacles you faced when you attempted to find information for your area.
- If your professor had not required you to do this research, would you have done it?
- Do you think the average citizen will be able to find meaningful information on this site?

WRITING IN CHEMISTRY

Introduction by Darla McCarthy, Professor of Chemistry

We all know that the pollution of our environment by toxic chemicals is a serious matter. Several types of cancer and birth defects, as well as increased incidences of miscarriage, infertility, and other physical and developmental maladies, have been linked to exposure to toxic chemicals. Leukemia and prostate cancer, for example, occur more frequently in people who have been exposed to dioxins—by-products of industrial processes such as pulp and paper bleaching, waste incineration, and pesticide manufacturing. Billions of pounds of pesticides, themselves toxic or contaminated with other toxins, are used annually in the United States; hazardous chemicals are accidentally spilled on roadways or fields; and some manufacturers and users of toxic chemicals fail to dispose of them properly. In other words, do not make the mistake of thinking that a highly specialized review in a chemistry journal has no bearing on you.

The review essay reprinted here does not take what you might think is the predictable line on environmental clean-up. Rather, author Martin Alexander argues that we might be wasting money cleaning some sites that do not pose real threats. His purpose, of course, is scientific, not political. His argument is a summary of the available scientific evidence. (And I hope you will notice how this review essay erases the line between summary and argument.)

Let me step back about forty years in order to place Alexander's work in its historical context. A review essay is, after all, a kind of history of science. Public awareness of the hazards associated with chemical pollutants was raised in the mid-1960s with the publication of *Silent Spring* (a section of which is reprinted in this chapter). In this landmark book, Rachel Carson discussed the decline of the American robin in certain regions of the United States due to its consumption of worms laden with the pesticide DDT, which was used in massive amounts to combat Dutch elm disease. Public attentiveness to chemical pollutants was further heightened in 1978, when Love Canal, a neighborhood in Niagara Falls, NY, was evacuated due to concerns regarding endemic health problems linked to soil and water contamination by various toxins that had leaked from a chemical waste disposal site. Because of mounting public pressure, the U. S. Congress passed several laws regulating the production, use, and disposal of hazardous chemicals. They also passed laws that provided funding and regulations for cleaning up, or remediating, contaminated sites.

Since the publication of *Silent Spring*, billions of dollars have been spent to remediate contaminated soil and water. And it is estimated that as many as 350,000 contaminated sites will require clean-up over the next 30 years, at a cost of as much as $250 billion.[*] With such astronomical costs, there is currently a great deal of interest in developing more efficient, cost-effective methods for remediation. One trend is a move toward more accurate descriptions of contaminated sites.[*]

This is the point at which Alexander enters the story. Currently, chemists use very rigorous methods for extracting chemical pollutants from soil samples taken from contaminated sites. Then they use various chemical analyses to determine the amount of toxin extracted from soil samples and determine the total amount of toxin contaminating the site. Sites with larger total amounts of contaminants are given higher priority for remediation. Scientists have recently become aware, however, that the total amount of contaminant present at a site is not necessarily a good indicator of the potential danger of that contaminant to the environment—some contaminants become so adsorbed, or stuck, to the soil that the organisms that live on or in the soil are not likely to ingest or absorb the toxin. So, even though there might be a high total amount of contaminant at a site, there may be little danger. Alexander summarizes those scientific findings and argues that they call for improved methods for characterizing contaminated sites.

Alexander, like any author of a scientific review essay, has two main goals: to summarize all of the pertinent literature related to his topic (to identify all of the puzzle pieces), and to suggest an answer to the question "what next?" (to tell us how the pieces fit together and what's missing). The most effective way to accomplish these goals is to craft the review as a thesis-based essay. However, as opposed to other types of thesis-based writing, in which data might play a supporting role in defending an argument based primarily on experience, logic, or reason, here the main emphasis is placed on data, as if the data inevitably leads to the conclusions the author draws. The data, not the argument, is the focus. The same could be said of hypothesis-driven scientific research papers (as in Chapters 8 and 9); we scientists pride ourselves on our objectivity, and the best way to remain objective is to stay focused on the data. To write a review confidently, a scientist must know the material, the research data, thoroughly. Notice that Alexander has 75 references in his bibliography. That's actually not much for a review essay—I've read some with more than 300 references!

---

[*] *New Report Projects Number, Cost and Nature of Contaminated Site Cleanups in the U.S. Over Next 30 Years.* United States Environmental Protection Agency, 11 Feb. 2005. http://www.epa.gov/superfund/news/30years.htm

The author of a review gains additional confidence—and credibility with the audience—by showing that he or she has been a participant in the area of science that is under review. It is almost universally the case that a review essay will make reference to the reviewer's published work. In other words, one earns the right to review a field of science only through building expertise in the field. Alexander cites his own publications 22 times.

You may find it helpful to scan over my marginal notes before you begin reading each section of the essay. I've defined terms that I think might be unfamiliar to you, and I've highlighted the main points of Alexander's argument. With that information you should find the article much easier to read.

✓ *READING TIPS*

Remember that this review essay is based on a thesis (see the first sentence after the abstract), is also data-based, and concludes with a suggested course of action (the sentence just before the "Relevance" section). That means, first, that you will be reading to find the support for a thesis, which is an argument and not a proven fact or set of facts. But because the paper is data-based (and not, for example, driven by emotion or personal appeal) the support for the thesis comes in the facts. Make sure that you judge the effectiveness of the paper by its fair and clear use of scientific data as grounds for the thesis. Finally, look for the author's suggestion of what to do next. Each of these features should be easy for you to find; don't let yourself get bogged down in the technical information. The marginal notes should help you to understand all of the science, but if you need to push past some complex chemistry to get the main points and structure of the argument, do so.

Aging, Bioavailability, and Overestimation of Risk from Environmental Pollutants

Martin Alexander

Bioavailability is the ability of a chemical to be ingested or absorbed by living organisms. Bioavailability affects the toxicity of chemicals and impacts their potential for biodegradation (degradation by organisms) and/or bioremediation (complete degradation or detoxification by organisms).

Environmental Science & Technology 2000; 34 (20): 4259–65

[Abstract] As they persist, or age, in soil, organic compounds become progressively less available for uptake by organisms, for exerting toxic effects, and for biodegradation and bioremediation by microorganisms. This declining bioavailability is not reflected by currently used methods for the chemical analysis of soils for determining concentrations of organic pollutants. As a result, such methods overestimate exposure, and thus risk, from toxic chemicals in contaminated sites.

Organic chemicals contain carbon.

The validity of current methods for analyzing soils to assess the risk from organic pollutants has been cast in doubt by recent research. The focus of much of the concern with analytical methods has been increasing the recovery and sensitivity of chemical procedures, and the relevancy of these procedures to living organisms has been largely ignored. However, a primary reason for performing these analyses is to provide information on the exposure of living organisms to, and hence the risk from, these pollutants. The underlying issue is one of bioavailability. . . .

The traditional method for analyzing polluted soil is to extract, or remove, the pollutant from the soil and then to identify and quantify the pollutant by various chemical procedures. Chemists are always trying to improve their analyses either by increasing the amount of pollutant recovered from the soil in the extraction process or by increasing the sensitivity, or precision, of their chemical procedures.

In this review, information will be presented to show that the bioavailability of organic pollutants in soil declines with time and that current analytical methods, because they measure total and not bioavailable concentrations, may overestimate the magnitude of the environmental and societal problem from these pollutants. Both early and recent evidence for these changes in accessibility will be presented, and the toxicological significance of these observations will be considered. The relevance of current analytical methods will then be evaluated. Differences in bioavailability among species, environments, and compounds and the consequent need for new analytical methods will be reviewed. . . .

The toxicological significance is a measure of how changes in the accessibility of chemicals to organisms affects the toxicity of the chemicals to the organisms.

Many of the organic pollutants in soil were introduced years or sometimes decades ago at a time when industry and the public were not adequately aware of the scope, magnitude, and importance of soil pollution. Even early research, which has largely been forgotten, provided evidence that the availability of certain chemicals that have been in soil for some time is less than freshly added compounds, and hence the term aging (or weathering) was applied to the phenomenon. Although the early findings and their importance have been obscured with the passage of time, awareness now is growing among environmental toxicologists, risk assessors, and regulatory agencies that the total concentration of a toxicant in a contaminated environment frequently overestimates the risk of pollutants to humans, animals, and plants.

Early Evidence

The heading reminds us that a review essay is partly history of science.

Data showing the time-dependence of changes in bioavailability are now compelling. The early information came from studies of concentrations of pesticides in the field measured for long periods of time and from measurements of toxicity of pesticides to invertebrates and plants.

For example, long-term monitoring of soil revealed that DDT, aldrin and its epoxide (dieldrin), heptachlor and its epoxide, and chlordane disappeared slowly at first, but then the rate of loss fell to such an extent that further loss was either extremely slow or ceased (1). Although the initial disappearance might be partially the result of volatilization or abiotic degradation as well as biodegradation by soil microorganisms, the fact that the disappearance was almost imperceptibly slow after several years indicates that those insecticides had become poorly available to the indigenous microorganisms; otherwise, these biodegradable compounds should have continued to disappear. The results of several long- and short-term monitoring studies are presented in Figure 1, which shows that the period when little or none of the insecticides is available to soil microorganisms may occur either soon or long after the compounds were introduced into the soil. Such results also show that the percentage of the compound that is poorly or no longer bioavailable differs markedly among the several soils and sites that were examined. This failing on the part of the soil microflora cannot be attributed to low winter temperatures, periods of drought, or other adverse conditions because the monitoring often extended for

> Volatilization is evaporation.

> Abiotic degredation is disappearance of a chemical caused by non-biological events such as reaction with oxygen in the air or decomposition initiated by sunlight.

> a population of microscopic organisms including algae, bacteria, and fungi

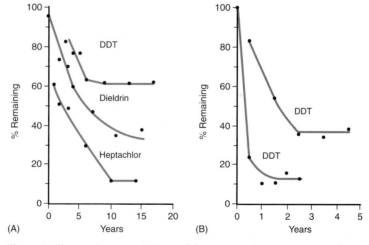

Figure 1 Changes in concentrations of three insecticides in longterm (A) and short-term (B) monitoring of several field sites. Calculated from data of Nash and Woolson and Lichtenslein et al. (1). In other field sites, the monitoring period was not sufficiently long to show the possible existence of a phase with little or no further disappearance of the insecticides.

several years and was done in fields or experimental plots where crops were growing. . . .

Recent Evidence

Organic compounds that have aged in the field are less bioavailable, often appreciably so, than the same compounds freshly added to samples of the same soil. In a field treated with DDT 49 years earlier, approximately 30, 12, and 34% of DDT and the DDE and DDD formed from the added insecticide were available for uptake by the earthworm *Eisenia fetida* compared to newly added chemicals, and 28 or 43% of dieldrin applied at the same time was available based on concentration in the worms or percentages assimilated, respectively. Similar reduced bioavailabilities of DDT, DDE, and DDD but not dieldrin were observed in soil from a waste disposal site in which the insecticides had aged for some 30 years (4). Field aging also diminishes the availability to microorganisms of 1,2-dibromoethane that persisted for 3 years (5), simazine applied for 20 consecutive years (6), and polycyclic aromatic hydrocarbons (PAHs) in soils from a closed coking plant (7) and manufactured-gas plant (8).

Laboratory tests confirm the lesser availability to microorganisms of aged than un-aged compounds in highly dissimilar soils (Table 1). The bioavailability to microorganisms decreases with time but reaches a value below which a further decline is no longer detectable. How long it takes to reach that value and the final percentage availability vary among soils and compounds. The process may be complete in days or weeks or may take in excess of 200 days, and the loss in availability may be small or large (9, 10). . . .

Table 1 Compounds Shown to Become Less Available for Microbial Degradation as a Result of Aging

Compound	Soil	Aging period (d)	Ref
naphthalene	Colwood loam	365	(73)
naphthalene	Mt. Pleasant silt loam	68	(17)
phenanthrene	Mt. Pleasant silt loam	110	(74)
phenanthrene	16 soils	200	(9)
anthracene	Lima loam	203	(18)
fluoranthene	Lima loam	140	(18)
pyrene	Lima loam	133	(18)
atrazine	Ravenna silt loam	90	(75)
atrazine	16 soils	200	(9)
4-nitrophenol	Lima loam	103	(10)
4-nitrophenol	Edwards much	103	(10)

In the previous two sections, Alexander established that pollutants do indeed become less available for uptake by small organisms over time. In this section Alexander reviews data that show that as pollutants age in soil, their toxicity to larger plants and animals also decreases.

acute toxicity: causing an immediate toxic effect such as paralysis or suffocation

chronic toxicity: causing long-term effects such as cancer or emphysema

Genotoxic compounds modify DNA and thus have potential to alter genes and eventually cause cancer. Here Alexander explains that the ability of certain compounds to modify DNA decreases as the compounds age in soil. He refers to a "solid-phase assay," which is just a fancy way of saying that researchers exposed organisms to genotoxins in the soil—or on a *solid* surface—and then determined if modifications had been made to the organisms' DNA.

Carcinogens are cancer-causing substances.

Toxicological Significance

Aging is toxicologically significant because the assimilation and acute and chronic toxicity of harmful compounds decline as they persist and become increasingly sequestered with time. Studies with mammals, for example, have shown that less 2,3,7,8-tetra-chlorodibenzo-*p*-dioxin (TCDD) was absorbed after it had been in soil for 8 days than after a contact period of 10–15 hours. The number of fruit flies (*D. melanogaster*), house flies (*Musca domestica*), and German cockroaches (*Blatella germanica*) killed by DDT and dieldrin declined markedly with increasing times of residence of these compounds in soil (13). Similar but largely forgotten data were obtained many years earlier by Peterson et al. (14), who found a marked and progressive reduction in toxicity to *D. melanogaster* as DDT persisted for 108 days in soil. An effect of aging on plants has also been noted with three herbicides: napropamide, simazine, and atrazine (3, 6, 15). In each instance, toxicity was less than that anticipated. . . . Aging also reduces the effectiveness of at least some genotoxic compounds in soil. Thus, by means of a solid-phase assay, it has been found that the genotoxicity of the carcinogens benzo(*a*)pyrene and 9,10-dimethyl-1,2-benzanthracene diminished rapidly and to a great extent within a 15-day period, although analysis following vigorous extraction showed only a slight decline in concentration after about 2 months (16). . . .

Nevertheless, a time-dependent decline in bioavailability does not always occur. This may be related to properties of the soil or of the compound. Instances in which bioavailability did not diminish include the biodegradability of simazine (6), the dermal and oral availability of TCDD and dieldrin to rodents (27, 28), and the uptake of DDE by earthworms in one soil (4). Only a small loss in bioavailability of certain compounds in sediments may occur with aging; witness that the rate of microbial dechlorination of polychlorinated biphenyls in Hudson River sediments contaminated for at least 15 years was only about 20% slower than compounds freshly added at 20 ppm (29). In addition, toxic compounds may exist in pockets or in nonaqueous-phase liquids within the soil, and after some physical disturbance, they may be released and become bioavailable. Although such compounds are aged in the sense of time, they have not been sequestered in a fashion to reduce their bioavailability to living organisms.

Incorrect Analytical Methodologies

The widely used protocols of federal and state regulatory agencies rely on analytical methods that entail vigorous extraction of soils and sediments with organic solvents. The aim is to remove

Here Alexander emphasizes that current methods focus only on chemical analysis—they aim to extract as much pollutant as possible out of the soil in order to determine the *total* amount of chemical pollutant in the soil. This type of analysis does not account for changes in the bioavailability of pollutants as they age; thus, risks are often overestimated.

Environmental scientists are well aware of the fact that certain chemicals are more accessible to organisms in one type of soil (environmental matrix) than another. So, they account for the differences by including a "correction factor," or "default value."

all, or as much as possible, of the pollutant from the environmental sample. Each method is carefully evaluated to assess its accuracy, as well as its precision and sensitivity, but the accuracy is interpreted in purely chemical terms. The relevancy of such methods to the toxicity of the compound in the form in which it exists in nature is generally not considered in carrying out risk analyses, except that a default value is sometimes included to relate to the particular environmental matrix. The fact that the compound may become progressively less bioavailable as it persists, even in a single environmental matrix, is not considered in assessing risk. Thus, the regulator is not making use of information that bioavailability may decline with little or no reduction in the concentration as determined by procedures that rely on initial vigorous extractions. Hence, such methods are often not relevant for prediction of potential exposures to, and thus risks from, contaminated soils or sediments.

The evidence is compelling that the quantities recovered by vigorous extraction fail to predict declining bioavailability as compounds persist in soil. For example, despite the marked diminution in effectiveness in killing three species of insects as dieldrin and DDT aged in soil, >90% of the dieldrin and ca. 85% of the DDT could still be recovered by vigorous extraction (13). . . .

If the total concentration at a polluted site is greater than the regulatory level but the bioavailable concentration is below that value, a site that might be slated for expensive cleanup might, instead, be deemed to present an acceptable risk. The public concern about a contaminated location might be allayed by the more meaningful assessment. Moreover, a site that was bioremediated but still contained concentrations of one or more contaminants above the target levels may have indeed been successfully cleaned up, even though conventional analysis suggested that the remediation was inadequate. This is true both of engineered and intrinsic bioremediation, which frequently do not destroy all of the targeted compounds. Because such bioremediation treatments act on the fraction that is bioavailable, to microorganisms at least, the accessibility of the portion that remains may be so low that the site presents little or no risk to higher organisms. . . .

New Assay Methods

Here Alexander addresses the key question: If bioavailability changes over time and can't be predicted, how can you predict the risk of exposure? This is his "what next?" question.

The regulator is faced with a major dilemma because the magnitude of reduction in bioavailability resulting from aging is different for a single compound in different soils, for different compounds in the same soil, and for different periods of time that a compound has remained in soil. How does one predict the degree of exposure and risk from an aged compound? Bioassays are an obvious means of performing assessments, but biological

Bioassays analyze the effects of pollutants on living organisms, while chemical and physical assays simply analyze the amounts and types of pollutants in the soil.

Here is Alexander's proposed answer to the "what next?" question— use mild extraction techniques for chemical assays. Notice that he does not overemphasize his solution; Alexander's purpose in writing the review is to highlight the issue of bioavailability, and not to solve the resulting problems. He does, however, suggest a direction that others could pursue to solve the problem.

In his conclusion, Alexander simply summarizes his review and reminds his audience of why they should be concerned about bioavailability.

measurements frequently do not have adequate precision for regulatory purposes, and they are time-consuming and expensive. An alternative is a chemical or physical assay, but the results of that assay must correlate well with the results of bioassays. . . .

Several chemical and physical methods have been considered as ways to measure the bioavailability of organic compounds in soil. The results of analyses by such procedures have been correlated with bioavailability to earthworms, springtails, nematodes, and microorganisms (31, 39–43). The observation that the time-dependent decline in bioavailability is accompanied by a time-dependent decline in the quantity of compounds extracted from soil by a mild procedure (9, 10, 31, 44) suggests that a mild-extraction technique might serve as the basis for a surrogate assay for bioavailability. . . .

Relevance

Because exposure to persistent compounds is overestimated by currently used chemical methods, the risk is likewise being overestimated. Inasmuch as aging appears to occur in many and possibly most contaminated soils, the bioavailability of aged chemicals probably is being overestimated very frequently. As a consequence, current approaches to evaluating sites for cleanup sometimes may alarm people in localities where the risk is small. They probably lead to choosing some sites for remediation where little such need exists and thus delay the cleanup of polluted areas where the risk is greater. They also probably result in requirements for cleanup that are unnecessarily stringent and thus lead to expenditure of funds that could be used to decontaminate additional areas. Therefore, a more widespread recognition of bioavailability of aged compounds is necessary—among scientists, environmental engineers, regulators, and the public at large.

Acknowledgments

Portions of the work were supported by National Institute of Environmental Health Sciences grants ES05950 and ES07052 with partial funding from the U.S. Environmental Protection Agency, U.S. Air Force Office of Scientific Research grant F49620–95–1–0336, the U.S. Department of Agriculture, and GRI. I thank R. C. Loehr, J. W. Gillett, and E. L. Madsen for helpful comments.

Literature Cited

1. Alexander, M. In *Environmentally Acceptable Endpoints in Soil*; Linz, D. G., Nakles, D. V., Eds.; American Academy of Environmental Engineers: Annapolis, MD, 1997; 43–136.

4. Morrison, D. E.; Robertson, B. K.; Alexander, M. *Environ. Sci. Technol.* **2000**, *34*, 709.

5. Steinberg, S. M.; Pignatello, J. J.; Sawhney, B. L. *Environ. Sci. Technol.* **1987**, *21*, 1201.

6. Scribner, S. L.; Benzing, T. R.; Sun, S.; Boyd, S. A. *J. Environ. Qual.* **1992**, *21*, 115.

7. Weissenfels, W. D.; Klewer, H. J.; Langhoff, J. *Appl. Microbiol. Biotechnol.* **1992**, *36*, 689.

8. Erickson, D. C.; Loehr, R. C.; Neuhauser, E. F. *Water Res.* **1993**, *27*, 911.

9. Chung, N.; Alexander, M. *Environ. Sci. Technol.* **1998**, *32*, 855.

10. Hatzinger, P. B.; Alexander, M. *Environ. Sci. Technol.* **1995**, *29*, 537.

13. Robertson, B. K.; Alexander, M. *Environ. Toxicol. Chem.* **1998**, *17*, 1034.

14. Peterson, J. R.; Adams, R. S., Jr.; Cutkomp, L. K. *Soil Sci. Soc. Am. Proc.* **1971**, *35*, 72.

15. Bowmer, K. H. *Aust. J. Soil Res.* **1991**, *29*, 339.

16. Alexander, R. R.; Alexander, M. *Environ. Toxicol. Chem.* **1999**, *18*, 1140.

27. Shu, H.; Teitelbaum, T.; Webb, A. S.; Marple, L.; Brunck, B.; Dei Rossi, D.; Murray, F. J.; Paustenbach, D. *Fundam. Appl. Toxicol.* **1988**, *10*, 335.

28. Midwest Research Institute. *Oral Bioavailability of Soil Associated Aldrin/Dieldrin*; Project 9849-F; Midwest Research Institute: Kansas City, MO, 1991.

29. Abramowicz, D. A.; Brennan, M. J.; Van Dort, H. M.; Gallagher, E. L. Environ. *Sci. Technol.* **1993**, *27*, 1125.

31. Kelsey, J. W.; Kottler, B. D.; Alexander, M. *Environ. Sci. Technol.* **1997**, *31*, 214.

39. Loibner, A. P.; Gartner, M.; Schlegl, M.; Heutzenberger, I.; Braun, R. In *In Situ and On-Site Bioremediation*; Battelle Press: Columbus, OH, 1997; Vol. 5, 617–622.

40. Cornelissen, G.; Van Noort, P. C. M.; Parsons, J. R.; Govers, H. A. J. *Environ. Sci. Technol.* **1997**, *31*, 454.

41. Houx, N. W. H.; Aben, W. J. M. *Sci. Total Environ. Suppl.* **1993**, 387.

42. Ronday, R. *Commun. Soil. Sci. Plant Anal.* **1997**, *28*, 777.

43. Tang, J.; Robertson, B. K.; Alexander, M. *Environ. Sci. Technol.* **1999**, *33*, 4346.

44. Tang, J.; Alexander, M. *Environ. Toxicol. Chem.* **1999**, *18*, 2711.

READING RESPONSES

1. As Professor McCarthy notes in her introduction, Martin Alexander summarizes a great deal of research in this review essay. How does he join it all together? To answer that question, analyze the structure of three of Alexander's paragraphs (choose paragraphs that include at least four references). For each paragraph, answer these three questions: 1) What seems to be the task of the first sentence? 2) Where in the paragraph do the references appear? 3) Why are these references in this order? Note any similarities you see in the structure of these paragraphs.

2. Alexander's thesis is "that current analytical methods, because they measure total and not bioavailable concentrations, may overestimate the magnitude

of the environmental and societal problem from these pollutants." How does this thesis fit with the research he summarizes in his essay? Relying on Alexander's summary of the research, count up the number of studies he cites for two topics: the bioavailability of aging chemicals and the effectiveness of analytical procedures. Compare your counts with Alexander's thesis, and evaluate Alexander's focus. Does all the research he cites support his thesis? If so, how does it do so? If not, what would you eliminate?

3. Professor McCarthy notes that Alexander is a well-respected scholar on the topic he reviews in this essay. How does his ethos as a respected scholar affect his review essay? As you answer that question, consider how he uses his own research, the information he provides citations for, and the information that he does not cite.

NOTES ON GRAMMAR, STYLE, AND RHETORIC:
USES OF OLD INFORMATION IN A CRITICAL REVIEW

One illuminating approach to the style of Martin Alexander's "Aging, Bioavailability, and Overestimation of Risk from Environmental Pollutants" is to examine the kinds of information his sentences convey. Most sentences can be divided into two parts, one of which conveys what linguists call old information, the other of which conveys what linguists call new information.

Old information in a sentence is information that readers know on the basis of the particular rhetorical situation, that readers with even minimal experience of the world are aware of, that appears prior to that sentence, or that can be inferred from material leading up to that sentence. For example, certain bits of information become old information after they appear once. Consider the following short text:

Professor Alexander has written a review essay on toxic chemicals in various kinds of soil. This essay should attract some serious attention.

In the second sentence, "This essay" carries old information since it refers to Alexander's review essay, which is mentioned in the first sentence.

New information in a sentence is information that is not obvious from the particular rhetorical situation, that is not known to all people with even minimal experience of the world, that is not mentioned prior to that sentence, or that cannot be inferred from material leading up to that sentence.

Consider again the sample text from above. I have already noted that in the second sentence "This essay" conveys old information. Now I can add that "should attract some serious attention" conveys new information. If these words were blacked out, no one could guess what they are. Therefore, in the second sentence, "This essay" makes a connection to earlier material, and "should attract some serious attention" moves the message into new territory. This sentence exemplifies what is true of the old and new information in many sentences: The old information appears early in a relatively short sentence subject, and the new information follows in a longer predicate.

Alexander's sentences use old information in at least three specific ways: (1) by using sentence subjects that package up information from fairly extensive prior sections of his essay, (2) by using introductory adverbial clauses to remind readers of information presented earlier, and (3) by including entire sentences that convey only old information.

Consider first Alexander's tactic of using sentence subjects to package up old information from extensive prior sections of his essay. One really good example of this appears in the section labeled "Recent Evidence." Alexander begins this section with two substantial paragraphs dealing with studies of the bioavailability of organic compounds that have aged in the field. After these two paragraphs, Alexander begins a new sentence and a new paragraph with these words: "These investigations with individual compounds. . . ." This phrase is made up entirely of old information, pointing backwards in the essay to keep all the details fresh in his readers' minds.

He does similar work with some adverbial clauses that introduce sentences. For example, in the first section of the essay, Alexander includes the following clauses: "Even early research, which has largely been forgotten, provided evidence that the availability of certain chemicals that have been in soil for some time is less than freshly added chemicals. . ." (106). He then begins the very next sentence with the following adverbial clause: "Although the early findings and their importance have been obscured with the passage of time. . ." (106). This clause conveys mainly old information, since it refers to the early research and how it has largely been forgotten.

Finally, at the end of this essay Alexander includes a short section that he labels "Relevance." The first sentence of this section reads as follows: "Because exposure to persistent compounds is overestimated by currently used chemical methods, the risk is likewise being overestimated" (111). Appearing where it does, this sentence is made up entirely of old information; everything in this sentence has come up earlier in the essay. In fact, most of the information in the section labeled "Relevance" is old. This section summarizes the major claims in Alexander's overall presentation.

You might worry that some readers could find these sentences repetitious, or they might feel condescended to when they encounter such sentences. Why should anyone be asked to read a sentence that doesn't add something new?

Alexander might well answer that he is writing a review essay, an essay that by its very nature covers lots of information. One of his priorities, therefore, almost certainly would be to help his readers keep all that information straight, something that the prominent examples of old information can help with. Further, he might argue that he is not just listing all sorts of research findings on toxic chemicals but is using these findings to build an argument.

Because his argument is based on extensive and complex details, Alexander cannot afford to allow his readers to forget all the accumulated information. Readers' memory is critical for the success of the argument, so frequent reminders are necessary. And the upshot of this argument—that we might not have to invest time and money in cleaning up some toxic waste sites—is important and even startling. If he is right in his argument, then we are probably wasting time and money trying to clean up some toxic sites. If he is wrong, the results of following his advice could well be disease, deformity, and death.

In Your Own Writing. . .

- When you revise your writing, pay attention to how you use old and new information.
- Use old information in your sentence subjects to "package" information that you've already provided.
- Include old information in introductory phrases and clauses to contextualize new information.
- Put new information in the predicates of your sentences.
- When you want to help the reader make connections among topics, use entire sentences that include old information. Use entire sentences to help the reader connect new information to the argument you're building.

STUDENT WRITING IN CHEMISTRY

Introduction by Arianne Folkema, chemistry major

The Assignment. My class was asked to conduct original research (in other words, no one else had previously determined the answers to the questions I was researching) and write a research report. The report was supposed to be similar to a published research report. To justify the validity of the questions I chose to research, my report's introduction had to summarize what was already known about the topic I was researching. My introduction also had to define the questions I was trying to answer. That is a lot like a review essay: first summarize what's known, then ask the "what next?" question.

The Content. My report is on the bioremediation of PCP—the use of live organisms to clean up ("bioremediate") sites contaminated by PCP, pentachlorophenol, a toxic compound that was formerly used as an industrial wood preservative and is now a banned substance. My argument in my introduction follows this outline: (1) PCP is a toxic compound; (2) research has proven that PCP can be degraded by some microbes (bacteria and fungi) occurring naturally in the environment; (3) very little is known about PCP degradation by other microbes, specifically, a microbe called *M. chlorophenolicum* PCP-1; (4) what little is known about PCP degradation by *M. chlorophenolicum* PCP-1 indicates that it degrades PCP in a different manner than do other microbes; (5) it would be beneficial to conduct further research on *M. chlorophenolicum* PCP-1 with the hope of learning if it could be more widely used to bioremediate PCP.

Learning to Write an Introduction to a Scientific Report: Lessons from Review Essays. My first exposure to original laboratory research was certainly a turning point in terms of understanding science in the "real world." I had taken many lab courses, following the protocols written in lab manuals: basic "recipe science" where the outcome is already known. I soon found out this was not the case in independent research, where the purpose is to first look at all the information available on a subject, and from there to figure out where the holes, the missing data, are . . . and to figure out ways to fill in those holes.

I spent two summers and a school year doing lab research on PCP degradation. An introduction to a scientific report must be confident in its summary, and a scientific writer only gains confidence through thorough research. So I began my project at the library. A search engine located abstracts for recently published articles containing information on everything from the metabolism of PCP by bacteria isolated from mushroom compost to observations about the degradation of pesticides by fermented sausages—hmm! That helped me to decide what publications were relevant to my project. My task was to summarize the published data clearly and use it to justify the argument that my research questions were worthwhile.

As I was drafting my paper and thinking about writing style, I took special care to be very specific and concise. One of the best ways for a scientist to be concise is to use figures, and the two figures in my introduction demonstrate the key points of the argument. Figure 1 shows a sequence of chemical changes (a pathway) that is known to break down PCP. Figure 2 shows a pathway with a question mark in the middle. That question mark was the key question for my research: How does the microbe *M. chlorophenolicum* PCP-1 break down PCP? When you see the question mark in the middle of that figure, you know just what my research is after.

Creating Change through Writing in Chemistry. When I first started reading professional research reports and reviews, I was amazed at how much research goes on, producing scientific knowledge and guiding scientists to new research. When scientists write about their research (or summarize the research published by others), their readers think of new ideas for their own research. For example, I read an article about an enzyme produced by certain types of bacteria. The enzyme catalyzes the formation of a molecule that the bacteria need in order to cause infection in mice (and presumably, in humans); bacteria that lack the enzyme are not infectious. I remember thinking that a researcher in the pharmaceutical industry would read the article and try to find a drug that would inhibit the enzyme and thus prevent the bacteria from forming the molecule and causing infections. Research in science always leads to more research; scientists create change as part of the unending process of trying to understand the natural world.

Introduction to "Bioremediation of Pentachlorophenol"

Arianne Folkema

> Bioremediation is the process of breaking down, or detoxifying, a toxic substance by biological organisms, in this case, the detoxification of the wood preservative, pentachlorophenol, or PCP.

Since the beginning of the industrial revolution, many xenobiotic chemicals have been introduced into the environment for a variety of purposes, with little attention paid to their potential long-term effects. The ecological consequences of some of these substances involve substantial damage to both aquatic and terrestrial ecosystems. In today's society, environmental, political, social and regulatory pressures demand that the use of xenobiotics be carefully monitored and that past mistakes be remedied. One technique that holds unique promise for remediation is bioremediation—the use of live organisms to clean up contaminated sites. One common technique for bioremediation is the culture of select bacteria which possess specific enzymes that have the ability to metabolize industrial waste components. These bacteria are then added to contaminated soil.

> Xenobiotic chemicals are foreign to biological systems, not naturally-occurring.

> A culture is the growth of bacteria under controlled conditions in a laboratory. The idea here is to grow large quantities of pollutant-degrading bacteria in the lab, and then to spread the bacteria on contaminated soil.

> Metabolism is the biological process of breaking down a large molecule into smaller molecules.

Pentachlorophenol (PCP) is one example of a xenobiotic compound that can be bioremediated. PCP was initially produced in the 1930s for use as an industrial wood preservative and was mass-produced for this purpose, leading to the production of 45 million pounds in 1983 alone (1). The use of PCP was banned for commercial purposes in 1987 due to its extreme toxicity, which is known to damage the lungs, liver, kidney, gastrointestinal tract, nervous system, and immune system. PCP is currently listed as a priority pollutant by the US Environmental Protection Agency (EPA) (2). Fortunately, in contaminated sites where PCP had previously been used, it has been discovered that there are a number of microbes that have the unique capability to degrade PCP into less toxic substances.

There are numerous reports of the attempted bioremediation of PCP-contaminated sites. One example of natural bioremediation on an actual field site was witnessed in contaminated groundwater near sawmills in Finland, which were reported to contain up to 190mg of chlorophenols per liter of water. Upon study of the site, a variety of chlorophenol-degrading bacteria were isolated and characterized (3). Reports of successful artificial bioremediation are scarce, however, due to the compromised survival of bacteria *in situ*. This is illustrated by an attempt to clean up contaminated soils via the introduction of *Mycobacterium chlorophenolicum* PCP-1, a bacterium known to degrade PCP, directly to PCP-contaminated soil. In this field study, PCP degradation was observed to be 5mg of PCP per kg of soil during the first two weeks after inoculation. However, this was only a slight improvement over the rate of PCP degradation by indigenous bacteria (2). This poor performance is possibly due to the method of inoculation, the soil properties, and/or the presence of toxic contaminants other than PCP in the soil. Additional studies have been carried out in more controlled settings such as bioreactors (vats in which microbes are grown in the presence of the compounds they metabolize), where soil properties and the presence of contaminants are not likely to be an issue. For example, the fungus *Panus tigrinus* was introduced to a mixture of chlorinated phenols at 500mg/L in a 72L bioreactor and was reported to have completely removed the PCP after three weeks (4).

Due to their potential (although often inefficient) bioremediation capabilities, research has been performed on a variety of PCP-degrading microbes. These include *Sphingobium chlorophenolicum* (4), a bacterium, and *Phanerochaete chrysosporium* (5), a fungus, on which thorough research has been done and for which the pathway of PCP degradation is known. Degradation of PCP by these microbes involves hydroxylation of PCP to form tetrachlorohydroquinone (TCHQ) (in which a hydroxyl—an oxygen atom, OH—replaces a chlorine atom, Cl). Then comes a reaction in which TCHQ produces trichlorohydroxyquinone (TriCHQ). TriCHQ is further degraded into dichlorinated and monochlorinated compounds. The benzene

---

Natural bioremediation is carried out by organisms that are already present at a site prior to contamination.

Artificial bioremediation is carried out by organisms that are added to a site after it has been contaminated.

In situ means at the original site of contamination.

M. chlorophenolicum PCP-1. is the scientific name of a particular strain of bacteria.

Inoculation is the introduction of bacteria to a medium; soil, in this case.

Indigeneous means living naturally in a particular area.

During metabolism, organisms break down compounds via a series of reactions to form the final product (often carbon dioxide). The set of reactions, with the accompanying intermediate compounds, is called a metabolic pathway. Figure 1 visualizes this concept.

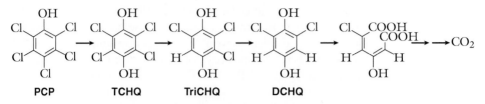

Figure 1 PCP Degradation Pathway for *S. chlorophenolicum* and *P. chrysosporium*.
The PCP degradation pathway for *S. chlorophenolicum* and *P. chrysosporium* is known to proceed through the intermediates TCHQ, TriCHQ, and DCHQ via a series of hydroxylations and reductive dehalogenations. PCP = pentachlorophenol; TCHQ = tetrachlorohydroquinone, TriCHQ = trichlorohydroquinone; DCHQ = dichlorohydroquinone.

ring is eventually cleaved and ultimately, carbon dioxide is formed (Fig. 1).

Figure 1 is a schematic diagram showing the chemical structures of PCP and the product of each reaction in the PCP metabolic pathway. Each of the chemical structures after PCP represents an intermediate in the pathway. The important thing to notice here is the minor differences between the structures. In the first reaction, we see that the chlorine atom (Cl) at the bottom of the molecule is removed and replaced by a hydroxyl group (OH). In the second reaction, the chlorine atom on the lower-left side of the molecule is replaced by a hydrogen atom. The last part of the pathway is not well understood, so after the fifth structure two arrows are shown to indicate multiple reactions leading to CO_2 (carbon dioxide).

Less research has been conducted on another bacterium with the potential to bioremediate PCP; *Mycobacterium chlorophenolicum* PCP-1. Fewer concrete details are known about its metabolism of PCP, although it is clear that PCP metabolism by *M. chlorophenolicum* PCP-1 differs significantly from PCP metabolism by other organisms. The first step in PCP degradation by *M. chlorophenolicum* PCP-1, is the hydroxylation of PCP to form TCHQ (6). The identity of the second intermediate in PCP degradation by *M. chlorophenolicum* is unknown (Fig. 2). Incubation of cells extracts with TCHQ results in the formation of dichlorotrihydroxybenzene (DTHB) and monochlorotrihydroxybenzene (MTHB); a trichlorinated intermediate is not observed. DTHB could be formed by first hydroxylating TCHQ to form trichlorotrihydroxybenzene (TTHB), followed by reductive dechlorination of TTHB (bottom pathway, Figure 2). Alternatively, DTHB could be formed by reducing TCHQ to form TriCHQ, and then hydroxylating TriCHQ (top pathway, Figure 2). It has been reported that TCHQ undergoes a hydroxylation reaction yielding TTHB (7). However, the basis for that

When molecules containing chlorine are degraded by microbes, generally only one chlorine atom is removed in each reaction of the pathway. So, when PCP, which contains five chlorines, is degraded, we expect there to be intermediates with four, three, two, and one chlorine atoms. The intermediate containing three chlorines in the PCP metabolic pathway utilized by *M. chlorophenolicum* PCP-1 was not identified in the experiment described here.

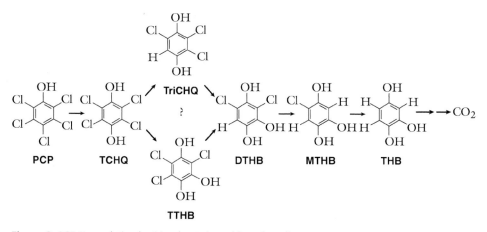

Figure 2 PCP Degradation by *Mycobacterium chlorophenolicum*

The PCP degradation pathway utilized by *M. chlorophenolicum PCP-1* is not completely defined and could either proceed through the intermediate TriCHQ or TTHB. PCP = pentachlorophenol; TCHQ = tetrachlorohydroquinone, TriCHQ = trichlorohydroquinone; TTHB = trichlorotrihydroxybenzene; DTHB = dichlorotrihydroxybenzene; MTHB = monochlorotrihydroxybenzene; THB = trihydroxybenzene.

> Look at the question mark in the third stage of the pathway; that question was the reason for my research. In order to understand this figure, compare each structure to the one that appears before it in the pathway. Notice that in some reactions Cl is replaced by OH, and in others Cl is replaced by H.

conclusion is questionable. The conclusion was made after observing that the bacteria are not able to convert TriCHQ to DTHB. However, the complementary experiment involving the other possible intermediate, TTHB, was not attempted. Thus, it has never been conclusively shown that the cells do indeed convert TTHB to DTHB.

Therefore, the purpose of my research was to characterize the degradation pathway of PCP by *M. chlorophenolicum* PCP-1; to confirm the identity of the second intermediate in the pathway, and to identify which reductive cofactors are involved in the metabolism of PCP.

The characterization and purification of the enzymes and cofactors necessary for degradation of PCP is important because it provides information that can be used to further characterize the genes encoding the enzymes involved in PCP degradation. It may then be possible to clone those genes into more robust bacteria capable of growing at more rapid rates and surviving in harsher soil environments. These genetically engineered microbes may ultimately be useful in the improved bioremediation of PCP-contaminated sites.

References

1. *Pentachlorophenol Facts.* PANNA – Pesticide Action Network North America http://www.panna.org/resources/documents/factsPentachlorophenol.dv.html May, 2004.

2. Miethling, R. and U. Karlson. "Accelerated Mineralization of Pentachlorophenol in Soil upon Inoculation with *Mycobacterium chlorophenolicum* PCP1 and *Sphingomonas chlorophenolica* RA2." *Appl. Environ. Microbiol.* **1996**, *62*: 4361–66.

3. Mannisto, M. and M. Tiirola. "Diversity of chlorophenol-degrading bacteria isolated from contaminated boreal groundwater." *Arch. Microbiol.* **1999**, *171*: 189–197.

4. Leontievsky, A. A. and N. M. Myasoedova. "Adaptation of the white-rot basidiomycete *Panus tigrinus* for transformation of high concentrations of chlorophenols." *Appl. Microbiol. Biotechnol.* **2002**, *59*: 599–604.

5. Reddy, G. and M. Gold. "Purification and Characterization of Glutathione Conjugate Reductase: A Component of the Tetrachlorohydroquinone Reductive Dehalogenase System from *Phanerochaete chrysosporium*." *Arch. Biochem. Biophys.* **2001**, *391*: 271–77.

6. Apajalahti, J. and M. Salkinoja-Salonen. "Dechlorination and *para*-Hydroxylation of Polychlorinated Phenols by *Rhodococcus chlorophenolicus*." *J. Bacteriol.* **1987**, *169*: 675–81.

7. Apajalahti, J. and M. Salkinoja-Salonen. "Complete Dechlorination of Tetrachlrohydroquinone by Cell Extracts of Pentachlorophenol-Induced Rhodococcus chlorophenolicus." *J. Bacteriol.* **1987**, *169*: 5125–30.

READING RESPONSES

1. As Arianne Folkema notes in her introduction, students find themselves in an odd position when they write summaries of research: these are usually written by an expert in a field of research, not a novice. Compare the first three paragraphs of Folkema's review with Alexander's. List the similarities and the differences that you find. For each difference, consider if it might be a result of Folkema's status as a novice researcher.

2. In her review, Folkema typically includes more information about the research she's summarizing than Alexander does. What additional information does Folkema include? Who might value this information? Why is it/isn't it worth including?

3. If you were a professor of chemistry, would you require students to include a review of literature in their research reports? Provide a set of reasons to support your answer.

PUBLIC WRITING IN CHEMISTRY

Introduction

The publication of Rachel Carson's *Silent Spring* is often credited with launching the environmental movement. Carson, after earning a master's degree in zoology, wrote radio scripts for the U.S. Bureau of Fisheries, later becoming an aquatic biologist and then chief editor of publications for the bureau. She turned to full-time independent writing, and, after four years of research for the book, published *Silent Spring* in 1962. Chemical companies tried to prevent its publication, and Carson was threatened with lawsuits and accused of being unprofessional, an "hysterical woman," and a communist. It became, nonetheless, an international bestseller.

Silent Spring begins with a three-page chapter entitled "A Fable for Tomorrow." The chapter's opening sentence, "There once was a town in the heart of America where all life seemed to live in harmony with its surroundings" draws readers into a story of an idyllic town that is beset by unimaginable biological horrors—birds and bees disappear, vegetation withers and dies. Carson concludes the chapter by telling us that no town had suffered all the blight that she visited upon her fictional town but that "every one of these disasters has actually happened somewhere." The final paragraph of the chapter reads, "What has already silenced the voices of spring in countless towns in America? This book is an attempt to explain."

The opening chapter tells us that Carson is offering a natural history—a history of nature assaulted by humans. It is very important to recognize that history is a kind of summary, here enlivened in skin and bone and bark and root. Through this recognition Carson's "review" of the environmental record enriches our sense of the vast usefulness of summary.

There are obvious differences between this piece and a scientific review. It is grounded in thorough research, but the references sit quietly off stage so as not to "burden the text with footnotes," as Carson explains. It is passionate and personal (note language such as "fantastic," "menace," and "endless problems").

Yet the kinship to a scientific review is evident. The first sixteen chapters of the book discuss the evidence that pesticide use is damaging nature. The last chapter, "The Other Road," answers the "what next?" question. In it she discusses the benefits of biological control over pests, identifying several particular methods, each of which has now been the subject of scientific research. In other words, *Silent Spring* follows the form and purpose of a review essay, and it brought about the field-shaping results that review writers hope for.

Realms of the Soil

Rachel Carson

Chapter 5, *Silent Spring*, 1962

. . . The problem that concerns us here is one that has received little consideration: What happens to these incredibly numerous and vitally necessary inhabitants of the soil **[worms, microbes, and all life forms that inhabit the soil]** when poisonous chemicals are carried down into their world, either introduced directly as soil "sterilants" or borne on the rain that has picked up a lethal contamination as it filters through the leaf canopy of forest and orchard and cropland? Is it reasonable to suppose that we can apply a broad-spectrum insecticide to kill the burrowing larval stages of a crop-destroying insect, for example, without also killing the "good" insects whose function may be the essential one of breaking down organic matter? Or can we use a nonspecific fungicide without also killing the fungi that inhabit the roots of many trees in a beneficial association that aids the tree in extracting nutrients from the soil?

The plain truth is that this critically important subject of the ecology of the soil has been largely neglected even by scientists and almost completely ignored by control men. Chemical control of insects seems to have proceeded on the assumption that the soil could and would sustain any amount of insult via the introduction of poisons without striking back. The very nature of the world of the soil has been largely ignored.

From the few studies that have been made, a picture of the impact of pesticides on the soil is slowly emerging. It is not surprising that the studies are not always in agreement, for soil types vary so enormously that what causes damage in one may be innocuous in another. Light sandy soils suffer far more heavily than humus types. Combinations of chemicals seem to do more harm than separate applications. Despite the varying results, enough solid evidence of harm is accumulating to cause apprehension on the part of many scientists.

Under some conditions, the chemical conversions and transformations that lie at the very heart of the living world are affected. Nitrification, which makes atmospheric nitrogen available to plants, is an example. The herbicide 2,4-D causes a temporary interruption of nitrification. In recent experiments in Florida, lindane, heptachlor, and BHC (benzene hexachloride) reduced nitrification after only two weeks in soil; BHC and DDT had significantly detrimental effects a year after treatment. In other experiments BHC, aldrin, lindane, heptachlor, and DDD all prevented nitrogen-fixing bacteria from forming the necessary root nodules on leguminous plants. A curious but beneficial relation between fungi and the roots of higher plants is seriously disrupted.

Sometimes the problem is one of upsetting that delicate balance of populations by which nature accomplishes far-reaching aims. Explosive increases in some kinds of soil organisms have occurred when others have been reduced by insecticides, disturbing the relation of predator to prey. Such changes could easily alter the metabolic activity of the soil and affect its productivity. They could also mean that potentially harmful organisms, formerly held in check, could escape from their natural controls and rise to pest status.

One of the most important things to remember about insecticides in soil is their long persistence, measured not in months but in years. Aldrin has been recovered after four years, both as traces and more abundantly as converted to dieldrin. Enough toxaphene remains in sandy soil ten years after its application to kill termites. Benzene hexachloride persists at least eleven years; heptachlor or a more toxic derived chemical, at least nine. Chlordane has been recovered twelve years after its application, in the amount of 15 per cent of the original quantity.

Seemingly moderate applications of insecticides over a period of years may build up fantastic quantities in soil. Since the chlorinated hydrocarbons are persistent and long-lasting, each application is merely added to the quantity remaining from the previous one. The old legend that "a pound of DDT to the acre is harmless" means nothing if spraying is repeated. Potato soils have been found to contain up to 15 pounds of DDT per acre, corn soils up to 19. A cranberry bog under study contained 34.5 pounds to the acre. Soils from apple orchards seem to reach the peak of contamination, with DDT accumulating at a rate that almost keeps pace with its rate of annual application. Even in a single season, with orchards sprayed four or more times, DDT residues may build up to peaks of 30 to 50 pounds to the acre; under trees, up to 113 pounds.

Arsenic provides a classic case of the virtually permanent poisoning of the soil. Although arsenic as a spray on growing tobacco has been largely replaced by the synthetic organic insecticides since the mid-'40s, *the arsenic content of cigarettes made from American-grown tobacco increased more than 300 per cent* between the years 1932 and 1952. Later studies have revealed increases of as much as 600 per cent. Dr. Henry S. Satterlee, an authority on arsenic toxicology, says that although organic insecticides have been largely substituted for arsenic, the tobacco plants continue to pick up the old poison, for the soils of tobacco plantations are now thoroughly impregnated with residues of a heavy and relatively insoluble poison, arsenate of lead. This will continue to release arsenic in soluble form. The soil of a large proportion of the land planted to tobacco has been subjected to "cumulative and well-nigh permanent poisoning," according to Dr. Satterlee. Tobacco grown in the eastern Mediterranean countries where arsenical insecticides are not used has shown no such increase in arsenic content.

We are therefore confronted with a second problem. We must not only be concerned with what is happening to the soil; we must wonder to what extent insecticides are absorbed from contaminated soils and introduced into plant tissues. Much depends on the type of soil, the crop, and the nature and concentration of the insecticides. Soil high in organic matter releases smaller quantities of poisons than others. Carrots absorb more insecticide than any other crop studied; if the chemical used happens to be lindane, carrots actually accumulate higher concentrations than are present in the soil. In the future it may become necessary to analyze soils for insecticides before planting certain food crops. Otherwise even unsprayed crops may take up enough insecticide merely from the soil to render them unfit for market.

This very sort of contamination has created endless problems for at least one leading manufacturer of baby foods who has been unwilling to buy any fruits or vegetables on which toxic insecticides have been used. The chemical that caused him the most trouble was benzene hexachloride (BHC), which is taken up by the roots and tubers of plants, advertising its presence by a musty taste and odor. Sweet potatoes grown on California fields where BHC had been used two years earlier contained residues and had to be rejected. In one year, in which the firm had contracted in South Carolina for its total requirements of sweet potatoes, so large a proportion of the acreage was found to be contaminated that the company was forced to buy in the open market at a considerable financial loss. Over the years a variety of fruits and vegetables, grown in various states, have had to be rejected. The most stubborn problems were concerned with peanuts. In the southern states peanuts are usually grown in rotation with cotton, on which BHC is extensively used. Peanuts grown later in this soil, pick up considerable amounts of the insecticide. Actually, only a trace is enough to incorporate the telltale musty odor and taste. The chemical penetrates the nuts and cannot be removed. Processing, far from removing the mustiness, sometimes accentuates it. The only course open to a manufacturer determined to exclude BHC residues is to reject all produce treated with the chemical or grown on soils contaminated with it.

Sometimes the menace is to the crop itself—a menace that remains as long as the insecticide contamination is in the soil. Some insecticides affect sensitive plants such as beans, wheat, barley, or rye, retarding root development or depressing growth of seedlings. The experience of the hop growers in Washington and Idaho is an example. During the spring of 1955 many of these growers undertook a large-scale program to control the strawberry root weevil, whose larvae had become abundant on the roots of the hops. On the advice of agricultural experts and insecticide manufacturers, they chose heptachlor as the control agent. Within a year after the heptachlor was applied, the vines in the treated yards were wilting and dying. In the untreated fields there was no trouble; the damage stopped at the border between treated and untreated fields. The hills were replanted at great expense, but in another year the new roots, too, were found to be dead. Four years later the soil still contained heptachlor, and scientists were unable to predict how long it would remain poisonous, or to recommend any procedure for correcting the condition. The federal Department of Agriculture, which as late as March 1959 found itself in the anomalous position of declaring heptachlor to be acceptable for use on hops in the form of a soil treatment, belatedly withdrew its registration for such use. Meanwhile, the hop growers sought what redress they could in the courts.

As applications of pesticides continue and the virtually indestructible residues continue to build up in the soil, it is almost certain that we are heading for trouble. This was the consensus of a group of specialists who met at Syracuse University in 1960 to discuss the ecology of the soil. These men summed up the hazards of using "such potent and little understood tools" as chemicals and radiation: "A few false moves on the part of man may result in destruction of soil productivity and the arthropods may well take over."

READING RESPONSES

1. Carson opens her chapter with three questions. Interestingly, each question serves a distinct function in her essay. Re-read each question and analyze

how that question relates to the rest of the chapter. Describe the function of each question.

2. When Carson discusses particular topics, she describes first old ways of thinking and then new research. Choose one paragraph that contains both old and new information. Analyze the purpose of old information in this paragraph. What "work" does it do?

3. Carson's chapter summarizes previous scientific research just as Alexander's does. But Carson is writing to a general audience, not other experts in the field. Compare Alexander's style with Carson's. What stylistic strategies does Carson use to make her essay more readable?

MORE WRITING IN CHEMISTRY

Introduction

The readings in this chapter have focused on issues related to soil contaminated by chemicals that humans have purposely, or in some cases, accidentally applied. Contaminated soil and water are significant contributors to the exposure of humans to toxic substances, but natural and man-made disasters also result in human exposure to toxins. This reading reviews scientific data regarding the types of exposure, and the consequences of that exposure, caused by the attack on the World Trade Center. The essay is written by a large team of scientists from seven institutions. The intended audience is toxicologists and other scientists who study human exposure to toxins, and, to a lesser extent, physicians who are interested in environmental exposure to toxins.

The review essay documents the types and amounts of toxins that were released into the atmosphere as a result of the disaster and the observed health consequences of human exposure to those toxins. Most of the information regarding the types and amounts of toxins produced during the disaster has been omitted from this abridged version because it is highly technical and difficult for a non-expert to follow. We include, however, studies of the health consequences of exposure to those toxins.

The review follows a logical argument: (1) the types and amounts of toxins released as a result of the disaster; (2) the health consequences observed; (3) the consequent need to continue monitoring the health of those exposed to the toxins. In other words, its structure is typical of a review essay, moving from a summary of what has been learned to a projection of what yet needs to be studied.

Health and Environmental Consequences of the World Trade Center Disaster

Philip J. Landrigan,[1] Paul J. Lioy,[2] George Thurston,[3] Gertrud Berkowitz,[1] L.C. Chen,[3] Steven N. Chillrud,[4] Stephen H. Gavett,[5] Panos G. Georgopoulos,[2] Alison S. Geyh,[6] Stephen Levin,[1] Frederica Perera,[7] Stephen M. Rappaport,[8] Christopher Small,[4] and the NIEHS World Trade Center Working Group

[1]Mount Sinai School of Medicine, New York, New York, USA; [2]Environmental and Occupational Health Sciences Institute of New Jersey, New Brunswick, New Jersey, USA; [3]New York University School of Medicine, Nelson Institute of Environmental Medicine, Tuxedo, New York, USA; [4]Lamont-Doherty Earth Observatory of Columbia University, Palisades, New York, USA; [5]U.S. Environmental Protection Agency, Office of Research and Development, Research Triangle Park, North Carolina, USA; [6]Johns Hopkins University Bloomberg School of Public Health, Baltimore, Maryland, USA; [7]Mailman School of Public Health of Columbia University, New York, New York, USA; [8]School of Public Health, University of North Carolina, Chapel Hill, North Carolina, USA

Environmental Health Perspectives 2004, vol. 112(6), pp. 731–39

[Abstract] The attack on the World Trade Center (WTC) created an acute environmental disaster of enormous magnitude. This study characterizes the environmental exposures resulting from destruction of the WTC and assesses their effects on health. Methods include ambient air sampling; analyses of outdoor and indoor settled dust; high-altitude imaging and modeling of the atmospheric plume; inhalation studies of WTC dust in mice; and clinical examinations, community surveys, and prospective epidemiologic studies [**studies of diseases**] of exposed populations. WTC dust was found to consist predominantly (95%) of coarse particles and contained pulverized cement, glass fibers, asbestos, lead, polycyclic aromatic hydrocarbons (PAHs), polychlorinated biphenyls (PCBs), and polychlorinated furans and dioxins [**various poisons**]. Airborne particulate levels were highest immediately after the attack and declined thereafter. Particulate levels decreased sharply with distance from the WTC. Dust pH was highly alkaline (pH 9.0–11.0). Mice exposed to WTC dust showed only moderate pulmonary inflammation but marked bronchial hyperreactivity. Evaluation of 10,116 firefighters showed exposure-related increases in cough and bronchial hyperreactivity. Evaluation of 183 cleanup workers showed new onset cough (33%), wheeze (18%), and phlegm production (24%). Increased frequency of new onset cough, wheeze, and shortness of breath were also observed in community residents.

Follow-up of 182 pregnant women who were either inside or near the WTC on 11 September showed a 2-fold increase in small-for-gestational-age (SGA) infants **[that is, smaller in size than the average human fetus of the same age]**. In summary, environmental exposures after the WTC disaster were associated with significant adverse effects on health. The high alkalinity of WTC dust produced bronchial hyperreactivity, persistent cough, and increased risk of asthma. Plausible causes of the observed increase in SGA infants include maternal exposures to PAH and particulates. Future risk of mesothelioma **[cancer of some internal membranes, in this case lung cancer]** may be increased, particularly among workers and volunteers exposed occupationally to asbestos. Continuing follow-up of all exposed populations is required to document the long-term consequences of the disaster. *Key words:* air pollution, airway hyperresponsiveness, asbestos, occupational lung disease, PM2.5, PM10, small for gestational age (SGA).

[Introduction] The destruction of the World Trade Center (WTC) on 11 September 2001 caused the largest acute environmental disaster that ever has befallen New York City (Claudio 2001; Landrigan 2001). The combustion of more than 90,000 L of jet fuel at temperatures above 1,000°C released a dense and intensely toxic atmospheric plume containing soot, metals, volatile organic compounds (VOCs), and hydrochloric acid. The collapse of the towers pulverized cement, glass, and building contents and generated thousands of tons of particulate matter (PM) composed of cement dust, glass fibers, asbestos, lead, polycyclic aromatic hydrocarbons (PAHs), polychlorinated biphenyls (PCBs), organochlorine pesticides, and polychlorinated furans and dioxins (Clark et al. 2003; Lioy et al. 2002; McGee et al. 2003). These materials dispersed over lower Manhattan, Brooklyn, and for miles beyond. They entered nearby office, school, and residential buildings. Much remained at the site to form Ground Zero, a six-story pile of smoking rubble that burned intermittently for more than 3 months.

Populations at greatest risk of exposure included firefighters, police, paramedics, other first responders Prezant et al. 2002; Centers for Disease Control and Prevention (CDC) 2002, and construction workers and volunteers who worked initially in rescue and recovery and then for many months cleared rubble at Ground Zero. Others at potentially elevated risk included workers who cleaned WTC dust from nearby buildings, women who were pregnant on 11 September and succeeding weeks in lower Manhattan and adjacent areas of Brooklyn, and community residents, especially the 3,000 children who resided within 1 km of the towers and the 5,500 who attended school there.

Previous studies have documented the acute traumatic consequences of the attacks on the WTC, most notably the occurrence of 2,726 deaths, including 343 deaths among firefighters and 60 among police officers (CDC 2002). Early clinical and epidemiologic assessments documented a high prevalence of respiratory symptoms, particularly, persistent cough in firefighters and rescue workers exposed to WTC dust (CDC 2002; Prezant et al. 2002). The prevalence of those symptoms was related to intensity and duration of smoke and dust exposure. Studies of the mental health consequences of the disaster have documented a high prevalence of posttraumatic stress disorder (PTSD) (Galea et al. 2002b; Fairbrother et al. 2003) and other psychological sequelae [**disease consequences**], including increased rates of drug and alcohol abuse (Boscarino et al. 2002; Galea et al. 2002a; Stuber et al. 2002; Vlahov et al. 2002a, 2002b).

In this report we summarize a comprehensive assessment of the impacts on human health and the environment of the chemical contaminants generated by destruction of the WTC. The work was undertaken by a consortium of six research centers supported by the National Institute of Environmental Health Sciences (NIEHS) in collaboration with the New York City Department of Health, the U.S. Environmental Protection Agency (EPA), and the CDC. . . .

Health Risk Assessment

Overview. Health risk assessments by the NIEHS Centers began by identifying populations at high risk of exposure to WTC contaminants and then undertaking clinical and epidemiologic studies within these groups (Landrigan 2001). Future analyses will seek to relate health outcomes data to geocoded information on contaminant levels (McCurdy et al. 2000).

Firefighters. Firefighters were among the most heavily exposed populations. They also suffered the greatest loss of life of all occupational groups. In the first 24 hr after the attack on the WTC, 240 New York City firefighters sought emergency medical treatment; of these, 50 (20.8%) received treatment of acute respiratory symptoms caused by inhalation of airborne smoke and dust (Prezant et al. 2002; Spadafora 2002). Firefighters described walking through dense clouds of dust and smoke in the hours immediately after the attack, in which "the air was thick as soup" (CDC 2002).

Follow-up medical evaluation of 10,116 firefighters was conducted over the 6 months after the attack (Prezant et al. 2002). Persistent cough accompanied by other respiratory symptoms so severe as to require at least 4 weeks' leave of absence, termed "World Trade Center cough," was diagnosed in 332 firefighters (Chen and Thurston 2002; Scanlon 2002). Prevalence of WTC cough was related to intensity of smoke exposure, and occurred in 128 (8%) of 1,636 firefighters with a high level of exposure, in 187 (3%) of 6,958 with moderate exposure, and in 17 (1%) of 1,320 with low-level exposure (Figure 4). Among firefighters without WTC cough, bronchial hyperreactivity was present in 77 (23%) of those with a high level of exposure, and in 26 (8%) of those with moderate exposure (Prezant et al. 2002). One case of eosinophilic pneumonia was diagnosed in a firefighter (Beckett 2002; Rom et al. 2002). Induced sputum analysis of New York City firefighters showed increases in sputum PM [**particulate matter: dust, fibers, etc.**] levels as well as in neutrophil and eosinophil counts [**white blood cell counts**]. Those abnormalities were positively correlated with levels of exposure to WTC dust and combustion products, as well as with levels of PAHs in the bodies of firefighters (Edelman et al. 2003).

Cleanup and recovery workers. Many hundreds of workers were involved in clearing rubble and transporting it off-site. To assess the occupational exposures and health status of these workers, many of whom were truck drivers, a team from the Bloomberg School of Public Health at Johns Hopkins University and the

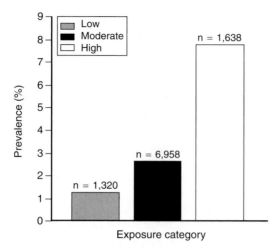

Figure 4 Prevalence of persistent cough in New York City firefighters exposed to smoke and dust from the WTC, September 2001 through March 2002.
Data from Prezant et al. (2002).

Mailman School of Public Health at Columbia University undertook area air monitoring, personal exposure assessment, and health studies.

Air monitoring was conducted in October 2001 and April 2002. It focused on PM, asbestos, and VOCs. Monitoring was conducted across both day and night shifts, 7 days/week. Personal monitoring was conducted for 69 truck drivers. A total of 458 personal and area air samples were collected.

In October 2001, the highest concentrations of total dust were found at the debris pile (median, 1,603 µg/m3 [**micrograms per cubic meter of air**]). Total dust levels on the pile in October were approximately five times higher than at the perimeter. By April 2002, total dust concentrations of the site had become significantly lower and were more uniformly distributed. In October 2001, median personal particulate exposure was 323.7 µg/m3. By April 2002, median exposure had fallen to 137.7 µg/m3. Airborne asbestos concentrations were found to be generally low. The fibers detected were mostly very short. Concentrations of VOCs were generally low. . . .

Among the 183 workers surveyed, a high proportion (32.8%) reported experiencing cough that began after the start of employment at the WTC site; 24.0% reported new onset of phlegm production; and 17.5% reported new onset of wheeze. Approximately half of all workers reported that they had experienced at least one new symptom since they had begun working at the WTC site. . . .

Community residents. To assess prevalence of new-onset respiratory symptoms after 11 September 2001 among previously healthy persons in lower Manhattan as well as in residents with preexisting asthma, a team from NYU Medical Center in collaboration with the New York State Department of Health and the New York Academy of Medicine conducted a clinical and epidemiologic survey (Reibman et al. 2003). Symptoms were assessed by questionnaire, and pulmonary function was evaluated in a subset of the study population by standard screening spirometry [a method for determining lung air capacity].

A total of 2,166 residents of lower Manhattan living within a 1.6-km radius of the WTC were enrolled in this survey and compared with 200 persons living 1.6–8.0 km distant. Spirometry was performed in 52 residents. Preliminary data indicate that previously healthy persons living near Ground Zero had a greater increase in prevalence of respiratory symptoms after 11 September than did more distant residents. These symptoms were predominantly cough, wheeze, and shortness of breath. Symptoms were not associated with abnormal screening spirometry.

Preexisting asthmatic residents in the exposed area also reported a higher prevalence of respiratory symptoms after 11 September. They also reported an increased use of asthma medication relative to controls. . . .

Pregnant women and their offspring. Many pregnant women were either working in the WTC or working or residing in the communities of lower Manhattan on 11 September 2001. To assess pregnancy outcomes in these women and impacts on their infants, teams from the Mount Sinai School of Public Health of Columbia University established complementary prospective epidemiologic cohort studies. . . .

Pregnancy outcomes. In the Mount Sinai cohort, no significant differences were found between the groups in mean gestational age or mean birth weight. There were no significant differences in frequency of preterm births (< 37 weeks of gestation) or in incidence of low birth weight (Table 2) (Berkowitz et al. 2003).

However, the Mount Sinai WTC cohort had a 2-fold increased risk of small-for-gestational-age (SGA) infants, defined as infants with a birth weight below the 10th percentile for gestational age in the nomogram of Brenner et al. (1976) (Table 2). This statistically significant difference was still evident after controlling for relevant covariates and potential confounders, including maternal age, parity, race/ethnicity, sex of the infant, and maternal smoking history. No significant difference in the frequency of SGA infants was observed according to the trimester of pregnancy on 11 September. No associations were evident between symptoms of posttraumatic stress, based on the PTSD Checklist (Schlenger et al. 2002), and frequency of preterm birth, low birth weight, or SGA infants.

Table 2 Pregnancy outcomes in relation to the attack on the WTC, September 2001 through June 2002

	WTC group	Control group	p-Value
No.	187	2,367	—
Mean gestational age (weeks)	39.1	39.0	0.55
Mean birth weight (g)	3,203	3,267	0.14
Frequency of preterm birth (%)	9.9	9.2	0.76
Frequency of low birth weight (%)	8.2	6.8	0.47
Frequency of SGA infants (%)	8.2	3.8	<0.01

Data from Berkowitz et al. (2003).

Discussion

This report presents the most comprehensive summary to date of the environmental exposures resulting from the attack on the WTC and of their effects on human health. Our main focus was on chemical exposures. Our findings complement earlier reports describing the acute physical consequences of the disaster (CDC 2002; Prezant et al. 2002) and its psychological impacts (Boscarino et al. 2002; Fairbrother et al. 2003; Galea et al. 2002a, 2002b; Stuber et al. 2002; Vlahov et al. 2002a, 2002b).

Our assessments show that exposures to chemical contaminants were not uniform in New York after 11 September (Clark et al. 2003; Lioy et al. 2002; McGee et al. 2003; Offenberg et al. 2003). Instead, there were sharp gradients by time after the attack and by distance from Ground Zero (Table 1). **[Table 1 appears here for the first time because in the published review it was part of a section that we deleted in this abridged version of the essay.]** In the first few hours, extremely heavy exposures to high levels of dust and smoke as well as to gaseous products of combustion predominated. This pattern continued for the next 2 days, when there occurred rapid decline of smoke and dust levels and continuing decline in levels of combustion products as jet fuel and flammable building contents were consumed. A large fraction of the outdoor dust was eliminated over the first weekend after the

Table 1 Sequence of environmental exposures after the attack on the WTC, September through December 2001

Time period	Predominant sources of pollution	Airborne pollutants
First 12 hr after collapse (11 September 2001)	Burning jet fuel	Combustion products: gaseous and particulate
	Fires	Evaporating gases from the collapse of towers
	Collapse of the Twin Towers	Coarse particles
Days 1 and 2	Burning jet fuel	Combustion products: gaseous and particulate
	Resuspension of settled dust/smoke	Gases evaporating from piles
		Resuspended coarse particles
Days 3–13	Smoldering fires	Combustion products: gaseous and particulate
	Resuspension of settled dust/smoke	Coarse particle resuspension
		Diesel exhaust
Day 14 through 20 December 2001	Smoldering fires with occasional flareups	Combustion products: gases and particulates
	Removal of debris by trucks and other heavy equipment	Diesel exhaust

Data from Lioy et al. (2002).

disaster by rain that fell on Friday, 14 September, and by the U.S. EPA's cleanup of the Wall Street area. Over the next several weeks, airborne particulate levels in lower Manhattan continued to decline but rose intermittently at night and when the air was still. Transient increases were noted also when the pile was disturbed and fires flared. Diesel exhaust became an important contaminant with the arrival on site of scores of cranes, heavy trucks, and other construction equipment. For weeks, an acrid cloud hung over lower Manhattan and areas of Brooklyn until the fires were finally extinguished on 20 December.

Asbestos was of great concern to the public in New York City and to government agencies after 11 September. Asbestos, principally chrysotile, was used in the early 1970s in construction of the WTC as fireproofing up to the 40th floor of the North Tower (Nicholson et al. 1971; Reitze et al. 1972). Asbestos was not used beyond that point because of the recognition of its hazard and its replacement in the remainder of the construction with nonasbestiform fireproofing materials. Although some of this asbestos had been removed over the preceding 30 years, hundreds of tons remained on 11 September 2001 and were blasted free. Ambient air samples showed that asbestos exposures were initially elevated but fell to within U.S. EPA standards after the first few days (U.S. EPA 2004). Asbestos was found in settled dust at Ground Zero in concentrations ranging from 0.8 to 3.0% (Lioy et al. 2002). Asbestos was found in dust in nearby apartments, sometimes at higher levels than in the outside environment (Lioy et al. 2002).

Airborne lead levels were elevated in the first days after 11 September, but never highly. There is little indication that ambient air lead exposures posed substantial health risks to the population of lower Manhattan (U.S. EPA 2004).

Airborne dioxin levels were elevated substantially above normal urban background levels in the initial days after 11 September. The U.S. EPA's initial risk analysis suggests that these elevations did not result in a significant elevation in cancer or non-cancer risk (U.S. EPA 2003). Further follow-up of exposed populations will be required to evaluate the accuracy of that assessment.

Risks to health were determined by the timing, duration, and chemical composition of exposures as well as by proximity to Ground Zero. Firefighters, police, and other first responders sustained heaviest initial exposures. Studies of firefighters confirmed the presence of a positive relationship between intensity and duration of exposure and severity of pulmonary effects (Figure 4) (Prezant et al. 2002) as well as of PM levels in sputum. Prolonged exposures occurred among firefighters and other public safety personnel who remained at Ground Zero as well as among construction workers, volunteers, and workers removing rubble (Levin et al. 2002; Lippy 2002). Workers cleaning nearby buildings may also have sustained potentially serious exposures (Malievskaya et al. 2002).

Health data from the study of rubble removal workers confirm that these workers, many of whom worked at Ground Zero for many months, had sustained clinically significant exposures to airborne irritants, resulting in symptoms consistent with upper and lower airway inflammation (Levin et al. 2002). To extend these initial studies, the team at Mount Sinai has initiated the World

Trade Center Worker and Volunteer Medical Screening Program. This program, supported by NIOSH, has already examined more than 10,000 workers. These workers will be followed prospectively to assess long-term and delayed effects. . . .

Airborne exposures in the residential and business communities of lower Manhattan beyond Ground Zero were much lower than those sustained by workers (U.S. EPA 2004). Daily average levels of fine particulate pollution in these communities were generally within U.S. EPA limits when averaged over a 24-hr period. Higher short-term peaks were, however, observed especially at night and could have contributed to reported health effects, especially in susceptible populations such as children, the elderly, and persons with respiratory or cardiac disease. Indoor exposures to resuspended dust may have added to total exposures (Lioy et al. 2002). Residents in these communities reported an increased frequency of new-onset pulmonary symptoms (Reibman et al. 2003) but had no abnormalities on pulmonary function testing. These findings are consistent with the observed gradient of exposures. . . .

Important questions about possible future risks to health of persons exposed to contaminants from the WTC remain unanswered:

- Will pulmonary disease persist in workers exposed to dust, especially in those who sustained very heavy exposures in the first days after 11 September and those with prolonged exposures?
- Will an increased incidence of mesothelioma result from exposures to asbestos? All types of asbestos fibers have been shown in laboratory as well as clinical studies to be capable of causing mesothelioma (Nicholson and Landrigan 1996). Pathologic studies have found short chrysotile fibers, the predominant type of fiber in WTC dust, to be the predominant fiber in mesothelioma tissue (Dodson et al. 1991; LeBouffant et al. 1973; Suzuki and Yuen 2002). Mesothelioma has been reported in persons with relatively low-dose, nonoccupational exposure to asbestos (Anderson 1982; Camus et al. 1998; Magnani et al. 2001). The greatest future risk of mesothelioma would appear to exist among first responders who were enveloped in the cloud of dust, other workers employed directly at Ground Zero, and workers employed in cleaning asbestos-laden dust from contaminated buildings. The risk of mesothelioma to residents of lower Manhattan must be considered to be extremely low but may still be elevated above background.
- Will exposure to airborne dioxin in lower Manhattan in the days and weeks after 11 September increase risk of cancer, diabetes, or other chronic disease (Kogevinas 2001)?
- Will the increased frequency of SGA observed in babies born to women who were within or near the WTC on 11 September result in long-term adverse effects on growth or development (Berkowitz et al. 2003)?

Full elucidation of these and other questions concerning the long-term and delayed health effects of exposures resulting from the attack on the WTC will require continuing, prospective, multiyear clinical and epidemiologic follow-up and further refinement of exposure assessments. That work is under way.

References

Beckett WS. 2002. A New York City firefighter overwhelmed by World Trade Center dust. *Am J Respir Crit Care Med* 166:785–6.

Berkowitz GS, Wolff MS, Janevic TM, Holzman IR, Yehuda R, Landrigan PJ. 2003. The World Trade Center disaster and intrauterine growth restriction [Letter]. *JAMA* 290:595–6.

Boscarino JA, Galea S, Ahern J, Resnick H, Vlahov D. 2002. Utilization of mental health services following the September 11th terrorist attacks in Manhattan, New York City. *Int J Emerg Ment Health* 4:143–55.

Brenner WE, Edelman DA, Hendricks CH. 1976. A standard of fetal growth for the United States of America. *Am J Obstet Gynecol* 126:55–64

CDC (Centers for Disease Control and Prevention). 2002. Injuries and illnesses among New York City Fire Department rescue workers after responding to the World Trade Center attacks. *Morbid Mortal Wkly Rep* 51(special issue):1–5.

Chen LC, Thurston G. 2002. World Trade Center cough. *Lancet* 360(suppl):S37–8.

Clark RN, Green RO, Swayze GA, Meeker G, Sutley S, Hoefen TM, et al. 2003. Environmental Studies of the World Trade Center Area after the September 11, 2001 Attack. Available: http://pubs.usgs.gov/of/2001/ofr-01-0429/ [accessed 25 March 2004].

Claudio L. 2001. Environmental aftermath. *Environ Health Perspect* 109:528–36.

Edelman P, Osterloh J, Pirkle J, Caudill SP, Grainger J, Jones R, et al. 2003. Biomonitoring of chemical exposure among New York City firefighters responding to the World Trade Center fire and collapse. *Environ Health Perspect* 111:1906–11.

Fairbrother G, Stuber J, Galea S, Fleischman AR, Pfefferbaum B. 2003. Posttraumatic stress reactions in New York City children after the September 11, 2001, terrorist attacks. *Ambul Pediatrics* 3:304–11.

Galea S, Ahern J, Resnick H, Kilpatrick D, Bucuvalas M, Gold J, et al. 2002a. Psychological sequelae of the September 11 terrorist attacks in New York City. *N Engl J Med* 346:982–7.

Galea S, Resnick H, Ahern J, Gold J, Bucuvalas M, Kilpatrick D, et al. 2002b. Posttraumatic stress disorder in Manhattan, New York City, after the September 11th terrorist attacks. *J Urban Health* 79:340–53.

Landrigan PJ. 2001. Health consequences of the 11 September 2001 attacks [Editorial]. *Environ Health Perspect* 109:A514–15.

Levin S. Herbert R, Skloot G, Szeinuk J, Teirstein A, Fischler D, et al. 2002. Health effects of World Trade Center site workers. *Am J Ind Med* 42:545–7.

Lioy PJ, Weisel CP, Millette JR, Eisenreich S, Vallero D, Offenberg J, et al. 2002. Characterization of the dust/smoke aerosol that settled east of the World Trade Center (WTC) in Lower Manhattan after the collapse of the WTC 11 September 2001. *Environ Health Perspect* 110:703–14.

Lippy BE. 2002. Safety and health of heavy equipment operators at Ground Zero. *Am J Ind Med* 42:539–42.

Malievskaya E, Rosenberg N, Markowitz S. 2002. Assessing the health of immigrant workers near Ground Zero: preliminary results of the World Trade Center Day Laborer Medical Monitoring Project. *Am J Ind Med* 42:548–9.

McGee JK, Chen LC, Cohen MD, Chee GR, Prophete CM, Haykal-Coates N, et al. 2003. Chemical analysis of World Trade Center fine particulate matter for use in toxicological assessment. *Environ Health Perspect* 111:972–80.

Nicholson WJ, Rohl AN, Ferrand EF. 1971. Asbestos air pollution in New York City. In: *Proceedings of the Second International Clean Air Congress* (Englund HM, Beery WT, eds.) New York:Academic Press, 36–139.

Offenberg JH, Eisenreich SJ, Chen LC, Cohen MD, Chee G, Prophete C, et al. 2003. Persistent organic pollutants in the dusts that settled across lower Manhattan after September 11, 2001. *Environ Sci Technol* 37:502–8.

Prezant DJ, Weiden M, Banauch GI, McGuinness G, Rom WN, Aldrich TK. 2002. Cough and bronchial responsiveness in firefighters at the World Trade Center site. *N Engl J Med* 347:806–15.

Reibman J, Lin S, Matte T, Rogers L, Hoerning A, Hwang S, et al. 2003. Respiratory health of residents near the former World Trade Center: the WTC Residents Respiratory Health Survey [Abstract]. *Am J Respir Crit Care Med* 167:A335.

Reitze WB, Nicholson WJ, Holaday DA, Selikoff IJ. 1972. Application of sprayed inorganic fiber containing asbestos: Occupational health hazards. *Am Ind Hyg Assoc J* 33:178–91.

Rom WN, Weiden M, Garcia R, Yie TA, Vathesatogkit P, Tse DB, et al. 2002. Acute eosinophilic pneumonia in a New York City firefighter exposed to World Trade Center dust. Am *J Respir Crit Care Med* 166:797–800.

Scanlon MD. 2002. World Trade Center cough—a lingering legacy and a cautionary tale. *N Engl J Med* 347:840–2.

Schlenger WE, Caddell JM, Ebert L, Jordan BK, Rourke KM, Wilson D, et al. 2002. Psychological reactions to terrorist attacks: findings from the National Study of Americans' Reactions to September 11. *JAMA* 288:81–88.

Spadafora R. 2002. Firefighter safety and health issues at the Word Trade Center site. *Am J Ind Med* 42:532–38.

Stuber J, Fairbrother G, Galea S, Pfefferbaum B, Wilson-Genderson M, Vlahov D. 2002. Determinants of counseling for children in Manhattan after the September 11 attacks. *Psychiatr Serv* 53:815–22.

U.S. EPA. 2003. Fact Sheet: Release of Reports Related to the World Trade Center Disaster. Exposure and Human Health Evaluation of Airborne Pollution from the World Trade Center Disaster. Toxicological Effects of Fine Particulate Matter Derived from the Destruction of the World Trade Center. Washington, DC: U.S. Environmental Protection Agency.

U.S. EPA. 2004. EPA Response to September 11. Washington, DC: U.S. Environmental Protection Agency. Available: http://www.epa.gov/wtc/ [accessed 25 March 2004].

Vlahov D, Galea S, Frankel D. 2002a. New York City, 2001: reaction and response. *J Urban Health* 79:2–5.

Vlahov D, Galea S, Resnick H, Ahern J, Boscarino JA, Bucuvalas M, et al. 2002b. Increased use of cigarettes, alcohol, and marijuana among Manhattan, New York, residents after the September 11th terrorist attacks. *Am J Epidemiol* 155:988–96.

READING RESPONSES

1. A scientific review rarely evokes an emotional response from readers, but this review may do exactly that. Who might have an emotional response to this review? What kind of emotions might it call up? What about the review encourages an emotional response?

2. These researchers review the extensive effects of the WTC attacks on the environment and human health. Which of these topics receives more attention? Develop a research method that will help you answer that question and apply it to the text. Describe your research method and display your results.

3. This research review is written by scientists for scientists, but the topic is of great concern to all Americans. Create a set of guidelines that could help these authors write about this information for a general audience. What can they keep the same? What must they change?

WRITING ASSIGNMENTS

ASSIGNMENT 1: APPLYING THE PORTABLE RHETORICAL LESSON

Background: It's difficult to find a summary of the environmental quality of your neighborhood from the epa.gov website. And yet this information is important for everyone who lives (or is considering living) in your neighborhood.

Your task is to create a summary of the environmental quality of your neighborhood. Consult the EPA's website as well as other sources of information: your local EPA office, other local governmental offices (city and state), non-governmental organizations, and journalist investigations. Introduce your summary with an overview that describes the general environmental quality for your neighborhood. Include information on several features of environmental quality as well as a list of sources of information on environmental quality in your area.

ASSIGNMENT 2: MAKING CONNECTIONS

Background: Summaries matter. They do more than describe something—they set a path for future action. This is certainly true in the business world. For example, in Chapter 14, Marketing, you will find a simple ad for a new office chair, but the simplicity is deceptive. The ad relies on summaries of research about the target audience—the people most likely to purchase the chair; and Steelcase, the company that designed the chair, considered this audience from the very beginning.

Your task for this assignment is to complete one of the following two tasks for the new line of cars, the Scion, that Toyota has designed and marketed to appeal to "Generation Y" buyers. Both require you to speculate about how summary information shaped Toyota's business practice. Before choosing one of these two tasks, search the Internet for summaries of "Generation Y" (you can start with the terms "Generation Y" and "summary"). List the features of your generation that these summaries identify.

1. Analyze the Toyota Scion's website, www.scion.com, looking for ways that the creators of this Web page may have tried to attract Generation Y car buyers. Report on your analysis, being sure to describe features of Generation Y you found in the summaries as well as descriptions of specific parts of the Web page that seem to respond to these features of Generation Y.
2. Analyze one of the Scion car models, looking for features of the car that designers may have included to appeal to Generation Y car buyers. Report on your analysis, being sure to describe features of Generation Y you found in the summaries as well as descriptions of aspects of the Scion car that seem to respond to these features of Generation Y.

ASSIGNMENT 3: DOING THE RESEARCH

Most writers, in academics and beyond, review previous research as part of their own writing. How they do this reviewing differs, though, across different academic disciplines and rhetorical situations.

Your task for this assignment is to compare Martin Alexander's review essay from the beginning of this chapter with that from another discipline to create a guide for students who have to write summaries in a variety of disciplines. Select an academic discipline that is or might be your major, and ask a professor or a reference librarian for help determining the major scholarly journals in that field.

1. Locate the back issues of one of these journals in the library, and page through them, looking for a review essay. Once you have found an essay that primarily reviews previous research in an area, copy the essay.

2. Read the essay through once so that you understand its scope and the author's argument. Then, analyze how the author crafted the review. How does the author group research on similar topics? What information about the research does the author provide? How does the author arrange the essay? What is the rhetorical effect of that arrangement? What is the author's reason for reviewing this body of research?

3. Determine the most interesting or important points of similarity and contrast between the chemistry review essay and the review essay in your discipline.

As you begin drafting, consider how description and examples from both essays can help you detail the most effective strategies for writing reviews.

ART HISTORY:
INTERPRETING CULTURE
THROUGH VISUAL ARTS

Art historians write to enrich our understanding of and appreciation for both art and culture. Like all other writers, they write to change the world, but they do so in subtle ways. In their writing, art historians help you better understand a piece of art, the artist, and the human culture that influenced the artist. First, they direct your attention to the most significant elements of a piece of art; under their guidance you notice what you might otherwise have ignored. In this way, they shape what you deem important—a powerful rhetorical move. Second, they offer background information about the artist, the artistic genre, the historical period, and the cultural context. When you understand this information, you can comprehend what the artist was trying to convey and why she made the artistic choices that she did. Finally, art historians suggest how you might interpret the art. Art historians do all this because they value the messages that art conveys—messages to the viewer about art and the artist's culture. Reading the writing of art historians expands our understanding of human nature and culture; in turn, as you learn more about how humans create culture you gain an even richer understanding of art, others, and yourself. The long-term effect of such change—reshaping your understanding of people and their cultures—is powerful.

➡ A Portable Rhetorical Lesson:

Looking, Pointing, and Interpreting

In this chapter we focus on how you can use images and words to clarify and enrich an interpretation. The chapter's portable rhetorical lesson is the strategy of pointing and saying, "If you want to understand, look—but look purposefully and knowledgeably." The images do more than merely illustrate the words; words and images collaborate to help the reader develop a fuller understanding of a complex idea.

Wise writers have always combined words and images to communicate effectively when things get complicated. If you need to explain how to wire an electrical outlet, you will use both a list of steps and a diagram rather than asking your audience to imagine what the inside of an outlet looks like. Furthermore, the extensive visual capabilities of word processing software and electronic slideshows such as PowerPoint have made it simple to combine words and images—so easy that many writers slap words and images together without considering how they work together or how they relate to the topic of the presentation. These are the presentations that bore some viewers and confuse others. Art historians can teach you much about how to do this work more intelligently.

Chapter Topics: Power is the common theme here: power of kings, divine power that is balanced by human limits, the power of a proverb as seen through the eyes of common people, political power, the power of images to tell stories and soothe or excite emotions, and even the power of an observer, of one who points, to shape meaning.

To Think About. . .

Middle school history teachers commonly assign their students to create a family crest as a way of engaging them in the distant world of medieval England. Typically, these family crests are comprised of three parts: a shield (the background shape), a set of images, and a motto. Think back to middle school. If you had been asked to create a family crest for your own family, what would it have looked like? What images would you have selected to represent your family's best qualities? What words would you use to represent what your family believes most dearly?

WRITING IN ART HISTORY

Introduction by Henry Luttikhuizen, Professor of Art History

As the old saying goes, a picture is worth a thousand words. Visual images and objects are extremely helpful in teaching us about the world and ourselves. One only needs to consider the medical use of magnetic resonance imaging (MRIs), an architect's use of blueprint, or a good hiking map to see the value of pictures. Diagrams, charts, and illustrations enable us to convey our ideas more clearly and with greater depth. The problem with the old saying is that it equates words and images: 1 image = 1,000 words. And that badly oversimplifies the rhetoric of art history.

Art historians work to develop the observational skills of their readers, helping them to be better at understanding images, but using both pictures and words to do that. Art historians point out particular features of the art and suggest how those features might be interpreted. They put those interpretive suggestions in the context of historical and cultural information, and they keep their reader's eyes fixed on the art and not on the art historian.

In the following short essay, a chapter from an exhibition catalogue, Linda Schele and Mary Ellen Miller provide an excellent model of art-historical writing. Their words do not attempt to reproduce an entire picture; rather, their writing enables us to focus on important visual elements and therefore think about the art more clearly. (And the words are frequently necessary complements to the art because in some of the sculpture it is hard to understand what we see without the authors' explanations.) The authors effectively address such things as the materials used to make the art, the location, and the cultural conventions exhibited by art objects, helping readers to understand the connection between ritualistic bloodletting and mystical vision in ancient Maya civilization.

The practice of art history requires us to bring verbal and visual modes of communication together; it is, in a sense, an occasion for "show and tell." Words do not merely describe pictures; they point out certain characteristics of the pictures. They suggest that particular aspects of a work are noteworthy. Schele and Miller do not try to explain everything they possibly can about specific images. They draw our attention to particular details in hopes of supporting their argument concerning the connections among visual imagery, divine bloodletting, and mystical vision. For instance, in their discussion of Lintel 25 (Plate 63, page 146), Schele and Miller concentrate on the relationship between the depiction of Lady Xoc's bloody gift and the evocation of the Vision Serpent, who makes it possible to communicate with the gods. Throughout the text, the authors direct us to the visual features of objects and connect those features to their social, political, and religious function. The figurine of a noble lord piercing himself (Plate 69, page 152), for example, reveals how mighty Maya leaders must also serve as sacrificial victims on behalf of their people.

Interpreting the symbolic content of art fosters greater cultural and aesthetic appreciation and understanding, but it is important not to overlook other artistic features, such as the style, the size of the work, its physical location, and the materials used to create it. As Schele and Miller point out, precious stones were carved in the form of stingray lancets. Although these objects were not used to perforate human flesh (other materials could serve this ritualistic task more effectively), these cut stones worked as powerful symbols that possessed more strength than an actual stingray spine. The spine-like appearance of the carved object conveyed bloodletting, while the use of precious stones suggested permanence and value.

Good art historiography does more than just point to the art; it is also always contextual. That is to say, it takes the original historical setting into account. Ideas from other disciplines are often imported to strengthen points in the argument. Schele and Miller, for instance, bring biology into the discussion by addressing the power of endorphins, which can be released by blood loss, to induce hallucinogenic visions, such as those depicted in Maya art. They also attempt to describe what the setting of a ritual would have looked like: "The rising clouds of swirling smoke provided the perfect field in which to see the Vision Serpent; gazing into the smoke, the celebrants may have actually seen it."

Because art history is like "show and tell," sometimes students confuse it with creative writing. Although every experience of art is subjective, art history writing should not be understood as an opportunity for personal expression. The focus needs to remain on the visual image or object instead of on the writer. For example, Schele and Miller may have been deeply moved by ancient art in Mexico, but they do not concentrate on their own experiences or on how these objects have touched their lives. On the contrary, they address how these works affected their initial audience, the people who looked at these images and used them.

In summary, art historians' words about pictures are rhetorical tools intended to guide viewers in a particular interpretive direction. Schele and Miller effectively direct the reader's eyes to visual characteristics that support and clarify their ideas. They successfully link the appearance of visual images and objects to their intended meaning and use within Maya society. Their careful descriptions of Maya art encourage readers to look more closely at the images, to become more engaged with what they are seeing and what they are reading. Perhaps this is the greatest strength of Schele and Miller's writing. They are able to entice readers to learn more about these powerful pictures in conjunction with Maya bloodletting rituals. Simply put, the authors are able to use their words to open their reader's eyes to see fascinating qualities of Maya art. And opening our eyes to others helps us better to see and understand ourselves.

✓ READING TIPS

Look at the pictures on pages 145–153. Try to imagine their textures, their size in real life, their stories, their characters, their sense of realism and fantasy. When you read the text, regularly flip to the pictures to see first-hand what the authors are pointing out to you. Finally, read for two elements: (1) descriptions of the art itself, (2) historical information about the art and culture. Remember that art history is the study of the interconnections of art and history; lose yourself in the art, but remember that the art also helps you understand the culture and history of the Mayans.

Bloodletting and the Vision Quest
Linda Schele and Mary Ellen Miller

Chapter 4, *The Blood of Kings: Dynasty and Ritual in Maya Art*

Think about the rhetorical effect of starting with this quotation: It focuses immediately on a historical account of blood sacrifice. So it both catches your interest with the words and conjures up very vivid, gruesome images.

They offered sacrifices of their own blood, sometimes cutting themselves around in pieces and they left them in this way as a sign. Other times they pierced their cheeks, at others their lower lips. Sometimes they scarify certain parts of their bodies, at others they pierced their tongues in a slanting direction from side to side and passed bits of straw through the holes with horrible suffering; others slit the superfluous part of the virile member leaving it as they did their ears.[1]

Yucatan is a large peninsula in southeastern Mexico.

Thus did Diego de Landa, the first bishop of Yucatan, describe the blood-letting of the Yucatec Mayas. During the early years after the Conquest, similar ritual practices were reported from all the regions occupied by Mayan-speaking peoples. Bloodletting imagery pervades Classic Maya art as well. Archaeological evidence for it is abundant, although much of the regalia made of perishable materials is lost. Beginning in the Late Preclassic period, lancets made of stingray spines, obsidian and flint are regularly found in burials and caches. Stingray spines, for example, are often found in the pelvic regions of the dead and were perhaps originally contained in bags hung from belts. It is clear that bloodletting was basic to the institution of rulership, to the mythology of world order, and to public rituals of all sorts. Through bloodletting the Maya sought a vision they believed to be the manifestation of an ancestor or a god. Thus the Maya expressed piety by letting blood from all parts of the body. Blood was the mortar of ritual life from Late Preclassic times until the arrival of the Spanish, who were shocked by the practice and discouraged it as idolatrous worship.

Classic Maya is the period from roughly, A.D. 200–900.

The Late Preclassic Period went from 300 B.C, to A.D. 200.

Obsidian and flint are stones used to make sharp-edged tools— which could be used for cutting flesh.

This sentence is the simple version of the thesis of the whole book. The three sentences that precede this statement outline the particulars of the thesis as it is developed in this chapter. So, as is common in humanities essays, you find the thesis at the end of the first paragraph.

While the importance of blood sacrifice in Mesoamerican societies has long been recognized, the practice was considered to be Mexican rather than fundamentally Maya. The recognition of event glyphs and the deciphering of iconography associated with bloodletting in the last twenty years has changed this view radically.[2] The Spanish reaction was not exaggerated: bloodletting did permeate Maya life. For kings, every stage in life, every event of political or religious importance, every significant period ending required sanctification through bloodletting. When buildings were dedicated, crops planted, children born, couples married or the dead buried, blood was given to express piety and call the gods into attendance.

Event glyphs are visual markers depicting historical events.

Consequently, the lancet—the instrument for drawing blood—became a sacred object infused with power. Models of stingray spines were manufactured from precious stone, not for use as lancets but rather as symbols of the power inherent in the spine. The Maya carved bone awls with bloodletting imagery to declare their function as lancets and to use in the costuming that signaled the rite. The concept of the lancet itself was personified in the form of the Perforator God, although this personified lancet is perhaps more accurately considered a sacred power object rather than a deity. The triple and double cloth knots tied around the forehead of the Perforator God became the most pervasive symbol of the bloodletting rite. The Maya wore cloth strips and knotted bows on their arms and legs, through pierced earlobes, in the hair and in clothing. Sacrificial paper made from the felted bark of the fig tree was used as cloth; unlike all other kinds of cloth, both this paper cloth and cotton cloth were cut and torn when used in the bloodletting rite. After the paper cloth became saturated with blood, it was burned in a brazier, for the gods apparently required that blood be transformed into smoke in order to consume it. Thus the icons of smoke and blood came to be indistinguishable in visual form; both are rendered as a bifurcated scroll, the specific reference for which is determined by context or by the addition of modifying signs.[3] In order to make this scroll understood indisputably as blood, the Maya added precious signs, such as bone beads or shells, to its basic configuration. Maya cosmological symbolism suggests that the building element of the Middleworld was blood; it was certainly the most precious and sacred substance of this world.

The creation story of the Popol Vuh provides a context for the rite of bloodletting. At the beginning of all things, when the creator gods finished their work, they wanted to be recognized by their living creations. The birds and beasts of the fields answered them with only a meaningless cacophony of sound, and for that they were forever destined to be the food of man and of one another. The gods tried several times to create special creatures who would know them, but nothing worked. Finally, using maize for flesh and water for blood, they created human beings who could recognize them and understand their relationship to the creator gods. The gods' prolonged efforts are central to the understanding of bloodletting: they wanted creatures to "name [their] names, to praise them" and to be their providers and nurturers.[4] The gods wanted creatures who could worship them, but—more important—they also needed men to give them sustenance.

Margin notes:

piercing instruments

a metal container

a scroll divided into two parts

The sacred text of the Maya, recorded after the Spanish conquest. Note how the way the authors tell the story in this paragraph evokes the tone of ancient mythology. The rhetorical effect is to put the reader in the mindset of the people who made and viewed the art.

Permeating this creation myth as well as many parallel myths from other Mesoamerican peoples is the concept of a reciprocal relationship between humans and the gods. The earth and its creatures were created through a sacrificial act of the gods, and human beings, in turn, were required to strengthen and nourish the gods. Gods and humans cannot exist without each other. It is clear from Classic Maya art and inscriptions, as well as from the Popol Vuh, that blood drawn from all parts of the body—especially from the tongue, earlobes, and genitals—was sustenance for the gods.

Some of the most dramatic representations of the Maya act of ritual bloodletting occur on two series of lintels found in buildings at Yaxchilan. The three lintels in each series are designed as a single program encoding one level of information into the imagery and another into the inscriptions. The scenes portray different points in the same ritual that compose a narrative whole, much like sequential frames in a comic strip. The inscriptions, however, record widely separated dates, implying that the same ritual occurred on several different occasions. This approach to narrative programming was attempted first by the artist called the Cookie Cutter Master during Shield Jaguar's reign, then repeated thirty years later, in the reign of his son, Bird Jaguar.[5]

The sequence of lintels featuring Shield Jaguar . . . begins over the left doorway of Structure 23 with a scene of bloodletting (Plate 62, Lintel 24, page 145).[6] Elegantly dressed, Shield Jaguar wears the shrunken head of a past victim tied to the top of his head, signaling his sacrificial role. His principal wife, Lady Xoc, kneels before him in a *huipil* of finely woven, complex design. Her headdress, with its tassels, bar, trapeze and Tlaloc signs[7] signal that she is engaged in a very special bloodletting rite that will eventually include captive sacrifice. She pulls a thorn-lined rope through the wound in her perforated tongue, letting the rope fall into a woven basket full of blood-spotted paper strips. Lady Xoc's lips and cheeks are covered with the dotted scrolls that signify the blood streaming from her wounded mouth.

Lintel 25, the second in the series, shows the consequence and purpose of the bloodletting rite (Plate 63, Lintel 25, page 146). The same woman, still kneeling, gazes upward at an apparition, a Tlaloc warrior, emerging from the gaping mouth of a Vision Serpent. In her left hand, she holds a bloodletting bowl with the bloody paper, a stingray spine and an obsidian lancet; in the right hand, a skull and serpent symbol. The Vision Serpent rises from a separate bowl placed on the ground in front of her. The

architectural elements supporting the weight above doors

ruler of Yaxchilan from A.D. 681 to 742

a garment worn by Maya noblewomen

Mesoamerican god of rain and storms

a mystical symbol associated with rebirth

Plate 62 (Lintel 24)

serpent is double headed, perhaps as a reminder of the royal scepter and the fact that the occasion of the rite is Shield Jaguar's accession. The serpent's writhing body surges upward through a blood scroll, declaring that the vision materializes from blood itself. The Tlaloc god and warrior brought forth refer to a special sacrificial complex that the Maya associated with the god of the

Plate 63 (Lintel 25)

evening star and with war. During the accession rites of the king, his wife underwent bloodletting so that she could communicate with this warrior, who may have been a dead ancestor or a symbol of the king's role as warrior in this cult. The warrior is not named, but it is clear that the purpose of the bloodletting rite was to cause this vision to materialize.

Note the explicit reminder of the chapter's point of focus: bloodletting and the vision quest.

Today, scientists acknowledge that endorphins—chemically related to the opiates and produced by the brain in response to massive blood loss—can induce hallucinogenic experiences. But the Maya also knew that drawing large amounts of blood would, without the help of other drugs, produce visions that were the raison d'etre of their rituals. Through such visions, the Maya came directly into contact with their gods and ancestors. The great rearing serpent—the physical manifestation of visions arising from blood loss and shock—was the contact between the supernatural realm and the world of human beings. The precise supernatural being contacted by the rite is manifested by the image in the mouth of the Vision Serpent.

a site of Maya wall paintings

Note this characteristic feature of writing in art history—describing the visual contexts of the visual objects being examined. This helps readers to imagine seeing the objects as they were seen by the people for whom they were constructed.

The Vision Serpent may have been more than a symbolic manifestation of hallucination. Information from Room 3 at Bonampak as well as from other pictorial records makes it possible to reconstruct some parts of the rituals that took place in the great open plazas of Maya cities. Against a backdrop of terraced architecture, elaborately costumed dancers, musicians, warriors, and nobles entered the courts in long processions. Dancers whirled across the plaza floors and terrace platforms to music made on rattles, whistles, wooden trumpets and drums of all sizes. A crowd of participants wearing bloodletting paper or cloth tied in triple knots sat on platforms and terraces around the plaza. According to Bishop Landa, these people would have prepared themselves with days of fasting, abstinence, and ritual steam baths. Well into the ceremony, the ruler and his wife would emerge from within a building high above the court, and in full public view, he would lacerate his penis, she her tongue. Ropes drawn through their wounds carried the flowing blood to paper strips. The saturated paper—perhaps along with other offerings, such as rubber (the chicle resin from which chewing gum is made)—were placed in large plates, then carried to braziers and burned, creating columns of black smoke. The participants, already dazed through deprivation, public hysteria and massive blood loss, were culturally conditioned to expect a hallucinatory experience. The rising clouds of swirling smoke provided the perfect field in which to see the Vision Serpent; gazing into the smoke, the celebrants may have actually seen it.

At Yaxchilan, the final act in Shield Jaguar's sequence is recorded on Lintel 26 (photo not included). Shield Jaguar, already dressed in cotton armor, carries a short stabbing knife. Lady Xoc stands silently beside him with blood still oozing from her wounded mouth. In her hands, she holds her husband's jaguar helmet and flexible shield. She is helping him prepare for battle, perhaps to take captives for the final sacrificial act.

Bird Jaguar, Shield Jaguar's son, came to the throne in A.D. 752, ten years after his father's death. He constructed a building to house lintels showing the same three scenes commissioned by his father; however, he ordered the scenes

Plate 65 (Lintel 15)

Plate 64 (Lintel 17)

differently by centering the war scene on Lintel 16, then flanking it on the left with the vision scene (Plate 65, Lintel 15, page 148) and on the right with the bloodletting scene (Plate 64, Lintel 17, above). The capture recorded in Lintel 16 occurred only eight days before the bloodletting depicted on Lintel 17, which was, according to its inscription, conducted in celebration of the birth of Bird Jaguar's heir, on 9.16.0.14.5, or February 18, A.D. 752.

These numbers refer to the complex dating system of the Maya, known as the Long Count calendar.

Lady Balam-Ix, the woman who lets blood on Lintel 17 (Plate 64), is not the mother of the newborn but apparently a second wife of Bird Jaguar who publicly lets blood in celebration of the birth of her husband's heir. She wears the same costume Lady Xoc wears in the earlier narrative sequence, which suggests that these rituals were closely regulated by tradition. The rope she uses to draw blood from her tongue, however, is not lined with thorns, perhaps because the artist neglected to represent them or because the thorn-lined rope was used only by Lady Xoc as a special gesture of piety. Bird Jaguar is shown preparing for his self-mutilation, thus confirming that the king and his wife both performed the mutilation rite and offered blood. Interestingly, by wearing a skull and snake headdress identical to those used by Lady Xoc on Lintel 25 (page 146), Bird Jaguar seems to be emphasizing a special association with his father's principal wife, even though she was not his own mother.

On Lintel 15 (page 148), Lady 6-Tun, yet another of Bird Jaguar's wives, stares at the vision she has brought forth through bloodletting (Plate 65). Her *huipil* repeats the one Lady Xoc wore in this rite a generation before, although she contacts a different, unidentified person. He may embody the idea of sacrifice, just as the Tlaloc warrior on Lintel 25 personifies sacrifice and the Tlaloc war complex.

Both of these series of lintels are associated with accession. The vision scene on Lintel 25 took place on the day of Shield Jaguar's accession, and the bloodletting and capture scenes of Bird Jaguar's series occurred only seventy-five days before his accession. The Maya had long practiced bloodletting rituals as a required preparation for, or conclusion to, accession rites. . . .

The association of bloodletting with accession was carried into a variety of media. A Late Classic cylindrical pot from the Dumbarton Oaks collection (Plate 68, page 151) shows an episodic narrative of accession. In the primary scene, Balam-Pauahtun, the new king, is seated on a bench in his palace surrounded by members of his court. In the smaller and more important scene, the king, standing outside the palace, aims a lancet at his penis, while one of his nobles pulls a rope through his own tongue. The noble takes on the role performed by the king's wife at Yaxchilan. Furthermore, the nobleman participant on this pot wears the same type of headdress as the wives at Yaxchilan. Thus, the ritual role rather than the gender or rank of the practitioner determines the headdress.

In his seventeenth-century account of the ceremony, Fray Delgado, a Spanish priest, vividly described the method of drawing blood from the penis, as practiced among the Manche Chol Maya:

In Vicente Pach's ranch I saw the sacrifice. They took a chisel and wooden mallet, placed the one who had to sacrifice himself on a smooth stone slab, took out his penis, and cut it in three parts two finger breadths [up], the largest in the center, saying at the same time incantations and words I did not understand. . . .[9]

An extant figurine (Plate 69, page 152) displays the exact procedure. A seated lord, who is cutting his penis with a sharp blade held in his right hand, sheds drops of blood onto blue

Plate 68

paper. The rope collar he wears symbolizes his acceptance of the role of penitent; he is a lord, but for this rite he has taken on the symbolic trappings of the lowliest of humans, the captive whose destiny is to die in sacrifice. His face, like that of the seventeenth-century Manche Chol practitioner, does not reveal pain, although other figurines show victims screaming in agony. Perhaps the ability to bear pain stoically was admired as both courageous and pious. . . .

Bloodletting had one final function for the Maya: to bring the gods into man's presence. This aspect is best conveyed by the imagery of the scattering rite. Long thought to symbolize either the beneficent distribution of bounty to the people or the casting of maize seeds in augury, the scattering rite is named simply for the action shown—the scattering of what looks like pellets or streams, which are now recognized as blood. This rite was performed to celebrate the period endings in the Long Count calendar, especially the katun, the hotun (five years) and the lahuntun (ten years).

fortune telling

twenty Maya calendar years, which lasted 360 days

Plate 69

La Pasadita Lintel 2 (Plate 76, page 153) is a particularly good illustration of the scattering rite. Bird Jaguar, the king of Yaxchilan, is marking a period ending (9.16.10.0.0) with the *cahal* or underlord, who ruled La Pasadita for him. Dressed in the symbolic array of Chac-Xib-Chac and wearing his father's name on his belt to declare his line of descent, Bird Jaguar drops a dotted stream of blood into a knot-shrouded brazier. His groin is covered with the Perforator God, marking the source of the blood offering he drops. The *cahal* stands nearby, ready to assist him in performing the rite.

During both the Early and the Late Classic periods, this rite is recorded either in images or inscriptions at most sites; around A.D. 780, however, the Maya of the central Peten began depicting it in a new way. Although, as before, the king wears an elaborate costume and drops blood from his hands, new elements—gods wrapped in blood scrolls—float

a region in northern Guatemala

Plate 76 (Lintel 2)

around his head. Some of these floating gods are presently unidentified, although the principal ones are the two Paddler Gods. That the scrolls surrounding the gods are blood seems certain, since they are identical in form to the material through which the Vision Serpents of Yaxchilan rise and identical to the substance scattered by Bird Jaguar. One aspect of the scattering rite, then, is that gods are found to float in blood scrolls—much as the Vision Serpent rises through blood in other rituals. . . .

The declaration of these births is explained by the symbolism of the period ending rites that the monument commemorates. Scattering was the principal period ending rite throughout Late Classic Maya history; scattering was a bloodletting rite; the Paddlers are the gods in the blood scrolls above the king's head; and the Paddlers are the gods born. The conclusion is inescapable—the act of bloodletting literally gave birth to the gods. The Maya believed that bloodletting brought the gods as well as their ancestors into

ancient delties who travel through life in canoes

Here we see an expansion of the chapter's thesis. The vision achieved through bloodletting has consequences beyond personal vislonary experience. And the language of the typically cautious authors becomes bold: "The conclusion is inescapable. . . ."

physical existence in human space and time. Thus the Vision Serpents were more than symbolic representations of hallucinations; they were the bodily fulfillment of those visions. The god or ancestor contacted in ritual actually appeared, and when the ritual ended, he was gone.

The power of ritual to incarnate the supernatural may also explain why the king could appear in so many different guises. It appears that the king was conceived to be a vessel of sorts and that through ritual, a god was brought into his body. At the end of a ritual, the god would depart, but in the next ritual, another god would come to reside within the vessel. This ability to host the supernatural may have been shared by all Maya, for masks and body suits are worn by many participants of public ritual. For the duration of a ritual, they would become the gods they impersonated.

Inscriptions associated with bloodletting rites imply other birthing symbolism: the king became "the mother of the gods" by giving them birth through ritual. This relationship is explicitly stated at Palenque, where the gods of the Palenque Triad are called "the children of Pacal and Chan-Bahlum." The glyph that records this relationship is one that stands between a mother and her child in all other contexts. The king is the mother of the gods because he gives them birth and nourishes them through his gift of blood. The blood scrolls and Paddler figures that float above the scattering king are pictorial representations of the result of bloodletting—the physical manifestation of the gods.

The ability to give birth to the gods through ritual is an awe-inspiring concept, for it means that ritual was far more than role playing. As the bearer of the most potent blood among humankind, the king was the focus of tremendous power—thus the pervasiveness of scenes showing his bloodletting in Maya art. Through his gift of blood, the king brought the gods to life and drew the power of the supernatural into the daily lives of the Maya.[13]

> This closing restatement of the thesis shows how a writer can stay focused on the thesis and yet lend it depth and richness. Visions gained through bloodletting were a form of piety that also benefited the king's people—and thus his standing with them. Sacred ritual is thus also political in its aims.

Notes

1. Alfred M. Tozzer, ed. and trans., "Landa's Relación de las cosas de Yucatan: A Translation," *Papers of the Peabody Museum of American Archaeology and Ethnology, Harvard University* 18 (New York: Kraus Reprint Corp., 1966), 113–4.

2. J. Eric S. Thompson first identified ritual bloodletting in Classic-period Maya iconography in "A Blooddrawing Ceremony Painted on a Maya Vase," in *Estudios de Cultura Maya*, vol. 1 (Mexico City: Universidad National Autónoma de Mexico, 1961), 13–20. David Joralemon focused attention on the iconography of bloodletting by identifying indisputable

scenes of the act, the Perforator God and other regalia in his article "Ritual Blood-Sacrifice among the Ancient Maya, Part 1," in the *Primera Mesa Redonda de Palenque, Part 2*, edited by Merle Greene Robertson (Pebble Beach, Calif.: Robert Louis Stevenson School, 1974), 59–77. Using this iconography as a base, epigraphers were able to identify verbs, tides and other written expressions recording the rite, which in turn led to the recognition of related pictorial representations.

3. In his study of the meaning of color in Late Preclassic architectural sculpture, David Freidel first suggested that scroll symbols for blood and smoke were identical, and he correlated an interrelationship between these two symbols and those of water and mist or clouds ("Polychrome Facades of the Lowland Maya Preclassic," in *Painted Architecture and Polychrome Monumental Sculpture in Mesoamerica* [Washington, D.C.: Dumbarton Oaks, 1985], 5–30).

4. Dennis Tedlock, *Popal Vuh: The Definitive Edition of the Mayan Book of the Dawn of Life and the Glories of Gods and Kings* (New York: Simon and Schuster, 1985), 77–80.

5. J. Alfred Maudslay, *Biologia Centrali-Americana: Archaeology* (London: Dulau & Co., 1889–1902).

6. Shield Jaguar's lintels were placed in Structure 23, a double-galleried, north-facing building on the lower level of the city. Lintels 24 and 25 were taken to The British Museum by Maudslay in 1882, and Lintel 26 was removed to Mexico City's Museo Nacional de Anthropologia in 1964. Originally the top member of a door, each lintel was carved with a text on the outer surface and with a scene on the underside, facing the floor.

7. Archaeological evidence suggests a strong interaction between Teotihuacán and the Lowland Maya, beginning about A. D. 400 and lasting for some two hundred years. During that period the Maya absorbed a complex of symbols, including this headdress and the so-called Tlaloc imagery, but it is increasingly clear that the Maya redefined this symbol complex for their own purposes, thereafter associating it with bloodletting rites, both self-inflicted and involving captives. Lady Xoc's usage of this Teotihuacanoid symbol does not mean that Teotihuacanos dominated Yaxchilan or that she was from that city; rather, it signals that this particular bloodletting ritual is being enacted.

9. Alfred M. Tozzer, "Landa's Relación," 114.

12. David Stuart was the first epigrapher to recognize the pattern of the Paddler names in Maya inscriptions and to realize their great import to the scattering rite. He was also the first to propose the interpretation of the Dos Pilas inscriptions presented here. See David Stuart, "Blood Symbolism in Maya Iconography," RES 7/8 (1984), 6–20.

13. In "Fertility, Vision Quest and Auto-Sacrifice: Some Thoughts on Ritual Blood-Letting Among the Maya," (in *Art, Iconography, and Dynastic History of Palenque, Part III, Proceedings of the Segunda Mesa Redonda de Palenque*, ed. Merle Greene Robertson [Pebble Beach, Calif.: Robert Louis Stevenson School], 181–193). Peter Furst first suggested the interpretation of Maya bloodletting as a "vision quest: like the young Indian in the ordeals associated with the Sun Dance on the Great Plains, under certain specific circumstances the Maya may have sought to obtain divine guidance from deified ancestors or guardian spirits in an alternate state of consciousness or ecstatic trance triggered not by psychoactive plants but rather by a massive physical jolt to the system" (184). He also discusses "non-hurtful pain" and its documentation in rituals and other experience around the world.

READING RESPONSES

1. Reading this chapter, you probably learned as much about Maya culture and religion as you did about Maya art. What seems to be the role of the Maya art in this chapter? That is, does the historical and cultural information help you "see" the Maya art better or is the Maya art "evidence" of Maya cultural practices? What evidence in Schele and Miller's chapter supports your choice?

2. Review Schele and Miller's chapter, paying special attention to the way they shift topics between the cultural context for the art and the art itself. Choose one shift that you think is particularly effective and describe why it is effective. Choose another shift that you find to be particularly ineffective and revise it so that it's more effective.

3. Choose one of the lintels that Schele and Miller describe. Study the image closely and then re-read what they have to say about the lintel. Do you accept everything they say about this lintel? Make a list of the claims they make about the lintel, ordering them from the claim that you are most willing to accept to the claim that you are least willing to accept. For claims that you find somewhat suspicious, what is it that makes you suspicious?

Notes on Grammar, Style, and Rhetoric:
Assertiveness and Honesty in Interpretation

One striking aspect of "Bloodletting and the Vision Quest" is that Linda Schele and Mary Ellen Miller present their statements with different levels of force or confidence. They present many of their statements as we would probably expect them to—in a straightforward manner as facts. For example, at an early point in their chapter, they write that "When buildings were dedicated, crops planted, children born, couples married or the dead buried, blood was given to express piety and call the gods into attendance" (p. 142). They present several other statements, however, with what many linguists call "modality markers," which allow writers to show how committed they are to the truth of their statements—an honest admission that they are offering only one possible suggestion.

With the kind of modality markers called "hedges," writers reveal a cautious commitment to the truth of their statements. Writers can hedge in many different ways (see the Notes on Grammar, Style, and Rhetoric essay in the biotechnology chapter for additional examples of hedges). They can use adverbs such as *perhaps* and *possibly*, modal verbs such as *might* and *may*, main verbs such as *seem* and *appear*, and phrases such as *to our knowledge* and *to a certain degree*. In addition, writers can use different kinds of clauses to introduce their statements: *I think*, *I guess*, *I suppose*, *It is possible that*, *I find it possible that*, and *It's thought that*.

When writers explicitly indicate how committed they are to the truth of their statements, they do not always give a cautious assessment. Sometimes they add punch to their statements by using what are called "emphatics." Many specific forms can function as emphatics. Writers can use adverbs such as *certainly* and *assuredly* as well as phrases such as *without a doubt* and *with no hesitation whatsoever*. They can insert clauses such as *I am certain* within other clauses: *The Maya, I am certain, continued this practice for years.* Similarly, they can introduce their statements with clauses such as *I am certain that*, *It is clear that*, *There is the certainty that*, and *It is surely the case that*.

As noted above, Schele and Miller use a large number of modality markers. Some of these are emphatics. It is interesting that some emphatics are linked to claims that appear immediately after Schele and Miller sound a note of doubt or ignorance: "The warrior is not named, but it is clear that the purpose of the bloodletting rite was to cause this vision to materialize" (147). It is also interesting that some emphatics are linked to explicit indications of the evidence Schele and Miller use to justify a certain statement: "It is clear from Classic Maya Art and inscriptions, as well as from Popul Vuh, that blood drawn from all parts of the body—especially from the tongue, earlobes, and genitals—was sustenance for the gods" (144). Finally, it is interesting that emphatics introduce some of the statements most central to this chapter: "It is clear that bloodletting was basic to the institution of rulership, to the mythology of world order, and to public rituals of all sorts" (142).

But Schele and Miller are not certain about all of their statements, and thus they do not present them all as facts or include emphatics with them. With some statements they use hedges. In one situation they hedge lightly with the adverb *apparently*: "After the paper cloth became saturated with blood, it was burned in a brazier, for the gods apparently required that blood be transformed into smoke in order to consume it" (143). In another situation they hedge lightly by using the introductory clause *It appears that*: "It appears that the king was conceived to be a vessel of sorts and that, through ritual, a god was brought into his body" (154).

These hedges sound relatively light notes of uncertainty. But Schele and Miller also use some hedges that signal a greater degree of uncertainty. For instance, at one point they use the modal verb *may*. In a sentence referring to an unidentified person brought forth in a vision, they write that "He may embody the idea of sacrifice, just as the Tlaloc warrior on Lintel 25 personifies sacrifice and the Tlaloc war complex" (150). But the most prominent of the hedges signaling fairly significant uncertainty is the adverb *perhaps*; it appears more than six times in this chapter. Here is one example: "Stingray spines, for example, are often found in the pelvic regions of the dead and were perhaps originally contained in bags hung from belts" (142).

What we find in this chapter, then, are statements lying all along the continuum of authorial certainty. Why do the authors move through such a wide range of expressed certainty? The range of their expression accurately reflects the range of knowledge in their field at the time of their writing. It is clear that Schele and Miller are confident that some of the statements they make about the Maya and their culture are facts. Moreover, they regard some of these facts as very important. But it is also clear that Schele and Miller are not absolutely certain about what some aspects of Maya culture meant to the Maya themselves. Thus Schele and Miller often hedge statements having to do with why the Maya might have performed certain rituals and depicted them in certain ways. And if you read the endnotes for this chapter, you will notice that such statements have been debated in the interpretation of Maya culture for years; you will even notice that scholars working in this area of interpretation can point to specific dates when people made breakthroughs in understanding Maya inscriptions or drawings.

Thus the emphatics that Schele and Miller use express enthusiasm about aspects of Maya culture and about interpretive progress in the study of Maya culture. And their hedges signal respect for the complex and distant culture that they study. This is respect for difference, for the alien, in that Schele and Miller do not assume that they can interpret all aspects of Maya culture in the ways we typically interpret other cultures—easily and quickly by comparing other cultures to our own.

In Your Own Writing . . .

The writing you do in college will not always be about cultures that are alien to you. But some of the writing you do will probably deal with subjects about which you do not have complete knowledge. As you write, remember the pattern that Schele and Miller follow:

- If some of your statements can clearly be shown to be based on facts, state them directly.
- If some of your statements are based on facts and are close to the heart of your overall message, consider using an emphatic with them.
- But if some of your statements cannot be shown to be based on facts, and if these statements are controversial, use a strategically placed hedge with them.

STUDENT WRITING IN ART HISTORY

Introduction by Rebecca Merz, art history major

The Assignment. I wrote the research paper that is reprinted here for a class on African art. The assignment was very open-ended; we were instructed to write about any topic pertaining to African art, such as a specific artistic tradition among a group of people, a contemporary African artist, or even a broader theme spanning many culture groups. Since I am particularly interested in how art serves as a means of promoting royal authority, I knew that I wanted to write my paper on this theme. To narrow the topic, I chose to focus on the obas (rulers) of the Benin kingdom in Africa (in an area that is in present-day Nigeria).

The Content. The Edo people of the Benin kingdom consider their obas to be semi-divine rulers, but this is a position of much complexity, laden with many fascinating contradictions and paradoxes. This complexity is abundantly manifest in the art of the Benin people. As the central authority of the Benin kingdom, the oba has control over the production of art. Thus, the majority of Benin art was produced for the use of the oba, and for distribution according to his will. Consequently, much Benin art promotes the authority of the oba both through empowering motifs, which serve as a sort of visual "propaganda," as well as through the innate power of the objects themselves.

The longer I looked at the images I found in my research, the more intriguing I found it and the more insight I received into the nature of Benin kingship. That gave me the confidence to point out important features of the images to my readers and offer interpretations.

Learning to Write in Art History. Once I asked my sister to read through one of my art history papers to give me some feedback, and as I read through her comments, I noticed that she asked several questions, the answers to which I thought should have been obvious. When I questioned her about this, I was appalled to find that she had not even glanced at the images included in the paper. The images are the most important part; they are what set an art history paper apart from any other kind of paper. The images and the words work together to illuminate cultural history.

Writing a good art history paper is, however, more than just carefully looking at, describing, and pointing out the features of an image. It does take careful research. It is important to know the historical context in order to understand fully what is happening in a work of art. Religion, politics, the economy, personal relationships, and so many other factors all need to be taken into account when analyzing a work of art. The more information that can be known about the artist and the context in which he or she worked, the better that the image can be understood.

In the end, though, it is impossible to know what was in the mind of the artist as he or she created the image—or in the minds of those who have viewed the art. The best that can be done is to make an interpretation based upon visual clues and historical context. Inevitably there will be many different theories about a work of art, and it is impossible to discern which are correct and which are not. Often all that can be done is to lay out all of the arguments and allow the reader to carefully examine the image for themselves. This is what I have tried to do in my paper, for example, with the two plaques. After briefly describing the image, I offer several interpretations on the meaning of the object. Not any one of these interpretations is correct—rather they are all at work simultaneously to make the image that much more complex. I leave the reader with these various contextual details and interpretations which comprise a potential meaning for the object.

Creating Change through Writing in Art History. Every day we are bombarded by images, many of which we interpret subconsciously. They become so commonplace that we do not even pay them much thought. There is much to learn, though, by training ourselves to really think about what we are looking at. Images play an integral role both in the formation of culture as well as the reflection of culture. Images reveal society's beliefs and values, and they are manipulated for specific ends, including the creation of political and cultural beliefs. This is certainly true of the Benin society. Examining Benin royal art reveals that art has a great deal of power.

Writing art history helps to develop a critical understanding of the various roles that images play as well as the power that they have to reflect and shape society, whether that be in the past or in the present. The ability to intelligently describe, explain, and interpret images leads to not only a greater insight into culture, and a greater appreciation for the visual arts, but also to a greater ability to discern the important role that images play in society. And that has certainly changed the way I experience and understand culture.

Images of the Oba: A Study in the Paradoxical Nature of Benin Kingship

Rebecca Merz

According to the legend of the Edo people, the Ogiso, or sky kings, were the first rulers of the Benin kingdom. At the end of the thirteenth century the Uzama, a powerful political group in

> It helps in writing to start with stories, especially since art history is often a mix of cultural mythology and art. You can't understand one without the other.

Benin, overthrew the Ogiso with the help of their Yoruba neighbors in Ife. The king of Ife sent his son, Oranmiyan, to Benin. Oranmiyan married an Edo maiden, and their son became the first oba of Benin, the first oba in a dynasty that continues to the present.

This legend illustrates well the complex nature of the office of the oba. Through marriage to an Edo woman, the divine nature of the Yoruba kings fused with the political authority of the native Benin rulers to form a new dynasty. Thus the oba of Benin is both human and divine. As such, he not only occupies the highest position in the Benin social hierarchy, but he is also able to act as a mediator between the physical and spiritual realms. The oba has the power over life and death, and is capable of both great wrath and great benevolence. Yet for all of his supernatural ability, the oba does not wield complete and absolute authority. He is dependent upon the many chiefs and court officials who check his power. The art produced by the

> my thesis statement

Benin court reflects the complicated nature of the oba, which is, in essence, a composite of paradoxes.

The oba of Benin has many supernatural powers. He is not thought to participate in ordinary human activities like sleeping and eating. These actions are not even alluded to in his presence.[1] The oba is believed to have psychic ability, and is considered so powerful that his feet cannot touch the ground without causing great devastation. He controls the forces that affect all aspects of Benin life and culture. Ritual and regalia enhance the oba's innate power. Coral, an important material in Benin, was controlled by the oba, who distributed it to various court officials as a sign of their loyalty as well as his power over them. The royal coral, which is only worn by the king, consists of an elaborate headdress and often includes netted coral beads that cover the oba's entire person. The coral is more than mere ornamentation; it is believed to make everything spoken in its presence come true. It gives the oba mystical abilities, the right to issue punishment, and the power to utter an irrevocable curse.[2]

> The brass heads, although a progression of style can be seen over time, all show certain characteristic features. The features are somewhat simplified and do not necessarily show a direct representation of actual human facial features. In particular, the eyes are larger than they are in actuality and they are reduced to simple geometric shapes. That's what I mean by "stylized."

The immense power of the oba is evident in the commemorative brass heads, which are an important class of Benin art. The brass head shown in Figure 1 is characteristic of Benin brass heads. It portrays the oba wearing royal regalia, in particular, the elaborate coral headdress. A comparison of this brass sculpture to the photograph of Oba Akenzua II shows the continuity between Benin sculpture and the actual regalia worn by the kings. The brass heads, while they were likely intended to represent a specific oba, are not individualized portraits, rather, they are a stylized depiction of the king.

Figure 1 Brass head.

That the image is in itself a generalization of the oba rather than an individual portrait speaks to the ritual nature of the office itself. The oba is a unique individual, but more than that, he is venerated as the embodiment of a political institution. He is a person, but his very existence is symbolic and ritual. For the Edo people, the head represents the seat of wisdom. Ceremonies to strengthen the head of the oba take place yearly.[3] Brass, the material from which the heads are cast, also has complex symbolism. Because it neither rusts nor corrodes, brass represents the continuity and permanence of the monarchy. In addition, its reddish color is thought to keep evil forces at bay.[4] These heads are kept on ancestral altars and usually represent the oba or the queen mother. Brass heads served as a base for elaborately carved elephant tusks. Ivory was a substance to which the oba had exclusive claim. He had rights to one tusk from every elephant killed, and since the oba served as the controller of the ivory trade with Europeans, the material represented great wealth. The white color of ivory is a sign of purity, and the possession of elephant tusks gives the oba the physical power of the elephant as well as its associations with leadership, longevity, and wisdom.[5] Finally, the elephant tusk forms a vertical projection from the top of the head, which the Edo consider to be the threshold between the physical and spiritual realms, and thus, the place where spirit possession takes place. This vertical axis is important in Benin culture, and it also appears in palace architecture and the coiffures of the queen mother. The spiritual qualities of ivory carved with empowering motifs, coupled with the sacrifices made on the altar and the placement of the tusk on the top of the head, works to channel power from the commemorative image of the king through the spiritually charged tusk and into the air, which represents the spiritual realm.

This function of the brass commemorative heads reflects one of the most important aspects of Benin kingship. Since the oba is both human and divine, he is the perfect mediator between the physical and spiritual worlds. His position places him in contact with the spirits, gods, ancestors, and even the forces of nature. He is able to communicate with these inhabitants of the other realm, act as an intermediary on behalf of the Edo people, and harness their powers for the good of his kingdom. The oba serves as the representative of the ancestors, but also as the channel for ancestral spirits, which protect and empower Benin society. Indeed, much of the oba's ritual function centers on the ancestors, and the first action of every oba upon coronation is to erect an altar to his predecessor. The

> Although the tusk is not included in Figure 1, you can see the circle on top of the head into which a tusk would have been inserted. Examples of heads with tusks appear in Figure 2.

> My point here is to connect the art, the significance of the material of the art, and the cultural meaning of the whole.

Figure 2 Benin palace altar.

ancestral altar of Oba Ovonramwen in the palace in Benin City
is a surviving example of such an altar (Figure 2). The oba is at
the center of Benin society, which is symbolically represented by
the fact that his palace lies at the heart of Benin City, which in
turn lies at the heart of the Benin kingdom. The oba is at the
pinnacle of the Benin socio-political hierarchy as well as at the
physical and symbolic the center of the kingdom.

By "iconography"
I am referring to a
set of images which
symbolically represent
the oba, and his
characteristics. These
images serve as a sort
of visual metaphor for
the oba. For example,
the Portuguese traders
represent the oba's
control of wealth.
The leopard represents
his strength.

Another important aspect of the oba's supernatural persona
and mediating position relates to his tie to the god Olokun.
Olokun, the god of the waters, was one of the most important
deities in the Edo pantheon. The oba was closely tied to the
deity, who acted both as a royal patron as well as a divine alter-
ego. Olokun was associated with trade and wealth. This was an
important aspect of the oba's power, for he controlled all trade
of precious materials like ivory, coral and brass. In addition, it
was the oba who controlled the trade with Europeans, and
images of Portuguese traders play an important role in Benin
royal iconography.

More important, though, was Olokun's association with
the waters. Olokun is the lord of the sea, and the oba is the lord
of the land; together they represent control over the whole.
They are deity and divine king, and their control is absolute and

complete. It is not only, however, that they rule the separate realms, but also that the oba takes on the characteristics of Olokun and receives power from the deity. Animals associated with the god Olokun, including mudfish and crocodiles, frequently serve as royal motifs. The Edo saw the riverbank as a place of transition between realms, and creatures that dwell both in and out of water are associated with the ability to travel between realms.

One of the most important dualities present in the person of the oba is his simultaneous role as life-giver and death-dealer. Since the oba has the power over life and death, he is seen as both benevolent and fearsome. The oba brings well-being to the nation.[6] Early obas were military heroes, who expanded and defended the kingdom. Later obas took on a more ceremonial role, and through their ritual actions brought well-being to the nation. During the yearly Igue festival, the mystical power of the oba is renewed, and his strength to guarantee the well-being of the community during the coming year is ensured.

Despite this positive role of the oba, there is also a violent and dangerous side that is greatly feared. Not only does the oba have the power to bring life to the community, he also has the power to deal out death. The Edo people refer to the oba as "child of the Sky whom we pray not to fall and cover us, child of Earth whom we implore not to swallow us up."[7] The oba presides over all capital offenses, and he is the only person able to deal out the death sentence.[8] This power over life and death is spiritual as well as political. The oba has a great deal of occult power and knowledge and is capable of using this as well as his political authority to deal out his judgment. The oba is capable of great violence, as is evident in his ability to perform human sacrifice. This highest form of sacrifice was controlled by the oba, and the violence of the action signified his great power.[9]

Even though I am not here referring to any examples of art, I try to keep my readers' attention focused on images that reinforce my thesis.

The oba was identified with a number of animals that illustrate this royal paradox of simultaneous benevolence and malevolence. As king of the forest, the leopard is one of the most common animal motifs in royal iconography. Killing leopards was the privilege of the oba, and these slain leopards are sacrificed to the cult of the oba's head. Tamed leopards are used in royal processions to show the oba's power over the king of the forest. The oba gave out leopard teeth and skins to military leaders as a symbol of their loyalty to him, his control over them, and his power to delegate the right to take life. In addition, the leopard possesses the innate qualities of leadership. Leopards possess a cruel side which is tempered

Figure 3 Bronze plaque, Oba with animals.

by reserve and moderation. Like the oba, the leopard is both "menacing and moderating."[10] The elephant also is symbolic of this dual nature. The elephant possesses great physical strength and is, like the oba, a formidable creature, but the elephant also possesses the leadership qualities of longevity and wisdom.[11] The crocodile, associated with the god Olokun, acted as a sort of "policeman" sent by Olokun to punish the wicked. According to the Edo people, the "power of the crocodile represents the power of the oba, whose hand has the strength of the crocodile."[12] The oba possesses the same dangerous ferocity as the crocodile in his ability to strike the wicked. The oba, as the highest authority in the Benin state, is responsible for insuring justice in his kingdom. A bronze plaque from the palace provides a telling example of the association of the oba with powerful animals (Figure 3). Here the oba is portrayed holding two leopards and having the feet of two mudfish. The pairing of these two particular animals represents the oba's control over both the land and the sea. Both animals show his strength and ferocity, but they also allude to his moderation and justice as the supreme authority in the Benin kingdom.

This enormous power wielded by the oba does not go unrestrained, however, for the hierarchy of the Benin political system offers many checks on the oba's power. The oba may be the highest member of the Benin kingdom, and the possessor of divine nature, but is in many ways dependant upon those around him. In numerous examples of Benin art, the oba is depicted surrounded by chiefs and attendants. He may have supreme authority, but he does not rule alone. Perhaps one of the greatest checks on the oba's authority comes from the Uzama. The seven members of the Uzama are an old political group in Benin. The Uzama existed before the oba, and it was they who ended the corruption of the previous dynasty and initiated the founding of the present. The Uzama are the kingmakers and the "keepers of tradition." Unlike many of the political positions in Benin, theirs is hereditary rather than appointed, and as such, they are somewhat beyond the control of the king. From the very beginning of the dynasty there was tension between the oba and the Uzama.[13] The oba is of the divine line of Ife, but he receives his authority to rule from the kingmakers. The oba needs the Uzama's cooperation in order to perform the rituals of his office, and their ability to withhold cooperation is a great weapon against tyranny.[14]

This simultaneous dependence upon the members of his court and authority over them can be seen in another brass plaque from the palace in Benin City (Figure 4). This plaque offers many insights into the complexity of Benin kingship and the variety of paradoxes that it presents. On this plaque are three figures; the central figure, who is depicted at a slightly larger scale, is the oba. Two attendants stand on either side of the oba, and as they

Figure 4 Brass plaque, Oba with attendants.

turn towards him, they act as a framing device, drawing the viewer's attention to the central figure. They hold his arms in a supportive manner that almost seems to impart a sense of weakness to the oba. This is a good example of the oba's reliance upon the members of his court. It is a visual reminder that, although the oba is the most important and powerful member of Benin

Just looking at the plaque in Figure 4 without any explanation, you probably would not be able to tell what it represents, but the people of the culture in which it was produced would know. The function of the art historian is to bring readers the knowledge that lets them see art from the viewpoint of a historical culture.

society, he does not rule alone. He is at the same time all-powerful and utterly dependant.

The apparent weakness of the oba is tempered by the portrayal of his divine nature. This is done through the depiction of mudfish legs. This is a common motif in Benin royal iconography, and its connotations are particularly rich. The mudfish is highly valued by the Edo people. It is a principal source of food, and it represents peace, prosperity and fertility.[15] Moreover, it is associated with Olokun. The divine attribute of mudfish appendages alludes to the fact that the oba's feet are never allowed to touch the ground because the divine power of the oba can cause terrible destruction. Mudfish are valued as sacrificial animals because they are thought to possess the "ability to overcome all obstacles." This is due to their ability to survive outside of water for substantial stretches of time by closing their gills. In this way, the mudfish, like the crocodile, is able to survive both in and out of water, and therefore, serves as a symbol of mediation between the physical and spiritual realms. In addition to these positive qualities, however, the mudfish is also dangerous. Some species of mudfish are capable of delivering an electric shock, and because of this dangerous potential, the mudfish serves as an apt metaphor for the simultaneously malevolent and benevolent powers of the oba.

Mudfish legs were first used in royal iconography during the reign of Oba Ohen in the fifteenth century. According to history, Ohen was struck with paralysis for having committed an act of adultery. Since physical perfection was demanded of kings, Ohen attempted to hide his infirmity. When he appeared in public he was carried and his legs remained covered. Images of him with mudfish appendages called attention to his divine power rather than his human frailty. After some time, the Iyase, an important official and military commander, became suspicious and decided to spy on the king. The Iyase discovered Ohen's secret, but the oba had him put to death. When the truth of the matter surfaced, the officials of the kingdom cast judgment on Ohen for his duplicitous actions, and they had him stoned to death.[16] This account reveals much about Benin kingship. It shows that although the oba is divine, he is not invulnerable. He is capable of wielding terrific power, but that power must be used within bounds. When the oba exceeds these bounds, he too is subject to judgment. This is evident in the U-shaped brass plaque (Figure 4), where the two attendants standing on either side of the oba function as checks on the power of the oba. They not only support the oba, but they keep him from misusing his power to the detriment of the kingdom.

This plaque represents the duality of Benin kingship. It portrays the oba as both human and divine, and therefore the mediator between the physical and spiritual realms. It depicts him as both powerful and vulnerable, capable of great benevolence and peace, as well as great violence and danger. Here, the oba is the most important and powerful member of Benin society, but he leans on his court for support. He possesses the ultimate authority, but it is authority within bounds. His power is both absolute as well as utterly fragile. It is this composite of paradoxes that creates an incredibly complex and multifaceted image of the oba.

Notes

1. Armand Duchâteau. *Benin: Royal Art of Africa from the Museum fur Volkerkunde, Vienna*. (Houston: Museum of Fine Arts, 1994), 27.
2. Ibid., 31.
3. Suzanne Preston Blier. *The Royal Arts of Africa: The Majesty of Form*. (New York: H. N. Abrams, 1998), 44.
4. Duchâteau, 31.
5. Ibid., 89.
6. Paula Ben-Amos and Arnold Rubin, eds. *The Art of Power, the Power of Art: Studies in Benin Iconography*. (Los Angeles, CA: Museum of Cultural History, UCLA, 1983), 21.
7. Kate Ezra. *Royal Art of Benin: The Perls Collection in the Metropolitan Museum of Art*. (H. N. Abrams, 1992), 4.
8. Paula Ben-Amos. *Art, Innovation and Politics in Eighteenth-Century Benin*. (Bloomington, Indiana: Indiana University Press, 1999), 70.
9. Ibid., 75–6.
10. Duchâteau, 89.
11. Ibid., 89.
12. Ibid., 64.
13. Ezra, 5.
14. Duchâteau, 27.
15. Ibid., 71–3.
16. Ezra, 113.

List of Illustrations

Figure 1: Head of an Oba, Brass, 19th century

Figure 2: Benin palace ancestral altar of Oba Ovonramwen, Benin City, Nigeria

Figure 3: Plaque depicting Oba with leopards and crocodiles, Brass, 18th–20th century

Figure 4: Plaque depicting mudfish-legged king and supporters, Brass, 18th–20th century

READING RESPONSES

1. At the end of her opening paragraph, Rebecca Merz claims that "The art produced by the Benin court reflects the complicated nature of the oba...." If read one way, this sentence would imply that Merz will examine art to understand a cultural role—that of the oba. Is this what Merz does? If you think so, list evidence from her text that would support you. If not, list evidence from her text that indicates she's doing something else.

2. Merz does a particularly good job of connecting information about the Benin culture to the art she's examining. Note the spot in the text where she makes this connection most skillfully. How would you describe the technique she uses to link cultural information and artistic artifact?

3. Create two lists of the places where Merz shows how committed she is to the truth of her statements, one list of places where Merz indicates she is cautiously committed and another list of places where she confidently asserts the truth.

PUBLIC WRITING IN ART HISTORY

Introduction

Michiel Plomp's essay on *The Beekeepers* appeared originally in an exhibit catalog for the Metropolitan Museum of Art in New York City. In this entry, Plomp accomplishes a great deal. First, he directs the attention of those viewing this drawing to the enigmatic features that make it such an object of curiosity for art historians. For example, in his opening paragraphs he draws the viewer's attention to the distant water mill and church. Second, he provides viewers with historical and cultural background so that they fully understand what the artist Pieter Bruegel was representing—for example, the contemporary viewer might not recognize the central figures as beekeepers or their baskets as bee hives. Third, he presses the viewer to question the relationship of the Flemish proverb located in the lower left corner to the scene Bruegel depicts. Finally, he summarizes recent attempts by art historians to discern what Bruegel was trying to communicate in this sketch. In all of these tasks, Plomp demonstrates the fine work that art historians do: he uses words to interpret artistic images and uses artistic images to interpret distant cultures.

Plomp demonstrates the enigmatic nature of this famous drawing by laying out at least three radically different interpretations of this drawing. While he notes the weaknesses of the first interpretation, he does not critique the other interpretations. Rather, he leaves it up to viewers to judge for themselves. In this way, Plomp encourages viewers to puzzle about Bruegel's *The Beekeepers*, just as art historians have for centuries.

Pieter Bruegel the Elder, *The Beekeepers*
Michiel C. Plomp

In a hilly farmyard in the vicinity of a village church three beekeepers appear with beehives, probably preparing to catch a swarm of insects. On the right, a boy or a young man has climbed a tree. To the left of center, in the background, a brook with a water mill can be seen. . . .

The text in the lower left corner of *The Beekeepers*—in all likelihood written by Bruegel himself[1]—reads: "He who knows where the nest is has the knowledge / he who robs it has the nest." This Flemish proverb, still in use today, alludes to the futility of having knowledge unless it is accompanied by action. It should explain the image but in fact, it obscures the meaning of this ostensibly simple peasant scene, making it mysterious and difficult to interpret.

Interestingly, in 1568—about the same time Bruegel drew *The Beekeepers*—he painted the *Peasant and the Bird Nester* (Kunsthistorisches Museum, Vienna), whose subject clearly relates to the proverb, and about forty years later two

The Beekeepers, ca. 1567–68
Pen and brown ink
20.3 × 30.9 cm (8 × 12 1/8 in.)
Signed and dated at lower right: *BRVEGEL MDLXV. . .*; inscribed, probably by the artist, at lower left: *dije den nest Weet dije[n?] Weeten / dijen Roft dij heeten*
(He who knows where the nest is has the knowledge / he who robs it has the nest)

etchings bearing the text of the saying and made after a composition by David Vinckboons ... were issued. Although the boy in the tree is the only element of the present drawing that appears in the *Peasant and the Bird Nester* and the etchings, one scholar has attempted to show that Bruegel's drawing carries the same meaning as the other works.[2] He noticed that just as in Vinckboons's composition a young lad strips the nest while peasants merely watch and allow themselves to be robbed, so in Bruegel's drawing activity and passivity are contrasted in the form of the boy who steals a swarm of bees while the oblivious beekeepers concern themselves with their work.[3] This argument founders, however, because there is no swarm of bees in Bruegel's image,[4] nor does the boy seem to have a receptacle for the insects, and, furthermore, the proverb speaks of nests rather than beehives.

Recently *The Beekeepers* has been the subject of several other studies. One of these suggests that the sheet illustrates the deadly sin of avarice and unwittingly revives the earliest identifications of the subject, which date from the late eighteenth and the early nineteenth century, in maintaining that the figures are robbers who are looking for a treasure (the nest) in the beehives.[5] The boy in the tree is the lookout and the thief on the right is still searching for the prize. The villain on the left has found it and is trying to flee without sharing the spoils; the man in the center knows this and grabs at a dagger with which to threaten his partner and prevent his escape.

Another recent analysis views the image as symbolic rather than as a straightforward representation of a real activity and considers its message to be religious and political.[6] According to this interpretation, Bruegel's beehives stand for the Catholic parish churches, for in the sixteenth century the Church was frequently compared to a beehive. After the iconoclastic raids of August 1566, many churches in Flanders had been emptied of their clergy (bees) and their contents (honey). Thus, in Bruegel's picture three faithful Catholics (the beekeepers) are attempting to restore the hives and put them back in their proper places,[7] while an iconoclast (the boy in the tree) turns his back on them, doing nothing. The work of the beekeepers, the action alluded to in the inscribed proverb, is action that benefits the Church. The study also suggests other possible readings—for example, that the boy sees how a Catholic hive and a Protestant church can coexist peacefully—and concludes with the rather farfetched idea that the image may present a Protestant point of view as well.[8]

Whether there is truth in any of these theories remains to be seen. It also remains to be seen whether *The Beekeepers* is the sole survivor of a group of Bruegel's drawings with sensitive religious and political content that Karel van Mander asserted the dying master asked his wife to burn because "he was afraid that on their account she would get into trouble or she might have to answer for them."[9] Clearly Bruegel's *The Beekeepers*, "one of the most enigmatic drawings" of the sixteenth century, has not yet yielded all its secrets.[10]

Notes

1. Vanbeselaere (1944, p. 85) and Boström (1949, pp. 79, 88) had doubts about whether Bruegel inscribed the text.
2. Boström 1949.

3. Renger (in Berlin 1975, no. 100) suggested that the drawing might also contrast audacity and caution, as symbolized by the unprotected boy and the covered-up beekeepers.

4. Admittedly, as Kavaler (1999, p. 235) has noted, the drawing may have been trimmed along the upper edge, which would perhaps have eliminated this crucial detail.

5. See Brandt 1989. The early identifications appear in two Dutch auction catalogues: Van der Schley and Yver, Amsterdam, April 28, 1783, Album A, no. 40 ("A Landscape . . . with some disguised persons who are stealing beehives . . ."); Daniel van Diepen, Amsterdam, April 8, 1805, Album H, no. 41 (same description).

6. Sybesma 1991.

7. According to Sybesma (ibid., p. 472), the three beekeepers may be agents of the Inquisition, since the Dutch word *corfdrager* can mean "hive or basket carrier" and also "secret informer."

8. Sybesma (ibid., pp. 476, 478) notes that the source for any presumed Protestant content would have been *De Biënkorf der H. Roomsche Kercke* (The Beehive of the Holy Roman Church) of 1569 by Philips van Marnix van Sint Aldegonde, in which the Catholic Church is ridiculed. However, this was published after the drawing was made, a fact that Sybesma explains away by hinting that Bruegel deliberately misdated his sheet to protect himself from the Inquisitors. Sybesma proposes that the proverb as well as the image can be interpreted as a Protestant message. Another recent interpretation suggests that *The Beekeepers* contrasts the communal ethic (as represented by the beekeepers) to individual enterprise (symbolized by the boy in the tree); see Kavaler 1999, pp. 233ff.

9. Van Mander 1994–99, vol. I, pp. 193–94 (1604, fols. 233v–234r) describes these sheets as "neatly and carefully drawn with some captions on them."

10. Sybesma 1991, p. 467.

READING RESPONSES

1. The author describes different interpretations of Bruegel's drawing. Which interpretation seems the most plausible to you? What facts, argumentation, or language did you find most persuasive?

2. Describe how your understanding of the Bruegel drawing changed from the first time you saw it until you finished reading Plomp's essay. What features of the drawing did Plomp's essay draw your attention to? What features of the drawing still confuse you?

3. Find three places in the text where Plomp uses modality markers to soften the strength of his claim. Rewrite these three, using a different method for signaling uncertainty for each one. Note the method you use.

MORE WRITING IN ART HISTORY

Introduction

Written for students, this "profile" of an important contemporary artist demonstrates the characteristic rhetorical choices of art historians. To begin, it points readers' attention to the artwork itself. It describes various features of the art and their significance: the prominent canoe image as an enduring symbol of Native American culture but also a symbol of movement and change, or the "trinkets" that represent stereotypes and commercialism but also a "trade" (the ironic title of the artwork) that is offered back to contemporary American culture. In short, the description and interpretation aim to bring out the rich complexity of the art itself.

The authors also talk about the physical presence of the artwork. Its size (over thirteen feet long by five feet tall) dramatic colors, and mixture of painting and various kinds of objects make a powerful, and possibly confrontational, impression on a viewer.

Furthermore, the authors introduce the historical context by writing about the tragic relationships between white settlers and Native Americans and by noting that the painting was composed in response to the five-hundredth anniversary of Columbus's first voyage to the "New World."

Finally, the authors write about the artist—her own history as a Native American and her philosophy of art. When they quote Smith as saying, "Dying cultures do not make art. Cultures that do not change with the times will die," they not only help us to understand *Trade*, they reinforce the message that art not only helps the viewer interpret culture; it *is* culture.

Profile: Jaune Quick-to-See Smith
Craig McDaniel and Jean Robertson

In *Themes of Contemporary Art: Visual Art after 1980*

In 1992 the United States recognized the five hundredth anniversary of Columbus's first voyage to the Americas. While most public events designed to mark the anniversary were planned as proud celebrations, Native Americans offered their reactions from a more somber vantage point. For them, Columbus's arrival in the Western hemisphere is remembered as the initial encounter of European and Indian civilizations, an encounter that resulted in violent contact and tragic results. Over a span of some four hundred years (from 1492 until the closing of the American frontier at the end of the nineteenth century), Native Americans lost their rights to land, Indian cultures were uprooted, and indigenous peoples suffered subjugation (especially in South America). Horrific numbers became victims to diseases the Europeans brought with them. The colonial era of European discovery and settlement meant increased warfare and displacement for the indigenous peoples who were already in the Americas.

In response to the Columbian quincentenary, Jaune Quick-to-See Smith, a prominent contemporary artist and enrolled member of the Flathead Salish, created a monumental oil painting. Measuring over thirteen feet wide, *Trade (Gifts for Trading Land with White People)* is a multi-layered artwork. The representation of a canoe dominates the image. The canoe's abstract simplicity is reminiscent of a pictographic image—a flat, abstracted style of representation that was used in many Indian cultures prior to the twentieth century. In the context of Quick-to-See Smith's art, the canoe shape serves as an icon symbolizing Native American people—their culture, history, and ongoing existence. Constructed on three

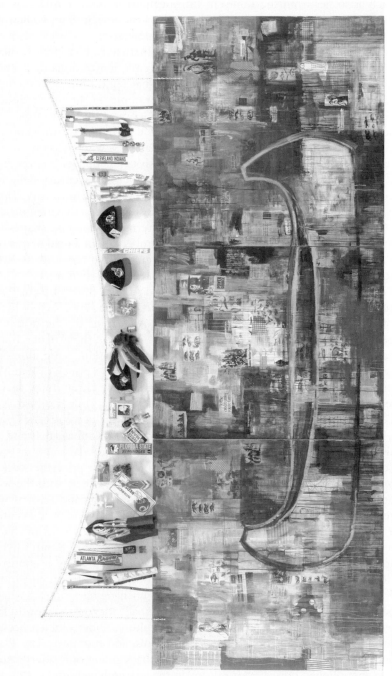

Trade (Gifts for Trading Land with White People)
Oil and mixed media, 60 × 170 inches
Chrysler Museum of Art, Norfolk, VA

separate canvases, *Trade* is a triptych, a tripartite format often reserved for sacred imagery (such as scenes from the Bible) in European art in the late fifteenth century, the time of Columbus's voyage. Smith employs the image of an Indian war canoe as a sacred object, worthy of veneration and meditation.

Around and within the image of the canoe, Smith affixed a plethora of collage material, including photographic images of news events, illustrations of animals, and snippets of text from current newspapers and magazines. She also incorporated imagery culled from other artists' work. For example, in the upper right of Smith's painting, we find a copy of a drawing by George Catlin (an artist who accompanied expeditions into Indian territories in the early nineteenth century); the image in the drawing juxtaposes an Indian in headdress with the same Indian wearing European-style clothing. The various newspaper clippings incorporated into *Trade* provide tidbits of information about late-twentieth-century daily life, such as a culture fair on an Indian reservation and an event at a university. Taken as a whole, the painting expresses Smith's understanding of the dynamic process of history: while earlier ways of life are lost, other patterns of living take shape. The canoe endures. The artwork's entire composition is embedded in a field of gestural brushstrokes. The overriding color scheme of bold greens and reds calls to mind the world of nature as well as the bloody conflicts of earlier Indian wars.

A row of trinkets (including a toy tomahawk and Atlanta Braves baseball cap) is festooned above the three canvases. Smith's tongue-in-cheek approach holds up evidence of the commercial exploitation of Native Americans by the dominant capitalist culture. Stereotyped portrayals of Indians, such as the Atlanta Braves baseball team's mascot with his huge grin and bright red skin, hang alongside consumer goods featuring a racialist use of nicknames, such as a pouch of Red Man tobacco. In her painting, Smith seems to offer to trade these cheap items *back* to white America; doing so, Smith offers an ironic commentary on the history of European colonialism, which perpetrated a long litany of "peace treaties" and "trades" with Indians—such as the purported purchase of Manhattan Island for the equivalent of twenty-four dollars' worth of cheap trade goods.

Some critics, collectors, and viewers of Native American art prize the work of artists who continue to utilize styles and subjects that identify closely with the work of their ancestors. Exemplifying this approach are current artists and artisans who create pottery and jewelry that look almost identical to objects made over a century ago. Other artists foster an approach to making art that signals the vitality of change and emphasizes the reality of the present. For example, Quick-to-See Smith's hybrid approach to the use of disparate materials and modes of image making is consistent with her identity as a contemporary artist educated in both mainstream and Indian cultures. For these artists, to insist on preserving an unchanging vision of what it means to be Indian would be to foster a romantic, essentialist view of the past. In fact, history shows that tribal cultures were never static; all cultures underwent a process of change, including the incorporation of new ideas, tools, and resources. The Plains Indians, for instance, adopted (and adapted to) horseback riding only after Spanish conquistadors first shipped horses from Europe in the sixteenth century.

Quick-to-See Smith explains, "Dying cultures do not make art. Cultures that do not change with the times will die."[1] The pastichelike quality of Smith's approach to painting—combining found objects with oil paint—matches the hybrid character of her expression of Indian identity. Today's Native Americans live complex lives, embedded in a rich mixture of cultural influences. Like most, Quick-to-See Smith's life has involved interactions with the world of mainstream culture and commerce; like other Americans, she has watched television, experienced her own direct encounters with the natural world, and heard stories passed down from her ancestors.

Trade exemplifies an activist approach to art-making. Activist art is an art of conscience, of creating for a cause. Donald Kuspit describes the preferred stance of activist artists as a willingness to "confront rather than console."[2] In this painting, the artist critiques mainstream American culture's tendency to pigeonhole Native American identity. . . .

As an artist, Smith could be described as a postmodernist: she appropriates and combines styles of imagery from other cultures and periods of history. Smith's approach to painting references the mark-making bravura of the Abstract Expressionists of the 1950s and 1960s, the irony of 1960s Pop Art, the energy of 1980s Neo-Expressionism, and the collage strategy of many modern and postmodern artists. Smith's work emphasizes deeply felt ideas about topical social issues, and her output also seems to be made in a spontaneous burst of emotion and creativity. What separates Smith's approach from many postmodernists' is that in undertaking her work she refuses to employ the products of culture as if objects and images were only arbitrary signs without any underlying significance. Smith insists that actions have real consequences. She examines some of the consequences of Native Americans' and newer arrivals' shared historical legacy and calls on all of us to reexamine the past and face the future without blinders.

Born 1940, on the Indian Mission Reservation in Saint Ignatius, Montana, Quick-to-See Smith received a masters in art from the University of New Mexico, Albuquerque. She now lives and works in Corrales, New Mexico.

Notes

1. Jaune Quick-to-See Smith, quoted in Lucy Lippard, *Mixed Blessings: New Art in a Multicultural America* (New York: Pantheon Books, 1990), 28.
2. Donald Kuspit, quoted in Allan M. Gordon, "George Longfish and Jaune Quick-to-See Smith at DC Davis," *Artweek*, April 1997, 21.
3. Jaune Quick-to-See Smith, quoted in Erin Valentino, "Coyote's Ransom: Jaune Quick to-See Smith and the Language of Appropriation," *Third Text* 38 (Spring 1997): 25.

READING RESPONSES

1. Authors McDaniel and Robertson describe "activist" art as "art of conscience, of creating for a cause." What cause is Quick-to-See Smith promoting with *Trade*? In your own words, describe the understanding that you gain from Quick-to-See Smith's art.
2. Consider how McDaniel and Robertson convey confidence in what they're writing. Note three places where they use either emphatics or hedges.

Finally, note three places where you believe the authors should have added a hedge or an emphatic.
3. In his introduction to the first reading, Professor Luttikhuizen draws on the adage "A picture is worth a thousand words." After looking at Quick-to-See Smith's artwork and reading McDaniel and Robertson's essay about it, agree or disagree with the adage. Be sure to include examples from your own experience with Quick-to-See Smith's art to support the points you make.

WRITING ASSIGNMENTS

ASSIGNMENT 1:
APPLYING THE PORTABLE RHETORICAL LESSON

Background: In art history, writers interpret art, making connections between the artist, her relationship to her culture(s), her selection and use of particular artistic media, and the skill with which she expresses herself. Often, however, living artists are called upon to interpret their own work; although art critics will not accept the artist's interpretation uncritically, this interpretation is the artist's opportunity to persuade people to view her art and its significance her way.

Your task is to create and explain a piece of art so that readers are inclined to interpret your art as you would like them to.

To begin, you'll need to create a piece of art that represents, honors, or critiques the culture around you, using media of your choice. Rest assured: since this is not an art course, you will not be assessed on your artistic skills. It's worth remembering, though, that your art should be complex enough to support extensive interpretation. Once you have completed your piece of art, note for yourself the dominant theme you want to express in your art and how particular aspects of the art help you communicate that theme.

As you begin drafting, think carefully about how you want to shape the reader's experience of your art—what aspect do you want him to attend to first? Next? How will you help the reader understand the connections among aspects of your art? How much description—of the culture, of the piece of art—will your reader need? Think carefully, too, about the level of confidence you want to use when you describe what your art means. How sure are you that you understand exactly what you meant to express? How much freedom do you want to give the reader to interpret the meaning of your art for himself?

ASSIGNMENT 2: MAKING CONNECTIONS

Background: When most people hear the name brand "Tupperware" they think of leftovers in a refrigerator rather than an art exhibit in a museum. But according to the Tupperware company's website, "The graceful form of Tupperware products and their quality and functionality have been recognized and acquired by a number of the world's art museums and industrial design collections, and have won design awards in the United States, Europe, and Japan." It seems that the Tupperware company values both design and functionality as two of the available means of persuading consumers to purchase their product. Contrasting Tupperware's attention to design to Steelcase's use of words and numbers from its ergonomic study of the Leap Chair in Chapter 14, Marketing, you might conclude that Steelcase cares more about functionality and less about design. In that report, the words and numbers from a study of employee productivity consistently draw the reader's attention to how the chair functions. But the images that accompany those words and numbers suggest that Steelcase cares about design, too.

Your task is to analyze the relationship between the images, the words, and the numeric information in the ergonomic study of the Leap Chair. You should pay careful attention to the images, words, and numbers that appear on the same page, analyzing how the images add design elements to the report and function to reinforce the information conveyed by the words and numbers. You should also carefully attend to the additional information that the images convey. Which design features does Steelcase emphasize? Why might consumers (business owners) value those features?

As you draft, you will want to decide how much information about the ergonomic study you need to convey to your reader, how to order your reader's experience of the ergonomic study, how you will draw your reader's attention to those design features, and the certainty with which you make your claims about the design features.

ASSIGNMENT 3: DOING THE RESEARCH

Background: One way a culture defines itself is through its art. This is undoubtedly true of the cultures of which you are a part, such as your local community, your ethnic group, or your country. Furthermore, as we have seen in the readings for this chapter, one way that others define a culture is by interpreting its art.

Your task for this assignment is three-fold: (1) to select a piece of art or a type of art from a culture in which you are a part, (2) research what others, such as art historians and cultural critics, have said about this piece or the type of art that this piece represents, and (3) analyze how these critics have defined your culture through their analysis of its art. This last aspect of the assignment will require you to read the words of others carefully, speculating about what they assume to be true about your culture—beliefs that they may be unaware of themselves. And this kind of reading will challenge you to consider the beliefs you hold about your own culture, too.

As you begin drafting, decide on the function of the art in your essay. Will it serve as a touchstone so that the reader can compare the analysis of the art to the piece of art itself? Will it be illustrative, giving the reader a general sense of the type of art? How will you connect your claims about the analysis of others to the art that they've analyzed? Consider, too, the level of confidence you use as you make your claims about the analysis of others.

PART THREE

REPORTING KNOWLEDGE

Each of the chapters in Part Three includes writing that reports knowledge—knowledge collected from other research, knowledge discovered through experimentation, knowledge constructed from logic and evidence. All of this is knowledge that people can put to good use.

We don't need to persuade you that knowledge is a good thing, but you may not be aware of how it improves your confidence and credibility as a writer. We hope you have had professors whom you respect because they know so much. Political scientist Christopher Layne (Chapter 7) writes compellingly, in large part, because his knowledge seems so vast. His readers feel compelled to take him seriously because he *knows* what he's talking about.

And knowledge is, of course, useful. When Tim Gabbett (Chapter 8, Biology) reports the findings of his study of rugby injuries, rugby coaches gain information they can use to adjust training regimens. When Shelley Correll (Chapter 9, Sociology) shares the knowledge of how gender affects career choices, school administrators can build better programs to educate young women. When Gordon Conway and Gary Toenniessen bring together their massive expertise about the biotechnology of food production (Chapter 10), politicians can forge intelligent international agreements.

When you write papers that require research, you develop skills in building and reporting knowledge. You see ways that new knowledge grows out of and adds to established knowledge. You read sources that change you as you see how they have changed others. You gain motivation to seek knowledge because knowledge matters.

7

POLITICAL SCIENCE:
BUILDING KNOWLEDGEABLE
ARGUMENTS

"The End of History," a 1989 article by Francis Fukuyama (currently deputy director of the U.S. State Department's policy planning staff), argued that the notion of history (defined as the coherent evolutionary process of human society) had found its "end" in liberal democracy. Fukuyama recognized much that is wrong with present democratic states, but he argued that those problems exist because individual democracies have not yet fully enacted their two foundational principles: liberty and equality. Fukuyama judged democracy to be the "endpoint of mankind's ideological evolution" and the "final form of human government."

You can easily imagine the storm of response that such claims would provoke. Both theoretical and concrete political change followed from "The End of History." In fact, each of the essays in this chapter has been somehow influenced by Fukuyama's paper and thus shows how writing in political science can create change. Christopher Layne's essay on the "Myth of Democratic Peace," for example, delivers a blow at an idealized image of democracy. Robin King's student essay argues for "consolidated" democracy as the preferred government for Israel, and he concludes his introduction by saying, "Perhaps my research will inspire some of my readers to investigate this issue further, or even to take action." The critical point for you, as a student trying to improve your writing, is that writing in political science self-consciously attempts to create change—sometimes dramatically so.

➤ A Portable Rhetorical Lesson:

Developing a Credible Authorial Voice

If you hope to inspire readers to take action because you believe that values such as equality, economic stability, or justice are at stake, your arguments will breathe with passion for the topic. You will use all available means to convince your opponents, and you will arm your supporters with compelling information and persuasive arguments. You will write, in short, like a good political scientist.

The writers of the essays in this chapter enhance their own credibility in three ways. They begin with an evident zeal for their topic—a passion to persuade because change is, the writers believe, necessary. This passion for their topic becomes evident in the words they choose, the sentence structures they craft, and the force of their claims. Second, they do thorough research, and they cite that research frequently. Layne's article in its original version contains a staggering 150 citations. Even Robin King uses 29 footnotes in an essay of less than 3,000 words—impressive for a college student. Third, they signpost the logical structure of their arguments to keep readers oriented as their argument unfolds. The extent to which both Layne and King take the time to give readers a map to their argument is remarkable. The combination of zeal, thorough and well-cited research, and a crystal clear knowledge of the structure of the argument builds a credible authorial voice—a voice that can argue for change.

A NOTE ON THESES, HYPOTHESES, AND RECOMMENDATIONS

Writers use three primary strategies to convey their main point: *thesis statements* (you see many examples of these in Part Two), *hypotheses* (examples appear in Part Three), and *recommendations* (Part Four). Political scientists make frequent use of all three strategies.

In these readings you will encounter thesis statements and hypotheses, both commonly used in academic writing. The Greek word from which we derive *hypothesis* means a proposal or supposition. In other words, those who use hypotheses are in the business of supposing: "Suppose that atoms—or nations, or cultures—are bound together in a particular way. What experiments could we conduct to see if the hypothesis is true?" A hypothesis implicitly says, "If we suppose this, how can we test it and prove whether it offers a better explanation than any other hypothesis?" A thesis, on the other hand, says, "Here's what I believe; let me explain why." Thesis statements are claims that can be argued about; hypotheses are tentative answers to research questions—answers that can be tested and proven valid or invalid.

Christopher Layne eases into his paper with an implicit thesis (basically, "I believe democratic peace theory is wrong"), but he focuses the reader's attention on two competing hypotheses—his own and one commonly used by American politicians. If Layne's hypothesis proves to better explain historical events than the common explanation, the reader is likely to accept Layne's implicit thesis. In this way, Layne enhances his credibility in the eyes of political *scientists* by using a *scientific* method.

Chapter Topics: Democracy, peace, and the relations between the two are the primary topics.

To Think About...

Where do you draw the line?

Ever heard of Koguryo? Most Americans haven't, but most people in China and South Korea have. Some of the territory that was once ancient Koguryo is now in China; the rest is in North Korea. According to Korean history, Koguryo was one of the three ancient kingdoms of Korea and the site of a famous battle. Thus, modern Koreans claim this ancient region and its history as their own. But China claims it, too. The Chinese *English People's Daily Online* describes Koguryo as "the ancient Koguryo Kingdom of China" and quotes the Chinese scholar Wei Cuncheng: "Koguryo was a regime established by ethnic groups in northern China some 2,000 years ago, representing an important part of Chinese culture."*

But this is ancient history. Why are the Chinese or Koreans passionate about it now? Two reasons: first, tombs in the region are now World Heritage sites. Prestige and tourism dollars are sure to follow. Second, some political scientists speculate that China is looking to the future. If North and South Korea ever re-unify, Koreans might claim all of the ancient Koguryo territory for this new, powerful Korea.

If you were Korean, what kinds of evidence could you use to claim Koguryo as a part of your national history? Create a list of at least five different types of evidence, ordering the list from most persuasive type of evidence at the top to least effective evidence at the bottom. You might find it helpful to do an Internet search on the word "Koguryo" to see what kinds of evidence political scientists have used.

---

*"China's ancient Koguryo Kingdom site added to World heritage List," http://english.people. com.ch/200407/01/eng20040701_148209.html.

WRITING IN POLITICAL SCIENCE

Introduction by Simona Goi, Professor of Political Science

Political scientists study politics in all its forms: governments, public opinion, the role of the media, the workings of social movements, the distribution of power in a region or the world at large, and so on. Christopher Layne's article is part of the scholarly research on the relationship between a country's type of government and that country's willingness to go to war. Political analysts have noted that democracies do not normally fight other democracies, even though they *do* go to war against non-democratic states. But *why* won't democracies go to war with other democracies? Are democratic governments inherently more moral than their non-democratic counterparts, and therefore less likely to use war to accomplish political ends? Or do democratic governments listen more carefully to their citizens who hope to avoid the human and financial costs of a war? One answer to these research questions is "democratic peace theory," the dominant theory regarding the relationships between democratic states. The article by Christopher Layne addresses the topic in two ways: first he summarizes scholarly explanations for why democratic states do not go to war against other democratic states, and then he tests those explanations against an alternative hypothesis that he proposes.

Generally speaking, scholars of political science write to accomplish three goals: to explain why something happened in the past, to predict what might happen in the future, or to influence/change what might happen in the future. Layne's essay explicitly addresses the first goal, but he does so because he hopes to lead people to see how to accomplish the other two: if we understand why some states chose not to go to war, we might be able to prevent war in the future. This is the passion that drives Layne's research. In this light, we can see that Layne is motivated not just by academic interest, but also by a belief that what he writes can help prevent future wars.

Sometimes this passion spills into word choice. For example, Layne describes democratic peace theory as a "myth" in his title and "wishful thinking" in the conclusion of his essay. Most readers would be surprised (and maybe a little offended) by such strong words. Although their passion for the subject sustains them during their research, political scientists usually use more restrained and precise language. Because political problems are complex and are always affected by the historical and geographic context, political scientists rarely suggest simple, clear-cut answers; rather, they state their conclusions as provisional, or subject to certain limitations or conditions.

Despite its strong language, Layne's essay is an excellent example of how political scientists develop complex logical arguments. First, Layne introduces the topic and notes its importance. Democratic peace theory is important, according to Layne, because it shapes American foreign policy in crucial ways: American politicians "who have embraced democratic peace theory see a crucial link between America's security and the spread of democracy" (page 186). Next he reviews two prominent versions of democratic peace theory, and he introduces a competing theory to explain how nations get along with each other: what he calls "realism." Then, Layne tests democratic peace theory and realism by applying them to historical events with known outcomes. Using four historical conflicts (only one appears in this shortened version of his essay) as case studies, Layne analyzes how well democratic peace theory and realism each explain the actions of these combating democratic states. Layne concludes that democratic peace theory cannot account for the historical evidence. Instead, realism better explains why these democratic countries avoided war with each other.

When political scientists write, they make good use of the passion that propels them to choose a particular research topic and sustains them through the hard work of collecting and analyzing large amounts of historical and analytical evidence. They write knowing that other scholars, using different evidence or a different method for analyzing the evidence, will likely come to different conclusions. Their various explanations compete with one another. In fact, the same journal issue in which Layne's article appears includes an article entitled "How Liberalism Produces Democratic Peace." It analyzes the same historical period that Layne does, but looks at it from a different perspective and, thus, produces different conclusions. Both writers try to convince others to see this topic as they do because they believe that their research will improve the chances for peace in the world.

✓ READING TIPS

Because the writing of political scientists is often long and complex, you'll read more efficiently if you map out the logical progression of ideas. So, for example, in Layne's essay, you might list the features of both democratic peace theory and realism and then match those features to the historical events that Layne describes in the Trent affair. Also, Layne's essay contains a thesis statement (something that is arguable), explicitly announces its hypothesis (something to be tested by analyzing the case studies), and adds recommendations (ways to respond to the argument and test). If you look for all three ways of stating the point of the essay, you will understand why this hybrid form of writing is so rich with rhetorical lessons.

> Democratic peace theory is based on the philosophy of Immanuel Kant. The title lets you know that Layne doesn't believe in the theory.

Kant or Cant: The Myth of the Democratic Peace

Christopher Layne

International Security, 1994 19(2): 5–49

Policymakers who have embraced democratic peace theory[1] see a crucial link between America's security and the spread of democracy, which is viewed as the antidote that will prevent future wars.... Because of its theoretical claims and policy implications, the democratic peace theory merits careful examination.[3] In this article, I focus primarily on a critique of the persuasiveness of democratic peace theory's causal logic and ask whether democratic peace theory or realism is a better predictor of international outcomes. I then briefly assess the robustness of democratic peace theory's empirical evidence in light of my conclusions about the strength of its explanatory power.

> In the first four paragraphs, Layne summarizes his entire article. Because this is a summary, these paragraphs are difficult to read. Consider re-reading these four paragraphs after you finish the entire essay.

I begin by reviewing the explanations of the Democratic Peace advanced by democratic peace theorists. There are two strands to the theory's causal logic. One attributes the absence of war between democracies to institutional constraints: the restraining effects of public opinion, or of the checks and balances embedded in a democratic state's domestic political structure. The other posits that it is democratic norms and culture—a shared commitment to the peaceful adjudication of political disputes—that accounts for the absence of war between democratic states. As I demonstrate, the institutional-constraints argument fails to provide a compelling explanation for the absence of war between democracies. Thus, democratic peace theory's explanatory power rests on the persuasiveness of the contention that democratic norms and culture explain why, although democratic states fight with non-democracies, they do not go to war with each other.

This article's centerpiece is a test of the competing explanations of international outcomes offered by democratic peace theory and by realism. This test is based on case studies of four "near misses"—crises where two democratic states almost went to war with each other. These four cases are well-documented instances of democratic great powers going to the brink of war without going over it. As such, they present an opportunity to determine which of the competing hypotheses advanced respectively by democratic peace theory and realism best account for international political outcome. . . .

I conclude that realism is superior to democratic peace theory as a predictor of international outcomes. Indeed, democratic peace theory appears to have extremely little explanatory power in the cases studied. Doubts about the validity of its causal logic suggest that the empirical evidence purporting to support democratic peace theory should also be revisited. Democratic peace theorists contend that the theory is validated by a large number of cases. However, a powerful argument can be made that the universe of cases from which it can be tested is actually quite small. This is a crucial issue, because if the theory's empirical support is based on a small-N universe, this magnifies the importance of possible exceptions to the rule that democracies do not fight each other (for example, World War I, the War between the States, the War of 1812). I conclude by discussing democratic peace theory's troublesome implications for post–Cold War American foreign policy.

The Case for a Democratic Peace: Its Claims and Its Logic

Democratic peace theory does not contend that democratic states are less war-prone than non-democracies; they are not. The theory does, however, make two important claims, first, that democracies never (or rarely; there is a good deal of variation about this) go to war with other democracies.[5] As Jack S. Levy observes, the "absence of war between democracies comes as close as anything we have to an empirical law in international relations."[6] Second, when democracies come into

---

Marginal notes:

Layne states his reason for writing—to test which theory better predicts known, historical outcomes.

In an article as long and complex as this, it is a rhetorical advantage for Layne to be bold and up-front about his point.

A small N means that there are very few cases to study. With too few numbers a statistical study may yield questionable results. So Layne chooses a "case-study" method, looking very closely at a small number of key cases.

An empirical law is a law that all observable evidence supports—like the law of gravity.

conflict with one another, they only rarely threaten to use force, because it is "illegitimate" to do so. Democratic peace theory explicitly holds that it is the very nature of democratic political systems that accounts for the fact that democracies do not fight or threaten other democracies.

The Causal Logic

> Causal logic refers to the relationship between an event, its causes, and its effects.

Democratic peace theory must explain an anomaly: democracies are no less war-prone than non-democratic states. Yet, while they will readily threaten and fight non-democracies, they do not threaten or fight other democracies. The key challenge for the theory, then, is to identify the special characteristics of democratic states that restrain them from using coercive threats against, or actually going to war with, other democracies. The theory advances two alternative explanations: 1) institutional constraints; and 2) democratic norms and cultures.[8]

There are two major variants of the institutional constraints argument. Michael Doyle, building on Immanuel Kant, explains that democratic governments are reluctant to go to war because they must answer to their citizens.[9] Citizens pay the price for war in blood and treasure; if the price of conflict is high, democratic governments may fall victim to electoral retribution. Moreover, in democratic states, foreign policy decisions carrying the risk of war are debated openly and not made behind closed doors, which means that both the public and policymakers are sensi-

> The U.S. fits this description: the president is elected by the people, we have political parties that compete with each other, and the power of the government is distributed among three branches: the executive, the legislative, and the judicial.

tized to costs of fighting. A second version of the institutional constraints argument focuses on "checks and balances"; it looks at three specific features of a state's domestic political structure: executive selection, political competition, and the pluralism of the foreign policy decision making process.[10] States with executives answerable to a selection body, with institutionalized political competition, and with decision making responsibility spread among multiple institutions or individuals, should be more highly constrained and hence less likely to go to war.

> In other words, the same things that promote peace within a country will promote peace between that country and others.

The democratic norms explanation holds that "the *culture, perceptions, and practices* that permit compromise and the peaceful resolution of conflicts without the threat of violence *within countries* come to apply across national boundaries toward other democratic countries."[11] Democratic states assume both that other democracies also subscribe to pacific methods of regulating political competition and resolving disputes, and that others will apply these norms in their external relations with fellow democracies. In other words, democratic states develop positive perceptions of other democracies. Consequently, Doyle says, democracies, "which rest on consent, presume foreign republics to be also consensual, just and therefore deserving of accommo-dation."[12] Relations between democratic states are based on mutual respect rooted in the fact that democracies perceive each other as dovish (that is, negotiation or the status quo are the only possible outcomes in a dispute). This perception, it is argued, is based on a form of learning. Democratic states benefit from cooperative relations with one another and they want to expand their positive interactions. In turn, this desire predisposes them to be responsive to the needs of other democratic states, and ultimately leads to creation of a community of interests. As democracies move towards community, they renounce the option to use (or even to threaten to use) force in their mutual interactions.[13]

The democratic ethos—based on "peaceful competition, persuasion and compromise"—explains the absence of war and war-like threats in relations between democratic states.[14] Conversely, the absence of these norms in relations between democracies and non-democracies, it is said, explains the paradox that democracies do not fight each other even though in general they are as war-prone as non-democracies: "When a democracy comes into conflict with a nondemocracy, it will not expect the nondemocratic state to be restrained by those norms [of mutual respect based on democratic culture]. It may feel obliged to adapt to the harsher norms of international conduct of the latter, lest it be exploited or eliminated by the nondemocratic state that takes advantage of the inherent moderation of democracies."[15] Thus it is a fundamental postulate of democratic peace theory that democracies behave in a qualitatively different manner in their relations with each other than they do in their relations with non-democracies.

The Realist Case: The Same Things Over and Over Again

In this section, Layne describes realism, an alternative way of explaining how countries get along with each other.

If history is "just one damn thing after another," then for realists international politics is the same damn things over and over again: war, great power security and economic competi-tions, the rise and fall of great powers, and the formation and dissolution of alliances. International political behavior is characterized by continuity, regularity, and repetition because states are constrained by the international system's unchanging (and probably unchangeable) structure.

The realist paradigm explains why this is so.[16] International politics is an anarchic, self-help realm. "Anarchy," rather than denoting chaos or rampant disorder, refers in international politics to the fact that there is no central authority capable of making and enforcing rules of behavior on the international system's units (states). The absence of a rule-making and enforcing authority means that each unit in the system is responsible for ensuring its own survival and also that each is free to define its own interests and to employ means of its own choice in pursuing them. In this sense, international politics is fundamentally competitive. And it is competitive in a manner that differs crucially from domestic politics in liberal societies, where the losers can accept an adverse outcome because they live to fight another day and can, therefore, ultimately hope to prevail. In international politics, states that come out on the short end of political competition face potentially more extreme outcomes, ranging from constraints on autonomy to occupation to extinction.

In other words, if a politician loses one battle, she can re-group and try again. If a country loses a battle to another country, it is less likely to remain autonomous.

It is anarchy that gives international politics its distinctive flavor. In an anarchic system, a state's first goal is to survive. To attain security, states engage in both internal and external balancing for the purpose of deterring aggressors, and of defeating them should deterrence fail. In a realist world, cooperation is possible but is hard to sustain in the face of the competitive pressures that are built into the international political system's structure. The imperative of survival in a threatening environment forces states to focus on strategies that maximize their power relative to their rivals. States have powerful incentives both to seek the upper hand over their rivals militarily and to use their edge not only for self-defense but also to take advantage of others. . . .

In the international system, fear and distrust of other states is the normal state of affairs. . . .

Testing Democratic Peace Theory

Institutional constraints do not explain the democratic peace. If democratic public opinion really had the effect ascribed to it, democracies would be peaceful in their relations with all states, whether democratic or not. If citizens and policymakers of a democracy were especially sensitive to the human and material costs of war, that sensitivity should be evident whenever their state is on the verge of war, regardless of whether the adversary is democratic: the lives lost and money spent will be the same. Nor is democratic public opinion, *per se*, an inhibitor of war. For example, in 1898 it was public opinion that impelled the reluctant McKinley administration into war with Spain; in 1914 war was enthusiastically embraced by public opinion in Britain and France. Domestic political structure—"checks and balances"—does not explain the democratic peace either. "This argument," as Morgan and Schwebach state, "does not say anything directly about the war-proneness of democracies," because it focuses on an independent variable—decisional constraints embedded in a state's domestic political structure—that is associated with, but not exclusive to, democracies.

Because these explanations fall short, the democratic norms and culture explanation must bear the weight of the democratic peace theory's causal logic. It is there we must look to find that "something in the internal makeup of democratic states" that explains the democratic peace.[18]

Democratic peace theory not only predicts a specific outcome—no war between democracies—but also purports to explain why that outcome will occur. It is thus suited to being tested by the case study method, a detailed look at a small number of examples to determine if events unfold and actors act as the theory predicts. The case study method also affords the opportunity to test the competing explanations of international political outcomes offered by democratic peace theory and by realism. To test the robustness of democratic peace theory's causal logic, the focus here is on "near misses," specific cases in which democratic states had both opportunity and reason to fight each other, but did not. . . .

Democratic peace theory, if valid, should account powerfully for the fact that serious crises between democratic states ended in near misses rather than in war. If democratic norms and culture explain the democratic peace, in a near-war crisis, certain indicators of the democratic peace theory should be in evidence: First, public opinion should be strongly pacific. Public opinion is important not because it is an institutional constraint, but because it is an indirect measure of the mutual respect that democracies are said to have for each other. Second, policymaking elites should refrain from making military threats against other democracies and should refrain from making preparations to carry out threats. Democratic peace theorists waffle on this point by suggesting that the absence of war between democracies is more important than the absence of threats. But this sets the threshold of proof too low. Because the crux of the theory is that democracies externalize their internal norms of peaceful dispute resolution, then especially in a crisis, one should not see democracies threatening other democracies. And if threats are made, they should be a last-resort option rather than an early one. Third, democracies should bend over backwards to accommodate each other in a crisis. Ultimata, unbending hard lines, and big-stick diplomacy are the stuff of Realpolitik, not the democratic peace.

A realist explanation of near misses would look at a very different set of indicators. First, realism postulates a ratio of

---

Margin notes:

"Institutional constraints" explanations

Now Layne takes on the second claim of democratic peace theory, norms and culture.

Social scientists, like natural scientists, always identify their methods for testing their hypotheses.

"Ultimata" is the plural of "ultimatum"—an all-or-nothing demand that offers no room for negotiation. In "big-stick diplomacy," a country threatens to use its superior military power as a way to coerce another country to do something. *Realpolitik* focuses on self-interest and what is practical over what is moral.

national interest to democratic respect: in a crisis, the more important the interests a democracy perceives to be at stake, the more likely that its policy will be shaped by realist imperatives rather than by democratic norms and culture. When vital interests are on the line, democracies should not be inhibited from using threats, ultimata, and big-stick diplomacy against another democracy. Second, even in a crisis involving democracies, states should be very attentive to strategic concerns, and the relative distribution of military capabilities between them should crucially—perhaps decisively—affect their diplomacy. Third, broader geopolitical considerations pertaining to a state's position in international politics should, if implicated, account significantly for the crisis's outcome. Key here is what Geoffrey Blainey calls the "fighting waterbirds' dilemma," involving concerns that others watching from the sidelines will take advantage of a state's involvement in war; that war will leave a state weakened and in an inferior relative power position vis-a-vis possible future rivals; and that failure to propitiate the opposing state in a crisis will cause it to ally with one's other adversaries or rivals.[21]

> Because of space limitations, we have included only the first case study.

I have chosen to study four modern historical instances in which democratic great powers almost came to blows: 1) the United States and Great Britain in 1861 ("the Trent affair"); 2) the United States and Great Britain in 1895–96 (the Venezuela crisis); 3) France and Great Britain in 1898 (the Fashoda crisis); and 4) France and Germany in 1923 (the Ruhr crisis).[22]

Anglo-American Crisis I: The *Trent* Affair, 1861

> The Civil War. A rhetorical advantage of the case-study method is that people like to read stories. Beginning this story in the context of what may be America's most captivating story—the Civil War—is smart rhetoric.

In 1861, tensions arising from the War Between the States brought the Union and Britain to the brink of war. The most important causes of Anglo-American friction stemmed from the Northern blockade of Confederate ports and the consequent loss to Britain of the cotton upon which its textile industry depended. The immediate precipitating cause of the Anglo-American crisis, however, was action of the USS *San Jacinto* which, acting without express orders from Washington, intercepted the British mail ship *Trent* on November 8, 1861. The *Trent* was transporting James M. Mason and John Slidell, the Confederacy's commissioners-designate to Great Britain and France; they had boarded the *Trent*, a neutral vessel, in Havana, Cuba, a neutral port. A boarding party from the *San Jacinto*, after searching the *Trent*, placed Mason and Slidell under arrest. The *Trent* was allowed to complete its voyage while the *San Jacinto* transported Mason and Slidell to Fort Warren in Boston harbor, where they were incarcerated.

When word was received in Britain, the public was overcome with war fever. "The first explosion of the Press, on receipt of the news of the Trent, had been a terrific one."[28] An American citizen residing in England reported to Secretary of State William H. Seward, "The people are frantic with rage, and were the country polled I fear 999 men out of 1000 would declare for war."[29] From Edinburgh, another American wrote, "I have never seen so intense a feeling of indignation in my life."[30]

The British government was hardly less bellicose than the public and the press. Fortified by legal opinions holding that Mason and Slidell had been removed from the *Trent* in contravention of international law, the Cabinet adopted a hard-line policy that mirrored the public mood. Prime Minister Lord Palmerston's first reaction to the news of the *Trent* incident was to write to the Secretary of State for War that, because of Britain's "precarious" relations with the United States, the government reconsider cuts in military expenditures planned to take effect in 1862.[31] At the November 29 Cabinet meeting, Palmerston reportedly began by flinging his hat on the table and declaring to his colleagues, "I don't know whether you are going to stand this, but I'll be damned if I do!"[32]

The Cabinet adopted a dual-track approach towards Washington: London used military threats to coerce the United States into surrendering diplomatically, while on the diplomatic side, Foreign Secretary Lord John Russell drafted a note to the Union government in which, while holding firm to the demand that Mason and Slidell be released, he offered Washington an avenue of graceful retreat by indicating that London would accept, as tantamount to an apology, a declaration that the *San Jacinto* had acted without official sanction. Nevertheless, the note that was actually transmitted to Washington was an ultimatum. Although the British minister in Washington, Lord Lyons, was instructed to present the communication in a fashion calculated to maximize the chances of American compliance, his charge was clear: unless within seven days of receipt the Union government unconditionally accepted Britain's demands, Lyons was to ask for his passports and depart the United States. As Russell wrote to Lyons: "What we want is a plain Yes or a plain No to our very simple demands, and we want that plain Yes or No within seven days of the communication of the despatch."[33]

Although some, notably including Russell, hoped that the crisis could be resolved peacefully, the entire Cabinet recognized that its decision to present an ultimatum to Washington could lead to war. The British believed that there was one hope for peace: that Washington, overawed by Britain's military power and its readiness to go to war, would bow to London's demands rather than resisting them.[34] As the Undersecretary of State for Foreign Affairs stated, "Our only chance of peace is to be found in working on the fears of the Government and people of the United States."[35]

Driven by the belief that Washington would give in only to the threat of force, London's diplomacy was backed up by ostentatious military and naval preparations. Anticipating a possible conflict, the Cabinet embargoed the export to the United States of saltpeter (November 30) and of arms and ammunition (December 4). Underscoring the gravity of the crisis, for only the fourth time in history the Cabinet created a special war committee to oversee strategic planning and war preparations. Urgent steps were taken to reinforce Britain's naval and military contingents in North America. Beginning in mid-December, a hastily organized sealift increased the number of regular British army troops in Canada from 5,000 to 17,658, and Royal Navy forces in North American waters swelled from 25 to forty warships, with 1,273 guns (compared to just 500 before the crisis).[36] These measures served two purposes: they bolstered London's diplomacy and, in the event diplomacy failed, they positioned Britain to prevail in a conflict.

> an ingredient in gunpowder

London employed big-stick diplomacy because it believed that a too-conciliatory policy would simply embolden the Americans to mount increasingly serious challenges to British interests.[37] Moreover, British policymakers believed that England's resolve, credibility, and reputation were at stake internationally, not just in its relations with the United States. The comments of once and future Foreign Secretary Lord Clarendon were typical: "What a figure . . . we shall cut in the eyes of the world, if we lamely submit to this outrage when all mankind will know that we should unhesitatingly have poured our indignation and our broadsides into any weak nation . . . and what an additional proof it will be of the universal . . . belief that we have two sets of weights and measures to be used according to the power or weakness of our adversary."[38] Thus "the British were prepared to accept the cost of an Anglo-American war . . . rather than sacrifice their prestige as a great power by headlong diplomatic defeat."[39]

London's hard-line policy was fortified by its "general optimism about the ultimate outcome" of an Anglo-American war.[40] Queen Victoria said a war would result in "utter destruction to the North Americans" and Secretary of State for War George Cornewall Lewis said "we shall soon iron the smile out of their face."[41] Palmerston was therefore untroubled by the discomfiture imposed on the Union by London's uncompromising policy. In his view, regardless of whether the crisis was resolved peacefully or resulted in war, Britain's interests would be upheld. He wrote to Queen Victoria:

If the Federal Government comply with the demands it will be honorable to England and humiliating to the United States. If the Federal Government refuse compliance, Great Britain is in a better state than at any former time to inflict a severe blow upon, and to read a lesson to the United States which will not soon be forgotten.[42]

In late 1861, the war against the Confederacy was not going well for Washington and the one major engagement, the first Battle of Manassas, had resulted in a humiliating setback for the Union army. Whipped up by Secretary of State Seward, who was a master at "twisting the lion's tail" for maximum domestic political effect, Northern opinion was hostile in London and resented especially Queen Victoria's May 1861 neutrality proclamation, which Northerners interpreted as *de facto* British recognition of Southern independence. News of the seizure of Mason and Slidell had a double effect on Northern public opinion. First, it was a tonic for sagging Northern morale. Second, it was seen as a warning to Britain to refrain from interfering with the Union's prosecution of the war against the Confederacy. Thus, although some papers (notably the *New York Times* and the *New York Daily Tribune*) urged that Washington should placate the British, public opinion strongly favored a policy of standing up to London and refusing to release Mason and Slidell.[43] In response to Britain's hard line, "a raging war cry reverberated across the Northern states in America."[44] Charles Francis Adams, Jr., whose father was U.S. minister in London at the time, wrote later of the affair: "I do not remember in the whole course of the half-century's retrospect ... any occurrence in which the American people were so completely swept off their feet, for the moment losing possession of their senses, as during the weeks which immediately followed the seizure of Mason and Slidell."[45]

The Lincoln administration was aware of the strength of anti-British sentiment among the public and in Congress (indeed, in early December, Congress passed a resolution commending the *San Jacinto*'s captain for his action). There is some evidence that in order to placate public opinion, President Lincoln was inclined toward holding on to Mason and Slidell, notwithstanding the obvious risks of doing so.[46] Nevertheless,

in actual fact

after first toying with the idea of offering London arbitration in an attempt to avoid the extremes of war or a humiliating climb-down, the United States elected to submit to Britain's demands. Given that Washington "could not back down easily," it is important to understand why it chose to do so.

The United States bowed to London because, already fully occupied militarily trying to subdue the Confederacy, the North could not also afford a simultaneous war with England, which effectively would have brought Britain into the War Between the States on the South's side.[47] This was clearly recognized by the Lincoln administration when the cabinet met for two days at Christmas to decide on the American response to the British note. The cabinet had before it two critical pieces of information. First, Washington had just been informed that France supported London's demands (ending American hopes that Britain would be restrained by its own "waterbird" worries that France would take advantage of an Anglo-American war).[48] Second, Washington had abundant information about the depth of the pro-war sentiment of the British public....

Facing the choice of defying London or surrendering to its demands, Washington was compelled to recognize both that Britain was serious about going to war and that such a war almost certainly would result in the Union's permanent dissolution. During the cabinet discussions, Attorney General Edward Bates suggested that Britain was seeking a war with the United States in order to break the Northern blockade of Southern cotton ports and he worried that London would recognize the Confederacy. The United States, he said, "cannot afford such a war." He went on to observe, "In such a crisis, with such a civil war upon our hands, we cannot hope for success in a . . . war with England, backed by the assent and countenance of France. We must evade it—with as little damage to our own honor and pride as possible."[51] Secretary of State Seward concurred, stating that it was "no time to be diverted from the cares of the Union into controversies with other powers, even if just causes for them could be found."[52] When the United States realized that Britain's threat to go to war was not a bluff, strategic and national interest considerations—the "waterbird dilemma"—dictated that Washington yield to Britain.

The *Trent* affair's outcome is explained by realism, not democratic peace theory. Contrary to democratic peace theory's expectations, the mutual respect between democracies rooted in democratic norms and culture had no influence on British policy. Believing that vital reputational interests affecting its global strategic posture were at stake, London played diplomatic hardball, employed military threats, and was prepared to go to war if necessary. Both the public and the elites in Britain preferred war to conciliation. Across the Atlantic, public and governmental opinion in the North was equally bellicose. An Anglo-American conflict was avoided only because the Lincoln administration came to understand that diplomatic humiliation was preferable to a war that would have arrayed Britain with the Confederacy and thus probably have secured the South's independence. . . .

Policy Conclusions: Why It Matters

The validity of democratic peace theory is not a mere academic concern. Democratic peace theory has been widely embraced by policymakers and foreign policy analysts alike and it has become a lodestar that guides America's post-Cold War foreign policy. Michael Doyle's 1983 conception of a democratic "zone of peace" is now routinely used in both official and unofficial U.S. foreign policy pronouncements. Following the Cold War, a host of commentators have suggested that the export or promotion of democracy abroad should become the central focus of American's post-Cold War foreign policy.[140] From Haiti to Russia, America's interests and its security have been identified with democracy's success or failure. National Security Adviser Anthony Lake said that America's post-Cold War goal must be to expand the zone of democratic peace and prosperity because, "to the extent democracy and market economics hold sway in other nations, our own nation will be more secure, prosperous and influential." [141]

A guiding star. Layne uses the term to indicate that democratic peace theory directs U.S. foreign policy. He then considers the problems that result from the U.S. using this flawed theory as a guide.

Those who want to base American foreign policy on the extension of democracy abroad invariably disclaim any intention to embark on a "crusade," and profess to recognize the dangers of allowing policy to be based on excessive ideological zeal."[142] These reassurances are the foreign-policy version of "trust me." Because it links American security to the nature of other states' internal political systems, democratic peace theory's logic inevitably pushes the United States to adopt an interventionist strategic posture. If democracies are peaceful but non-democratic states are "troublemakers" the conclusion is inescapable: the former will be truly secure only when the latter have been transformed into democracies, too.

That is, following democratic peace theory, the U.S. intervenes in the internal affairs of other countries to press them to adopt a democratic form of government.

Indeed, American statesmen have frequently expressed this view. During World War I, Elihu Root said that, "To be safe democracy must kill its enemy when it can and where it can. The world cannot be half democratic and half autocratic."[143] During the Vietnam War, Secretary of State Dean Rusk claimed that the "United States cannot be secure until the total international environment is ideologically safe." These are not isolated comments; these views reflect the historic American propensity to seek absolute security and to define security primarily in ideological (and economic) terms. The political culture of American foreign policy has long regarded the United States, because of its domestic political system, as a singular nation. As a consequence, American policymakers have been affected by a "deep sense of being alone" and *they* have regarded the United States as "perpetually beleaguered." Consequently, America's foreign and defense policies have been shaped by the belief that the United States must create a favorable ideological climate abroad if its domestic institutions are to survive and flourish. . . ."[145]

> That is, the U.S. must create democracies abroad so that its own democracy will flourish.

Democratic peace theory is dangerous in another respect, as well: it is an integral component of a new (or more correctly, recycled) outlook on international politics. It is now widely believed that the spread of democracy and economic interdependence have effected a "qualitative change" in international politics, and that war and serious security competitions between or among democratic great powers are now impossible.[147] There is therefore, it is said, no need to worry about future great power challenges from states like Japan and Germany, or to worry about the relative distribution of power between the United States and those states, unless Japan or Germany were to slide back into authoritarianism.[148] The reason the United States need not be concerned with the great-power emergence of Japan and Germany is said to be simple: they are democracies and democracies do not fight democracies. . . .

> a change in the nature, character, or degree of something

If American policymakers allow themselves to be mesmerized by democratic peace theory's seductive—but false—vision of the future, the United States will be ill prepared to formulate a grand strategy that will advance its interests in the emerging world of multipolar great power competition. In-deed, as long as the Wilsonian worldview underpins American foreign policy, policymakers will be blind to the need to have such a grand strategy, because the liberal theory of international politics defines out of existence (except with respect to non-democracies) the very phenomena that are at the core of strategy: war, the formation of power balances, and concerns about the relative distribution of power among the great powers. But in the end, as its most articulate proponents admit, liberal international relations theory is based on hope, not on fact.[150] In the final analysis, the world remains what it always has been: international politics continues to occur in an anarchic, competitive, self-help realm. This reality

> A belief typical of President Woodrow Wilson, who thought that the U.S. should promote democracy in other countries and peace among nations.

must be confronted, because it cannot be transcended. Given the stakes, the United States in coming years cannot afford to have either its foreign policy, or the intellectual discourse that underpins that policy, shaped by theoretical approaches that are based on wishful thinking.

Notes

1. I use the term "democratic peace theory" because it is a convenient shorthand term. However, strictly speaking, the claim that democracies do not fight democracies is a proposition, or hypothesis, rather than a theory. Democratic peace "theory" proposes a causal relationship between an independent variable (democratic political structures at the unit level) and the dependent variable (the asserted absence of war between democratic states). However, it is not a true theory because the causal relationship between the independent and dependent variables is neither proven nor, as I demonstrate in this article, adequately explained. See Stephen Van Evera, "Hypotheses, Laws and Theories: A User's Guide," unpub. memo, Department of Political Science, MIT.

3. In this article, I build upon and expand the criticisms of democratic peace theory found in John J. Mearsheimer, "Back to the Future: Instability in Europe After the Cold War," *International Security*, Vol. 15, No. 1 (Summer 1990), pp. 5–56; and Kenneth N. Waltz, "America as Model for the World? A Foreign Policy Perspective," *PS* (December 1991), pp. 667–670.

4. Other cases of crises between democratic great powers that might be studied include Anglo-French relations during the Liberal entente cordiale of 1832–48, Franco-Italian relations during the Late 1880s and early 1890s and, if Wilhelmine Germany is classified as a democracy, the Moroccan crises of 1905–06 and 1911 and the Samoan crises of 1889 and 1899. These cases would support my conclusions. For example, from 1832 to 1843, the Foxite legacy disposed England's Whigs to feel a strong commitment to France based on a shared liberal ideology. Yet Anglo-French relations during this period were marked by intense geopolitical rivalry over Belgium, Spain, and the Near East, and the threat of war was always a factor in the calculations of policymakers in both London and Paris. Foreign Minister Lord Palmerston profoundly distrusted French ambitions and constantly urged that England maintain sufficient naval power to defend its interests against a French challenge. See Kenneth Bourne, *Palmerston: The Early Years, 1784–1841* (New York: Macmillan, 1982), p. 613. Also see Roger Buller, *Palmerston, Guizat and the Collapse of the Entente Cordiale* (London: Athlone Press, 1974); and Sir Charles Webster, *The Foreign Policy Palmerston, Vol. I: 1830–1841, Britain, The Liberal Movement and The Eastern Question* (London: Bell & Sons, 1951). Italy challenged France for Mediterranean ascendancy although the two nations were bound by liberalism, democracy, and a common culture. The two states engaged in a trade war and came close to a real wax. France apparently was dissuaded from attacking Italy in 1888 when the British Channel Fleet was sent to the Italian naval base of La Spezia. Italy was prevented from attacking France by its military and economic weakness. See C.J. Lowe and F. Marzari, *Italian Foreign Policy, 1870–1940* (London: Routledge & Kegan Paul, 1975), chap. 4; C.J. Lowe, *The Reluctant Imperialists: British Foreign Policy 1879–1902* (London: Routledge & Kegan Paul, 1974), Vol. I, pp. 147–150; John A.C. Conybeare,

Trade Wars: The Theory and Practice of International Commercial Rivalry (New York: Columbia University Press, 1987), pp. 183–188.

5. Melvin Small and J. David Singer first observed the pattern of democracies not fighting democracies in a 1976 article: Small and Singer, "The War-proneness of Democratic Regimes, 1816–1865," *Jerusalem Journal of International Relations*, Vol. 1, No. 4 (Summer 1976), pp. 50–69. Their finding has been the subject of extensive further empirical testing which has produced a consensus around the propositions stated in the text. See Stuart A. Bremer, "Dangerous Dyads: Conditions Affecting the Likelihood of Interstate War, 1816–1865," *Journal of Conflict Resolution*, Vol. 36, No. 2 (June 1992), pp. 309–441; Steve Chan, "Mirror, Mirror on the Wal. . . Are the Freer Countries More Pacific?" *Journal of Conflict Resolution*, Vol. 28, No. 4 (December 1984), pp. 617–648; Zeev Maoz and Nasrin Abdolali, "Regime and International Conflict," *Journal of Conflict Resolution*, Vol. 33, No. 1 (March 1989), pp. 3-35; R.J. Rummel, "Libertarianism and International Violence," *Journal of Conflict Resolution*, Vol. 27, No. 1 (March 1983), pp. 27–71; Erich Weede, "Democracy and War Involvement," *Journal of Conflict Resolution*, Vol. 28, No. 4 (December 1984), pp. 649–664.

6. Jack S. Levy, "Domestic Politics and War," in. Robert I. Rotberg and Theodore K. Rabb, eds., *The Origin and Prevention of Major Wars* (Cambridge: Cambridge University Press, 1989), p. 88.

7. Russett, *Grasping the Democratic Peace*, p. 33; Michael W. Doyle, "Kant, Liberal Legacies and Foreign Affairs," Part I, *Philosophy and Public Affairs*, Vol. 12, No. 3 (Summer 1983), p. 213.

8. This is the terminology employed by Russett, *Grasping the Democratic Peace*; also see Bruce Russett and Zeev Maoz, "Normative and Structural Causes of Democratic Peace," *American Political Science Review*, Vol. 87, No. 3 (September 1993), pp. 624–638. Russett points out (pp. 40–42) that, although analytically distinct, these two explanations are intertwined.

9. Doyle, "Kant, Liberal Legacies, and Foreign Affairs," pp. 205–235. See also Doyle, "Liberalism and World Politics," *Antedate Political Science Ravine*, Vol. 80, No. 4 (December 198b), pp. 1151–1169; Russett, *Grasping the Democratic Peace*, pp. 38–40.

10. T. Clifton Morgan and Sally N. Campbell, "Domestic Structure, Decisional Constraints and War: So Why Kant Democracies Fight?" *Journal of Conflict Resolution*, Vol. 35, No. 2 (June 1991), pp. 187–211; and T. Clifton Morgan and Valerie L. Schwebach, "Take Two Democracies and Call Me in the Morning: A Prescription for Peace?" *International Interactions*. Vol. 17, No. 4 (Summer 1992), pp. 305–420.

11. Russett, *Grasping the Democratic Peace*, p. 31 (second emphasis added).

12. Doyle, "Kant, Liberal Legacies, and Foreign Affairs," p. 230. It is also argued that the predisposition of democratic states to regard other democracies favorably is reinforced by the fact that liberal democratic states are linked by mutually beneficial ties of economic interdependence. Democracies thus have strong incentives to act towards each other in a manner that enhances cooperation and to refrain from acting in a manner that threatens their stake in mutually beneficial cooperation. Ibid., pp. 230–232; Rummel, "Libertarianism and International Violence," pp. 27–28. For the "interdependence promotes peace" argument see Richard Rosecrance, *The Rise of the Trading State* (New York: Basic Books, 1986). In fact, however, for great powers economic interdependence, rather than promoting peace, creates seemingly important interests that may be defended by overseas military commitments. . . .

13. Doyle, "Kant, Liberal Legacies, and Foreign Affairs"; and Harvey Starr, "Democracy and War. Choke, Learning and Security Communities," *Journal of Peace Research*, Vol. 29, No. 2 (1992), pp. 207–213.

14. Maoz and Russett, "A Statistical Artifact?" p. 246.

15. Russett, *Grasping the Democratic Peace*, p. 33.

16. Classic explications of realism are Kenneth N. Waltz, *Theory of International Politics* (Reading, Mass.: Addison-Wesley, 1979) and Hans J. Morgenthau, rev. by Kenneth W. Thompson, *Politics Among Nations: The Struggle for Power and Peace*, 6th ed. (New York: Knopf, 1985).

18. Manz and Russett, "Normative and Structural Causes," p. 624.

21. Geoffrey Blainey, *The Causes of War*, 3rd ed. (South Melbourne: Macmillan Co. of Australia, 1988), pp. 57–67. As the parable goes, while the water-birds fight over the catch, the fisherman spreads his net.

22. My classification of the United States in 1861 and 1895 and of Germany in 1923 as great powers might be challenged. By the mid-nineteenth century British policymakers viewed the United States, because of its size, population, wealth, and growing industrial strength (and latent military power), as "a great world power," notwithstanding the fact that it was not an active participant in the European state system. Ephraim Douglass Adams, *Great Britain and the American Civil War* (New York: Russell and Russell, 1924), Vol. I, p. 10. In 1895 the perception of American power had heightened in Britain and in other leading European powers. In 1923, Germany, although substantially disarmed pursuant to Versailles, remained Europe's most economically powerful state. As most statesmen realized, it was, because of its population and industry, a latent continental hegemon. Democratic peace theorists have classified all eight states as having been democracies at the time of their involvement in the crises under discussion. See Doyle, "Kant, Liberal Legacies, and Foreign Affairs," part I, pp. 214–215. Russett, *Grasping the Democratic Peace*, pp. 5–9, briefly discusses the Venezuela and Fashoda crises, but his bibliography has few historical references to these two crises (and related issues), and omits most standard sources.

28. Adams, *Britain and the Civil War*, Vol. I, p. 216.

29. Quoted in Gordon H. Warren, *Fountain of Discontent: The Trent Affair and Freedom of the Seas* (Boston: Northeastern University Press, 1981), p. 105.

30. Quoted in Adams, *Britain and the Civil War*, Vol. I, p. 217.

31. Quoted in Norman B. Ferris, *The Trent Affair: A Diplomatic Crisis* (Knoxville: University of Tennessee Press, 1977), p. 44.

32. Ibid., p. 109; Howard Jones, *Union in Peril: Tice Crisis Over British Intervention in the Civil War* (Chapel Hill: University of North Carolina Press, 1992), pp. 84–85.

33. Quoted in Jones, *Union in Peril*, p. 85.

34. Jenkins, *War for the Union*, p. 214.

35. Quoted in Kenneth Bourne, *Britain and the Balance of Power in North America, 1815–1908* (Berkeley: University of California Press, 1967), p. 219.

36. The figures are from Warren, *Fountain of Discontent*, pp. 130, 136. For an overview of British military and naval activities during the Trent crisis see Kenneth Bourne, "British Preparations for War with the North, 1861–1862," *English Historical Review*, Vol. 76, No. 301 (October 1961), pp. 600–632.

37. Ferris, *Trent Affair*, p. 56; Wilbur Devereux Jones, *The American Problem in British Diplomacy, 2841–2861* (London: Macmillan, 1974), p. 203. In international relations theory terms, London's view of Anglo-American relations was based on a deterrence model rather than a spiral model. See Robert Jervis, *Perception and Misperception in International Politics*

(Princeton: Princeton University Press, 1976), pp. 58–111. Coexisting uneasily with the positive view of an Anglo-American community was the British image of the United States as a vulgar "mobocracy" that, unless firmly resisted, would pursue a rapacious and bullying foreign policy. Warren, *Fountain of Discontent*, pp. 47–51.

38. Quoted in Bourne, *Balance of Power*, p. 247.
39. Bourne, "British Preparations," p. 631.
40. Bourne, *Balance of Power*, p. 247.
41. Quoted in ibid., pp. 245–246, emphasis in original.
42. Quoted in Jenkins, *War for the Union*, p. 216.
43. Ferris, *Trent Affair*, pp. 111–113.
44. Norman B. Ferris, *Desperate Diplomacy: William H. Seward's Foreign Policy, 1861* (Knoxville: University of Tennessee, 1976), p. 194.
45. Quoted in Adams, *Britain and the Civil War*, Vol. I, p. 218.
46. Warren, *Fountain of Discontent*, pp. 184–185; Adams, *Britain and the Civil War*, p. 231. Howard Jones, however, suggests that Lincoln probably intended to give up Mason and Slidell and that he may have been posturing in order to shift to other members of his cabinet the onus of advancing the argument for surrendering them. Jones, *Union in Peril*, pp. 91–92.
47. Ferris, *Trent Affair*, pp. 177–182; Jenkins, *War for the Union*, pp. 223–226; Warren, *Fountain of Discontent*, pp. 181–182.
48. See Jenkins, *War for the Union*, pp. 225–226.
51. Quoted in ibid., p. 182.
52. Quoted in Jenkins, *War for the Union*, p. 224.
140. See for example Joshua Muravchik, *Exporting Democracy: Fulfilling America's Destiny* (Washington, D.C.: AEI Press, 1991); and Larry Diamond, "Promoting Democracy," *Foreign Policy*, No. 87 (Summer 1992), pp. 25–46.
141. "Remarks of Anthony Lake," Johns Hopkins School of Advanced International Studies, Washington, D.C., September 21, 1993 (Washington, D.C.: National Security Council Press Office).
142. Lake stated that the Clinton administration does not propose to embark on a "democratic crusade." Both Doyle and Russett acknowledge that democratic peace theory could encourage democratic states to pursue aggressive policies toward non-democracies, and both express worry at this. Doyle, "Kant, Liberal Legacies, and Foreign Affairs," part II; Russett, *Grasping the Democratic Peace*, p. 136.
143. Quoted in Russett, *Grasping the Democratic Peace*, p. 33.
145. Uoyd C. Gardner, *A Covenant With Power: America and World Order from Wilson to Reagan* (New York Oxford University Press, 1984), p. 27. For an excellent critique of the notion that America's domestic ideology must be validated by its foreign policy, see Michael H. Hunt, *Ideology and U.S. Foreign Policy* (New Haven: Yale University Press, 1987).
147. Robert Jervis, "The Future of World Politics: Will It Resemble the Past?" *International Security*, Vol. 16, No. 3 (Winter 1991–92), pp. 39–73.
148. For an example of this argument see James M. Goldgeier and Michael McFaul, "A Tale of Two Worlds: Core and Periphery in the Post-Cold War," *International Organization*, Vol 46, No. 3 (Spring 1992), pp. 467–491.
150. Russett, *Grasping the Democratic Peace*, p. 156, argues that, "understanding the sources of democratic peace can have the effect of a self-fulfilling prophecy. Social scientists sometimes create reality as well as analyze it. Insofar as norms do guide behavior, repeating those norms helps to make them effective. *Repeating the norms as descriptive principles can help to make them true.*" (Emphasis added.)

READING RESPONSES

1. Summarize the central claim of democratic peace theory and the causal logic that supports it. In other words, what's the chain of reasoning that supports democratic peace theory?

2. Assess Layne's use of the case-study method to test democratic peace theory. Did you find his analysis of the Trent Affair (1861) persuasive? Would you have found statistics more effective? What are the limitations of case-study evidence?

3. Near the end of his essay, Layne describes democratic peace theory as "dangerous." What in his article would most persuade you to agree with him—what evidence? What logical reasoning? Why do you think that some readers would respond passionately to this description of democratic peace theory?

NOTES ON GRAMMAR, STYLE, AND RHETORIC:

TEXTUAL COHERENCE

One striking aspect of the introductory paragraphs of Christopher Layne's "Kant or Cant: The Myth of the Democratic Peace" is that they include several prominent text connectives. Text connectives help show readers how the parts of a text relate to one another, how the overall text is organized, and sometimes how the text relates to its context. Specific examples of text connectives are elements that indicate sequences (*first, in the third place, finally*) as well as those that indicate logical or temporal relationships (*consequently, at the same time*). Other text connectives are reminders about material presented earlier (*as I demonstrated in Chapter Two*) and previews of forthcoming material (*as I will show in the next section*).

In his early paragraphs Layne uses several statements to preview how his essay will unfold. These preview statements begin already at the end of the first paragraph. There he uses two general statements to give an overview of much of his article. One of these begins with "In this article, I focus primarily on . . .," and the other begins with "I then briefly assess. . . ."

Then he moves to previews of the specific steps he will take in his essay. At the start of the second paragraph he writes, "I begin by reviewing. . . ." Shortly thereafter he adds, "As I demonstrate. . . ." And then in the third and fourth paragraphs, he adds still other preview statements, introduced as follows: "I deduce . . .," "Using a process-tracing approach, I examine . . .," "I conclude . . .," and finally "I conclude by discussing. . . ."

Since all these preview statements occur within a handful of lines of one another, you might be inclined to ask, "Why does Layne spend so much time telling readers what he is going to do? Why doesn't he just go ahead and start his presentation?" Speculating about how Layne might respond to these questions is instructive. He could, for instance, appeal to aspects of his rhetorical situation and formulate a defense that would include several points.

First, he could note that in the United States we generally place much responsibility on the writer for signaling how texts are organized. Probably all of us, at some point in school, have been advised to use transitions, especially as we begin paragraphs. Our print culture tells us that we should take care to mark the way clearly for readers as they move through our texts. Not all cultures convey this message. In the print culture of some European countries—Germany and Finland, for example—writers are encouraged to let readers discover organizational patterns of texts on their own.

Second, he might note that his essay is long. What is reprinted of Layne's essay in this textbook is only a portion of his overall piece. To make his essay fit within the scope of a chapter in this book, the editors have had to cut several of his case studies. Similarly, Layne's argument is quite complex. He is rejecting a popular view of the democratic peace and offering a different view in its place. To lay out the essence of the view he opposes as well as of the view that he supports involves some careful explaining. In this process he gives the details of several case studies and shows how those details support his view and work against the popular one.

When writers have long and complex presentations, they have good reason to use preview statements to help readers see where they are headed. Similarly, when readers have little knowledge about the writer's subject matter, writers have good reason to use preview statements to keep them from getting lost.

In Your Own Writing . . .

- When your writing is long and complex, consider using preview statements.
- When your topic is new to your reader, consider using preview statements.
- When you write in a new discipline or a new culture, try to determine the level of text connectives that your reader expects.

STUDENT WRITING IN POLITICAL SCIENCE

Introduction by J. Robin King, political science major

The Assignment. I wrote the following essay as the final project for a political science class on the topic of democracy—theories about democracy as well as political states, worldwide, that follow democratic principles. My professor asked us to write a research paper that analyzed one country's attempts at democratic consolidation. Prior to this project, I had developed an interest in the Arab–Israeli conflict. I was certain that I wanted to write a paper on the status of Arab citizens of Israel, but I was unsure where that would lead.

The Content. Although it may seem obvious, the key to writing a quality political science paper is to become knowledgeable about your topic. When you become aware of the range of opinions that people have about your topic, you can more easily spot the bias of the researcher, and you can better sort out fact from opinion. I had to be well-versed on the subject of Israeli democracy. As I read a number of online and journal articles and books and spoke with my professors, I started to figure out exactly what I wanted to argue. I developed my thesis that because of Israel's heavy emphasis on its Jewish character, it cannot be considered a fully consolidated democracy. As I wrote, I continued to do research, allowing my thesis to evolve, leaving myself open to its possible changes. But, building this initial foundation was essential to the completion of this kind of controversial piece.

Learning to Write about Political Issues. Although writers in all fields must think about the audience for their essays, I think that political scientists—because everyone argues about politics—have to pay especially careful attention to their readers. I decided that I would like to publish this essay to convince people (in addition to my professor) to pay attention to the plight of Israeli-Palestinians, so I kept a secondary audience in mind as I wrote—those potential readers in an academic journal or an online publication.

Appealing to this secondary audience, I knew, would be much more difficult than writing for my professor. In my experience, most people bring strongly held opinions to the issues surrounding Israel and the Middle East; very few people come to an essay on this topic eager to be persuaded. I was aware that regardless of what I said, many of the readers of my paper would not change their views. Therefore, throughout the actual writing process, I chose to focus on the readers who, although perhaps initially uncomfortable with criticism of the state of Israel, might accept my thesis if I provided convincing evidence. I felt that if I could persuade them, then I could certainly convince any readers who were neutral on this issue.

So I set for myself the goal of convincing a slightly biased yet relatively uninformed reader. To reach out to this audience, I relied on three methods most heavily: First, in doing my research, I looked at a wide variety of sources, both in terms of the type of sources (whether a book, academic journal, news source, think tank report, etc.) and especially the political leanings of the author. I knew that it was especially critical that my research not be perceived as (or actually be) biased or one-sided. For example, I cited such well-respected sources as the *New York Times* and the BBC, and I employed quotes and statistics from the former mayor of Jerusalem, a non-partisan Israeli research institute, and official Israeli government studies.

Second, I sought to incorporate some of the obvious objections to my thesis into the paper. I knew that the uninformed, slightly biased reader would certainly have a number of reservations about my thesis, so I included specific questions readers might have about the paper. By asking—and answering—the imagined audience's questions, I proved that I had thought deeply about the topic and that I had proposed a strong, well-supported thesis, a thesis I hoped they would accept as their own.

Finally, I used a blend of theoretical and factual analysis when I argued for my thesis. The theory helps the reader understand the overall significance of the given idea, while the facts and statistics effectively display the significance. I had to demonstrate that Israel's theory of "ethnic democracy" does not fit the definition of democracy. While certainly some people will disagree with my interpretations of facts, by using statistical evidence, I tried to illuminate tensions within Israeli democracy. After reading this combination of theoretical and factual analysis, my readers ought to have a more complete understanding of the problems facing Arab citizens of Israel and Israeli democracy; as a result, they should be more willing to agree with my thesis.

Creating Change through Writing in Political Science. Being able to argue for an issue that you're passionate about is an important skill for any citizen in a democracy. A single political act, such as declaring war, can affect the lives of millions of people; it is vital that political leaders—and citizens in a democracy—are able to argue effectively about political acts. Perhaps my research will inspire some of my readers to investigate this issue further, or even to take action. Maybe it will inspire you.

Democratic Consolidation in Israel?: The Situation of Arab Citizens of Israel and the Implications for Larger Israeli Democracy

J. Robin King

In 2003, the Israeli Democracy Institute (IDI), an Israeli non-partisan research institute that analyzes the status of Israeli democracy, presented its Democracy Index to Israeli President Moshe Katsav. The report stated that "Protection of human rights in Israel is poor; there is serious political and economic discrimination against the Arab minority; there is much less freedom of religion than in other democracies; and the socioeconomic inequality indicator is amongst the highest in the sample."[1] Ori Nir, the Washington Bureau Chief for *The Forward*, and former correspondent to *Ha'aretz* newspaper, provided a number of disturbing statistics to a conference sponsored by the Foundation for Middle East Peace and the Middle East Institute:

> I used statistics to convince the reader that Arab-Israelis do not receive equal treatment.

- On a per capita basis, the Government [of Israel] spends two-thirds as much for Arabs as for Jews.
- Most [Israeli government] ministries have less than 5% Arabs on their payroll, and mostly in minor positions. The Ministries of Housing, Transportation, and Trade and Industry all had representation of less than 1% of Arabs in their workforce.
- The budget for the Ministry of Religious Affairs for 2000 only allocated 2.9% of its resources to the non-Jewish sector, although Muslims, Christians, and Druze constituted approximately 20% of the population.
- Between 1975 and 2000, only 0.3% of public construction initiated and subsidized by the Israeli government was for Arabs.

- No Arab community has been created since 1948, except for seven towns created for Bedouins in the Negev, whereas something like 1,000 towns have been created for Israeli Jews.
- Only 30% of Arab communities have an adequate sewage system (approximately 95% of the communities in the Jewish sector do).[2]

Nevertheless, Israel is considered by many Americans to be the only functioning democracy in the Middle East.[3] In a troubled region where democracy has largely failed to develop, this statement certainly has some merit. In the first part of this essay, I will analyze Israeli democracy generally, especially how and why it functions well, despite its relatively recent establishment and the difficult circumstances it has faced throughout its brief history. After this important recognition, however, the majority of the essay will examine areas in which Israeli democracy has failed to consolidate. I will contend that Israel, in fact, is not nearly as democratic as is often purported.

This essay will focus primarily on the explicit and inherent Jewish character of the Israeli state and how that affects the minority Arab citizens of Israel, the Israeli-Palestinians.[4] Does the fact that Israel, both as a state and in the beliefs of its Jewish citizens, sees itself ideologically (as well as in law and practice) as an ethnic state, a state for Jews worldwide, necessarily present problems for its non-Jewish citizens? Does Israel's emphasis on its "Jewishness" over its functioning as a democratic state for all its citizens, render it undemocratic, or lacking and in need of democratic transition? Or, is Israel's situation merely the result of unique circumstances? I argue that the Israeli situation is certainly unique, thus requiring different and probably more generous analysis; nonetheless, to better consolidate its democracy, Israel must move from its fundamental and all-pervasive Zionist ideology, one based on security, domination, and ethnic exclusivism, to a post-Zionist statehood that strives for a peaceful, pluralist society that is democratic before it is ethnic.

On the surface and certainly for its Jewish citizens, Israel does sustain a thriving democracy. Israel's bicameral parliament, the Knesset, is comprised of not only two main parties but also a large number of smaller parties, including Arab parties. The current Knesset, elected in 2003, contains eight Arabs, out of 120 total members. All Israeli citizens have voting rights, including women and Israeli-Palestinians.[5] Israeli law guarantees civil liberties for both individuals and groups, including minorities. Certainly, much of Israeli democracy is impressive, especially when one considers Israel's relatively

---

Margin notes:

It's common in political science writing to describe the organization of the essay first and then introduce the claim.

Rhetoric in political science calls for directly stating the point of your argument—even if it is controversial. Almost any political argument is going to be controversial, so it helps to be humble but straightforward.

I begin with evidence that seems to contradict my thesis.

Bicameral means having two chambers, houses, or branches.

recent establishment (1948) and the instability that results from war with its neighbors and the continued military presence in the Occupied Territories. However, I maintain that many aspects of Israeli government and society, both in structures and attitudes, in fact the very foundation of the state, demonstrate a lack of democratic consolidation. The most obvious manifestation of this failure is the condition of the Israeli-Palestinian, a complicated and under-analyzed situation.

Israeli-Palestinians, representing roughly twenty percent of the total Israeli population, are both Arab-Palestinians and Israeli citizens. They are those Palestinians (or descendents of those) who remained within the post-1948 borders of the newly created state of Israel and were granted Israeli citizenship. Common scholarship tends to view this Israeli-Palestinian minority as parallel to other minority groups in Western liberal democracies. According to this sort of "normal development model," Israeli-Palestinians are moving along in a gradual process of development and normalization in Israeli society.[6]

Although there is some validity in this model, it fails to recognize the fundamental and inescapable tension between the values of an *ethnic* state and the principles of a *democratic* one. While democratic process should promote equality by negating the ascendancy of one group or the state's identification with it,[7] Israel, as an ethnic state, "sets its goals with no thought for nationalities other than the dominant group and its members in all sorts of legally-sanctioned ways. The discrimination against other ethnic groups derives from the state's refusal to respond to demands for equality, affiliation, and identification."[8] As opposed to the model of a liberal democracy, where equal citizens compete to collectively determine the "common good,"[9] the commitments of Israeli democracy are first and foremost to its Jewish citizens, even if the policy in question is detrimental to the Arab minority.

Because Israel was founded as a safe haven for Jews worldwide, it became, necessarily, a Jewish state. Beginning in the 1870s, Jews from all over the world immigrated to Israel, with the explicit intention of establishing a Jewish state. After the horrific events of the Holocaust, this immigration project became a priority of the Western states. Finally, in 1948 Israel was founded as a Jewish democracy. From Israel's founding until now, Arabs have been isolated from the project of Israeli statehood; in fact, many within the Palestinian population (and arguably the Palestinians as a collective group) have been unwillingly forced to sacrifice their homes, their land, and their rights for this cause of a Jewish state. Foundational Israeli law,

> In this paragraph the history of Israel seems to support a claim that contradicts my thesis. But I focus on aspects of that history that support my claim.

especially the legal definition of the state as the "state of the Jewish people," has also reflected the ethnically exclusive nature of the Israeli state. For example, the Law of Return and the Citizenship Law grant any Jew from anywhere in the world automatic citizenship into the state of Israel, while a Palestinian refugee cannot claim that automatic citizenship.

The current exclusion of Arabs from full democratic participation is rooted in Israel's refusal to acknowledge Arab culture. The former mayor of Jerusalem, Meron Benvenisti, in his book *Sacred Landscape: The Buried History of the Holy Land Since 1948*, argues that Israel established the distinctly Jewish character of the newly established homeland by attempting to disguise its former Arab identity. According to Benvenisti, after 1948 the Jewish state suppressed Arab history by creating a new, Hebrew map of the region. On the map, Israel altered the place names of virtually all Arab villages and geographical features, officially changing them to Hebrew names or to names that were particularly meaningful to Jews. Benvenisti maintains that by changing the long-standing Arabic names, the Jewish state was essentially declaring a war on Arab culture, announcing that it was no longer interested in living side-by-side in a bilingual or bicultural state.[10]

Unfortunately for the Palestinian-Israelis and for Israeli democracy, the unwillingness to integrate the Palestinian population and their culture into the new state certainly continued after Israel's establishment. By appealing almost entirely to this Zionist cultural, religious, and historical heritage, a heritage that Palestinians often associate with war, displacement, and exclusion, modern Israeli symbols such as the national anthem, state flag, and official state holidays[11] have made it painfully clear to Palestinian-Israelis that Israel remains a Jewish state. Eliezer Ben-Rafael and Stephen Sharot, in their book *Ethnicity, Religion, and Class in Israeli Society* recognize the dual nature of the Palestinian-Israeli's situation: "On the one hand, Arabs are granted full citizenship and legal equality. On the other hand, the Jewish-Zionist character of the state has led to the exclusion of Arabs at a number of symbolic and material levels."[12] Ghanem argues that Israel relies on two key policies to maintain this Jewish character. First, the state supports policies that reinforce Jewish superiority in all spheres. Second, the state limits the democratic character of the state and thereby minimizes Arab incorporation. Because this latter policy encourages democracy at some level, it often gives the false appearance of true democracy.[13]

It is obvious, then, that Palestinian-Israelis are isolated from their state in a number of critically important ways, in many cases as a direct result of state intentions to exclude them. Of course, this intentional exclusion results in tangible experiences of discrimination for Palestinian-Israelis. Although a number of areas could be analyzed (remember some of the statistics listed at the beginning of the essay), the remainder of this essay will look to the unequal treatment of Palestinian-Israelis in terms of land expropriation, political involvement, economics, and the popular sentiment of Jewish-Israelis. In these four areas, it will be further demonstrated that Israel has failed to develop the workings of a consolidated democracy.

Founding a Jewish state on a land that was occupied primarily by Palestinians was an extremely formidable task, one that, according to Benvenisti, did not end when the state of Israel was established in 1948. Israel continues to expropriate Arab land for state and Jewish use. Much of the land has been used to enable immigrant Jews (from under the Law of Return and the Citizenship Law) to acquire land in Israel. The Jewish Agency and the Jewish National Fund have largely succeeded in turning much of Israel into state land, or at least land distributed by the state, land that is designed to benefit only Jews. In fact, over 93% of Israeli land is state owned; Arabs own only approximately 3.5% of the land in Israel.[14]

Despite the fact that they constitute roughly twenty percent of the total Israeli population, Palestinian-Israelis are greatly underrepresented in the Israeli government. While Palestinian-Israelis do have full voting rights and some Arabs serve in the Knesset, Arab parties tend to play the permanent role of opposition. A *New York Times* article on Arab involvement in Israeli government states that "No Israeli prime minister has ever given leaders of the Arab parties significant positions of power."[15] This has been a common pattern in Israeli politics. Palestinian-Israelis are systematically excluded from the most important Knesset committees, like Finance, Defense, and Foreign Affairs.[16] Many Israeli government ministries have special departments dealing with matters of the Arab minority, but with a Jewish head.[17]

Amendment 9 to the Basic Law also excludes Arabs from full participation in Israeli government. In January of 2003, Israel's Central Election Committee disqualified two of the most prominent Arab members of the Knesset, Ahmad al-Tibi and Azmi Bisharah, from running in the election. The committee justified their decision based on al-Tibi's and Bisharah's opposition to the existence of a Jewish state (an opposition which is illegal under Amendment 9), and their promotion of an Israeli state for all citizens, regardless of ethnicity. The committee reviewed the candidacy of another controversial figure, Jewish politician Baruch Marzel, because of his open anti-Arab racism; but, amidst assurances that he no longer promoted racist policies (despite his open support for transferring Palestinians out of the West Bank and Gaza), the committee allowed Marzel to run. Eventually, this decision was overturned by the Israeli High Court of Justice.[18] According to a *New York Times* article, however, the message to Palestinian-Israelis was clear: "If you are a Jewish extremist, you can go on the campaign trail. But if you belong to the Arab minority and do not openly toe the government line, you cannot be part of the election game."[19]

The economic situation of Palestinian-Israelis remains quite dire as well, reflecting both their lack of integration into Israeli society and the Israeli government's apathy towards their plight. Statistics provide the best indicator of the difficult economic situation of the Palestinian-Israelis. These statistics were provided by the International Crisis Group, an international advocacy group, in its report entitled "Identity Crisis: Israel and its Arab Citizens"[20]:

- In 2003, some 44.7% of Arab-Israeli families lived in poverty, as opposed to roughly 20% of Israeli Jewish families;[21]
- 27 of the 30 communities in Israel with the highest unemployment rates are Arab, including the top fourteen;[22]
- The average gross hourly income of an Arab wage earner is 60% that of a Jewish counterpart.[23]

According to Sarah Kreimer, co-director of The Center for Jewish-Arab Economic Development, the Israeli Ministry of Education spends nearly twice as much per Jewish child as per Arab child. This has led to an infant mortality in the Arab sector that is nearly double that among Jews.[24]

Certainly, statistics cannot tell the entire story of the current situation of the Palestinian-Israelis. The economic depravity of Israel's Arab population cannot be attributed wholly to government discrimination, as a number of factors have contributed to their poor economic situation. It is clear, however, that the Israeli government has discriminated against this minority group, and it is also clear that this discrimination is supported by a majority of Israel's population. The popular opinion of Jews in Israel regarding their fellow Arab citizens might, in fact, be the most disturbing aspect of Israeli democracy, as it shows an obvious lack of democratic value within the population.

A number of popular opinion surveys have recorded attitudes of Israel's Jewish population toward their fellow Arab-Palestinian citizens. These surveys indicate that a large majority of Jews in Israel emphasize Israel's Jewish identity before and often times against its democratic identity. In a survey conducted in 1995 by Jewish scholar Sammy Smooha of the University of Haifa eighty-five percent of Jews surveyed said that they were opposed to any change to the Israeli state symbols to make them less offensive to the Arab minority, and seventy-four percent believed that the state should manifest great or some preference to Jews over Arab citizens. Ninety-five percent of the Jewish Israelis opposed the idea of Israel as a liberal democratic state in which Arabs can compete freely and live wherever they wish. In fact, fifty-one percent said that the term "Israeli" applies only to Jews and not Arabs.[25] The 2003 Israel Democracy Index revealed that fifty-three percent of Jewish-Israelis are openly against full equality for the Arabs, only thirty-one percent support having Arab parties in the government, and fifty-seven percent agree that Arabs should be encouraged to emigrate.[26] The popular opinions of Israelis indicate that many of the core values of a liberal democracy have failed to take hold, undoubtedly a sign of incomplete democratic consolidation.[27]

In this essay, I have shown how Israeli democracy has largely failed to consolidate in relation to its ethnic minority, the Palestinian-Israelis. In nearly all areas of Israeli society, including land distribution, political participation, the economic sphere, and general attitudes of Israeli's dominant Jewish population, Palestinian-Israelis remain marginalized and discriminated against. However, even if their status in these areas improves, Palestinian-Israelis will remain isolated from their fellow citizens in Israel. Because Israel has established itself in law, symbol, and practice as an inherently and explicitly Jewish state, Palestinian-Israelis will always face the fundamental tension of being Arab and living in a Jewish state.[28] They will remain what Dan Rabinowitz terms a "trapped minority," both Arab and Israeli, accepted by neither world.

To transition to a functioning, fully consolidated democracy, Israel must shift its focus away from its ethnic statehood. In his article, "Israel in Transition from Zionism to Post-Zionism," Herbert C. Kelman argues that Israel must begin to see itself as a state for *all* its citizens, not a state for Jews worldwide. Israel has successfully become a safe haven for persecuted Jews around the world; the Zionist project has largely been completed. Now, he argues, "The primary feature of a post-Zionist state must be to protect and advance the interests and well-being of its citizens, regardless of ethnicity."[29] Israel must regard itself as a democratic state, a state that treats all citizens equally. Only when

Israel shifts away from an exclusively Jewish ethnic state to that of a liberal democracy, one that includes both Jews and Arabs, can it be considered a fully transitioned democracy.

Notes

1. "The State of Israeli Democracy," *The Democracy Index.* Israel Democracy Institute.<http://www.idi.org.il/english/article.php?id=1466>. (18 September 2004).
2. Ori Nir, "Israel's Arab Minority," The Foundation for Middle East Peace, Current Analysis, Speech given on April 30, 2003, <http://www.fmep.org/analysis/ori_nir_israels_arab_minority.html>, (25 April 2004).
3. It should be noted that the definition of what states comprise the Middle East is its own topic of debate. Many, for example, would include Turkey and Iran as a part of the Middle East. These states are certainly democratic on a number of levels.
4. "Israeli-Palestinian" is the preferred name for Arabs who are citizens of the state of Israel. They are also known as Arab-Israelis, although this name is not preferred.
5. "Political Parties and Platforms," *Israeli Democracy in Action*, <http://www.israelvotes2003.com/>, (22 April 2004).
6. As'ad Ghanem, *The Palestinian-Arab Minority in Israel, 1948–2000*, (Albany, NY: State University of New York Press, 2001), 5–7.
7. As'ad Ghanem, "State and minority in Israel: the case of ethnic state and the predicament of its minority," *Ethnic and Racial Studies*, Volume 21, No. 3 (May 1998), 429.
8. Ibid., 439.
9. Ghanem, *The Palestinian-Arab Minority in Israel*, 7.
10. Meron Benvenisti, *Sacred Landscape: The Buried History of the Holy Land Since 1948*, (Berkeley, CA: University of California Press, 2000.)
11. Ghanem, "State and Minority in Israel," 432.
12. Eliezer Ben-Rafael and Stephen Sharot, *Ethnicity, religion, and class in Israeli society*, (Cambridge, England: Cambridge University Press, 1991), 233.
13. Ghanem, *The Palestinian-Arab Minority in Israel*, 9.
14. "Identity Crisis: Israel and its Arab Citizens," The International Crisis Group, *ICG Middle East Report*, Number 25 (4 March 2004), <http://www.crisisweb.org//library/documents/middle_east__north_africa/arab_israeli_conflict/25_identity_crisis_israel_arab_citz.pdf>, (26 April 2004), 14.
15. David Newman, "A Decision That Hurts Israeli Democracy," *The New York Times*, January 6, 2003, (A, 21).
16. Ghanem, "State and Minority in Israel," 433.
17. Eliezer Ben-Rafael and Stephen Sharot, 235.
18. "Israeli Arabs urged to vote after disqualifications overruled," *BBC News Online*, 10 January 2003, (8 March 2004).
19. Newman, *New York Times*.
20. The full report can be found at <http://www.crisisweb.org//library/documents/middle_east__north_africa/arab_israeli_conflict/25_identity_-crisis_israel_arabcitz.pdf>.
21. From "Identity Crisis: Israel and its Arab Citizens," (Mossawa Center, "Socio-Economic Report on Arab Citizens and Local Councils." <www.mossawacenter.org/eng/reports/summaryeng.htm>).
22. Ibid., (National Security Council, "The Arab Citizens of Israel—Organising Ideas for Addressing the Issue").

23. Ibid., (Central Bureau of Statistics, op. cit.).
24. Sarah Kreimer, The Center for Jewish-Arab Economic Development, <http://www.cjaed.org.il/news_161000_b.html>. (26 April 2004).
25. Ghanem, *The Palestinian-Arab Minority in Israel*, 160–163.
26. "The State of Israeli Democracy."
27. This could also include the public's relative apathy to government corruption, the lack of rule of law in the Occupied Territories, and the frequent undemocratic measures carried out even within Israel, among other things.
28. Mark Tessler and Audra K. Grant, "Israel's Arab Citizens: The Continuing Struggle," *The Annals of the American Academy of Political Science*, Volume 555 (January 1998), 97–113.
29. Herbert C Kelman, "Israel in Transition from Zionism to Post-Zionism," *The Annals of the American Academy of Political and Social Science*, Volume 555 (January 1998), 46–61.

READING RESPONSES

1. In his introduction, Robin King notes that he intentionally included objections to his thesis. Review King's essay and list the objections that he includes. Do you have additional objections to King's thesis? What are they?

2. Both Professor Goi and Robin King emphasize the passion that political scientists bring to their topics. Where in the essay can you detect King's passion for this topic? Is his use of emotion-laden discourse appropriate?

3. What strategies does King use to "map" his argument for his reader? Note the kind of preview statements he uses and record their location. Where in his essay do these most commonly appear?

PUBLIC WRITING IN POLITICAL SCIENCE

Introduction

Bowling? Democracy? Can these two topics have anything to do with each other? In "Bowling for Democracy," an editorial that appeared in the *New York Times*, Orlando Patterson and Jason Kaufman make the connection. In the first paragraph of this editorial, Patterson and Kaufman, both Harvard professors, pose two questions about the game of cricket (the "pitcher" in cricket is called the "bowler"):

> Why, on the one hand, does the game flourish in lands like Pakistan and India, where a hard-fought series can transfix two nations and even lead to improved diplomatic relations? (Last month's series, in which Pakistan defeated India by 159 runs, concluded with a historic meeting between Pakistan's president and India's prime minister.) And why, on the other hand, is cricket not much played in other former British colonies like Canada—or, for that matter, in the United States, with its heritage and special relationship with Britain?

By asking these questions, Patterson and Kaufman set their readers to wondering about differences between how things work in other parts of the world and in North America. They devote most of their editorial to part of the last question—why don't Americans play cricket anymore? And they find their answer in the nature of American culture.

Patterson and Kaufman connect the history of cricket and democracy in the final two paragraphs of their editorial. Once again they use a question to help the reader make the transition from sports to politics: "What broader lessons might the history of cricket have for the globalization of Western cultural practices?" Answering this question, they summarize their history of cricket to argue that other cultural practices—such as a democratic political system—can enter a culture by way of a colonizing power or an upper class. Democracy does not come about exclusively from a groundswell of popular feeling.

So what about bowling? Why is bowling in the title when the authors can guess that most American readers will not catch the reference to cricket? Although you and other readers may answer this question differently, we believe that Patterson and Kaufman use the word "bowling" to tap into an assumption that many Americans hold. When most Americans read "bowling" they assume it refers to a game of tenpin. This game of tenpin, bowling, is one of the few sports that Americans associate with social status; Americans presume that bowling is a sport of the lower classes. In essence, Patterson and Kaufman argue that democracy can enter a society as easily through "the cricket classes" as through "the bowling classes." In other words, the United States can pressure other countries to adopt democratic reforms without manufacturing an uprising of the general population.

Why do Patterson and Kaufman care so much about how the United States influences political practices in other countries? The final two paragraphs indicate to us that they hope to offer Americans a new way to influence the politics in other countries—not top-down at the point of a gun, not bottom-up by fanning popular unrest, but top-down by fostering a passion for the game.

Bowling for Democracy
Orlando Patterson and Jason Kaufman

New York Times, May 1, 2005, p. WK15(L)

Cricket, the quintessential English game, is nonetheless one of the most international of sports. It is a dominant game in more countries than any other sport except soccer, in lands as varied as Australia, India, Pakistan, South Africa and the Commonwealth Caribbean. But a glance at the global map of cricket poses a remarkable cultural puzzle. Why, on the one hand, does the game flourish in lands like Pakistan and India, where a hard-fought series can transfix two nations and even lead to improved diplomatic relations? (Last month's series, in which Pakistan defeated India by 159 runs, concluded with a historic meeting between Pakistan's president and India's prime minister.) And why, on the other hand, is cricket not much played in other former British colonies like Canada—or, for that matter, in the United States, with its heritage and "special relationship" with Britain?

The puzzle only deepens when one considers that cricket was once popular in both Canada and the United States. It rivaled baseball for most of the 19th century, with as many stories in the sports pages of The *New York Times* until 1880. Indeed, the world's first international test match was played between Canada and the United States in 1844. So the puzzle is not so much why it was never adopted in North America, but why in the early 20th century it was subsequently rejected.

Many popular explanations are flawed. Climate has nothing to do with it; cricket emerged as a summer game, and is easily played in North America during mild weather. North American multiculturalism is hardly a factor, given the game's popularity in the multicultural societies of the Caribbean and South Africa. Ethnicity cannot be the answer: while the Scots, with their preference for curling, predominated among early Canadian immigrants, there was a far greater proportion of English in North America than in India or the Caribbean; meanwhile, the preponderance of the Irish in Australia did not prevent cricket from becoming that country's national pastime. Why is it, then, that hockey and baseball eventually trumped cricket in Canada and the United States?

The most common argument is that cricket was too long and slow for fast-paced North America; formal test matches last for five days. This explanation at least has some merit—though not in the manner usually understood.

Cricket lost ground in North America because of the egalitarian ethos of its societies. Rich Americans and Canadians had constant anxiety about their elite status, which prompted them to seek ways to differentiate themselves from the masses. One of those ways was cricket, which was cordoned off as an elites-only pastime, a sport only for those wealthy enough to belong to expensive cricket clubs committed to Victorian ideals of sportsmanship. In late 19th-century Canada, according to one historian, "the game became associated more and more with an older and more old-fashioned Anglo-Saxon elite."

This elite appropriation played into the hands of baseball entrepreneurs who actively worked to diminish cricket's popularity. A.G. Spalding, described in the Baseball Hall of Fame as the "organizational genius of baseball's pioneer days," was typical. "I have declared cricket is a genteel game," he mocked in "America's National Game," his 1911 best seller. "It is. Our British cricketer, having finished his day's labor at noon, may don his negligee shirt, his white trousers, his gorgeous hosiery and his canvas shoes, and sally forth to the field of sport, with his sweetheart on one arm and his cricket bat under the other, knowing that he may engage in his national pastime without soiling his linen or neglecting his lady."

Baseball, in contrast, was sold as a rugged, fast-paced, masculine game, befitting a rugged, fast-paced economic power. Americans of all classes swallowed the chauvinistic line. It was also great business for Spalding. By inventing elaborate baseball gear and paraphernalia, he created a market for his new sporting-goods company.

In the remaining British colonies, however, the opposite happened. In these rigidly unequal societies the colonial elites and their native allies never had any anxieties about their status, and the British actively promoted the game—first to native elites, then to the masses.

In India, the wealthy Parsis first took up the game in emulation of their British masters. Soon, royalty throughout the subcontinent adopted it. English-style grammar schools were an important source of exposure to upwardly mobile native men. In the Caribbean, grammar schools made the imperial game a core feature of their education and made competition possible between different classes and ethnic groups without disrupting the social fabric. As C.L.R. James, the famed Trinidadian intellectual and cricket enthusiast, wrote in his memoir: "I haven't the slightest doubt that the clash of race, caste and class did not retard but stimulated West Indian cricket."

Both colonizer and colonized developed a stake in the popularization of the game. To the British colonists, the "imperial game" was the perfect vehicle for civilizing the colonial masses (as it had previously, they imagined, civilized generations of upwardly mobile British schoolboys). For elite members of the colonized, it was a way to curry favor. And for the masses, who quickly mastered the game, it was a symbolically powerful and clandestine form of political liberation as they soon learned to literally beat the British and their native surrogates at their own game.

The game itself partly facilitated this process. Cricket requires no contact between players, and its strict and complex rules, dress code and officiating largely eliminate any risk of embarrassment in play with those of different ranks or castes. So did the careful allocation of positions; less glamorous roles like bowling and fielding were assigned to social inferiors while those of specialist batsmen and team captain were reserved for elites.

Much the same was true of 19th-century Australia, at the time a highly stratified colony whose masses were descended from prisoners. Cricket helped antipodean elites cultivate their Englishness, but the size and isolation of their European settlements limited the extent to which they could be truly exclusive. North American-style upper-class appropriation of the game was out of the question. Cricket became a powerful unifying force, and prowess at the game, according to one cricket historian, was "the mark of an amateur gentleman" from any class.

As in the Caribbean, cricket was also a major element in the formation of Australian nationalism. The biennial matches with England solidified the link between colony and mother country even as it fostered Australian national pride when the Australians increasingly came to whip the British at their imperial game.

What broader lessons might the history of cricket have for the globalization of Western cultural practices? It shows that such practices can be promoted or discouraged from the top down; it is not necessarily a bottom-up process, as is commonly believed. Nor does such downward dissemination require the point of a gun. The passion for cricket in places like Pakistan and India also shows that a complex Western cultural practice can be adopted in its entirety by very different cultures, even when highly identified with its country of origin.

Might the same be true of other Western cultural practices, like democracy?

READING RESPONSES

1. Authors Patterson and Kaufman end their editorial with a question: "Might the same be true of other Western cultural practices, like democracy?" How would you answer that question? What logic would you use to support your answer?
2. Why do you think the authors chose to compare politics to sports? How does the topic of sports help them engage the interest, and maybe even passions, of their readers?
3. Patterson and Kaufman devote a good deal of their editorial to summarizing the global history of cricket. How does this summary build their credibility with readers?

MORE WRITING IN POLITICAL SCIENCE

Introduction

People sometimes say that professors "live in an ivory tower," by which they mean that professors focus on abstract questions and ignore real-world problems. In this brief essay, John Owen reviews *Electing to Fight: Why Emerging Democracies Go to War*, a scholarly book published by two well-known political scientists—Edward Mansfield and Jack Snyder. Owen uses his review to persuade his readers not only that *Electing to Fight* is an important book but also that "ivory-tower" research in political science can speak to real-world political problems like U.S. policy in the Middle East.

Owen begins by describing a profound irony: political scientists usually fume that American presidents pay no attention to academic research when they forge foreign policy, but President George W. Bush has relied on a prominent theory—democratic peace theory—to justify the war with Iraq, a war that makes most academics fume. The problem, according to Owen, is that President Bush, like most politicians, relied on an over-simplified version of democratic peace theory, namely the presumption that democracies go to war less frequently than other forms of government. Applied to the Middle East, the simplified thinking goes like this: if Iraq becomes a democracy it will no longer fight with its neighbors; it will begin to stabilize this politically troubled region. Such thinking is flawed, according to Owen, because it does not pay attention to nuances in what counts as a "democracy," nuances that profoundly affect a democracy's appetite for war. In essence, Owen reminds politicians that "the devil is in the details."

Owen builds his argument that politicians should pay attention to the complexity by describing one in-depth study of democratic peace theory, *Electing to Fight*. Authors Mansfield and Snyder categorize democracies and then examine the war-lust among the different types of democracies. They conclude that "incomplete democracies," countries that have some but not all features of a democracy, are actually more likely to go to war than authoritarian states. Young democracies are also highly likely to instigate war. Because Iraq is both a young and an incomplete democracy, Mansfield and Snyder's research suggests that it will likely retain its appetite for war. Rather than stabilize the region, a democratized Iraq is likely to continue to cause trouble for its neighbors and for the United States.

In this review Owen does not merely summarize Mansfield and Snyder's book; he uses the book to make his own argument. Owen argues that the U.S. presidents should take the time to understand the complexities of political science research before they use it as the basis for going to war.

Iraq and the Democratic Peace: Who Says Democracies Don't Fight?

John M. Owen IV

Foreign Affairs 2005 84(6): 122–7. Review of *Electing to Fight: Why Emerging Democracies Go to War*. By Edward D. Mansfield and Jack Snyder. MIT Press, 2005.

Seldom if ever has the hostility between academics and the U.S. president been so pronounced. Of course, political scientists always seem to complain about the occupant of the White House, and Republicans fare worse than Democrats: Herbert Hoover was called callous, Dwight Eisenhower a dunce, Richard Nixon evil, Ronald Reagan dangerous, and George H.W. Bush out of touch. But professors have consigned George W. Bush to a special circle of their presidential hell. And the White House seems to return the sentiment.

According to the academics, Bush's chief transgressions have had to do with foreign policy, especially the Iraq war—a mess that could have been avoided if only the president and his advisers had paid more attention to those who devote their lives to studying international relations.

The irony of this argument is that few other presidents—certainly none since Woodrow Wilson, a former president of the American Political Science Association, scribbled away in the Oval Office—have tied their foreign policies more explicitly to the work of social science. The defining act of Bush's presidency was grounded in a theory that the political scientist Jack Levy once declared was "as close as anything we have to an empirical law in international relations," namely, that democracies do not fight one another.

The theory, which originated in the work of the eighteenth-century philosopher Immanuel Kant and was refined in the 1970s and 1980s by several researchers working independently, has, since the 1990s, been one of the hottest research areas in international relations. Although some skeptics remain and no one agrees about why exactly it works, most academics now share the belief that democracies have indeed made a separate peace. What is more, much research suggests that they are also unusually likely to sign and honor international agreements and to become economically interdependent.

The administrations of Presidents George H.W. Bush and Bill Clinton made frequent appeals to the theory in public, and it seems to have informed their support for democratization in former communist lands and in Haiti. The current Bush administration, however, has gone much further in its faith in the idea, betting the farm that the theory holds and will help Washington achieve a peaceful, stable, and prosperous Muslim world as, over time, Iraq's neighbors, following Iraq's example, democratize. The United States' real motives for attacking Iraq may have been complex, but "regime change"—the replacement of Saddam Hussein's gruesome tyranny with a democracy—was central to Washington's rhetoric by the time it began bombing Baghdad in March 2003.

Why has a president who set his defining policy around one of political science's crown jewels come in for so much venom from the same academics who endorse the idea? After all, a host of peer-reviewed journal articles have implicitly supported the president's claim that a democratic Iraq would not threaten the United States or Israel, develop weapons of mass destruction, or sponsor terrorism. Are professors simply perpetual critics who refuse to take responsibility for the consequences of their ideas? Or does Bush hatred trump social science?

The Bush administration's desire to break with its predecessors and alter the authoritarian status quo in the Middle East was admirable. But the White House got its science wrong, or at least not completely right: the democratic peace theory does not dictate that the United States can or should remake Iraq into a democracy. In *Electing to Fight: Why Emerging Democracies Go to War*, the veteran political scientists Edward Mansfield and Jack Snyder make two critical points. Not only is turning authoritarian countries into democracies extremely difficult, much more so than the administration seems to have anticipated. The Middle East could also become a much more dangerous place if Washington and the rest of the world settle for a merely semi-democratic regime in Baghdad. Such an Iraq, Mansfield and Snyder imply, would be uncommonly likely to start wars—a bull in the Middle Eastern china shop. Unfortunately, such an Iraq may also be just what we are likely to end up with.

Illiberal Democracies

At first glance, the realists' critique of the Iraq war is easier to understand than that of the democratic peace theorists. Indeed, realism—which holds that a country's type of government has no systematic effects on its foreign policy—is enjoying a revival in Washington these days, precisely because of the war. According to the realists, the best way to have dealt with Saddam would have been not to overthrow him but to use coercive bargaining: to have threatened him with annihilation, for example, if he ever used nuclear weapons.

Even the democratic peace theory, however, does not necessarily prescribe the use of force to transform despotisms such as Iraq into democracies. Indeed, by itself, the argument that democracies do not fight one another does not have any practical implications for the foreign policymaker. It needs an additional or minor premise, such as "the United States can make Iraq into a democracy at an acceptable cost." And it is precisely this minor premise about which the academy has been skeptical. No scholarly consensus exists on how countries become democratic, and the literature is equally murky on the costs to the United States of trying to force them to be free.

This last part of the puzzle is even more complicated than it first appears. Enter Mansfield and Snyder, who have been contributing to the democratic peace debate for a decade. Their thesis, first published in 1995, is that although mature democracies do not fight one another, democratizing states—those in transition from authoritarianism to democracy—do, and are even more prone to war than authoritarian regimes. Now, in *Electing to Fight*, the authors have refined their argument. As they outline in the book, not only are "incomplete democratizing" states—those that develop democratic institutions in the wrong order—unlikely ever to complete the transition to democracy; they are also especially bellicose.

According to Mansfield and Snyder, in countries that have recently started to hold free elections but that lack the proper mechanisms for accountability (institutions such as an independent judiciary, civilian control of the military, and protections for opposition parties and the press), politicians have incentives to pursue policies that make it more likely that their countries will start wars. In such places, politicians know they can mobilize support by demanding territory or other spoils from foreign countries and by nurturing grievances against outsiders. As a result, they push for extraordinarily belligerent policies. Even states that develop democratic institutions in the right order—adopting the rule of law before holding elections—are very aggressive in the early years of their transitions, although they are less so than the first group and more likely to eventually turn into full democracies.

Of course, politicians in mature democracies are also often tempted to use nationalism and xenophobic rhetoric to buttress their domestic power. In such cases, however, they are usually restrained by institutionalized mechanisms of accountability. Knowing that if they lead the country into a military defeat or quagmire they may be punished at the next election, politicians in such states are less likely to advocate a risky war. In democratizing states, by contrast, politicians know that they are insulated from the impact of bad policies: if a war goes badly, for example, they can declare a state of emergency, suspend elections, censor the press, and so on. Politicians in such states also tend to fear their militaries, which often crave foreign enemies and will overthrow civilian governments that do not share their goals. Combined, these factors can make the temptation to attack another state irresistible.

Mansfield and Snyder present both quantitative and case-study support for their theory. Using rigorous statistical methods, the authors show that since 1815, democratizing states have indeed been more prone to start wars than either democracies or authoritarian regimes. Categorizing transitions according to whether they ended in full democracies (as in the U.S. case) or in partial ones (as in Germany in 1871–1938 or Pakistan throughout its history), the authors find that in the early years of democratic transitions, partial democracies—especially those that get their institutions in the wrong order—are indeed significantly more likely to initiate wars. ... In most of these cases, the authors find what they expect: in these democratizing states, domestic political competition was intense. Politicians, vying for power, appeased domestic hard-liners by resorting to nationalistic appeals that vilified foreigners, and these policies often led to wars that were not in the countries' strategic interests.

Although their argument would have been strengthened by a few comparative studies of democratizing states avoiding war and of full democracies and authoritarian states starting wars, Mansfield and Snyder are persuasive. In part this is because they carefully circumscribe their claims. They acknowledge that some cases are "false positives," that is, wars started by states that have wrongly been classified as democratizing, such as the Iran–Iraq War, started by Iraq in 1980. They also answer the most likely objections to their argument. Some skeptics, for example, might counter that Mansfield and Snyder get the causality reversed: it is war or the threat of it that prevents states from becoming mature democracies. Others might argue that democratizing states become involved in more wars simply because their internal instability tempts foreign states to attack them—in other words, that democratizers are more sinned against than sinning. Analyzing data from 1816 through 1992, Mansfield and Snyder put paid to these alternative explanations. Bad domestic institutions usually precede wars, rather than vice versa, and democratizing states usually do the attacking. . . .

The authors' conclusions for foreign policy are straightforward. The United States and other international actors should continue to promote democracy, but they must strive to help democratizing states implement reforms in the correct order. In particular, popular elections ought not to precede the building of institutions that will check the baleful incentives for politicians to call for war. Mansfield and Snyder are unsparing toward well-intentioned organizations that have pressured authoritarian governments to rush to elections in the past—often with disastrous consequences. As the authors show, for example, it was organizations such as the World Bank and the National Democratic Institute that pushed Burundi and Rwanda to increase popular sovereignty in the early 1990s—pressure that, as Mansfield and Snyder argue, helped set off a chain of events that led to genocide. Acknowledging their intellectual debt to writers such as Samuel Huntington (particularly his 1968 book *Political Order in Changing Societies*) and Fareed Zakaria, Mansfield and Snyder have written a deeply conservative book. Sounding like Edmund Burke on the French Revolution but substituting statistics and measured prose for rhetorical power, the authors counsel against abruptly empowering people, since premature elections may well usher in domestic upheavals that thrust the state outward against its neighbors.

Back in Baghdad

This brings the conversation back to Iraq, and in particular the notion that the United States can turn it into a democracy at an acceptable cost. In effect, Mansfield and Snyder have raised the estimate of these costs by pointing out one other reason this effort may fail—a reason that few seem to have thought of. Forget for a moment the harrowing possibility of a Sunni-Shiite-Kurdish civil war in Iraq. Set aside the prospect of a Shiite-dominated state aligning itself with Iran,

Syria, and Lebanon's Hezbollah. What if, following the departure of U.S. troops, Iraq holds together but as an incomplete democratizer, with broad suffrage but anemic state institutions? Such an Iraq might well treat its own citizens better than the Baathist regime did. Its treatment of its neighbors, however, might be just as bad.

Although Saddam was an unusually bellicose and reckless tyrant, attacking Iran in 1980 and Kuwait in 1990 and engaging in foolish brinkmanship with the United States, as Mansfield and Snyder imply, a democratic Iraq may be no less bellicose and reckless. In the near future, intensely competitive elites there— secularists, leftists, moderates, and both Shiite and Sunni Islamists—could compete for popularity by stirring up nationalism against one or more of Iraq's neighbors. And Iraq lives in a dangerous neighborhood. Already, Iraqi Shiite parties have been critical of Sunni-dominated Jordan; Iraqi Sunni parties, of Shiite-dominated Iran; and Iraqi Kurdish parties, of Turkey.

One hopes that the White House contemplated this scenario prior to March 2003. Whether it did or not, the possibility must be considered now, by U.S. civilian and military leaders, academics, and U.S. allies who agree with those academics. If Mansfield and Snyder are correct about the bellicose tendencies of young, incompletely democratized states, the stakes of Iraq's transition are higher than most have supposed. . . . The odds may be long that Iraq will ever turn into a mature democracy of the sort envisaged by the Bush administration. But those odds are lengthened by the refusal of those states in Europe and the Middle East that could make a difference actually to do so.

READING RESPONSES

1. Owen begins his review by focusing his readers' attention to the fact that President George W. Bush relied on democratic peace theory to justify going to war with Iraq. How will his audience likely respond to that claim? How passionate do you expect they will be?
2. How does Owen establish Mansfield and Snyder's credibility? How does he establish his own?
3. Did Owen persuade you? What aspects of his argument did you find persuasive? What aspects did you find less so?

WRITING ASSIGNMENTS

ASSIGNMENT 1: APPLYING THE PORTABLE RHETORICAL LESSON

Background: For his research paper, Robin King chose a political topic that he already knew and cared about. But his passion for the topic didn't blind him to the rhetorical context of his essay. While reading previous research on his topic, King made sure to read what had been written by those who might disagree with his opinions, and he included information from those sources in his essay.

Your task for this assignment is to write a research-based essay on a political topic that you already know something about. Your essay should include a thesis that you really believe in, one you'd be willing (maybe even eager) to defend in public. You might choose to use hypotheses to help you prove your thesis or a set of recommendations to sharpen the point of your thesis. Start brainstorming by creating a list of three topics that you've recently discussed with others. For your own benefit, narrow the scope of each topic as much as possible. So, for example, instead of researching "environmentalism" research "ground water contamination" or even better "Los Angeles ground water contamination." For each of these topics, use research databases to complete the following lists. Keep track of the sources you find by listing them in a bibliography:

- List the words or search terms that research databases use to describe this topic.
- List the issues that people are currently discussing.
- List the "camps" or groups of people who share opinions about this topic. Be sure to look for more than just groups that oppose each other. Record the opinions of these scholarly groups.
- Note the kind of evidence that authors use: statistics, expert opinions, case studies, scientific experiments, quotes from authorities or authoritative texts, etc.

As you begin drafting, create a working version of a thesis that you believe in, one you can support and defend with scholarly evidence and logic. Be sure to include scholarly research from those who might disagree with your thesis, those who will seem impartial, and those who agree with your thesis. Provide logical reasoning that connects your research to your point. In other words, do everything you can to create a credible voice for yourself—and thereby increase your chances of actually changing your reader's mind.

ASSIGNMENT 2: MAKING CONNECTIONS

Background: Approximately 40 million people are infected with HIV/AIDS, and over 25 million of those people live in developing countries such as Botswana, Zimbabwe, Haiti, and Thailand. In western countries people with HIV can live almost normal lives thanks to new anti-retroviral drugs. These drugs are rarely available to those in developing countries, though, because they are expensive, complex to administer, and require careful supervision by trained medical personnel. Some have suggested that developing countries forget about trying to treat those infected with HIV/AIDS and, instead, concentrate on preventing new infections. What gets lost in these statistics is the patient—the person suffering the effects of this ravaging disease. The readings in Chapter 12, Nursing, on the other hand, demonstrate the rhetorical power of personal experience to counter the potentially numbing effect of numeric evidence. When personal experience is not possible—because of geographic or historical distance—examples and case studies can produce a similar rhetorical effect.

Your task is to research the topic of HIV/AIDS in developing countries, looking for both numeric information and information about individuals who suffer the effects of HIV/AIDS. Using both numeric and case study information, write an essay that ends in a set of recommendations. You can start your research with two websites that provide reliable information—www.unaids.org (the U.N. website for HIV/AIDS) and *www.who.int/hiv/en* (the World Health Organization website for HIV/AIDS). As soon as possible, limit your focus to a particular developing country or a particular aspect of the HIV/AIDS crisis in developing countries. Decide on the claim you want to make and frame that as the working draft of your thesis.

As you begin drafting, list the likely responses that readers will have to your thesis. Include some of these in your essay and answer these questions or criticisms with evidence and reasoning. Consider the relationship between your working thesis and your recommendations, and revise both to enhance the relationship.

ASSIGNMENT 3: DOING THE RESEARCH

Background: In Christoper Layne's fourth endnote, he lists political conflicts, other than the Trent conflict, between democracies that also support his claim that realism better predicts historical outcomes than democratic peace theory.

Your task for this assignment is to select one of the political conflicts that Layne lists in his fourth endnote and write a case study of the conflict that emphasizes the features of the conflict that make it good evidence for the value of realism. Consult reference librarians for help finding detailed descriptions of these historical events.

As you being drafting, consider how you will describe the theory of realism to emphasize the features that your case study will demonstrate. Decide where in your essay you will help the reader make connections between the historical events and how realist theory accounts for them. And think about how you will document the information you include in your essay.

8

BIOLOGY:
DESCRIBING NATURE

In this chapter you will read four different kinds of scientific writing that share the purpose of reporting discoveries about the natural world of biology. The first reading (on rugby injuries) offers a glimpse into the workaday world of science. A scientist asks a specific question about the natural world, designs a reliable method, and gathers experimental data. If the data prove statistically sound, those results can lead both to further studies and perhaps to some practical application (a change in athletic training). In the chapter's fourth reading, on the other hand, you witness an example of the kind of science writing that rarely happens. The knowledge presented in Watson and Crick's one-page paper introduced the world to the structure of DNA... and changed everything from the way we understand our biological history to the way we prosecute crimes. In brief, science writing changes the world by informing us of new knowledge and thus reforming what we know. Reading about science can produce feelings of both awe and terror (think of atomic weapons or genetic engineering) because scientific knowledge has been one of the primary agents of change in human history.

We include these readings in a writing textbook because the simple but powerful rhetorical tools of the natural sciences are available to all writers.

➤A Portable Rhetorical Lesson:

Using Visual Aids to Make Information

Accessible

In the introduction to the paper on rugby injuries, Prof. Howell writes, "A scientific paper begins with data." The literal truth is that the data appear somewhere in the middle of a scientific paper—in the Results section. However, when scientists actually write and read reports of experimental research, they begin with the data.

To understand why that is the case, recognize that every successful writer has to write with confidence. Scientists earn confidence when they discover reliable data and can present their data in visually accessible forms. Tables, graphs, illustrations, and photographs are probably the most common graphic "figures" in scientific writing. They all make factual data visually accessible. This information then says to other scientists, "Here is what we learned—in a nutshell." When scientists read such reports, they typically jump straight to the data in the "Results" section, and what first catches their attention are the figures. The data in figures are the foundation of the essay; everything else interprets and contextualizes that data. Our aim in this chapter is to enable you to bring scientists' expertise to your writing tasks—expertise in constructing information-carrying figures and in anchoring those figures to the words.

Writers in any field occasionally face a writing task in which their audience wants clear, concise, accessible information, obligating the writer to tell the audience, "Here's the information we collected—in a nutshell." Suppose, for example, that your supervisor has asked you to gather information about your company's electric bills over the past five years and explain reasons for any significant changes. If, however, you took a lesson from scientists, you would use a figure to present the data. You would also refer to and offer some explanation of the figure, thereby "anchoring" it in your words. The combination of the data table and your words would provide the most effective mix of direct access to the essential information with the explanations necessary to understand the context of that information—just what your supervisor needs.

How to display information is a key rhetorical question for scientists. *Tables* present facts—in columns and rows; they are especially useful for presenting a lot of numbers that can be categorized (put into the rows and columns) for comparison. Thanks to spreadsheet software, the numbers in a table can be converted to a graph, and, as Professor Howell says, "I think using a table when you can have a graph is, well, perhaps not a sin, but at least a shame." *Graphs* allow the eye to detect patterns (Figures 1 and 2, page 238 of the rugby paper, are good examples), which are more important for gaining scientific knowledge than discrete facts. *Illustrations* (drawings) can create simplified versions (models) of the natural world's complex systems and processes, revealing patterns in nature. And sometimes there's no substitute for a *photograph*: if you want to explain how a spider can hang upside down from a slick glass surface, trust an electron microscope photo of the incredibly delicate hairs on a spider's foot to demonstrate.

Chapter Topics: Topics in the chapter include sports, injuries, and genetics—and connections among these.

To Think About . . .

Annual Survey of Football Injury Research, 1945–2004

Head and Cervical Spine Fatalities

Year	Head Frequency	Percent	Cervical Spine Frequency	Percent
1945–1954	87	17.2	32	27.3
1955–1964	115	22.8	23	19.7
1965–1974	162	32.1	42	35.9
1975–1984	69	13.7	14	12.0
1985–1994	33	6.5	5	4.3
1995–2004	40	7.9	1	0.8
Totals	506	100.0	117	100.0

National Center for Catastrophic Sport Injury Research Data Tables
http://www.unc.edu/depts/nccsi/ SurveyofFootballInjuries.htm

Scan this report on the number of football players who died as a result of head and spine injuries and answer the following questions:

- Which kind of injury has caused the most deaths?
- During which time period did the most football players die from head and spine injuries? During which time period did the fewest die?
- What conclusions can you draw from this data?
- What information is missing from this chart?
- If the NCAA (National Collegiate Athletic Association) were to add a written explanation of this chart, what three things should they explain in writing?

WRITING IN BIOLOGY

Introduction by Elizabeth Howell, Professor of Biology

Imagine that you are the coach of a semi-professional ice hockey team. Your players train for two months before competing and then play matches for eight months while still keeping up their training. What information might you need to make decisions about a training program that would minimize injury while maximizing wins? Will you rely on your own past experience, anecdotal stories from other coaches, or some other, more objective source?

Imagine now that you have a scientist friend who researches sports and exercise. He is also interested in the relationship between athletic activity and injury. You're in luck! He's just published a paper on a topic that may help you out: "Influence of training and match intensity on injuries in rugby league."

You would then read this paper with the same objectives that motivate scientists, seeking an objective, unbiased answer to a specific question. And the answer to that question appears in the data, particularly as they are represented in the paper's data tables and "figures."

Any scientific paper begins with data. That is not to say that the first thing a reader encounters in the Introduction are facts and figures, but rather that the paper is written inside out, with the Results section first. In fact, the very first step in writing a paper doesn't involve writing at all. A scientist first designs a study to answer a specific research question; the study then yields data, and the scientist's primary job is to construct a figure—typically a table or graph—that makes the data clear and accessible. In the case of this paper, the specific question at hand is this: How does the intensity and duration of training and play affect the injury rate of rugby players? It doesn't ask whether the players win or lose, or if they are content or miserable, or even if they get stronger as they train and play. Reading this paper explains only injury rates; scientific writing focuses narrowly on a specific research question.

Note also that the data must be quantifiable; that is, you have to be able to measure what you study. If you study the effect of a particular soil additive on plant growth, you will need to measure plant height. If you study the effect of day length on reproductive success of robins, you'll be snooping in a lot of nests come spring. In this study, the author explains the objective methods he used to measure injury rates, training intensity, and player exertion during matches. The figures (tables and graphs) in the Results section present an accessible summary of those measurements.

You should now begin to understand why the Results section is written first. The figures represent the complete answer to the specific question asked. In fact, scientists typically look at the figures before we even read the text. Unlike an illustration in a critical paper about a novel, a figure does not simply amplify or enhance the text. The figure (or the data it presents) is the reason that the paper exists. A scientific paper with good figures can be accepted for publication even though the text is muddy and poorly written, but even the most elegant, crystal-clear prose can't cover for bad data and confusing figures. That's why scientists write, and read, their figures first.

Turn to the graphs from Figure 1 (one of the two central figures of the paper, page 238). They compare the rate of injury to the training duration, intensity, and "load" (duration plus intensity) during a season. On the X axis at the bottom of the graphs we find a spot for each month of the season. We can see at a glance that the training intensity rose over the first three months, then fell until May, and then rose again a bit, finally tapering off at the end of the season. The solid line indicates injury incidence over that same period. By following the line, we can see that as training increased, so did injury. Figure 2, which allows almost instant comparison to Figure 1, then pictures an increase in injuries that accompanies longer and tougher games.

Having discovered the heart of the paper in the Results, a reader who finds the data potentially useful will read the rest of the paper, all of which supports and contextualizes the data figures. Scientists use Abstracts to quickly scan an almost overwhelming body of literature and determine which papers are relevant to their own research. Abstracts are rife with the jargon and dense prose that are understood by experts.

The Introduction of the paper has several goals. It provides enough *background* about a possibly esoteric topic to make the point of the paper understandable to the reader and to allow the reader to see how it fits into a larger body of work on the subject. More subtly, by reviewing the history of previous work on the subject, the author *credentials* himself and his study. Gabbett shows us that he has done his homework and is an expert by citing over twenty-five publications (many written by him) in just the first two paragraphs. He also demonstrates that since many other scientists have worked on similar problems, his own research has validity. Most importantly, the introduction *points directly to the results*. The organization of the introduction moves from the broader background and context, to the particular system studied, and finally to the specific question. It is easy to imagine the last sentence of the introduction posed as the central research question: "What is the influence of training and match intensity, duration and load . . . on . . . injury . . . in rugby league players?"

The Methods section describes in great detail the specific techniques used in the study. Any flaw in the methods will cast doubt on the data. (This is the section that non-experts would be most likely to scan quickly).

The Discussion both explains and expands upon the results. In many ways it mirrors the introduction, except in reverse. Discussions start with the specific findings of a study (as in the first paragraph of Gabbett's Discussion section) and then expand outward, interpreting findings in order to explain their broader significance: My marginal annotations in Gabbett's Discussion section point out examples of this practice.

Once you have finished reading the paper, imagine the author asking the specific question, designing the experiment, collecting the data, generating graphs and tables, then writing the results, methods, discussion, and finally introduction. Do you see why many scientists write their papers inside-out? It allows them to tie everything into the story: asking an important question, using methods that produce reliable data, and presenting the data figures as the main characters of the story.

✓ READING TIPS

You probably should not read a scientific article straight through, front to back. Instead, read as a scientist would. Start with a quick scan of the Abstract; then go to the Results section, focusing first on Figures 1 and 2 and the part of the text that explains those figures. When you know what the main findings are, you might next want to look at the Discussion section—to see why the data matter and what might be done to further the research. Then scan the Introduction and Methods sections to get a broader context. Headings and visual aids allow you to scan and quickly pick out the information you are eager to find. And anytime you need help understanding some of the science, the marginal annotations should clarify things for you. Remember that the main point is not to learn the science but to learn how scientists think and write to achieve their purpose.

Influence of training and match intensity on injuries in rugby league

Tim J. Gabbett

Journal of Sports Sciences, 2004, 22: 409–17. Accepted 2 October 2003.

[Abstract]

The range of numbers gives the average value and the range that most of the data fell into. CI refers to confidence interval: the researchers are 95% confident that their data falls in this range (confidence is determined by a mathematical formula). In this case, the average training load in December was 278.3 units, but there was a broader range, with the vast majority of loads being between 262.2 and 294.5 units.

The aim of this study was to examine the influence of perceived intensity, duration and load of matches and training on the incidence of injury in rugby league players. The incidence of injury was prospectively studied in 79 semi-professional rugby league players during the 2001 season. All injuries sustained during matches and training sessions were recorded. Training sessions were conducted from December to September, with matches played from February to September. The intensity of individual training sessions and matches was estimated using a modified rating of perceived exertion scale. Training load was calculated by multiplying the training intensity by the duration of the training session. The match load was calculated by multiplying the match intensity by the time each player participated in the match. Training load increased from December (278.3 [95% confidence interval, CI 262.2 to 294.5] units) to February (385.5 [95% CI 362.4 to 408.5] units), followed by a decline until September (98.4 [95% CI 76.5 to 120.4] units). Match load increased from February (201.0 [95% CI 186.2 to 221.8] units) to September (356.8 [95% CI 302.5 to 411.1] units). More training injuries were sustained in the first half of the season (first vs second: 69.2% vs 30.8%, $P < 0.001$), whereas match injuries occurred more frequently in the latter stages of the season (53.6% vs 46.4%, $P < 0.001$). A significant relationship

P is known as the P-value; it is a measure of the quality of the statistics. These statistical results are quite good.

(P <0.05) was observed between changes in training injury incidence and changes in training intensity (r = 0.83), training duration (r = 0.79) and training load (r = 0.86). In addition, changes in the incidence of match injuries were significantly correlated (P <0.05) with changes in match intensity (r = 0.74), match duration (r = 0.86) and match load (r = 0.86). These findings suggest that as the intensity, duration and load of rugby league training sessions and matches is increased, the incidence of injury is also increased.

Keywords: collision sport, football, performance, rugby league, semi-professional.

> Scientists include keywords so that their readers can easily search the databases for related studies.

Introduction

> Note that the introduction gives the broader context for the research and the reasons for this particular study.

Rugby league is an international 'collision' sport played by amateurs (Gabbett, 2000a,b), semi-professionals (Gabbett, 2002a,b,c; Courts et al., 2003) and processionals (Gissane et al., 1993; Brewer and Davis, 1995). The game is physically demanding, requiring players to compete in a challenging contest involving frequent bouts of high-intensity activity (e.g. running and passing, sprinting) separated by short bouts of low-intensity activity (e.g. walking, jogging) (Meir et al., 1993). During the course of a match, players are exposed to many physical collisions and tackles (Brewer and Davis, 1995; Gissane et al., 2001a,b). As a result, musculoskeletal injuries are common (Gibbs, 1993; Hodgson-Phillips et al., 1998).

> In scientific papers the references are listed in parenthesis with the authors' names and the year of the paper. The full citation will be found at the end of the article. Experts will recognize the names of other experts.

Several researchers interested in rugby league have reported a higher incidence of injury as the playing level is increased (Gissane et al., 1993; Stephenson et al., 1996; Gabbett, 2000a, 2001). These findings have often been attributed to the higher intensity of elite competition (Gissane et al., 1993; Stephenson et al., 1996). It has also been shown that rugby league training injuries occur more frequently in the earlier stages of a season when training intensity and duration are high (Gabbett, 2003), while match injuries increase progressively throughout the course of a season (Gabbett, 2000a, 2003). Collectively, these results suggest that training and match intensity influence injury rates in rugby league players (Gissane et al., 1993; Stephenson et al., 1996; Gabbett, 2000a, 2003). However, no research has quantified the intensity and duration of training sessions and matches for comparison with injury rates over the course of a rugby league season.

> This is the motive for the study: what is new and noteworthy about this project in relationship to previous work. Note that the motive is restated succinctly in the last sentence of this section.

The intensity, duration and overall training and match load (i.e. the product of intensity and duration) may impact to differing degrees on injury rates, and therefore warrant individual consideration for injury management throughout the season. The aim of the present study was to examine the influence of training and match intensity, duration and load on the incidence of injury over the course of a season in rugby league players.

Methods

Participants

The incidence, site, nature, cause and severity of training and match injuries were studied prospectively in 79 semi-professional rugby league players over the 2001 season. The season lasted from December 2000 to September 2001 inclusive, with matches played from February 2001 to September 2001 inclusive. All players were registered with the same semi-professional rugby league club, and were competing in the Gold Coast Group 18 senior rugby league competition (New South Wales Country Rugby League, Australia). The players were considered to be 'semi-professional' as they were receiving moderate remuneration to play rugby league, but were also relying on additional employment to generate income. The participants in the present study could be distinguished from amateur players (who do not receive match payments) and professional players (who generate their entire income from their involvement in rugby league) (Gabbett, 2001). The playing roster for the season included 57 players, with the remaining players relegated to the amateur team affiliated with the club. Depending on age and skill, players competed in one of three teams (First Grade, Second Grade or Under 19). The Second Grade and Under 19 teams consisted of a squad of 20 players, while the First Grade team consisted of a squad of 17 players. All participants received a clear explanation of the study, including the risks and benefits involved, and written consent was obtained. The Institutional Review Board for Human Investigation approved all experimental procedures.

Matches

The players participated in 69 matches, which included trial ('friendly'), fixture and finals matches. Trial matches were 60 min in duration. Fixture and finals matches were either 60 min (Under 19), 70 min (Second Grade) or 80 min (First Grade) in duration. One finals match (Second Grade) required 2 × 10-min 'extra-time' periods (i.e. 90 min in duration) because of level scores at the end of regulation time. All matches were played under the unlimited interchange rule.

Training sessions

Each player participated in two organized field-training sessions per week. A periodized, game-specific training programme was

---

Sidebar notes (left margin):

The methods section provides precise detail of the way in which the experiments were done and how the data were collected. Other scientists who study very similar topics will read this section very carefully, partly to learn new research methods but also to critically evaluate the experiments: Were they set up well? Was enough data collected? Were controls (untreated samples) included? Note that in this paper, the methods never identify the gender of the subjects. Since you might expect men and women to get different types of injuries and react to them differently, identifying gender is pretty important and should have been done.

First Grade are the top players.

Experiments involving human subjects must be presented to and approved by a committee of other scientists (including psychologists), and non-scientists to ensure they are safe and worthwhile. A similar board (with a veterinarian) reviews experiments involving other (non-human) animals.

Substitute players can enter the game to replace injured players whenever necessary.

implemented, with training loads being progressively increased in the preparatory phase of the season (i.e. December to February) and reduced during the competitive phase of the season (i.e. March to September). The duration of training sessions was recorded, with sessions typically lasting between 60 and 100 min. Players participated in a total of 82 training sessions, which included all pre-season and in-season training sessions that corresponded with pre-season, fixture and finals matches. . . .

Results

Site of injury

A total of 389 training injuries were recorded, with an overall incidence of injury of 105.9 [95% CI 95.4 to 116.4] per 1000 training hours. More than 35% of the training injuries sustained were to the thigh and calf. Injuries to the ankle and foot (23.9%), knee (12.1%), and thorax and abdomen (12.6%) were less common. Over the course of the season, a total of 948 match injuries were recorded, with an overall incidence of injury of 917.3 [95% CI 857.9 to 976.6] per 1000 playing hours. Approximately 19.0% of the injuries sustained during matches were to the thigh and calf. Injuries to the face (14.2%), knee (13.8%), and arm and hand (12.9%) were less common (Table 1) .

Nature of injury

The types of injuries sustained during training and match-play are shown in Table 2. Muscular injuries (haematomas and strains) were the most common type of training injury (45.2%),

Table 1 Site of injury

	Match injuries			Training injuries		
Site of injury	Number	Incidence	95% CI	Number	Incidence	95% CI
Thigh and calf	160	174.2	148.7 to 199.6	142	38.6	32.3 to 45.0
Face	135	130.6	108.7 to 152.6	13	3.5	1.6 to 5.5
Arm and hand	122	118.0	97.0 to 139.1	21	5.7	3.3 to 8.2
Knee	131	126.8	105.0 to 148.5	47	12.8	9.1 to 16.5
Shoulder	90	87.1	69.1 to 105.1	13	3.5	1.6 to 5.5
Head and neck	89	86.1	68.3 to 103.9	10	2.7	1.0 to 4.4
Thorax and abdomen	100	96.8	77.8 to 115.7	49	13.3	9.6 to 17.1
Ankle and foot	91	88.1	70.1 to 106.1	93	25.3	20.2 to 30.4
Other	10	9.7	3.6 to 15.8	1	0.3	0.0 to 0.8

Note: Match injuries: incidence expressed per 1000 playing hours. Training injuries: incidence expressed per 1000 training hours. 95% CI = 95% confidence interval.

Table 2 Type of injury

Type of injury	Match injuries			Training injuries		
	Number	*Incidence*	*95% CI*	*Number*	*Incidence*	*95% CI*
Contusions	191	184.8	158.6 to 211.0	38	10.3	7.0 to 13.7
Muscular strains	166	160.6	136.1 to 185.1	160	43.5	36.8 to 50.3
Joint injuries	155	150.0	126.3 to 173.7	88	24.0	18.9 to 29.0
Abrasions	170	164.5	139.8 to 189.2	31	8.4	5.4 to 11.4
Haematomas	135	130.6	108.7 to 152.6	16	4.4	2.2 to 6.5
Lacerations	32	31.0	20.1 to 41.8	4	1.1	0.0 to 2.2
Concussion	36	34.8	23.4 to 46.3	1	0.3	0.0 to 0.8
Fractures and dislocations	18	17.4	9.5 to 25.4	3	0.8	0.0 to 1.7
Unspecified medical conditions	20	19.4	10.8 to 27.9	15	4.1	2.0 to 6.2
Respiratory disorders	14	13.5	6.5 to 20.6	8	2.2	0.7 to 3.7
Blisters	9	8.7	4.7 to 14.4	20	5.4	3.1 to 7.8
Overuse	—	—	—	2	0.5	0.0 to 1.3
Other	2	1.9	0.0 to 4.6	3	0.8	0.0 to 1.7

Note: Match injuries: incidence expressed per 1000 playing hours. Training injuries: incidence expressed per 1000 training hours. 95% CI = 95% confidence interval.

> Tables 1–4 give the raw data in great detail; by studying them, you can see exactly what type of injury occurs when in the season, and how severe the injuries are. Note that the tables are not designed to clearly and easily answer his question: Is there a direct relationship between intensity of exertion and rate of injury?

while joint injuries (22.6%) and contusions (9.8%) were less common. Muscular injuries were also the most common type of injury sustained during match-play (31.8%), while contusions (20.2%) and abrasions (17.9%) were less common.

Cause of injury

The causes of injuries sustained during training and match-play are shown in Table 3. Overexertion was the most common cause of training injury (35.2%). The incidence of training injuries sustained while making direct contact with another player (18.8%) or falling and stumbling (13.1%) were less common. Most injuries sustained during matches were the result of tackles (38.2%). In addition, physical collisions with fixed objects (11.8%) and direct contact with another player (22.7%) were also common causes of injury.

Severity of injury

The majority of training (97.9%) and match (92.9%) injuries were transient, resulting in no loss of playing time. Minor, moderate, and major training injuries were uncommon (Table 4).

Table 3 Cause of injury

Cause of injury	Match injuries			Training injuries		
	Number	Incidence	95% CI	Number	Incidence	95% CI
Being tackled	209	202.2	174.8 to 229.7	3	0.8	0.0 to 1.7
While tackling	153	148.0	124.5 to 171.6	2	0.5	0.0 to 1.3
Collision with fixed object	112	108.4	88.2 to 128.5	30	8.2	5.2 to 11.1
Struck by opposition player	159	153.8	130.0 to 177.8	12	3.3	1.4 to 5.1
Overexertion	75	41.6	56.0 to 89.1	137	37.3	31.1 to 43.5
Fall or stumble	66	63.9	48.5 to 79.3	51	13.9	10.1 to 17.7
Collision with player	56	54.2	40.0 to 68.4	51	13.9	10.1 to 17.7
Overuse	19	18.4	10.1 to 26.7	72	19.6	15.1 to 24.1
Temperature-related disorder	1	1.0	0.0 to 2.9	—	—	—
Twisting to pass or accelerate	2	1.9	0.0 to 4.6	—	—	—
Slip or trip	—	—	—	1	0.3	0.0 to 0.8
Scrum collapse or scrum contact	3	2.9	0.0 to 6.1	—	—	—
Struck by ball	2	1.9	0.0 to 4.6	5	1.4	0.2 to 2.5
Other	91	88.1	70.1 to 106.1	25	6.8	4.1 to 9.5

Note: Match injuries: incidence expressed per 1000 playing hours. Training injuries: incidence expressed per 1000 training hours. 95% CI = 95% confidence interval.

Table 4 Severity of injury

Severity of injury	Match injuries			Training injuries		
	Number	Incidence	95% CI	Number	Incidence	95% CI
Transient	881	852.4	796.1 to 908.8	381	103.7	93.3 to 114.1
Minor	27	26.1	16.3 to 36.0	4	1.1	0.0 to 2.2
Moderate	30	29.0	18.6 to 39.5	4	1.1	0.0 to 2.2
Major	10	9.7	3.6 to 15.8	—	—	—

Note: Match injuries: incidence expressed per 1000 playing hours. Training injuries: incidence expressed per 1000 training hours. 95% CI = 95% confidence interval.

Month of injury

The frequencies of injuries sustained during training (x^2= 121.5, d.f. = 9, P < 0.001) and match play (x^2= 117.3, d.f. = 8, P < 0.001) were significantly different throughout different months of the season (Figs. 1, 2). At the beginning of the season (December) the incidence of training injuries was 105.2 [95% CI 55.7 to 154.8] per 1000 training hours. Training injury rates increased progressively from December to February, and then declined through to the end of the season. Expressed relative to training hours, the highest number of training injuries was recorded in February (205.6 [95% CI 162.1 to 249.0] per 1000), near the beginning of the season. When injuries at the beginning and end of the season were compared (by dividing each season in half), more training injuries occurred in the first half of the season (first vs second: 69.2% vs 30.8%; x^2=103.9, d.f =1, P <0.001).

At the beginning of the competitive season (February), the incidence of match-play injuries was 935.5 [95% CI 721.9 to 1148.2] per 1000 playing hours. Match injury rates increased from February to September. The highest number of match injuries sustained in a month was 187, recorded in July. Expressed relative to playing hours, the highest number of match injuries was recorded in September (1338.5 [95% CI 058.5 to 1618.51] per 1000), at the end of the season. When injuries at the beginning and end of the season were compared (by dividing each season in half), more injuries sustained during matches occurred in the second half of the season (second vs first: 53.6% vs 46.4%; x^2= 16.2, d.f. = 1, P <0.001)....

*Relationship between incidence of injury
and training and match intensity, duration
and load*

A significant relationship (P < 0.05) was observed between changes in the incidence of training injuries and changes in training intensity (r = 0.83), training duration (r = 0.79) and training load (r = 0.86). In addition, changes in the incidence of match-play injuries were significantly correlated (P < 0.05) with changes in match intensity (r = 0.74), match duration (r = 0.86) and match load (r = 0.86).

Discussion

This is the first study to document the intensity and load associated with rugby league training sessions and matches. In addition, the relationships between training and match intensity, duration and load and the incidence of injury in rugby

---

Here are the figures we've been waiting for (or, the ones we should have started with). In clear, direct graphics, Figure 1 demonstrates that as the training intensity and duration (training load) decreases, so the training injury rate (Figure 2), we see the match intensity and duration (match load) increases. The visual demonstration of the data offers instant and convincing evidence of how the experimental results add up to useful knowledge.

The first paragraph of this section is a nice summary of the results. It says why the study is important and how it's produced knowledge not previously available.

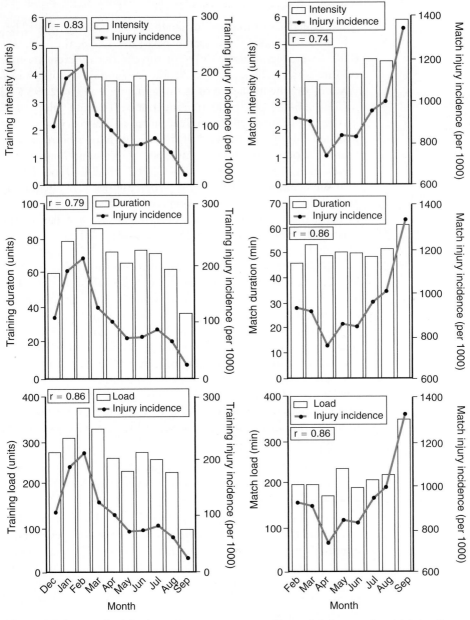

Figure 1 Influence of training intensity, duration and load on the incidence of training injuries in rugby league. Training load calculated from the product of training intensity and training duration. Units for training intensity and training load are reported as arbitrary units.

Figure 2 Influence of match intensity, duration and load on the incidence of match injuries in rugby league. Match load calculated from the product of match intensity and the time each player participated in the match. Units for match intensity and match load are reported as arbitrary units.

league has not previously been addressed. The findings of the present study demonstrate a significant positive relationship between the incidence of training injuries and the intensity, duration and load of training sessions. In addition, the incidence of match-play injuries was highly correlated with the intensity, duration and load of matches. These findings provide further support for the suggestion that injury rates in rugby league are increased with increased training and playing intensity (Gissane et al., 1993; Stephenson et al., 1996).

The incidence of training injuries was highly correlated with the intensity, duration and load of training despite the implementation of a game-specific, periodized training programme. Periodization refers to the application of sport science principles to training programme design (Bompa, 1983). The application of periodization to team sports such as rugby league is a relatively new concept (Meir, 1994), although its role in preventing unnecessarily high injury rates, and enabling athletes to reach peak performance at an appropriate stage of competition, has been well documented for individual sports (Bompa, 1983). The 38.5% increase in training load from December through to February corresponded with a 95.4% increase in the incidence of injuries sustained during training. These findings suggest that the prescribed increase in training load over the 12-week period (i.e. from December to February) was greater than was tolerable for the musculoskeletal system. Despite the significant increase in injury rates in the initial phases of the training programme, the majority of injuries were transient, resulting in no significant loss of match time. In addition, given that all three teams in the present study were successful in reaching the finals series, it could be suggested that the training programme employed was successful in attaining its goal of improving player performance. However, it should be recognized that the relationship between injury incidence and training intensity, duration and load may not be applicable to other rugby league teams who use different training programmes to the present cohort of players.

The finding that injury rates increased with the applied training load raises the question of the appropriate training stimulus required to elicit improvements in physical fitness and performance. While most injuries in the present study were transient, all injuries have the potential to impact on sporting performance (Watson, 1993). It would appear that a given training load designed to elicit improvements in performance will result in a given number of injuries and, as a consequence, will inadvertently lead to some decrement in performance. However, it is unclear if the improvement in performance provided by the

> In other words, the very program designed to get athletes in shape so they don't get injured later in the season is giving them injuries during the training itself, because it is too intense.

training stimulus is adequate to compensate for the potential reduction in performance resulting from injuries sustained while training under that same stimulus. Conversely, a poor preparation, as a result of an inadequate training stimulus, may lead to an excessive increase in match-play injuries. Therefore, the obvious challenge for rugby league conditioning coaches is to develop game-specific programmes that provide an adequate training stimulus to enhance physical fitness and performance, without unduly increasing the incidence of injury.

One function of the Discussion section is to suggest practical application of the results.

In the present study, the incidence of match-play injuries increased from the beginning to the end of the season. In addition, the incidence of these injuries was significantly correlated with the intensity, duration and load of matches. These findings are to be expected given that the intensity of matches would be expected to increase as a 'finals' series approaches. Furthermore, the lower match intensity and load associated with early season matches most probably reflects the less competitive nature of pre-season trial matches. Rugby league teams devote a significant amount of training time to the development of defensive communication skills and cohesion in attack. It is to be expected that it may take several matches for the development of these team skills to the point where playing performance is enhanced. It is unclear if the injuries sustained in the latter stages of the season impacted significantly on the playing performance of the teams in the present study. While the present study provides important information regarding the influence of match intensity on the incidence of injury, it is equally important to determine the influence of injuries on the playing performance of rugby league players.

Here the author mentions the limitations of his study. A Discussion section will tell the reader the significance of what was found but also what was not able to be determined. That's a characteristic of scientific ethics.

In the present study, the perceived intensity of training and matches was higher in Under 19 players than First Grade and Second Grade players. This finding may be expected given that Under 19 players have lower physiological capacities than First Grade and Second Grade players (Gabbett, 2002b) and, as a result, any absolute training stimulus would pose a higher relative physiological strain on these players. However, while perceived match intensity was higher in Under 19 players, the overall match load was highest in First Grade players, reflecting the sustained exposure to high-intensity activity for a longer duration in these players. The match injury rates also closely tracked the overall match load, with higher intensity matches resulting in the highest injury rates. These findings are consistent with previous studies that found higher rates of injury as the playing level and match intensity was increased (Gissane et al., 1993; Stephenson et. al., 1996). Although the match intensity and match injury rates of First Grade, Second Grade and Under 19 players were closely related, the training loads and training injury rates of the three teams were inversely related. First Grade players had the lowest perceived training intensity and load, but the highest training injury rates. A high training injury rate in First Grade players may have resulted in a higher number of training stoppages, thereby reducing active training time in these players.

A subjective measurement tool (i.e. RPE scale) was used in the present study to quantify training and match intensity. Although subjective RPE scales have been shown to have good agreement with other objective physiological indicators of intensity (e.g. heart rate, blood lactate concentration) (Foster et al., 1995; Foster, 1997), it is possible that the relationship between training and match intensity and injury incidence may have been different with a different measurement of intensity. Future studies could utilize heart rate, blood lactate concentration or other physiological markers to quantify the relationship between injury incidence and intensity. Alternatively, recent evidence has shown that the speed of matches may influence the incidence of injury in team sport athletes (Norton et al., 2001). The use of video analysis would permit the quantification of training and match speed, thereby providing a more objective estimate of training and match intensity.

In summary, the present study examined the influence of training and match intensity, duration and load on the incidence of injury over the course of a season in rugby league players. The findings suggest that as the intensity, duration and load of rugby league training sessions and matches is increased, the incidence of injury is also increased. Further studies are required to determine the appropriate training stimulus required to enhance the physical fitness and performance of rugby league players, without unduly increasing the incidence of injury.

Side notes:

In other words, the matches seemed harder for the younger, less experienced players, but in fact the older, better players were working harder during their (more intense) matches.

Researchers often critique their own methods to reveal more limitations of the study. While they did the work, they need to be objective about the strengths and weaknesses of their experiments.

The suggested studies could be done by this researcher or others who are interested in the study.

References

Bompa, T.U. (1983). *Theory and Methodology of Training. The Key to Athletic Performance*. Dubuque, IA: Kendall-Hunt.

Brewer, J. and Davis, J. (1995). Applied physiology of rugby league. *Sports Medicine*, 20, 129–135.

Coutts, A., Reaburn, P. and Aht, G. (2003). Heart rate, blood lactate concentration and estimated energy expenditure in a semi-professional rugby league team during a march: a case study. *Journal of Sports Sciences*, 21, 97, 103.

Dunbar, C.C., Robertson, R.J., Baun, R. et al. (1992). The validity of regulating exercise intensity by ratings of perceived exertion. *Medicine and Science in Sports and Exercise*, 24, 94–99.

Finch, C.F., Valuri, G. and Ozanne-Smith, J. (1999). Injury surveillance during medical coverage of sporting events—development and testing of a standardised data collection form. *Journal of Science and Medicine in Sport*, 2, 42–56.

Foster, C. (1997). Monitoring training in athletes with reference to over-training syndrome. *Medicine and Science in Sports and Exercise*, 30, 1164–1168.

Foster, C., Hector, L.L., Welsh, R. et at. (1995). Effects of specific versus cross-training on running performance. *European Journal of Applied Physiology*, 70, 367–372.

Foster, C., Florhaug, J.A., Franklin, J. et at. (2001). A new approach to monitoring exercise training. *Journal of Strength and Conditioning Research*, 15, 109–115.

Gabbett, T. J. (2000a). Incidence, site, and nature of injuries in amateur rugby league over three consecutive seasons. *British Journal of Sports Medicine*, 34, 98–103.

Gabbett, T. J. (2000b). Physiological and athropometric characteristics of amateur rugby league players. *British Journal of Sports Medicine*, 34, 303–307.

Gabbett, T. J. (2001). Severity and cost of injuries in amateur rugby league: a case study. *Journal of Sports Sciences*, 19, 311–347.

Gabbett, T. J. (2002a). Influence of physiological characteristics on selection in a semi-professional rugby league team: a case study. *Journal of Sports Sciences*, 20, 399–405.

Gabbett, T.J. (2002b). Physiological characteristics of junior and senior rugby league players. *British Journal of Sports Medicine*, 36, 334–339.

Gabbett, T.J. (2002c). Training injuries in rugby league: an evaluation of skill-based conditioning games. *Journal of Strength and Conditioning Research*, 16, 236–241.

Gabbett, T.J. (2003). Incidence of injury in semi-professional rugby league players. *British Journal of Sports Medicine*, 37, 36–43.

Gibbs, N. (1993). Injuries in professional rugby league. a three-year prospective study of the South Sydney professional rugby league club. *American Journal of Sports Medicine*, 21, 696–700.

Gissane, C., Jennings, D.C. and Standing, P. (1993). Incidence of injury in rugby league football. *Physiotherapy*, 79, 305–310.

Gissane, C., Jennings, D., Jennings, S., White, J. and Kerr, K. (2001a). Physical collisions and injury rates in professional super league rugby. *Cleveland Medical Journal*, 4, 147—155.

Gissane, C., White, J., Kerr, K. and Jennings, D. (2001b). Physical collisions in professional super league: the demands of different player positions. *Cleveland Medical Journal*, 4, 137–146.

Hodgson-Phillips, L., Standen, P.J. and Batt, M.E. (1998). Effects of seasonal change in rugby league on the incidence of injury. *British Journal of Sports Medicine*, 32, 144–148.

Meir, R. (1994). A model for the integration of macrocycle and microcycle structure in professional rugby league. *Strength and Conditioning Coach*, 2, 6–12.

Meir, R., Arthur, D. and Forrest, M. (1993). Time and motion analysis of professional rugby league: a case study. *Strength and Conditioning Coach*, 1, 24–29.

Norton; K., Schwerdt, S. and L.ar:ge, K (2001). Evidence for the aetiology of injuries in Australian football. *British Journal of Sports Medicine*, 35, 418–423.

Stephenson, S., Gissane, C. and Jennings, D. (1996). Injury in rugby league: a four year prospective study. *British Journal of Sports Medicine*, 30, 331–334.

Watson, A. S. (1993). Incidence and nature of sports injuries in Ireland: analysis of four types of sport. *American Journal of Sports Medicine*, 21, 137–143.

READING RESPONSES

1. When you read the Results section, which presentation of data was easiest for you to understand—the written version or the tables? Why?
2. In the Results section, the author presents some data in tables and some in bar graphs. Present the information in Table 1 as a bar graph and compare the two: which presentation is more effective? Now create a bar graph for the information in Table 4. Which presentation is more effective? Based on your experience, what factors would you consider when choosing a table or a bar graph for information?
3. Re-read the "Nature of Injury" paragraph in the Results section and Table 2. What function do the words fulfill? What function does the table fulfill?

NOTES ON GRAMMAR, STYLE, AND RHETORIC: PASSIVE VERBS

One significant controversy about scientific prose centers on the question of whether scientists should use verbs in the passive voice. What kind of verbs are these? To begin, they are transitive verbs, verbs that signal the transfer of action from an agent onto some kind of recipient. When transitive verbs appear in the active voice, the agent is expressed as the subject of the sentence, and the recipient is expressed as the direct object:

The head trainer [agent] *classified* [action] *the injury* [recipient].

When these verbs appear in the passive voice, the recipient is expressed in the subject, and the agent is usually expressed after the verb in a prepositional phrase:

The injury [recipient] *was classified* [action] *by the head trainer* [agent].

Sometimes, however, writers choose to delete the reference to the agent:

The injury was classified.

When writers are deciding between the active and the passive voice of a verb, they choose whether to focus on the agent (active voice) or on the recipient (passive voice) of the action.

Writers should be cautious about using passive verbs for several reasons. First, a sentence with a passive verb will typically be longer than the corresponding sentence with an active verb (as in first two of the earlier examples).

Second, passive verbs do not depict actions as directly and energetically as active verbs do:

Active: *Reckless players sometimes break an arm or a leg.*

Passive: *An arm or a leg is sometimes broken by reckless players.*

Although both sentences depict the same activity, the passive sentence has more of a static quality than does the active sentence.

Third, studies of language processing have shown that a sentence is easier to read when it presents the agent before the action and the action before the recipient. Sentences with passive verbs, you recall, move from the recipient through the action to the agent.

Finally, when writers use passive verbs and omit references to agents, they can mask responsibility:

The toxic chemicals were marketed as environmentally safe.

Who marketed the chemicals? No one can tell. In some cases, then, writers intentionally use passives to avoid revealing who the agents of actions are. And when these actions fall into the realm of the unethical, so does the use of passive verbs.

On the basis of these and related cautionary notes, the fifth edition of *The Council of Biology Editors Style Manual* advises scientists to avoid passive verbs in their writing. But why is this advice ignored by so many scientists? And is it possible that you could have good reasons to use some passive verbs in your own scientific writing?

You can take a significant step toward answering these questions by examining the functions of passives in the scientific report on rugby injuries. This report contains over sixty verbs in the passive voice. These verbs appear in every major section of the report, but most of them appear in the Methods section. What kinds of functions does the author use passive verbs to fulfill?

First, he uses passive verbs to present what he views as facts of the world of rugby. For instance, early in the report he writes, "During the course of a match, players are exposed to many physical collisions and tackles ..." (page 232). The effect of this sentence is clear: Injuries occur; to whom they occur does not matter, so passive voice is the right choice.

A second function of passives has to do with how the author presents the details of his own research. That is, he presents his preparations for research, the steps involved in that research, the results of that research, and his interpretation of those results as if there were no agent at all associated with any of these activities. For example, he uses subject–verb combinations such as these: "The intensity of individual training sessions was estimated," "Training load was calculated," "Injury rates were calculated," "A total of 389 training injuries were recorded" (234), "A subjective measurement tool (i.e. RPE scale) was used" (241), and "Further studies are required" (241). In all these statements, references to the author and experimenter do not occur. In fact, in the entire report the words *I* and *me* never appear. (Quotations not followed by a page reference come from parts of the paper not reproduced here.)

When scientists report on their research and leave out all or almost all references to themselves as the agents, they are usually aiming for at least two effects. For one thing, they hope to keep their readers focused on the scientific objects and processes, an effect that would be difficult to achieve if some sentences included references to agents (as in *We classified almost 400 training injuries*). For another thing, they imply that whatever preparing, experimenting, calculating, and interpreting they do would come out exactly the same way even if other researchers took these tasks over. The implied invitation to other researchers is to try out the described experiment for themselves and see that their repetition of the experiment will in fact turn out exactly as the original did. In this way, many people argue, passive verbs reflect and even support the fundamental practices of science.

But as I have indicated from the start, not everyone accepts this argument. Some people, for instance, say that behind every experiment there are real experimenters and that it would be more honest if they were to come right out and refer to themselves as the agents of the experimental actions.

So ... the most important style guide for biologists advises the use of active voice, but most publications in biology contain many passive voice constructions. Assume that the debate doesn't continue out of stubbornness; there are good and bad reasons for using passive voice in the sciences. It's clear that you will need to be purposeful in your choices.

In Your Own Writing ...

• Be alert for passive verbs that mask responsibility for unethical actions. Point them out in what you read, and avoid them in your own writing.

- Determine your reader's attitude toward passive verbs and take that into consideration as you draft.
- Use passive verbs when you want to focus the reader's attention on the action or the recipient of the action rather than on the agent of the action.

STUDENT WRITING IN BIOLOGY

Introduction by Stephanie McElroy, biology major

The Assignment. My genetics teacher asked us to produce a standard lab report, based on the model of a published research paper in a scientific journal. We worked in teams to generate experimental data and then wrote a report in a standard introduction, materials and methods, results, and discussion format. In this way we learned to produce, analyze, and present experimental data in the same way that professional scientists do—and learned some lessons about genetics along the way.

The Content. Of course our "writing" began well before we sat at our computers to generate our reports. All scientific papers begin with the collection of data from an experiment. The first week of the semester, we set up our genetic experiment. We wanted to test the linkage between three mutant genes in fruit flies. That is, we wanted to see if the genes are near each other on the chromosome—and therefore inherited together. The mutations affect the appearance of the flies. Normal flies have long wings, red eyes, and yellow bodies. One mutation causes the wings to be vestigial (stunted), another causes the eyes to be brown, and the last one makes the flies' bodies black. Other scientists had already proven that the genes were linked, but we wanted to replicate their data. The first four weeks were spent mating mutant and normal flies with each other: first learning how to anesthetize flies without killing them, then identifying males and females, and finally putting them together so they would mate. The flies mated and laid eggs, eggs hatched and larvae grew, and then mature flies appeared. We took some of these mature flies and mated them back to mutant flies, and then let their offspring develop. The appearance of these second generation flies would tell us if the mutant genes are linked to each other. In the fifth week of the experiment we looked at these flies and scored their appearance for all three traits: wing shape, eye color, and body color. The numbers we found formed the central part of the paper.

Just like in a "real" scientific paper, we each started actually writing our reports by generating and analyzing figures. In this case, the main figure is a data table that lists the number of each type of fly found (see Table 1). (The tables and graphs are so important that some professors have us turn in the tables and graphs weeks before the formal lab report is due, to check our work). In our experiment, we found mostly two types of flies: those with yellow bodies, normal wings, and red eyes, or those with black bodies, vestigial wings, and brown eyes (see the left column of Table 1). These flies looked just like their parents. We also found very few flies that had a mixture of the characteristics, like red eyes, normal wings, and black bodies. Since we were studying genetics, we knew already that if genes are linked, their characteristics would travel together most of the time. So since most of the time if a fly had red eyes she also had normal wings, the genes for these two traits are next to each other in her mother's DNA, so she gets them together. If the genes were far apart from each other, she'd be just as likely to have red eyes and vestigial wings. Once we finished making the table of our data, we could easily see that the three genes are linked.

Learning to Write Lab Reports in Biology. After our data tables were created, I sat down to write my report. In the Results section, I simply presented the data that my partner and I collected, with a descriptive title. I also learned to "anchor" each table or figure, which means to include at least one sentence that refers to it in the text. (I had a high school teacher who went crazy if tables weren't anchored and would take several points off and then make you fix it, so anchoring is a habit now.)

The Results tell *what* data I found; the Discussion section tells *why* they are worth finding—the greater significance. My Discussion referenced the data presented in the Results section and reported that it supports my hypothesis. Finally, good research leads to more research, so I gave suggestions for new experiments based on the conclusions of this study or what I would do better if I had to do this again.

In general, I found the Methods section easiest to write; I pretended I was explaining the experiment to a friend from class who missed the lab.

The Introduction can be the hardest part. I had to learn to throw my old notions of creativity out the window. I asked myself the relevance of the experiment outside of this class and answered that question in the first few sentences of the Introduction. The next part of the Introduction explained the background concepts that the experiment studies, which are what we were discussing in the lecture part of class. Then, I described the actual questions asked by the study.

Creating Change through Writing in Biology. When I first started thinking about being a science major, I was in awe of the great things science does—finding cures, unraveling the mysteries of DNA. When I had to do my first lab reports, they felt like busywork. But eventually I learned to love labs. They let me see the way scientists really work. Science is mostly adding little bits of highly specialized information to a bigger picture (in this case, the big picture of genetics). Once you see how all the little results add up to major fields of knowledge, then you believe that the little pieces you add contribute to important changes. Theories get clarified and knowledge gets applied and you end up with better medicine, technology, etc. You really cannot have change in science without the little pieces.

Writing up labs also reminds me of how amazing nature is, which is how studying science has changed me. You study these crazy little fruit flies, and genetics starts to make sense. That makes me love science and want to add more of those little pieces to the big pictures. And those little pieces, even by themselves, are wonderful. Knowing that I can figure out how and why a fruit fly ends up with mutated wings and does or doesn't pass them on to offspring . . . it just doesn't get much cooler than that.

Lab Report: Linkage between 3 Genes in Drosophila

Stephanie McElroy

Introduction

Inheritance is at work everywhere in the world around us. From a human family resemblance to a tree that drops seeds that grow into more of the same tree, we see that organisms reproduce to create offspring similar to themselves. The field that studies this phenomenon is known as genetics.

Parent organisms replicate their own genetic information and pass a portion or all of it to their offspring. In sexually reproducing organisms, half of the parent's information is packaged in a haploid gamete (the product of merging egg and sperm), which unites with another gamete to form a diploid offspring. So, the offspring contains genetic information from both parents.

In this experiment, we studied the linkage of three mutant genes in *drosophila melanogaster* (fruit flies). The mutations in the flies caused a black body, vestigial wings, and brown eyes. The experiments showed that all three genes are linked. The vestigial wings gene is in the middle on the chromosome, with the black body 13 map units (a measure of distance between genes on a chromosome) away on one side and the brown eyes 17 map units away on the other.

Materials and Methods

We obtained triple mutant flies (black bodies, vestigial wings, and brown eyes) and wild-type flies (yellow bodies, normal wings, and red eyes). We made two new tubes of media (in which to breed and nourish the flies) and crossed mutant males with wild type virgin females and wild type males with mutant virgin females in separate tubes. We stored the flies on the bench top. One week later, we checked for larvae in the tubes and removed and disposed of the parent flies to prevent offspring from mating with parents.

One week later we scored the sex and phenotypes (a measurable characteristic such as eye color) of the F1 generation for each tube. We discarded all of the flies and made a new tube with two fully mutant males (from stock, the flies we started with) in it. We collected two newly hatched virgin females from the F1 cross and added them to this tube the next day. In the next mating, we mated flies with one mutant and one normal

---

Using first-person and active verbs felt strange at first, but we got used to telling the story of the experiment as if we were talking to our teacher.

Most complex animals and plants are diploid: they have two copies of every gene (one from each parent). When they reproduce, they make haploid eggs and sperm: they only have one copy of each gene. When an egg and sperm join, they make a new, diploid organism.

Linkage tells us how close different genes are to each other on a chromosome. If genes are close together, they will be inherited together more often.

To determine if the genes are linked, we mated nine crossed normal flies with mutant flies. The offspring will have one normal and one mutant copy of each gene. How these copies are passed on to their offspring (the next generation) will tell us how close the genes are to each other.

F1 is the first generation: offspring of the first parents mated.

copy of each gene with a fly that had all mutant genes. If two normal genes end up in the offspring (red eyes and normal wings) more often than not, then the red eye gene and the normal wing gene are probably near each other. A few days later, we checked for larvae from this cross and discarded the flies in the tube.

One week later, we removed any flies that had hatched and placed them in a separate tube for scoring after further maturation. The week after that, we scored those flies and again moved any flies that had hatched in the original tube to a new one. We discarded the original tube. Two days later, we scored those flies.

Results

The F1 flies' phenotypes were comparable for both of the reciprocal crosses. There was a 1:1 ratio of males to females, and all F1 flies were wild-type for all three traits, which shows that the wild-type traits were dominant to the mutants and were not sex linked. F1 females were crossed with mutant males to produce the results for gene mapping shown in Table 1.

Since the number of flies in each phenotype in the table is not evenly distributed, we can see that the genes are indeed linked. The results in Table 1 also allow us to determine the order of the genes and the map-distance between them. The double crossover flies are those with b vg+ bw or b+ vg bw+, which means that vg is the middle gene on the chromosome. The distance between genes was calculated using the following equation: (number of crossovers/total number scored) x 100. This formula uses the raw data (number of flies scored) to calculate map distance.

The distance from vg to b is: $3/23 \times 100 = 13$ map units.

The distance from vg to bw is: $4/23 \times 100 = 14$ map units.

Discussion

If genes are linked, they will consistently appear in offspring together. In the test cross (the second mating), the offspring have an expected ratio of 1:1 for each trait. Since the combination of all three wild-type genes and all three mutant genes (like the parents) are the most common phenotypes, it appears that all three genes are linked. The data in the left column of Table 1 show this linkage. This can be further tested since genes that are not linked will be calculated at 50 map units apart.

The least common combinations were the black body, normal wings, and brown eyes and its sister phenotype yellow

---

Sidebar notes:

In the first cross, whether it was the mother or father that was mutant, we always got the same result: all the flies are normal. So we know that the genes for brown eyes, black body, and vestigial wings are not on the sex chromosomes, and the mutations are recessive: a fly with one normal and one mutant copy of a gene will still look normal. In other words the normal copies of the gene are dominant over the recessive copies.

Double crossover refers to a chromosomal rearrangement during the formation of gametes. This type of rearrangement is very rare; its occurrence can tell us which of the three linked genes is in the middle (between the other two).

That is, to mix up the genes this much, the chromosomes had to be altered twice, which is very rare.

Table 1 Number of Flies with Each Phenotype

Phenotype	Flies	Phenotype	Flies	Phenotype	Flies	Phenotype	Flies
b+ vg+ bw+	13	b vg+ bw+	1	b vg bw+	2	b vg+ bw	0
b vg bw	4	b+ vg bw	1	b+ vg+ bw	1	b+ vg bw+	1

Key: b = black body, b+ = yellow body, vg = vestigial wings,
vg+ = normal wings, bw = brown eyes, bw+ = red eyes.
A b+ vg+ bw+ fly is black bodied, normal winged, red eyed.
A b vg+ bw+ fly is black bodied, normal winged, red eyed.

body, vestigial wings and red eyes. Since it is hardly seen at all, it is probably the result of the rare double crossover. The trait that differs from the parents is the switch of vg and vg+. The gene for vestigial wings is the middle gene. To determine the distance between two genes, we counted the number of flies that exhibited the opposite phenotype of the parents, a sign of crossing over. The more crossing over that occurs, the farther the genes are apart. By calculating the crossing over between vg and b, the distance is calculated to be 13 map units. There is more crossing over between vg and bw, and those genes are further apart on the chromosome.

One difficulty in this part of the experiment was scoring the eye color. It was difficult for us to distinguish between red and brown. This problem affected our results. Since the F1 female parent is heterozygous (having one normal and one mutant gene for all three characteristics), half of her offspring should have brown eyes and half should have red eyes. Looking at our data, it seems that we erred on the side of red since regardless of body color and wing shape, there are more flies with red eyes than with brown eyes (17 red vs. 6 brown). The data would be better if in further experiments flies were able to develop even further or eye color was tagged with another closely linked phenotype. Our map distances would also probably be closer to the actual distances if we had scored more flies.

By mating flies and scoring their offspring, we were able to study the inheritance of three mutant genes in Drosophila: vestigial wings, black body, and brown eyes. We learned that the genes are linked and so travel together in offspring. As we did our crosses, we also learned about experimental techniques and how do improve our experimental design. Finally, we were able to observe first hand the way in which all organisms pass genetic material on to their offspring, continuing their characteristics to the next generation.

READING RESPONSES

1. Re-read McElroy's introduction. Then compare her introduction to the introduction to "Influence of training and match intensity on injuries in rugby league." How does each author introduce the topic? How are these introductions similar? What differences do you notice? Which introduction do you prefer?
2. McElroy says that Table 1 is the most important part of her lab report. What is the most important information in this table? Describe that information in your own words.
3. Consider McElroy's Discussion section. List the recommendations she makes for future research. What is the relationship between these recommendations and her results?

PUBLIC WRITING IN BIOLOGY

Introduction

"The Female Hurt," a paper published in the magazine *Scientific American*, uses a mixture of illustrations and figures to explain why female athletes have a different rate and pattern of injuries than male athletes. In some ways, the article looks very different than the other articles in this chapter. It begins with a "catchy" title that gives very little specific information, and it also has anatomical drawings that are "artist renderings" of the human body. In other ways, it looks a lot like the other papers in this chapter. The author quotes scientific studies that involve experimental and control subjects, cites specific numbers, and embeds three graphs in the text. The hybrid nature of the paper reflects its intended audience. *Scientific American* articles are written for non-experts who have a general interest in news-making science.

Keeping in mind the chapter's portable rhetorical lesson, think about the figures in the article. You will notice how clearly and effectively the results are conveyed by the figures. The difference between male and female injury rate and participation in sports is made obvious, at a glance, by the bar graphs.

The figures in this paper share another characteristic with figures in journals published for experts. While the author of this paper did not collect the data and did not design her paper around her lab work, she still would have started with these figures, as they tell the core of the story. The paper is centered on the following observation: female athletes have a higher rate of ACL injury. This fact (and the graph that conveys it) comprises what amounts to the "results" section: explanations of why the injury rate is higher are equivalent to the introduction and discussion.

The Female Hurt

Marguerite Holloway

Scientific American 2000, 11(3): 32–37.

"I don't want to hear a bunch of thuds," bellows Deborah Saint-Phard from her corner of the basketball court. Several dozen young women and girls, some barefoot, some in jeans and tank tops, some in full athletic regalia, look sheepish. They jump again, trying to keep their knees slightly bent and facing straight forward, trying to make no noise when their feet hit the floor. "I can hear you landing," Saint-Phard nonetheless admonishes, urging them into a softer touchdown. "Control your jump."

Saint-Phard is a doctor with the Women's Sports Medicine Center at the Hospital for Special Surgery in New York City. She and several colleagues have traveled to this gymnasium in Philadelphia for "Hoop City"—a National Collegiate Athletic Association (NCAA) event—to teach young women how to jump safely. Female athletes, particularly those playing basketball, volleyball and soccer, are between five and eight times more likely than men are to injure their anterior cruciate ligament, or ACL, which stabilizes the knee. Some 20,000 high school girls and 10,000 female college students suffer debilitating knee injuries each year, the majority of which are ACL-related, according to the American Orthopedic Society for Sports Medicine. Tearing the ligament can put an athlete out of the game for months, if not forever.

"This is a huge public health problem for women," says Edward M. Wojtys, an orthopedic surgeon at the University of Michigan. "Fourteen- to 18-year-olds are subjected to injuries that many of them will never recover from, that will affect whether they can walk or exercise at 40 and 50." For this reason, physicians are placing new emphasis on teaching female athletes how to jump in such a way that they strengthen their knees and protect their ACLs. "We have to get them when they are young," Saint-Phard says.

Torn ACLs are just one of the medical problems that plague female athletes. Injuries and ailments that occur with higher incidence in women than in men are garnering more attention as women enter sports in record numbers—not only as Olympians and professionals but for fitness and recreation. Today 135,110 women participate in collegiate athletics, according to the NCAA, up from 29,977 in 1972. The number of girls playing high school sports has shot up from 294,015 to 2.5 million in the same time frame. As a result, researchers, physicians and coaches are increasingly recognizing that girls and women engaged in sports have some distinct medical concerns.

This makes perfect sense. Women's bodies are shaped differently than men's, and they are influenced by different hormones. They may be at greater risk not only for ACL tears but for other knee problems, as well as for certain shoulder injuries. Women are also uniquely threatened by a condition called the female athlete triad: disordered eating habits, menstrual dysfunction or the loss of their menstrual cycle,

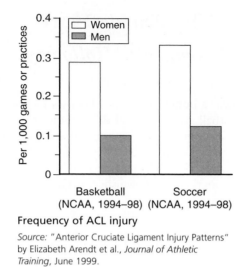

Frequency of ACL injury

Source: "Anterior Cruciate Ligament Injury Patterns"
by Elizabeth Arendt et al., *Journal of Athletic
Training,* June 1999.

and, as a consequence of these two changes, premature and permanent osteoporosis. "We are seeing 25-year-olds with the bones of 70-year-olds," Saint-Phard says.

Although the passage of Title IX legislation in 1972 required that institutions receiving federal funding devote equal resources to men's and women's
sports, it has taken a while for the particular needs of female athletes to emerge.
As an example, Wojtys points to the ACL: "It took us 15 to 18 years to realize
that this problem existed." Women entering sports even a decade and a half after
Title IX received less care from coaches and physicians than male athletes did,
says Saint-Phard, who competed in the 1988 Olympic shot-put event. When she
was in college, she recalls, "the men's teams got a lot more resources and a
different level of coaches than the women's teams."

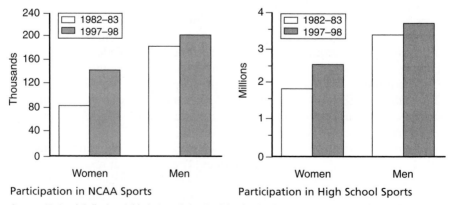

Participation in NCAA Sports   **Participation in High School Sports**

Sources: National Collegiate Athletic Association Participation Statistics Report, 1982–98; National Federation
of State High School Associations Participation Study.

And today even those conditions that are increasingly well recognized as more problematic for women are not fully understood, and their etiology and treatment remain controversial at times. "There is not enough awareness of the differences," says Regina M. Vidaver of the Society for Women's Health Research. For most of the people treating sports injuries, she explains, "their predominant history is with men.". . .

Tearing into ACL Injuries

The most obvious musculoskeletal difference between men and women is the breadth of their hips. Because a woman's pelvis tends to be wider, the muscles that run from the hip down to the knee pull the kneecap (the patella) out to the side more, sometimes causing what is called patellofemoral syndrome—a painful condition that appears to occur more frequently in women. In men, the muscle and bone run more directly vertically, putting less lateral pull on the patella. Some studies also indicate that women's joints and muscles may tend to be more lax than men's; although this adds to greater flexibility, it may mean that female joints and muscles are not necessarily as stable.

Increased laxity and differences in limb alignment may contribute to ACL injuries among female athletes. And yet, even though physicians and coaches first recognized in the 1980s that female athletes were more prone to this injury, there is still no resolution about the cause. "It is an area of controversy," observes Joseph Bosco, an orthopedic surgeon at New York University. . . .

Recent studies indicating that ACL injuries can be prevented by training women to jump differently and to develop their hamstring muscles suggest that inadequate training is at least a large part of the problem. "We train and condition women in the same way that we do the men," says Wojtys, who showed in a 1999 study that women tend not to bend their knees as much as men do when they land a jump, thereby increasing the pressure of the impact on the joints. "They probably need their own training programs."

The Cincinnati Sportsmedicine and Orthopaedic Center focuses on just such an approach. In 1996 Frank R. Noyes and his colleagues there followed 11 high school girl volleyball players who went through Sportsmetrics, a grueling six-week jump-training program the researchers had created. They found that all the participants improved their hamstring strength and that all but one were able to reduce their landing forces, placing less stress on their knees as a result (and achieving the "quiet landing" Saint-Phard was looking for in Philadelphia).

The investigators went on to follow two new groups of female athletes—those who did this strength training and those who did not—as well as a group of male athletes without Sportsmetrics. In an article published last year in the *American Journal of Sports Medicine*, the authors, led by Timothy E. Hewett, reported that only two of the 366 trained female athletes (and two of the 434 male athletes) suffered serious knee injuries, whereas 10 of the 463 untrained women did. They concluded that specially trained female athletes were 1.3 to 2.4 times more likely to have a serious knee injury than the male athletes were, whereas the untrained females were 4.8 to 5.8 times more likely.

The idea that better, or perhaps more, training could have a strong effect on injury rates is supported by work with another set of women: army recruits. According to a recent study by Nicole S. Bell of the Boston University School of Public Health, female recruits were twice as likely to suffer injuries during basic combat training than men were—and two and a half times more likely to have serious injuries. . . .

Noyes is also working to redress another sports medicine imbalance. Historically, men have been more likely than women to have knee surgery. Noyes believes that there are two reasons. First, knee surgery used to be a difficult procedure with often poor outcomes, so it was limited to athletes who really "needed" it—in other words, professional male athletes. Second, there has been a perception among physicians that women would not fare as well during the often painful surgery and recovery. So Noyes and his colleagues decided to examine the responses of both men and women to ACL surgery. They determined that although women took slightly longer to heal, both sexes fared equally well in the long run.

Noyes's work on surgery outcomes and the growing consensus about the importance of neuromuscular control appear to have shifted some attention away from another area of ACL injury investigation: hormonal influences. Researchers have found that the ACL has estrogen and progesterone receptors—target sites that respond to those two hormones. In studies in animals and in vitro, they have discovered that the presence of estrogen decreases the synthesis of collagen fibers, the building blocks of ligaments. It also increases the levels of another hormone, relaxin, which in turn adds to the disorganization of collagen fibers. This change in the ligaments makes the ACL more flexible and, according to the hypothesis, more vulnerable to injury.

This view seems supported by some studies, including one by Wojtys published two years ago in the *American Journal of Sports Medicine*. He and his team questioned 40 women with ACL injuries; the majority of the tears occurred during ovulation, when estrogen levels were highest. Other studies show some increased muscle laxity in ovulating women, but nothing dramatic. . . .

"Estrogen probably has some role," notes Jo A. Hannafin, orthopedic director at the Women's Sports Medicine Center. But, she says, no one is applying the studies' findings to the court—limiting, say, what time of month a player should or should not play. The hormonal result "just reinforces old stereotypes," Bosco adds. "It takes weeks and weeks for the effects [of estrogen] to be seen, so it doesn't make sense. We still strongly encourage women to participate in athletics over the whole month."

Treating the Triad

Estrogen's role in the other major health threat to female athletes is not at all controversial. Exercise or poor eating, or both, can cause an athlete's body to develop an energy deficit, become stressed and lose essential nutrients. Any or all of these changes can cause levels of follicular-stimulating and luteinizing hormones to fall and ovulation to therefore cease. Absent their menstrual cycles, young athletes do not have the requisite estrogen at precisely the time they need the hormone the most to help retain calcium and lay down bone. By the age of 17, nearly all a

young woman's bone has been established, explains Melinda M. Manore, a professor of nutrition at Arizona State University. If an athlete's level of estrogen
remains low, she can start to lose bone mass at a rapid rate, which can lead to stress
fractures and, if the process is not curbed, premature osteoporosis.

The phrase "female athlete triad" was coined in 1992 by participants at an
American College of Sports Medicine meeting. Since then, anecdotal reports have
indicated that the occurrence of the triad is on the rise. "I think young women are
more and more aware of their body size," Manore says. Furthermore, female
athletes are especially vulnerable.

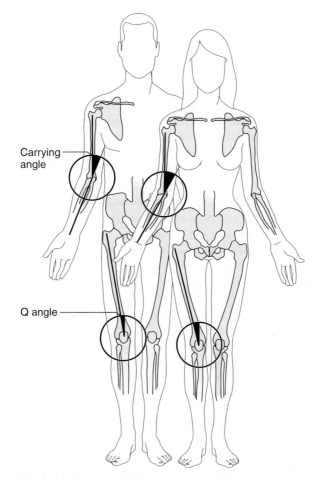

The Inside Story on Injury

The skeletons of women differ from men's most visibly in the
width of the pelvis. As a result, women have a wider Q angle
(a measure of bone alignment from hip to knee) and carrying
angle (from upper to lower arm), which can lead, respectively,
to higher rates of knee and elbow or shoulder injuries.

Eating disorders—such as obsessive dieting, calorie restriction or aversion to fat (all labeled disordered eating), as well as anorexia and bulimia (the so-called classic eating disorders)—are disproportionately high in girls and women who participate regularly in sports. Averaged across various sports, some 30 percent of these individuals have an eating problem, as opposed to 10 to 15 percent of the general population— although no one knows for sure, because no large-scale studies on prevalence have been conducted in the U.S. The proportion may be as high as 70 percent in some sports. "High achievers, perfectionists, goal setters, people who are compulsive and determined—those are the things that characterize our best athletes," says Margot Putukian, a team physician at Pennsylvania State University. Those are also the very qualities that often lead people into problem eating.

And athletic culture—particularly for swimmers, runners, skiers, rowers and gymnasts—only continues to reinforce these behaviors and expectations. Many coaches encourage their athletes to lose weight so they can be faster or have less mass to move through acrobatic maneuvers. According to a recent study, female gymnasts weigh 20 pounds less than those in the 1970s did. And many female athletes at all levels see losing their period as a badge of honor.

"They don't see it as a negative," Putukian explains. "They see it as something that happens when you get in shape, a sign that you are training adequately." What they also don't see is what is happening to their bones—until they develop stress fractures. "They fly through their adolescent years with no knowledge of why being too thin is dangerous," Saint-Phard says.

Treating the triad is challenging, and, as Putukian notes, "there is not a lot of great data to tell us what is the best thing." Researchers now recognize that female athletes experiencing these problems need the combined talents of a physician, a nutritionist and, if they have bulimia or anorexia, a psychologist—a multidisciplinary team that most schools and colleges lack. "When you have a kid who has an eating disorder, it is very frustrating," Putukian says. "It is reversible if you catch it early on, irreversible if you don't." She tells her athletes—who are all questioned about their menses and their eating habits during their initial physical—that if they haven't had their period for three months, they are in danger.

Putukian tries to get them on a birth-control pill and works with them to change their eating habits if they have a problem. But although the pill restores some hormonal activity, it does not provide the requisite levels for normal bone development. And hormone replacement therapy, which is used by some physicians, has not been extensively tested in young women. Nevertheless, Putukian notes that athletes may be easier to treat than women in the general population because there is an incentive: competition. "It is an incredible tool," she says. "You can help kids come back." Putukian has refused to let several athletes compete until they got their weight up to healthy levels; their desire to participate drove them to improve their eating habits.

Putukian, Manore and others would like to see young women better educated about the consequences of excessive dieting and amenorrhea. They admit that little can be done about the cultural pressures facing young women—the unrealistic icons of emaciated beauty that destroy many self-images.

But they believe that if girls understand that they may be jeopardizing their freedom to take a simple jog in their 30s without fracturing their osteoporotic hips or leg bones, they will change their behavior.

The investigators hope that athletes will focus on how they feel and how they perform, rather than on how much they weigh. But as with the jump-training program to prevent ACL injuries, there remains a great divide between the medical community's recommendations and the reality of the track or court or gymnasium. Only when those are fully integrated will Title IX have truly fulfilled its promise.

READING RESPONSES

1. Introductions to the first two readings in this chapter indicate that graphics need to be "anchored" in the text. That is, the writers use words to explain the tables, graphs, figures, etc. Note two places in this article where the author fails to do this and describe why each is ineffective.
2. In this article, the author and others make two claims that seem to be contradictory. First, female athletes have been hurt because they have been treated like male athletes. Second, female athletes have been hurt because they have not been treated like male athletes. How have they been treated like males? How have they not? Are these two claims contradictory after all?
3. Compare the introduction to this article to the introduction to "Influence of training and match intensity on injuries in rugby league" and to McElroy's introduction to her lab report. Which two are most alike? Why do you think these authors chose the rhetorical strategies they used for their introductions?

MORE WRITING IN BIOLOGY

Introduction

In 1953, two relatively unknown scientists published a one-page scientific paper that changed the future of biology. It had only one figure, a simple line drawing showing two intertwined spiraling lines with horizontal bars connecting them. Although the figure appears to be a quickly-sketched doodle on the margin of a paper, the drawing's simplicity is deceptive. Rather than being an attractive illustration that enhances the main points of the paper, the drawing *is* the entire reason for the paper. This drawing marks the first time that a DNA molecule was correctly described, and the authors, James Watson and Francis Crick, won the Nobel Prize for their work.

It's hard for us to believe that the structure of DNA was once a mystery, but in the early 1950s, several different scientific groups were locked in a heated race to determine exactly how DNA is put together.* Watson and Crick won the race by combining sophisticated analysis of detailed chemical data (provided by Rosalind Franklin) with good old-fashioned ingenuity. They first determined what was known about the size and shape of nucleotides; these building blocks are individual molecules that are linked together to make longs chains of DNA. (The different sequences of nucleotides determine different genes, the same way different sequences of letters signify different words.) Next, they built models by assembling the nucleotides to see how best they fit together in a way that matched the data about DNA. It turns out that the only way they can be assembled is in two twisting chains (a "double helix"), one upside-down relative to the other, with strong chemical bonds holding nucleotides in their own chains and weak chemical bonds holding the chains together. By correctly proposing this model, Watson and Crick were also able to explain how cells copy their DNA, and by extension, how genetic information is passed from one cell to another.

The mathematical rationale for their model forms the text of the paper, but their diagram says it all: you can see there are two chains with steps (these are the nucleotides) connecting them; the small arrows indicate that one chain is upside-down relative to the other. (Note that the drawing was meticulously prepared to accurately reflect the mathematical data. The number of nucleotides per turn of the helix, the angle of the bases, and the distance between the helices are all accurately represented.) Perhaps because of its elegant simplicity, this figure is one of the most recognizable images of modern biology.

Molecular Structure of Nucleic Acids

Watson, J. D. & Crick, F. H. C.

Nature (1953), 171: 737–738

A Structure for Deoxyribose Nucleic Acid

We wish to suggest a structure for the salt of deoxyribose nucleic acid (D.N.A.). This structure has novel features which are of considerable biological interest.

A structure for nucleic acid has already been proposed by Pauling and Corey.[1] They kindly made their manuscript available to us in advance of publication. Their model consists of three intertwined chains, with the phosphates near the fibre axis, and the bases on the outside. In our opinion, this structure is unsatisfactory for two reasons:

(1) We believe that the material which gives the X-ray diagrams is the salt, not the free acid. Without the acidic hydrogen atoms it is not clear what forces would

---

*For details of the race, read James D. Watson, *The Double Helix: a personal account of the discovery of the structure of DNA*, 1968, New York, Atheneum.

hold the structure together, especially as the negatively charged phosphates near the axis will repel each other.

(2) Some of the van der Waals distances appear to be too small.

Another three-chain structure has also been suggested by Fraser (in the press). In his model the phosphates are on the outside and the bases on the inside, linked together by hydrogen bonds. This structure as described is rather ill-defined, and for this reason we shall not comment on it.

We wish to put forward a radically different structure for the salt of deoxyribose nucleic acid. This structure has two helical chains each coiled round the same axis (see diagram). We have made the usual chemical assumptions, namely, that each chain consists of phosphate diester groups joining ß-D-deoxyribofuranose residues with 3',5' linkages. The two chains (but not their bases) are related by a dyad perpendicular to the fibre axis. Both chains follow right-handed helices, but owing to the dyad the sequences of the atoms in the two chains run in opposite directions. Each chain loosely resembles Furberg's[2] model No. 1; that is, the bases are on the inside of the helix and the phosphates on the outside.

The configuration of the sugar and the atoms near it is close to Furberg's "standard configuration," the sugar being roughly perpendicular to the attached base. There is a residue on each chain every 3.4 A. in the z-direction. We have assumed an angle of 36° between adjacent residues in the same chain, so that the structure repeats after 10 residues on each chain, that is, after 34 A. The distance of a phosphorus atom from the fibre axis is 10 A. As the phosphates are on the outside, cations have easy access to them.

The structure is an open one, and its water content is rather high. At lower water contents we would expect the bases to tilt so that the structure could become more compact.

The novel feature of the structure is the manner in which the two chains are held together by the purine and pyrimidine bases. The planes of the bases are perpendicular to the fibre axis. They are joined together in pairs, a single base from one chain being hydrogen-bonded to a single base from the other chain, so that the two lie side by side with identical z-co-ordinates. One of the pair must be a purine and the other a pyrimidine for bonding to occur. The hydrogen bonds are made as follows: purine position 1 to pyrimidine position 1; purine position 6 to pyrimidine position 6.

If it is assumed that the bases only occur in the structure in the most plausible tautomeric forms (that is, with the keto rather than the enol configurations) it is found that only specific pairs of bases can bond together. These pairs are: adenine (purine) with thymine (pyrimidine), and guanine (purine) with cytosine (pyrimidine).

In other words, if an adenine forms one member of a pair, on either chain, then on these assumptions the other member must be thymine; similarly for guanine and cytosine. The sequence of bases on a single chain does not appear to be restricted in any way. However, if only specific pairs of bases can be formed, it follows that if the sequence of bases on one chain is given, then the sequence on the other chain is automatically determined.

It has been found experimentally[3,4] that the ratio of the amounts of adenine to thymine, and the ration of guanine to cytosine, are always very close to unity for deoxyribose nucleic acid.

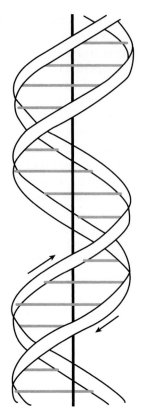

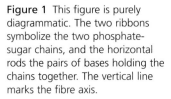

Figure 1 This figure is purely diagrammatic. The two ribbons symbolize the two phosphate-sugar chains, and the horizontal rods the pairs of bases holding the chains together. The vertical line marks the fibre axis.

It is probably impossible to build this structure with a ribose sugar in place of the deoxyribose, as the extra oxygen atom would make too close a van der Waals contact. The previously published X-ray data[5,6] on deoxyribose nucleic acid are insufficient for a rigorous test of our structure. So far as we can tell, it is roughly compatible with the experimental data, but it must be regarded as unproved until it has been checked against more exact results. Some of these are given in the following communications. We were not aware of the details of the results presented there when we devised our structure, which rests mainly though not entirely on published experimental data and stereochemical arguments.

It has not escaped our notice that the specific pairing we have postulated immediately suggests a possible copying mechanism for the genetic material. Full details of the structure, including the conditions assumed in building it, together with a set of co-ordinates for the atoms, will be published elsewhere.

Acknowledgements

We are much indebted to Dr. Jerry Donohue for constant advice and criticism, especially on interatomic distances. We have also been stimulated by a knowledge of the general nature of the unpublished experimental results and ideas of

Dr. M. H. F. Wilkins, Dr. R. E. Franklin and their co-workers at King's College, London. One of us (J. D. W.) has been aided by a fellowship from the National Foundation for Infantile Paralysis.

References

1. Pauling, L., and Corey, R. B., *Nature*, 171, 346 (1953); Proc. U.S. Nat. Acad. Sci., 39, 84 (1953).
2. Furberg, S., *Acta Chem. Scand.*, 6, 634 (1952).
3. Chargaff, E., for references see Zamenhof, S., Brawerman, G., and Chargaff, E., *Biochim. et Biophys. Acta*, 9, 402 (1952).
4. Wyatt, G. R., *J. Gen. Physiol.*, 36, 201 (1952).
5. Astbury, W. T., *Symp. Soc. Exp. Biol.*, 1, *Nucleic Acid*, 66 (Camb. Univ. Press, 1947).
6. Wilkins, M. H. F., and Randall, J. T., *Biochim. et Biophys. Acta*, 10, 192 (1953).

READING RESPONSES

1. Order the features of the DNA molecule as Watson and Crick describe them. What do they describe first? Next? After you've listed them all, propose a rationale for describing the features in this order.
2. Think about the history of science. Describe three other models that have reformed scientific understanding as profoundly as the DNA model has.
3. In the opening paragraphs of their paper, Watson and Crick analyze earlier models of the DNA molecule, but they provide no illustrations for these models. Why do you think they used only words to describe the models?

WRITING ASSIGNMENTS

ASSIGNMENT 1: APPLYING THE PORTABLE RHETORICAL LESSON

Background: So, how much of your athletic ability results from your genetics? Australian researchers have discovered that our muscles contain a protein, alpha-actinin 3, that helps them make fast, strong contractions, like those you make sprinting to class. In some people, a different protein substitutes for alpha-actinin 3; this abnormal protein helps muscles in sustained exercise, such as a three-mile run. The researchers wondered whether these muscle proteins are present in different ratios in the muscles of different types of athletes, and whether these differences could account for their Olympic success. The researchers presented their data in a paper which can be found at this site: http://www.inmr.com.au/articles/ACTN3AmJHumGenetics.pdf.

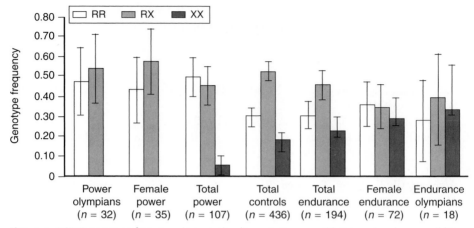

Figure 1 *ACTN3* genotype frequency in controls, elite sprint/power athletes, and endurance athletes. Compared with healthy white controls, there is a marked reduction in the frequency of the *ACTN3* *S77*XX genotype (associated with αa-actinin-3 deficiency) in elite white sprint athletes; remarkably, none of the female sprint athletes or sprint athletes who had competed at the Olympic level (25 males and 7 females) were αa-actinin-3 deficient. Conversely, there is a trend toward an increase in the *S77*XX genotype in endurance athletes, although this association reaches statistical significance only in females. Error bars indicate 95% CIs.

The central figure of the paper is presented above; just as in the rugby paper, the figure tells most of the story. For you to understand this story, you need to know that in the figure the scientists have nicknamed the normal version of apha-actinin 3 "R" and the abnormal version "X." Humans, like all complex animals and plants, have two versions of every gene. So, a given person could have two versions of the normal protein ("RR"), one normal and one abnormal ("RX"), or two abnormal versions ("XX"). The graph measures what percentage of each group has each pattern of genes: RR, RX, and XX. The numbers are represented as the gray, black, or white boxes. (You can ignore the narrow lines. They show the range of high and low values for statistical purposes only.)

Your task for this assignment is to create a verbal explanation of the figure. First, describe the topic a bit so that your reader understands the context for the information that the table and figure provide. Then summarize the data in the figure, drawing your reader's attention to the most important results. Finally, help the reader understand the implications of the results—how does this research affect the reader or others in the world?

As you begin drafting, you'll want to draw the reader's attention to how the pattern of genes in "Total Power" athletes (short distance runners, swimmers, and cyclists, speed skaters, and judo athletes) differs from those in "Total Endurance" athletes (long-distance runners, swimmers, and cyclists, and cross-country skiers). And you'll want to help the reader understand how the pattern of genes in "Endurance Olympians" and "Power Olympians" differs from the other athletes and from the general population.

ASSIGNMENT 2: MAKING CONNECTIONS

Background: The chart on football injuries at the beginning of the chapter contains a great deal of information, too much for a reader to comprehend at a glance. Often, though, it's important for people to understand complex information like this in a hurry. In marketing, a common way of presenting complex information quickly and effectively is a PowerPoint presentation because you can easily blend visual representations of information (tables, figures, images) with verbal representations. To create an effective PowerPoint presentation, you must present data effectively so that the audience understands the information and can see the connection between the information and the author's central point.

Your task for this assignment is two-fold:

A. Create a PowerPoint presentation that supports a claim about head and cervical spine fatalities in American football. Using the information from the chart on pg. 228 as data, design figures and write text that present data in a clear, convincing way.

B. In a two-page report, justify your choices.
   • Why did you choose to use figures to represent certain information?
   • Why did you choose text for other information?
   • Why did you arrange your figures and text as you did?
   • What does your PowerPoint presentation emphasize about the data? What does it de-emphasize?

ASSIGNMENT 3: DOING THE RESEARCH

Background: Marguerite Holloway provides a valuable service by using graphs to help professionals interpret the complex biological data produced by scientific experiments. Trainers and coaches are most likely to influence the behavior of female athletes, but they can do so only if they understand the data.

Your task for this assignment is to provide the same kind of service for trainers and coaches of a sport you played as a child (or still play!). Using research databases that cover biological journals, locate several research articles on your sport. Select one that includes useful information and interpret that information so that trainers, coaches, and athletes can easily understand the data contained in some of the article's tables, graphs, and figures.

As you begin drafting, review the strategies that Holloway uses to help her readers understand complex data and lay out all the options available to you (verbal, visual, design) for displaying information clearly. Think, too, about how you can use options together to achieve a common effect.

SOCIOLOGY:
SEARCHING FOR CAUSES OF
SOCIAL PROBLEMS

Sociologists conduct research because they're curious to discover the factors that influence how people live in their communities. They write because they want to improve life for the people they've studied. Sometimes sociologists write to describe the hidden social pressures on particular groups of people so that others—politicians, social workers, and the general public—better understand them. Often sociologists write to encourage politicians and others to improve social programs. Thus, sociologists provide reasons and evidence that change laws—and, sometimes, lives. Because sociologists believe that their research can create change, they are highly motivated to conduct their research responsibly.

As social scientists, sociologists attempt to research human communities as objectively as possible. They find it doubly difficult to achieve objectivity because human interactions are exceedingly complex and because sociologists—like all of us—are part of human society. Their life experiences shape how they see the world—from what they consider to be important problems to what they assume to be "good" for society. Because human society is so complex, sociologists very carefully narrow their focus to one or a small set of factors that they define clearly. To keep things objective, they try to use the same definitions and the same procedures that previous researchers have used, always documenting this previous research so that the reader understands the scholarly context for a new study. For this reason, as writers and readers, sociologists devote a great deal of attention to the Methods section.

To get beyond the limitations of their own life experience, sociologists harness the curiosity that leads them to wonder about particular aspects of human society to develop "sociological imagination," a way of thinking about the world that relies on both creative thought and objective scientific practices. This enables them to see past cultural stereotypes. When faced with the question from the final reading in this chapter, (Why do young women have babies and yet remain unmarried?), for example, cultural stereotypes provide easy answers. But sociological imagination encourages researchers to consider different and more complex answers. Those potential answers form hypotheses that can be tested by reliable social science research. The results of this research can improve social policy and relations between different social communities.

A Portable Rhetorical Lesson:

Limiting a Research Topic

The rhetorical lesson for this chapter is the process of limiting a research topic. You may find it useful in research situations that make you want to throw up your hands and say, "This problem is too complicated. I don't even know where to begin." In this situation, the strategies that sociologists use could help you get past this paralysis. The following outline oversimplifies the components of sociological method, but it should help you to see the basic parts.

- After you identify the general topic of your research, use imagination and previous research on the topic to help you get outside your own experience so that you can see the topic more completely and analyze it more objectively.
- Narrow your focus to one aspect of the topic or one specific problem so that you will not be overwhelmed by the complexity of the topic. For example, in the first reading Shelley Correll investigates why so few women enter careers like engineering. She narrows her focus to a small set of factors regarding how men and women assess their own competence, and then tests the effect of those factors empirically.
- Develop a theoretical framework that describes the lens you are using to view the topic. Your theoretical framework will describe what you believe to be true about the world (your cultural assumptions), the perspective you take on the topic (the ideology or values you apply), and the line of scholarship that you follow. So, for example, Correll believes that women and men are equally intelligent and that cultural assumptions significantly shape women's career choices, and she aligns herself with existing scholarship on effects of social status.
- Focus in on one or a small number of factors for your research, remembering that scholars work on complex problems collaboratively—each scholar tackles one part of the problem; collectively scholarship provides a full picture.
- Develop one or more hypotheses—provisional explanations—that can be tested.
- Develop a research design, using proven methods to test the hypotheses.
- Assess the research data collected to determine if it does or does not support the hypotheses.

An agile imagination and reliable research methods will be your most valuable tools for those impossibly complex situations you will surely face as a writer.

Chapter Topics: Gender is the main topic of the chapter, but it branches into the ways gender influences career choices, politics, sexuality, marriage, and parenthood.

To Think About . . .

The following chart, compiled by the National Science Foundation, illustrates the changes in the percentage of science and engineering degrees granted to female students.

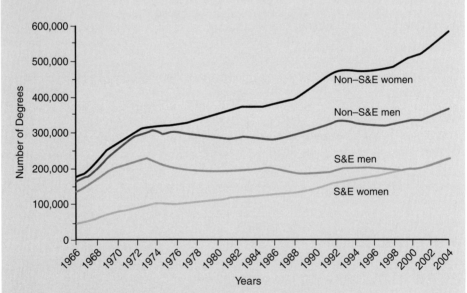

The Changing Representation of Women in Science and Engineering

Note: National data not available for 1999. "S & E" refers to bachelors degrees in science and education.

Source: National Science Foundation, Division of Science Resources Statistics, special tabulations of U.S. Department of Education, National Center for Education Statistics, Integrated Postsecondary Education Data System, Completions Survey, 1966–2004.

The more recent information comes from 2004. If you collected the same information today, what would you expect to find?

- What kind of change (increase, decrease, no change) would you expect for each of the four categories?
- How large of a change would you expect for each?
- What social forces might account for each of these changes?

WRITING IN SOCIOLOGY

Introduction by Cheryl Brandsen, Professor of Sociology

Sociologists use scientific research methods to study human society and social interaction. They focus their work on how human behavior is shaped by the people with whom we interact (family or neighbors) and social structures that shape those relationships (economic policies or social conventions). Sociologists use a variety of research methods to study social life, including field work, questionnaires and surveys, historical documents and census data, and experiments. Sociologists use all these methodologies to help them see the world objectively. They follow a scientific method of collecting, observing, and thinking about evidence that is designed to minimize any bias emerging from the researcher's personal values and experiences.

How sociologists go about gathering information on their research questions is shaped by how they already envision the world, their theoretical framework (which is a more formal way of envisioning the world), and the findings of previous research studies. Consequently, while sociologists attempt to be objective, they do so with the understanding that they will never perceive society in a purely objective way.

In the preceding paragraph I spoke of sociologists "envisioning" the world. Sociologist C.W. Mills argues that in order to understand human behavior and social interaction, researchers must cultivate a "sociological imagination." This kind of imagination, says Mills, focuses on the relationship between "private troubles" and "public issues," between our personal, everyday life experiences and the larger structural arrangements of society. Decisions or problems that seem to be solely personal and intimate—unemployment, suicide, or career choice, for instance—are shaped by larger social, economic, historical, and political forces.

Most people think about divorce, for example, in personal terms. A woman wonders where she "went wrong" or ruminates about her partner's bad habits. To prevent a subsequent divorce, the woman will focus on individual adjustments: "I will work fewer hours," "I will choose more wisely," or "I will manage money more effectively." That nearly fifty percent of marriages end in divorce, however, suggests that divorce might be more than an individual trouble. A sociological imagination pushes sociologists to wonder whether something in society influences marriages . . . and divorces. When sociologists view divorce through the lens of social pressures, they begin to wonder about the effects of high rates of unemployment, geographic mobility, changing gender roles and sexual norms, or unrealistic emphases on romantic love on the stability of marriages.

Sociologists construct theoretical frameworks—about social situations such as marriage and divorce—to help them describe how social pressures shape individual lives. A useful theoretical framework identifies these social pressures and helps researchers analyze the relationships between them. It provides a lens—a formalized framework for seeing, imagining—through which they can more fully understand human experiences like divorce.

In "Constraints into Preferences: Gender, Status, and Emerging Career Aspirations," Shelley Correll uses sociological imagination to better understand why men and women aspire to different careers. Particularly, she's curious about how cultural beliefs about gender affect the ways people assess their own competence, and how that shapes the careers that people choose.

Correll's essay follows a conventional research structure that is familiar to even the novice social scientist: (1) Introduction, (2) Review of literature/ Theoretical framework for the study, (3) Methods, (4) Results, (5) Discussion, and (6) Conclusion. Although she doesn't label it as such, Correll's introduction is really a statement of the problem that she investigated. In her first three paragraphs, Correll's inquisitiveness about gender differences in regard to career choice is clear. Rather than accepting people's career choices as individual decisions, Correll imagines and asks a foundational question: Why do men seem more attracted to some careers and women to others?

Her curiosity motivates her to analyze the theoretical frameworks that previous researchers have used. She reviews previous research on this problem, she identifies the gaps in such research, and she shows how this study connects with the prior research. Taking on the question herself, Correll focuses on the cultural beliefs (an aspect of social structure) that men and women hold about gender. In particular, she targets research that suggests that men are more likely to attribute their performance to their personal abilities than women are. Correll wonders if this level of confidence in personal abilities eventually funnels men and women into different career tracks. Career choice is perhaps constrained or enhanced by cultural factors that shape such self-assessments.

Correll then crafts hypotheses. Formally defined, a hypothesis is a provisional explanation for a particular phenomenon that can be empirically tested. Informally defined, hypotheses put sociological imagination into specifics: Correll imagines what factors might explain the situation, and she suggests two hypotheses: (1) When a particular task is believed to be "more masculine," men, in contrast to women, will make higher self-assessments of their abilities to perform the task competently; (2) cultural beliefs about competence will influence career choices.

Correll tests her hypotheses through methodologically sound experiments, ensuring that her findings are reliable, valid, and generalizable. These three qualities determine the persuasiveness of sociological research. *Reliable* means that there is a high likelihood that the results would be verified if the experiment were repeated; *valid* means that the results are very likely to represent something true about the social situation; and *generalizable* means that the truth of the results can be applied to situations beyond those of the experiment. These kind of findings will help other social scientists understand the complex links between individuals and society, and decide if and how to intervene.

The data support both of her hypotheses.

Finally, Correll's sociological imagination is apparent in her "Summary" and "Conclusion and Implications" sections. The "Summary" provides a "big picture" overview of the research (again note that the words *picture* and *overview* refer to seeing), and the "Conclusion and Implications" review the intent of the project. Correll affirms tentative support of her hypotheses, and re-states her commitment to understanding how gender inequality is reproduced by larger structural factors (cultural beliefs about gender) that are not immediately visible in something as personal as career choice.

✓ *READING TIPS*

Because sociologists achieve objectivity by carefully limiting the focus of their study and by describing their methods, their writing can seem exceedingly complex. To comprehend complex texts like those that sociologists write, you must pause to interpret what you've read and record your interpretation. Begin by jotting down the topic of the research, paying special attention to how the author narrows her focus to a particular aspect of the topic. Then read with an eye open for the author's theoretical framework (marginal annotations will help you to identify that). As you analyze the author's theoretical framework, consider how alternative theoretical frameworks might produce different results. In studies that sociologists write for other sociologists this theoretical framework usually appears as an independent section or as a part of the Literature Review. When sociologists write for a general audience they usually describe their theoretical framework in the introduction or in an appendix. If you take notes like these, you'll avoid getting entangled in the complexities of the text.

Constraints into Preferences: Gender, Status, and Emerging Career Aspirations

Shelley J. Correll

American Sociological Review, 2004, 69: 93–113

[Abstract] This study presents an experimental evaluation of a model that describes the constraining effect of cultural beliefs about gender on the emerging career-relevant aspirations of men and women. The model specifies the conditions under which gender status beliefs evoke a gender-differentiated double standard for attributing performance to ability, which differentially biases the way men and women assess their own competence at tasks that are career relevant, controlling for actual ability. The model implies that, if men and women make different assessments of their own competence at career-relevant tasks, they will also form different aspirations for career paths and activities believed to require competence at these tasks. Data from the experiment support this model. In one condition, male and female undergraduate participants completed an experimental task after being exposed to a belief that men are better at this task. In this condition, male participants assessed their task ability higher than female participants did even though all were given the same scores. Males in this condition also had higher aspirations for career-relevant activities described as requiring competence at the task. No gender differences were found in either assessments or aspirations in a second condition where participants were instead exposed to a belief that men and women have equal task ability. To illustrate the utility of the model in a "real world" (i.e., nonlaboratory) setting, results are compared to a previous survey study that showed men make higher assessments of their own mathematical ability than women, which contributes to their higher rates of persistence on paths to careers in science, math, and engineering.

How do gender differences in career choices emerge? Understanding the gendered nature of the career choice process is important since, to the extent that men and women make different career-relevant choices throughout their lives, the labor force will continue to be segregated by gender. Gender segregation in paid work is stubbornly resilient, persisting despite other structural changes in society, changes such as the vast movement of women into paid work in recent decades (Jacobs 1989, 1995a; Jacobsen 1994; Reskin 1993) and the transformation of work content due to technological changes and the increase in service sector jobs (England 1981; Game and Pringle 1983; Reskin and Roos 1990; Tienda and Ortiz 1987). The distribution of men and women into different kinds of occupations, firms, and establishments is consequential, explaining the majority of the gender gap in wages (Peterson and Morgan 1995).

Many explanations of this continued segregation have examined the impact of "demand-side" processes, a phrase referring to processes that lead to a greater demand for men

---

Sidebar annotations (left margin):

This is the central idea of the study: When men are told that men are better at a task than women, men assess their competence at that task more highly than if they believe that gender is not a factor.

When told that men are better at a given task than women, women rated their ability to perform that task lower than men did—even when their scores for ability were the same as the men's.

If men and women are told that gender does not influence ability to perform a task, men and women assess their ability to perform that task the same.

In short, we believe what culture tells us about ourselves, even when there is no evidence to back those beliefs—and we act on what we are told to believe.

Correll begins her introduction with a simplified version of her research question.

"Demand side" refers to the employers and their demand for employees.

By "supply side,"
Correll means the
number of men and
women who have
prepared for certain
kinds of careers—the
"supply" of employees.
Why is it, for instance,
that those who study
nursing are usually
women, and those who
study engineering are
usually men? When
companies hire
employees, the supply
of potential employees
is already skewed
by gender.

when filling more desirable jobs (Anker 1997; England 1992; Nelson and Bridges 1999; Reskin and Roos 1990). This paper focuses instead on the "supply side" of the issue by addressing how men and women develop preferences or aspirations for different kinds of work.[1] Most scholars of gender inequality have been reluctant to develop supply-side explanations because these explanations often "blame the victim" (Browne and England 1997). However, by developing models that are truly sociological (i.e., that explicate how macro-level variables constrain individual action) it should be possible to understand how gender differences in career choices emerge without simultaneously suggesting that women voluntarily choose less advantageous positions in the labor market.

Macro-level variables
are large-scale social
conditions such as
gender prejudice.

This paper, which is part of a larger project to develop a theory about gender and the career choice process, presents an experimental evaluation of one model that describes the constraining effects of cultural beliefs about gender on the emerging career-relevant preferences or aspirations of men and women. The main hypothesis is that cultural beliefs about gender that accord men higher status in society than women (i.e., status beliefs) can evoke gender-differentiated standards for attributing performance to ability, which differentially biases the assessments men and women make of their own competence at career-relevant tasks. This paper uses status characteristics theory and the empirical literature on stereotype threat to explain how and when this biasing effect is likely to occur. The implication is that, if individuals act on gender-differentiated evaluations of their own competence when forming aspirations for activities that lead to different careers, then status beliefs about gender will also differentially impact the career-relevant choices that men and women make. In the aggregate, if men and women systematically make different career-relevant choices, the gender-segregated labor force is necessarily reproduced. Before developing the model further, I briefly review supply-side explanations of gender segregation in paid work.

Here Correll introduces
her theoretical
orientation: that she will
root her study in the
research on personal
characteristics (like
gender) that people
associate with a
person's social status.

When data is
aggregated, it is
analyzed for a group
(not an individual)
that shares a similar
characteristic—in this
case, gender.

[I] Supply-Side Explanations of Gender Segregation

Early on the path to many careers, men and women—indeed, even boys and girls—begin to differentially commit themselves to activities that are career relevant. As early as high school, and even more strikingly by college, young men and women elect to take different kinds of courses and choose different college majors, which produces gender differences in the kinds of jobs that are later seen as plausible options for students (AAUW 1992; Jacobs 1995b; National Science Board 1993; National Science

Foundation 1994). Given this early gender divergence, it is probably not surprising that those who study labor market matching processes (i.e., the processes by which prospective employees become matched with employers) find that the supply networks from which employers recruit are highly segregated by gender (Granovetter and Tilly 1988). The gender segregation of job supply networks means that, even if all gender discrimination at the point of hire and subsequent promotion were removed, considerable gender segregation would still remain in paid work due to the different and seemingly voluntary career choices men and women make.

Human Capital Explanations

Human capital theory suggests that gender discrimination exists because men and women differ in what they value (their personal capital). Women, according to this theory, choose careers that allow them to move in and out of the paid labor force so that they can attend to other priorities.

Scholars studying labor market matching processes tend to downplay the issue of gender differences in job supply networks. They assume that men and women have different tastes, preferences, or ways of maximizing utility, which leads to differences in men's and women's choices in careers and/or jobs. For example, human capital theorists have argued that women choose jobs with flatter rates of wage growth, because these jobs, which are primarily in female-dominated occupations, have smaller wage penalties for sustained periods of absence from the paid labor force and have higher starting wages (Polachek 1976, 1981; Zellner 1975). According to these theories, women know they will likely need to take an extended absence for child birth and/or care, so they choose jobs with the above characteristics to maximize their lifetime earnings. However, England and colleagues (1984; 1988) demonstrate that, contrary to the predictions of human capital theory, women employed in male-dominated occupations actually have higher lifetime earnings.

Correll presents a contradictory study in order to demonstrate the weakness of the human capital theoretical model.

When human capital theorists are confronted with evidence that men and women with equivalent human capital are found in jobs with different wages or different lifetime earning potential, they often expand their model of individual choice (Glass 1990). The most common expansion of this model is that women choose jobs that maximize their ability to coordinate family and paid work responsibilities (Marini and Brinton 1984; Polachek 1976). However, Glass (1990) shows that male-dominated jobs—compared with female-dominated jobs—are actually associated with more flexibility and autonomy, thus allowing a person, for example, to more easily leave work to tend to a sick child. In sum, women maximize neither earnings nor their ability to coordinate family and paid work duties by working in female-dominated occupations, leaving the question of why women and men

Another contradiction, proving that human capital research is not a good theoretical model for gender segregation of career choice.

Culture is understood to include language, beliefs, norms, values, behaviors and practices, and material objects. We often take our cultural context for granted until we experience a culture very different from our own. Correll suggests that our culture, in ways we might not even be aware of, shapes our preferences and aspirations for particular careers. It is a statement that reflects a sociological imagination at work.

choose different kinds of careers unanswered by the human capital perspective.

Cultural Constraints on Choice

What is needed is a supply-side approach that recognizes that the culture in which individuals are embedded constrains or limits what these individuals deem possible or appropriate, thereby shaping the preferences and aspirations that individuals develop for activities leading to various careers, often starting early in the life course. . . .

[Such an approach should also] specify *how* choices are induced. One goal of the current project is to develop a model that can account for this type of constraint on choice and that can be evaluated empirically. While there are undoubtedly many reasons why individuals develop preferences for one career or another, my model assumes that, as a minimum, individuals must believe they have the skills necessary for a given career in order to develop preferences for that career. I refer to a person's understanding of his or her own competence as a "self-assessment." The model explains how cultural beliefs about gender bias the formation of self-assessments of their competence at career-relevant tasks. I use "career-relevant" to refer to tasks, activities, decisions, and aspirations that, when performed, enacted, or held, impact the trajectory or path of an individual's job or career history. For example, going to graduate school is a career-relevant activity. . . .

For instance, a cultural belief that women are "natural caregivers" might make a man think that he would not be a very good nurse. A cultural belief that men are better at mathematics and science might bias women against choosing engineering.

[II] Status Beliefs, Self-Assessments, and Emerging Aspirations

I rely on status characteristics theory and the empirical literature on "stereotype threat" to develop a model that describes the constraining effect of cultural beliefs about gender on self-assessments of task competence and emerging career-relevant aspirations. . . .

Status Characteristics Theory

An attribute that differentiates people is a *status characteristic* if there are widely held beliefs in the culture attaching greater social value and competence with one category of the attribute (men, computer expert) than another (women, computer novice) (Berger et al. 1977). . . .

Gender as a Status Characteristic

Gender is commonly described as a *diffuse* status characteristic, meaning that widely shared cultural beliefs about gender include expectations that men are diffusely more competent or capable at most things, as well as specific assumptions that men are better at some particular tasks (e.g., mechanical tasks) while women are better at others (e.g., nurturing tasks) (Conway, Pizzamiglio, and Mount, 1996; Fiske et al. 2002; Wagner and Berger 1997; Williams and Best 1990). Beliefs about gender and competence have changed over time; however, empirical studies continue to find that men are thought to be generally more capable (Williams and Best 1990:334) and competent (Fiske et al. 2002:892) than women. For example, Fiske et al. (2002:892) surveyed nine diverse samples, from different regions of the United States, and found that members of these samples, regardless of age, consistently rated the category "men" higher than the category "women" on a multidimensional scale of competence. . . .

Both sociologists and psychologists often note that gender beliefs reflect a cultural system, representing what we think "most people" believe or accept as true about the categories of "men" and "women" (Ridgeway 1997; Deaux and Kite 1987). As such, status beliefs, and stereotypes more generally, operate as schemas for interpreting and making sense of the social world (Fiske 1998; Ridgeway 1997). Viewing status beliefs as cultural schemas implies that their effect is potentially far reaching: even individuals who do not personally endorse beliefs that men are generally more competent than women are likely to be aware that these beliefs exist in the culture and expect that others will treat them according to these beliefs. This expectation, or what we think "most (other) people" believe, has been shown to modify behavior and bias judgments (Foschi 1996; Lovaglia et al. 1998; Steele 1997).

> Correll claims that both status beliefs and stereotypes are so basic to human thinking that they operate as schemas—ways of making sense of the world.

> In other words, people determine if they are competent at a given task by determining if they possess the *diffuse status* characteristics that are most important for that task.

> That is, if others do not expect you to do well because of your diffuse status characteristics, they will carefully scrutinize your performance. For example, when a male successfully teaches preschool, people scrutinize his performance more carefully because such tasks are not consistent with status-based expectations for males.

Double Standards for Assessing Competence

In an extension of status characteristics theory that is highly relevant for understanding how gender differences in self-assessments emerge, Foschi (1989) incorporates insights from the psychological literature on attribution to develop a theory about how individuals attribute performance to ability (or lack of ability). The main claim is that the standards individuals use to determine if a given performance is indicative of ability are a function of the diffuse status characteristics that are salient in a setting. When people who possess the lower state of a salient diffuse status characteristic (symbolized as $D-$) perform well at the group's task, their performances are critically scrutinized, because a good performance is inconsistent with status-based expectations for them. When people with the more valued state ($D+$) perform equally as well, their performances are consistent with expectations and are, therefore, less scrutinized. Since their performances are less scrutinized, higher status group members are judged by a more lenient standard than lower status group members. As a result, higher status group members are more likely to be judged as having task ability even when no "objective" performance differences exist....

When individuals assess their own competence at a task, they undoubtedly rely on performance information provided by legitimate evaluators (e.g., teachers, testing agencies, and employers). More positive evaluations of performance should lead to higher self-assessments of task competence. However, if we apply the double standard argument presented above in settings where individuals make assessments of their own competence, we would expect that, if gender is salient in the setting, gender will impact the performance expectations men and women hold for themselves. As long as the task is not one for which beliefs specifically advantage women, men will have higher performance expectations for themselves than otherwise similar women will. Men will, therefore, use a more lenient standard when assessing their own task competence. If individuals are provided with equal performance evaluations of their competence (e.g., have equal scores on a test), but men use a more lenient standard, then men will overestimate and women will underestimate their actual task ability. In this way, cultural beliefs about gender can lead to biased self-assessments of task competence. However, this prediction assumes that the status process just described occurs in the kind of setting where individuals assess their own competence.

> In other words, because American culture presumes men to be generally more competent than women, men will expect to perform well, and they will use more lenient standards to evaluate their own performance. Women, on the other hand, expect to perform less well and will more stringently evaluate their own performance.

> Note how Correll continues to refine the predictive ability for her theoretical model—a key feature of sociological rhetoric.

Status Processes in Individual Settings

Applying status characteristics theory to develop this argument requires explaining why the theory should hold in settings where individuals commonly assess their own task competence. For instance, individuals likely assess their competence in settings where they take socially important mental ability tests, such as intelligence quotient (IQ) tests, scholastic aptitude tests (SATs), and graduate record examinations (GREs). In these situations... individuals are highly task oriented (i.e., they are focused on performing well on the task), but since they are not participating in a group, they are not collectively oriented....

Empirical Evidence

> In this section, Correll continues her theoretical model-building by supporting the model with empirical research.

A growing body of empirical evidence is consistent with the idea that status generalization occurs in individual evaluative settings, such as those where individuals take socially important mentally ability tests....

... [P]sychologist Claude Steele (1997) theorizes that individuals experience a self-evaluative threat in the presence of salient negative stereotypes about their group's intellectual ability. This threat of social devaluation generates anxiety, arousal, and/or task-irrelevant processing that interferes with intellectual functioning and leads to decreased test performance (Steele and Aronson 1995). Although those who study "stereotype threat" use the more general term, "stereotype," these studies actually focus on the status element of stereotypes. They claim the belief that one category of the characteristic (African Americans, women) is less competent or capable than another (whites, men) causes the threat.[3]

Steele and Aronson (1995) show, for example, that when a difficult, standardized verbal exam is described as diagnostic of ability, African American students perform more poorly than white students. However, when the same test is not characterized as diagnostic of ability, African American and white students perform at the same level. Defining a test as ability-diagnostic primes a stereotype about race and verbal ability and makes race salient in the setting. Likewise, Shih, Pittinsky, and Ambady (1999) show that Asian women experience a stereotype threat, which reduces their mathematical performance when the stereotype that women have lower mathematical ability is primed, but they experience what might be called a stereotype "bonus," raising their mathematical performance, when the stereotype that Asians have superior mathematical ability is primed instead. As this study shows, the very same group of people, Asian women, can be advantaged or disadvantaged when performing the same task (a mathematics test) by varying what belief is described as relevant in the setting. Although beliefs about women and Asians are widely available in the culture, the impact of these beliefs in a given setting varies with the relevance of the belief in that setting, as status characteristics theory would predict.

Collectively, these studies indicate that status beliefs impact task performance in settings where individuals are task oriented, but are not members of a group. Based on these empirical results and the theoretical justification given, I make predictions about the effects of status beliefs on self-assessments of task competence in individual evaluative settings, identifying the conditions under which we would expect to see these effects.

Empirical Predictions

Based on the argument developed above, if status generalization occurs in individual evaluative settings, status beliefs will impact

> Correll cites this research for two reasons: (1) the context is academic test-taking—the same context as her study—and (2) to establish that individuals accept the negative status characteristic of an entire group—women, for example, or members of a particular race.

> Researchers "prime" subjects when they tell them information before a test.

So D is a broadly held (or diffuse) belief about a social characteristic that affects one's status, or sense of worth. A D + characteristic is a positive belief and a D− a negative belief.

Hypothesis 1. When subjects believe that men (D+) do better on a particular "masculine" task than women (D), men will make higher self-assessments of their own competence than women who perform at the same level.

Hypothesis 2. In other words, cultural beliefs about competence will shape emerging career aspirations. In the interests of brevity, we have not included the portion of Correll's study that addresses this second hypothesis.

An independent variable is a condition that is a relatively stable belief; here, an independent variable is the cultural presumption that there are gender-specific abilities.

A dependent variable is the behavior or attitude that can be explained or predicted by the independent variable. American culture believes that abilities depend on gender, that independent variable would explain why women tend not to choose careers in a field such as engineering (that choice is the dependent variable).

the self-assessments of individuals in these settings. This will occur when individuals are task oriented and anticipate that they will receive a socially important and socially valid performance evaluation. Under these conditions and if a diffuse status characteristic (D) is defined as relevant to the task at hand, performance expectations will vary positively with the state of D. Those with + states of D will have higher performance expectations than those with − states of D, assuming the task is not one for which cultural beliefs specifically advantage those with − states of D. In turn, higher performance expectations will lead to lower (more lenient) performance standards for inferring task ability (Foschi 1989).

Therefore, I present the following hypotheses:

Hypothesis 1: In the presence of a belief making D task relevant and given an equal task outcome and differing states of D, those with a + state of D will assess their competence at the task higher than those with a − state of D.

Hypothesis 2: If competence at the task is perceived to be necessary for persisting on a particular career path, then higher self-assessments of competence lead to higher aspirations for activities that are associated with that career path. . . .

[III] The Experiment

Overview

The experiment was designed primarily to evaluate hypothesis 1, regarding the bias that status beliefs impose on self-assessments of task competence. A test of the hypotheses calls for an experimental setting in which task performance can be controlled and the relevance of cultural beliefs about gender can be manipulated by associating or dissociating gender with task performance. The gender belief associated with the task and the gender of the subject are independent variables; self-assessment of task competence and the standard used to infer ability are the primary dependent variables. Task performance was experimentally held constant.

In one condition of the experiment, I manipulate gender belief associated with the task to advantage males (the "male advantaged" or "MA" condition). I provide subjects in this condition with evidence that males, on average, have more ability at the experimental task. This association between gender and task performance is intended to make gender salient and task relevant, leading to the prediction that men will use a more lenient standard than women when assessing their own task competence, resulting in higher male self-assessment levels.

Correll leads subjects in this group to believe that gender does not affect people's performance of the task. In this case, Correll hypothesizes that men and women will assess their performance similarly.

The final design includes four groups of subjects: males who have been led to believe that men are more competent in performing the task at hand, females who have been led to believe that men are more competent at the task, men who have been led to believe that gender is not associated with ability to perform the task, and women who have been led to believe that gender is not associated with ability to perform the task.

In the contrasting condition, I specifically dissociate gender beliefs from the task (the "gender dissociated" or "GD" condition) by providing subjects with evidence that there are no gender differences in task ability. The explicit dissociation of gender from the task should eliminate the task relevance of gender in the setting and, consequently, the effect of gender on self-assessments. . . .

The final design, based on procedures drawn from Foschi (1996) and Erickson (1998), crosses the gender of subject with the "male advantaged" or "gender dissociated" presentation of the task, yielding four conditions. The subjects were male and female first-year undergraduates, who were paid for their time and randomly assigned to either the MA or GD condition. Analysis is based on a sample of 80 subjects (20 subjects per condition). . . .

Procedures

Subjects came to the lab individually and were told that they were participating in the pretesting of a new set of graduate admissions examinations for a national testing service, purportedly measuring their "contrast sensitivity" ability. To establish that the task is socially important and would be used to legitimately rank "test-takers," as is required by the theory, subjects were informed verbally by an undergraduate experimenter and by reading a passage on their computer screen, that a national testing organization developed the contrast sensitivity exam and that both graduate schools and Fortune 500 companies have expressed interest in using this exam as a screening device. To further emphasize that individuals would be ranked based on their scores, subjects were also told that participants who scored in the top 25 percent of the scoring distribution would be entered into a drawing for a 50-dollar cash prize.

Next, the gender task belief manipulation was introduced. As a part of the initial verbal script delivered by the experimenter, participants were told either that males, on average, perform better on tests of contrast sensitivity (the MA condition) or that there is no gender difference in scores on tests of contrast sensitivity (the GD condition). To further emphasize the association or dissociation of gender with the task, subjects read more about gender and contrast sensitivity on their computer screen. In particular, the cover story described the interest of social science researchers in understanding either the gender difference or the lack of gender difference in performance on this task. This manipulation was intended to either make gender relevant to the goals of the situation (i.e., scoring high on the test) or to explicitly break the bond of relevance between gender and task performance.

Participants then completed two, 20-item rounds of the computer-administered contrast sensitivity test, in which subjects have five seconds to judge which color (black or white) predominates in each of a series of rectangles (Troyer 2001). The contrast sensitivity task is a reliable instrument commonly used in experimental social psychology. The task has no discernable right or wrong answers, yet subject suspicion in regard to the task is low. . . . Since the amounts of white and black area are either exactly equal or very close to equal in each rectangle, it is impossible for subjects to actually derive correct solutions to the problems. All subjects were told that they correctly answered 13 of the 20 items during round one and 12 of 20 in round two. The scores were similar between rounds to convey that the test reliably measures contrast sensitivity ability. Mid-range scores, such as these, should allow for a wider range of self-assessment values than more extreme scores would (Foschi 1996). Giving all subjects identical test "scores" ensures that they assess their ability from objectively identical performance information.

> Researchers asked questions that measured ability, self-assessment, and likelihood of engaging in activities requiring this ability. They were also asked questions that assessed how seriously the subjects took the test. Correll's original article lists the specific questions.

After receiving their scores at the end of each round, participants answered a series of questions designed to first provide ability standard and then self-assessment measures. After the second round, they also answered a set of questions about how likely they would be to engage in activities that required high levels of task ability. They then answered questions to assess the extent to which the experimental manipulations were successful. Before leaving, they were debriefed and paid. . . .

[IV. Results and Discussion]. . .

Summary of Results

> Because of space limitations, we have eliminated most of Correll's "Results and Discussion" section. At the end of the section, however, she provides the following "Summary of Results."

The main hypothesis was strongly supported. Men use a more lenient standard to infer ability and assess their task competence higher than women when exposed to a belief about male superiority, but no gender differences in self-assessments or ability standards were found when gender was defined as irrelevant to the task. Further, these differences were produced relatively easily. Although subjects had not heard of the task before participating in the study, after minimal exposure to a belief about male superiority and two rounds of testing, significant gender differences in self-assessments of task competence emerged. Finally, the results provide empirical support for the theoretical claim that status generalization occurs in individual evaluative settings under the conditions previously described. . . .

The experimental data also rule out the alternative explanation described earlier for higher male self-assessments. Recall that, according to this alternative logic, self-assessments tap an additional component of unmeasured "real" ability, leading to the explanation that, in the case of mathematics, men make higher assessments of their mathematical ability, not because of the biasing effect of cultural beliefs about gender and mathematics, but because men "really are better" at mathematics. However, because correct solutions to the experimental task are impossible to derive, men cannot "really" be better at the experimental task. Nevertheless, when subjects, who were all given the same score on the task, were told that, on average, men perform better on the test, male subjects rated their task ability higher than female subjects did, consistent with the hypothesis advanced in this study. . . .

Correll's results support her theoretical model, refuting an earlier argument that suggests men make higher self-assessments of mathematical ability because they indeed do possess such abilities. Correll's experimental task had no correct solution; therefore, it was impossible for men to be better at the task.

[V] Summary

The main contribution of this study is to develop and evaluate a theoretical model that describes the constraining effect of cultural beliefs about gender on the emerging career-relevant aspirations of men and women. Using status characteristics theory and the empirical literature on stereotype threat, I argue that gender status beliefs will lead men and women to use different standards to judge their own task competence in individual evaluative settings, such as testing situations, when gender is salient and defined as relevant to performance in the setting. In this situation, I hypothesize that gender differences in self-assessments of task competence will emerge and lead to gender differences in emerging aspirations for career paths and activities that require task competence. The theoretical model is evaluated with data from an experiment that was designed to permit the manipulation of the relevance of gender in the setting, thereby providing for a strong test of the causal argument. Importantly, the experimental data support the model. A comparison of the experimental results with results from a probability sample illustrates the utility of the model and suggests that the causal process operates similarly in a "real world" setting.

Because Correll's study is so complex, she provides a summary to give readers the big picture: readers can see how all the parts fit together to support her theoretical model.

This paragraph recaps the highlights of the whole paper: its purpose, theoretical frame, hypotheses, research design, and findings. It thus serves as a reminder of what is most essential in sociological research.

More generally, the experimental results, along with the work on stereotype threat and the recent study by Lovaglia et al. (1998), indicate that the impact of status processes on the reproduction of inequality might be more far reaching than status characteristics theory has considered. Extending the scope of the

Correll reminds us of a unique contribution her work makes: it extends the theory to include a variety of individual educational, occupational, and testing settings.

theory to include individual evaluative settings, such as those described here, is an important advancement, since this setting is both very common and highly consequential in its impact on educational and occupational attainment. It includes most standardized test settings, including those that are used to determine college, graduate school, and professional school admissions and those used for certification in a wide range of professional occupations.

[VI] Conclusion and Implications

The motivation for this study was to better understand how gender segregation in paid labor persists over other structural changes in society by focusing on the supply-side of the issue, examining how cultural beliefs about gender differentially constrain the emerging career-relevant aspirations or preferences of men and women. The implication of the theory is that if gender differences in aspirations emerge, men and women will likely make different career-relevant choices, which will funnel them into supply networks for different types of jobs. Rather than examining how men and women's aspirations emerge, many previous supply-side explanations simply document or assume that men and women have different aspirations or different career-relevant preferences.

In sociology, "macro" often refers to larger-scale patterns of society, such as cultural beliefs about gender.

Economic models, in particular, tend to view aspirations or preferences as exogenous to labor market matching processes (England 1993). However, as I have shown, individuals form aspirations by drawing on perceptions of their own competence at career-relevant tasks, and the perceptions men and women form are differentially biased by cultural beliefs about gender. In this way, macro belief structures constrain emerging preferences and aspirations and, to the extent that individuals act on their aspirations, individual choice. The

Here Correll applies her research to a social problem: if we don't pay attention to how gender influences student's career choices, we will never be able to solve the gender segregation in careers or the inequity in men's and women's pay.

failure to recognize the constrained aspect of choice obscures some of the processes by which gender inequality is perpetuated. It either defines the problem away or locates its source in the individualistic actions of those already disadvantaged by their position in the labor market.

Notes

1. In taking a supply-side approach, I am not suggesting that demand-side approaches are not important. To the contrary, this has been and continues to be a very important line of work. My argument is that demand-side process cannot fully account for gender segregation in paid labor (see England 1992 and Reskin and Roos 1990 for a review).

3. One common criticism of the stereotype threat literature and the larger literature on stereotype activation is that there are inconsistencies in the mecha-

nisms proposed to explain how stereotypes produce their effects depending on whether the stereotypes are negative or positive and whether the stereotypes are about one's own group or about other groups (see Wheeler and Petty 2001 for a review). Status characteristics theory, by contrast proposes one mechanism for the effects of status beliefs (regardless of whether the beliefs are advantaging or disadvantaging) on the behaviors and evaluations of both self and others.

References

American Association of University Women. 1992. *How Schools Shortchange Girls.* Washington DC: American Association of University Women Educational Foundation.

Anker, Richard. 1997. "Theories of Occupational Segregation by Sex: An Overview." *International Labour Review* 136:315–39.

Berger, Joseph, Hamit Fisek, Robert Norman, and Morris Zelditch. 1977. *Status Characteristics and Social Interaction.* New York: Elsevier.

Browne, Irene and Paula England. 1997. "Oppression from Within and Without in Sociological Theories: An Application to Gender." *Current Perspectives in Social Theory* 17: 77–104.

Conway, Michael, M. Teresa Pizzamiglio and Lauren Mount. 1996. "Status, Communality and Agency: Implications for Stereotypes of Gender and Other Groups." *Journal of Personality and Social Psychology* 71: 25–38.

Correll, Shelley J. 2001. "Gender and the Career Choice Process: The Role of Biased Self-assessments." *American Journal of Sociology* 106: 1691–730.

Deaux, Kay and Mary Kite. 1987. "Thinking About Gender." 92–117 in *Analyzing Gender: A Handbook of Social Science Research*, edited by Beth Hess and Myra Marx Ferree. Newbury Park, CA: Sage.

England, Paula. 1981. "Assessing Trends in Occupational Sex Segregation, 1900–1976." 273–95 in *Sociological Perspectives on the Labor Market*, edited by I. Berg. New York: Academic Press.

———. 1984. "Wage Appreciation and Depreciation: A Test of Neoclassical Economic Explanations of Occupational Sex Segregation." *Social Forces* 62:726–49.

———. 1992. *Comparable Worth: Theories and Evidence.* New York: Aldine.

———. 1993. "The Separative Self: Andocentric Bias in Neoclassical Economics." Pp. 37–53 in *Beyond Economic Man: Feminist Theory and Economics*, edited by Marianne A. Ferber and Julie A. Nelson. Chicago: The University of Chicago Press.

England, Paula, George Farkas, Barbara Stanek Kilbourne and Thomas Dou. 1988. "Explaining Occupational Sex Segregation and Wages: Findings from a Model with Fixed Effects." *American Sociological Review* 53:544–58.

Erickson, Kristan G. 1998. "The Impact of Cultural Status Beliefs on Individual Task Performance in Evaluative Settings: A New Direction in Expectation States Research." Ph.D. dissertation. Department of Sociology, Stanford University, Stanford, CA.

Fiske, Susan T. 1998. "Stereotyping, Prejudice, and Discrimination." Pp. 357–411 in *The Handbook of Social Psychology*, 4th edition (volume 2), edited by D.T Gilbert, S.T. Fiske, and G. Lindsey. Boston: McGraw-Hill.

Fiske, Susan T., Amy J.C. Cuddy, Peter Glick and Jun Xu. 2002. "A Model of (Often Mixed) Stereotype Content: Competence and Warmth Respectively Follow from Perceived Status and Competition. *Journal of Personality and Social Psychology* 82: 878–902.

Foschi, Martha. 1989. "Status Characteristics, Standards, and Attributions." Pp. 58–72 in Sociological *Theories in Progress: New Formulations*, edited by Joseph Berger, Morris Zelditch, Jr. and Bo Anderson.

———. 1996. "Double Standards in the Evaluation of Men and Women." *Social Psychology Quarterly* 59: 237–54.

Game, Ann and Rosemary Pringle 1983. *Gender at Work*. Boston: Alien and Unwin.

Glass, Jennifer. 1990. "The Impact of Occupational Segregation on Working Conditions." *Social Forces* 68:779–96.

Granovetter, Mark and Charles Tilly. 1988. "Inequality and Labor Processes." Pp. 175–220 in *The Handbook of Sociology*, edited by Neil J. Smelser. Newbury Park, CA: Sage Publications.

Jacobs, Jerry A. 1989. "Long-term Trends in Occupational Segregation By Sex." *American Journal of Sociology* 95:160–73.

———. 1995a. "Trends in Occupational and Industrial Sex Segregation in 56 Countries, 1960–1980." Pp. 259–93 in *Gender Inequality at Work*, edited by Jerry A. Jacobs. Thousand Oaks, CA: Sage Publications.

———. 1995b. "Gender and Academic Specialties: Trends Among Recipients of College Degrees in the 1980s." *Sociology of Education* 68: 81–98.

Jacobsen, Joyce P. 1994. "Trends in Work Force Segregation, 1960–1990." *Social Science Quarterly* 75 (1): 204–11.

Lovaglia, Michael I, Jeffrey W. Lucas, Jeffrey A. Houser, Shane R. Thye, and Barry Markovsky. 1998. "Status Processes and Mental Ability Test Scores." *American Journal of Sociology* 104: 195–228.

Marini, Margaret Mooney and Mary C. Briton. 1984. "Sex Typing in Occupational Socialization." Pp. 192–232 in *Sex Segregation in the Workplace*, edited by Barbara Reskin. Washington DC: National Academy Press.

National Science Board. 1993. *Science and Engineering Indicators: 1993*. Washington DC: (NSB No. 87–1).

National Science Foundation. 1994. *Women, Minorities and Persons With Disabilities in Science and Engineering: 1994*. Arlington, VA (NSF 94–333HL).

Nelson, Robert L. and William P. Bridges. 1999. *Legalizing Inequality: Courts, Markets and Unequal Pay for Women in America*. Cambridge: Cambridge University Press.

Peterson, Trond and Laurie A. Morgan. 1995. "Separate and Unequal: Occupation-Establishment Sex Segregation and the Gender Wage Gap." *American Journal of Sociology* 101: 329–65.

Polachek, Solomon. 1976. "Occupational Segregation: An Alternative Hypothesis." *Journal of Contemporary Business* 5: 1–12.

———. 1981. "Occupational Self Selection: A Human Capital Approach to Sex Differences in Occupational Structure." *Review of Economics and Statistics* 58: 60–9.

Reskin, Barbara. 1993. "Sex Segregation in the Workplace." *Annual Review of Sociology* 19: 241–70.

Reskin, Barbara and Patricia A. Roos. 1990. *Job Queues, Gender Queues: Explaining Women's Inroads into Male Occupations*. Philadelphia: Temple University Press.

Ridgeway, Cecilia. 1997. "Interaction and the Conservation of Gender Inequality: Considering Employment." *American Sociological Review* 62: 218–35.

Shih, Margaret, Todd L. Pittinsky and Nalini Ambady. 1999. "Stereotype Susceptibility: Identity, Salience and Shifts in Quantitative Performance." *Psychological Science* 10: 80–3.

Steele, Claude M. 1997. "A Threat Is in the Air: How Stereotypes Shape Intellectual Identity and Performance." *American Psychologist* 52: 613–29.

Steele, Claude M. and J. Aronson. 1995. "Stereotype Threat and Intellectual Task Performance of African Americans." *Journal of Personality and Social Psychology* 69: 797–811.

Tienda, Marta and Vilma Ortiz. 1987. "Intraindustry Occupational Recomposition and Gender Inequality in Earnings." Pp. 23–51 in *Ingredients for Women's Employment Policy*, edited by Christine Bose and Glenna Spitze. Albany, NY: State University of New York Press.

Troyer, Lisa, 2001. *SES v 7.2: A Computerized Version of the Expectation States Research Program's Standardized Experimental Setting.*

Wagner, David G. and Joseph Berger. 1993. "Status Characteristics Theory: The Growth of a Program." Pp. 23–63 and 454–63 in *Theoretical Research Programs: Studies in the Growth of Theory*, edited by Joseph Berger and Morris Zelditch Jr. Stanford, CA: Stanford University Press.

Williams, John E. and Deborah L. Best. 1990. *Measuring Sex Stereotypes: A Multinational Study.* Newbury Park, CA: Sage.

Zellner, Harriet. 1975. "The Determinants of Occupational Pay." Pp. 44–70 in *Sex, Discrimination and the Division of Labor*, edited by Cynthia B. Lloyd. New York: Columbia University Press.

READING RESPONSES

1. Describe your career goal (if you haven't decided, describe the type of career you hope to have). Now try to list as many factors as you can that affected your choice, specific things that might fit the following general categories:
   - Family relationships
   - Economic considerations
   - Physical skills
   - Emotional capacities
   - Intellectual abilities
   - Geographic location
   - Lifestyle options
   - Gender

2. Look at Correll's first hypothesis. Prior to reading Correll's research, would you have expected that men would assess their competence at a given task more highly if they believe that men perform the task better than women do? What personal experiences shape your opinion?

3. Correll begins to research gender differences in career choices because she's curious about the "stubborn" segregation of men and women into different careers. As she reviews the previous research on this topic and builds the theoretical framework for her own study, Correll reviews many sociological factors that influence people when they are choosing their careers. Scan Correll's review of the literature (pages 271–77). Which factors seem most influential to you? Least influential?

NOTES ON GRAMMAR, STYLE, AND RHETORIC: NOUN PHRASES

Shelley J. Correll's "Constraints into Preferences: Gender, Status, and Emerging Career Aspirations" offers a striking mix of sentences that were easy to read and those that are much more challenging.

Consider some sentences that seem easy. Here is one from the abstract: "In this condition, male participants assessed their task ability higher than female participants did even though all were given the same scores" (page 270). Here is one from the literature review: "According to these theories, women know they will likely need to take an extended absence for child birth and/or care, so they choose jobs with the above characteristics to maximize their lifetime earnings" (272). Finally, here is an example from later still in the report: "I provide subjects in this condition with evidence that males, on average, have more ability at the experimental task" (277).

These examples contrast to many other sentences in the article. For example, consider the first sentence of the abstract: "This study presents an experimental evaluation of a model that describes the constraining effect of cultural beliefs about gender on the emerging career-relevant aspirations of men and women" (269). This sentence is not quite as long as the longest of the three earlier examples, yet many readers may have to read it more than once to figure out the meanings of its various parts and to relate those meanings to one another. Sentences like this last example significantly challenge even expert readers.

What lies at the heart of this challenge? Long and densely informative noun phrases, especially the noun phrases that contain one or more nominalizations. The main ingredient of a noun phrase is a noun, often accompanied by *a*, *an*, or *the*: *the nature*. But such noun phrases can have one or more modifiers before the noun: *the gendered nature*. They can have one or more modifiers after the noun: *the nature of the career-choice process*. And they can have one or more modifiers both before and after the noun: *the gendered nature of the career-choice process*.

Since writers can include several modifiers both before and after a noun, they can produce long noun phrases that carry a great deal of information. Consider two that Correll uses: "a gender-differentiated double standard for attributing performance to ability" (270), and "the constraining effect of cultural beliefs about gender on self-assessments of task competence and emerging career-relevant aspirations" (273). Moreover, since a noun phrase can appear wherever a noun can appear (for example, as the subject and the direct object), it is possible to find sentences and clauses in this report that consist almost entirely of noun phrases (the noun phrases in the following clause are underlined): "... gender differences in self-assessments of task competence play a mediating role in producing gender differences in emerging aspirations" (from a section of the paper not reproduced for you).

But there is more to the story of why some sentences in this article are challenging to read and understand. Many of the noun phrases contain nominalizations, and most nominalizations pack up a lot of information in one word. A nominalization is a noun derived from a verb or an adjective. From the verb *analyze*, for example, we have derived the nominalization *analysis*. And from the adjective *murky* we have derived the nominalization *murkiness*.

Now consider how writers can use a nominalization to pack up a great deal of information. Early in her article, Correll writes that already in high school, young men and women decide to take different kinds of courses and later in college select different majors. She goes on to note that once they select different majors, they see different kinds of jobs as possible options for themselves. Shortly thereafter, she packs all that meaning up in one noun phrase with the nominalization *divergence* as the main noun: "this early gender divergence" (272). It is easy to see that if writers build lots of sentences around noun phrases that are as packed with meaning as "this early gender divergence" is, they can put a strain on their readers' abilities to understand their work. But when they are writing for other experts, the density of information carried by nominalizations and noun phrases is efficient. Technical jargon can be useful among the experts, but even if you are an expert, be very cautious about making readers work too hard to unpack your meaning.

In Your Own Writing. . .

How do you know when to use long and dense noun phrases and when to avoid them?
- Use long noun phrases when you need a short-hand way of referring to a complex idea. Describe the complex idea once (including the noun phrase you will use subsequently) and afterward refer to the idea with the noun phrase.
- Use long noun phrases to refer to information that your reader already understands.
- Avoid long noun phrases when your reader is unfamiliar with the subject matter in general or the long complex idea that the noun string specifically refers to.
- Avoid long noun phrases when you do not know how well your reader can read. Long noun strings pose significant challenges for weaker readers.

STUDENT WRITING IN SOCIOLOGY

Introduction by Joy Van Marion, sociology major

The Assignment. In my Sociology 151 class, our professor often encouraged us to imagine possible relationships among aspects of human society. When we conducted our own sociological research we tested one of those potential relationships with a hypothesis-driven study. Since we were amateur social science researchers, our professor gave us a list of narrow topics with well-established theoretical frameworks. I picked "acceptance of cohabitation" (basically, whether or not people approve of unmarried people in a sexual relationship living together).

The Content. Since I was also taking a political science course that semester, I was doing a lot of thinking about how people identify with a particular political party. I began to wonder if these two aspects of human society related to each other, so I decided to research how students' political views related to their views about cohabitation. This gave me an independent variable (a person's established, chosen political views) and a dependent variable (a person's views on cohabitation). To break these independent and dependent variables down further, I created categories for both variables. For example, I categorized political views as liberal, moderate, and conservative. I categorized reasons to cohabitate as economics, safety, and sex.

From there, I used surveys to gather information from a sample of college students. The survey method was ideal since the surveys didn't take long to fill out, and that left me time to interview students. Once I collected all of the student surveys, my professor ran statistical tests through the computer on the data, and I discovered if my hypothesis was right.

Learning to Write in Sociology. Sociologists use the structure of their report to emphasize their objectivity. The first part of my sociology report, the abstract, provided a short summary of the whole project. Then I included my problem statement, which includes my questions and why they are important. In this section, I tried to grab the reader's interest and show why the questions I asked were good ones. Next, in the "Literature Review," I laid out my theoretical framework. I described what I had found in the scholarship on cohabitation and, in particular, how people's political perspectives relate to their views on cohabitation. In this way, the reader can see how my research fits into a bigger scholarly conversation on the subject.

By this point, I was ready to talk about how I conducted my study: in "Research Design," I show the reader how I tested my hypothesis—with a survey. A section of my report called "Sampling and Data Collection" describes the characteristics of the people we studied and the strengths and weaknesses of my research design. In the "Data Analysis" (results) section I used tables to show the relationship between my independent variables and dependent variables. For social scientists, tables are like pictures in a story; they present everything at a glance. In my conclusion, I described what I had learned and what my study can offer to other scholars.

Creating Change through Writing in Social Work. When I signed up for Sociology 151 as a freshman, I thought, "Yes, an easy class!" I imagined that I would read and write interesting stories about far-away human cultures; I really didn't expect to learn much about the people around me. Doing sociological research showed me that I have plenty to learn about the human culture that I'm a part of. As a senior majoring in social work, I feel ready to use my writing to improve the world around me. Writing is one of the primary tools that social workers use to help others. Social workers write assessments so poor families can get enough to eat; they write home studies so that foster families can provide safe homes for needy children; they write petitions to the court so that battered women can receive protection from their abusive husbands. Social workers write to make people's lives better.

But social workers use writing to make a different kind of change, too. Designing research projects and then writing about them reminds me (and my readers) to think differently—more critically—about the nature and causes of social problems like poverty or unequal pay for male and female workers. When students take on complex research questions like sociologists do, they learn how to use a theoretical framework to limit a research topic. They begin to ask questions and test answers; they begin to make a difference in the world.

The Politics of Cohabitation
Joy Van Marion

Abstract

The purpose of this research project is to survey a sample of the student body at a small, Midwestern college to determine their views on cohabitation. Students were given the opportunity to relay personal information such as political identification and opinions on cohabitation. The data were then reviewed and patterns noted. The following paper specifically analyzes survey data regarding students' political associations and their feelings about cohabitation.

The problem statement explains the need or purpose for the study, offering some background context, and sparking interest in the subject.

Problem Statement

Cohabitation is reshaping the structure of family life and society on the whole. Statistics show that this specific relationship is on the rise. In 1970, 523 thousand American couples cohabitated. In 1993 that number rose to 3.5 million (Wilhelm, 1998, 289). Two questions might be asked: "For what reasons do people choose to cohabitate?" and "How do their political views correlate to their willingness to cohabitate?" To answer these questions, researchers must explore the reasons people choose to cohabitate rather than form another relationship such as marriage. Furthermore, they must study the attitudes that members of American society hold toward the social practice of cohabitation. This study attends to possible connections between people's political views and their attitudes toward the practice of cohabitation. By researching the relationship between people's political stances and their acceptance of cohabitation, we may start to better understand people's attitudes toward cohabitation.

I learned the importance of proper citation, to verify statistics and give the author credit. Many of the social sciences use the American Psychological Association's formatting method (APA) to cite sources, and that is what was required for this course.

The literature review explores what other studies have been done on and/or relate to your research subject. This helps you decide where your study fits into the research, what it might verify or disprove that other studies have already looked at, or what it might accomplish that other studies have not yet set out to do. The literature review is therefore the theoretical foundation for my research design.

Literature Review

Cohabitation is a popular and growing development in social relationships across the United States. Cohabitation in this study specifically refers to a mutual relationship of emotional and/or physical intimacy between two members of the opposite sex who, though not married, share the same residency. This social relationship appeals to heterosexual couples for economic, safety, and physical reasons. Yet cohabitation remains controversial, as evidenced by two articles on this topic that appeared in magazines for the general public.

According to Carin Gorrell, "about half of American couples today live together before marrying" (2000, 16). In her article Gorrell describes the relationships of couples who cohabitate prior to marriage and those who do not. Gorrell summarizes a study by Catherine Cohan, Ph.D., to suggest that couples who cohabitate before marriage face more difficulties in marriage than those who don't. According to Cohan's research, cohabitating couples do not problem-solve or communicate as well as other couples (2000, 16). Cohan speculates that perhaps the people who choose to cohabit before marriage have weak communication skills prior to cohabitation, and thus their weaker communication skills are not a result of cohabitation. Cohan also suggests that possibly the lack of commitment in a cohabitating relationship weakens a couple's investment in the relationship and diminishes their attempts to improve their communication patterns (2000, 16). Gorrell's attitude toward cohabitation become clear when she concludes with this statement from Cohan: "There is no evidence that living together before marriage benefits couples" (2000, 16).

On the other hand, Gunnell argues in favor of cohabitation, claiming that individuals should not be required to limit themselves to marital relationships alone. Furthermore, according to Gunnell, social relationships like cohabitation will evolve to meet society's needs; since social relationships evolve, people should be free to live and love as they like. While Gunnell expresses concern that the children resulting from male/female relationships are cared for in a healthy environment, she argues that all other decisions regarding the characteristics of the relationship should be left to the adults involved (Gunnell, 2000).

These two views appear to suggest a population divided over cohabitation. Lye and Waldron (1997) offer four main hypotheses as to why people hold the beliefs that they do about cohabitating. First, they offer the Consumerism Hypothesis that focuses on people's lifetime goals as a factor that shapes their attitudes about cohabitation. According to this hypothesis, "high aspirations for material goods and living standards contributes to non-traditional family and gender role behavior and attitudes" (1997, 201). In other words, people who want to prosper financially would tend to cohabitate and would, as a result, have positive attitudes regarding cohabitation.

Second, Lye and Waldron describe the Higher Order Needs Hypothesis. This hypothesis focuses on a pattern of human reasoning as the source for people's attitudes toward the

Hypotheses mark the research method of many social sciences. It all begins with potential answers to a question about human society.

social practice of cohabitation. This hypothesis suggests that people's desire for "personal fulfillment, self-actualization and individual autonomy" could cause them to choose a type of relationship (such as cohabitation) that satisfies their sexual needs but does not limit their personal freedom (1997, 201). Thus, the hypothesis predicts that people who focus more intensely on their personal needs and goals are more likely to cohabitate and, in turn, to accept cohabitation as an acceptable (perhaps even preferable) social practice.

Next, Lye and Waldron describe the Political Ideology Hypothesis. This hypothesis proposes a correlation between people's political views and their acceptance or rejection of cohabitation as a social practice. The hypothesis suggests that people who hold liberal views about political issues would be inclined to approve of cohabitation. People who hold more conservative views about political issues would be negatively disposed toward this relationship (1997).

Fourth, Lye and Waldron discuss the Social Concerns Hypothesis. This explanation suggests that a combination of "traditional" and "non-traditional" views shape a person's social interactions, and consequently, their attitudes toward cohabitation (1997, 203).

Interestingly, the results of Lye and Waldron's research most closely supported the Political Ideology Hypothesis. Their research seems to suggest that people's political beliefs strongly correlate to their attitudes regarding cohabitation (Lye and Waldron, 1997). Wilhelm (1998) offers supporting data for the relationship between people's political beliefs and their attitudes toward cohabitation. She concludes, "Participation in left-oriented activism strongly affects the likelihood of cohabitation" (1998, 310).

For college students in particular, three central factors seem to influence their attitudes toward cohabitation. Knox (1999) outlines these: age, hedonistic sexual values, and interracial dating experiences. He argues that the evidence suggests those students who are older, believe in hedonist practices, and do or would date people of different ethnicities are more likely to enter a cohabitating relationship (Knox, 1999).

In the following report, cohabitation will be studied from the perspective of students enrolled in a small, Midwestern college. The data that were collected for this study are meant to confirm the young adult's attitude toward cohabitation and determine who favors it, who objects to it, and whether the political views of the individual correlates with her or his attitude toward cohabitation.

Hypothesis

> This is where I get to make a statement about what I think the answers to my questions will be, where I put my theory to the test.

There is a significant correlation between an individual's political views and his/her stance on cohabitation. People who hold conservative political views are more likely to disapprove of cohabitation. Persons who have liberal political ideologies are more likely to approve of cohabitation. People with "middle-of-the-road" political ideologies are more likely to approve of cohabitation in some circumstances and disapprove of it in others. The independent variable is the political identity of each individual. The dependent variable is the individual's response toward cohabitation. The assumption is that the independent variable affects the dependent variable.

Research Design

> This is my methods section.

Surveys were used to collect data on cohabitation. The advantages of this research method include its time efficiency, cost efficiency, and ability to examine a wide range of subjects. Surveys study a representative sample of the population in a relatively small amount of time (Tischler, 2000). People are asked direct questions and given the opportunity to respond in short answers. However, the answers received from the population are not always accurate. People may not be truthful in their responses if they are uncomfortable with the questions or feel

> Here I explain some research limitations to help the reader know how to interpret the study's findings.

threatened by them. Also, if the respondents misinterpret a question's meaning, their answers may not be accurate reflections of what they really think or believe. Consequently, the results will be skewed. Researchers must recognize the potential for error in a survey (Tischler, 36).

Sampling and Data Collection

> I tried to use active verbs as opposed to passive verbs so that readers could more easily follow my writing, but I did not use first-person pronouns (*I* or *we*) that would call attention to me rather than the study.

The target for study was the student body of a small, Midwestern college. The sample of subjects drawn from the population at this college included 478 students. Of the 478 respondents, 237 were males and 241 were females. The total number consisted of 143 freshmen, 143 sophomores, 101 juniors, and 91 seniors. Participants ranged from 17 years of age to 24 years of age. The population size was small enough to study carefully and large enough to monitor for results and significant patterns. The surveys were distributed to specific individuals in an attempt to gather data from an equal number of first, second, third, and fourth year students as well as an equal number of male and female students. Though the final sample of students did not match the original outline for the sample, the sample obtained is still valid for study.

These explanations help show how the data are skewed. Later, I learned that some student subjects were confused about the definition of cohabitation. This confusion may have affected their answers.

Certain limitations of the sampling and data collection did occur. An equal number of first, second, third, and fourth year students were not contacted. It is important to note, too, that the actual respondents could only choose between the answers provided for them and may not have been able to provide the fullest explanations. Furthermore, participants may have been confused about the meaning of questions and been unable to provide the most accurate information. Those who answered the questions may have purposely given a false reply if they felt ashamed or were offended by a question. In short, the survey did not reach equal populations of the student body and could not extract the most honest or complete data.

Data Analysis

the results section

Cross-tabs are statistical tests.

The cross-tabs necessary to test this hypothesis address the political views and the social views on cohabitation of 478 college students. In Table 1, the data establish a foundation of political ideologies, distinguishing between liberal, middle-of-the-road, and conservative participants. Tables 2, 3, and 4 show which respondents approved of cohabitation for economic reasons, safety reasons, and the satisfaction of sexual desires. Finally, the data in Tables 2, 3, and 4 also depict the individuals' political views next to their estimation of whether or not there is a chance that they would cohabitate before marriage.

Looking back, I think I might give a bit more of an explanation about this table by summarizing the test results in words instead of relying on the table alone to illustrate the findings.

Based on survey data, the 478 respondents are divided into three categories: liberal, middle-of-the-road, and conservative as shown in Table 1.

Table 2 identifies student views on cohabitation for economic reasons. Of the 85 liberal respondents, 76.5% approve of cohabitation for economic reasons and 23.5% disapprove. Of the 214 middle-of-the-road respondents, 71.5% approve of cohabitation and 28.5% disapprove. Of the 174 conservative respondents, 37.5% approved of cohabitation and 62.5% disapproved.

Table 1   Frequency Count Percentage Table

	Frequency	Percent
Liberal	85	17.8
Middle-of-the-road	215	45.0
Conservative	177	36.8
No Response	2	0.4
Total	n = 478	100.0

n = number of respondents

Table 2 Cross-tabs Correlating Political Affiliation with Views on Cohabitation for Economic Reasons

	Yes, I agree with cohabitation for economic reasons	No, I do not agree with cohabitation for economic reasons	Total
Liberal	76.5%	23.5%	100%
Middle-of-the-road	71.5%	28.5%	100%
Conservative	37.5%	62.5%	100%

The numbers suggest that for economic benefits the liberal students are more approving of cohabitation and the conservatives are less approving.

Regarding cohabitation for security purposes (Table 3), of the 85 liberal respondents, again, 76.5% agree with cohabitation and 23.5% disagree. Of the 214 middle-of-the-road respondents, 70.1% agree and 29.9% disagree. And of the 174 conservative respondents, 39.1% agree while 60.9% disagree. Here, too, there is a decreasing amount of support for cohabitation as the political status of an individual shifts from liberal to conservative.

In response to cohabitation for sexual desires as outlined in Table 4, 8.5% of the 85 liberal respondents approve while 91.5% disapprove. Of the 214 middle-of-the-road respondents, 2.8% approve while 97.2% disapprove. Of the 174 conservative respondents, 1.2% approve and 98.8% disapprove. In this case, too, the liberals were more supportive of cohabitation for sexual purposes than were conservatives.

Finally, respondents were asked to indicate whether there is a chance they might cohabitate before marriage, based on their personal experience. Among liberal students, 63.9% said yes and 36.1% said no. Among middle-of-the-road students, 45.1% of the middle of the road respondents said yes and 54.9% said no.

Table 3 Cross-tabs Correlating Political Affiliation with Views on Cohabitation for Safety Purposes

	Yes, I agree with cohabitation for safety purposes	No, I do not agree with cohabitation for safety purposes	Total
Liberal	76.5%	23.5%	100%
Middle-of-the-road	70.1%	29.9%	100%
Conservative	39.1%	60.9%	100%

Table 4   Cross-tabs Correlating Political Affiliation with Views on Cohabitation to Satisfy Sexual Desires

	Yes, I agree with cohabitation to satisfy sexual desires	No, I do not agree with cohabitation to satisfy sexual desires	Total
Liberal	8.5%	91.5%	100%
Middle-of-the-road	2.8%	97.2%	100%
Conservative	1.2%	98.8%	100%

> I wondered if another table would have helped to clarify these results.

Among conservative students, 19.3% of the conservatives said yes while 80.7% said no.

The results were as expected and the hypothesis made at the beginning of this study is supported. There appears to be a connection between people's political ideals and their views on cohabitation. The liberals strongly favored cohabitation in more circumstances than the conservatives did. Interestingly, the middle-of-the-road respondents were very supportive of cohabitation for economic or safety reasons while they were almost completely disapproving of it for sexual purposes. And overall the liberals were the most likely to cohabitate before marriage, followed by the middle-of-the-road participants, with the conservatives least likely to cohabitate of them all.

The information provided here is valid and reliable for the purposes of a research analysis in an introductory course in sociology. It evaluates a sample of the student body as they understood the questions concerning cohabitation and then reacted from personal opinion. The data are unreliable to the extent that participants may have misinterpreted questions and consequently responded incorrectly, intentionally lied, or chosen not to answer at all. The results of this survey cannot be generalized to all college student populations.

Conclusions

In summary, the findings are consistent with the original hypothesis. If these patterns are representative of the college's student body, researchers may begin making predictions about the future social relationships within this local society based on the connections drawn here between the political ideals of students and their views on cohabitation. A greater number of liberals in the community may indicate the potential for a rise in the practice of cohabitation; whereas a greater number of conservatives may suggest the potential for a decline in cohabitating relationships.

On a broader scale, political identification may be taken as an indicator of one's standing on cohabitation. Liberals tend to embrace tolerance of new and developing social relationships that appear appropriate to the present day culture. If a relationship is financially and physically satisfying, then they tend to approve. Conservatives tend to cling to traditional family structures and reject changes to these relationships. They are strongly tied to their historical and often religious roots, which make little or no room for relationships of cohabitation.

In closing, it is impossible to state from the evidence found here that an individual's political standing will confirm their position on cohabitation. However, the data strongly suggest that there is some association between political ideology and one's stand on cohabiting. The research and findings from this study form a base of empirical evidence on which to build future sociological studies.

> Out of the collective knowledge base come creative and resourceful applications.

Works Cited

Gorrell, C. (2000, Nov/Dec). Live-in and Learn. *Psychology Today*, 33, 16.

Gunnell, B. (2000, Aug, 28). "I Do"—But Not for Long, Thanks. *New Statesman*, 129, 13.

Knox, D. (1999, Dec). Characteristics of College Students Who Cohabit. *College Student Journal*, 129 (4), 510–12.

Lye, D. N. and Waldron, I. (1997). Attitudes Toward Cohabitation, Family, and Gender Roles: Relationships to Values and Political Ideology. *Sociological Perspectives*, 40 (2), 199–225.

Wilhelm, B. (1998, Sept). Changes in Cohabitation Across Cohorts: the Influence of Political Activism. *Social Forces*, 77 (1), 289–313.

READING RESPONSES

1. Review the research by Lye and Waldron on pages 289–90. Prior to reading Van Marion's results, which did you believe to be the most influential factor on people's attitudes toward cohabitation? Did her study change your mind? If not, why not?

2. In her review of literature, Van Marion does more than present all the scholarly research on cohabitation; she builds the theoretical framework for her own study. Analyze how Van Marion builds this framework: What research does she begin with? What research does she end with? And recommend revisions: Which additional topics should she have researched? Which topics could she have eliminated from her review of the literature?

3. Working from Lye and Waldron, Van Marion looks only for a correlation between political affiliation and attitudes toward cohabitation, not for all the causes of students' attitudes toward cohabitation. Using sociological imagination, list possible factors that account for the correlation between students' political affiliation and their attitudes toward cohabitation. Then, rank-order your list from what you suspect to be the most significant factor to least significant factor.

PUBLIC WRITING IN SOCIOLOGY

Introduction

Stephanie Coontz, a professor of history and women's studies, has published several books and many scholarly articles on the history of marriage, global perspectives on marriage, and the nature of modern, Western marriages. Coontz's theoretical framework consists, in part, of the presumption that marriage is shaped by cultural factors that change across time and cultures. She looks at cultures from long ago or far away to help her readers more easily see how social structures such as economics, politics, or gender expectations shape the relationship between marriage partners. After considering marriage from this distance, readers are better able to critically examine the factors that affect marriage relationships in their own time and culture. This kind of creative thinking sets the stage for hypothesis building and testing.

In this article, Coontz focuses on self-help books about marriage and critiques the advice they offer, advice directed primarily to women. Coontz provides a brief historical overview of marriage in the Western tradition to bolster her argument that contemporary marriage advice is a remnant from a previous time and inadequate to meet the needs of modern marriage partners; in fact, the nature of marriage has changed so much that this old-fashioned advice actually causes more problems than it solves. Blending historical overview and sociological research on contemporary marriages, Coontz suggests that modern marriages take more work from both partners, but that these marriages are ultimately more satisfying.

Why marriage today takes more love, work—from both partners

Stephanie Coontz

The Christian Science Monitor, (June 28, 2005): 9

For hundreds of years, marital advice books have been written for women rather than men, because women were responsible for making a marriage work. And over all that time, their advice to women could be summed up in a single word: submit.

Church officials in the 12th century declared that only God could own a woman's soul, but her husband had a leasehold over her body and she could not deny him its use. The tale of "Patient Griselda" was a staple of the marital advice industry in the 14th century. Its moral, one author explained, was that if a husband makes outrageous demands, do not refuse one's "ruler," for "greater good cometh by obeying." In the 16th century, ministers rebuked wives who used endearing nicknames for their husbands, because such familiarity undermined a man's authority. . . .

Beginning in the 1920s, professional psychologists replaced physicians and ministers as advice givers, but otherwise little changed. The premier marital therapy association of the 1950s, the Institute of Family Relations, handled the popular *Ladies' Home Journal* feature, "Can This Marriage Be Saved?" The answer was almost always yes, but only if, after counseling, the wife allowed her husband "to feel, as she now feels, that he is the head of the family."

The "rules" for a successful marriage in the 1950s were clear-cut—and still directed at women. Marry early. Say no to sex before marriage, but afterwards, never say no to anything again. Act dependent and a little dumb. One prominent 1950s marriage therapist told wives to express an interest in their husband's work, but never act as though they were truly knowledgeable about it. If your marriage is in trouble, "pretend ineptitude" at tasks like balancing the checkbook and invent little tasks to make your husband feel needed, such as fraying a lamp cord to produce a short, so he can step in and rescue you.

Today we may find such advice appalling, but back then it actually worked. Until the end of the 1950s, girls with the most conventional views about women's roles and the least economic independence were the ones who got and stayed married. A woman who postponed marriage to pursue a college degree might never marry at all, and if she did she had a much higher risk of divorce.

But this rule, and most others like it, no longer applies. For females born since 1960, college graduates and women with higher earnings are more likely to marry than women with less education and lower wages. Men are much more likely than in the past to want a partner who is equally educated. And studies show that marriages in which wives are not afraid to ask their husbands to change and where men respond favorably to such requests have the greatest chance of turning into long, happy relationships.

Yet many marriage-advice books still claim that the secret to a successful marriage is for women to "surrender" to their husbands' traditional views about gender roles. But recent research shows that this is a bad idea. Today men with traditional ideas about male and female roles are more likely to divorce than men with non-traditional views. It's particularly bad advice to tell women to play games to catch a man, because women tend to grow more discontented with their marriages over time, while men grow more content, even if they initially resisted pressure to change their behavior.

I once asked my students to review the marital advice books in our town's bookstores and determine how many were based on actual research data and peer-reviewed studies. Only 34 percent—one in three—passed that test. One student went a step further and researched the family history of marital-advice experts. Half of them had been through a divorce, a track record no better than the non-experts!

Of course, there are many well-researched books that provide tested methods for improving a marriage. And divorced experts may even bring a special insight to their work because they've personally experienced how a marriage can go wrong. But the role of marriage in society and personal life has changed more in the past 30 years than in the previous 3,000, primarily because of the new opportunities for women to live independent lives. In consequence, everything we used to think we knew about who marries and how marriage works—and why it doesn't work—is changing.

Marriage was a lot more stable when women had to give in to everything their husbands wanted. But it was also less satisfying, not just for women but for many men who never quite understood why their wives were so unhappy or withdrawn.

Over the past century, a good marriage has steadily become fairer, more fulfilling, and better at fostering the well-being of adults and children than ever before in history. At the same time, an unsatisfactory marriage has become less bearable and more brittle. These two seemingly contradictory changes stem from the same source—the breakdown of husbands' legal domination over wives and of women's economic dependence on men.

Today, marriage takes more time, more love, more work, and more daily negotiation—from both partners, not just the wife—than it did in the past. There is no magic formula, weekend encounter, or set of "rules" that can bypass the hard work it takes to make a marriage succeed. The bad news is that if negotiations break down, there are few constraints forcing unhappy partners to stay together. Yet if they could speak, a lot of couples who lived in the "old days" would tell you that this is also the good news.

READING RESPONSES

1. Describe a marriage portrayed on a television show or in a movie, paying special attention to how the two partners interact. Have the screenwriters portrayed the marriage as a contemporary marriage, a marriage out of the 1950s, or a mix of traditional and contemporary elements?
2. Describe Coontz's theoretical framework. What aspects of marriage does it help Coontz focus in on? What aspects of marriage does it ignore?
3. What argument is Coontz making when she reports on her students' analysis of marriage advice books? What argument could be made to disagree with her? Would you make such an argument?

MORE WRITING IN SOCIOLOGY

Introduction

Many people are surprised by the number of poor women who become mothers when they are very young, some as early as 14 or 15. Some policy makers have proposed that fewer young women will get pregnant if these women have access to good sex education and effective birth control. Others seem to blame the girls themselves, pointing to lax morals or the breakdown of the nuclear family. Rather than rely on speculation, two professors of sociology, Kathryn Edin and Maria Kefalas examine the sociological factors behind the number of poor, young mothers by asking two questions: Why do poor women have children when they are very young? Wouldn't it be wiser for them to wait until marriage to have children?

It might seem that previous research has already answered that last question. In the 1990s social scientists discovered a number of negative outcomes for children raised in mother-only families. Relying in part on these studies, some politicians reformed welfare in 1996 (The Personal Responsibility and Work Opportunity Reconciliation Act) and, even more to the point, politicians authorized nearly two billion dollars in 2003 to encourage welfare recipients to marry. The logic of this bill goes something like this: Because families of single mothers are more likely to be poor than families with two parents, if "welfare mothers" married (and stay married), poverty would disappear and children would face fewer challenges in life. Of course, someone with a sociological imagination recognizes that many factors may contribute to the number of mother-only families and the challenges faced by children in those families. Poverty is only one factor. Nevertheless, "wedfare" is currently a poverty policy favored by many in the United States.

Edin and Kefalas find it striking that in the midst of these policy discussions the voices of young, unwed mothers—those most affected by poverty and early childbearing—are seldom heard. So they interviewed single mothers from low-income communities in Philadelphia. Edin and Kefalas focus on the answers from one of their interviewees, Jen Burke. Through rich description and Jen's own words, they paint a full picture of her life as a young, poor, single mother. As readers come to understand Jen's life and perspective more fully, they are better able to imagine how Jen's social setting within a larger political and economic context, shapes the complicated choices she makes. Through this informal case study, Edin and Kefalas let readers hear Jen's story for themselves.

Unmarried with Children
Kathryn Edin and Maria Kefalas

Contexts: Understanding People in Their Social Worlds, 2005, 4(2):16–22.

Jen Burke, a white tenth-grade dropout who is 17 years old, lives with her stepmother, her sister, and her 16-month-old son in a cramped but tidy row home in Philadelphia's beleaguered Kensington neighborhood. She is broke, on welfare, and struggling to complete her GED. Wouldn't she and her son have been better off if she had finished high school, found a job, and married her son's father first?

In 1950, when Jen's grandmother came of age, only 1 in 20 American children was born to an unmarried mother. Today, that rate is 1 in 3—and they are usually born to those least likely to be able to support a child on their own. In our book, *Promises I Can Keep: Why Poor Women Put Motherhood Before Marriage*, we discuss the lives of 162 white, African American, and Puerto Rican low-income single mothers living in eight destitute neighborhoods across Philadelphia and its poorest industrial suburb, Camden. We spent five years chatting over kitchen tables and on front stoops, giving mothers like Jen the opportunity to speak to the question so many affluent Americans ask about them: Why do they have children while still young and unmarried when they will face such an uphill struggle to support them?

Romance at Lightning Speed

Jen started having sex with her 20-year-old boyfriend Rick just before her 15th birthday. A month and a half later, she was pregnant. "I didn't want to get pregnant," she claims. "*He* wanted me to get pregnant. As soon as he met me, he wanted to have a kid with me," she explains. Though Jen's college-bound suburban peers would be appalled by such a declaration, on the streets of Jen's neighborhood, it is something of a badge of honor. "All those other girls he was with, he didn't want to have a baby with any of them," Jen boasts. "I asked him, 'Why did you choose me to have a kid when you could have a kid with any one of them?' He was like, 'I want to have a kid with *you*'." Looking back, Jen says she now believes that the reason "he wanted me to have a kid that early is so that I didn't leave him."

In inner-city neighborhoods like Kensington, where child-bearing within marriage has become rare, romantic relationships like Jen and Rick's proceed at lightning speed. A young man's avowal, "I want to have a baby by you," is often part of the courtship ritual from the beginning. This is more than idle talk, as their first child is typically conceived within a year from the time a couple begins "kicking it." Yet while poor couples' pillow talk often revolves around dreams of shared children, the news of a pregnancy—the first indelible sign of the huge changes to come—puts these still-new relationships into overdrive. Suddenly, the would-be mother begins to scrutinize her mate as never before, wondering whether he can "get himself together"—find a job, settle down, and become a family man—in time. . . .

Most poor, unmarried mothers and fathers readily admit that bearing children while poor and unmarried is not the ideal way to do things. Jen believes the best time to become a mother is "after you're out of school and you got a job, at least, when you're like 21. . . . When you're ready to have kids, you should have everything ready, have your house, have a job, so when that baby comes, the baby can have its own room." Yet given their already limited economic prospects, the poor have little motivation to time their births as precisely as their middle-class counterparts do. The dreams of young people like Jen and Rick center on children at a time of life when their more affluent peers plan for college and careers. Poor girls coming of age in the inner city value children highly, anticipate them eagerly, and believe strongly that they are up to the job of mothering—even in difficult circumstances. Jen, for example, tells us, "People outside the neighborhood, they're like, 'You're 15! You're pregnant?' I'm like, it's not none of their business. I'm gonna be able to take care of my kid. They have nothing to worry about." Jen says she has concluded that "some people . . . are better at having kids at a younger age. . . . I think it's better for some people to have kids younger."

When I Became a Mom

When we asked mothers like Jen what their lives would be like if they had not had children, we expected them to express regret over foregone opportunities for school and careers. Instead, most believe their children "saved" them. They describe their lives as spinning out of control before becoming pregnant—struggles with parents and peers, "wild," risky behavior, depression, and school failure. Jen speaks to this poignantly. "I was just real bad. I hung with a real bad crowd. I was doing pills. I was really depressed. . . . I was drinking. That was before I was pregnant." "I think," she reflects, "if I never had a baby or anything, . . . I would still be doing the things I was doing. I would probably still be doing drugs. I'd probably still be drinking." Jen admits that when she first became pregnant, she was angry that she "couldn't be out no more. Couldn't be out with my friends. Couldn't do nothing." Now, though, she says, "I'm glad I have a son . . . because I would still be doing all that stuff."

Children offer poor youth like Jen a compelling sense of purpose. Jen paints a before-and-after picture of her life that was common among the mothers we interviewed. "Before, I didn't have nobody to take care of. I didn't have nothing left to go home for. . . . Now I have my son to take care of. I have him to go home for. . . . I don't have to go buy weed or drugs with my money. I could buy my son stuff with my money! . . . I have something to look up to now." Children also are a crucial source of relational intimacy, a self-made community of care. After a nasty fight with Rick, Jen recalls, "I was crying. My son came in the room. He was hugging me. He's 16 months and he was hugging me with his little arms. He was really cute and happy, so I got happy. That's one of the good things. When you're sad, the baby's always gonna be there for you no matter what." Lately she has been thinking a lot about what her life was like back then, before the baby. "I thought about the stuff before I became a mom, what my life was like back then. I used to see pictures of me, and I would hide in every picture. This baby did so much for me. My son did a lot for me. He helped me a lot. I'm thankful that I had my baby."

Around the time of the birth, most unmarried parents claim they plan to get married eventually. Rick did not propose marriage when Jen's first child was born, but when she conceived a second time, at 17, Rick informed his dad, "It's time for me to get married. It's time for me to straighten up. This is the one I wanna be with. I had a baby with her, I'm gonna have another baby with her." Yet despite their intentions, few of these couples actually marry. Indeed, most break up well before their child enters preschool.

I'd Like to Get Married, But . . .

The sharp decline in marriage in impoverished urban areas has led some to charge that the poor have abandoned the marriage norm. Yet we found few who had given up on the idea of marriage. But like their elite counterparts, disadvantaged women set a high financial bar for marriage. For the poor, marriage has become an elusive goal—one they feel ought to be reserved for those who can support a "white picket fence" lifestyle: a mortgage on a modest row home, a car and some furniture, some savings in the bank, and enough money left over to pay for a "decent" wedding. Jen's views on marriage provide a perfect case in point. "If I was gonna get married, I would want to be married like my Aunt Nancy and my Uncle Pat. They live in the mountains. She has a job. My Uncle Pat is a state trooper; he has lots of money. They live in the [Poconos]. It's real nice out there. Her kids go to Catholic school.... That's the kind of life I would want to have. If I get married, I would have a life like [theirs]." She adds, "And I would wanna have a big wedding, a real nice wedding."

Unlike the women of their mothers' and grandmothers' generations, young women like Jen are not merely content to rely on a man's earnings. Instead, they insist on being economically "set" in their own right before taking marriage vows. This is partly because they want a partnership of equals, and they believe money buys say-so in a relationship. Jen explains, "I'm not gonna just get into marrying him and not have my own house! Not have a job! I still wanna do a lot of things before I get married. He [already] tells me I can't do nothing. I can't go out. What's gonna happen when I marry him? He's gonna say he owns me!"

Why is Jen, who describes Rick as "the love of my life," so insistent on planning an exit strategy before she is willing to take the vows she firmly believes ought to last "forever?" If love is so sure, why does mistrust seem so palpable and strong? In relationships among poor couples like Jen and Rick, mistrust is often spawned by chronic violence and infidelity, drug and alcohol abuse, criminal activity, and the threat of imprisonment....

Trust has been an enormous issue in Jen's relationship with Rick. "My son was born December 23rd, and [Rick] started cheating on me again . . . in March. . . ." Things finally came to a head when Rick got another girl pregnant. "For a while, I forgave him for everything. Now, I don't forgive him for nothing." Now we begin to understand the source of Jen's hesitancy. "He wants me to marry him, [but] I'm not really sure.... If I can't trust him, I can't marry him, 'cause we would get a divorce. If you're gonna get married, you're supposed to be faithful!" she insists. To Jen and her peers, the worst thing that could happen is "to get married just to get divorced.". . .

These Are Cards I Dealt Myself

. . . Jen clearly sees how her life has improved since Rick's dramatic exit from the scene. "That's when I really started [to get better] because I didn't have to worry about what he was doing, didn't have to worry about him cheating on me, all this stuff. [It was] then I realized that I had to do what I had to do to take care of my son. . . . When he was there, I think that my whole life revolved around him, you know, so I always messed up somehow because I was so busy worrying about what he was doing. Like I would leave the [GED] programs I was in just to go home and see what he was doing. My mind was never concentrating." Now, she says, "a lot of people in my family look up to me now, because all my sisters dropped out from school, you know, nobody went back to school. I went back to school, you know?. . . I went back to school, and I plan to go to college, and a lot of people look up to me for that, you know? So that makes me happy. . . because five years ago nobody looked up to me. I was just like everybody else."

Yet the journey has not been easy. "Being a young mom being 15, it's hard, hard, hard, you know." She says, "I have no life. . . . I work from 6:30 in the morning until 5:00 at night I leave here at 5:30 in the morning. I don't get home until about 6:00 at night." Yet she measures her worth as a mother by the fact that she has managed to provide for her son largely on her own. "I don't depend on nobody. I might live with my dad and them, but I don't depend on them, you know." She continues, "There [used to] be days when I'd be so stressed out, like, 'I can't do this!' And I would just cry and cry and cry. . . . Then I look at Colin, and he'll be sleeping, and I'll just look at him and think I don't have no [reason to feel sorry for myself]. The cards I have I've dealt myself so I have to deal with it now. I'm older. I can't change anything. He's my responsibility—he's nobody else's but mine—so I have to deal with that."

Becoming a mother transformed Jen's point of view on just about everything. She says, "I thought hanging on the corner drinking, getting high— I thought that was a good life, and I thought I could live that way for eternity, like sitting out with my friends. But it's not as fun once you have your own kid. . . . I think it changes [you]. I think, 'Would I want Colin to do that? Would I want my son to be like that. . .?' It was fun to me but it's not fun anymore. Half the people I hung with are either. . . . Some have died from drug overdoses, some are in jail, and some people are just out there living the same life that they always lived, and they don't look really good. They look really bad." In the end, Jen believes, Colin's birth has brought far more good into her life than bad. "I know I could have waited [to have a child], but in a way I think Colin's the best thing that could have happened to me. . . . So I think I had my son for a purpose because I think Colin changed my life. He saved my life, really. My whole life revolves around Colin!"

Promises I Can Keep

There are unique themes in Jen's story—most fathers are only one or two, not five years older than the mothers of their children, and few fathers have as many glaring problems as Rick—but we heard most of these themes repeatedly in the stories of the 161 other poor, single mothers we came to know. Notably, poor women do not reject marriage; they revere it. Indeed, it is the conviction that marriage is forever that makes them think that divorce is worse than having a baby outside of marriage. Their children, far from being liabilities, provide crucial social-psychological resources—a strong sense of purpose and a profound source of intimacy. Jen and the other mothers we came to know are coming of age in an America that is profoundly unequal—where the gap between rich and poor continues to grow. This economic reality has convinced them that they have little to lose and, perhaps, something to gain by a seemingly "ill-timed" birth.

The lesson one draws from stories like Jen's is quite simple: Until poor young women have more access to jobs that lead to financial independence—until there is reason to hope for the rewarding life pathways that their privileged peers pursue—the poor will continue to have children far sooner than most Americans think they should, while still deferring marriage. Marital standards have risen for all Americans, and the poor want the same things that everyone now wants out of marriage. The poor want to marry too, but they insist on marrying well. This, in their view, is the only way to avoid an almost certain divorce. Like Jen, they are simply not willing to make promises they are not sure they can keep.

READING RESPONSES

1. Did Edin and Kefalas offer you a new way of understanding why young, poor women have children? What surprised you most?
2. Because they use a case study methodology, the authors never state their theoretical framework explicitly. How would you describe their theoretical framework?
3. What in Jen's story most sparked your own curiosity? What aspect of Jen's story would you research in greater depth, if you had the opportunity?

WRITING ASSIGNMENTS

ASSIGNMENT 1: APPLYING THE PORTABLE RHETORICAL LESSON

Background: The research report "Unmarried with Children" is extracted from a larger project that sociologists Kathryn Edin and Maria Kefalas completed entitled *Promises I Can Keep: Why Poor Women Put Motherhood Before Marriage*. In the introduction they offer their research as fresh and important information that can help the U.S. government create better social welfare policies.

Your task in this assignment is to offer a recommendation for further research on a governmental policy, noting in particular who has new and important information about the social issue that the government is trying to influence.

To begin, select a specific city, state, or federal governmental policy, like those described in the introduction to "Unmarried with Children." With the help of a reference librarian who specializes in government documents, research the history of policy: When was it enacted? By whom? What was the desired outcome? Which aspects were most contested as lawmakers debated the policy? How did the public respond? Research the outcomes of the policy: Has the policy had the effect that its creators anticipated? Has it had other, unanticipated effects? Analyze the history of the policy with sociological imagination to discover the voices that were not heard in discussions on the policy. In your report, describe the policy and its consequences. Then recommend further research on the policy that will target otherwise muted voices.

ASSIGNMENT 2: MAKING CONNECTIONS

Background: Because of the complexity of human relationships, sociologists are careful to detail the theoretical framework of their research. But our focus on theoretical framework in this chapter should not imply that researchers in other disciplines do not root their research in theory; it may be that in their published work they do not make those roots as obvious as sociologists do.

Your task for this assignment is to show the theoretical roots in a piece of academic scholarship from one of three fields: religion, biotechnology, or nursing. In the first part of your report, describe what serves as an equivalent for the socio-logical imagination—the focus of the researcher's curiosity. In the second part of your report, evaluate the research, noting its strengths by answering questions like these: "What kind of information can this research reliably tell us?" and "What sources of information does it make good use of?" And then note the weaknesses of the report by answering questions like these: "What sources of information does this research ignore?" "What vital information does it not provide?"

To complete this task, choose one of the following texts:

- "Civil Religion in America" by Robert Bellah (Chapter 4)
- "Feeding the World in the Twenty-first Century" by Gordon Conway and Gary Toenniessen (Chapter 10)
- "A Phenomenologic Study of Chronic Pain" by Sandra P. Thomas (Chapter 12)

To begin, read the piece carefully and describe as specifically as possible what it is that the researcher is curious about. You may find it helpful to formulate this as a research question or a hypothesis. Then, describe the theoretical frame for this research. You may need to do some careful analysis here since the researcher may have left this somewhat or nearly completely unstated. Note the research (if any) that grounds the theoretical frame. Finally, list the conclusions that result from the research as well as the limitations of the research—both those the researcher notes and additional limitations that you note.

ASSIGNMENT 3: DOING THE RESEARCH

Background: Correll's research relies on a collection of studies that establish the existence of a social stereotype: men are "naturally" better at math than women are. Based on research she conducted in 2001, Correll concludes the following: "students, parents, and teachers perceive mathematic skills to be associated with masculinity." (page 282) This assignment requires you to engage your sociological imagination as Joy Van Marion did when she researched attitudes regarding cohabitation.

Your task for this assignment is to report on a sociological study that you have conducted, paying special attention to the relationship between your theoretical model and your hypothesis. If your teacher allows it, consider collaborating with a partner on this project.

To begin, propose a list of possible answers to the following question: What sociological factors correspond to a person's belief that men are inherently superior at mathematics? Once you have isolated one or two factors that you suspect to be especially important, do some library research to build a theoretical model for your study. The most efficient way to conduct this research is to work from Correll's bibliography with the help of a reference librarian. If you prefer to research on your own, use search terms like "gender" and "mathematical skills" in research databases that cover the fields of sociology, education, and psychology.

As you review this research, analyze how the research studies relate to each other, noting studies that build on other research as well as those that produce findings that contradict the findings of previous research. As you describe your theoretical model in your research report, be sure to help your reader see these relationships. Cite your sources in APA style.

Choose one of the sociological factors you researched and draft a hypothesis about the relationship between this factor and people's assumptions about men's superior math abilities. Simplify your hypothesis as much as possible, and be sure that you will be able to gather information about your hypothesis through a simple methodology. Design a methodology to test your hypothesis, conduct your study, and analyze the results (You may find it helpful to consult the Biology chapter for help with this part of your project).

In your report, describe the theoretical model that supports your hypothesis, your methodology, and your results. When you discuss your results, be sure to (1) show the relationship between your study and those that comprise your theoretical model, (2) note the limitations of your study, and (3) describe future research that could provide more information about your hypothesis.

BIOTECHNOLOGY: BUILDING CONSENSUS WITH KNOWLEDGE

The readings in this chapter break traditional disciplinary boundaries. Because biotechnology draws evidence and readers from a variety of academic and professional fields, the essays here are part objective science, part impassioned ethics, and part policy-making. In that way, the chapter lets you think about how your writing will constantly change and adapt to fit the expectations of different academic disciplines and to respond to unique rhetorical situations.

The authors in this chapter argue with caution, reason, and respect for the opinions of others, but they do not flinch from making specific and bold claims for action. For example, in the first reading Conway and Toenniessen argue for a partnership between higher education and industry. Such a partnership would foster responsible research for agricultural biotechnology, which could help to protect environments and produce sufficient healthy food. The student-written essay calls for a major overhaul of the health-care insurance industry. And Lempert and Dixon, co-authors of the chapter's "public" reading, reason that only a democratic process—a vote—will open a way out of the immovable battle between two equally reasonable and irreconcilable positions on stem cell research.

➤ A Portable Rhetorical Lesson:

Persuading with Balanced Arguments

The authors in this chapter write for blended audiences: people from various academic fields (scientists, philosophers, politicians, sociologists, business people), each of whom prefers different kinds of evidence. They also hold various ethical allegiances and moral assumptions (secular and religious, conservative and liberal), and they work in different settings (government, industry, social action). Because the audiences are so varied, the authors cannot target specific interests and expectations to advocate for change.

Furthermore, the issues are extremely volatile. Often people disagree vehemently about topics such as genetic engineering. As you probably know from experience, when people argue from extreme positions, they invite extreme responses. Talk shows encourage hot-tempered arguments over complicated and emotionally charged topics—with lots of shouting. However, while shouting may get high ratings for talk shows, it does not generate workable solutions to complex problems.

Therefore, if you have to suggest solutions for a complex problem, you would do well to imitate the writing of the biotechnologists in this chapter, balancing (1) a moderate tone that respects the views of opponents; (2) evidence that everyone respects, in this case scientific data; and (3) practical solutions. The fair and balanced argumentation style that results from combining these features is the chapter's main rhetorical lesson.

Regarding moderation: When no single solution resolves a problem, people can either hold stubbornly to their own positions and make no progress, or they can treat one another's positions respectfully and compromise on solutions. Writers establish themselves as reasonable and balanced by using these rhetorical strategies: they begin an argument by respecting those with whom they disagree, they admit the limits of their own claims, and they honestly acknowledge their opponents' worthwhile objections. These are the kind of people who can create positive change. The "Notes on Grammar, Style, and Rhetoric" demonstrates how "hedges" help you convey this moderate tone.

Regarding evidence: Both scientists and non-scientists respect the relative objectivity of scientific data. Consequently, the writers in this chapter use scientific data extensively—and they present the data in forms (tables, graphs, figures) that scientists and others recognize. These facts are elements of the argument about which all parties can agree, so they form the foundation for mutual understanding and respect.

Regarding practicality: The authors aim to persuade their readers that their solutions are the best available options—not necessarily perfect, but the best currently available. To argue for the best available solution, authors use data to establish the urgency of the problem, describe possible solutions, and demonstrate the superiority of one of them.

Chapter Topics: The chapter readings are about the confrontations between science and ethics that appear in biotechnology–in food production, genetics, and health care.

To Think About . . .

How 'bout a steaming cup of genetically engineered FrankenLatte? According to the Organic Consumers Association (www.organicconsumers.org), that's what you might be sipping next time you purchase a beverage from Starbucks. On its website the OCA offers advice for effective protesting, publicizes information about upcoming Starbucks protests around the nation, and provides a downloadable leaflet. The leaflet begins like this:

Consumer Warning

Do you want your coffee beverages and food to be free of genetically engineered ingredients and dangerous hormones?

Do you want to support fair wages and living conditions for coffee farmers and plantation workers?

If so here are some things you should know about Starbucks:

The rest of the brochure includes information about Starbucks' ingredients and its relationship with those who grow its coffee beans. Under the header "Starbucks or Frankenbuck$: Take Action Now!" the brochure recommends strategies for pressuring Starbucks to change its business practices.

- Do you worry about the biotechnology that might have produced the ingredients in your coffee, or milk, or breakfast cereal? Should you worry?
- What do you think of the kinds of protests that OCA promotes? Are they legal? Are they ethical? Under what circumstances would you participate in such protests?

WRITING IN BIOTECHNOLOGY

Introduction by David Koetje, Professor of Biology

"People on both sides of the debate are unwittingly collaborating to create a very considerable threat indeed. The threat is that the debate over the pros and cons of genetically modified crops may become so acrimonious that the sides cease speaking to each other altogether. . . . Through our rhetoric, we may erode the foundation of mutual trust apart from which democratic institutions fail."

Gary Comstock, *"The Threat That Biotechnology Is"*

In the heat of debate it can be difficult to maintain a moral high ground. Well-known people have capitulated to the temptation to "fight fire with fire." One sure-fire way to infuriate your critics is to call their motives into question. Consider this quote from biotechnology proponent Norman Borlaug: "I think the researchers at Cornell who fed Bt corn pollen to monarch butterflies were looking for something that would make them famous and create this big hullabaloo that's resulted."* Put-downs are another conversation buster. In response to a challenge from an environmentalist who was questioning the need for transgenic crops, one biotechnologist retorted, "Well, I live in the *real* world." Lest you think that biotechnology's proponents have a corner on bad behavior, consider this Ralph Nader quote: "This is an industry with no sense of humility or caution. The biotech industry is intent on turning the entire consuming public into guinea pigs. For those not interested in participating in such an involuntary experiment, the time to act is now."** Though cheap shots like this may be normal in national politics, it can hardly be considered good persuasive writing because it further entrenches existing conceptions and misconceptions rather than "reaching across the aisle" to build consensus.

The following essay, "Feeding the world in the twenty-first century," addresses widely-held concerns about genetically modified foods and other forms of agricultural biotechnology. The authors, Gordon Conway and Gary Toenniessen, have served, respectively, as the president and the director of the food security program at the Rockefeller Foundation, a philanthropic organization that funds scientific and social research to improve the lives of poor people. The Rockefeller Foundation has funded efforts to advance agricultural science and biotechnology throughout the world. Naturally, Conway and Toenniessen see a lot of promise in biotechnology. Yet their respect for diverse ethical concerns and accurate scientific knowledge makes their writing persuasive.

Scholars in biotechnology typically write to a mixed audience of scientists, policy wonks, advocacy groups, and the general public. To communicate with this diverse group of readers, authors must examine thoroughly, explain carefully, and refute gently.

Context and Content of the Argument. Concern about transgenic crops, which have a gene borrowed from some other species, has spread worldwide. Can transgenic crops alleviate problems of hunger and death from starvation? Biotechnology proponents claim that transgenic crops are more resistant to insect infestation, disease, drought, flooding, and pollution. Therefore, they can boost food production, especially in developing countries where soils tend to be poorer. Critics counter that the poor and hungry will never reap the benefits of transgenic crops because much of biotechnology is now controlled by for-profit corporations.

Conway and Toenniessen published this article in *Nature*, a leading scientific journal headquartered in the U.K. and read by scientists and policy analysts

---

*"Billions Served: Norman Borlaug," interview by Ronald Bailey. *Reason Magazine,* April 2000.
**"Changing the Nature of Food: Genetically Engineered Food," by Ralph Nader. *San Francisco Bay Guardian,* January 8, 2001.

worldwide. The authors argue that transgenic crops help humanity; they "ensure that the world's poorest people do not still go hungry in the twenty-first century." Of course, some readers strongly disagree. But even if they disagree, they may like, for example, the authors' proposal of a partnership between the public sector (universities and international research centers) and the private sector (industry) to ensure that transgenic technologies are accessible to developing countries.

Conway and Toenniessen strive to make peace by appealing first to proponents, then to critics. First they discuss the benefits of transgenic crops and validate proponents' passionate advocacy of them; then they validate critics' concerns and admonish the proponents of biotechnology to take these concerns seriously.

Rhetorical Strategies for Balancing Passion, Reason, and Scientific Evidence. Good persuasive writing in bioethics must carefully balance scientific knowledge and ethical considerations. Conway and Toenniessen cite numerous published essays to frame their contributions within the wider conversation. These references point the reader to what has already been written about the topic, but more importantly, they acknowledge the important contributions that others— including critics—are making to the debate. Reference #15 is one such book. Environmentalists praise it for its well-reasoned summary of the ecological risks of transgenic crops, particularly those with the enhanced fitness traits identified above. Conway and Toenniessen refer to these criticisms as "genuine concerns." They also are careful to cite primary sources whenever possible. Information passed on secondhand by way of a website posting, or even published in a review article, is not as reliable as the original source. This general rule applies to all persuasive writing.

Conway and Toenniessen include figures to present scientific data that underscore some of their primary points: the worrisome drop in crop yields in developing countries (Figure 1) and the diversity of biotechnology research in developing countries (Table 1 and Figure 2). A key question is whether these data help explain a complex point or give scientific support to the argument. Keep in mind that readers may respond to the data in different ways. For example, Figure 1 assumes a type of agricultural production that makes extensive use of high-energy inputs (fertilizers and fuels) to support monocultures (fields devoted to one species). For those who support alternative methods (such as organic farming), these data may underscore their contention that modern production agriculture, and biotechnology by extension, cannot sustain agriculture in developing countries. For a scientifically sophisticated audience, the data represent important talking points.

Finally, note how Conway and Toenniessen maintain the scientific sophistication of their arguments for a very diverse audience. Although most *Nature* readers are scientists, the authors recognize that not every reader will be. So they take care to avoid excessive use of scientific jargon. Most college graduates should understand most of the scientific terms and concepts. That the authors have been considerate of their audience's diversity—both in terms of their familiarity with the science and their ethical value systems—is another earmark of a good persuasive article.

✓ *READING TIPS*

The visual components in this article may lure your attention away from the words, but you must pay attention to the words if you want to see how the authors reach out to a variety of readers, balance competing ideas, and develop a moderate tone. The headings indicate that the authors begin with background to the problems before they consider solutions. The graphics display the evidence that supports the writers' argument. Readers who are expert on the topic might jump immediately to the solutions. Others scan the article to orient themselves and then proceed to read it thoroughly.

Feeding the world in the twenty-first century

Gordon Conway and Gary Toenniessen

Nature 1999, 402(suppl): C55–C58

The gains in food production provided by the Green Revolution have reached their ceiling while world population continues to rise. To ensure that the world's poorest people do not still go hungry in the twenty-first century, advances in plant biotechnology must be deployed for their benefit by a strong public-sector agricultural research effort.

This abstract lays out the basic premise of the paper.

The Green Revolution was one of the great technological success stories of the second half of the twentieth century. Because of the introduction of scientifically bred, higher-yielding varieties of rice, wheat and maize beginning in the 1960s, overall food production in the developing countries kept pace with population growth, with both more than doubling. The benefits of the Green Revolution reached many of the world's poorest people. Forty years ago there were a billion people in developing countries who did not get enough to eat, equivalent to 50 per cent of the population of these countries. If this proportion had remained unchanged, the hungry would now number over two billion— more than double the current estimate of around 800 million, or around 20 per cent of the present population of the developing world. Since the 1970s, world food prices have declined in real terms by over 70 per cent. Those who benefit most are the poor, who spend the highest proportion of their family income on food.

Critics disagree strongly with this statement . . .

. . . and this one. However, proponents of agricultural biotechnology typically use this argument to justify their cause.

The Green Revolution brought benefits too for the industrialized world. The high-yielding varieties of staple crop plants bred by the international agricultural research centres of the CGIAR (the Consultative Group on International Agricultural Research) have been incorporated into the modern varieties grown in the United States and Europe. The additional wheat and rice produced in the United States alone from these improved varieties is estimated to have been worth over \$3.4 billion from 1970 to 1993.[1]

Yet today, despite these demonstrable achievements, over 800 million people consume less than 2,000 calories a day, live a life of permanent or intermittent hunger and are chronically undernourished.[2] Most of the hungry are the women and young children of extremely poor families in developing countries. More than 180 million children under five years of age are severely underweight: that is, they are more than two standard deviations below the standard weight for their age. Seventeen million children under five die each year and malnourishment contributes to at least a third of these deaths.

As well as gross undernourishment, lack of protein, vitamins, minerals and other micronutrients in the diet is also widespread.[3] About 100 million children under five suffer from vitamin A deficiency, which can lead to eye damage. Half a million children become partly or totally blind each year, and many subsequently die. Recent research has shown that lack of vitamin A has an even more pervasive effect, weakening the protective barriers to infection put up by the skin, the mucous membranes and the immune system.[4] Iron deficiency is also common, leading to about 400 million women of childbearing age (15–49 years) being afflicted by anaemia. As a result they tend to produce stillborn or underweight children and are more likely to die in childbirth. Anaemia has been identified as a contributing factor in over 20 per cent of all maternal deaths after childbirth in Asia and Africa.

If nothing new is done, the number of the poor and hungry will grow. The populations of most developing countries are increasing rapidly and by the year 2020 there will be an additional 1.5 billion mouths to feed, mostly in the developing world. What is the likelihood that they will be fed?

The end of the Green Revolution

The prognosis is not good. As indicated in Fig. 1, there is widespread evidence of decline in the rate of increase of crop yields.[5–7] This slowdown is due to a combination of causes. On the best lands many farmers are now obtaining yields close to

---

Margin notes:

In other words, 97.7% of kids their age weigh more than these hungry kids.

The authors point this out to set up their argument that biotechnology, which offers tools to address such needs, is essential.

Supporting data lend scientific credibility to their argument. Note, however, that the root cause of this rate of deceleration is open to speculation.

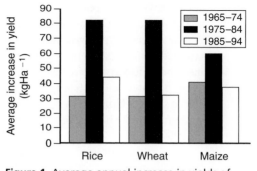

Figure 1 Average annual increase in yields of rice, wheat and maize in developing countries by periods.

those produced on experimental stations, and there has been little or no increase in the maximum possible yields of rice and maize in recent years. A second factor is the cumulative effect of environmental degradation, partly caused by agriculture itself.

Simply exporting more food from the industrialized countries is not a solution. The world already produces more than enough food to feed everyone if the food were equally distributed, but it is not. Market economies are notoriously ineffective in achieving equitable distribution of benefits. There is no reason to believe that the poor who lack access to adequate food today will be any better served by future world markets. Food aid programmes are also no solution, except in cases of specific short-term emergency. They reach only a small portion of those suffering chronic hunger and, if prolonged, create dependency and have a negative impact on local food production.

About 130 million of the poorest 20 per cent of people in developing countries live in cities. For them, access to food means cheap food from any source. But 650 million of the poorest live in rural areas where agriculture is the primary economic activity, and as is the case in much of Africa, many live in regions where agricultural potential is low and natural resources are poor.[8] They are distant from markets and have limited purchasing power. For them, access means local production of food that generates employment and income, and is sufficient and dependable enough to meet local needs throughout the year, including years that are unfavourable for agriculture.

All these arguments point to the need for a second Green Revolution, yet one that does not simply reflect the successes, and mistakes, of the first. In effect, we require a 'Doubly Green

In this paragraph the authors make these claims to support their contention that biotechnology offers the best solution. Critics may contend that market intervention may offer a better approach.

Cheap food has come to imply "industrial agriculture," which many claim is at the heart of food security problems.

Local food is often touted as a remedy for the economic ills of global industrial agriculture.

Revolution', an agricultural revolution that is both more productive and more 'green' in terms of conserving natural
resources and the environment than the first. We believe that
this can be achieved by a combination of: ecological approaches
to sustainable agriculture; greater participation by farmers in
agricultural analysis, design and research; and the application
of modern biotechnology directed towards the needs of the
poor in developing countries, which is the subject of the rest of
this article.

> Those who argue for sustainable agriculture will like these first two points. Conway and Toenniessen are probably hoping this will foster acceptance of their third component.

The price of biotechnology

The application of advances in plant breeding—including tissue
culture, marker-aided selection (which uses DNA technology
to detect the transmission of a desired gene to a seedling arising from a cross) and genetic engineering—are going to be
essential if farmers' yields and yield ceilings are to be raised,
excessive pesticide use reduced, the nutrient value of basic
foods increased and farmers on less favoured lands provided
with varieties better able to tolerate drought, salinity and lack
of soil nutrients.

> For many, this stretches the definition of "plant breeding." The authors are no doubt doing this to make a point: there's more to biotechnology than just genetic engineering.

In the industrialized countries the new life-science
companies, notably the big six multinationals—Astra-Zeneca,
Aventis, Dow, Dupont, Monsanto and Novartis—dominate the
application of biotechnology to agriculture. In 1998, 'genetically modified (GM)' crops, more accurately referred to as
transgenic or genetically engineered crops, mostly marketed by
these companies or their subsidiaries, were grown on nearly
29 million hectares worldwide (excluding China).[9] That year,
40 per cent of all cotton, 35 per cent of soya beans and 25 per
cent of maize grown in the United States were GM varieties.

> Noting this problem will gain some support among biotechnology's critics.

> 1 hectare = 10,000 square meters = 2.47 acres

So far, the great majority of the commercial applications of
plant genetic engineering have been for crops with single-gene
alterations that confer agronomic benefits such as resistance to
pests or to herbicides. These agronomic traits can reduce costs
to the farmer by minimizing applications of insecticides and herbicides. However, as with many agricultural inputs, the benefits
received by farmers vary from year to year.

Most of the GM crops currently being grown in developing
countries are cash crops; Bt cotton, for example, has reportedly
been taken up by over a million farmers in China. But despite
claims to be 'feeding the world', the big life-science companies
have little interest in poor farmers' food crops, because the
returns are too low. National governments, the international
research centres of the CGIAR, and a variety of western donors
are, and will continue to be, the primary supporters of work that

> Bt is shorthand for *Bacillis thuringiensis*, a common soil bacterium that produces Bt toxin, which kills caterpillars. It has no effect on humans and is therefore used in organic farming. Biotechnologists have placed the gene for Bt toxin in various crops to deter insect infestations. This may, however, speed insect resistance to Bt toxin.

produces advances in biotechnology useful to poor farmers. New forms of public–private collaboration could help to ensure that all farmers and consumers benefit from the genetic revolution and, over time, this should increase the number of farmers who can afford to buy new seeds from the private sector.

The cost of accomplishing this will not be insignificant but it should not be excessive. For example, over the past 15 years, the Rockefeller Foundation has funded some US$100 million of rice biotechnology research and trained over 400 scientists from Asia, Africa and Latin America. In several places in Asia there is now a critical mass of talented scientists who are applying the new tools of biotechnology to rice improvement. To date, most of the new varieties are the result of tissue culture and marker-aided selection techniques. For example, scientists at the West Africa Rice Development Association have used anther culture to cross the high-yielding Asian rices with traditional African rices. The result is a new plant type that looks like African rice during its early stages of growth (it is able to shade out weeds, which are the most important constraint on crop production in Africa; . . .) but becomes more like Asian rice as it reaches maturity, thus giving higher yields with few inputs. Marker-aided selection is being used to breed rice containing two or more genes for resistance to the same pathogen, thereby increasing the durability of the resistance, and to accumulate several different genes contributing to drought tolerance.

> Plants can be regenerated from tissues grown in artificial media supplemented with plant growth hormones. Although such plants are typically clones, some can have new useful genetic traits.

> DNA fragments can serve as "markers" to identify plants that have certain genes even before the plant displays the trait associated with that gene. This expedites breeding.

> Anthers are the male parts of a flower.

Potential of genetic engineering

For some time to come, tissue culture and marker-aided selection are likely to be the most productive uses of biotechnology for cereal breeding. However, progress is being made in the production of transgenic crops for the developing countries. As in the industrialized countries, the focus has been largely on traits for disease and pest resistance, but genes that confer tolerance of high concentrations of aluminium (found in many tropical soils) have been added by Mexican scientists to rice and maize . . ., and Indian scientists have added two genes to rice which may help the plant tolerate prolonged submergence. There is also the possibility of increasing yield ceilings, through more efficient photosynthesis, for example, or by improved control of water loss from leaves through regulation of stomatal opening and closing.[10]

> That is, submergence under water during floods.

> Stomata are the specialized openings on the surfaces of leaves that allow gas and water exchange with the environment.

In addition to generating new traits that enable the plant to grow better (input traits), which are useful to poor farmers, GM technology can also generate plants with improved nutritional features (output traits) of benefit to poor consumers. One of the most exciting developments so far has been the introduction of genes into rice that result in the production of the vitamin A precursor β-carotene in the rice grain.[11] β-carotene is a pigment required for photosynthesis and is synthesized in the green tissues of all plants, including rice, but is not usually present in

A key implication from Table 1: Biotechnology will positively affect subsistence farming in developing countries.

Table 1 Biotechnology research useful in developing countries

Traits now in greenhouse or field tests	Traits now in laboratory tests
Input traits	*Input traits*
Resistance to insects, nematodes, viruses, bacteria and fungi in crops such as rice, maize, potato, papaya and sweet potato	Drought and salinity tolerance in cereals
	Seedling vigour in rice
Delayed senescence, dwarfing, reduced shade avoidance and early flowering in rice	Enhanced phosphorus and nitrogen uptake in rice and maize
Tolerance of aluminium, submergence, chilling and freezing in cereals	Resistance to the parasitic weed *Striga* in maize, rice and sorghum, to viruses in cassava and banana, and to bacterial blight in cassava
Male sterility/restorer for hybrid seed production in rice, maize, oil-seed rape and wheat	Nematode resistance and resistance to the disease black sigatoka in banana
New plant types for weed control and for increased yield potential in rice	Rice with the alternative C, photosynthetic pathway and the ability to carry out nitrogen fixation
Output traits	*Output traits*
Increased β-carotene in rice and oil-seed rape	Increased β-carotene, delayed post-harvest deterioration and reduced content of toxic cyanides in cassava
Lower phytates in maize and rice to increase bioavailable iron	Increased vitamin E in rice
Modified starch in rice, potato and maize and modified fatty-acid content in oil-seed rape	Apomixis (asexual seed production) in maize, rice, millet and cassava
Increased bioavailable protein, essential amino acids, seed weight and sugar content in maize	Delayed ripening in banana
Lowered lignin content of forage crops	Use of genetically engineered plants such as potato and banana as vehicles for production and delivery of recombinant vaccines to humans
	Improved amino-acid content of forage crops

non-photosynthetic tissues such as those of seeds. Traditional plant breeding has given us some plants that produce β-carotene in non-photosynthetic tissue, such as the roots of carrots, but despite decades of searching no rice mutants had been found that produce β-carotene in the grain, so conventional breeding was not an option. To get the cells of the grain to produce β-carotene, genetic engineers added three genes for key enzymes for β-carotene biosynthesis to the rice genome. The grain of the transgenic rice has a light golden-yellow colour . . . and contains sufficient β-carotene to meet human vitamin A requirements from rice alone. This 'golden' rice offers an opportunity to complement vitamin A supplementation programmes, particularly in rural areas that are difficult to reach. These same scientists and others have also added genes to rice that increase the grain's nutritionally available iron content by more than threefold.

> This is a contentious claim. Critics argue that beta-carotene levels are too low and require sufficient body fat for its absorbance via our digestive tract. Conway and Toenniessen should have addressed or acknowledged this issue.

Over the next decade we are likely to see much greater progress in multiple gene introductions that focus on output traits or on difficult-to-achieve input characteristics (Table 1).

The potential benefits of plant biotechnology are considerable, but are unlikely to be realized unless seeds are provided free or at nominal cost. This will require heavy public investment by national governments and donors, at times in collaboration with the private sector, both in the research and in the subsequent distribution of seed and technical advice. Breeding programmes will also need to include crops such as cassava, upland rice, African maize, sorghum and millet, which are the food staples and provide employment for the 650 million rural poor who need greater stability and reliability of yield as much as increased yield.

> That the authors are talking about the poor is implied in this comment on potential benefits.

The role of the public sector

None of this will happen through marketing by multinational seed companies, particularly if they decide to deploy gene-protection technologies, commonly referred to as terminator gene technologies, which will mean that farmers cannot save seed from the crop and sow it to get the next crop. In developing countries roughly 1.4 billion farmers still rely on saving seed for their planting materials and many gain access to new varieties through farmer-to-farmer trade. Much of the success of the Green Revolution was due to the true-breeding nature of the higher-yielding rice and wheat varieties.

> In subsequent generations of the crop, these gene technologies would prevent reproduction via seeds or prevent expression of the novel genes. Some are now proposing these technologies as a strategy to reduce genetic pollution from transgenic plants.

While terminator technology is clearly designed to prevent rather than encourage such spread of proprietary varieties among poor farmers, some argue that it will do them no harm because they can still use and replant new varieties from the public sector. But if the companies tie up enabling technologies

> Enabling technologies include methods and instruments, some of which are patented.

and DNA sequences of important genes with patents, and then use terminator technologies to control the distribution of proprietary seed and restrict its use for further breeding, the public sector will be severely constrained in using biotechnology to meet the needs of the poor.

Rather than using the terminator technology to protect their intellectual property in developing countries, it would be better if seed companies focused on producing hybrid seed combined with plant variety protection (PVP) to protect the commercial production of the seed. Hybrid plants do produce viable seed but it is not genetically identical to the original hybrid seed; it may lack some of the desirable characteristics. Hence, there is still an incentive (for example, increased yield) for farmers to purchase hybrid seed for each planting. However, if such purchase is not possible, farmers can still use a portion of their harvest as seed and obtain a reasonable crop. Such recycling of hybrids is not uncommon in developing countries and is an important element of food security. And with PVP, new varieties can be protected while also becoming a resource that both the private and public sectors can use in further breeding for the benefit of all farmers.

> Hybrid seed is used extensively in developed countries.

> Plant variety protection is more limited than typical biotechnology patents. It would allow farmers to grow it, but not sell it for seed.

Intellectual property rights

Even assuming that terminator technologies are not used, there is cause for concern about the rights of developing countries to use their own genetic resources, the freedom of their plant breeders to use new technologies to develop locally adapted varieties, and the protection of poor farmers from exploitation. In part, these concerns result from the privatization of crop genetic improvement, the rapid expansion of corporate ownership of key technologies and genetic information and materials, and the competitive pressure on these companies to capture world market share as rapidly as possible.

It is only recently that intellectual property rights (IPR) have become an important factor in plant breeding, primarily through the greater use of utility patents. Such patents have stimulated greater investment in crop improvement research in industrialized countries, but they are also creating major problems and potentially significant additional expense for the already financially constrained public-sector breeding programmes that produce seeds for poor farmers.

> Utility patents confer broad rights to patent holders. They might cover, for example, any use of a certain useful gene. University scientists are pursuing these patents too.

The success of the Green Revolution was based on international collaboration which included the free exchange of genetic diversity and information. Most of the "added value" present in modern crops has been accumulated over the centuries by

> Another appeal from biotechnology's critics: crops are a common heritage that should be freely exchanged.

farmers themselves as they selected their best plants as the source of seed for the next planting. These "land races" have traditionally been provided free of charge by developing countries to the world community. The CGIAR centres add value through selective breeding, and the superior varieties they generate are widely distributed without charge, benefiting both developing and developed countries.

Patents on biotechnology methods and materials, and even on plant varieties, are complicating and undermining these collaborative relationships. Public-sector research institutions in industrialized countries no longer fully share new information and technology. Rather, they patent and license and have special offices charged with maximizing their financial return from licensing. Commercial production of any genetically engineered crop variety requires dozens of patents and licenses. It is only the big companies that can afford to put together the IPR portfolios necessary to give them the freedom to operate. And now, under the TRIPS (Trade-Related Aspects of Intellectual Property Rights) agreement of the World Trade Organization, most developing countries are required to put in place their own IPR systems, including IPR for plants. Furthermore, all of this 'ownership' of plant genetic resources is causing developing countries to rethink their policies concerning access to the national biodiversity they control, and new restrictions are likely.

So far, international negotiations relevant to agricultural biotechnology and plant genetic resources have not been effectively coordinated. There are inconsistencies, and the interests of poor farmers in developing countries have not been well represented. The days of unencumbered free exchange of plant genetic materials are no doubt over, and agreements and procedures need to be formulated to ensure that public-sector institutions have access to the technological and genetic resources needed to produce improved crop varieties for farmers in developing countries who will not be well served by the for-profit sector. If the big life-science companies wish to find a receptive and growing market in developing countries, they will need to work with the public sector to make sure this happens.

Some solutions

While negotiations are underway, there are a number of things that should be done. With little competitive loss, seed companies could agree to use the PVP system (including provisions allowing seed saving and sharing by farmers) in developing countries in cooperation with public plant-breeding agencies,

---

The open exchange of ideas has historically been a critical component of the philosophy of science. This appeal is common among public sector scientists.

A key question not adequately addressed here: what does it mean to "own" biodiversity?

Here, Conway and Toenniessen are proposing a big change in the way biotechnologists typically think about their enterprise. Following it up with some suggestions in the next paragraph lends practical support.

rather than using patents or terminator technologies to protect their varieties.

To speed the development of biotechnology capacity in developing countries, companies that have IPR claims over certain key techniques or materials might agree to license these for use in developing countries at no cost.

We would also like to see an agreement to share the financial rewards from IPR claims on crop varieties or crop traits of distinct national origin, such as South Asian Basmati rice or Thailand's Jasmine rice. The granting of free licenses to use such materials in breeding programmes in the country of origin of the trait might gain the appreciation of developing country researchers and governments.

Finally, the current opposition to GM crops and foods is likely to spread from Europe to the developing countries and maybe even to North America unless there is greater public reassurance. At the heart of the debate about the safety of GM crops and their food derivatives is the issue of relative benefits and risks. The debate is particularly impassioned in Europe. Some of it is motivated by anti-corporate or anti-American sentiment, but underlying the rhetoric are genuine concerns about lack of consumer benefits, about ethics, about the environment and about the potential impact on human health.[12–16]

Much of the opposition tends to lump together the various risks—some real, some imaginary—and to assume there are generic hazards.[17] However, GM organisms are not all the same and each provides different potential benefits to different people and different environmental and health risks. Calls for general moratoria are not appropriate. Each new transgene and each new GM crop containing it needs to be considered in its own right. Well planned field tests are crucial, particularly in the developing countries where the risks of using, or not using, a GM crop may be quite different from those in industrialized countries.

The multinational companies could take a number of specific decisions in this area that would improve acceptance of plant biotechnology in both the developing and the industrialized world. First, consumers have a right to choose whether to eat GM foods or not and although there are serious logistic problems in separating crops all the way from field to retail sale, the agricultural seed industry should come out immediately and strongly in favour of labelling. Second, the industry should disavow use of the terminator technology in developing countries and, third, it should phase out the use of antibiotic-resistance genes as a means of selecting transgenic plants. Alternatives exist and should be used.

Risks and benefits are important, but here Conway and Toenniessen are at risk of over-simplifying critics' multifaceted concerns — as you will see in the paper by Sagar et al. at the end of this chapter.

North American biotechnologists typically support the view that GM crops are "substantially equivalent" to their non-GM counterparts and do not need extra-ordinary testing. This is lumping of a different kind, which critics strongly assail. Conway and Toenniessen imply that GM crops must be considered on a case-by-case basis. Thus, they contend that both camps have adopted the wrong strategy.

These three points will play well with critics, but cause concern among proponents. Clearly, throughout the paper Conway and Toenniessen are relying on their clout among proponents to win their support.

The Rockefeller Foundation and other donors have invested significant sums in helping developing countries put in place biosafety regulations and the facilities necessary for biosafety testing of new crops and foods, but much more needs to be done. The big life-science companies could join forces and establish a fellowship programme for training developing country scientists in crop biotechnology, biosafety, intellectual property rights and international negotiations administered by a neutral fellowship agency.

> This claim has far-reaching implications. In this paper they have tried to set the tone by identifying points of discussion from both sides of the debate. If you've been keeping tally, you know that they have placed the ball in the biotechnologists' court. Theirs is primarily a call to heed critics' concerns.

Most important of all, a new way of talking and reaching decisions is required. We believe a global public dialogue is needed which will involve everyone on an equal footing— the seed companies, consumer groups, environmental groups, independent scientists, and representatives of governments, particularly from the developing nations.

Agriculture in the twenty-first century will need to be more productive and less damaging to the environment than agriculture has been in the twentieth. An increased effort is needed to assure that the benefits of agricultural research reach the hundreds of millions of poor farmers who have benefited little from previous research. We believe that biotechnology has significant potential to help meet these objectives but that this potential is threatened by a polarized debate that grows increasingly acrimonious. We need to reverse this trend, to begin working together, to share our various concerns, and to assure the new technologies are applied to agriculture only when this can be done safely and effectively in helping to achieve future food security for our world.

Note added in proof: We commend the Monsanto Company's recent public commitment not to commercialize sterile seed technologies and encourage other companies to follow their lead.

Notes

1. Pardey, P. G. Alston, J. M., Christian, J. E. & Fan, S. *Summary of a Productive Partnership: The Benefits from U.S. Participation in the CGIAR* (International Food Policy Research Institute, Washington DC, 1996).
2. Conway, G. R. *The Doubly Green Revolution: Food for All in the 21st Century* (Penguin Books, London/Cornell University Press, Ithaca NY, 1999).
3. UNICEF. *The State of the World's Children 1998* (Oxford Univ. Press, Oxford/New York, 1998).
4. Somer, A. & West, K. P. *Vitamin A Deficiency: Health, Survival and Vision* (Oxford Univ. Press, New York and Oxford, 1966).
5. Mann, C. C. *Science* **283,** 310–314 (1999).
6. Cassman. K. G. *Proc. Natl Acad. Sci. USA* **96,** 5952–5959 (1999).
7. Pingali, P. L. & Heisey, P. W. *Cereal Productivity in Developing Countries: Past Trends and Future Prospects.* CIMMYT Economics Paper 99–03 (CIMMYT, Mexico, 1999).

8. Leonard, H. J. in *Environment and the Poor: Development Strategies for a Common Agenda* (ed. Leonard, H. J.) 3–45 (Overseas Development Council, Washington DC, 1989).

9. James, C. *Global Review of Commercialized Transgenic Crops: 1998.* ISAAA Briefs No. 8. (International Service for Acquisition of Agri-biotech Applications, Ithaca NY, 1998).

10. Mann, C. C. *Science* **283,** 314–316 (1999).

11. Ye, X. D. et al. *Science* (submitted).

12. The Royal Society of London. *Genetically Modified Plants for Food Use* (The Royal Society, London, 1998).

13. Nuffield Council on Bioethics. *Genetically Modified Crops: The Ethical and Social Issues* (Nuffield Council on Bioethics, London, 1999).

14. UN Food and Agriculture Organization. *Biotechnology and Food Safety.* FAO Food and Nutrition Paper 61. (World Health Organization/FAO, Rome, 1996).

15. Rissler, J. & Mellon, M. *The Ecological Risks of Engineered Crops* (MIT Press, Cambridge MA/London, 1996).

16. May, R. *Genetically Modified Foods: Facts, Worries, Policies and Public Confidence* (http://www.2.dti.gov.uk/ost/ ostbusiness/gen.html, 1999).

17. Pretty, J. *The Biochemist* (in the press).

Acknowledgements

We thank M. Lipton, S. Dryden, R. May and colleagues at the Rockefeller Foundation for comments on an earlier draft of this article.

READING RESPONSES

1. How much did you know about biotechnology before you read Conway and Toenniessen's essay? Did they persuade you that biotechnology is a safe and effective way to combat world-wide poverty? What parts of their essay did you find most convincing?

2. On a scale of 1–10 (where 1=simple and 10=impossible) where would you plot the difficulty of reading this essay? Note specific places in the text where the authors go out of their way to help readers who know little about biotechnology.

3. In a marginal comment, Professor Koetje notes that Conway and Toenniessen direct most of their recommendations to those in favor of biotechnology solutions to world hunger. In what ways is this an effective persuasive strategy? How will critics of biotechnology respond to these recommendations?

NOTES ON GRAMMAR, STYLE, AND RHETORIC:
HEDGES IN PERSUASIVE WRITING

A student teacher was introducing a group of high-school seniors to the nature of persuasive writing. As she neared the end of the session, she paused briefly and said, "One last thing— what do you think you should do if you suspect that some readers will have a position opposed to yours? If you have a good idea about what their position is, should you bring it up? Or would you maybe want to soften how you state your position to avoid alienating those readers?"

A young man slouching in a desk responded immediately: "Soften it? You've got to be kidding. If some readers are opposed to your view, you've got to crush them. State your position as if any other view would be stupid." Several of his classmates turned toward him and grinned in agreement.

That teacher would do well in a future class on persuasive writing to show her students Gordon Conway and Gary Toenniessen's "Feeding the world in the twenty-first century." For in this persuasive essay, the authors clearly acknowledge that some readers will be opposed to their position. And they express their position in such a way that those opposed to it will probably not get angry or dismissive. In part, Conway and Toenniessen do this work through skillful uses of what linguists call *hedges*.

Hedges are linguistic elements that help us to soften positions, to be somewhat tentative about them, to pull back from expressing them as if we were certain about them. We can hedge with adverbs such as *possibly* and *perhaps*, with modal auxiliary verbs such as *may* and *might*, with main verbs such as *seem* and *suggest*, and with phrases such as *to a certain extent* and *to our knowledge*. In addition, we can hedge clauses that express parts of our position by introducing them with other clauses such as *We believe that*, *We suggest that*, and *It is possible that*.

In "Feeding the world," Conway and Toenniessen use two kinds of hedges at prominent points of their essay. At the end of their opening subsection, they include this sentence, which is the most general statement of their overall position: "We believe that this [having a "Doubly Green Revolution"] can be achieved by a combination of: ecological approaches to sustainable agriculture; greater participation by farmers in agricultural analysis, design and research; and the application of modern biotechnology directed towards the needs of the poor in developing countries, which is the subject of the rest of this article" (page 315). Note that this statement is introduced with the prominent hedge "We believe that," which Conway and Toenniessen also use to introduce some other clauses near the end of their essay. If you have some doubt about the hedging effect of "We believe that," read the sentence once with the "We believe that" where it appears in the essay and once with the "We believe that" omitted. You should notice a striking difference in the force of these two sentences.

In the last section of their essay, which carries the modest title "Some solutions," Conway and Toenniessen do quite a bit of hedging with modal verbs. For instance, here is a controversial claim that is hedged with the modal verb *might*: "To speed the development of biotechnology capacity in developing countries, companies that have IPR [intellectual property rights] claims over certain key techniques or materials might agree to license these for use in developing countries at no cost" (321). In several other sentences in this section, Conway and Toenniessen hedge with the modal verb *could*. Here is one example: "The multinational companies could take a number of specific decisions in this area that would improve acceptance of plant biotechnology in both the developing and the industrialized world" (321).

At this point, you might ask whether such obvious hedges in such prominent positions actually weaken Conway and Toenniessen's argument, making it appear hesitant or wordy. In fact, a hedged passage can be especially persuasive because its reasonable moderation invites readers to respond in kind. Hedges, in other words, can help writers communicate to readers, "We are reasonable people. Why not consider our view seriously?"

Besides, no one can accuse Conway and Toenniessen of being weak in their overall presentation. Indeed, they include many direct statements of what they clearly regard as facts, as when they introduce their final paragraph by writing that "Agriculture in the twenty-first century will need to be more productive and less damaging to the environment than agriculture has been in the twentieth" (322).

In Your Own Writing. . . .

- If a claim can be shown to be based on facts, state it directly.
- If a claim cannot clearly be shown to be based on facts or if a claim is controversial, use a strategically placed hedge.
- Where it's especially important that your audience agree with you, use a hedge to create a claim that your audience is more likely to find acceptable.

STUDENT WRITING IN BIOTECHNOLOGY

Introduction by Meghan Sheehan, biotechnology major

The Assignment. What follows is a persuasive paper I wrote for a course titled "Perspectives in Biotechnology." The professor assumed that students had a strong laboratory background and thus could understand the technical terms. Interestingly, though, we also had to have completed prerequisite liberal arts classes before we enrolled in this class. The assignment for this paper asked us to describe a problem associated with biotechnology and provide a solution.

The Content. I chose one of the most troublesome issues in biotechnology—the proper use of genetic testing. Genetic testing, particularly universal genetic testing (that is, testing everyone) raises all sorts of concerns, from worries about private medical information becoming public knowledge to concerns that genetic testing will be used to discriminate against people. I narrowed the focus of my research to the function of genetic testing in the field of medical insurance. I was able to highlight the principle problems associated with the use of genetic testing by medical insurance companies, but providing a solution proved more complicated. Because health care is an issue of public concern that nonetheless involves private companies, I realized that any solution I offered would have political implications. I think that my solution is a good one, but I worry that those who disagree with my political leanings might disagree with my solution, too.

Learning to Write in Biotechnology. When I was writing my essay, I focused on two goals. First, given the controversial nature of my topic, I knew that I could expect both friendly and hostile readers, and I wanted to gain the respect of both. To gain their respect and to encourage them to consider my ideas, I had to respect not only the scholars I cited in my essay, but also my readers, those who disagree with me as well as those who see things my way. I knew that I wouldn't be able to convince every reader, but I hoped that I'd at least be able to make them consider my arguments, instead of angering them and causing them to dismiss my ideas. Additionally, I hoped to revise this essay and publish it in a journal, so reader respect became an absolute necessity. I tried to accomplish this goal primarily by using non-inflammatory diction (which was hard) and by not mocking any of the views that I discussed in my essay (also hard, but not as hard as the first part).

The second goal was that my argument had to be practical; I wanted my readers to agree with me because I suggested reasonable solutions. This arose from my personality as much as from the class. We read a number of essays by many different authors for the class, and I disliked the essays that simply named and expounded on a problem without offering suggestions for fixing it. It is well and good to recognize a flaw, but I had no patience (and therefore no respect) for authors who couldn't suggest a way to mend it. Worst of all were the suggestions that were unworkable because they were either too vague or simply impractical. Because of this, I took great pains in my essay to include detailed and practical solutions for the problems I studied.

I kept both of these lessons in mind while I was writing this essay. I hope that you are able to see how I tried to win my audience's respect and consideration through a careful critique of the situation described in the essay. I was not ignorant or arrogant enough to think that I could win every individual over to my way of thinking. I aimed instead for a well-reasoned argument that most readers could respect and find thought-provoking. I hope I persuaded some of my readers, too.

Creating Change through Writing in Biotechnology. It seems to me that everyone has a vested interest in what happens in the field of biotechnology. After all, it affects not only the food we eat but the environment in which we live. Because biotechnology offers the potential for such great good and such significant harm, people often take radical stances. Too often people are more eager to speak than they are to listen; more eager to win an argument than to find a solution that everyone can live with. By writing to build consensus rather than writing to win, I not only serve as a mediator between opposed groups I also move us closer to implementing a workable solution rather than continuing an argument. I entered the field of biotechnology because I hope to improve people's lives and protect the environment. By working with people rather than against them, I am better able to achieve those goals.

The Insurance Industry and Adult Preventative Genetic Screening: An evil beast using awesome powers for harm?

Meghan Sheehan

Abstract

In this paper, the issue of genetic screening in the insurance industry is discussed, particularly the practice of predictive screening prior to issuing health and life insurance. Predictive screening raises concerns that some clients will not be able to find insurance and that the use of genetic screening raises the risk of genetic determinism. To exemplify these concerns this paper considers attempts by the Association of British Insurers at self-regulation, regulation by the state of Michigan, and one ethicist's call for a system that circumvents the problems associated with genetic screening. Rather than perform genetic screening, the insurance industry should perform as any business would. Since the current insurance system is maladapted to absorb the influx of genetic information and yet insure everyone regardless of genetic condition, this paper presents a new system of insurance more able to handle the claims of *every* individual.

Current Issues in Genetic Screening and Insurance, an Introduction

Currently, outside of reproductive therapies, most genetic screening done on asymptomatic adults is termed predictive or presymptomatic testing. This type of screening is done to judge whether an adult with a familial history of a disease has a genotype conducive to the disease. For example, patients who have a family history of Huntington disease (HD) can have a genetic test performed to determine whether they have the excessive genetic DNA repeat that causes HD long before they show any sort of symptoms of the disease. Again, this type of test is typically performed only on patients who have an established familial history of the disease. Screening of this sort is not currently performed on the population at large.

Many people are concerned, though, that this sort of screening may eventually become a universal prerequisite for receiving health and life insurance.[1] These people worry that if a test reveals a person's genetic disposition towards a disease, especially a chronic disease, that person may face greatly increased insurance premiums or even find herself uninsurable. Along the same lines, some worry that universal predictive screening will produce a class of patients who are deemed genetically superior, from a medical stand point, and who would therefore pay a miniscule premium. In both supposed scenarios, the results of such a screening are unfair: in the first case those patients who have a greatly increased need for insurance would not receive it and in the second society at large does not benefit from the reduced rate of a few "lucky" individuals.

I would argue that we should be concerned about universal predictive screening for another reason—the risk of genetic determinism. If people overly value the results of these tests, they might de-emphasize lifestyle choices that affect the length and

---

WHAT?!? WHERE IS THE THESIS?!? Not every essay begins with a thesis. Ordering this essay in sections, marked with headings, allows me to describe the problem before I get to my main point—my solution. Without this background information, my audience would be less likely to accept the plan I'm proposing.

I broke my paper into parts, using headings to increase the overall readability of the essay. This section, "Current Issues," provides background information on the problem. The reader needs this information to understand both the nature of the problem and how my solution can fix it.

Depending on your philosophical tradition, you could argue that fairness for society at large is irrelevant. This is an argument I did not think of at the time, so I did not address the point. In general, though, I'm trying to reach out to readers who might otherwise disagree with me by voicing their concerns in a respectful way.

Genetic determinism can mean that your biological fate is caused by your genes and nothing you can do will change this fate.

quality of their lives. Furthermore, people might presume that if a person is genetically inclined towards a disease he is certain to develop that disease. Socio-economic and environmental factors play a large role in whether a person actually succumbs to the potential disease. A classic example of other factors determining the onset of disease is the case of diabetes mellitus in genetically identical twins; only one-in-three times do both twins develop diabetes mellitus.[2] Two thirds of the time the second twin (with the exact same genes as the first twin) is able to avoid the disease by changing his exercise regimen and diet. Furthermore, many genetic diseases are not simple monogenic diseases. Therefore, screening for multigenic diseases must account for several factors, both genetic and non-genetic, before it can be fairly concluded, "yes/no, this patient has/does not have a high probability of disease." If an insurance company does not consider all factors, both genetic and non-genetic, when it interprets the results of genetic screening, it may unfairly charge an increased premium throughout the entire life of a person, even if he never develops the disease. The basis of these charges could lie solely in the interpretation of one test showing that he is an increased risk because of his propensity for a disease.

> Monogenic diseases are caused by a single genetic problem.

Addressing These Concerns

These are very valid concerns and both the insurance industry at large and the government have tried to address them. The Association of British Insurers (ABI), a non-government organization which 96% of insurance companies in the United Kingdom are part of, has drafted an extensive code outlining what the member companies may and may not do regarding genetic screening.[3] The guidelines address many topics and specifically state:

> I think my argument would be stronger if I used statistics from an American insurance association. These statistics would appeal more to readers throughout the U.S.

- Applicants must not be asked to undergo a screening in order to obtain insurance.
- If results from a screening are obtained, the insurer must consult a specialist for interpretation of the results.
- The screen must be ruled valid by the ABI genetics board before insurers can use it to cause premium increases.
- Informed, adult consent is required for all types of genetic screening.
- Policyholders are not required to reveal the results of a blood relative's test.
- Insurers must not offer lower than standard premiums on the basis of genetic test results.
- Insurers in the ABI are required to offer a minimum life insurance policy of £100,000 that cannot be affected by a genetic test.

- Each year the insurance company must demonstrate that they are following the Genetics Code set forth by ABI to renew membership status.

I couldn't find evidence from an American insurance association, but I did find information on the laws pertaining to the state where my professor lives.

In the state of Michigan, citations SB590 and SB593 attempt to address some of the same issues that the ABI regulated in the United Kingdom. Specifically, these laws prohibit health insurers from requiring an asymptomatic applicant or insured person to submit to genetic testing before issuing, renewing or continuing a policy. Additionally, applicants are under no obligation to discuss whether previous testing has been performed, and physicians are prohibited from performing predictive genetic tests without the written, informed consent of the adult subject.[4]

From these examples, we see that both industry associations and government agencies are trying to address the very real concerns discussed above. Especially admirable are the efforts of ABI to ensure that genetic screenings do not unfairly limit a person's access to life insurance and health insurance.

What about industry regulation of insurance in the United States? Will for-profit insurance agencies in corporate America regulate themselves as the ABI does? Already people have complained that some U.S. insurance companies are labeling some people as "medically uninsurable,"[5] especially patients with chronic conditions such as Huntington disease and cystic fibrosis. Would a for-profit industry allow regulation that requires it to insure the "uninsurable"? James Peterson argues that this is unlikely. Furthermore, he calls for an undefined health care system in which all people are guaranteed basic health care.[6] A universal health care system would avoid the potential problems of the current insurance system, and would offer health care to all people, including those who most need the insurance because of their genetic conditions. He does not explain how such a system could be implemented, but he argues that universal, basic health care would ensure that everyone received treatment, regardless of their genes. In Peterson's argument, this concern for the "uninsurable" is the only reason why a system of universal health care is necessary.

Peterson wrote one of the essays we read for class. I tried to summarize his proposed solution. In retrospect, I think I may have been too brief.

I bring up this point here to prepare my audience to see an advantage of my solution—my plan takes into account other considerations in addition to patient need.

Realistically Addressing the Concerns in the United States—A Radical Approach

Is the insurance industry truly evil? Is a universal health care system necessary to ensure that each person, regardless of genetic status, is treated? Should genetic status be a factor, i.e., should genetic screening be required for insurance?

No, the insurance industry is not evil. But insurance companies are in business to make a profit; they exist primarily to make money for shareholders and only secondarily to benefit the insured. If industry companies do not make a profit, they will cease to exist; someone, presumably individuals, will have to pick up the tab for our health expenses. What does this mean for you and me? It means that when I buy health insurance from an agency, I buy a policy from a company that also insures hundreds or thousands of other people. All of us pay a premium to keep our policy active. This money is pooled together, and the company draws from this pool when one of us files a claim. Whatever is leftover in the pool is the company's profit. As a for-profit institution, an insurance company is always looking for ways to maximize the amount of money left in the pool—their profit ratio. Therefore, insurance companies seek to insure low-risk applicants because they are less likely to draw heavily from the pool. People who have no chronic health conditions have fewer regular health expenses, and with few exceptions for unforeseen catastrophic events, their claims take less from the pool than a high-risk applicant who takes out more money, and takes it out more often. To put it very simply, insurance is a business of risk-management—insurance companies seek to minimize their risks to maximize their profits. If they used genetic screening to evaluate potential policyholders, companies could further minimize their risks.

This mysterious person could suffer from a range of diseases—from sickle cell anemia or genetically determined hypertension to diseases like Huntington disease or cystic fibrosis.

Rather than focusing on universal health care system, we should consider the possibilities for a universal *insurance* system. If we agree that morally and ethically *all* people should have access to affordable health care, we must create a system to make health care affordable. If we agree that businesses have a right to make a profit and that all people deserve affordable healthcare, we must create a system that allows companies to make a profit while still insuring high-risk people. The government can ill-afford to subsidize insurance companies, so we must seek another solution. Extremely large, privately operated insurance companies that operated under a stringent government oversight system and an unheard of profit distribution system could effectively insure all of us, low- and high-risk alike.

Here I link together the two propositions I've carefully established. This lays the groundwork for my proposed solution.

Very, very large companies would be necessary, so large that there could be only a few in the entire country. Because insurance companies must be very large to efficiently absorb the costs of high-risk people, there is room in the U.S. for only a few companies. I propose a few companies rather than a monopoly or a government agency because I do not believe that a monopoly would benefit either the insured or the insurance companies.

Currently, health insurance is distributed between multiple companies in the United States. For a condition such as Tay-Sachs disease, one in 250 people in the population at large is a carrier while one in 27 people in the Ashkenazi Jew population is a carrier.[7] Imagine one large company with a statistically average percentage of Ashkenazi Jews in their client pool. Only 1 in ~63,000 births will be a child with Tay-Sachs. Now imagine a small company that, through fate of location, insures primarily Ashkenazi Jews. Because 1 in ~800 births will be a child with Tay-Sachs, the company would have an at least 8x larger chance of paying out on Tay-Sachs claims for children of those they insure. Statistically speaking, it does not matter to that smaller company that Tay-Sachs is a rare disease; because they have a comparatively small client pool, statistics simply do not work in their favor. However, if there was a very, very large (i.e., multi-regional) client pool, statistics would be restored to the 1 in ~63,000 births. Additionally, because there would be a large clientele, their pool of money would be quite large. Indeed, the pool would be so large that the payment on large claims would be a smaller percentage and hurt the company much less. Insurance companies with large pools can afford to insure those who are currently "medically uninsurable" because the statistics regarding genetic disorders actually work in their favor—the good news is that most people are not genetically predisposed to catastrophic diseases that require expensive medical treatment.

> Tay-Sachs is a wasting disease of the neurological system. Babies born with it appear normal at first and seem to develop quite well. Slowly, though, they start to regress and most die by age five.

These large insurance companies should be privately operated because the current system of distributed power and government bureaucracy could not effectively process medical claims. Additionally, for reasons to be discussed below, these companies should be privately operated to ensure that they still turn a profit. Decisions about what is best for the company would still need to be made by the executives within the company to ensure that it remained vital. Additionally, incentives such as profit sharing and bonuses would encourage employees to work efficiently, and these incentives are unheard of from government employers.

The policy decisions of these large companies would require strict governmental oversight to ensure that the veritable monopoly of a few companies does not abuse the people that they serve. The government oversight should also include an independent panel of genetic counselors who interpret the results from genetics tests. In this way, the counselors can avoid the ethical dilemma of trying to serve two contrary masters (the people whose tests they read and the insurance company that employs them). Finally, the government should regulate profit distribution in the companies. Because the companies would operate in near-monopoly conditions, they could potentially make obscene profits. To combat this and to further the cause of benefiting people through advancements in medicine, a large percentage of the profits from the companies (perhaps as large as 50%, although this may not be realistic) should be *donated* to medical research. This would benefit society at large and also the company through more effective, cheaper treatments of their clients in the future.

Returning to the issue that opened this essay—should these companies perform genetic screening? I believe that they should perform genetic screening only for diseases where genetic tendency plays a role equal to other environmental factors and the genetic tendency can be flagged by a simple test. In the spirit of promoting better health for the client and keeping costs for the company down, this kind of testing would allow the company to provide incentives to help clients stay healthy. If, for example, through screening a client is discovered to have the CHD2 gene (the gene that can cause high cholesterol[8]), the insurance company can offer the client a lower premium if she can demonstrate that she lives a healthy lifestyle (through independently administered doctor physical results). In this case, government oversight would ensure two things: (1) the premium rates for those who do and do not live healthy lifestyles and (2) what would count as the minimum physical results for the lower premium. In the end, the first policyholder would benefit from a more healthy lifestyle (even if she never developed the disease), the second policyholder would exercise personal autonomy, and the insurance company would benefit from the desire of policyholders to be healthy.

> Here, at the end, is the thesis. The insurance system I describe is the necessary context for this claim. Without the system, my claim is unworkable.

Only this type of universal insurance system offers the necessary controls on universal predictive genetic screening. In this system, selective screening for a few manageable diseases benefits all people. The use of any type of predictive genetic screening outside such an insurance system and government oversight creates the potential for unethical use of this technology.

References

1. "Genetic Testing." Genetics and Public Policy Center. 22 Jan. 2004 http://www.dnapolicy.org/genetics/testing.jhtml.
2. Peterson, James C. *Genetic Turning Points: The Ethics of Human Genetic Intervention*. Grand Rapids: Eerdmans, 2001. p 206–211.
3. Drell, Daniel. "FAQs." *Human Genome News* 9. p 4: nos 1–2. 1998.
4. "Genetic Testing – ABI Code of Practice." Association of British Insurers. 22 Jan. 2004. http://www.abi.org.uk/Display/default.asp?Menu_ID=946&Menu_All=1,946,0&Child_ID=203.

5. "Genetic Information and Health Insurance Enacted State Legislation." National Human Genome Research Institute. 22 Jan. 2004 http://www.genome.gov/page.cfm?pageID=10002338.

6. Peterson. p 210–211.

7. "Tay-Sachs Disease." Jewish Genetic Diseases MazorNet. 22 Jan. 2004 http://www.mazornet.com/genetics/tay-sachs.asp

8. "Gene Responsible for High Cholesterol." *Applied Genetics News.* (2001). Retrieved 22 Jan 2004 http://www.findarticles.com/cf_dls/m0DED/ 11_21/76142147/p1/article.jhtml

READING RESPONSES

1. Note three places in her essay where Meghan Sheehan tries to accommodate her audience's prior knowledge and assumptions. For each place, describe the strategy she uses to reach out to her audience. Find two places where you believe Meghan should have worked harder to reach out to her audience.

2. Sheehan intentionally delays presenting her thesis until the last paragraph of her essay. In what ways does this organization treat the reader respectfully? In what ways might it be disrespectful to the reader? Do you think this is an ethical way to organize the essay? List your reasons.

3. List three adjectives to describe Sheehan's tone in this essay. For each adjective you've listed, jot down an example or two from her essay.

PUBLIC WRITING IN BIOTECHNOLOGY

Introduction

August 9, 2001, stands out as a watershed date in U.S. policy concerning human embryonic stem cell research. On that day, President George W. Bush announced a new policy limiting federally-funded research to a handful of existing embryonic stem cell lines. This followed months of wrangling over the ethics of using embryonic stem cells, cells that are removed from a non-implanted embryo in a procedure that destroys the embryo. The president's policy was touted as a compromise between two opposing sides of the issue: (1) those who believe that human life begins at conception and claim that destroying an embryo is morally wrong, and (2) those who believe that human life begins at a later stage in the uterus and claim that limiting research on potential cures for human diseases is morally wrong. The president's policy allowed some federally-funded research to proceed with existing cells, but it disallowed federal funds for research that uses new embryonic stem cell lines.

This editorial was written by a prominent social scientist and a prominent life scientist at the University of Michigan in the days following the president's press conference. The authors published this editorial on the webpage of the U of M's Life Sciences program. In this editorial, the authors clearly disagree with the president's decision, in part, because the University of Michigan is a leader in federally-funded life science research. The authors are passionate about this topic, but they temper that passion with evidence, sound reasoning, and respect for others' views. Note, for example, the care the authors take in presenting both sides in the best possible light, and how their solution seeks to respect the values of those with whom they disagree. By creating a credible argument, the authors open the door for readers to agree with their claim.

Stem Cell Research
Richard O. Lempert and Jack E. Dixon

http://www.lifesciences.umich.edu/pdf/StemEdit.pdf, August 28, 2001

The debate over whether the federal government should fund research on stem cells derived from human embryos has been made to appear as a conflict between science and ethics, with science arguing for the funding of stem cell research to cure currently incurable diseases and ethics arguing against it. But ethically it may be more problematic not to fund human embryo stem cell research than to fund it, and scientifically no one can guarantee that cures for the currently incurable will soon be at hand.

Under most ethical schemes, including many religious ones, helping fellow human beings is often an ethical imperative, and curing the sick is a classic example of what it means to help other people. A state that impedes or does not actively support attempts to heal illness is arguably acting immorally. Moreover, morality requires responsibility. By failing to fund human embryo stem cell research while allowing privately funded research to proceed, the federal government is abrogating its responsibility to think carefully about the conditions under which such research should proceed and forfeiting any chance to lead the private sector and other nations in thinking about the conditions under which such research can morally proceed. Indeed, the government would be taking more ethical responsibility if it outlawed human embryo stem cell research entirely rather than allowing it to proceed only with private funding. This, at least, would be taking a moral stance rather than ducking the issue in political compromise.

Yet morality is also about means: no matter how desirable the end may be, some ways of achieving it could be morally impermissible. This is the argument of those who believe that stem cell research, which destroys human embryos, regardless of the stage of development, is always a moral wrong. Most Americans reject this position. They fail to see anything distinctively human about a frozen fertilized embryo, which has not yet begun to differentiate into tissues that make people human. Human life for us, and many others, begins in a mother and not in a petri dish. Other proponents of human embryo stem cell research point out that most embryo sources of stem cells have to date been the byproducts of in vitro fertilization procedures, and they will at some point be discarded. Using their stem cells in an effort to save lives is no more morally problematic than using organs of the accidentally killed for transplants. For people who take either of these positions, morality not only permits human embryo stem cell research and federal funding, but also is promoted by it because the research may lead to discoveries that save or substantially improve the lives of indisputably human beings.

The division between the moral opponents of human embryo stem cell research and its moral and scientific proponents is not of a sort that can be compromised. If a fully human life exists the moment sperm fuses with egg, whether within a woman or in a petri dish, there is no way of doing human embryo stem cell research that does not take a human life or use humans as means to ends. The majority supporting stem cell research cannot demand that people who believe a fully human life exists at conception give up this belief, nor can they claim that this belief, and the case against stem cell research that follows from it, is unreasonable. At the same time the minority opposed to this research can point to no failures of reason in the majority's position that human stem cell research takes no human lives that would otherwise exist nor in the majority's sense of the ethical desirability of using stem cells to cure disease. We have in the opposed groups different starting points that yield different ethical conclusions that cannot be compromised.

A policy that allows human embryo stem cell research to proceed privately but withholds federal funds is not a compromise. From the opponents' point of view this allows human life to be taken while the government turns a blind eye, and from the proponents' point of view, this not only retards progress toward under-standing how stem cells may be used to fight disease but also channels stem cell research along lines made attractive by potential profits while raising the likely price of therapies that are generated.

We have in this country a way of proceeding despite such fundamental conflicts: it is called politics. In the stem cell controversy, the majority should prevail. It should not seek to compromise fundamental issues, for that is impossible, but it should respect the views held by opponents of this research and recognize them not only as widespread, but also reasonable and rooted in religious and moral values as admirable as the value of curing disease. The spirit of respect yields some of the same policy prescriptions as those that have been presented as compromises and some that are different. For example, respect for those who equate the life of embryos with that of babies justifies special efforts to ensure that any embryos that might mature into babies are not destroyed. Thus, federal rules governing stem cell research might provide that embryo adoption takes priority over embryo research, and that embryo research can only proceed on embryos that are not wanted, either by donors or by potential adoptive mothers.

Federal funding should continue and perhaps even increase for adult and fetal cord stem cell research. Should there ever come a time when science is satisfied that human embryo stem cells offer no therapeutic advantages over adult or fetal cord stem cells, respect for the moral opponents of embryo stem cell research means that it should stop. Respect also suggests federal funding should not encourage the creation of embryos simply for their stem cells. Hence unless stem cells from specially created embryos offer scientific advantages over stem cells from embryos already existing and fated for degradation or destruction, creating embryos for their stem cells should not be supported by federal funds and might even be precluded in the private sector. But if there are good scientific reasons for creating embryos for research purposes, a clash of ethical values cannot be avoided, and the majority's preferred values, which at the moment seem to favor curing disease, should prevail. The same is true of proposals to limit federally funded stem cell research to cell lines already in existence, that is, cells from already destroyed embryos. It is not a compromise; rather, it is a limit that respect can justify, but only if science tells us that stem cell research will not thereby be hampered.

One of the promises of embryonic stem cell research is that it will provide a means of treating diseases like Alzheimer's and Parkinson's. At this time, such treatments are only a plausible suggestion. Research is needed to determine how effective adult stem cells and embryonic stem cells can be in treating these diseases. This is no small task. In order to determine which stem cells to use, it is necessary to understand their properties, how they function, and how long they live. This information is needed prior to using these cells to treat human diseases. Uncovering this information will take time, and no one can say with any certainty what the best source of stem cells will be or when we will be ready to treat specific diseases with stem cell therapy. What is clear, is that, in the absence of federal funding, progress in understanding the properties of stem cells will be slower, in fact, much slower. There are many examples of how federal funding has had a major impact on progress made in treating human diseases. Some of us are old enough to remember that federal funding hastened the development of the vaccine that prevented polio. To argue that one should not use federal funding to support research on fertilized embryos, that would be destroyed if not used, is to put the treatment of incurable diseases, like Alzheimer's and Parkinson's, far, far in the future. This in our view is a morally indefensible position for ourselves and for our government.

READING RESPONSES

1. Throughout their essay, authors Lempert and Dixon argue for compromise rather than for the victory of one side over the other. To emphasize compromise they establish several sets of oppositions that they then break down. List as many oppositions as you can find in the essay.
2. Lempert and Dixon make extensive use of careful, logical argumentation to persuade readers to accept their views. Review the essay and pin-point what you believe to be their most persuasive argument. Justify your choice.
3. It's clear that the authors favor federal funding for embryonic stem cell research, but they treat those who oppose funding this research with care and respect. What strategies do they use to ensure that those who disagree with them feel fairly treated?

MORE WRITING IN BIOTECHNOLOGY

Introduction

Published in *Nature Biotechnology*, a journal for professionals in biotechnology, this paper criticizes proponents for oversimplifying or neglecting the general public's concerns about transgenic crops and other contested issues in biotechnology. "Sustainable development of biotechnology will require renewed focus on stakeholders and their needs," conclude Sagar and his co-authors. Though few would argue against this claim, some might disagree with its implications. Furthermore, the authors argue that biotechnologists must come to grips with the complexities of the public's concerns. The StarLink corn fiasco, which led in 2000 to the recall of food products contaminated with transgenic corn approved for animal feeds but not for human consumption, supports these authors' contention that "lay individuals, unhindered by disciplinary boundaries, often display a remarkable sensitivity to issues that policy experts fail to address." While a scientific advisory panel at the Environmental Protection Agency was poring over allergenicity data, the public was concerned about issues of justice (Who benefits and who bears the risks?), globalization, and individual liberty (Why isn't this labeled?). Sagar et al. describe these public concerns thoroughly and respectfully, and in so doing they encourage scholars on both sides of the biotechnology debate to do the same.

Sagar et al. describe solutions to improve the ways that all stakeholders, especially those with traditionally marginalized voices, can join the conversation about biotechnology research and development. While some might object that this would increase costs and delay implementation, Sagar et al. rightly contend that "biotechnology's future ultimately relies on governing institutions listening and responding to the public." Could proponents object to strengthening public trust and support for biotechnology?

The tragedy of the commoners: biotechnology and its publics

Ambuj Sagar, Arthur Daemmrich, and Mona Ashiya

Nature Biotechnology 18(2000): 2–4

In pluralistic societies, innovations offering new ways to promote independence or individuality are generally rapidly embraced, whereas those that appear to centralize power and authority are either outright attacked, or accepted only after contentious debates. Biotechnology, however, has repeatedly broken this mold, offering the potential for remarkably individualized products while also appearing

to concentrate capabilities and power in the hands of a small number of global players. For example, biotechnology's promise to provide health care specific to individual needs goes hand in hand with giving corporations access to detailed genetic information. Likewise, its potential to fine-tune food production to local needs coincides with concentrating the capabilities to do so in a small number of institutions. Understandably, such scenarios have met with both support and opposition. The most recent, and perhaps the most contentious of the resulting controversies, has been the highly visible and ongoing debate on genetically modified (GM) agricultural products. Many observers seem to be surprised by the sudden rise of this issue, and its origin is often ascribed to a lack of public trust in regulatory institutions.

In one sense, the emergence of the GM issue should not be seen as surprising: it is only one of numerous debates over the applications of biotechnology. Scientists, politicians, and the public have also expressed concern about aspects of cloning, xenotransplantation [**developing organs in animals to be used as transplants for humans**], genetic testing, and gene prospecting, to name a few other prominent examples. We suggest that a major factor in the emergence of these controversies has been neglect of the needs, interests, and concerns of the primary stakeholders—the "commoners"—in the biotechnology arena. The sustainable development of biotechnology will require a renewed focus on stakeholders and their needs. This, in turn, demands a clearer understanding of public concerns as well as attention to issues of institutional structure and representation in decision-making processes. The framework presented in this paper suggests some steps in this direction. While many of the points raised in the following analysis are based on examples from agricultural biotechnology, our approach also applies to other areas where ongoing development hinges on proper process in the construction of new forms of governance.

The complexities of controversy

Observers of recent developments in the agricultural biotechnology arena often claim that different degrees of trust in regulatory institutions have shaped the lay public's response to the products of this new technology. Whereas protests have targeted GM foods in Europe, Americans have been comparatively quiet and accepting of such new foods. Some analysts have claimed that this difference emerges from greater regulatory transparency and an ability to modulate agency decisions (often through the courts) in the United States in contrast to the closed-door elite decision-making procedures employed in Europe. They further suggest that experiences with BSE **[mad-cow disease]** and dioxin-tainted foods have eroded the credibility of regulators in Europe to safeguard the public interest.

Whereas the above is true to some extent, a broader analysis of the factors governing debates over GM products shows limitations of reducing the controversy solely to degrees of trust in environmental and health safety agencies. A more textured account indicates that the public is also concerned with issues such as globalization and stratification of power, ethics, equity, and individual rights and choice. Such intertwined themes underlie not just the European public disquiet over GM products, they also cut across a number of issue areas in biotechnology (see Figure 1 for a representative list). Put another way, concerns of "commoners" focus not just on the narrow aspects of applications of individual technologies, but also on the broader institutional and political context in which they are introduced. As the sociologist Dorothy Nelkin has noted, "controversies over science

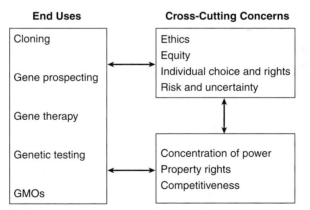

Figure 1 Concerns of "commoners" focus not just on the narrow aspects of applications of individual technologies, but also on the broader institutional and political context in which they are introduced.

and technology are struggles over meaning and morality, over the distribution of resources, and over the locus of power and control."[1] Lay individuals, unhindered by disciplinary boundaries, often display a remarkable sensitivity to issues that policy experts fail to address. As a result, risks that are reduced to narrow variables and deemed amenable to traditional "scientific/technical" analyses by experts are not resolved easily once they become public controversies. In the current policy discourse, attention is paid mostly to specific issues such as GM products, genetic testing, or gene prospecting as they become contentious. There is little systematic analysis of underlying currents that lead to controversies.

Concerns of the commoners

Public concerns must be understood as factors that shape the very discourse—the style and content of interactions—surrounding biotechnology around the globe. They determine the structure and boundaries of disputes and are key considerations for conflict resolution. Here we discuss two particularly important cross-cutting concerns to illustrate how they are germane to debates in biotechnology.

Risk and uncertainty. Recent public protests against GM foods are indicative of a divide between expert and lay perceptions of risk and uncertainty. Scholars of risk analysis have long noted that risk estimates vary significantly between experts and the public.[2] Public risk perception is influenced as much by social relations and feelings of power and powerlessness as by objective knowledge about the likelihood of large-scale accidents or individual harm. Furthermore, there is an increasing sense that the shift from an industrial era to the information age has produced a "risk society," characterized by self-inflicted dangers, increasing inter-dependence of human decisions, worldwide implications even of seemingly local events, and controversies that undermine the basis for calculating risk and insurance.[3] In such a society, regulatory institutions, corporations, and even scientists who base decisions regarding field trials or widespread marketing of GM foods on risk/benefit calculations fail to grasp the deeper ethical and social bases that shape public opinion.

Consequently, even when government officials in Europe, Asia, and Latin America respond to public concerns by instituting additional testing and regulatory requirements on biotechnology, they fail to account for the broader unquantifiable concerns of the "commoners." Attention has, instead, focused on environmental and human health risks alone. For example, this past June, the European Union's environment ministers adopted a decision imposing a *de facto* moratorium on new marketing approvals for GM organisms. Furthermore, ministers from Denmark, France, Greece, Italy, and Luxembourg independently insisted that they would block new applications to market GM seeds, plants, or foodstuffs until a new regulatory regime is put in place.[4] These announcements came two days after the Japanese Ministry of Agriculture, Forestry and Fisheries (MAFF) stated it would tighten safety regulations on GM crops in the wake of a Cornell University study showing that pollen from insect-resistant *Bt* (*Bacillus thuringiensis*) maize is potentially toxic to monarch butterfly larvae. MAFF will suspend approval of *Bt* crops in Japan until revised safety protocols are developed for GM crops. In a third example, the Brazilian state of Rio Grande do Sul has declared itself a "genetically modified free zone." This followed a Brazilian federal court decision in June barring the planting or distribution of GM soybeans in the country.

These events all illustrate the degree to which broad uncertainty is being examined in a traditional risk framework, making it amenable to testing and regulation under existing structures. But, in this process, moral and cultural unease as well as concerns about the unknown (or perhaps unknowable) consequences of some aspects of biotechnology are swept aside. Given this divide, the lay public is likely to increasingly demand "socially precautionary" principles in regulatory oversight. Decision makers should consider how they have represented the public and its concerns when making complex and often incommensurable calculations of economic benefits against ecological and health risks. All too often, key concerns are lost in the processes through which institutions model and represent stakeholders.

Globalization and its discontents. Current modes of exchanging knowledge, services, and consumer goods are rapidly reshaping the social, political, and economic structures of the world. This process of globalization is widening troubling gaps in access to knowledge and financial resources. In turn, these disparities are fueling criticism of new technologies—even within highly developed countries—based on several key features.

First among the issues to be considered are increasing income/resource disparities. The developing world, home to 80% of the world's population, generates less than 20% of the global gross domestic product, and there are few signs this divide will shrink in the foreseeable future. In 1997, the richest fifth of the world had an income 74 times that of the poorest fifth, more than double the inequality in 1960.[4]

Second, patterns of industrial ownership are changing. Recent mergers have led to the formation of transnational corporations of unprecedented size and wealth. Worldwide mergers in 1998 were worth $2.4 trillion and reflected a 50% increase over 1997, which itself was a record year.[5] In the biotechnology sector alone, mergers and acquisitions increased from $9.3 billion to $172.4 billion in the decade between 1988 and 1998.[4]

Third, there have been major shifts in the nature of financial flows to developing countries. Whereas public development aid dropped from $56.9 billion in 1990 to $47.9 billion in 1998, private flows to developing countries increased from $43.9 billion to $227.1 billion in the same period.[6] As a percentage of their combined gross national product, contributions from members of the OECD's Development Assistance Committee have fallen to their lowest level ever, from 0.33% in 1992 to 0.22% in 1997.[7]

Fourth, disparities are increasing in knowledge generation and utilization. North America, Europe, Japan, and newly industrialized countries accounted for 84.5% of the $470 billion spent on research and development worldwide in 1994 (the latest year for which data are available).[8] A similar trend is also evident when considering patent filings. Industrialized countries hold 97% of patents worldwide, and more than

80% of patents granted in developing countries belong to individuals or corporations based in industrialized countries.[4]

These disparities pose critical challenges to governments, particularly those of developing countries. In today's world where knowledge is considered the single "most important factor in determining the standard of living,"[9] the biotechnology pillar of the knowledge economy is often seen as increasing global divisions. For example, future applications of biotechnology may increasingly depend on genetic diversity. A substantial portion of the global genetic resources reside in the South, while the capabilities to commercially utilize them lie in the North. This raises serious concerns about appropriate benefit sharing. Furthermore, as developing countries become more dependent on private sources for capital, choices available to promote and expand research in biotechnology are constrained. Notably, even pragmatic analysts from the North are concerned that future innovations will be limited under an emerging industry structure where the top five biotechnology firms control more than 95% of gene transfer patents.[4]

More broadly, critical reactions to emerging applications of biotechnology are based on control of research agendas, access to useful technologies, influence in decision-making forums, and debates over who will benefit from new technologies. Biotechnology is expected to give further impetus to the current process of globalization. Given the aforementioned concerns, it often serves as a lightning rod for expressing disquiet about the apparent future of the world. While such public concerns may not be easy to face or assuage, downplaying their relevance will only exacerbate the current polarization.

Who speaks for the stakeholders?

Given the substantial social and economic consequences of biotechnology, a broad swath of society has become a stakeholder in discussions on its applications. At the same time, a variety of institutions are involved in these debates. Figure 2 presents some major categories of relevant institutions and stakeholders.

Importantly, while some stakeholders may be able to participate directly in discussions about the adoption of new technologies, most are unable to do so. For this reason, channels to incorporate stakeholder views into debates take on critical importance. To some extent, such perspectives are inserted into discussions and

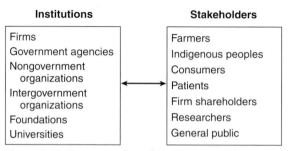

Figure 2 Major categories of institutions and stakeholders in biotechnology.

decision making about biotechnology through participating institutions. However, these have to balance a number of interests and agendas, including those of the institutions themselves, of their internal constituents, and of stakeholders they explicitly represent. For example, the views of a biotechnology firm may be shaped by the personal ambitions of the company officers and scientists, the obligation to ensure returns to shareholders, and the need to satisfy customers. Similarly, nongovernmental organization (NGO) positions reflect the passions of activists, the concerns of their donors, and their public support base.[10] Such balancing acts may often give short shrift to the already marginalized voices of external stakeholders and raise serious issues about the authenticity of representation, even though many institutions derive their legitimacy from "representing" stakeholders.

Even the most well-meaning organizations can view the interests of beneficiaries in a simplistic manner, or distort them unwittingly. Moreover, institutions may indulge strategically in a "virtual representation" of their stakeholders that offers both moral authority in defense of their own views and reduced costs of actual representation. The recent GM foods debate illustrates a situation where supporters and opponents of this technology have invoked their concern for the disenfranchised to defend their positions. Biotechnology firms, some government agencies, and other organizations cite the potential contribution of biotechnology to resolve world hunger, while NGOs highlight the potential adverse impacts of biotechnology on farmers and ecosystems in developing countries (see, for example, refs 11–13).

Thus, some hard questions should be asked of any institution that participates in a given debate: Whose interests does it purport to represent and whose interests does it actually represent through its actions? How does it model and understand stakeholders' interests? Is the institution's present mode of representation consistent with past actions and stances in other policy arenas? More broadly, are the interests of all stakeholders represented equally? Finally, how is the institution accountable to its stakeholders? Such questions apply equally to industry, advocacy groups and academia. Requiring institutions to provide answers should compel them to be more honest in their representation of stakeholders' views.

The issue of accountable representation is central to the biotechnology debate. Ultimately, stakeholders' interests should be given priority, not only for reasons of justice and fairness, but also because sustainable development of biotechnology will require widespread acceptance by the public of its goods and services. Accountable representation necessitates the integration of stakeholder interests into activities including basic and applied science, policy research, advocacy, and policy formulation and implementation.

Conclusion

The issue of trust certainly will continue to be of major significance for biotechnology in the coming years. But this issue is far more complex than generally portrayed, and not easily reduced to "trust in regulatory institutions." In our view, public trust—the ultimate arbiter of any technology in the marketplace—is based on perceptions of how a technology will influence the lives of various individuals, of how specific firms as well as the industry as a whole have represented public interests, and of the social, political, and economic landscape that serves as a backdrop for technological change. Thus, it becomes fundamentally important to pay attention to the "commoners" in the biotechnology debate, as well as to their needs and concerns.

Biotechnology's future ultimately relies on governing institutions listening and responding to the public, rather than discounting key stakeholders as irrational, scientifically illiterate, or technophobic. Institutions such as the biotechnology industry and government agencies stand to gain greater acceptance only by soliciting public input, implementing policies in a transparent and democratically representative fashion, and demonstrating their responsiveness to concerns raised by scientific experts, other organizations, and citizens and consumers around the world. New interactive approaches must be developed in order to bring stakeholders together and allow them to articulate cross-cutting concerns. Industry, given its stake in the debate, will need to go furthest by not merely recognizing "the public" as stakeholders, but by granting them some of the rights normally afforded citizens of modern states: open access to information, the opportunity to comment on proposed actions, the right to receive reasoned explanations, and above all, recognition that dissent can be bridged only through compromise.

Notes

1. Nelkin, D. Science controversies, in *Handbook of science and technology studies* (eds Jasanoff, S. et al.) 445 (Sage Publications, Thousand Oaks, CA; 1995).
2. Slovic, P. Beyond numbers: a broader perspective on risk perception and risk communication, in *Acceptable evidence: science and values in risk management* (eds Mayo, D.G. & Hollander, R.) 48–65, (Oxford Univ. Press, New York, NY; 1991).
3. Beck, U. *Risk society: towards a new modernity.* (Sage Publications, London; 1992).
4. United Nations Development Program. *Human development report 1999.* (Oxford Univ. Press, New York, NY; 1999), 36.
5. Anonymous. How to merge: After the deal. *The Economist*, January 9 (1999), 21–23.
6. World Bank. *Global development finance 1999.* (World Bank, Washington, DC; 1999).
7. Organization for Economic Cooperation and Development. Aid and private flows fell in 1997. (news release, June 18, 1998).
8. Barre, R. *World science report 1998.* (UNESCO, Paris; 1998).
9. World Bank. *World development report 1999.* (World Bank, Washington, DC; 1999).
10. Of course, institutions and individuals are shaped by their past experiences. Institutional and personal experiences with disparate issues such as nuclear power, pesticides, globalization, or individual privacy often shape current perceptions in the debate on GM foods.
11. Persley, G.J. & Doyle, J.J. *Biotechnology and developing-country agriculture: problems and opportunities.* Overview. (International Food Policy Research Institute, 2020 Focus 2: Brief No. 1, Washington, DC; 1999.)
12. AgrEvo. *To nourish ten billion people.* (AgrEvo Background Paper; Berlin,1998).
13. Rural Advancement Foundation International. *Traitor technology; the terminator's wider implications.* (RAFI Communiqué, Winnipeg; January/February 1999).

READING RESPONSES

1. The essay opens with a truism that most readers will accept. Why might Sagar and his co-authors begin their essay in this way? How do they move the reader's attention from that truism to the more complex issues that they'll consider in the essay?
2. To explain the forces shaping public thinking about biotechnology, Sagar and his co-authors focus on two issues: risk and uncertainty, and globalization and its discontents. In two or three sentences for each, summarize the information they provide.
3. Review the evidence that the authors provide. What about the evidence makes it effective for a wide range of readers?

WRITING ASSIGNMENTS

ASSIGNMENT 1: APPLYING THE PORTABLE RHETORICAL LESSON

Background: You will not be surprised to learn that Starbucks promotes itself as a socially and environmentally responsible company. A link to "Social Responsibility" under "About Us" on the company website (www.starbucks.com) proclaims that "It's the way we do business." The company's "Social Responsibility Newsletter" promotes the company's good work across the globe, but it does not acknowledge or respond directly to its critics.

Your task is to draft a Web article for either a global food company like Starbucks or an environmental watchdog organization like the Organic Consumers Association that addresses a difficult environmental issue in a way that builds trust among those who might otherwise think of themselves as adversaries. To complete this assignment you will have to conduct some research on the environmental issue that has polarized the adversaries. Consult a reference librarian for help with this research.

As you begin drafting, look for common ground: goals, methods, and evidence that the contending groups can agree on. Attempt to describe contentious issues in ways that all groups will accept as fair. Take advantage of strategies for writing on the Web that will help you emphasize ethical—and ultimately effective—arguments about these vital issues.

ASSIGNMENT 2: MAKING CONNECTIONS

Background: Some writing teachers restrict students from writing on topics that have a reputation for dividing people, topics such as abortion, euthanasia, gun control, partisan politics, prayer in public schools, and affirmative action. Writing teachers claim, rightly so, that people who hold strong opinions on a controversial issue often have a difficult time assessing the validity of evidence, identifying the range of assumptions that people bring to the topic, and treating opposing arguments respectfully.

Your task is to revise an essay or speech that takes a stance on a controversial subject like those listed above so that it better acknowledges the assumptions and concerns of those who might disagree with the author. You might consider selecting a text that takes a position that you oppose. Once you've selected your text, assess how well the author addresses the concerns of those who oppose her stance. Analyze the text for issues like the following:

- What evidence does the author use? Is this evidence that all rational people will accept?
- How does the author address the assumptions and concerns of those who oppose her?
- In what ways does the author reach out to audience members who disagree with her stance?

As you begin drafting, consider the progression of your argument carefully. What common ground can you start from? How can you address the concerns of those who will oppose point of your piece? What evidence will appeal to these readers?

ASSIGNMENT 3: DOING THE RESEARCH

Background: New advances in the field of biotechnology have sparked heated debate within the scholarly community and protests from citizens in many countries. One such advance is "Bt corn," so called because it contains *Bacillus thuringiensis* (Bt), a bacterium deadly to the caterpillars that feed on corn plants. People around the world are protesting the effects of Bt corn on the livelihoods of organic farmers, the animals who ingest the corn (and the people who eat those animals), the people who live near the Bt corn fields, and butterfly populations.

Your task is to research the problems associated with Bt corn and promote a solution to one, some, or all of those problems.

As you begin drafting, be sure to carefully assess the research you find, paying close attention to the credibility of the source. Since you likely do not have the expertise to develop your own solution, select a solution from your research and promote that solution in your own work. Be sure to provide citations for the research you use. Following the lead of Conway and Toenniessen, attempt to present the problem in a way that represents fairly the claims of all groups. When you present your solution, emphasize how it addresses the concerns of those who might initially be inclined to disagree with it.

PART FOUR

RECOMMENDING ACTION

Not all of the writers in Part Four make recommendations that are simple and straightforward, but all tell their readers how they should act. It is not enough for these writers to influence assumptions (though they do that); it is not enough for them to supply useful knowledge (though they do that as well). Most importantly, these writers attempt to change what people do.

The English education chapter (Chapter 11) is especially complex in its aims and strategy. We place it at the beginning of Part Four because it synthesizes strategies typical of all three sections: the authors analyze theory to reshape readers' assumptions, and they produce and report important knowledge. And, finally, they all recommend specific changes in how we teach and learn.

In Chapter 12 (nursing) and Chapter 13 (psychology) the authors make recommendations directly. Nurses advocate for particular changes in nursing practice, and they plot specific "care plans." Clinical psychologists diagnose their clients and recommend treatment. The marketing chapter (Chapter 14) includes many of the explicit recommendations you might expect in business settings: "buy this chair to save money for your company." It also makes more subtle recommendations: "implement this new marketing campaign."

As you move into professional and civic lives, you will frequently write in order to recommend. So use these chapters to prepare yourself to effectively recommend action—and change.

ENGLISH EDUCATION: CHALLENGING CONVENTIONS

Every one of the readings in this chapter argues explicitly that teachers should change how they teach so that they can better prepare students to change the world. In the last sentence of the first reading, Victor Villanueva urges, "look to how things might be—and ought to be—changed"; in the student-composed reading, Cherilyn Dudley claims, "students . . . can influence the world around them." Similar statements appear in the public reading by Hirsch ("we hope it [his plan] will help improve American public education") and the reading by Friere ("liberation [in education] is praxis: the action and reflection of men and women upon their world in order to transform it").

In short, expect that these writers will try to change you and expect that you will be called upon to respond to the challenge—accepting what they say, countering it, revising it, and putting it into practice as you take part in your own education. Expect many things, but don't expect to keep warming the La-Z-Boy.

You are familiar with the ways of teachers, so none of this high-intensity talk about change should surprise you. But what you read in this chapter about education will offer you practical—and possibly surprising—models for changing the ways you and your teachers practice education.

A Portable Rhetorical Lesson:
Challenging Conventions Purposefully

In this chapter, we examine how writers disrupt readers' expectations to accomplish a rhetorical goal. First, understand that all readers bring a set of expectations, based on past experience, to their reading of a text. You have no doubt had the experience of walking into a room when others are watching a TV show or movie; you can't figure out why the characters in the movie are acting so weird, but then someone notices the puzzled look on your face and explains, "It's a satire." Then everything becomes clear to you. We interpret what we see, hear, and read based on our expectations. Genres—comedies, tragedies, lab reports, movie reviews, whatever—communicate effectively because we know what to expect of them; we know the rules of their games (and satires surprise and entertain us by putting a twist on the familiar rules).

In a similar way, Villanueva keeps his readers teetering between the familiar and unfamiliar. *Bootstraps: From an American Academic of Color* is a scholarly discussion about educational philosophy. Readers might expect theses, topic sentences, and references to other scholarship. And Villanueva offers his readers these things— sometimes. Other times, however, he captures the reader's attention by challenging expectations. When you observe his experiments with form, you need to remember that he does not violate conventions of standard written English just to thumb his nose at convention. He surprises you to persuade you, and that is the core of the chapter's portable rhetorical lesson.

Breaking with convention can be effective because it surprises the reader and piques our curiosity. When Villanueva jumps from one point in time to another, he surprises us; we perk up and ask "What did you do that for?" We start to wonder, in other words, about the writer's rhetorical choices—especially when we know that the writer is capable of following convention and has chosen not to. As our student writer Cherilyn Dudley astutely observes, a writer needs to be sure that readers will recognize breaks with convention as "*choices* rather than *mistakes.*"

When we read texts that play with our expectations, we also become more aware of why we do or do not violate conventions in our own writing. Cherilyn Dudley explains why she rarely breaks with convention as a student writer. She helps us to understand why students shy away from experimental writing and brash creativity: it's too much of a risk to their grades.

Finally, the experience of reading unconventional texts teaches us that a little experimentation with convention goes a long way. Most of Villanueva's sentences would pass under the red pen of a picky grammarian unmarked. He creates no new forms of punctuation, his pronouns have clear referents, and his organization rarely requires re-reading to figure out what he's talking about. And yet he appears to be boldly innovative. If you observe how infrequently Villanueva breaks with convention, you may be more deeply impressed by the power of such breaks to capture a reader's attention.

Chapter Topics: Although the focus of the chapter is English education, the readings open doors to discussion of educational practice in general, with emphases on issues of social justice and equality of opportunity.

To Think About . . .

In *Cultural Literacy: What Every American Needs to Know*, E.D. Hirsch Jr. provides a list of 5,000 pieces of "basic information" that people need to "thrive in the modern world." Here are some of them:

1939–1945	Lunatic fringe
Aficionado	Madison Avenue
Bite the bullet	Nihilism
Chernobyl	O brave new world!
Danube River	Prime the pump
The Emperor's New Clothes	Quadratic equation
fetish	Realpolitik
genocide	Seamy side
Hoover Dam	Telemetry
Incumbent	Utilitarianism
Joie de vivre	Vicious circle
We are such stuff as dreams are made on	You can't take it with you
Xenophobia	Zero-sum game

- Make three lists: items you know, those that sound familiar but you couldn't use them in a sentence, and those you don't know.
- Consider your lists: would you argue that you should learn all these items in school? Which five items are most important for students to learn? Which five items are least important? How did you decide what was most and least important?
- Is there more to education than teaching information? If so, what else should education teach students?

WRITING IN ENGLISH EDUCATION

Introduction by William J. Vande Kopple, Professor of English

Bootstraps: From an American Academic of Color is the kind of book that students majoring in secondary English education would probably be asked to read toward the end of their college career, perhaps in a course on the teaching of writing or in a course on methods and materials in English education.

Villanueva's final sentences in the section reprinted here capture well his fundamental purpose for writing: "We can do critical literacy. And what better to be critical of than the cultural norms contained in tradition? Start with what students know or have been told they ought to know. Allow and encourage a questioning of the norms. And maybe look to how things might be—and ought to be—changed." In other words, Villanueva aims to move readers to examine the social, economic, and political forces that they have always taken for granted within their culture and to ask how these forces might need to be altered in order to promote justice and equity.

You might be surprised by some aspects of the form of *Bootstraps*. Villanueva calls his book "a postmodern text" and adds that "[i]t fits no specific genre; its presentation, on the surface, is fragmentary." Writers are certainly not afraid to experiment with the form of essays and books, going against conventions at times, but when it comes to experimenting with form, Villanueva probably wins a special prize. His experimentation is especially evident in what he calls the book's "alinearity"; even if you scan this book, you will notice that it includes several abrupt shifts. For example, Villanueva shifts from one time period to another; at one point readers learn about the autumn of 1984, while shortly thereafter they start reading about 1990. He also includes shifts in subject matter— leaping, for example, from a description of how he learned that he had been replaced as the director of a basic-writing program to some critical examination of E. D. Hirsch's *Cultural Literacy*. Further, he shifts his references to himself, sometimes using "Victor," sometimes "he," and still other times "I"; in other parts of the book, he refers to himself as the "graduate student," the "new Teaching Assistant," "Victor the Curiosity," "Dr. V. the Deadbeat," and "Papi." Sometimes he shifts from sentence fragments to grammatically correct sentences and then back to fragments. And although this practice is not fully evident in the pages reprinted here, in his book Villanueva some-times shifts in the kind of language he includes—from quotations in Spanglish to neighborhood chants to lines from poems to musings about his family to discussions of theory.

Running through the book, however, are five closely related lines of thought, all of which are represented in the pages reprinted here. In one line, Villanueva tells the story of his life, describing how he takes a few days away from his university for a job interview and returns to learn that he has been replaced as the director of the basic-writing program. In another line, he introduces readers to scholars like Freire and Gramsci who have affected his life, particularly his educational career. In a third line, he discusses theories of the social, economic, and political forces in the United States, especially as these forces affect persons of color. In yet another line, he connects the theoretical discussions to specific aspects of his own life. Finally, he includes several descriptions of classroom practices that he thinks will promote "critical dialogue within a cultural literacy."

Villanueva also goes against the convention forbidding the use of personal details in academic writing. This convention is not universally held among college teachers. Some urge you to use examples from your own life in your writing and to feel free to use the pronoun *I*. Still, I often hear of professors who prohibit any move into the personal realm. And students often call and e-mail me while they are preparing their papers for my class to double-check whether they can use *I* or not; they would not do this had they not heard many warnings against the personal in other classes. In this light, it is striking to examine how Villanueva effectively juxtaposes general theories of social, economic, and political forces with very specific details of his personal life.

As he discusses general theories of how privileged social classes do much to determine what kinds of language are approved of in a society, I follow his discussion and begin to evaluate the theories. But when I also encounter Villanueva's anecdote with the personal details about how one of the nuns from his primary school visited his home and warned his parents about how his English was marred by "an accent," my emotions start to come into play. And when my emotions are moved, I am more likely to respond to calls for action. So the move to the personal can be a very powerful tactic for writers who seek this effect.

I also believe that these pages from *Bootstraps* can teach a widely applicable lesson about ways of thinking. This lesson has to do with the general theories of social, economic, and political forces that I have already referred to. Too often, if we evaluate these theories at all, we evaluate them only in terms of our own experience ("Racism? Sure, when I was a kid and that African-American family wanted to move into a house on the next block, there was a lot of trouble. But you should see my neighborhood now—about half of the families are African-American. Racism is probably a thing of the past.").

One important way that *Bootstraps* can function is to alert us to how social, economic, and political forces actually affect other individuals' lives. In the light of these forces, Villanueva examines his own life and the lives of his relatives and friends. And he shows that, depending on background, temperament, and situation, different individuals will have different responses to powerful social forces. Racism, for example, does not mean exactly the same thing for everyone. If we look closely, we will find a mosaic of responses to such forces as racism, materialism, and individualism.

In conveying this general message, Villanueva implicitly passes on a set of specific emphases to us, his readers. We should learn humility and fight our tendency to see the entire world only in terms of our own experience. We should be eager to hear how others have been affected by powerful social forces. We should be willing to have our views of powerful social forces become more complex than we usually like them to be. And we should have the courage to evaluate theories about social forces on the basis of both our own and other individuals' experiences.

These emphases are important for everyone, not just for majors in secondary English education.

✔READING TIPS

Villanueva's writing combines different genres: story, which you can read at story pace, and analysis of theory, which you may have to read more slowly. But more importantly you need to look for ways that the two genres combine. Remember that

Villanueva's focus is on the goal of "Tradition and change for changes in traditions." So you need to pay attention to how his selection of genre affects what he says about tradition and change. As you're reading, watch out for the following style shifts so they don't confuse you: (1) talking about his story in the past and referring to himself in third person, (2) using first person to discuss theories of education, (3) going back to a past story and using third person, and (4) telling his personal story, including how he practices his teaching theory, in first person and in present tense.

Of Color, Classes, and Classrooms

Victor Villanueva

In *Bootstraps: From an American Academic of Color*, NCTE, 1993.

Villanueva begins this chapter with a long fragment, throwing his readers into the middle of his description of a televised panel discussion. This use of a story-teller's rhetoric makes us feel personally involved from the very first sentence.

Hot, bright, stage lights blaring down on the four teachers and two parents seated in a circle before a TV camera. The six are about to speak on the cable network's public access channel.

Channing is the ring leader. He is a big man, large, round face with a shock of rumpled gray hair, a large belly pressing on a gray vest, not the rotund of the sedentary, but the large of the powerlifter. He is big, blustery, and brilliant: a polymath, well-versed in everything it seems, another who had traveled the class system: a childhood of unusual affluence, son of a government ambassador, an adulthood of unusual poverty.

There is Jolinda. She is lovely, thin, with shoulder-length auburn hair, sparse make-up. She has a quick, critical mind—decisive, un-flinching. A long-time interracial marriage and a racially mixed child to raise keeps her decidedly active politically, a hard-working Democrat for Jesse Jackson's Rainbow Coalition, a hard-working advocate for her children's school.

David Zank, goatee, beret, an administrator and a teacher at Jolinda's and Channing's and Victor's children's school. He administers an alternative public school. It's an elementary school, one not divided into traditional grades, though the students tend to group themselves into the younger, the older, the middle kids. It's a school that attracts children from all of the city's classes and races. Instead of a set curriculum, children decide on projects of interest, the teachers providing all that is necessary to carry out the projects: the mechanics, say, of building an airplane, lessons on aerodynamics, on the history of experiments in flight, and so on, though this ideal isn't always reached. Discipline is handled through "forum": students, teachers, and parents in a circle to discuss injustices. Injustices, not rules—there are no rules, really, but infringements on what is generally held to be socially acceptable behavior. Anyone can call for a forum. Issues are discussed. The school is democracy in action, not the usual contradiction of an authoritarian structure preaching democracy. Zank is an instrumental part of that school.

There are also two teachers from one of the more traditional public schools in the area. Their names are now forgotten, our being together limited to that one show. Channing had found them. Silver gray hair on both, off the neck, tastefully curled atop heads, the look of professional coiffeurs. They have stylish glasses, pleasant faces. Both are part of this discussion before the camera because they are upset by recent changes in their curriculum, changes imposed from above, from higher administration.

> Villanueva lists some of his identities in the third person—as if he is joining his readers in observing himself from a distance.

And there is Victor, graduate student, parent.

Channing opens the discussion. At issue is a new curriculum the city has purchased from a major publishing house. It's a computerized package. Depending on how they perform on a standardized pretest, students are presented with a series of hierarchically ordered mastery tests. Versions of a mastery test are taken and retaken until a certain score is attained; then students are directed to the next test, which is taken, retaken again, until a certain score is reached; then onto the next, and so on. The guarantee of the package is that there will be a city-wide improvement on national standardized scores, a guarantee that will be made good, no doubt. But the teachers protest that all curricular decisions are thereby taken from them, that they will be able to do nothing but teach to tests.

Zank's school has annually refused to administer standardized tests on the grounds that even though they measure nothing but the ability to take tests they are too easily read as matters of intellectual ability by the students themselves. He tells the teachers to do the same as his school's teachers—refuse to take part. The teachers say that though they agree with Zank on principle, they cannot afford to jeopardize their jobs. They would not have the support of their principal, would not enjoy the support of Zank's teachers. Jolinda argues that their jobs are the education of children—matters of public responsibility more than personal security. Again, there is agreement on principle, but personal security is not confined to any one individual; there are families to care for. Victor suggests not teaching to the tests, but teaching test-taking. His life would have been easier, perhaps, if he had understood standardized test-taking and knew not to take what they actually measure (test-taking) seriously. Zank nods, saying "Paulo Freire kind of stuff."

Victor had never heard of Paulo Freire before Zank's comment. He reads *Pedagogy of the Oppressed*. The things written there make sense. He sees what has been working in his children's school: children believing in their humanity, willing and able to take social responsibility, even at the age of six. He sees the problem he has had with the school, despite being pleased in the main: "laissez-faire." Here's Freire:

> I cannot leave the students by themselves because I am trying to be a liberating educator. Laissez-faire! I cannot fall into laissez-faire. On the other hand, I cannot be authoritarian. I have to be radically democratic and responsible and directive. Not directive of the students. but directive of the process. the liberating teacher is not doing something to the students but with the students. (Shor and Freire 46)

Students cannot be left to their own devices totally, yet they cannot be handed everything.

Fall 1984. Victor is placed in charge of the English department's basic-writing program. He is the best candidate for the job in a number of ways; his fields are rhetoric and composition; he is doing research that focuses on basic writing; he is of color in a program replete with students of color; and he is willing, as were the directors of the program before him, to undertake the job at teaching-assistant pay. Administration denies the color aspect. Tokenism, stereotyping—sensitive issues.

He institutes a Freire-like dimension to the curriculum. He does away with the focus on sentence-combining, adopts the autobiography of Carolina Maria deJesus, *Child of the Dark*, the story of a woman from the *favelas* of Brazil, where Freire had spent his adolescence, the likely nurturing ground for his pedagogy. Her diary presents a view from the eyes of a barely literate woman, her political awareness and the contradictions she embodies, her understanding of social stratification, and her desire for what she believes she cannot have, the social stigma she suffers in having to provide for her children by collecting trash, and the pride she nevertheless feels, the way she is labeled a Marxist by a local politician when she complains about her living conditions in a system she somehow believes in. It's the story of an American of color and of poverty set in Brazil. It is a story that the basic-writing students might well understand. And, because she is barely literate, the writing is such that the students can be critical of her language use, can gain confidence in their own abilities with literacy.

After growing up in a poor family in Brazil, at a time when the ruling class oppressed the poor, Paulo Freire (1921–1997) was exiled. After his years in exile, he returned to Brazil to become Secretary of Education in Brazil's largest school district. His radical pedagogy, which calls for teachers and students to examine cultural practices in order to expose, critique, and change oppressive situations, has been adopted by numerous North American educators.

Pedagogy of the Oppressed is perhaps Freire's best-known book.

To be "laissez-faire" is to interfere in the affairs of others as little as possible.

If an organization were to engage in "tokenism," it would offer just enough opportunities to minorities so that it would avoid criticism and perhaps even look good.

Favela is a term used commonly in Brazil to describe slums.

Lisa Delpit grew up on the "wrong side of the tracks" in Baton Rouge, LA, where she was among the first African Americans to integrate the Catholic schools. She has devoted her life to challenging the educational system. She argues that linguistic and cultural standards must be taught to African Americans and other minorities to empower these oppressed groups. Rather than just teaching to one cultural norm, though, Delpit says that teachers need to take a critical approach to the dominant culture, while also recognizing and drawing on the cultural strengths that all of their students bring to the classroom.

The basic-writing teachers seem to enjoy teaching the book. But the political is downplayed. Discussions turn on the cultural: "Tell me 'bout the ghetto and I'll tell you 'bout the 'burbs." Students enjoy the dialogue. But there seems to be no dialectic, no sustained probing into the conditions that relegate certain peoples to the ghettos and others to the 'burbs in disproportionate numbers. In some sense, this is a minor problem, outweighed by the students' being heard at all.

Still there are problems, not with the material but with the relations between students and teachers, the kinds of problems discussed by Lisa Delpit. Students are being graded on their courage more than on how others at a university or elsewhere might regard their writing. Disgruntled students complain that they have been lied to, that they thought they really were "A" or "B" writers, only to find that others consider them barely literate. Irate professors say that the university is no place for remedial courses. Victor convinces the higher administration that the basic-writing program is a cultural education, not remediation. The program survives, eventually acquiring a regular, permanent administrator.

Louis Farrakhan (born 1933) currently serves as a leading Muslim thinker and teacher. He organizes groups for the political empowerment of black people in the U.S. and around the world.

But while Victor was still there, there were still the disgruntled and the irate to contend with. He prepares a memo that quotes Louis Faraq'an, a naive move. The memo notes that Faraq'an defines black power as the ability for black people to come to the table with their own food. The point is to have teachers stop proffering academic charity, no matter how well intentioned. Victor knew the pain of charity.

He goes on a job interview. He returns to find a memo announcing his replacement for the coming academic year. He had not been consulted. The rationale was that he would surely get a job. But he remembered the teachers' argument in that television show. He had gone too far.

There must be a way to go about doing our jobs in some traditional sense and meeting some of the potential inherent in our jobs, the potential for social change, without inordinately risking those jobs. Utopianism within pragmatism; tradition and change.

A professor and educational theorist, E. D. Hirsh (born 1928) is perhaps best known for his *Cultural Literacy: What Every American Needs to Know.* He's been accused of elitism for arguing that there is a single cultural literacy every student ought to learn.

When I think of tradition, I think of the literary critic turned compositionist, turned social critic—E. D. Hirsch. His *Cultural Literacy* is simplistic and politically dangerous, say his critics in English studies (e.g., Bizzell, Johnson, and Scholes). There is surely the sense that he's suggesting a return to halcyon days that never were, surely not wondrous bygone days for people of color, surely not for the poor. Hirsch is among those who believe that "multilingualism is contrary to our traditions and extremely unrealistic" (93). More myth than history. It is this mythic nostalgia that permeates his book that causes him to be read as advocating teaching a literary canon. He denies it (xiv). He says that he is advocating a national-cultural set of common assumptions to be learned through an understanding of national-cultural allusions, his list of "what literate Americans know," a list, he points out, containing relatively few references to literary works (146–215; xiv). But he apparently senses the superficiality, backing up his theory with references to broad reading (109, 23). What, then, to read? Seems like we're back to a canon.

> Arguments about a canon, a list of books that everyone should read, have been very common in discussions of literature in the last several decades.

And that canon has historically favored one gender and one race. That this is the case, says Hirsch, is an accident of history (106). He seems not to regard how that particular accident has had a high casualty count over time. And it keeps recurring—like the same fender-bender with the same car at the same intersection—time and again. But Hirsch does go on to argue that national-cultural allusions are subject to change, that as more women and people of color become literate, they will affect the norms. And there is something to this. There are more women in the canon nowadays, more people of color. But the changes are not proportionate to the accomplishments or the potentials of women or people of color, surely. And those who enter the canon tend to be those who are politically safe. We read Langston Hughes's "Theme for English B" more often than Hughes's more angry "The Negro Speaks of Rivers." We read Martin Luther King, Jr. but little of W. E. B. DuBois, Richard Rodriguez instead of Ernesto Galarza, Emily Dickinson more often than Virginia Woolf (see Aiken; West "Canon Formation"). Hirsch's hopes are for better test scores and for greater access to the middle class, not for making the class system more equitable.

> Note how Villanueva here—and elsewhere—strives to give opposing arguments the credit they deserve.

For all that, there *is* something to cultural literacy. One has to know how to be heard if one is to be heard. Those who rail the loudest against cultural literacy can afford to. They already have it. How, then, to exploit it without being subsumed by it?

Critical literacy, like that espoused by Paulo Freire and others, will lead to change, we're told. And I agree with that too. But what are the students to be critical of? How do they come to know what to be critical of? Why not cultural literacy, the national culture? Play out the polemic; develop the dialectic.

One theorist who has seen the necessity for both the cultural and the critical is Antonio Gramsci. His theories will provide the focus of the next chapter. For now, it's enough

Born into poverty in Sardinia, Italy, Antonio Gramsci (1891–1937) died in one of Mussolini's prisons, where he was being held for his socialist politics. Villanueva refers to Gramsci's belief that the ruling ideology or culture must be resisted by alternative cultural perspectives, an ideal that has been embraced by many educators and political theorists.

Stanley Aronowitz (born 1933) grew up in the Bronx, New York City. A proponent of radical social change, Aronowitz went on to study and participate in politics, community organization, and education, serving as a voice for activism while protesting the corporate nature of many educational institutions.

Henry Giroux is a leading critical theorist who has adopted Freire's notion of education as a process of uncovering political and cultural ideologies that will lead students and teachers to social activism. Currently he is the Waterbury Chair Professor in Secondary Education at Penn State University.

Here Villanueva shifts from the theoretical to the personal and familial.

just to mention that he was an advocate of teaching a national culture, of teaching the classics, of something that sounds a lot like cultural literacy. Yet Gramsci also added that the classics and the national-cultural should be taught in such a way as to expose what he called the folkloristic, the commonly accepted ways of the world, the things too often accepted as if they are a part of nature—in short, the ideological. This suggests to me that it is possible to provide what's needed for the commonly accepted notions of success but with a critical dimension that might foster social action among teachers and among students. This is what sociologist Stanley Aronowitz and educational theorist Henry Giroux call "the language of possibility" (138–62). This is likely what Freire alludes to when he writes of a pedagogy that pits permanence with change (Pedagogy 72). I prefer "tradition" to "permanence," given Hirsch's observation that traditions can and do change. Tradition and change for changes in traditions.

In a way, the graduate course on classical rhetoric I teach lends itself best to Gramsci's ideas. We read Plato, Aristotle, Cicero, Quintilian, and others. And we discuss and write about the ways in which some of the things they espoused are still with us—things like censorship for children's better good; things like the only meaningful language should be on abstractions rather than concretes. Plato and the rhetoric of the constitution. We find the first-century idea of proper oratorical arrangement and discover the basis for the five-paragraph theme. We find Cicero writing of writing as a mode of learning and Quintilian writing of peer-group work. We look at how the ancients are still with us and question the degree to which they ought to be. Students gather something of a classical education, a matter of some prestige, and they develop a critical perspective.

Something of the same ideas can be adapted for undergraduates, secondary students, elementary students.

1990, Flagstaff: Victor and Carol's younger children attend the public school. The school district has adopted a literacy package from a major publishing house that explicitly discourages individual instruction. All the children perform their drills in unison, do their reading together—everybody, every time, getting 100 percent on everything. This isn't a matter of collaboration. Just recitation. No talking to neighbors seated ten inches away; no looking at neighbors. The books contain color: drawings of kids with nappy hair or slant eyes, not caricatures, done respectfully; yet there is a single cultural norm being advanced—force-fed cultural literacy.

More than hints at racism start to crop up at home. The brown-skinned, curly haired five-year-old daughter asks whether an Indian woman (the largest number of people who are of color in the community) would care for a human baby if she found one. A human baby! Another daughter, seven at the time, considerably more immersed in this literacy package than the kindergartner, mentions in passing that she doesn't care for black people. She doesn't know any. And she fails to see her own sister's features, forgets the pictures of her aunt, on whom the West African comes out clearly.

Victor and Carol don't blame the school completely. Market forces have them living in a predominately white community, making for little exposure to the kind of cultural complexity Victor and Carol's older children had known in Seattle or that Victor had known as a child in New York. But even if the school was not completely to blame for the hints at racism Victor and Carol would now have to counter, there remained the school's blind acceptance of a reductive notion of cultural literacy, a presentation that did nothing to expose and glory in difference as well as similarity.

Home schooling becomes the only short-term (and economically viable) alternative. Victor and Carol expose the national-cultural, but with an eye to multiplicity. The seven-year-old reads Cinderella, for instance. But she doesn't just stop with the Disney version. She reads translations of the Grimm Brothers' version, Poirot's seventeenth-century French version, an older Italian version, an ancient Chinese version. They're readily available. Discussion concerns how different people, with different ways and living in different times, can see some of the same things differently. She writes her own Cinderella story, which inevitably includes characters and situations from her own life. Spelling comes from the words she's trying to use in her own writing. It has a context. Grammar comes from trying to make her stories sound like she wants them to.

Other subjects take a similar tact. For history and geography, for example, she reads stories of dragons from China and dragons of the middle ages and dragons of C. S. Lewis and even dragons of Homer. She writes dragon stories.

C.S. Lewis (1898–1963) is perhaps best known today for his *Chronicles of Narnia.*

Oral proficiency more or less takes care of itself; no need to impose doggedly the standard dialect. Victor's dialect changed without his being overtly conscious of it. The Spanish accent that Sister Rhea Marie had long ago warned his parents about disappeared, as did much of the black dialect he had acquired on the block. The more he became exposed to written discourse, the more his speaking came to reflect that exposure.

And exposure to different worldviews, even if written in one standard dialect, provided the critical perspective. Reading aloud would help hone speaking skills in the prestige dialect.

I take the Cinderella idea to high school and college. The only real difference in the high school and the college is that I have the college students look up and report on literary critics who write about fairy tales. They read people like Bruno Bettelheim, who comes up with crazy interpretations of Cinderella as going through Freudian puberty rites, or others who write about fairy tales and archetypes, or Plato and his notion that fairy tales should be used to indoctrinate children into proper attitudes about life and the gods. I have the students do research about the historical or cultural conditions which existed at the time and place of the various versions. They become exposed to academics and academic discourse using a kind of literature they know intimately. They feel comfortable being critical of the great authorities. With the junior high and high school kids I've visited on short stints, I have provided the histories and selected the critical analyses; otherwise, the assignments have been the same.

> Bruno Bettelheim (1903–1990) was a developmental psychologist who taught at the University of Chicago from 1944–1973 and who directed the Orthogenic School for children with emotional problems.

Students resist being critical of fairy tales. They want to say that fairy tales are simply diversions for children. And this is okay as a jumping-off point for discussion. Resistance is a good thing, an assertion of authority, an opening for dialogue (see Giroux). So it tends that through the dialogue some begin to question what else might be contained in those simple diversions. A student writes about Rosie the Riveter during World War Two, women not just entering male-dominated jobs, like business and medicine, but performing "man's work," physical labor—and doing well. Then she wonders at Disney's Cinderella, which promotes the house wench whose only hope for the future is to marry well. She wonders if Disney's version didn't help put Rosie's daughters "back in their place." Another writes about the Chinese version, about foot binding as a way to keep women in their place. She wonders if having Cinderella wear glass is a kind of modern foot binding. Another notices how Red Riding Hood's stories become more and more sexual as they approach the Victorian era. Another student: Is Jack and the Beanstalk a promotion of laissez-faire economics, get rich however you can? Is Robin Hood a proto-socialist? Students look at fairy tales and children's stories, and, in looking, begin to question the obvious and the natural, begin to question ideology.

> Roland Barthes (1915–1980) was a French structuralist-turned-poststructuralist critic who saw a text as "a fabric of quotations, resulting from a thousand sources of cultures." His book *Mythologies* (1957) contains 54 short pieces that demonstrate the presence of ideology and power structures in a variety of cultural situations. The book ends with a lengthier theoretical article in which Barthes deals with semiology, the study of signs and systems of signs.

Another way we look at ideology is by using Roland Barthes's little book *Mythologies*. The book contains a series of articles Barthes had written for a popular French magazine in the 1950s. Here, again, the idea works for high school and for college. The college students are asked to read and work with the theoretical essay at the end of the book, where Barthes explains semiology. Others get the idea without the thick theoretical language. But I want to introduce the college students to the esoteric language of "pure" theory. They resist—vehemently. There was outright mutiny in one class.

But, generally, they do tend to respond well to the essays. In one essay, for example, Barthes explains the popularity of professional wrestling as a spectacle, as containing the elements of ancient Greek plays. Students get the notion of the spectacle. One student writes about how wrestling in the 1990s exploits stereotypes, exploits and promotes existing prejudices. A video-tape of contemporary wrestling backs him up. In terms of ideological mythologies, another student, a retired policeman, writes about TV ads to help the hungry as maintaining the myth of American prosperity. The poor and hungry children are in Latin America or in Africa, never dying of hunger and disease in America's cardboard shacks. A sophisticated literary theory is introduced—traditional academic discourse—and critical questioning arises—a possibility for change.

The basic idea is to present the cultural in such a way as to have students question worldviews, become critical. Action presupposes a need for action. Questioning what is commonly accepted makes clear the need for action. Among the things that are commonly accepted is the canon.

Literature can be set up so as to create a dialectic between differing worldviews, between the national-cultural and the critical. Students read Hemingway, for example, as male, white, middle-class as they come, skeptical, perhaps, but no radical. Then they read Buchi Emecheta's *Double Yoke*—the story of a black African woman trying to get through different value systems, cultures, different ways of viewing the world, her struggles at gaining a college degree. Men and women are at issue, black and white; the tribal ways that the main character, Nko, was raised with against the modern Western ways of the university. White students confronting the college community, women, African American students, American Indian students—all have a portion of Nko's pains, and, since the story takes place far away, the defense of bigotries does not come up immediately, as it often does in more explicitly African American or Latino or American Indian literature (though it is good to have these prejudices present themselves). Nko and Hemingway's Nick Adams handle things differently, confront different obstacles. Ideologies peep out of the classroom discussions (which usually

Here Villanueva uses the passive voice to describe this pedagogy: he avoids attributing the success of the class to the teacher, the students, or the texts. He reinforces his belief that collaborative critical engagement produces both greater understanding and the potential for change.

begin with moral questions: Nick's sense of responsibility, Nko's integrity). What is it about where the characters come from that causes them to behave and believe in different ways? We can look at Steinbeck and Ayn Rand, Rodriguez and Galarza, Louis L'Amour and Leslie Marmon Silko. Students sometimes shock themselves with their own prejudice—anti-color *and* anti-white.

The students write about how they too must confront conflicts, and about the sources of those conflicts. These aren't always explained in grand cultural terms, but the cultural is always present, often coming out in discussions. They write autobiographies (or narratives if culturally uncomfortable with the autobiographic). The things they are to write about concern their own experiences, experiences that are tied to the things they are reading. Toward the end of the semester they are asked to downplay the autobiographical elements but keep them in mind. The autobiographical is an important assessment tool, even essential—always there, really. "[A]ll writing, in many different ways, is autobiographical," says Donald Murray, even "academic writing, writing to instruct, textbook writing" (67; 73). But outside the English classroom the autobiographical, the narrative, is not usually appreciated (Spellmeyer). So we look at how the personal is impersonally imparted in writing, still looking to different worldviews espoused in standard written form. We look at Booker T. Washington and W. E. B. DuBois, then find out about their backgrounds, how two African Americans living in the same time can come to polar viewpoints. Or we look at Martin Luther King, Jr. and Malcolm X. In a sense, the strategy is not much different from that proposed by David Bartholomae and Anthony Petrosky: an investing of the personal into what is read and an investigation into how what is read appears, its presentation. The difference is in the introduction of difference within convention. Throughout, there are the culturally literate and the critical, both in what they read and in what they write.

Some students—even a lot, even those who come from poor minority backgrounds—reject the critical views. This is to be expected. People are not turned around overnight. Floyd, back in Kansas City, showed that. But the goal is not necessarily to have students relinquish national-cultural myths. The goal is to expose them to differences and similarities within the literacy conventions they have to contend with, to know the traditional norms while also appraising them, looking at the norms critically. It's a directed process, not propaganda.

All of this is to say that it is possible to have our educational cake and eat it too. It is possible to do our jobs as others define

---

David Bartholomae and Anthony Petrosky both teach at the University of Pittsburgh. Villanueva refers to Petrosky and Bartholomae's pedagogy that combines personal experience with critical inquiry, a pedagogy made especially evident in their *Ways of Reading* (sixth edition 2002).

Villanueva had met Floyd earlier in his life, when he had conducted some ethnographic research in the Midwest. In Villanueva's words, Floyd tried "to promote a Freire-like pedagogy in a school designed exclusively for students who had been locked out of the public schools, mainly by the court system."

them: provide *haute couture*, "high literacy," literacy skills, standardized-test-ready cultural literacy. And it is possible to do our jobs as we believe they ought to be done: with students recognizing that education should carry social responsibility. We can do critical literacy. And what better to be critical of than the cultural norms contained in tradition? Start with what students know or have been told they ought to know. Allow and encourage a questioning of the norms. And maybe look to how things might be—and ought to be—changed.

READING RESPONSES

1. Villanueva begins this chapter by describing two events from his life: his appearance on a TV show and his directing of a basic writing program at a state university. Do you think he's described things even-handedly? List the people who come off looking good in Villanueva's description. List those who come off looking bad. For each person you've listed describe how he/she views the purpose of education. How does Villanueva use autobiography to make his argument?
2. List the goals that Villanueva has for education—that is, catalog the ways Villanueva hopes education will shape students. What goals do you have for your education? How closely do they match Villanueva's?
3. Consider the "interruptions" in Villanueva's writing—those surprising shifts in content, structure, and style. List three shifts that you found to be effective and the reasons they were effective. List three that you found to be ineffective and the reasons they were ineffective.

NOTES ON GRAMMAR, STYLE, AND RHETORIC:
SENTENCE FRAGMENTS AND SPECIAL EFFECTS

In *Bootstraps* Villanueva regularly violates conventions of formal, academic writing. Here we focus on his willingness to go against the convention that forbids the use of sentence fragments.

What is a sentence fragment? The third edition of *The Longman Handbook for Writers and Readers* states (294) that to qualify as a sentence, not a sentence fragment, a group of words must begin with a capital letter and end with an appropriate mark of end punctuation (most often, a period). Further, the group of words must meet all three of the following criteria:

1. It must have a subject.
2. It must contain a verb, not just a verbal (in the phrase *overflowing in the stream, overflowing* is a verbal).
3. And it must contain at least one clause that is not introduced with a subordinating word such as *although, if, because,* or *that*.

The Longman Handbook gives several examples of fragments (295 and 298):

1. A fragment because it lacks a subject: "Yet also needs to establish a family coun-seling program."
2. A fragment because it lacks a verb: "The new policy to determine scholarship size on the basis of grades rather than on the basis of need."
3. A fragment because it begins with a subordinating word: "Which has led to rapid population growth and a rise in property values."

You must take care never to leave unintentional fragments in your writing, especially your formal writing. If you leave unintentional fragments in such writing, readers might not take your ideas seriously. In fact, since the convention forbidding fragments is so strong, readers might start to question your ability to write.

But it is a fact that skilled writers sometimes use intentional fragments for special effects, even in formal writing. In the reading selection from *Bootstraps* Villanueva uses about a dozen fragments. And he uses them to try to achieve several kinds of effects. Here is a sampling:

1. At one point he uses a fragment to mark one of his abrupt shifts in topics: "Fall 1984" (355).
2. At another point he uses a fragment to make a biting comment about one of E.D. Hirsch's positions: "More myth than history" (357).
3. At the very beginning of the selection he uses a fragment to throw readers into the middle of a scene he will describe: "Hot, bright, stage lights blaring down on the four teachers and two parents seated in a circle before a TV camera" (353).
4. And in an anecdote about his family, he uses a fragment to add emphasis and drama to his reaction to a racist comment his five-year-old daughter had made: "A human baby!" (359). The use of fragments for special emphasis or drama is the most common use of intentional fragments. And this use is particularly interesting because it probably exemplifies something that Villanueva tries to accomplish throughout his book: facilitating "the reader's participation in creating the text" (quoted from a later chapter).

In Your Own Writing . . .

* Assess your relationship with your reader and consider the context of your writing before you decide to use sentence fragments to make a point.
* Edit your final work carefully to ensure that it contains only the sentence fragments that you've used intentionally.
* Be sure that you know what you are trying to achieve with a sentence fragment and that a sentence fragment is the best way to achieve that effect.
* Check that the sentence fragment does not overly confuse the reader.
* Be sure that your reader will think that the effect justifies breaking the convention forbidding fragments.

STUDENT WRITING IN ENGLISH EDUCATION

Introduction by Cherilyn Dudley, English education major

The Assignment. During my student teaching semester, all English education student teachers created a teaching portfolio. We had to include a statement of our philosophy of education and samples of materials we had developed during our student teaching experiences. We also were assigned to read Victor Villanueva's book *Bootstraps* and write an essay in which we critiqued Villanueva's perspectives on education. After writing the critique, we wrote a lesson plan that embodied our philosophy in light of Villanueva's ideas.

The Content. I feel strongly that education should raise awareness about social issues and that students should be enabled and encouraged to take action in these areas. So I focused on how and when students should be encouraged to think critically about the world around them. I also discussed the importance of writing style. Villanueva's unconventional method of writing is one way to communicate a passion for social justice, but there are other media through which students may feel more comfortable voicing their opinions and beliefs: art, poetry, music, narrative, non-fiction essay, journalism, etc. It is by identifying and articulating social critique that social inequalities can be brought into the light and publicly discussed.

The lesson plan, "Debatable Civil Rights," was the second part of my assignment. My goal was to encourage students to think critically about society and to realize that things are not as equal as they might seem. I also wanted them to explore some civil rights websites so that they would become familiar with the many organizations that tackle social inequalities in our society and so they could see the many ways in which they can bring about change in their communities.

Learning to Write in English Education. As an English education major, most of the books I've read and papers I've written have consistently followed the Standard English requirements that my professors so highly esteem. For this reason, reading *Bootstraps* was an unusual experience. Were I to write a paper for an English professor in the style of Villanueva, I know I would get much corrective feedback: sentence fragments underlined, misplaced or missing punctuation circled, and innumerable remarks about fluidity and continuity. Many English professors would either not accept Villanueva-style writing from their students, or they would give it a bad grade.

I wonder about two things: (1) the writing I have done as an English education student and (2) the challenges and benefits of stepping outside of those standard writing forms. To be honest, aside from an occasional introduction in which I tried to be creative, I have intentionally adhered to the conventions of academic English. Although I had some creative writing assignments in high school, only once did I take the chance to exercise such creativity in college. The professor of my English class gave us the option to write an essay in the same voice as that of the author we had read. Since the author had poured out his soul in his writing, I decided to be equally honest and vulnerable. Turning in the paper, I was terrified; I had not held back at all and had no idea how the professor would respond. When I got the paper back, I saw that the professor had made a few structural and stylistic notes and had given me an A-. But what really *horrified* me was the lack of comments about *what* I had written. Just like Villanueva, I had used the medium of an experimental style to communicate something that was very important to me. Although the professor had helpful things to say about my style, I felt as though the style was just a means to convey the most important part of the essay: my thoughts, beliefs, and experiences. I was satisfied with the grade, but I couldn't help feeling uncomfortable about knowing that my professor had scrutinized my deepest feelings—especially since I had no idea what his response to them had been.

I believe that Villanueva's style of writing makes people nervous because it is so genuine. Villanueva is passionate about what he writes because he has experienced it himself. These experiences shape not only the educational philosophy he recommends but also the practical suggestions he makes for teachers. Most students avoid this kind of genuine expression for several reasons: (1) we aren't passionate about every single topic we write about, (2) our life experiences don't always connect to the topics we're writing about, and (3) we don't have the same authority or confidence as Villanueva. He makes it clear that he has read and understands complex philosophies. And as an influential scholar in the field of English education, readers accept his unconventional choices as *choices* rather than as *mistakes*. He has gained enough academic respect to put unconventionality to good use. In a classroom, only one person has the final say about our writing—the professor. If the professor doesn't buy into our forms of individualistic expression, our own grades are at stake. So most students shy away from this option and continue to adhere to Standard English expectations.

Creating Change through Writing in English Education. I believe that writing in English education provides many opportunities to change society. English students can critique social inequalities, political corruption, environmental misuse, and many other things through comparative essays, research papers, journalism articles, poetry, drama, etc. Through class discussions, students can articulate and defend their beliefs about the world, strengthening and expanding their perceptions as they listen to others' justifications for differing opinions. Student teachers in English classrooms can help students change their societies as they write about issues of importance to their communities, debating policies and practices that promote injustice in society, volunteering for nearby humanitarian organizations, and seeking correspondence with other politically and socially active members of society.

One of the things I most appreciate about writing in education is the constant moving back and forth between the philosophical and the practical how-to questions. Writing in English education integrates these two impulses. This ongoing balance between philosophy and practicality provides depth and application to writing in English education for both students and teachers, and that makes change possible.

Who Cares?:
Analysis and Application of
Victor Villanueva's *Bootstraps*

Cherilyn Dudley

Some of the most frequently asked questions in high school include "Why does this matter?" and "Why should I care?" And many teachers can't give convincing answers. Because of these common student frustrations about a useless education, I decided to teach a unit in my student teaching classroom about the history of civil rights and the value of social action. I introduced these topics through biographies of liberation movement leaders like Martin Luther King Jr., César Chávez, Malcolm X, Fannie Lou Hamer, and Nelson Mandela.

On the first day of the unit, I asked students to complete a survey of their attitudes regarding civil rights. Students quickly completed the sheet on their own, and once we began sharing perspectives, the class erupted into debate. I hadn't expected students to respond so strongly to the statements on the sheet, but the school has a diverse student body, and many felt that their civil rights had been violated at one time or another. As we further examined and discussed civil rights in class, students moved from feeling angry to making specific plans to safeguard their rights. What I experienced as a student teacher convinces me that Victor Villanueva is right to promote the challenging of social norms as a goal for education. Through individual assignments as well as larger decisions about curriculum, teachers should strive to implement Villanueva's ideas about critical cultural literacy. At each stage of a child's education, we must encourage them to analyze how they see the world, to understand that different people perceive the world in different ways, to discuss sources and effects of these worldviews, and to put what they've learned into practice as actively engaged citizens.

As my experience proves, questioning norms and traditions can lead to controversy, so it is important that teachers consider when and how to encourage such questioning. In this endeavor, we can find guidance from child psychologist Jean Piaget. Piaget claims that children go through three main cognitive stages during the elementary and high school years. From the time they begin to talk until the age of seven, children are in a "preoperational" stage of development. During this stage, they perceive everything as "here and now" and nicely fitting what

A unit is a set of lesson plans on a particular topic or theme.

Although this essay is a "critique," I agree with most of the philosophies Villanueva advocates. Therefore, I analyze the *Bootstraps* excerpt by extending the application of his ideas and discussing practical ways to use his philosophies in the classroom.

Here I transition from the applied to the theoretical—from the classroom to Villanueva's philosophies—a transition that will reappear throughout the essay.

Education is a field in which the rhetoric of experience can carry weight in an argument.

they believe about the world. Although the egocentrism of infancy influences the early years of this stage, it is during this time that young children should be exposed to the idea that not everyone lives as they do. Villanueva describes how he accomplished this in his own family: his daughters read international versions of fairy tales and identified the similarities and differences among them. Teachers can accommodate this stage in the classroom by introducing literature and art from a variety of cultures, bringing in speakers or going on fieldtrips that showcase different ways of life, and teaching cultural units in which teachers and students affirm and celebrate cultural differences. Through mere exposure to diversity, young children will begin to realize that there is more than one way of seeing the world and that not everyone thinks the way they do.

> Although the next few paragraphs are mostly about the application of Villanueva's ideas, I occasionally reference specifics from his book so my reader doesn't think I'm getting too far away from the assignment to critique *Bootstraps.*

Between first grade and early adolescence, children transition into the "concrete operational" stage of development. During this time, they develop critical thought processes and begin to make rational judgments about concrete and abstract ideas. Using the preoperational observations they made in their younger years, students in later elementary and junior high school should learn to critique world literature, politics, history, and other subject matters. As the educational focus shifts from telling to asking, students can discuss why our society does things the way it does. Under the teacher's guidance, students can begin to formulate ideas and perspectives about what literature might reveal about cultures, both foreign and familiar. In junior high, students should be exposed to literature that raises questions and concerns about society. Students can begin to make connections between other cultures and their own as they wonder why their government and society operate as they do. Through this stage of critical analysis, students begin to define who they are and what they believe, and as they begin to make judgments about their own culture, they will learn to see it in a more objective light.

> In my mind, critical thought processes include weighing the positives and negatives of something and making a judgment about its value.

During adolescence, young adults apply the critical thinking of the concrete operational stage to an active "formal operational" stage of development. In this stage, they learn to use hypothetical and deductive reasoning to make conclusions about society and suggest solutions to problems in the world around them. In high school classrooms, teachers can foster this type of thinking through interdisciplinary studies. When students bring history and politics into their English classes, they can examine different models of cultures and societies in literature, comparing these structures to those found around the world. Students can research and debate social equality, economic opportunity, political infrastructure, and other aspects of life as they begin to articulate their own worldviews. Reading books such as *Lord of the Flies, The Jungle, Utopia, Animal Farm,* and other culturally, socially, and politically critical literature will nurture students' own critical consciousness. And making connections between books such as these and current events—i.e., newspaper or magazine articles—will turn the inevitable high school question "Who cares?" back to the students: Do *they* care enough about their world to express their ideas publicly and to act on them? As adolescents prepare to establish lives separate from their parents and enter the workforce, they must become confident enough to express unconventional opinions and disagree with mainstream society. This isn't an easy mindset for teachers to teach or for students to learn. Even in his college classes, Villanueva has to encourage students to become comfortable "being critical of the great authorities" (98). Rather than accepting everything the way it is, Villanueva advocates an education that encourages questioning, engagement, and reflection. Piaget agrees, and so do I.

By making a general statement that applies both to the application I've discussed as well as to Villanueva himself, I shift the focus back to *Bootstraps* after the discussion about applying his ideas.

Unconventional critical thoughts are often best represented by experimental, unconventional ways of communication. In *Bootstraps,* Villanueva defies Standard English grammatical and syntactical rules as he aims to convey not only knowledge and philosophies, but also emotionally-charged experiences and perceptions of the world. As students develop their own philosophies and perceptions, they must discover how to best express themselves genuinely. Taking a non-traditional approach to communication can be intimidating, but so is holding culturally critical viewpoints. Villanueva chooses to express himself through a varied narrative writing style, but students might choose a different medium to convey their thoughts: poetry, journalism, research essays, or even art or music. The important decision is not necessarily *how* an individual's beliefs are communicated, but rather *that* they are communicated in a genuine and effective manner.

Every good argument should include a counter-argument, and this paper is no different. In this paragraph I point out legitimate disadvantages of Villanueva's experimental style, while also sending a cautionary message to students: they need to be discerning about how, when, and with whom to use unique, creative forms of expression.

Although there are many benefits and strengths of authentic, unique self-expression, there are also draw-backs. Writing is only powerful when it meets the needs of its audience. Readers who want to learn about the demographics of education for minorities or the poor would seek statistics, charts, or clear organizational structure of most research articles. And Villanueva's unconventional style might encourage these readers to dismiss *Bootstraps* as unscholarly. On the other hand, Villanueva's descriptive, emotive writing style is more effective for readers who want to learn about someone's experiences with education and perspectives on educational philosophy. As students decide how to best express their developing worldviews, they must keep this tension in mind.

As students discover what issues to be critical of and what stylistic means they should use to communicate those concerns, they need to make the personal decision about how this criticism should affect their life and learning. Students should learn to put their convictions into action as they find ways to get involved in their communities. Teachers should encourage students to seek out information resources and organizations that challenge them to go beyond classroom learning. Through such venues, students can live out their ideals and discover that they can influence the world around them. And as long as students find a way to get involved that matches their talents and interests, they will continue to be active in those areas even after the school year ends.

> As this critique touches on many different aspects of Villanueva's philosophy and style, the concluding paragraph is meant to summarize and bring cohesion to the different areas of the paper's focus.

Although some may perceive Villanueva's ideals of educating for cultural criticism as radical or threatening to the classroom teacher's authority, I believe that evoking a critical consciousness in students is the most powerful and effective method of educating. Students too often feel that they can get away with passively regurgitating facts in the classroom. Quite often, they don't "care" about what is being taught; they think their voice doesn't matter because they are not as educated as the teacher or lack a position of authority. However, their experiences and perceptions about the world can and should be articulated and shared. Students need to know that each of them has something valuable to contribute to the world. And while they must be stylistically aware of how to effectively communicate their worldviews, they must also find a method of communication that accurately conveys their individuality. Whether they express themselves through art or music, narrative or non-fiction, conventional Standard English or experimental Villanueva-style reflection, when students critique and question the world around them, their critical thought will often lead to active promotion of positive, much needed changes in society.

> The objectives help the teacher, as well as anyone else who looks at the lesson plan, identify the main goals of the class period. Through them, the teacher articulates what he or she wants the students to learn.

Lesson Plan: Debatable Civil Rights

Cherilyn Dudley

Objectives:

1. Students will become familiar with the three main rights listed in the Declaration of Independence.
2. Students will be able to formulate definitions of words based on their nature and function.

3. Students will be able to examine and critique their own as well as one another's perspectives on the enactment of civil rights today both in society and in politics.
4. Students will be able to identify and articulate ways they can participate in promoting social justice and equality in today's society.

Materials:

You don't want to be standing in front of 30 expectant students before you realize you've forgotten the hand-outs and overheads you need for your lesson! The Materials section ensures that you'll be well-prepared for class.

Overhead with opening sentence of Declaration of Independence

Anticipation Guide: *Get it Right!*

Methods:

Introduction (10 minutes)

The Methods section describes the specific activities a teacher will do in class. It includes how the material will be introduced, how it will be developed as it is further explained, and how the class will be concluded.

1. Students will share what they know about the Declaration of Independence and the three rights it lists in its introduction.
2. Teacher will put up Declaration of Independence, and a student will read the first sentence aloud to the class:

   "We hold these truths to be self-evident, that all men are created equal, that they are endowed by their Creator with certain unalienable Rights, that among these are Life, Liberty and the pursuit of Happiness."

Anticipation Guides are a type of introductory activity designed to pique student interest in a subject before it is studied more in-depth.

3. Hand out Anticipation Guide; Students will write their own definitions for the three rights (Life, Liberty, pursuit of Happiness).
4. Student definitions for each of these rights will be listed on the board.

Development (40 minutes)

5. Students will read the Anticipation Guide statements and mark whether they agree or disagree.
6. The teacher will ask students to review the definitions they came up with for "Life, Liberty, and pursuit of Happiness." Class will discuss what makes a definition a "good definition": how to make it specific, yet broad enough so it doesn't exclude anything. Students will revise at least one of their personal definitions of the three rights to make it stronger and more effective.
7. Students will share the conclusions they reached for each of the Anticipation Guide statements, as well as justification for these differing conclusions. The class will debate statements that were more controversial.

> During the Conclusion of a lesson, class material is reviewed and the teacher gives the assignment.

Conclusion (5 minutes)

8. Class will review the Declaration of Independence sentence, and the teacher will reiterate how even in today's society, rights that may seem to be quite straight-forward and simple are not always valued and preserved.

9. Students will be assigned to use the Internet to research a specific area of Civil Rights that interests them (women's rights, minority rights, economic rights, etc.). They must write a journal describing 1) a recent event in today's news that demonstrates either respect or disrespect for others' rights, 2) how they think the rights listed in the Declaration of Independence were, or could have been, justly applied in that situation, according to their definition of those rights, and 3) what they can do to influence and/or promote the continued goal of equality (students may reference website suggestions for getting involved).

Assignment:

Journal, which will be discussed in class the next day

> It's amazing how students can pretend they're listening but never actually hear a thing. Prompting them to list the three rights is an easy way to make sure they specifically note which three we're talking about. Defining them gives them some ownership over the material and encourages them to think about the rights more in-depth.

Assessment:

Class participation with Anticipation Guide and debate

Journal

["Anticipation Guide"]

Get it Right!

What rights does the Declaration of Independence say everyone should have? List them here, and write your own definition of what each right means:

> I intentionally designed this activity to create some controversy and disagreement about civil rights so students would recognize the on-going debate that occurs over this issue. Numbers 2–5 are the most controversial, and student responses will be influenced by their individual beliefs and experiences. Number 5 encourages students to think critically about their own society and its practices.

    1.

    2.

    3.

Based on what you know and believe about Civil Rights, circle AGREE or DISAGREE next to each statement. Be prepared to justify your decisions, and remember there is no one right answer!

1. AGREE   DISAGREE   Regardless of ethnicity, religion, political preference, gender, or social class, all people should have access to the same rights.

2. AGREE   DISAGREE   U.S. citizens should have more rights in the U.S. than people who are not U.S. citizens.

3. AGREE   DISAGREE   Illegal immigrants should not be given any of the rights that U.S. citizens possess.

4. AGREE   DISAGREE   Even if they are U.S. citizens, convicted criminals should not have the same rights as other citizens.

5. AGREE   DISAGREE   It is the duty of the U.S. to make sure other countries provide their citizens with the same rights as those we enjoy in our country.

6. AGREE   DISAGREE   Regardless of ethnicity, religion, political preference, gender, or social class, all people *do* have access to the same rights in our society today.

READING RESPONSES

1. How does Dudley's reading of *Bootstraps* compare with yours? Do you think that she has been critical enough of Villanueva in her "critique"? Why or why not?
2. Review Dudley's essay, noting each time she describes her personal experience. How do her descriptions compare with Villanueva's?
3. Consider what Dudley asks her students to reveal on the "Get It Right!" survey. Do you think that some students might be uncomfortable with this activity? Is it necessary for teachers to make students uncomfortable? What do they accomplish by doing so? What do they risk?

PUBLIC WRITING IN ENGLISH EDUCATION

Introduction

At several points in *Bootstraps*, Villanueva refers to E.D. Hirsch's *Cultural Literacy, What Every American Needs to Know* (1987). When *Cultural Literacy* appeared, it quickly made its way to best-seller lists. It was a topic of conversation among educators and non-educators alike. People used it for everything from parlor games to office arguments. It is easy to imagine why it touched off such interest and conflict. Some readers believed that it promised equal educational footing and better educational results; others thought it was a reductive and arrogant approach to education, presuming to know "what every American needs to know."

Below we reproduce a short article that Hirsch uses as part of the introduction to a different book, *The New Dictionary of Cultural Literacy*, Third Edition (2002). The dictionary lists the specific facts that Hirsch and his collaborators think people in our culture should know. In it, Hirsch offers an abbreviated version of his famous argument for promoting cultural literacy through teaching common knowledge. Hirsch reasons that since we learn by associating something new with something we already know, learning requires "a knowledge of shared, taken-for-granted information."

Compared to Villanueva, Hirsch sounds like a thorough traditionalist. But does the larger project, the dictionary which this piece introduces, play with convention? Have you read any other books for your college courses that are made up of lists of facts—places, people, dates, slang words and phrases—that a culturally literate person should know?

The Theory Behind the Dictionary: Cultural Literacy and Education

E.D. Hirsch Jr.

From the Introduction to *The New Dictionary of Cultural Literacy*, Third Edition (2002)

The conceptions that underlie this dictionary are outlined in my book *Cultural Literacy*, published in 1987. But in fact, the dictionary project was begun before I thought of writing a separate book, and the book itself was first conceived merely as a technical explanation of the ideas that led us to undertake the dictionary.... So here, in brief compass, is why this project was undertaken, and why we hope it will help improve American public education and public discourse....

The novelty that my book introduced into this discussion is its argument that true literacy depends on a knowledge of the *specific* information that is taken for granted in our public discourse. My emphasis on background information makes my book an attack on all formal and technical approaches to teaching language arts. Reading and writing are not simply acts of decoding and encoding but rather acts of communication. The literal words we speak and read and write are just the tip of the iceberg in communication. An active understanding of the written word requires far more than the ability to call out words from a page or the possession of basic vocabulary, syntax, grammar, and inferencing techniques. We have learned that successful reading also requires a knowledge of shared, taken-for-granted information that is not set down on the page.

To grasp the practical importance of that point for our entire education system, we need to ask a fundamental question. Why is high national literacy the key to educational progress in all domains of learning, even in mathematics and natural sciences? We have long known that there is a high correlation between students' reading ability and their ability to learn new material in diverse fields. That sounds vaguely reasonable, even obvious, but why *exactly* should it be the case? Let's try to understand the no-so-obvious reason for the high correlation between reading ability and learning ability.

The true measure of reading ability is the ease and accuracy with which a person can understand *diverse* kinds of writing. All standardized tests of reading ability include samples from several different subject matters. But why isn't one long sample just as effective a test as several short ones? Well, if reading ability were a purely generalizable skill, one long sample would be an adequate diagnostic test. But in fact, reading ability is not a generalizable skill. If a young boy knows a lot about snakes but very little about lakes, he will make a good score on a passage about snakes, but a less good score on a passage about lakes. So to get a fairly accurate picture of his overall reading ability, we have to sample how he does on a variety of subjects.

But notice that this variability in a person's performance shows us something of utmost importance about reading ability. To have a good *general* reading ability, you need to know about a lot of things. If you know about lakes and snakes, and rakes and cakes, you will have a higher reading ability than if you just know about snakes. Aha! you might say, that simply means you will read better if you have a broad vocabulary. That is true. But remember what it means to have a broad vocabulary. Knowing a lot of words means knowing a lot of things. Words refer to things. Language arts are also knowledge arts.

We have now taken a first step in understanding the correlation between reading ability and learning ability. We have established that high reading ability is a multiplex skill that requires knowledge in a wide range of subjects. It turns out that the same is true of learning ability. A basic axiom of learning is that the easiest way to learn something new is to associate it with something we already know. Much of the art of teaching is the art of associating what kids need to learn with what they already know. The process of learning often works as metaphor does, yoking old ideas together to make something new. In the nineteenth century, when people wanted to describe the new transportation technology that went *chug-chug-chug*, they called the engine an "iron horse" and the rail system the "track way" (if they were Dutch) or "rail way" (if they were English) or "iron way" (if they were French, German, or Italian) or "narrow iron lane" (if they were Greek). All of these metaphors successfully conveyed a new concept by combining old concepts. . . .

It should now be clear why reading ability and learning ability are so closely allied. They both depend on a diversity of prior knowledge. You can easily read a range of new texts if you already know a lot; so too you can easily learn a broad range of knowledge if you already know a lot. It should not surprise us, therefore, that back in the 1950s the College Board found out that the best predictor of how well students would perform in school was their performance on a general knowledge test. "Reading, writing and arithmetic" and the general ability to learn new things all show a high correlation with broad background knowledge.

I must ask your indulgence to take another step along the path I am leading you. Reading and learning ability depend on something more definite than broad, unspecified knowledge. To a significant degree, learning and reading depend on *specific* broad knowledge. The reason for this goes back to my earlier point that reading is not just a technical skill but also an act of communication. When somebody is reading with understanding, communication is taking place between writer and reader. Conversely, if communication isn't taking place, the reader isn't accurately understanding what he or she is reading. Successful communication depends on understanding both the text's literal meanings and its implied meanings. These all-important implied meanings can only be constructed out of specific knowledge shared between writer and reader. Let me give a very brief example of why this is so. Here are the beginning words of a school textbook on chemistry:

> You are beginning your study of chemistry at a time when growing numbers of people are concerned about the declining quality of life. Chemistry can help you gain a deeper and more satisfying understanding of our environment than you have now. If you are curious and wish to know more about natural processes, minerals of the earth, water and solutions, and gases of the atmosphere, the activities in chemistry beckon to you.

That's it. As a child, I'm supposed to know before reading the passage that chemistry has to do with minerals, water, and solutions, that numbers of people are concerned about the quality of life, that quality of life has something to do with water and solutions. Understanding that passage will be easy if I already know what "chemistry," "solution," and "declining quality of life" are supposed to signify. . . .

Therefore, learning depends on communication, and effective communication depends on shared background knowledge. The optimal way to fulfill this requirement of communication is simply to insure that readers and writers, students and teachers do in fact share a broad range of specific knowledge. This makes good communication possible, which in turn makes effective learning possible, and also enables a society to work. In short, we have come round to the point of my book. An important key to solving the twin problems of learning and literacy is to attain the broadly shared background knowledge I have called "cultural literacy." My book argues that the content of this literate background knowledge is not a mystery, and that it can be taught systematically to all our students. The book further claims that if we do impart this content, we can achieve the universal literacy that is a necessary foundation for further educational, economic, and social improvements. No active reading researcher—that is to say, no one who is thoroughly conversant with the empirical data in cognitive research—has challenged this analysis. . . .

Publishers and schools need to direct their energies to enhancing the effectiveness with which core literate content is presented. They should not try to overhaul the entire content of literate culture, which cannot successfully be done in any case. Professional linguists have often remarked on the inherent conservatism of literacy. Some of its elements do not change at all. Spelling, for example is extraordinarily conservative, because so many people have learned the traditional forms, and so many books have recorded them, that successful spelling reform would require orthographical thought-police. This linguistic inertia induced by print and mass education also extends to other contents of literate culture.

But the conservatism of literate culture is far from total. New elements are constantly coming in, and the old ones falling out of use. Americans have successfully pressed for cultural reforms, including greater representation of women, minorities, and non-Western cultures. In addition, literate culture must keep up with historical and technical change. Yet the materials of literate culture that are recent introductions constitute about a fifth of its total. The disputed territory of literate culture is much smaller still—about 4 percent. Thus, 96 percent of literate culture is undisputed territory, and most striking of all, *80 percent of literate culture has been in use for more than a hundred years!*

Such cultural conservatism is fortunate and useful for the purposes of national communication. It enables grandparents to communicate with grandchildren, southerners with midwesterners, whites with blacks, Asians with Latinos, and Republicans with Democrats—no matter where they were educated. If each local school system imparts the traditional reference points of literate culture, then everybody is able to communicate with strangers. That is a good definition of literacy: the ability to communicate effectively with strangers. We help people in the underclass rise economically by teaching them how to communicate effectively beyond a narrow social sphere, and that can only be accomplished by teaching them shared, traditional literate culture. Thus the inherent conservatism of literacy leads to an unavoidable paradox: the social goals of liberalism *require* educational conservatism. We only make social and economic progress by teaching everyone to read and communicate, which means teaching myths and facts that are predominantly traditional.

Those who evade this inherent conservatism of literacy in the name of multicultural antielitism are in effect elitists of an extreme sort. Traditionally educated themselves, and highly literate, these self-appointed protectors of minority cultures have advised schools to pursue a course that has condemned minorities to illiteracy. The disadvantaged students for whom antielitist solicitude is expressed are the very ones who suffer when we fail to introduce traditional literate culture into the earliest grades. . . .

The real test of any educational idea is its usefulness. We hope this dictionary will be a useful tool. We also hope and expect that no one will be willing to stop with cultural literacy as a final educational aim. Cultural literacy is a necessary but not sufficient attainment of an educated person. Cultural literacy is shallow; true education is deep. But our analysis of reading and learning suggests the paradox that broad, shallow knowledge is the best route to deep knowledge. Because broad knowledge enables us to read and learn effectively, it is the best guarantee that we will continue to read, and read and learn, and deepen our knowledge. True literacy has always opened doors—not just to deep knowledge and economic success, but also to other people and other cultures.

READING RESPONSES

1. Describe times when teachers have pressed you to learn background information. How did you respond? When have you felt the need for this knowledge? When have you resisted learning this kind of information? Why did you resist?
2. Review Hirsch's argument, looking for places where he breaks with convention. For two places, describe how Hirsch breaks convention and what effect that has on the reader.
3. Summarize Hirsch's argument about the conservatism of literate culture, paying special attention to the advantages Hirsch describes. What disadvantages can you imagine?

MORE WRITING IN ENGLISH EDUCATION

Introduction

Throughout *Bootstraps* Villanueva shows how indebted he is to Paulo Freire's proposals about education in general and critical literacy in specific. Here we include the portion of Freire's well-known book *Pedagogy of the Oppressed* in which he develops his famous "banking concept of education." Freire robustly critiques the idea that students should merely passively receive knowledge from the teacher. Instead, he argues, students should learn to see their culture with new eyes. They should learn to pose new questions and solve them. The purpose of education is to prepare students to take an active role in their education and in their society. This reading selection should help you understand what Villanueva means when he includes such phrases as "Paulo Freire kind of stuff." It can also help you evaluate Hirsch's proposals about cultural literacy, for it raises the question of how much of Hirsch's program is actually a matter of "banking education."

As you read Freire, consider the conflict between the form of his writing and the point he's making. While Freire challenges students to become active creators of their education, does he provide opportunities for his readers to become active readers of his text? Does he pose problems that readers can take an active role in solving? Does Freire provide breaks in the text that offer the reader opportunities to challenge, question, refine, or extend his ideas?

Pedagogy of the Oppressed (Chapter 2)
Paulo Freire

30th Anniversary Edition, Continuum, NY: 2000. Translated by Myra Bergman Ramos.

A careful analysis of the teacher-student relationship at any level, inside or outside the school, reveals its fundamentally *narrative* character. This relationship involves a narrating Subject (the teacher) and patient, listening objects (the students). The contents, whether values or empirical dimensions of reality, tend in the process of being narrated to become lifeless and petrified. Education is suffering from narration sickness.

The teacher talks about reality as if it were motionless, static, compartmentalized, and predictable. Or else he expounds on a topic completely alien to the existential experience of the students. His task is to "fill" the students with the contents of his narration—contents which are detached from reality, disconnected from the totality that engendered them and could give them significance. Words are emptied of their concreteness and become a hollow, alienated, and alienating verbosity. . . .

Narration (with the teacher as narrator) leads the students to memorize mechanically the narrated content. Worse yet, it turns them into "containers," into "receptacles" to be "filled" by the teacher. The more completely she fills the receptacles, the better a teacher she is. The more meekly the receptacles permit themselves to be filled, the better students they are.

Education thus becomes an act of depositing, in which the students are the depositories and the teacher is the depositor. Instead of communicating, the teacher issues communiqués and makes deposits which the students patiently receive, memorize, and repeat. This is the "banking" concept of education, in which the scope of action allowed to the students extends only as far as receiving, filing, and storing the deposits. They do, it is true, have the opportunity to become collectors or cataloguers of the things they store. But in the last analysis, it is the people themselves who are filed away through the lack of creativity, transformation, and knowledge in this (at best) misguided system. For apart from inquiry, apart from the praxis, individuals cannot be truly human. Knowledge emerges only through invention and re-invention, through the restless, impatient, continuing, hopeful inquiry human beings pursue in the world, with the world, and with each other.

In the banking concept of education, knowledge is a gift bestowed by those who consider themselves knowledgeable upon those whom they consider to know nothing. Projecting an absolute ignorance onto others, a characteristic of the ideology of oppression, negates education and knowledge as processes of inquiry. The teacher presents himself to his students as their necessary opposite; by considering their ignorance absolute, he justifies his own existence. The students, alienated like the slave in the Hegelian dialectic, accept their ignorance as justifying the teacher's existence—but, unlike the slave, they never discover that they educate the teacher.

The *raison d'être* of libertarian education, on the other hand, lies in its drive towards reconciliation. Education must begin with the solution of the teacher-student contradiction, by reconciling the poles of the contradiction so that both are simultaneously teachers *and* students. . . .

Indeed, the interests of the oppressors lie in "changing the consciousness of the oppressed, not the situation which oppresses them";[1] for the more the oppressed can be led to adapt to that situation, the more easily they can be dominated. To achieve this end, the oppressors use the banking concept of education in conjunction with a paternalistic social action apparatus, within which the oppressed receive the euphemistic title of "welfare recipients." They are treated as individual cases, as marginal persons who deviate from the general con-figuration of a "good, organized, and just" society. The oppressed are regarded as the pathology of the healthy society, which must therefore adjust these "incompetent and lazy" folk to its own patterns by changing their mentality. These marginals need to be "integrated," "incorporated" into the healthy society that they have "forsaken."

The truth is, however, that the oppressed are not "marginals," are not people living "outside" society. They have always been "inside"—inside the structure which made them "beings for others." The solution is not to "integrate" them into the structure of oppression, but to transform that structure so that they can become "beings for themselves." Such transformation, of course, would undermine the oppressors' purposes; hence their utilization of the banking concept of education to avoid the threat of student *conscientização* [**This is not really a translatable word; it refers to a process of forming a critical character that encourages people to solve the problems they become aware of through critical thinking.**]. . . .

. . . If men and women are searchers and their ontological vocation is human-ization, sooner or later they may perceive the contradiction in which banking education seeks to maintain them, and then engage themselves in the struggle for their liberation.

But the humanist, revolutionary educator cannot wait for this possibility to materialize. From the outset, her efforts must coincide with those of the stu-dents to engage in critical thinking and the quest for mutual humanization. His efforts must be imbued with a profound trust in people and their creative power. To achieve this, they must be partners of the students in their relations with them.

The banking concept does not admit to such partnership—and necessarily so. To resolve the teacher-student contradiction, to exchange the role of depositor, prescriber, domesticator, for the role of student among students would be to undermine the power of oppression and serve the cause of liberation. . . .

Yet only through communication can human life hold meaning. The teacher's thinking is authenticated only by the authenticity of the students' thinking. The teacher cannot think for her students, nor can she impose her thought on them. Authentic thinking, thinking that is concerned about *reality*, does not take place in ivory tower isolation, but only in communication. If it is true that thought has meaning only when generated by action upon the world, the subordination of students to teachers becomes impossible.

Because banking education begins with a false understanding of men and women as objects, it cannot promote the development of what Fromm calls "biophily," but instead produces its opposite: "necrophily."

> While life is characterized by growth in a structured, functional manner, the necrophilous person loves all that does not grow, all that is mechanical. The necrophilous person is driven by the desire to transform the organic into the inorganic, to approach life mechanically, as if all living persons were things. . . . Memory, rather than experience; having, rather than being, is what counts: The necrophilous person can relate to an object—a flower or a person—only if he possesses it; hence a threat to his possession is a threat to himself; if he loses possession he loses contact with the world. . . . He loves control, and in the act of controlling he kills life.[4]

Oppression—overwhelming control—is necrophilic; it is nourished by love of death, not life. The banking concept of education, which serves the interests of oppression, is also necrophilic. Based on a mechanistic, static, naturalistic, spatialized view of consciousness, it transforms students into receiving objects. It attempts to control thinking and action, leads women and men to adjust to the world, and inhibits their creative power. . . .

Unfortunately, those who espouse the cause of liberation are themselves surrounded and influenced by the climate which generates the banking concept, and often do not perceive its true significance or its dehumanizing power. Paradoxically, then, they utilize this same instrument of alienation in what they consider an effort to liberate. Indeed, some "revolutionaries" brand as "innocents," "dreamers," or even "reactionaries" those who would challenge this educational practice. But one does not liberate people by alienating them. Authentic liberation—the process of humanization—is not another deposit to be made in men. Liberation is a praxis: the action and reflection of men and women upon their world in order to transform it. Those truly committed to the cause of liberation can accept neither the mechanistic concept of consciousness as an empty vessel to be filled, nor the use of banking methods of domination (propaganda, slogans—deposits) in the name of liberation.

Those truly committed to liberation must reject the banking concept in its entirety, adopting instead a concept of women and men as conscious beings, and consciousness as consciousness intent upon the world. They must abandon the educational goal of deposit-making and replace it with the posing of the problems of human beings in their relations with the world. "Problem-posing" education, responding to the essence of consciousness—intentionality—rejects communiqués and embodies communication. It epitomizes the special characteristic of consciousness: being *conscious of*, not only as intent on objects but as turned in upon itself in a Jasperian "split"—consciousness as consciousness *of* consciousness.

Liberating education consists in acts of cognition, not transferals of information. It is a learning situation in which the cognizable object (far from being the end of the cognitive act) intermediates the cognitive actors—teacher on the one hand and students on the other. Accordingly, the practice of problem-posing education entails at the outset that the teacher-student contradiction be resolved. Dialogical relations—indispensable to the capacity of cognitive actors to cooperate in perceiving the same cognizable object—are otherwise impossible.

Indeed, problem-posing education, which breaks with the vertical patterns characteristic of banking education, can fulfill its function as the practice of freedom only if it can overcome the above contradiction. Through dialogue, the teacher-of-the-students and the students-of-the-teacher cease to exist and a new term emerges: teacher-student with students-teachers. The teacher is no longer merely the-one-who-teaches, but one who is himself taught in dialogue with the students, who in turn while being taught also teach. They become jointly responsible for a process in which all grow. In this process, arguments based on "authority" are no longer valid; in order to function, authority must be *on the side of* freedom, not *against* it. Here, no one teaches another, nor is anyone self-taught. People teach each other, mediated by the world, by the cognizable objects which in banking education are "owned" by the teacher.

The banking concept (with its tendency to dichotomize everything) distinguishes two stages in the action of the educator. During the first, he cognizes a cognizable object while he prepares his lessons in his study or his laboratory; during the second, he expounds to his students about that object. The students are not called upon to know, but to memorize the contents narrated by the teacher. Nor do the students practice any act of cognition, since the object towards which that act should be directed is the property of the teacher rather than a medium evoking the critical reflection of both teacher and students. Hence in the name of the "preservation of culture and knowledge" we have a system which achieves neither true knowledge nor true culture.

The problem-posing method does not dichotomize the activity of the teacher-student: she is not "cognitive" at one point and "narrative" at another. She is always "cognitive," whether preparing a project or engaging in dialogue with the students. He does not regard cognizable objects as his private property, but as the object of reflection by himself and the students. In this way, the problem-posing educator constantly re-forms his reflections in the reflection of the students. The students—no longer docile listeners—are now critical co-investigators in dialogue with the teacher. The teacher presents the material to the students for their consideration, and re-considers her earlier considerations as the students express their own. The role of the problem-posing educator is to create, together with the students, the conditions under which knowledge at the level of the *doxa is* superseded by true knowledge, at the level of the *logos.*

Notes

1. Siméone de Beauvoir, *La Pensée de Droite, Aujord'hui* (Paris); ST, *El Pensamiento politico de la Derecha* (Buenos Aires, 1963), 34.
4. Fromm, *op. cit.,* 41.

READING RESPONSES

1. Describe when you have experienced "banking" education. Was it a good experience? In your opinion, was the teacher acting as an oppressor? What other factors may have affected the teacher's method?
2. Review Freire's chapter. What strategies does he use to encourage readers to become a "critical co-investigator" with him in developing the idea of liberal education?
3. Choose three places in Freire's text and disrupt it. Talk back to Freire, pose a question, provide a personal experience.

WRITING ASSIGNMENTS

ASSIGNMENT 1: APPLYING THE PORTABLE RHETORICAL LESSON

Background: In Freire's *Pedagogy of the Oppressed* he contrasts education that operates based on a banking metaphor and "liberatory pedagogy" that operates on a metaphor of "problem-posing."

Your task is to take on the role of student teacher and create two lesson plans for teaching high school students something about civil rights. One plan should rely on a banking metaphor for education and the other on liberatory pedagogy. Review the selection from Freire's book to determine the features that you should include in each of your lesson plans. Think about your own experience to determine what you most want American high school students to learn about civil rights. Then think about the students' experiences: What do they take for granted? What do you need to wake them up to? How can you break conventions to help them understand in a new way?

As you begin drafting, use Dudley's lesson plan as a template for your own, including all the features that she has in hers. Record your thoughts and emotional responses as you create the two lesson plans: Which was easiest to craft? Which do you expect to be more effective? Which best enacts what you believe should be the goals of a high school education? Consider how you might use your experience in introducing your lesson plans or comparing them.

ASSIGNMENT 2: MAKING CONNECTIONS

Background: An Internet search for "September 11," produces more than twenty million results. On many of those pages you will find references to the dramatic way those attacks changed life the United States. Most college students remember the events of September 11, 2001; they witnessed horrific scenes of roaring flames and collapsing buildings; they listened carefully to reports on the rescue efforts of New York police and firefighters; they experienced the surge of patriotism and a feeling of national unity that followed. In a few years, though, this will no longer be the case. For future students, the events of September 11 will be only history, an important, but long-past moment.

In Chapter 7, Political Science, Robin King describes how his personal interest in the political difficulties facing Arab-Israelis enlivened his research and writing. For Victor Villanueva and Cherilyn Dudley, personal experience does the same thing. Villanueva makes direct references to personal experiences in his writing: those experiences help the reader understand not only Villanueva's point but also why his point is important. While Villanueva refers directly to his personal experience, Cherilyn Dudley does not. In her introduction she mentions personal experiences that influenced both her philosophy of education and the lesson plan that she created, but she does not include these experiences in what she writes.

Your task for this assignment is to write a case study of American life—for a period of time just before, during, or soon after September 11, 2001—that will help future students understand what happened and why those events were important. Be sure to combine your personal experience and academic research in some way, even if one or the other does not appear in the final draft.

As you begin drafting, consider how your personal experience shapes what you want your reader to understand about September 11. Consider, too, how the scope you choose for your case study will affect your ability to use your personal experience. If you want to rely heavily on personal experience, consider focusing on your home town and local events rather than events in distant cities. Finally, experiment with ways you could use unconventional form, style, organization, evidence, etc., to bring these events to life for your readers.

ASSIGNMENT 3: DOING THE RESEARCH

Background: On January 8, 2002, the "No Child Left Behind" act (NCLB) became law; this federal law requires school districts to test students regularly to determine what they're learning and how well they're learning it. When students in a school district score poorly, the school district risks losing financial support from the federal government. An Internet search on the phrase "No Child Left Behind" produces over a million hits. One important website is maintained by the U.S. Department of Education (http://www.ed.gov/nclb/landing.jhtml? src=pbt). This site provides the full text of the NCLB act, data on how students in individual school systems have performed on standardized tests, and advice for teachers and parents. Not surprisingly, it describes the NCLB act in positive terms. An Internet search combining the phrases "No Child Left Behind" and "NCTE," the acronym for the National Council of Teachers of English, produces fewer than one thousand hits; among those is NCTE's critique of the NCLB act as well as descriptions of the effects of the NCLB act from English teachers across the country.

Your tasks for this assignment are three-fold:

1. List the standardized tests you remember taking in school. Describe your experience taking these tests, providing as much detail as possible. You might find it helpful to answer some or all of the following questions

when writing your description: How did you feel as you prepared for the test? As you took the test? How did your teachers seem to view the test? How did your classmates view it? How did your parents react to the test? Do you remember your score? What did you think when you received your score? If you did not take standardized tests in school, describe who assessed your academic work, how they did so, and how you and your parents responded to that assessment.

2. Read about the NCLB act on the Department of Education website and on other reputable websites such as NCTE's. Keep track of the websites you visit, jotting notes for yourself about the author of the website, the author's attitude about the NCLB act, and any information you find interesting. In about 50 words, write out your opinion about the NCLB act—overall, is it a good law or a bad one? What effects does it have on education in the U.S.? Which of these effects are positive? Which are negative?

3. Now write a thesis-based essay in which you support your claim about the NCLB act. As you begin drafting, develop and support your claim as Victor Villanueva does, by blending your autobiographical experience and your research. Expand your earlier autobiographical descriptions with vivid, effective specifics. Be sure to note the source of your research support. If you have good reason to do so, consider breaking conventions that readers associate with a thesis-based academic essay, conventions related to organization, type and presentation of evidence, logical structure, and grammar. Be prepared to justify your choices.

12

NURSING: OBSERVING TO IMPROVE PRACTICE

Nurses deal with highly technical medical information, observe subtle indicators of particular illnesses, and comfort people who are frightened and in pain. The readings in this chapter represent some of the kinds of writing that nurses write—scientific studies that aim to discover, test, and improve health-care practice; recordings of personal observation and professional health-care planning in everyday nursing practice, and a public plea for improved health-care policy. As you read, notice the many ways that nurses use their direct, personal experience of observing and treating patients in their writing.

Writing in nursing frequently begins with recording observations. The nurse and others treating a patient then use the written record to recall the observation. So you will in this chapter hear patients describe their pain, you will track their symptoms and treatments, and you will quite possibly become their advocates. One of the rhetorical benefits of recorded personal observations is that they allow readers to see through the writer's eyes. The writing of nurses can teach you how to do that—and thus how to use your writing to improve what you observe.

A Portable Rhetorical Lesson:
Using Personal Experience
for Rhetorical Purpose

One of the most difficult lessons for developing writers is learning when—and how—to use personal experience effectively. It is not uncommon to see student writers criticized for using personal experience when they shouldn't or failing to use it when they should. When you wonder whether or not to include something personal in a piece of writing, you should consider your relationship with your audience, the kind of evidence that is customary for the type of writing, and how personal experience would serve the *purpose* of your writing. Few writers answer these questions better than nurses.

A story illustrates our point. (To put this story in context, take a peek at the nursing "Care Plan" on pages 408–411, which is a version of the records and plans that nurses maintain for every patient.) As the team who worked on this book talked about the chapter on nurses' writing, one of our members told the group about how impressed he had been with a nurse who cared for him when he'd been hospitalized. He told us about a late night in intensive care when a nurse noticed he was awake and came over to talk. He was feeling unwell, alone, uninformed, and anxious; she looked him in the eye and asked him to tell her how he was feeling—physically, emotionally. After our colleague had finished telling his story, someone turned to the nursing professor on our team and asked, "So did the nurse go back to her station and write up the conversation in the care plan?" "Yes, of course," she answered. The team member who had told the story seemed surprised and a little disappointed, as if he had wanted to remember the incident as a moment of private care, extended from one human to another, and not calculated medical practice, but it was both. Listening carefully helped the nurse assess the physical and emotional state of the patient. Recording her observations, the nurse helped the medical team make a treatment plan that fit the patient's needs, both physical and emotional.

You will find times when your personal observations or experiences can help you build a relationship with your audience and accomplish your purpose for writing. To prepare yourself for those times, observe the ways nurses use personal experience to write more effectively.

Chapter Topics: Health care is the general topic, but most of the readings focus on the study of pain.

To Think About . . .

The Web site WebMD provides these statistics regarding people who are chronically in pain:

> It is estimated that 15% to 33% of the U.S. population, or as many as 70 million people, are affected by chronic pain. It disables more people than cancer or heart disease and costs the American people more than both combined.

This is a posting on a message board for people who are chronically in pain:

I am just about at the end of my rope. I am so sick of being in pain, sick of having to plan my life around my med schedule, sick of having people act like I am just using my "pain" to get attention or to get out of doing things and going places. I am sitting here now, have taken my meds and my back is still on fire, left leg and arm needing to be pulled off and I am just sick of it. I did not ask for this and I do not want to be in pain until I die . . . would rather just get it over with and be done with it.

I wake up every morning and swallow a handful of pills just to be able to get the day started, I grit my teeth to get thru those first agonizing hours of the day and then have to swallow handfuls of pills through-out the day to keep the day going, then a handful at night to be able to get what sleep I do get. I am so tired of being told that I am being grumpy . . . DUH . . . if those people could have my arm or leg or back for a rainy weekend I bet my last buck they would be grumpy too.

SO sick of this attitude that we are addicts . . . no one calls a diabetic an addict, or an epileptic one, yet because our problem is physical pain we are treated like shit!! I wish the parts that caused our pain would glow or beep so others would see that we are not being anti-social, we are being held in the grip of the demon pain. It really bothers me when those in pain refer to us and themselves as addicts. I take the meds, not because I want to but because I have to and not for the purposes of getting high but for the purposes of being able to get thru the damn day without blowing my brains out. Sorry to go on so . . . just not dealing with the pain well tonight. —Braz

What kind of information do the WebMD sentences provide? What kind of information does the message-board post provide? Combine the information from WebMD with the information contained in the post from Braz to build an argument about caring for people with chronic pain.

WRITING IN NURSING

Introduction by Mary E. Flikkema, Professor of Nursing

As a nurse, writer, and researcher, Dr. Sandra Thomas advocates for those who may not be able to speak for themselves. She desires that health professionals and others will hear the voices of those who are living in chronic pain. Dr. Thomas describes her writing as "giving a voice to the voiceless," a practice consistent with traditions and purposes of nursing research and writing. Nurses engage in a practice profession, and the focus of the profession is on the well-being of individuals, those who need support in achieving or maintaining their health. Nurses seek to understand the human response to health and illness, how a person's health may affect their everyday lives at work, with their families, and in society.

The practice of nursing is both an art and a science. It is necessary for nurses to have specific scientific knowledge—in this case, knowledge about the neurological basis of pain sensations, how pain travels through the body, knowledge about pain medications and alternative therapies. The factual, scientific data is part of a much larger picture of holistic care. Holistic care, the art of nursing practice, is the recognition and treatment of human beings as unique individuals with unique lives and health experiences. The art of nursing involves the application of scientific principles in a unique way for each person. The essence of nursing is the art of caring, creatively weaving holistic approaches for each individual person.

Thomas specifies the focus of the study in her abstract, writing that her findings argue against simple or idealized understandings of chronic pain. She hopes to gain insight from those who experience severe pain every day. The content of nursing papers is about interaction with clients, or interaction with health professionals, but the focus is always on improving the health experiences of those seeking care and support.

As nurse writers prepare a document, they begin with a problem or question, an inquiry about a health issue of concern. The nurse writer determines the best method to answer those questions or concerns. For credibility Thomas followed a specific method of research involving a series of carefully controlled steps to gather and report information. She selected a qualitative method of gathering information about individuals' experiences of pain, an examination of peoples' "lived experiences." This involves the process of allowing those experiencing chronic pain to tell their own stories about their lives and experiences. Listening to individuals' experiences provides the person-to-person contact that is the content of the research findings.

Thomas also follows a conventional format in nursing literature, providing an overview of chronic pain and why it is important to write about this topic. She explains the methods used, reports the findings, her interpretation of the findings, and her analysis of the findings.

But Thomas also uses words and images that are almost certain to evoke a response from others, describing how nurses talk about chronic pain sufferers as "difficult, demanding, manipulators and addicts," or the stereotyped "low back loser." Thomas's role is not simply that of the detached, objective observer. She hopes to convey the negativity that characterizes health-care professionals, those who should be the most compassionate, kind, and helpful. She creates these images so that her readers may understand, examine their own behavior, and thus provide more supportive care. The information gathered from the interviews of pain sufferers evokes personal response. She makes a good case for the fact that chronic pain sufferers do not have the support they need to cope with chronic pain, and she argues that change must occur in treating those with chronic pain.

In many professions, as well as in community and public life, it is necessary to provide a voice for the voiceless. For the nurse who writes, changing health care for the better is both motive and goal.

✓ *READING TIPS*

To read this paper as a nurse would read it, you should read as both a health-care scientist (looking for concrete, technical knowledge of chronic pain) and as a health-care practitioner (looking for ways to understand your patient's personal experience). Reading the abstract will give you the first clue that you need to read from both these perspectives, and the rest of the paper will reinforce that need. The section called "Gaps in Our Understanding of Chronic Pain" emphasizes the science background, and the Findings section emphasizes the human experience of the study subjects.

A Phenomenologic Study of Chronic Pain

Sandra P. Thomas

Western Journal of Nursing Research, 2000, 22(6): 683–705

This "phenomenologic study" is the type of research that holistically observes "lived experience" of the subjects.

[Abstract] Researchers have seldom invited patients with chronic pain to describe their lived experiences. This phenomenologic study involved in-depth interviews with nine women and four men with nonmalignant chronic pain. The essence of participants' experiences was unremitting torment by a force or monster that cannot be tamed. The body was altered and recalcitrant, the life world was shrunken, and the pain set up a barrier that separated them from other people. Time seemed to stop; the future was unfathomable. Findings of this study contribute to the phenomenological literature that explores the human body and its symbolic meanings and call into question the idealized positive depiction of chronic illness that is prominent in contemporary literature.

Pain . . . teaches us how unfree, transitory, and helpless we really are, and how life is essentially capable of becoming an enemy to itself.
                                    —*Buytendijk (1962, p. 27)*

Buytendijk's (1962) words aptly depict the helplessness of individuals with chronic pain, a disabling health problem that affects 75 to 80 million Americans (Matas, 1997). By the time they earn the diagnostic label of chronic pain, these individuals usually have tried to get relief from a variety of self-care measures as well as a host of medical interventions. As they endure the gamut of physical examinations, diagnostic tests, exploratory surgeries, and a bewildering array of remedies, chronic pain patients progressively become more discouraged, weary, and angry. Both patients and caregivers become frustrated with one another when treatments are ineffective and suffering becomes prolonged. The cryptic advice "learn to live with it" is often the final salvo of the health care provider to the departing chronic pain patient. The biomedical approach, with its focus on patho-physiology, does not address the complexity of chronic pain and does not provide adequate guidance for successfully living with it. From the perspective of nursing's holistic philosophy, extant literature has significant limitations, including the tendency to focus on discrete aspects of the chronic pain experience ("the parts") rather than on its interrelated wholeness. Researchers seldom invite patients to describe their lived experience. A multidisciplinary panel convened at the National Institutes of Health (NIH) in 1995 stated that "qualitative research is needed to help determine patients' experiences with . . . chronic pain" (NIH, 1995, p. 18). In this article, I present the findings of a pheno-menologic study designed to "give a voice to the voiceless" (Hutchinson, Wilson, & Wilson, 1994)—the men and women who live daily with chronic pain.

the study of physical illness

"Qualitative research" in this case is a method of gathering in-depth, holistic information about a topic of interest by interviewing those who are experiencing a particular phenomenon (thus "phenomenologic study").

Gaps in Our Understanding of Chronic Pain

The chronic pain literature is voluminous, including studies of its epidemiology and socioeconomic impact as well as its association with anxiety, depression, fatigue, immature defense style, helplessness, locus of control, and substance abuse (Ackerman & Stevens, 1989; Bates & Rankin-Hill, 1994; Covington, 1991; Elton, Hanna, & Treasure, 1994; Latham & Davis, 1994; Skevington, 1983). Notable gaps in our understanding remain nonetheless. Researcher bias is evident in the use of labels such as *immature defense style*, and numerous methodologic problems lessen reader confidence in the conclusions drawn. An excellent summary of these problems may be found in a review of 21 years of research on patients' beliefs, coping strategies, and adjustment to chronic pain (Jensen, Turner, Romano, & Karoly, 1991). Another critical analysis of the literature deplored researchers' heavy reliance on pain clinic samples and failure to use commensurable measures of pain experience (Dworkin, Von Korff, & LeResche, 1992).

Note the labels that the author has selected to use based on her review of the literature. These labels arouse the reader's sense of injustice.

Studies that illuminate the nature of interactions between pain patients and their caregivers are particularly relevant to nursing. This literature documents paternalistic staff stoicism (Edwards, 1989); labeling of patients as *difficult, demanding,*

Notice again the inflammatory words the author cites to arouse one's recognition of the injustice.

Health care professionals learn that the definition of pain is "what the person says it is." We are trained to believe what the individuals with pain say about their pain. But the author points out that those with chronic pain may not be believed.

manipulators, and *addicts* (Faberhaugh & Strauss, 1977); and adversarial relationships between patients and care providers (McCaffery & Thorpe, 1989). Nurse estimations of patients' pain intensity are often erroneous, especially when they are assessing the chronic patient. For example, in a study of 268 registered nurses, the chronic pain sufferer was negatively stereotyped and judged to have less intense suffering than an individual with acute pain (Taylor, Skelton, & Butcher, 1984). Particularly pejorative views of the chronic low back pain patient were noted, perpetuating the stereotype of the "low back loser."

This startling statistic about suicide implies that effective holistic perspective is often lacking in the treatment of chronic pain.

Although modern analgesic medications may provide episodic relief of the physical pain—at least temporarily—they fail to alleviate the profound suffering of these patients, which often is psychological and spiritual, not just physical. A survey of chronic pain patients who were members of a national self-help organization revealed that 50% of them had considered suicide—a particularly disturbing finding given that this was a select sample of well-educated and financially secure individuals who had actively sought out a group to help them manage their condition (Hitchcock, Ferrell, & McCaffery, 1994). I believe that nurses have a moral obligation to provide more skillful psychosocial care to these patients. According to Price (1996),

First person statements like this "I believe" are seldom used in professional health literature. Here the author indicates her strong feelings about the need to understand and attempt to improve the care provided.

The provision of skillful psychosocial care to patients suffering from chronic illnesses starts with an appreciation of what it is like to live with a chronic condition. . . . Getting inside the experience of such illness may be key to understanding patient motivation, noncompliance with therapy and altered patterns of social engagement. (p. 275)

Qualitative research (phenomenology) may be considered by some to be "soft" research with no "hard data" to support the findings. Those conducting qualitative research follow specified methods for sampling, data collection, and analysis. Qualitative research provides different, "rich" data, taken directly from those who are experiencing the phenomenon. The author identifies the procedure used in her study, giving others the opportunity to critique her report.

Research shows that nurses who have personally borne intense pain are more sympathetic to the patient in pain (Holm, Cohen, Dudas, Medema, & Allen, 1989). Qualitative studies that involve in-depth interviewing of patients could permit nurses to vicariously experience the life world of the chronic pain patient.

Although "getting inside the experience" is recommended, few qualitative studies have been conducted. One exception is a British interview study involving a large sample of 75 patients (Seers & Friedli, 1996). Despite its ambitious scope, this study has several significant limitations. The interviews were not audio-taped, and there is a possibility that the researchers' field notes may be subject to selection bias (i.e., tendency to record what the researchers were interested in or wanted to hear). At best, field notes must be regarded as incomplete accounts of parti-cipants' subjective experiences. Furthermore, the data-coding scheme was superficial (e.g., psychological state, social activities), and some themes, such as desperation of doctors, were not well supported by the quotations from study participants that the authors cited. In a phenomenological study by Bowman (1991) of 15 individuals with chronic low back pain, data were not plumbed deeply by the researcher; typical themes were varied psychological reactions and related physical symptoms. Although the interpretations were plausible, they were not highly illuminating. Semistructured interviews by Henriksson (1995) with 40 fibromyalgia patients yielded a useful typology of strategies for managing activities of daily living, but the researcher did not attempt to explore the deeper meaning of having continuous muscular pain.

Purpose of Study

Therefore, the purpose of this study was to explore the deeper meaning of what it is like to live with chronic pain, using a qualitative design. The method selected was eidetic (descriptive) phenomenology derived from the Husserlian (1913/1931) tradition, as elucidated by Pollio, Henley, and Thompson (1997). Within phenomenology, particularly within the writing of Merleau-Ponty (1945/1962), the body is viewed as a fundamental category of human existence. In fact, the world is said to exist only in and through the body. Therefore, phenomenology appeared particularly well suited for the exploration of pain phenomena.

Method

Sample

Thirteen individuals were interviewed for the study. Criteria for participants' inclusion in the study were as follows: willingness to talk about their lived experiences, older than age 18, and nonmalignant chronic pain consistent with the following North American Nursing Diagnosis Association (NANDA) definition: "Chronic pain is an unpleasant sensory and emotional experience arising from actual or potential tissue damage or described in terms of such damage . . . without a predictable end and a duration greater than 6 months" (NANDA, 1996, p. 76). Individuals were recruited for the study via a newspaper article and network sampling. No attempt was made to recruit patients with a particular diagnosis or disease trajectory. As noted by Dworkin et al. (1992, p. 7), "chronic pain conditions at different anatomical sites . . . may share common mechanisms of pain perception and appraisal, pain behavior, and social adaptation to chronic pain."

Moreover, variation in experience is considered desirable for phenomenological research because it "enhances the opportunity for the thematic structure of the phenomenon to reveal itself" (Hawthorne, 1988, p. 11).

Ages of the participants ranged from 27 to 79 years. Most were white. Nine were female, and 4 were male. Of the participants, 10 were married, and the remainder were single and/or divorced. Duration of pain ranged from 7 months to 41 years. Back pain was the Number 1 type, although shoulder, arm, neck, hip, leg, jaw, and ear pain were also reported by various participants. Pain was present at multiple sites for many of them.

Procedure

In-depth, nondirective phenomenological interviews, lasting 1 to 2 hours, were conducted with each participant after informed consent was given. Participants were asked to describe what it is like for them to live with chronic pain. Following this initial question, the interviewer sought to elicit richer description and clarification of the narrative. Interviews were audiotaped and transcribed verbatim by a professional transcriptionist who signed a confidentiality pledge. Transcripts of the interviews were analyzed according to the procedure of Pollio et al. (1997), which includes independent examination of the text by the researcher (reading, reflecting, intuiting) and thematizing in an interdisciplinary phenomenology research group in which transcripts are read aloud and discussed: "The group functions in a critical, rather than consensual, capacity" (Pollio et al., 1997, p. 49). Any proffered interpretations must be supported by citation of specific lines of text. . . .

Findings

Chronic pain patients described their experiences as an individualized dialogic process between themselves and their painful condition. Their *Lebenswelt* (life world) was shrunken and their freedom greatly constricted. The pain set up a wall or barrier that separated them from other people. Pain dominated their consciousness, as shown in the following exemplars from the transcripts.

"You can't think about anything else, really." "Pain is king. Pain rules." "The pain just rides on your nerves." "Pain dominates what you can do." "Pain is a monster. All I can say is that it's tormenting." Pain was a formidable opponent with whom they fought daily: "You're drowning and you got that will to fight to get to shore . . . to live with chronic pain is a challenge every day." "I tried to outlast it. I tried to just tough it out. But it was boss." The dyadic nature of the relationship was succinctly captured as follows: "Now it's me and this pain. It's a thing. And you've just got to fight it continuously." Feelings ran the gamut from irritability, anger, helplessness, and frustration to profound depression, despair, and exhaustion. Several participants blamed themselves for causing the original injury. Fear was pervasive: fear of the unknown, further incapacitation, and becoming a burden to the family.

In the following sections, we turn to elucidation of the figural themes—that is, those that stand out most prominently against the existential grounds of body, other people, and time. Participants' narratives included little awareness of the external world, which will soon become evident to the reader.

> Qualitative researchers look for similarities in what the study participants say. These are common "figural themes," experiences that several of the participants related to the interviewer(s).

The Altered, Recalcitrant Body. . . .

Invisibility of Pain

Despite the profound changes in their bodies, study participants ruefully acknowledged that the chronic pain was not readily apparent to other people. Chronic pain was invisible, a "secret disorder" with no outward manifestations. Because their bodies looked healthy in the eyes of others, they were accustomed to hostile glances when they disembarked from vehicles parked in spaces for the handicapped. Some longed for external manifestations of disability that could provide greater societal legitimacy: "You can't look at me and say, 'I guess she has rheumatoid arthritis.' You can't tell by looking." "It's so hard for people to understand if I say I'm in pain because they don't see it; I'm not in a wheelchair or walking with a cane." Ironically, a woman whose arm was in a sling—who conceivably might have welcomed the device as a badge of legitimacy— actually resented the attention it garnered: "I just want to wear a sign that says, 'Please don't ask.'"

Separation from Other People. . . .

Isolation

Isolation was thematic in all interviews. Dialogue took place between the study participants and their nonhuman tormentor, the pain, more so than with other human beings. Participants described their pain as imprisoning them. For example, they used terms such as locked off, roped off and caged off. Pain had somehow reset their interpersonal parameters, creating separation and distance from the world and other people, even family members. They felt that they no longer had much in common with others and no longer "fit in." Relationships in which they could be honest and authentic were few or nonexistent. Exemplars of the isolation theme included the following: "Pain separates you. It's really hard to be involved with people when you're in pain." "I feel like I'm on this little island all by myself." "My life is pulled in to where I have very little contact with anybody." "I am absolutely alone."

Trust and Mistrust of Physicians

The data indicated that when pain patients do make an effort to leave their solitary "island" to have contact with others, they are most likely to be keeping an appointment with a physician. Clearly, the most prominent others in narratives of pain patients, more significant than family members or friends, were physicians. Despite repeated experiences with doctors who were impersonal, unkind, or even cruel, participants could not abandon a fantasy that there was a caring doctor out there somewhere who could provide relief for them. Therefore, they were willing to entrust their bodies to the Magnetic Resonance Imaging (MRI) machines and scalpels again and again. But their fragile trust of physicians fluctuated, with considerable disillusionment and mistrust evident in some narratives, such as the following. "He didn't even want to listen to what I said. He just wrote out a prescription." "You wonder are they really trying to help or are they just trying to take the money?" "Some of them think females are just a bunch of walking complaints." "I still go to the library and check up on something a doctor has told me. Because I had lost a lot of trust [during the years before lupus was diagnosed]." "In every state we have moved to, I try to get a book telling me those doctors who have had some type of disciplinary action."

Lack of Support

The author emphasizes the lack of support from health-care professionals. Recognition of the need for holistic support may help to change treatment.

Only two chronic pain patients cited anyone to whom they could talk freely about their experience. One mentioned a supportive spouse and the other a sister, but the remainder of the sample did not describe any support persons. Exemplars of nonsupport, such as the following, were common in the data: "My wife wouldn't give me peace if I took a day off." "My ex [husband] couldn't understand." Nurses were virtually invisible in the narratives, a curious omission given the numerous contacts of the patients with both acute care facilities and doctors' offices. One individual spoke briefly about hospital nurses and their poor management of acute pain. Another made a vague statement of admiration for nurses and doctors but described no specific incidents or interactions. No participants mentioned nurses as part of their support system, and none of them were involved in nurse-led support groups.

Moments of Time, Existential Crisis, and Thoughts of Death

The chronicity of these patients' conditions obviously implies a disease process developing and continuing across a span of time. However, the unit of time that was most consequential to study participants was the moment, a diminutive unit but paradoxically also a lengthy, heavy one that does not correspond to customary notions of clock time. The moment contains not only the pain now but also the perceived possibility of an eternity of suffering, taking "pill after pill after pill." The pain was ever present: "I haven't had 2 days pain free in 6 years" "Constant, can't never get comfortable. Can't never rest. Can't do anything." "Wake up with it, go to bed with it, every time I move, something hurts." There is no assurance that the agony of this moment will end; the future is unfathomable. Time seems to stop. Life is on hold, its rhythms disrupted. One participant used the word limbo. Another wondered if he would "ever have a life again."

Hope and Hopelessness

The meaning of life itself was called into question by some study participants. As exemplified in the following transcript segments, participants were confronted with events that had radically revised their expectations: "I was just 25 years old when it happened. I didn't think anything like that could happen to me . . . . I'll probably never be able to carry a child." "What happened to me was quite existential. It made me very aware of my age, very aware of becoming less able, in the process of growing old. Becoming aware and accepting age and dying in all things." Strategies to maintain some hope were described in terms of "holding on" and "hanging on," but exacerbations of the painful condition often shattered tenuous hopes. A rheumatoid arthritis patient related, "I just got this area fixed and now I've got another [painful] area. Is this what it's going to be like forever for me?"

After a cyclical process of seeking the solution or cure for their problems, participants sometimes came to view treatment as futile. In a world of highly touted medical miracles and dramatic organ transplantations, they expressed bitterness about the lack of a definitive solution to their own distress: "Sometimes

The study participants related a fear of trying something new since hopes rise each time they try a different therapy. The continued disappointments may be worse than living with the pain.

I just want to quit taking everything 'cause it doesn't seem like anything's working." "After six surgeries, I am probably no better off than I was to start with." "We can go to the moon, but nobody can find something to change this."

Hopelessness and thoughts of death as liberating were revealed in some interviews. One participant expressed the feelings of many:

> Really don't fear death because one day I won't hurt. . . . On a day where you feel like things are hopeless, you wonder whether you want to go on . . . and whether the quality of your life is enough to keep plugging away.

Another admitted trying to imagine how his suicide could be made to look like an accident or a natural death. Another was acutely aware that a means of liberation from suffering was already available to him: "These pills are very tempting to take more than you're supposed to."

Only 3 participants mentioned any positive aspects of their chronic pain experience. One of these said, "Maybe there's a reason, maybe it's to slow me down [to] look around to see other people are in pain. I'm more and more interested and want to be involved with helping battered women."

Discussion

Here the author interprets her findings in light of other studies and emphasizes differences between the pain experiences and other chronic health concerns. The first paragraph is key in that it contrasts this study's findings with other, more "idealized" descriptions of chronic pain.

Most notably expressed in the powerful metaphors used by study participants, the essence of the chronic pain experience is unremitting torment by a force or monster that cannot be tamed. In contrast to popular pain management parlance, these patients say their pain cannot be managed. Data from this study call into question the idealized positive depiction of chronic illness that is prominent in contemporary literature. Thorne and Paterson (1998), having reviewed 15 years of qualitative research on chronic illness experiences, concluded that the early focus on themes of loss and burden had shifted by the mid-1990s to positive images of normality, courage, and self-transcendence. Patients were increasingly being depicted by researchers as strong, powerful, and competent. But few of my study participants with chronic pain perceived their position as one of strength or described any personal benefit of their suffering. The transformative elements within the chronic illness experience may have been overemphasized in the optimistic literature of the 1990s. On the other hand, there may be substantive differences between chronic pain and other chronic illnesses, precluding their comparison.

The grim, ongoing struggle with chronic pain is a very individual one ("Now it's me and the pain"), although the sufferer longs for a physician rescuer. Physicians are both trusted and mistrusted, with the pendulum swinging toward greater mistrust and alienation after repeated experiences of being unheard and unhealed. Not being listened to by doctors is a well-documented complaint of many types of patients but may be particularly galling to the pain patient. No electrocardiogram can reveal the pattern of the pain; only by talking can the patient describe his or her subjective sensations. But patients interviewed by Miller, Yanoshik, Crabtree, and Reymond (1994) all claimed that their physicians did not listen to them when they tried to describe pain and its impact on their daily lives. When the researchers interviewed the physicians, a different understanding of listening was discovered: It meant hearing words as diagnostic cues, not placing the words into the context of the patients' life world. This communication gap between physician and patient was the strongest theme in Miller et al.'s study and was alluded to by participants in this study as well. It logically follows that chronic pain patients begin to doubt that health professionals can help them. In one recent report, 78% of patients with chronic neuropathic pain resulting from breast cancer treatment declined an offer of free treatment in a pain center because they did not believe that treatment would alleviate the pain. Despite an average of 29 months of living with the pain and a significant decrease in quality of life, the women remained unconvinced that the pain center therapies were efficacious (Carpenter, Sloan, & Andrykowski, 1999).

Participants' doubts about the effectiveness of treatment lead some to refuse free treatment, believing the treatment for pain would not help. This appeals to readers'—nurses'—sense of professional experience and compassion.

Friedemann and Smith (1997) reported intense family involvement in the lives of their sample of 30 chronic pain patients. Such intense involvement was not evident in this study. However, Friedemann and Smith's interviews were conducted for the specific purpose of obtaining descriptions of family functioning, and the interviews took place after participants had completed a questionnaire about their family's stability and growth. In phenomenological interviewing, if the respondent does not volunteer information, the researcher does not probe. Participants in this study seldom mentioned family members except to deplore their lack of understanding. They concealed their discomfort from family rather than seeking sympathy or assistance. These findings are divergent from literature about the reinforcing "secondary gain" (i.e., attention and solicitude) that chronic pain patients allegedly receive from significant others.

The need to hide pain, a prominent element of study participants' narratives, has been noted by other researchers (e.g., Hitchcock et al., 1994). The culture does not offer a "natural home" for these patients, leaving them on the "amorphous frontier of nonmembership" in society (Hilbert, 1984, p. 375). The concept of internalized stigma, which Phillips (1994) examined in AIDS patients, is perhaps germane to the chronic pain patient as well. Other literature contains concepts and metaphors that are comparable to themes of this study. Existential philosopher Camus once referred to illness as a convent. If one takes his metaphor to mean closed off from the world and deprived of worldly pleasures, it seems relevant to the chronic pain patient. Participants' narratives of pain are consistent with its portrayal by philosopher Hannah Arendt as "a borderline experience between life...and death" (as cited in Engelbart & Vrancken, 1984). If there is no one who understands and no place where one fits, is this not a kind of living death?

Findings of this study contribute to the phenomenological literature that explores the human body and its symbolic meanings. In contrast to healthy individuals' relative lack of consciousness of their bodies, the body is the main focus of the chronic pain patient's existence: "Bodily events become the events of the day" (Merleau-Ponty, 1945/1962, p. 85). The life world, in fact, is virtually restricted to the patient's body, as described by Plugge (1967). Themes found in this study may be contrasted with a previous phenomenological study of 16 healthy adults who were interviewed about experiences when they were aware of their bodies (MacGillivray, 1986). One of the three figural themes of the lived body in that study was engagement in the world (i.e., the body as vitality and activity). Vitality involved feeling highly energetic and fully in control of the body while engaging in an absorbing project. For example, a runner spoke of the good feelings of stretching his legs and taking in breaths as he ran. Perhaps because volitional control over the body was largely absent in this sample of pain patients, there were no similar anecdotes of body as an instrument of mastery over the world. Participants' perceptions of their bodies were sharply discrepant from the "socially engaged, skilled bodies" described by Benner (1994, p. xvii) but consistent with MacGillivray's (1986) theme of body as object: "The body 'owns' the person, demands attention, and calls the person back from the world and projects" (as cited in Pollio et al., 1997, p. 79). The chronic pain patient

The author summarizes the world in which those with chronic pain live, a world of "I cannot." She has indeed "given a voice to the voiceless" and provided insight for health-care professionals into the needs of those whom they serve.

dwells in the world of "I cannot" instead of the world of "I can," like the cancer patients who were studied by Kesselring (1990).

These findings can assist health care providers to understand the chronic pain patient and provide more empathic, supportive care. The psychological pain of being disbelieved and stigmatized is surely as devastating to these patients as their bodily pain, perhaps more so. Therapeutic benefit was obtained by some of the study participants simply by talking to a respectful listener. As one put it, "I believe there has been a release here." Research is needed on nursing interventions that could help chronic patients cope and find meaning in their suffering.

Note

I am grateful to a number of individuals who assisted with the literature review, interviews, and data analysis for this project: Vicki Slater, Linda Hafley, Karen Heeks, Tracey Martin, Rebecca Ledbetter, Lisa Fleming, and Pam Watson. Linda Dalton transcribed all of the audio-tapes with commendable accuracy. The contributions of my mentor Howard Pollio and the University of Tennessee Phenomenology Research Group have been invaluable. Earlier versions of this article were presented at meetings of the Southern Nursing Research Society, the American Nurses' Association, and the European Health Psychology Society.

References

Ackerman, M., & Stevens, M. (1989). Acute and chronic pain: Pain dimensions and psychological status. *Journal of Clinical Psychology*, 45, 223–228.

Bates, M., & Rankin-Hill, L. (1994). Control, culture, and chronic pain. *Social Science and Medicine*, 39, 629–645.

Benner, P. (1994). Introduction. In P. Benner (Ed.), *Interpretive phenomenology: Embodiment, caring, and ethics in health and illness* (pp. xiii-xxvii). Thousand Oaks, CA: Sage.

Bowman, J. M. (1991). The meaning of chronic low back pain. *American Association of Occupational Health Nursing Journal*, 39, 381–384.

Buytendijk, F.J.J. (1962). *Pain: Its modes and functions*. Chicago: University of Chicago Press.

Carpenter, J. S., Sloan, P., & Andrykowski, M. (1999). Anticipating barriers in pain-management research. *Image: Journal of Nursing Scholarship*, 31, 158.

Covington, E. C. (1991). Depression and chronic fatigue in the patient with chronic pain. *Primary Care*, 18, 341–358.

Dworkin, S. F., Von Korff, M. R., & LeResche, L. (1992). Epidemiological studies of chronic pain: A dynamic-ecologic perspective. *Annals of Behavioral Medicine*, 14, 3–11.

Edwards, R. B. (1989). Pain management and the values of health care providers. In C. S. Hill Jr. & W. S. Fields (Eds.), *Advances in pain research and therapy* (Vol. 11, pp. 101–112). New York: Raven.

Elton, N., Hanna, M., & Treasure, J. (1994). Coping with pain: Some patients suffer more. *British Journal of Psychiatry*, 165, 802–807.

Engelbart, H. J., & Vrancken, M. A. (1984). Chronic pain from the perspective of health: A view based on systems theory. *Social Science and Medicine*, 12, 1383–1392.

Faberhaugh, S. Y., & Strauss, A. (1977). *Politics of pain management.* Reading, MA: Addison-Wesley.

Friedemann, M. L., & Smith, A. A. (1997). A triangulation approach to testing a family instrument. *Western Journal of Nursing Research*, 19, 364–378.

Giorgi, A. (1985). Sketch of a psychological phenomenological method. In A. Giorgi (Ed.), *Phenomenology and psychological research.* Pittsburgh: Duquesne University Press.

Hawthorne, M. C. (1988). The human experience of reparation: A phenomenological investigation. Unpublished doctoral dissertation, University of Tennessee, Knoxville.

Henriksson, C. M. (1995). Living with continuous muscular pain: Patient perspectives. *Scandinavian Journal of Caring Science*, 9, 77–86.

Hilbert, R. (1984). The acultural dimension of chronic pain: Flawed reality construction and the problem of meaning. *Social Problems*, 31, 365–378.

Hitchcock, L., Ferrell, B., & McCaffery, M. (1994). The experience of chronic nonmalignant pain. *Journal of Pain and Symptom Management*, 9, 312–318.

Holm, K., Cohen, F., Dudas, S., Medema, P. G., & Allen, B. L. (1989). Effect of personal pain experience on pain assessment. *Image: Journal of Nursing Scholarship*, 21(2), 72–75.

Husserl, E. (1931). *Ideas: General introduction to pure phenomenology* (W. Gibson, Trans.). New York: Collier Books. (Original work published 1913)

Hutchinson, S., Wilson, M., & Wilson, H. (1994). Benefits of participating in research interviews. *Image: Journal of Nursing Scholarship*, 26, 161–164.

Jensen, M. P., Turner, J. A., Romano, J. M., & Karoly, P. (1991). Coping with chronic pain: A critical review of the literature. *Pain*, 47, 249–283.

Kangas, S., Warren, N. A., & Byrne, M. M. (1998). Metaphor: The language of nursing researchers. *Nursing Research*, 47, 190–193.

Kesselring, A. (1990). The experienced body: When taken for-grantedness fails. Unpublished doctoral dissertation. University of California, San Francisco.

Latham, J., & Davis, B. D. (1994). The socioeconomic impact of chronic pain. *Disability and Rehabilitation*, 16, 39–44.

MacGillivray, W. (1986). Ambiguity and embodiment: A phenomenological analysis of the lived body. Unpublished doctoral dissertation, University of Tennessee, Knoxville.

Matas, K. E. (1997). Human patterning and chronic pain. *Nursing Science Quarterly*, 10(2), 88–95.

McCaffery, M., & Thorpe, D. (1989) Differences in perception of pain and the development of adversarial relationships among health care providers. In C. S. Hill & W. S. Fields (Eds.), *Advances in pain research and therapy*, 11, 113–125. New York: Raven.

Merleau-Ponty, M. (1962). *The phenomenology of perception* (C. Smith, Trans.). Boston: Routledge Kegan Paul. (Original work published 1945)

Miller, W. L., Yanoshik, M. K., Crabtree, B. F., & Reymond, W. K. (1994). Patients, family physicians, and pain: Visions from interview narratives. *Clinical Research and Methods*, 26, 179–184.

Munhall, P. L. (1994). *Revisioning phenomenology: Nursing and health science research*. New York: National League for Nursing Press.

National Institutes of Health Technology Assessment Conference Statement. (1995, October 16–18). Integration of behavioral and relaxation approaches into the treatment of chronic pain and insomnia. Bethesda, MD: U.S. Department of Health and Human Services.

North American Nursing Diagnosis Association. (1996). Nursing diagnoses: Definitions and classification 1997–1998. Philadelphia.

Phillips, K. (1994). Testing biobehavioral adaptation in persons living with AIDS using Roy's theory of the person as an adaptive system. Unpublished doctoral dissertation, University of Tennessee, Knoxville.

Plugge, H. (1967). *Der Mensch and sein Leib* (The person and human life). Tubingen: Max Neimeyer.

Pollio, H. R., Henley, T. B., & Thompson, C. J. (1997). *The phenomenology of everyday life*. New York: Cambridge University Press.

Price, B. (1996). Illness careers: The chronic illness experience. *Journal of Advanced Nursing*, 24, 275–279.

Seers, K., & Friedli, K. (1996). The patients' experiences of their chronic non-malignant pain. *Journal of Advanced Nursing*, 24, 1160–1168.

Skevington, S. M. (1983). Chronic pain and depression: Universal or personal helplessness? *Pain*, 15, 309–317.

Taylor, A. G., Skelton, J. A., & Butcher, J. (1984). Duration of pain condition and physical pathology as determinants of nurses' assessments of patients in pain. *Nursing Research*, 33, 4–8.

Thompson, C. J., Locander, W. B., & Pollio, H. R. (1989). Putting consumer experience back into consumer research: The philosophy and method of existential phenomenology. *Journal of Consumer Research*, 16, 133–146.

Thorne, S., & Paterson, B. (1998). Shifting images of chronic illness. *Image: Journal of Nursing Scholarship*, 30, 173–178.

READING RESPONSES

1. In her article Thomas notes, "Research shows that nurses who have personally borne intense pain are more sympathetic to the patient in pain." Do you believe that readers will be more sympathetic to people with chronic pain after they read the personal experiences Thomas includes in her article? Will her descriptions be enough to change reader's attitudes? Why or why not?

2. Thomas cites other scholarly research as well as the results of her own study. Analyze her use of other research. When does she refer to other studies? What purpose does this research serve in Thomas's essay? What is the relationship between this research and Thomas's own research?

3. What does Thomas want nurses to do differently after reading her article? That is, what is her purpose for writing? Where does she indicate that most clearly? How will the personal experiences in the essay persuade nurses to act differently?

NOTES ON GRAMMAR, STYLE, AND RHETORIC:
APPEALS TO THE GENERAL AND PARTICULAR

Many writing researchers believe that a good way to characterize texts involves determining to what extent those texts appeal to the general or the particular. Taking this approach to "A Phenomenologic Study of Chronic Pain" by Sandra P. Thomas shows it to be an interesting combination of appeals to both the general and the particular.

What do the terms *general* and *particular* mean? To answer this question, it helps to imagine a scale, with the uniquely particular on one end and the extraordinarily general on the other. As you approach the particular end of the scale, you come ever closer to focusing on one individual person, place, object, or phenomenon. For example, a writer might focus on his or her Aunt Margaret Marianna and the deep stab of pain she feels every morning because of the rheumatoid arthritis in her left shoulder. As you approach the general side of the scale, you focus on generalized people, places, objects, or phenomena. For example, a writer might focus on "thousands of adults suffering from long-term pain arising from multiple causes."

In "A Phenomenologic Study," Thomas focuses on the general by using three closely related kinds of noun phrases. First, she uses many phrases that refer to large groups. Thus we read about "nurses," "study participants," "patients and caregivers," and "men and women who live daily with chronic pain." Second, she uses phrases that refer to types; that is, a singular term represents many individuals or objects of a certain type. For example, we read about "the chronic low back pain patient," "the health care provider," and even "the human body." A closely related kind of phrase refers to characteristics and experiences that many of the subjects in her study have in common. We read about "Isolation," "the chronic pain experience," and "the profound suffering of these patients, which is often psychological and spiritual, not just physical" (392). All three of these kinds of phrases can appear in a single sentence. For example, in the following sentence, we first find a reference to a generalized experience, then a reference to a group, and finally a reference to a type: "Therapeutic benefit was obtained by some of the study participants simply by talking to a respectful listener" (401).

Such appeals are accompanied by numerous appeals to the particular. For example, the report includes many exact quotations from individuals. One person is quoted as saying that the pain is so bad that "I feel like I'm on this little island all by myself" (396). Another individual complains that "After six surgeries, I am probably no better off than I was to start with" (398). This last quotation clearly illustrates the degree of specificity with which Thomas presents unique individuals in that it provides details of personal history (the "six surgeries"). We even learn about some of the patients' relatives, in one case reading about "a supportive spouse" (396).

Sometimes we encounter appeals to both the very general and the uniquely particular in the same sentence. In the following example, for instance, we find references to a generalized experience (the "grim, ongoing struggle") and to types ("the sufferer" and "a physician rescuer"), but we also find a direct quotation from an individual: "The grim, ongoing struggle with chronic pain is a very individual one ('Now it's me and the pain'), although the sufferer longs for a physician rescuer" (399). Further, sometimes we find both kinds of appeals appearing within larger sections of the report. For example, in the first three paragraphs under "Findings," we first see appeals to the general with phrases such as "Chronic pain patients," "their painful condition," and "their freedom" (394–95). Then we encounter several exact quotations. And after the quotations we move on to generalized traits such as "irritability, anger, helplessness, and frustration . . ." (395). The pattern of appeals in these three paragraphs is the same as the pattern in the report as a whole—first come appeals to the general, then appeals to the particular, and finally some additional appeals to the general.

Why might Thomas have followed this pattern? The answer relates to her overall purpose, which she explains as follows: "I believe that nurses have a moral obligation to provide more skillful psychosocial care to these patients [with chronic pain]" (392). She wants to help nurses see how to "help chronic patients cope and find meaning in their suffering" (401). In other words, she is proposing significant changes in nursing practice. And she lays out the background to and rationale for that proposal with all the appeals to the general. But she also apparently knows that people do not accept significant changes—in medical care and most other endeavors—quickly and easily. If important aspects of nursing practice are to be changed, then nurses themselves will have to feel a sense of urgency about them. As Thomas puts it, nurses will have to get "inside the experience" (392) of long-term pain; they will have to imagine feeling such pain themselves. To help them do that, she includes all the appeals to the particular.

But there is a little more to this story. A respected writer once said that people respond to generalities with their reason and to particulars with their emotions. If he was largely correct, then we can understand even better what Thomas is doing. She uses the appeals to the general to get readers to understand and consider her proposals for changes in nursing. And she uses the appeals to the particular to get readers to feel how desperately each patient in pain needs nurses to care for him or her more sensitively. For the agenda that Thomas is pursuing, her combination of appeals works well.

In Your Own Writing . . .

- Consider how genre and field affect your use of general and particular appeals. Some genres—memoir, for example—do not include a great many appeals to the general. Some fields, such as economic theory, do not include a great many appeals to the uniquely particular.
- When you want readers not just to think about but also to act on a proposal, use appeals to the general to get them thinking and evaluating, but also include appeals to the particular to grip their emotions and move them to action.
- Use general appeals as a way to introduce particular appeals and to follow up appeals to the particular.

STUDENT WRITING IN NURSING

Introduction by Curt Gritters, nursing major

The two short pieces of student writing in this section each represent a different perspective on nursing.

   1. Care Plan Assignment. The objective of the assignment was to gather information regarding various aspects of the patient's history and current condition. After gathering the information, I had to establish goals for this patient's recovery and formulate a plan of care to achieve those goals (see page 409 of the care plan). When the care plan was filled out, I would have a list-style summary of the patient's situation and a fairly precise direction that I should take in providing care as a nursing student, and someday soon as a nurse.

The Content. By browsing the care plan shown here, you can see that I gleaned both objective and subjective data. Not only do nursing students need to know patients' medical or surgical diagnoses, they must also consider family concerns or barriers to healing and how the client will take care of himself and return to his usual lifestyle. The care plan shown here describes an 82-year-old man whose recovery from open-heart surgery was complicated by fluid accumulation in his lungs ("pleural effusion"). Since his blood was still "too thin" from anticoagulants, a procedure to remove some of that fluid was postponed (to prevent serious bleeding). Meanwhile, an infection was being treated with antibiotics.

Writing a Care Plan. To write effective care plans, I could not cut and paste portions of interest from the patient's medical record—an easy way out. Many areas in the assignment required a small amount of information, but the patient's medical record was hundreds of pages long. I knew that summarizing in a descriptive yet concise manner was going to be the key. Once I had compiled all of the lab results, for example, I could write down the ones that were especially important in his current situation.

However, not all of the information I needed was stated explicitly in the medical record. Writing as a nurse required me both to borrow some information gleaned by others and to retrieve much of the subjective or personal data on my own.

2. Reflection Paper Assignment. "Reflection paper...hummph. How hard can that be? There's no chart to fill out, questions to answer, or format to follow. How strictly can my professor grade something so opinionated?" But deep-down I knew the purpose. The assignment asked me to step back from the medical record and even from the patient, to analyze legal and ethical concerns, and to make suggestions for improved personalized care at the bedside or in the operating room.

The Content. One of my fellow clinical students wrote the reflection paper reproduced here. Her experiences in the operating room (OR) and critical care settings are surprisingly typical. Megan watched an "everyday" (in terms of the OR) back surgery and an "everyday" brain injury case. She wrote about what she saw, identified core virtues of nursing that were either utilized or violated, and made suggestions for improved practice.

Writing a Reflection Paper. A reflection paper starts with general observations and ends by giving specific suggestions for changing the patient's care. The nursing student must be descriptive regarding the situation he or she experienced, analytical and insightful regarding the broader issues involved, and concise in making practical suggestions for improvement in patient care. Writing reflection papers is another way of developing the critical thinking process of a nurse—a way in which nurses examine ethical issues in light of their own practice related to patient's rights (dignity, autonomy, consent, etc.) and the treatment of patients as unique human beings.

Learning to Write in Nursing. In general nursing writing is . . .

- concise, and writing concisely requires precise summary. For example, when explaining a heart problem which is directly related to the lungs and kidneys, the nurse must summarize concisely the heart problem, then move on to explain its involvement with the lungs and kidneys. Staying focused in a summary of a patient's condition and not diverging into unnecessary details is vital in a world where every second counts.

- both technically objective and descriptively subjective because the discipline uniquely stakes claims both in healthcare science and in the ailing patient's individual being.

- adaptive because patient conditions are always changing. When conditions change, goals change, and the written records and plans must change as well.

Consequently, good writing assignments for nursing students require them to put critical thinking processes onto paper. Though I realize that much of what I write as a nursing student is not what I will write as a nurse, I know that everything I do on paper now must be done mentally as a nurse. Nurses do not, for example, regularly write reflection papers on their practice, but the thought process that the reflection paper simulates must be continuous in nursing practice.

Nursing writing is a fascinating interplay between professional and personal writing styles. Care plans take the objective, scientific technicalities of health care and apply them to personalize care. Reflection papers complete the cycle by transforming personal and subjective ideas into professional practice—which is again made personal in individual care plans.

Creating Change through Writing in Nursing. The first changes I noticed occurred in myself as I became more aware of the power of writing. When I first wrote care plans, I simply answered questions, and filled in blanks. As I did more, I understood the purpose more, so I began to use the information I obtained in providing more holistic care for my patients (and this is where my growth began effecting change in others). Finally, taking it a step farther, I was able to use care plans as nurse-to-nurse communication to improve the consistency of this holistic care.

In a similar manner, I first approached reflection papers very superficially. I simply reflected back onto paper the situation I observed. Okay, I wasn't *that* shallow; I saw a suboptimal condition and recognized a need for something better. Naturally, one's mind drifts to "what can be done about this?" or "what would the ideal situation look like?" I began searching for solutions. Looking deeply into the assignment, I began to see the unwritten purpose . . . that of using reflection-paper writing as a means of effecting change. Therefore, in some of my later reflection papers, I began using some persuasive writing to convince others of the need to change, to strive for the ideal.

Nursing Care Plan
Curt Gritters

Nursing Care Plan: Patient Data

Your Name ————————————————— Date of Care —————————————————

Patient Initials ———————— Room Number ———————— Gender ———————— Age ————————

Admission Date ———————— Admitting Diagnosis —————————————————

Medical/Surgical Diagnosis (current reason for hospitalization and other potential compounding problems) 1. Cellulitis of L pleural effusion (empyema) 2. . . .	**Family/Significant Other Concerns** 1. Concern re husband's infection 2. . . .
Other health concerns/past medical/surgical history/allergies: MSO$_4$, ASA, CAD, MI in 82, A-fib, L, TKA, ACF, angiopla sty × 2	**Financial situation** retired, financially stable, excellent insurance, no concerns
Barriers/cultural considerations (e.g., deaf, indigent, illiterate, etc.) None apparent	**Activity level (why?)** BR c̄ BRP: rest so body can fight infection
Lab tests/diagnostic imaging/procedures (list those completed during the two days you are on the unit and why) Hgb: 10.4, BUN: 32 (azotemia), BNP: 334 (not pathognomic for CHF), INR: 2.8...	
Medications (list those received by the patient during the days you are on the unit and why) 1. Nesteritide: vasodilator/diuretic for acutely decompensated CHF (watch SBP > 90 mmHg and HR) 2. Cefazolin: antibiotic for cellulitis (watch interaction with loop diuretics (Lasix), I/O, BMqd?) . . . 3–14. . . .	

All patient care plans are made in light of the specific information about a patient. An actual data form would contain more technical information than what you see here; this just gives you examples of the contents.

The patient came into the unit after heart surgery and developed some problems that are common to those who undergo heart surgery—congestion in the lungs which makes breathing difficult; the difficulty breathing causes low levels of oxygen to be delivered to the tissues which heal the surgical wound and fight infections. Patients are routinely given drugs to prevent clots from forming which can lead to strokes or heart attacks. Unfortunately, the drugs also cause the patient to bleed more easily. The patient described in this care plan was being watched for all of the complications that can develop after an extensive surgery such as a CABG (open-heart surgery).

Nursing Care Plan
Current Plan of Care

What is the plan of care and why? _____

Maintain BP while waiting for INR [a blood test to indicate how long it will take for blood to clot] to determine whether fluid might be drained from the lung. Antibiotics until infection is relieved.

What potential barriers with compliance or healing do you foresee after discharge?

Compliance will be okay, but obesity, diabetes, high blood pressure and cholesterol will impair healing.

What are the most difficult issues/problems for this patient right now? _____

1. Cellulitis of sternal incision [an infection of the chest incision for his heart surgery]

2. Cellulitis of L pleural effusion [lung congestion]

3. DOE

How will this data influence your care of this patient (including eaching)? How will you approach this patient/family? _____

Pt [patient] very teachable, so encourage continuing weight loss, watching his diabetes (diet) → include wife with this teaching, encourage deep breathing techniques (to flow) to build R lung and compensate for L; encourage rest until infection is overcome; praise his quitting of smoking; good established relationship and conversational style willl facilitate encouragement/recommendations.

Nursing Diagnoses (list and prioritize)

1. Impaired gas exchange related to fluid accumulation in lungs as evidenced by ↓'d [decreased] lung sounds throughout and dullness upon percussion [indicates fluid in chest]

3. Infection risk for (further) related to inadequate primary defenses (broken skin) chronic disease (diabetes, etc), invasive procedures. [surgery]

2. Ineffective breathing pattern related to decreased lung expansion as evidenced by dyspnea [difficulty breathing] and lung field auscultation. [lung sounds]

4. Impaired skin integrity related to infection of skin/tissues.

Risk for imbalanced fluid volume.

Current Plan of Care, continued

Discussion and Reflection on:

Textbook Picture of Patient Diagnosis	Actual Patient Picture/Condition
Discuss the patient's illness/injury including • pathophysiology • common signs/symptoms • expected diagnostic tests and results • usual medical/surgical treatments • usual nursing diagnoses and interventions • reference(s)	Discuss your patient's actual condition including • assessment findings (related to the diagnosis) • diagnostic tests and results • medical/surgical treatments • nursing interventions
Pt has L pleural effusion (empyema). [infected fluid in the lung] This is an accumulation of fluid and pus in the pleural space caused by an infection of surgical wounds of the chest. Often this is manifest by progressive difficulty breathing and decreased mov't of the chest wall on affected side. Dullness to percussion, ↓'d breath sounds over the affected area, fever, night sweats, cough, weight loss.	Pt empyema may be complicated further by his high blood pressure which may force fluid into this space rather than out. Pt did have ↓'d breath sounds over his entire L lung. Pt also had difficulty breathing and cough and dullness upon percussion [tapping on the chest] to L lung field. However he was not running a fever and was actually gaining weight.
Diagnostic tests and results: chest x-ray show if effusion is > 250 mL; diagnostic thoracentesis to determine cause/type of fluid; therapeutic thoracentesis to relieve pressure build up from fluid (inserting needle into the lung to drain fluid.)	A thoracentesis (diagnostic but esp. therapeutic was on hold until his INR dropped into range (so the high Coumadin [a blood thinner] levels did not make him bleed uncontrollably)

Tx: therapeutic thoracentesis; drain pleural space via therapeutic thoracentesis or close thoracotomy tube, appropriate antibiotic treatment.	Pt was on appropriate antibiotic therapy
	
	Appropriate nursing diagnosis for RK included:
	    Impaired gas exchange
	    Ineffective breathing pattern
	    Excess fluid volume
	    Potential for (further) infection

Nursing diagnosis: Impaired gas exchange, ineffective breathing pattern, anxiety. References: Lewis, Ackley	

What is the correlation between the textbook pictures and your patient's actual condition? Why?
I think it fit rather well considering the thoracentesis was on hold for his INR to drop.

This part of the "plan of care" is critical because writing about the patient problems allows us to set goals for his recovery and for the health team to evaluate if those goals are met.

Nursing Care Plan
Nursing Process/Teaching Plan

Nursing Diagnosis	Plan/Outcome Criteria	Implementation	Rationale	Evaluation of Outcomes
Impaired gas exchange Related to pleural effusion as evidenced by dyspnea [difficulty breathing], irritability, somnolence [excessive sleepiness], tachycardia.	1. PaO_2 and $PaCO_2$ are maintained within patient's normal range by 9/17. [These indicate the patient's ability to exchange oxygen and carbon dioxide] 2. Normal breath sounds are maintained, and Pt remains free of signs of respiratory distress by 9/18.	1. Monitor SaO_2 for and administer as ordered to SaO_2 levels. 2. Monitor apical radial HR [heart rate] for irregular rhythm, tachy- [too fast], and brachycardia [too slow]. 3. Teach and encourage pursed-lip breathing to improve gas exchange. 4. Position Pt HOB [head of the bed], incline 30 degrees as tolerated.	1. SaO_2 under 90% indicates oxygenation problem. 2. Hypoxia may cause cardiac arrhythmias. 3. Pursed-lip breathing results in increased use of intercostal [between ribs] muscles, increased exercise perfromance, and ability of Pt to self-manage. 4. Semi-Fowler's [sitting] position allows lung expansion.	1. PaO_2 and $PaCO_2$ in normal range as of 9/17. "Goal met." 2. Breath sounds were improving on left side, but Pt was still experiencing DOE [difficulty breathing with activity]. "Goal partially met."

This plan teaches nursing students various elements that must become normal processes for planning and carrying out patient care.

Teaching—and encouraging—self-care is an important part of a care plan.

The numbers in this chart refer to the four "nursing diagnoses" listed at the bottom of the first page of the "Current Plan of Care."

Reflection Paper: Peri-Operative and Critical Care Experiences

Megan Nyenhuis

the time before and during surgery, and in the recovery room

This past week I had the opportunity to have my peri-operative and critical care experiences. During both of these experiences I was able to observe the role of the nurse and identify some ethical issues that exist and virtues necessary in that setting. During my peri-operative experience, I followed a 67-year-old woman through her surgical experience. I first saw her in pre-op where she was with her family, waiting to be taken back to surgery. I then watched her surgery, a lumbar laminectomy. I admit that I did not

removal of tissue pressing on nerves in the spine

really enjoy watching the surgery and hearing the surgeon break through some of the bone in her spine, but I made it through and so did my patient. I then followed her into the recovery room where she woke up from the anesthesia, and finally, was transferred to a medical-surgical floor.

This experience allowed me to somewhat understand what patients go through during their surgical experience. It also allowed me to see what the role of the peri-operative nurse is. I saw the pre-op nurse being an educator, communicator, advocator,

Nursing students are asked to describe how they see the nurse providing personal as well as technical aspects of care. Reflecting and writing are good ways to organize thoughts and impressions in order to evaluate them.

and comforter. She explained what would happen to the patient, spoke with and listened to the patient to decrease the patient's anxiety, advocated for the patient by making sure everything was in order for the surgery and making sure everything ran smoothly, and comforted the patient by reassuring her and letting her know someone would be with her at all times. The nurse served as advocate in the operating room by being the one to stop the surgeon from cracking jokes about the patient when the patient was starting to wake up.

I was also able to observe an ethical issue in the operating room. After my patient was unconscious from the anesthesia, they moved her into position for the surgery (positioned her on her stomach). She was a bigger lady, so moving her was not the easiest task. However, they really gave little attention to being careful and gentle with the patient. They just flipped her over and pushed her into the right position. Later in the surgery when the patient was

Student nurses are taught that an important principle of nursing is patient advocacy. Reflection papers allowed a forum to "recognize reality, search for solutions, and try to transform."

just starting to come to, the surgeon make some joke about the patient. I thought that these things were not appropriate actions in the operating room. Just because a patient is unconscious does not mean that the patient should be treated any differently.

Some basic virtues necessary for peri-operative nursing became evident to me as well. The ones that seem most important are courage, empathy, and compassion. Courage is necessary to confront co-workers who are not treating the patient like they should be treated as in the situation described above. Empathy is necessary because many nurses cannot understand what it is like to undergo surgery. The nurse must listen carefully and use therapeutic communication to show that she is trying to understand and that she truly cares for the patient. Compassion is necessary because surgery is a scary thing, and patients need to know that they are cared about and that someone is looking out for them and putting their needs first.

A subdural hematoma is a blood clot on the brain.

During my critical care experience in the surgical unit, I observed a nurse who was caring for a 64-year-old man who had suffered a traumatic brain injury from a 10–15 feet fall onto cement. He had suffered a left temporal subdural hematoma, rib fractures, left atelectasis, and a mediastinal hematoma. He was unconscious and showed response to very strong stimulus on his arms only. This patient had made little progress since his admission, and doctors were not too hopeful about his prognosis.

Atelectasis is lung congestion.

A mediastinal hematoma is a collection of blood around the area of the heart.

An ethical issue was evident during this experience as well. The wife of this patient was understandably very upset and teary-eyed. She came to visit her husband and said things to the nurse like, "When will he wake up? It might take a few weeks, right?" The nurse had told me previously that this patient's prognosis was very poor. However, she felt like it was not her place to give a prognosis especially since the prognosis was still somewhat unknown. But she told me that she also did not want to give false hope to this wife. This situation puts the nurse in a difficult position because she might either overstep her bounds and give the patient's prognosis or give false hope which could be devastating to the family. I thought that this nurse handled the situation well by hugging the wife and reassuring her that they were doing everything they could for the patient.

Virtues that seem especially important in the critical care setting are compassion and empathy. Even if the nurse cannot understand what the patient and family are going through, the nurse can listen and comfort the patient and family and show them that they are cared about.

READING RESPONSES

1. In reflecting on her experiences shadowing a nurse, Megan Nyenhuis focuses on the interactions that the nurses had with their patients. She does not record the times that the nurses performed clinical tasks like administering medication or recording data. Do you think some nurses would object

to this focus? On what grounds? How does Megan's purpose for writing affect the personal experiences she includes in her paper?

2. If you were experiencing severe pain, how important would a nurse's concern be to you? What would be the best way for a nurse to express concern for you?

3. Consider the information that Gritters includes on the patient data sheet. Where does he include emotional or social information? What strategies does he use in writing that must be both technical and abbreviated to showcase the humanness of his patient?

PUBLIC WRITING IN NURSING

Introduction

The *American Journal of Nursing* stands at the front of the line of prestigious journals in the nursing profession. It publishes articles about nursing care (such as the studies of chronic pain and the "faces scale" also reproduced in this chapter), but it also offers articles on the business and politics of nursing. Because of its prestige, it has gained an audience of hospital administrators, public policy makers, and others. These editors reach out to the "public" audience by defining—in large font right beneath the title—the term *palliative care*: "Care that's based on need rather than prognosis." It is, in other words, "comfort" care, given to people after curative care has been unsuccessful.

The structure of the editorial further opens a public conversation. The authors use bullet points to focus their readers' attention to the action that specific groups should take to improve care for extremely sick people. Because they have broad experience in nursing, the authors are keenly aware of the experiences that their readers have had. The authors invoke the experience of their readers by making strong claims about how end-of-life care currently is, and how it ought to be. They can expect that their readers will nod knowingly as they read because their own personal experiences convince them of the truth and the importance of the authors' claims.

Why Isn't All Care "Palliative Care"?

Diana Mason, PhD, RN, FAAN;
Nessa Coyle, PhD, NP, FAAN; and
Betty R. Ferrell, PhD, RN, FAAN

American Journal of Nursing, November 2004, Vol. 104, No. 11
"Those who learned to know death, rather than to fear and fight it," said the recently deceased Elisabeth Kubler-Ross, "become our teachers about life."

By discussing death and dying frankly when it was deemed unseemly to do so, she helped many to think about how they wanted to live, particularly when confronted with serious illness. Those who participated in her workshops or read her writings over the years came to recognize the obscenity of leaving a dying patient alone in a room at the end of the hall.

But have nursing thought and practice changed sufficiently? In the January 2004 issue of the *Journal of the American Medical Association*, Teno and colleagues reported on a survey of family members and others who knew the circumstances surrounding the end-of-life experience of people who had died. The final place of care for 69% of the sample was a hospital or nursing home, despite the fact that the majority of people would prefer to die at home. Regardless of setting, staff were reported by respondents to have inadequately addressed several areas of care: pain (24%), dyspnea **[difficulty breathing]** (22%), and emotional needs (50%).

A number of changes are required to remedy this situation:

- Providers, policymakers, and the public must discuss the need for a shift from a prolonging-life-at-any-cost approach to one that focuses on the patient's priorities, the quality of life, and the relief of suffering. Unfortunately, such conversation usually takes place only when a provider realizes that cure is no longer possible. But palliative care is not an either–or proposition.
- Reimbursement policies should follow suit. Regular Medicare benefits cover only care that follows the curative approach, while coverage for care that follows the quality of life approach falls under the rubric of hospice care. On March 10 the *Wall Street Journal* reported that the Virginia Commonwealth University Medical Center actually cut its costs of caring for cancer patients by 57% when patients were on its 11-bed palliative care unit, compared with care provided on traditional units. And yet, fewer than 20% of community hospitals have palliative care services. At a time when health care costs are rising, Medicare and all insurers must pay for care that addresses patients' goals, whether curative or not.
- Providers must address the difficulties of talking with patients and families about their wishes *before* death is near. The first step is asking why this is so difficult. Providers must continue to talk about these issues in their institutions; patients and families must be assured that the end of curative treatment does not mean the end of all treatment.
- Nurses must anticipate the risk of dying by using the instruments Matzo discusses in "Palliative Care: Prognostication and the Chronically Ill" (September). The point isn't predicting the exact moment of death but rather talking about dying and supporting patients and families as part of making informed treatment decisions.
- Family caregivers, who provide end-of-life care in the home, deserve more attention than they receive. To expect families to care for the dying without adequate training and support is harmful to all involved.

Teno and colleagues found that satisfaction with hospice care was higher than with care provided by hospitals, nursing homes, and home care providers. Undoubtedly, this is because in hospice care the patient and family define the goals of care and the care is truly interdisciplinary: all members of the health care team are valued participants.

So why isn't all health care "palliative care"—that is, care that's based on need rather than prognosis? Over the past 15 years, the Robert Wood Johnson Foundation has invested $150 million in projects designed "to bring attention to the need for improvements in end-of-life care." As a recipient of a grant under this initiative, *AJN* has published a series on palliative nursing care (available online at www.NursingCenter.com/AJNpalliative) over the past two and a half years, ending this month. We will continue to publish articles on this important topic and urge you to continue to teach yourself about best practices in palliative and end-of-life care.

READING RESPONSES

1. What does the opening quote by Elisabeth Kubler-Ross say about personal experience? Paraphrase her words, emphasizing personal experience.
2. This editorial addresses a broad range of readers who have a wide variety of personal experiences with palliative care. The authors do not refer to their own personal experience but the personal experiences of their readers. Describe three places where they refer to their readers' experiences. What is the effect of these references?
3. Most of the personal experiences that the editors use come in the form of quoted material from respected academic sources. Does this make this personal experience evidence more or less effective? What kinds of personal experience evidence would strengthen this editorial? Note three places in the text where you would insert such material.

MORE WRITING IN NURSING

Introduction

Like the study of chronic pain that is the first reading in this chapter, the paper on a "Faces Scale" is the report of nurses' research, written for an audience of nurses. The study examines the hypothesis that people possess an ability to read human faces, and that nurses can use this ability to determine the anxiety of people who cannot speak or write. Knowing the anxiety level of patients helps medical professionals create a better care plan for them. This scientific study, like most clinical trials, relies on the personal experiences of the people who will be most affected by the new medication or procedure. By sharing their personal experience with the researchers, the patients potentially improve the experiences of many others.

The second part of the study is interesting, too. The researchers examined the universality of the "faces scale" to see if health care professionals interpret personal experiences with anxious patients in similar ways. They conclude that indeed they do. This study, then, provides tantalizing evidence that personal experience is not always idiosyncratic—that while our experiences are personal, our observations are rooted in shared ways of interpreting what we see. And that is why readers trust an author's personal experience: it often resonates with their own observations and life experiences.

Development and testing of a faces scale for the assessment of anxiety in critically ill patients

Sharon McKinley, Katherine Coote, and Jane Stein-Parbury

Journal of Advanced Nursing, 2003, 41(1): 73–79.

[Abstract]

Background. Many patients experience anxiety during treatment in an intensive care unit, but intensive care patients are often not able to respond to existing validated measures of anxiety such as the Brief Symptom Inventory. We have developed a new single item Faces Anxiety Scale made up of drawings of five faces.

Aims. The aims of this study were to: (i) assess the ability of intensive care patients to respond to the Faces Anxiety Scale; and (ii) investigate whether the scale yields ordinal and interval data.

Ethics. The project was approved by two Human Research Ethics Committees. Patients were included in the study if they gave informed consent.

Instruments and methods. (i) Intensive care patients (n = 40) were asked to respond to the Faces Anxiety Scale, the anxiety subscale of the Brief Symptom Inventory, and a numerical analogue anxiety scale; and (ii) Hospital and University staff and students (n = 75) were asked to place the five faces in rank order. . . .

Results. The Faces Anxiety Scale elicited more responses from intensive care patients than the numerical analogue anxiety scale the or anxiety subscale of the Brief Symptom Inventory (36 vs. 25 vs. 17, respectively, P < 0.0001). In the testing of the order of the scale items, 93% of respondents independently placed the scale items in the order of least to most anxiety as intended in the design of the scale. . . .

Conclusion. The Faces Anxiety Scale has minimal subject burden, elicits self report from intensive care patients more often than other simple scales, and has evidence of the interval scale properties of rank order and equality between the points on the scale.

Introduction

Critically ill patients have life threatening conditions requiring life-support mechanisms and extensive treatments that necessitate close monitoring available exclusively within the intensive care unit (ICU). Despite receiving sedative drugs, many critically ill patients experience anxiety because of the seriousness of their condition and the nature of the procedures they undergo (McKinley et al. 2002, Puntillo et al. 2001). Stress and anxiety in acutely ill patients have harmful physiological consequences (Spielberger 1979). For example, patients with anxiety early after a myocardial infarction are more likely to have physical complications in hospital (Moser & Dracup 1996), and experimentally induced cognitive stress in cardiac surgical patients increases myocardial workload, which can jeopardise recovery (McFetridge & Yarandi 1997).

The measurement of anxiety in ICU patients is necessary for the evaluation of nursing actions to reduce anxiety and potentially enhance recovery, but is particularly difficult in this population. State anxiety is defined as a subjective experience which signals that a threat of some type has stimulated the stress response; the subjective feelings associated with anxiety include apprehension, feelings of uncertainty, uneasiness, dread and worry (Hill 1991). Approaches to the assessment of anxiety include observation of its physiological and behavioural signs and self report by patients. The physiological and behavioural signs of distress and anxiety, such as tachycardia, raised blood pressure and restlessness, are difficult to interpret in critically ill patients, who may have many

---

WHAT IS ALREADY KNOWN ON THIS TOPIC:

- Critically ill patients report afterwards that they had experienced anxiety and fear at times while in the intensive care unit.
- Stress and anxiety may have harmful psychological consequences.
- The complexity of these patients' conditions confounds assessment of anxiety during intensive care.
- Most intensive care patients are unable to respond to existing self-report measures of anxiety.

WHAT THIS STUDY ADDS:

- Many intensive care patients were able to respond to the Faces Anxiety Scale.
- The Scale is easily administered for clinical assessment and research purposes.
- There is evidence that the Scale provides continuous data.
- Ongoing research is evaluating the criterion and construct validity of the Scale.

competing explanations for such signs. Similarly, alterations in levels of the biochemical markers of stress, cortisol and catecholemines, may be attributable to physiological and psychological stress (Torpy & Chrousos 1997), and are difficult to interpret. In recent studies into the assessment of patient anxiety by North American critical care nurses it was found that there was commonly a reliance on behavioural and physiological signs, that assessment was usually not systematic, and that staff assessments of anxiety did not match patients' self ratings of anxiety (O'Brien et al. 2001, Frazier et al. 2002). Hence the patient's report of anxiety is potentially the most reliable approach to its measurement in critically ill patients, but is accompanied by other methodological problems.

Intensive care patients often are unable to communicate their emotions because of impaired cognition and mechanical aspects of the treatment they are receiving. Their metabolic states, the administration of sedative agents and the requirement for endotracheal intubation and mechanical ventilation frequently cause difficulty in the expression of emotions such as anxiety (Bergbom-Engberg & Haljamae 1989, Hafsteindottir 1996, Menzel 1997, Stein-Parbury & McKinley 2000). Most ICU patients are not able to respond to existing validated anxiety measures, such as the Spielberger State-Trait Anxiety Inventory (STAI) (Spielberger et al. 1983) and the Brief Symptom Inventory (BSI) (Derogatis & Melisaratos 1983). The STAI has 40 items, thus presenting a recognized barrier to its completion by some populations (Marteau & Bekker 1992). Similarly, the BSI has 53 items which measures several affective states including anxiety (Derogatis & Melisaratos 1983). Such instruments are therefore inappropriate for many ICU patients because they are too cognitively demanding. Studies in which anxiety has been measured by self-report in ICU patients have been limited, for example by the inclusion only of patients who were not intubated (Treggiari-Venzi et al. 1996) or alert and not receiving continuous sedatives if intubated (Chlan 1998), or by incomplete data collection because of the patients' need to rest (Menzel 1997). There is a recognized need for an anxiety measure that is sensitive, reliable and able to be understood and completed by critically ill patients (Chlan 1998). The purpose of the present research therefore was to develop and test a self report anxiety scale, the Faces Anxiety Scale, for use with critically ill patients in ICU....

Faces scales have been used for the self-report of pain in children for a number of years (Bieri et al. 1990). A scale of faces is appropriate for self-report in subjects with limited or impaired cognitive capacity in that it presents little cognitive complexity or metaphoric difficulty, as well as being relatively free from outside influences of explanation and interpretation (Bieri et al. 1990). The human face provides expression of emotions such as happiness, anger and anxiety (Ekman & Oster 1979). Ekman and colleagues have shown that facial muscle patterns can be used to reliably detect emotions and to distinguish between emotions, e.g. anger vs. fear (Ekman et al. 1983) Therefore it was speculated that a faces scale may be a suitable self-report measure of anxiety in critically ill adults.

Scale Development

The Faces Anxiety Scale is a single item scale with five possible responses ranging from a neutral face to one showing extreme fear (Figure 1). The faces were drawn by a graphic artist based on photographs of faces exhibiting fear, together with detailed descriptions of how facial muscles change as fear intensifies (Ekman & Friesen 1975). Faces showing fear were used to represent anxiety in this research. Fear and anxiety have the same physical manifestations but different causes; fear is generally a response to an actual and present danger, whereas anxiety is a response to something perceived to be dangerous on the basis of previous experience (Doctor & Kahn 1989).

Pictorial representations of photographs of facial expressions have been found to be a valid alternative to photographs in research using facial expression (Katsikitis 1997). Therefore a faces scale with line drawings developed in close accordance with photographs and descriptions of fearful expressions is potentially a suitable self-report measure of anxiety. However there is a need to confirm the utility of such an instrument for the measurement of anxiety of critically ill patients in ICU.

Research aims

The aims of this research were: (i) to compare the ability of ICU patients to respond to the Faces Anxiety Scale, the Brief Symptom Inventory anxiety subscale (Derogatis & Melisaratos 1983) and a numerical analogue anxiety scale; and (ii) to investigate whether the Faces Anxiety Scale yields data of ordinal and interval levels of measurement. **[Editors' note: We have deleted some parts of this paper (e.g., Tables 1–3) that discuss technical details related to aim #2.]**

Methods

The research aims were addressed in a series of four studies. Studies 1 and 2 addressed aim (i) and Studies 3 and 4 addressed aim (ii). All studies were approved by the Human Research Ethics Committees of the Hospital and the University. Data collection from patients commenced only after the aims and procedure were explained to them and they gave informed consent to participate; data collection was discontinued immediately if the patient became too tired to respond or wished it to stop for any reason. Data collection from non-patient volunteers occurred only after the aims and procedure were explained to them and they gave informed consent to participate, and in the case of students with the approval of the Dean of the Faculty. The studies were conducted during 1999 and 2000.

Studies 1 and 2

The purpose of Studies 1 and 2 was to assess the ability of patients to respond to the Faces Anxiety Scale compared with two other relatively brief anxiety scales.

Instruments. The Faces Anxiety Scale was produced in proportion on an 11 by 42 cm laminated card and presented to respondents with the following instructions: These faces are showing different levels of anxiety. This face shows no anxiety at all, this face shows a little bit more, a bit more (sweep finger along scale),

Figure 1 Faces Anxiety Scale.

right up to extreme anxiety. Have a look at these faces and choose the one that shows how much anxiety you are feeling at the moment.... Each of the six items on the anxiety subscale is rated on a 5-point scale (0–4) of distress ranging from "not at all" to "extremely." In this study, each item was read to the patient and the five alternative responses were held in large letters on a card where the patient could easily see and read them....

Participants. Intensive care patients eligible for the study met the following criteria: a score of 3 or better on the Ramsay Sedation Scale (opens eyes to name, opens eyes spontaneously, or awake) (Ramsay et al. 1974); conversant in English; normal or corrected vision; and no apparent neurological impairment. Patients who met these criteria were approached by the research assistant and asked if they would like to take part in the study. Those patients who indicated consent by nodding their heads were included in the study. The sample consisted of 40 general ICU patients (Table 1).

Procedure. The first 20 patients were presented with the faces scale.... [P]atients responded to questions by either nodding or shaking their heads or pointing to the appropriate answer. When it was confirmed that the Faces Anxiety Scale was comprehensible to critically ill patients by 18 of 20 patients responding to it, a further 20 patients meeting the entry criteria were studied using the same procedure....

Results. Of the first 20 patients tested, almost all [18 of 20] were able to respond to the faces scale....

Study 3

The purpose of Study 3 was to investigate whether the scale possessed the property of rank order, that is that the scale items displayed a consistent and recognizable ascension, from least to most fear or anxiety.

Participants and procedure. Non-patient volunteers, namely hospital and university staff and students were approached to be participants in this research. Seventy-five participants were given the five faces of the Faces Scale on individual cards, in a random order. Participants were asked to place the faces in the order which they believed best represented least to most fear or anxiety.

Results. Ninety-three per cent of respondents placed the faces in the order of the faces in the scale. This result confirmed the placement of the anchor faces at the lowest and highest points of the scale....

Discussion

The aim of this series of studies was to assess the utility and the scale properties of the Faces Anxiety Scale as an instrument to measure anxiety in ICU patients. . . . The Faces Anxiety Scale is accessible to a higher proportion of ICU patients, compared with two existing brief measures. . . .

In the testing of the order of the scale items almost all respondents independently placed the scale items in the order of least to most anxiety as intended in the design of the scale. This indicates that the Faces Anxiety Scale has the property of rank order. . . . Studies such as this and that of Bieri and colleagues have provided evidence of the interval properties of scales, which is of particular importance when the measure is to be used as a research instrument.

Conclusion

The newly developed Faces Anxiety Scale is easy to administer and subjects the respondent to minimal burden. It appears to elicit anxiety self-report from ICU patients, and this report provides good evidence that it has the interval scale properties of rank order and equality of intervals. The criterion validity of the Scale is currently being determined. The Faces Anxiety Scale is a promising instrument for research to rigorously evaluate interventions to reduce anxiety in ICU patients and further investigate the relationship between patient anxiety and recovery in the critically ill population.

References

Bergbom-Engberg I. & Haljamae H. (1989) Assessment of patients' experience of discomforts during respirator therapy. *Critical Care Medicine* 17, 1068–1072.

Bieri D., Reeve R.A., Champion G.D., Addicoat L. & Ziegler J.B. (1990) The Faces Pain Scale for the self-assessment of the severity of pain experienced by children: development, initial validation, and preliminary investigation of ratio scale properties. *Pain* 41, 139–150.

Chlan L. (1998) Effectiveness of a music therapy intervention on relaxation and anxiety for patients receiving ventilatory assistance. *Heart and Lung* 27, 169–176.

Derogatis I.R. & Melisaratos N. (1983) The brief symptom inventory: an introductory report. *Psychological Medicine* 13, 595–605.

Doctor R.M. & Kahn A.P. (1989) *The Encyclopedia of Phobias, Fears, and Anxieties.* Facts on File, New York.

Ekman P. & Friesen W.V. (1975) *Unmasking the Face: A Guide to Recognizing Emotions from Facial Clues.* Prentice Hall, NJ, USA.

Ekman P., Levenson R.W. & Friesen W.V. (1983) Autonomic nervous system activity distinguishes among emotions. *Science* 221, 1208–1210.

Ekman P. & Oster H. (1979) Facial expressions of emotion. *Annual Review of Psychology* 30, 527–554.

Frazier S.K., Moser D.K., Riegel B., McKinley S., Blakely W., Kim K.A. & Garvin B.J. (2002) Critical care nurses' assessment of patient anxiety: reliance on physiological and behavioral parameters. *American Journal of Critical Care* 11, 57–64.

Hafsteindottir T.B. (1996) Patients experiences of communication during the respirator period. *Intensive and Critical Care Nursing* 12, 261–271.

Hill F. (1991) The neurophysiology of acute anxiety: a review of the literature. CRNA 2, 52–61.

Katsikitis M. (1997) The classification of facial expressions of emotion: a multidimensional-scaling approach. *Perception* 26, 613–626.

McFetridge J.A. & Yarandi H.N. (1997) Cardiovascular function during cognitive stress in men before and after coronary bypass grafts. *Nursing Research* 46, 188–194.

McKinley S., Nagy S., Stein-Parbury J., Bramwell M. & Hudson J. (2002) Vulnerability and security in intensive care patients. *Intensive and Critical Care Nursing* 18, 27–36.

Menzel L.K. (1997) A comparison of patients communication-related responses during intubation and after extubation. *Heart and Lung* 26, 363–371.

Moser D.K. & Dracup K. (1996) Is anxiety early after myocardial infarction associated with subsequent ischemic and arrhythmic events? *Psychosomatic Medicine* 58, 395–401.

O' Brien J.L., Moser D.K., Riegel B., Frazier S.K., Garvin B.J. & Kim K.A. (2001) Comparison of anxiety assessments between clinicians and patients with acute myocardial infarction in cardiac critical care units. *American Journal of Critical Care* 10, 97–103.

Puntillo K.A., White C., Morris A.B., Perdue S.T., Stanik-Hutt J., Thompson C.L., Wild L.R. (2001) Patients' perceptions and responses to procedural pain: results from Thunder Project II. *American Journal of Critical Care* 10, 238–251.

Ramsay M.A.E., Savege T.M., Simpson B.J.R. & Goodwin R. (1974) Controlled sedation with alphaxalone-alphadolone. *British Medical Journal* 2, 656–659.

Spielberger C.D. (1979) *Understanding Stress and Anxiety*. Nelson, Melbourne, Australia.

Spielberger C.D., Gorsuch R.L., Lushene P., Vagg P.R. & Jacobs G.A. (1983) *Manual for the State-Trait Anxiety Inventory (Form Y)*. Consulting Psychologists Press, Inc., Palo Alto, CA, USA.

Stein-Parbury J. & McKinley S. (2000) Patients' experiences of being in an intensive care unit: a select literature review. *American Journal of Critical Care* 9, 20–27.

Torpy D.J. & Chrousos G.P. (1997) Stress and critical illness: the integrated immune/hypothalamic–pituitary–adrenal axis response. *Journal of Intensive Care Medicine* 12, 225–238.

Treggiari-Venzi M., Borgeat A., Fuchs-Buder T., Gachoud J.P. & Suter P.M. (1996) Overnight sedation with midazolam or propofol in the ICU: effects on sleep quality, anxiety and depression. *Intensive Care Medicine* 22, 1186–1190.

READING RESPONSES

1. Why do these researchers combine their study of patients' ability to use the Faces Anxiety Scale with the staff's placement of the faces on a scale? Why do they need to gather information about the personal experiences of both of these groups?

2. Try to place yourself in the position of an ICU patient, terribly sick and unable to communicate with words. How would using the Faces Anxiety Scale to communicate your anxiousness affect your anxiety level?

3. To what extent is facial expression of anxiety a biological (therefore universal) response to stress, fear, or pain? To what extent is facial expression of anxiety shaped by a person's culture? What other personal experiences might shape how a person shows anxiety on his or her face?

WRITING ASSIGNMENTS

ASSIGNMENT 1: APPLYING THE PORTABLE RHETORICAL LESSON

Background: One reason we chose Thomas's essay for this chapter is that we appreciate how her evidence fits her research problem. Thomas argues that doctors and nurses tend to dismiss pain because pain does not show up on x-rays, MRIs, blood tests, and other "objective" biomedical tests. To "picture" chronic pain, Thomas interviews thirteen people who are living with chronic pain. She uses quotes from those interviews as her evidence for the nature and significance of chronic pain. In this way, the personal experience of people in chronic pain bears witness to that pain in a way that medical tests often don't.

Your task for this assignment is to picture Thomas's use of personal experience by charting it. You may find it helpful to review Chapter 8, Biology, for advice on creating effective tables and figures. Re-read Thomas's essay, recording each time she uses personal experience as evidence. For each use of personal experience, describe how Thomas presents the personal experience: quote, paraphrase, summary, or narrative. How does Thomas introduce the personal experience to the reader? Does Thomas cluster examples of personal experience or does she allow them to stand alone? Once you've collected your data, analyze it. What patterns do you see? How do those patterns shape the reader's experience of Thomas's article? Based on your research and your experiences as a reader of Thomas's article, make recommendations about the use of personal experience evidence in science articles.

As you begin drafting, consider how your own personal experience reading and analyzing Thomas's article can help you explain the results of your study to your reader.

ASSIGNMENT 2: MAKING CONNECTIONS

Background: Chapter 11, English Education, contains an excerpt from *Bootstraps*, in which Victor Villanueva blends humanities scholarly research with his own experiences. Sandra Thomas, author of "A Phenomenologic Study of Chronic Pain" also blends academic research with descriptions of personal experience. But she does so in very different ways.

Your task for this assignment is to create a set of recommendations for using personal experience effectively. What are the issues that writers should consider regarding when and how to use personal experience? How does the situation in which they're writing affect their use of personal experience? What purposes do personal experiences serve in academic writing? What kinds of personal experiences are appropriate in academic writing? What are inappropriate? What strategies can writers use to present personal experience? To integrate it in their writing?

As you begin drafting, try to be very clear about the ways that context shapes the answers to the questions above and the means that writers can use to determine the appropriate use of personal experience in a given context.

ASSIGNMENT 3: DOING THE RESEARCH

Background: College students hear frequent warnings to avoid the "freshman fifteen," (weight gain supposedly experienced by first-year students), but recent research indicates that this warning itself can create trouble for students, especially female students.

Your task is to research and report on the effects of the myth of the "freshman fifteen" by targeting two sources of information: published research on the topic and the personal experiences of college students. A reference librarian can help you locate published research on the topic. To gather the personal experiences, create a set of interview questions and then interview five to ten students at your school (you might want to interview only women or only men). Record their answers carefully by taking thorough notes or using a tape recorder.

As you begin drafting, consider the relationship between the kinds of evidence that you collected—how can you present your evidence so that it all works together? Consider, too, the relationship between your evidence and the claims that you make in your report—what kind of evidence will best support a particular claim? If you found particularly compelling evidence, you might direct your report to university administrators who oversee student life and include a set of recommendations in your conclusion.

PSYCHOLOGY: LISTENING AND RECOMMENDING CARE PLANS

As in the other chapters in Part Four of this book, recommendations for action take center stage in this chapter. But clients' mental and physical health is at stake in these recommendations, so the authors exercise great caution in their research and their judgments. The first and second sets of readings, composed by a psychologist and two students who worked with her, form a fictional reproduction of documents that would be written by a psychologist as she works with a new client. The third and fourth readings report more traditional research in psychology; they build knowledge that they hope will create better understanding of human psychology and will thus eventually change the ways we try to improve mental health.

   If you pay careful attention to the rhetoric of the fictional clinical documents—and then listen for echoes of their rhetorical choices in the third and fourth readings, you will detect distinctive characteristics in the discipline of psychology. The authors demonstrate great skill in asking good questions, and they pay very close attention to the details of what they learn. Because they know how much is at stake, they exercise sensitivity in their research with clients, and they work hard to establish and honor trust between themselves, their clients, and their readers. In short, they ask questions purposefully, listen to responses carefully, and recommend cautiously: characteristics that can improve the work of any writer.

A Portable Rhetorical Lesson:

Respecting Your Sources

Writers operate within communities: we read others, respond to others, and write for others. Because we write in communities, teachers frequently advise writers to "Respect your readers." A complementary recommendation is the main rhetorical lesson for this chapter: "Respect your sources."

You have probably used research in your writing. You have, therefore, quoted, paraphrased, summarized, and cited information from sources. If you want to become better at using sources ethically, writing in psychology offers excellent models. Psychologists simply cannot function without respecting the communications of others. So they handle their sources—clients, professionals whom they consult, clinical records, and published research—with respect.

Clinical psychologists (those who work one-on-one with clients) seem especially bound to respect their clients' words.* But every professional in the field of psychology shares an ethical commitment to listening and observing carefully, and representing others' words and actions accurately.

A psychologist is therefore ideally suited to teach us how to treat sources with consideration. When using people as sources from your research, you should practice some of the strategies of clinical psychologists. As psychologists take notes during a session, write follow-up notes after a session, and later write more formal reports, they are constantly choosing whether to (1) summarize (when they are confident that they can comprehensively represent the gist of a larger group of things that a client has said or things that they infer from non-verbal communications), (2) paraphrase (when they need to capture the content of what a client has said but can do so more concisely or accurately than with a quotation), or (3) quote (when the clients' actual words present the most accurate or most telling version of their conversation).

Observing psychologists make particular choices should convince you that respect for your sources will make your writing more accurate and more ethical. It might even help you if you imagine that your sources, like the psychologist's clients, have the right to read what you have written. Realizing the nature of your responsibility to sources—and seeing it modeled in the writing samples in this chapter—will have the practical benefits of helping you know when and why to avoid plagiarism, spin, misrepresentation, and other unethical writing practices. It will also teach you how to make the most of your sources,

---

*A study has shown that as psychologists become more experienced they gradually rely more on clients' non-verbal communications—body language, for example. But the study also confirmed that psychotherapists always depend primarily on clients' words in order to understand and represent their clients. "Psychotherapists' Representations of Their Patients," Geller, Lehman, and Farber. *Journal of Clinical Psychology* 58 (2002): 733–45.

using the words and ideas from their writing to make your writing more human, credible, authoritative, and interesting.

Chapter Topics: The chapter focuses on mental health and brain function, including aging, depression, loneliness, and trauma.

To Think About . . .

Write for yourself: Use the form for Dr. VanderGoot's "Initial Assessment" (pages 431–433) to fill out assessment notes on yourself. Complete these exercises as if you are the psychologist asking the questions and filling out the forms. Read your notes to discover how well you respect yourself as a source of information. What evidence do you see that you trust your own assessment of yourself, including trusting your own words, your own interpretations, even your own uncertainties?

    Write for your instructor: Use the form to fill out an assessment of a fictional person. Next take the assessment of your fictional character and, without changing, adding, or deleting information, revise your word choice so that you describe the fictional person as positively as possible. Finally, rewrite the assessment a third time, revising your word choice so that you describe the fictional person as negatively as possible. Analyze the three versions and explain how your intentional biases in the second and third version change the assessment's accuracy and fairness.

WRITING IN PSYCHOLOGY

Introduction by Mary VanderGoot, Ph.D., Licensed Psychologist

The Importance of Clinical Writing. Written documents are essential to the therapist because in all mental health professions both legal standards and ethical standards require that professionals keep treatment records. Any professional who defies these standards is taking serious risks, including the risk of making mistakes that damage the client. Records also confirm that clients have been informed about the plans for their treatment and that they are true participants in the process.

    Psychologists, social workers, and counselors who work in agencies and clinics have a responsibility to their clients as well as their employers. Clients have a right to read their own files. Organizations which provide services must be licensed and accredited, and among the standards for accreditation is the requirement of adequate record-keeping. It is not unheard of for an employer to fire a therapist who does not keep records, because failure to do so creates too great a risk for the employer. The desire to help clients and to respect their rights is always foremost in a therapist's mind while writing about clients.

In short, mental health professionals are necessarily record-keepers. Clients have a right to expect that good records are kept, professionals are obligated to provide them, and employers will insist that this work is done.

Writing in clinical records must, therefore, be clear and concise. Clients as well as professionals should be able to understand the documents in a single reading, and professionals (other therapists, consulting physicians, lawyers, etc.) need quick and easy access to the information they want. Sometimes, psychologists use bullet points, highlighted words, and numbered lists to make information more easily accessible.

Audiences and Clinical Writing. While it's true that psychologists must remember that others will read their documents, the audience of those documents is quite small. The clinical record is like a very private letter. It is meant only for the eyes of the persons who are clearly designated to read it—other members of a medical team, the client, and perhaps the client's legal representative or the courts. (In 2003 the United States government passed a set of laws governing the privacy of all health-related records and documents. These laws are called HIPAA, Health Insurance Portability and Accountability Act).

Clinical documents are personal. A second and quite different situation might make your document available to non-professionals. Your client may ask for a copy of the record. When clients read their clinical documents, it is like looking in a mirror: the documents may give clients a painfully close-up look at themselves. Sometimes this image is of the person in difficult circumstances. It is important for the psychologist to *be respectful.* It is a good exercise to ask this question: "If I were in my client's circumstances, would it be acceptable to me if this document were written about me and shared with others?"

After you run the spell check, review your grammar, and check one more time to be sure that you have included everything that needs to be in your document, you might add the additional step of a *kind-hearted edit.* This edit does not require that you make your client look good, that you be flattering, or that you be dishonest. Rather it requires that you stick with the useful facts, and that you be careful to avoid judgments that are more opinionated than clinical.

Clinical documents should not reveal whether or not you like your client. Even when clients' choices or actions do not speak well of them, you should not add your *personal* opinions to clients' records. It may be difficult to withhold your opinion if you are assessing someone who, for example, injured a family member. Nevertheless, your stance must remain objective. When all is said and done, you must be fair, and you must show respect. This is essential.

Types of Clinical Writing. In the student writing section of this chapter you will find examples of a letter and memo, two types of writing that therapists regularly write when they need to consult with other health care professionals. In this first section of the chapter, I have created (using fictitious characters and information) three other common clinical documents: (1) intake notes (more formally called an "initial assessment"), (2) progress notes, and (3) an official clinical report.

When composing "intake notes," psychologists use a standardized form to ensure that all of the usual topics are addressed. The therapist must also avoid making any premature judgments, so therapists try to be as objective as possible in recording what clients say and what we observe.

"Progress notes" are the least structured of all clinical documents. Clinical psychologists write progress notes to themselves. Progress notes are like a series of answers to unwritten questions that the therapist knows to ask (are there signs of depression? of abuse? of dementia?). The two progress notes produced in this chapter record "Jane Doe's" first two visits with her therapist. In this case, Jane Doe's relatives described symptoms that would lead her therapist to ask about appetite, self-esteem, history of mental illness, substance abuse, etc.

At the end of the second progress note, notice the shift in the tone. The paragraph that begins with the words "Jane is positive. . . ." uses the answers to the unwritten questions in order to make a diagnosis. When Rose first brought her mother for treatment, she might have asked: "My mother's behavior has changed, and we are worried about her. What is going on with my mother?" The diagnosis is the therapist's answer.

The last part of the second progress note outlines an action plan. The goal of the progress note is to record the therapist's thoughts, moving from observation to diagnosis to a treatment plan.

In the "clinical report" you will see the same progression—from the presenting problem, to observations and assessment, to the conclusion and recommendations. Because the therapist cannot know who might read a clinical report, however, the therapist must include more detail, define technical terms, and explain procedures. Shortcuts do not work in the clinical report. The style of the writing in a clinical report tends to be impersonal and thorough. A therapist's clinical report is the most important document of record. It must reflect precision, objectivity, and respect for the client—all with the purpose of effective treatment for the client.

✓ *READING TIPS*

Try an experiment. First read these documents as if you are a psychologist, called in to consult with the primary psychologist and looking for information to help you understand Jane Doe's case. Then read as if you are the patient, Jane Doe. Ultimately you will understand these writing samples best if you can see them simultaneously through the eyes of the professional therapist and the eyes of the patient. You need to balance the expertise and objectivity of the former and the human individuality of the latter.

A Case History in Clinical Psychology

Mary VanderGoot

Initial Assessment ("Intake Notes")

Note that this is addressed to no one. I write these notes for myself only.

Date: 8/1/05

Client(s) Name: Jane Doe   **Age:** 76   **Units:** 2

Participants: daughter, Rose, present

Employee Assistance Program is a mental health referral system set up by an employer to allow initial referral of employees for assessment. Sometimes when there is an incident on the job the employer will require an employee to see the EAP for an assessment. This would be a mandatory EAP intake.

1. **Presenting Problem** (symptoms, duration, why now. **If Mandatory EAP**, address presenting problem, its relationship to job performance, and other work related issues):

   Family concerned about Cx's possible depression. Has shown recent signs of confusion. May now have difficulty living independently. Symptoms recent duration - not specified by family. May also have some complicated grief reaction following death of sister/best friend six months ago

Cx=patient. To help keep my objectivity, I do not use the patient's name in intake notes.

2. **Previous Mental Health Problems/Services:**

   None

3. **Physical Health** (underline remarkable areas only and detail below):

   medical   appetite   <u>activity</u>   sex

   <u>sleep</u>   <u>energy</u>   exercise   <u>other</u>

When writing for yourself, you must be brief and to the point; complete sentences are not necessary. This is my summary of what has been reported to me and what I have observed.

   Sleeping more during daytime; difficulty with night sleep

   Activity may be impacted by dementia

   Less social activities now than previously

4. **Medications:**

Rx=prescription

   Cx reports taking Rx for thyroid

   Daughter reports Cx takes Rx for heart

   Report unclear; there may be a problem with compliance

indicating whether there is evidence for the possibility of death

5. **Lethality** (ideation, attempts, plan):

   None - none - none

6. **Mental Status:**

   Appearance: immaculate   <u>well-groomed</u>   <u>neat</u>   casual   unkempt   sloppy

Anergic=low energy, inactive

WNL=within normal limits

Behavior: agitated restless relaxed anergic WNL
slightly passive in interview

Orientation: person: Y N place: Y N time: Y N
oriented X3

Insight: good fair poor questionable

Memory: short term: impaired unimpaired / long
term: impaired unimpaired

Speech: coherent intelligible unintelligible difficulty:
(_____)

Judgment: good fair poor questionable

Mood/affect: anxious depressed flat angry manic
tearful labile WNL

Intellectual functioning: below average average
above average

Perceptual Processes: intact not intact

Thought content: unremarkable problematic

Thought processes: unremarkable fragmented
perseverated paranoid

Homicide: none ideation intent plan

Suicide: none ideation intent plan

Motivation for treatment: good fair poor

Comments:

I hint at my uncertainty about how aware Jane is of the problems that have brought her into therapy.

*Cx cooperative but how fully aware of presenting
problem? Family is motivated for treatment, and she
agrees to their decisions for her.*

7. **Family of Origin/Developmental** (relationships, dynamics):

*Fifth born of six. Raised on farm. Older brother died
in WWII. Other three siblings deceased: brother, lung
cancer; sister, complications of auto accident; sister,
stroke six months ago. This sister was best friend.
Younger brother lives in Ohio.*

8. **Present Marital & Family Relationships:**

This is a fairly dramatic moment during the session with Jane and Rose, but I refrain from stating anything more than summarizing the simple facts that I observe.

*Widowed for 22 yrs. Married at 18. Daughter
suggests Cx's husband was alcoholic. Cx downplays
this and emphasizes he was a good provider. Cx had
four children; one died at age four. One son lives in
AZ, other son lives in CA. Daughter Rose and her
children are Cx's primary family system.*

9. **Family Mental Health/Substance Abuse History:**

*Not significant overall, some history of alcohol abuse
by deceased spouse.*

10. **Alcohol/Drug Problems** (blackouts, overdoses, withdrawal, consequences, other adverse effects, impact on family and friends, cultural factors):

Limited social use in past. Some self-medicating for sleep difficulty recently. Alcohol removed from home; Cx agrees not to use alcohol. No history of using controlled substances.

11. **Physical/Sexual Abuse/Trauma:**

None

12. **Education:**

High School

13. **Employment** (current, patterns, problems, military):

Retired. Has been homemaker. Seven years employment doing billing for insurance agent.

14. **Support Systems** (friends, spiritual):

Strong family support by daughter and her children. Less contact with friends recently.

15. **Finances:**

Adequate and managed by family.

16. **Legal/Arrests:**

None

17. **Other Information/Diagnostic Impressions & Strengths:**

Family may need help evaluating current living situation
Provisional Dx: 309.28

18. **Recommendations & Referrals:**

See physician to review for Rx
Assess re: appropriate medication for depression
Evaluate for dementia, stroke, organicity

> Dx=diagnosis. Diagnoses in mental health use the *Diagnostic and Statistical Manual of Mental Disorders,* which is published by the American Psychiatric Association. Each diagnosis has a number. This one (309.28) is a diagnosis called "Adjustment Disorder with Mixed Anxiety and Depressed Mood." What distinguishes Adjustment Disorders is that they are usually in response to a life circumstance that causes stress.

Progress Notes

> Describing the scene as if in a story helps me to remember the details that may later help in diagnosis.

Jane Doe

August 1, 2006, 9:00–10:00 am, First Session

Present: Jane Doe and her daughter, Rose

Jane Doe is a 76-year-old female presenting with signs of depression. Neatly dressed, walks with a straight and steady gait, and makes good eye contact. She is accompanied by her daughter, Rose, who appears to be more concerned about Jane's well being than Jane herself is. Rose feels that her mother's behavior has declined, and the family would like to have an assessment of Jane's condition.

> Since these are notes for myself, I include my interpretation of the situation, but I also am careful to qualify my comments by saying that this "appears" to be the case.

Jane admits to some feelings of sadness, denies that she is anxious or has been in the last thirty days or during the last year. She denies that she has ever had hallucinations, violent thoughts, assaultive behavior, or thoughts of suicide. She denies any history of abuse or domestic violence. She does admit that recently she sometimes feels confused and that her memory and concentration are not as good as they used to be. She says that this has not happened before in her life. Her daughter claims that the decline in her concentration and clarity of thought is recent, and that it has been noticeable during the last year. Rose reports that she frequently calls her mother during the day and finds that her mother has been sleeping. She also reports that her mother has lost weight.

> This is an example of a response from Jane to a question that any professional therapist would ask of a patient who was presenting signs of depression.

> Almost every verb in this paragraph indicates that I am paraphrasing what Jane and Rose have said.

Jane will reschedule for an individual visit next week to continue history and assessment.

Jane Doe

August 7, 2006, 9:00–10:00 am, Second Session

Present: Jane Doe

Jane reports that she has withdrawn from friends and prefers to stay at home. Jane makes statements that suggest that she does not feel that anyone needs her: "It probably won't turn out anyway." "There is no one who would care anyway." "It doesn't matter." Jane says that she has lost interest in cooking and sometimes does not prepare food for herself. Her appetite is poor.

> Using quotations rather than paraphrasing helps me to remain objective. My professional judgment comes in my choice of what quotes I choose to record.

During a brief cognitive assessment Jane showed memory for events in the distant past and in the previous week. She knew the name of the city where her son lives and could describe his house. She reports her own age, the current date, the season of the year, her address, and how long she has lived there She could not add a column of six two-digit numbers. She could not describe the way from her house to her daughter's. She could not tell when the mail is delivered to her house. When asked if it is delivered in the evening she said, "Maybe." She knows that she gets the newspaper, but she does not know what she does with old ones. She could not explain how or where she would do laundry or wash dishes. In summary, she has difficulty with computation and sequencing. She has no obvious problems with memory.

> I come to this conclusion by asking Jane about common events in her life and observing her thought process as she formulates an answer. Recording this string of observations in my records makes them work as a brief assessment.

Jane is positive for five criteria of depression. No history of mania, melancholia, cyclothymia, schizophrenia, delusional disorder, or psychosis reported. Provisional diagnosis: Major Depressive Disorder, Single Episode. Rule out dementia, disorder due to other organic cause, substance abuse.

> In this paragraph my tone changes as I move from recording what I observe to making a diagnosis.

Treatment Plan:

1. Med review by physician.
2. Assess for antidepressants.
3. Assess for stroke or organic causes of cognitive decline.
4. Psychotherapy to explore grief reactions.
5. Assess for alcohol use and education re this.
6. Family involvement in providing temporary support in living situation.
7. Family commitment to reassess independent living in three months.

Clinical Report

Name: Jane Doe

D.O.B or SS #: SS: 123–45–6789

Date of Assessment: August 1 and 7, 2006

Means of Assessment: Case history and clinical interview

Reason for Referral: Family concerns with client's decline in functioning

> The report is not addressed to anyone in particular. That is because so many different people might read it.

Presenting Problem

Mrs. Jane Doe came to an initial meeting at the urging of her daughter, Rose. In this interview Rose reported that the family is concerned because Mrs. Doe has not been taking care of her home. Rose describes it as "messy" and says that her mother has always been a very responsible and tidy homeowner in the past. In preparation for this interview Rose had prepared a written list of "recent problems." Included on this list were the following: although her mother has been a non-drinker in the past, there were two empty wine bottles in the trash when she emptied it for her mother. Utility bills have not been paid consistently. Mrs. Doe drove into the side of the garage when she was bringing the car inside late one evening. Mrs. Doe has locked herself out of the house and on one of those occasions appears to have lost both her house keys and her car key.

> This first paragraph of the report shows two features that are different from my progress notes: more detail from my notes and a more impersonal tone. It is mostly summary, with a couple of key words in quotes.

History

Much of the history and description of the presenting problem were offered by Rose in the initial visit. Mrs. Doe did not voice concerns about herself, but she also did not disagree with anything that Rose was saying. It was clear to Mrs. Doe that the appointment was for her, and she did not object to seeing a psychologist, although she did state that this was something that she has never done before.

This is a word I use frequently. I report, as paraphrase, what a patient says; I do not interpret or analyze except as is necessary to make a diagnosis.

Born in 1928, Mrs. Doe is currently seventy-six years old. She was the fifth born of six children and was raised in Michigan where her family owned and ran a farm. She reports that her childhood was happy, although she remembers working hard and that the family had limited financial means. Her one older sibling was a brother who died while serving in the military during World War II. In Mrs. Doe's description of her childhood this stands out by far as the most difficult family event.

Of Mrs. Doe's remaining siblings the youngest, a brother, is still living and resides in Ohio. The other three siblings are deceased: her brother died of lung cancer at age forty-four, one sister died at age sixty-seven as a result of complications during surgery for a hip fracture which occurred during an automobile accident, and her other sister died of a stroke about six months ago at the age of seventy-three. Mrs. Doe describes this sister as her best friend; they were both widows and spent considerable time together. Both of Mrs. Doe's parents are deceased. Her father died of pancreatic cancer in his late sixties. After having several strokes her mother died at the age of eighty-one.

Mrs. Doe was married at age eighteen, and she and her husband had just celebrated their fortieth anniversary at the time of his death in 1982. He was sixty-one years old. She reports that he died of some kind of "sickness of the liver," but she is not able to say exactly the nature and the cause of it. Rose suggests that her father was alcoholic and his liver disease was a result of his drinking. Mrs. Doe agrees that her husband "drank more than was good for him," but she says that he was a quiet man and his drinking was not a problem for her or the family. He held a steady job, was a good provider, and "never treated her bad." Rose does not agree with her mother's evaluation of her father's drinking and says that except for bringing in an income her father left all of the responsibilities to her mother. In her words, "Mom did everything: Dad did nothing." Since the time of her husband's death Mrs. Doe has lived alone and independently in her own home.

During her twenties Mrs. Doe gave birth to four children. She reports that her youngest child was born with a "bad heart" and died at age four. She has two surviving sons: one lives in California and the other has recently retired and moved to Arizona. According to Mrs. Doe she has regular contact with her sons. Rose reports that her brothers visit their mother every few years, and their wives call her every few weeks. Rose is Mrs. Doe's oldest child and also her primary support. They see each other several times each week. Rose is married, has three grown children and four grandchildren. Mrs. Doe reports that she enjoys her grandchildren very much, particularly her two grand-daughters who live nearby and sometimes take her on errands.

> A detail like this helps to remind readers that Jane is a human being, to be treated with respect.

When asked about her education and work history, Mrs. Doe reports that she completed high school and has been a homemaker most of her adult life. For about seven years after her children were grown she worked part-time doing billing for an insurance agent. She describes this work as enjoyable because she liked the contact with people. She discontinued the work because she "got too busy" as she describes it. Rose says that her mother became busy because she was providing childcare when her granddaughters were working.

Assessment

Mrs. Doe's health history was somewhat unclear during her initial interview. She does report that during the last fifteen years she has taken something for "thyroid," but she was not able to tell the name of the medication. She claims that she has run out of it. Rose reports that her mother is "supposed to take three pills everyday," and that two of them are for her heart. Rose is concerned that her mother has not been taking her medication recently.

Because Rose does not feel that Mrs. Doe can drive safely in her present condition she has taken away her keys, and Rose's husband has disabled the car so that it cannot be driven. Rose reported this in Mrs. Doe's presence, and Mrs. Doe did not object. In fact she said that she does not feel confident driving now.

It is not clear whether the incident involving damage to her car and the garage occurred when Mrs. Doe was using alcohol. According to Rose, it could have occurred after Mrs. Doe drank wine in the evening to help her sleep, and then noticed that she had not put the car inside. Rose does not believe that there have been any occasions when her mother has taken her car out on the street after she has been drinking. Mrs. Doe has not used alcohol socially in the past. She has kept some in the house to serve to her guests, but she has always been outspoken about drinking and driving. There is no longer alcohol in the house, and because Mrs. Doe will not be driving and does all of her grocery shopping with Rose it is unlikely that Mrs. Doe will be able to replace her supply of alcohol. She agreed willingly that she will not drink.

While Mrs. Doe does admit that she has been having difficulty sleeping, she tends to attribute it to warm summer weather. She does not recognize that there is a problem with her housekeeping. Recently she has had less contact with her friends and neighbors; she says that she would rather stay at home and read or watch television. Rose suspects that Mrs. Doe is not reading much, and that her mother sleeps in front of the television.

With increasing frequency Rose finds that when she calls during the day her mother has been sleeping and seems confused when she answers the phone. Rose often suggests to her mother some activity or chore and her mother's responses are quite negative. "It doesn't matter." "There is no one here who would care anyway." "It probably won't turn out anyway." Mrs. Doe seems to have lost interest in cooking, doing handywork, or visiting with her friends by phone. These are all activities that she used to do with enthusiasm.

> I use these quotations so that readers can hear the client's degree of negativity and not have to depend on my attempt to describe that degree.

In a second interview during which Rose was not present, Mrs. Doe was asked for specific facts in the recent past and in the distant past. Her memory for events in the news in the previous weeks was quite good, she was able to report the name of the city to which her son has moved and was able to describe the sort of house in which he now lives. She accurately reported her own age, the current date, the season of the year, her address and how long she has lived there. When given a column of six two-digit numbers to add she was not able to complete the task. Similarly when asked what streets she takes to go from her home to her daughter's home she was not able to answer the question. She was not able to tell what time the mail is delivered to her house. When asked if it is delivered in the evening she replied, "maybe." She was able to report that she receives a newspaper at her house, but she was not able to tell what she does with the old ones. She was not able to verbalize a sequence of activities for completing simple household tasks: for example, she could not explain what she would do if she wanted to do a load of laundry or wash the dishes.

Diagnosis and Summary

Mrs. Doe has symptoms of depression (sleep difficulty, low level of motivation, loss of confidence in ordinary tasks, cognitive impairment, withdrawal from social contact). It appears that she may have been using alcohol as a medication to help her sleep. There is some evidence that Mrs. Doe requires medications that have been prescribed in the past but which she is not taking with any consistency now. There is evidence also that she has cognitive impairment particularly with sequencing, computational tasks, and behavioral strategies. In comparison to her level of functioning one year ago there appears to be a decline in Mrs. Doe's ability to care for herself. Her family has legitimate concerns about

> Even in my diagnosis I try to remain cautious and not state possibilities as if they are facts.

her ability to function adequately in an independent living situation.

Recommendations

All of the report up to this point has been building toward these recommendations. They are the most important part of the report and have to be very specific.

1. That Mrs. Doe be referred to Dr. John Soandso for the following:
   a. A review of her current medications and her compliance taking them, particularly the thyroid medication.
   b. An evaluation of her need for an antidepressant medication to address sleep disturbances and her low motivation.
   c. An evaluation for dementia, stroke, or other organic conditions which may underlie her cognitive decline.
2. That Mrs. Doe continue in psychotherapy to address the following:
   a. Whether her depression is related to grief reactions following the loss of important persons and important roles in her life.
   b. Whether there is an issue with alcohol use. This can be assessed in the course of her psychotherapy and psycho-education may include family members.
3. That Mrs. Doe's family organize to support her regarding:
   a. The safety of her present living situation. While her medical condition is being evaluated some short-term assistance would seem advised. For example, a family member might stay with her at night, and help her with some housework, food preparation, and medications.
   b. The need for a reassessment in three months to determine if Mrs. Doe's level of self-care has improved or whether she needs a supported living environment.

Sincerely,
Mary VanderGoot, Ph.D.
Licensed Psychologist

READING RESPONSES

1. Use a metaphor to describe each of the three documents that Dr. VanderGoot provides: the Initial Assessment, the Progress Notes, and the Clinical Report. Describe why you chose the metaphor you did for each one. Then, attempt to find a metaphor that describes how the three pieces relate to each other.

2. The Initial Assessment contains information about Jane Doe that is arranged topically; the Progress Notes describe Jane Doe's behavior and abilities in a way that has a slightly narrative feel to it; the Clinical Report emphasizes the history of Jane Doe's life and thus relies heavily on narration. Which of these three documents seems most "objective" to you? What effect do you think the narrative organization has on the feel of objectivity?

3. Choose one adjective to describe Dr. VanderGoot's attitude toward Jane Doe. Provide quotations from her three documents to demonstrate the attitude you describe.

Notes on Grammar, Style, and Rhetoric: Source Attributors

The three primary documents in this chapter—the "Initial Assessment," the "Progress Notes," and the "Clinical Report"—are not aimed at exactly the same audience and do not seek to accomplish precisely the same purpose. Yet the three are strikingly similar in that they all have a large number of what many linguists call "attributors."

Attributors are phrases and clauses that writers use to introduce material that we have heard from others or that we have read in others' work. They include phrases such as *according to the doctor* and *in the client's words*. They also include clauses such as *the psychologist noted that* and *the caseworker suggested that*. Attributors can be associated with either paraphrase or quotation. An example of an attributor using paraphrase is *The psychologist said that the patient's response might be a complex grief reaction*. An attributor introducing a quotation is quite similar: *The psychologist said, "The patient's response might be a complex grief reaction."*

As noted above, in the three primary documents in this chapter, attributors play a prominent role. For example, in the "Initial Assessment," attributors introduce words from both the client, Jane Doe, and her daughter, Rose. At one point, we read that the "Cx [client] reports taking Rx [a prescription] for thyroid." At another point we read that the "Daughter suggests Cx's husband was alcoholic."

In the "Progress Notes," we learn more about Jane Doe, from both paraphrase and quotations. In the "Progress Notes" for August 1, we read that "She [Jane Doe] does admit that recently she sometimes feels confused and that her memory and concentration are not as good as they used to be. She says that this has not happened before in her life." In the "Progress Notes" for August 7, we find that "Jane reports that she has withdrawn from friends and prefers to stay at home." In the same set of progress notes, the psychologist includes some quotations to shed additional light on Jane's feelings and actions: "Jane makes statements that suggest that she does not feel that anyone needs her: 'It probably won't turn out anyway.' 'There is no one who would care anyway.' 'It doesn't matter.'"

In the third document, the "Clinical Report," we can find attributors in many sentences. In fact, it is easy to imagine using them as conversational tags, and re-casting part of this report as a script. Again, attributors introduce words that reveal important things about Mrs. Doe's actions: "According to Mrs. Doe she has regular contact with her sons" (463). Attributors also introduce words that reveal Mrs. Doe's feelings: "Mrs. Doe reports that she enjoys her grandchildren very much, particularly her two granddaughters who live nearby and sometimes take her on errands" (436–37). Finally, in this section attributors once again introduce words from Rose, who provides some of the explanatory framework for her mother's life: "Rose says that her mother became busy because she was providing childcare when her granddaughters were working" (437).

Why do you think attributors appear so often in documents associated with counseling and psychotherapy? Consider at least three points.

First, the primary purpose of this kind of writing is not to display the psychologist's intelligence, wit, interpretive ability, or writing style. The main point is to focus on the client: in this case to try to understand what feelings and actions have led Jane Doe's closest relatives to be concerned about her, to try to understand what has caused those feelings and actions, and to seek to find helpful responses to those causes. In such writing, it is wise to keep the client as close to the center of readers' attention as possible. And probably the most effective way of doing that—short of videotaping her—is to refer to and cite many of her own words.

Second, doing that work is complex and challenging, so the psychotherapist must proceed cautiously. You can get a good idea of the strength of the forces moving psychotherapists to be cautious by looking closely at the paragraph labeled "Diagnosis and Summary." There you will find expressions such as "It appears that," "she may have been," "There is some evidence that," "There is evidence also that," and "there appears to be." This is a paragraph with a very guarded tone. Therefore, in a situation in which it is truly challenging to understand what lies behind a woman's not entirely healthful feelings and actions, perhaps the best response is to try to get as close to the roots of those feelings and actions as possible. And that can be done by focusing at length on her own words.

A closely related point is that if a psychotherapist makes an error in the work of diagnosing and treating, he or she can in fact do harm to people, sometimes significant harm. Patients who have gone through damaging experiences because of misdiagnoses are sometimes inclined to sue the person or persons responsible for the faulty diagnoses and treatments. Thus the attributors and all the client's words that they introduce also function potentially to decrease legal liability. They take the focus off the therapist as an interpreter and medical agent and put that focus on the client's detailed descriptions of her own feelings and actions. In that situation, a particular therapist could defend the prescribed course of treatment by saying something like "Look at all these detailed and specific symptoms as laid out by the client herself. Doesn't it seem as if the evidence points overwhelmingly to the kind of disorder that the patient was treated for?"

In Your Own Writing . . .

You might never be asked to write anything like the three primary documents in this chapter. But in the message that these documents convey of great respect for and care with others' words, these documents strongly reinforce two points that we hear often but probably do not take seriously enough:

- Whenever you quote others' words, quote the words accurately, and include enough words to ensure that the point you are borrowing is not distorted.
- If you cite others' words, attribute the citations clearly and fully.
- Generously and accurately use attributors ([the source] claims, concurs, affirms, denies, reports, suggests, etc.) when summarizing, paraphrasing, or quoting.

STUDENT WRITING IN PSYCHOLOGY

Introduction by Janette Curtis, psychology major

The Assignments. When Dr. VanderGoot contacted Ben Fiet and me (both senior psychology majors) about helping with this chapter, we were happy that she was letting us use the same file notes that she used for her parts of the chapter, but we did not know that we would be using them to write a memo and letter. We had written clinical observations and traditional research papers, but the memo and letter assignments asked us to practice another type of professional writing in psychology.

We had to read the case files, summarize the key issues, and then imagine ourselves writing to a particular audience to ask for help with the case. Ben wrote a letter to a doctor, asking for medical advice, and I wrote to a fellow therapist in our hypothetical office to ask for a consultation.

The Content: Letter of Referral. The letter gives just enough of the clinical history to explain to Dr. Soandso why Ben (the therapist) wants a physical exam for Jane Doe. It then lists the four questions that Ben hopes that a physical exam will help to answer.

The Content: Memo. My memo asks for advice on the same four questions that Ben's letter asks about. The big difference is in style, since the memo is written to a fellow worker in the same office. Asking these questions of health care professionals reminds us that decisions about treatment combine physical and psychological points of view.

Learning to Write in Psychology. Each of those assignments presented the same pair of challenges: (1) to find the right way to ask questions of each particular audience, (2) to figure out the right questions to ask. So we had to think like professionals in terms of the ways we spoke to other professionals—in the language of the business of psychology. You have to respect your sources when you are asking them questions just as much as you do when you report their answers. Neither of us thought that a one-page paper would be so hard, but we were wrong.

I wondered: how do I write professionally—that is, concisely—and not come across as rude? In the professional world time is limited and valuable. I needed to politely ask for insight but also make it easy for my colleague to answer my questions without wasting time trying to figure out what I was asking or why. With that in mind, I knew I had to get to the point. Having to get to the point taught me that a psychologist writes for a specific purpose—to make good decisions about treatment.

Creating Change through Writing in Psychology. Writing can sometimes, especially at the end of a semester when many assignments are due, seem like just another huge undertaking that needs to be completed only for a grade. Only your professor is going to read and care about it. This should *not* be the case, but it probably will be unless you understand that your assignments really can help you to learn skills that you can someday use to create change.

Writing the memo and letter of referral reminded us that no individual professional has all the answers. Memos and letters are for the explicit purpose of exchanging ideas and creating change. It is only though dialogue and the exchange of ideas—and respecting one another's ideas—that we are able to gain greater understanding and provide better diagnoses and treatment plans.

Letter of Referral

Family Counseling
1234 Any Street
Anytown, USA 12345

August 1, 2005

John D. Soandso, MD
1234 Main Street
Anytown, USA 12345

Dr. VanderGoot pointed out that the two addresses and the date at the beginning of a letter remind us that the letter is about an exchange of information between two professionals in order to accomplish a task efficiently—for the patient's sake. The formality of the letter also shows respect for a fellow professional.

Dear Dr. Soandso:

I am writing to you today on behalf of Jane Doe. She was recently referred to me for psychological counseling because her family has become concerned for her health. I am requesting that you meet with her for a consultation.

She is seventy-six years old, lives alone, and because of the decrease in social, physical, and cognitive functioning observed by her family, they have sought medical and psychological advice. Mrs. Doe has been prescribed three drugs to be taken daily, two for her heart and one for her thyroid. Her daughter, Rose, fears that Mrs. Doe is not taking her medications. Rose has observed evidence of alcohol consumption, lackadaisical maintenance of her house, and general loss of social interest. Mrs. Doe appears to suffer from memory loss, depression, cognitive impairment and a general decline in her ability to take care of herself.

Even in this letter the writer has to show that the family's observations, not the therapist's judgments, are primary.

I am requesting a physical examination of Mrs. Doe to determine the following:

1. Whether Mrs. Doe's decline in condition can be attributed to her neglect of medication use, particularly the thyroid medication.
2. Whether Mrs. Doe suffers from an organic depression and would benefit from antidepressant medication(s).

> In my first draft, I listed these without numbers and just as part of the paragraph. The accessible visual design of the revision clarifies why I made the change.

3. If Mrs. Doe has suffered from stroke(s), dementia, or other organic precipitators of her cognitive decline.
4. Whether Mrs. Doe's alcohol consumption has negatively affected her health.

I hope this brief summary is sufficient. If you require a more comprehensive history, or if there is any way I can be of service to you in this regard, feel free to contact me. Thank you very much for this consultation.

Sincerely,
Benjamin Fiet
Therapist

> Because most people use e-mail for memos, they make a convenient electronic record.

Memo to Colleague Requesting a Consultation

Family Counseling
1234 Any Street
Anytown, USA 12345

To: Dr. Carin Finity
From: Janette Curtis
Date: August 1, 2004
Subject: Referral of Jane Doe

> Since I'm writing to someone that I know, it's easier for me to just get straight to the point.

Thanks for agreeing to see Mrs. Jane Doe for a consultation. These are my questions:

- Do you think that Mrs. Doe's decline in functioning is related to her not using the medications previously prescribed for her, more specifically the thyroid medications?
- Do you think that the difficulty she has been having with sleep could be related to depression? Please evaluate her for an antidepressant medication.
- Could you assess Mrs. Doe for dementia, stroke or other organic conditions, which may underlie her cognitive decline? Are her symptoms related to a depressive disorder or another medical condition?
- Do you see any evidence that Mrs. Doe has an alcohol problem that could also be causing some of the symptoms related to depression and cognitive decline?

Thanks again for your consultation on this case. If you need any more information from me, let me know. I would be grateful for a response within ten days.

READING RESPONSES

1. Read the Letter of Referral carefully and make a list of information that is attributed to a particular person. How often does the author attribute information to himself?
2. In the Memo, Janette asks for the professional opinion of a colleague on four questions she has about her client, Jane Doe. The memo is so tightly focused that it contains little more than the four questions. What effects do you expect that that tight focus will have on her colleague's response?
3. In the Letter of Referral and the Memo, the authors use questions to focus the reader's attention on the specific information that they're asking for. How do you think these questions will function for the reader?

PUBLIC WRITING IN PSYCHOLOGY

Introduction

Many organizations attempt to keep their work in the public eye by issuing "press releases." These tell the stories that the organization hopes are newsworthy. News media frequently use press releases as the basis for their reports. A press release is therefore part news and part public relations.

The American Psychological Association (APA) issued this press release. As the most important organization of psychologists and the publisher of the premier journals in psychology, the APA sends out press releases that summarize research reports, bringing specialized professional research to public attention.

The press release also practices psychologists' traditions of representing the words of others through paraphrase (see paragraph 3 of the press release) and quotation (third paragraph from the end, beginning, "The independence of social network size . . . "). And the authors of the research being summarized are shown the respect of not only being named, but one is even called a "pioneering health psychologist."

The press release, on the physical effects of loneliness in college students, uses standard press-release rhetoric. It provides a synopsis of the research report, giving-credit to the researchers (the sources for the press release) and stating the findings. It makes no mention of hypotheses, research methods, statistical analyses. It simply summarizes the news for the public. It is presented in a form the public can understand, but it also carries a tone of formal respect for the authority and importance of the research and researchers.

Press Release: First-Year College Students Who Feel Lonely Have a Weaker Immune Response to the Flu Shot
Loneliness and social network appear to make independent contributions to immunity.

American Psychological Association, May 1, 2005

WASHINGTON – A new study at Carnegie Mellon University in Pittsburgh confirms how college challenges both mind and body, by demonstrating that lonely first-year students mounted a weaker immune response to the flu shot than did other students. The study appears in the May issue of *Health Psychology*, which is published by the American Psychological Association (APA).

The research team, headed by doctoral student Sarah Pressman and pioneering health psychologist Sheldon Cohen, PhD, also found that social isolation, measured by the size of a student's social network, and feelings of loneliness each independently compromised the students' immunity. Thus both objective and subjective aspects of social life appear related to health.

In the multi-faceted study, 37 men and 46 women, mostly 18–19 years old, were recruited in their first term at Carnegie Mellon. They got their first-ever flu shots at a university clinic and filled out questionnaires on health behavior. For two weeks starting two days before vaccination, they carried palm computers that prompted them four times a day to register their momentary sense of loneliness, stress levels and mood. For five days during that period, they also collected saliva samples four times a day to measure levels of the stress-hormone cortisol.

To assess loneliness, the students took questionnaires at baseline and during the four-month follow-up. Researchers calculated social-network size at baseline by having the students provide the names of up to 20 people they knew well and with whom they were in contact at least once a month.

The researchers assessed blood samples drawn just before the flu shot and one and four months later for antibody levels, which indicated how well the students' immune systems mounted a response to the multi-strain flu vaccine, which included three different antigens.

Sparse social ties were associated at a level of statistical significance with poorer immune response to one component of the vaccine, A/Caledonia, independent of feelings of loneliness. Loneliness was also associated with a poorer immune response to the same strain—as late as four months after the shot. This supports the argument that chronic loneliness can help to predict health and well-being.

The independence of social-network size and loneliness as factors in immunity is supported by the observation that, says Pressman, "You can have very few friends but still not feel lonely. Alternatively, you can have many friends yet feel lonely."

The finding could also help to explain why first-year students tend to visit student health centers more than older classmates; they can be unmoored socially as they adjust to their new circumstances.

Researchers will continue to study these interrelated variables to isolate the specific pathway by which social factors can alter immunity. Among other things, they speculate that stress may be a go-between because loneliness is "stressful and stress impairs health." In any case, the findings reinforce the knowledge that social factors are important for health, in part because, says Pressman, "they may encourage good health behaviors such as eating, sleeping and exercising well, and they may buffer the stress response to negative events."

Article: "Loneliness, Social Network Size and Immune Response to Influenza Vaccination in College Freshman," Sarah D. Pressman, MS and Sheldon Cohen, PhD, Carnegie Mellon University; Gregory E. Miller, PhD, University of British Columbia; Anita Barkin, DrPH, CRNP, Carnegie Mellon University; Bruce S. Rabin, MD, University of Pittsburgh; John J. Treanor, MD, University of Rochester; *Health Psychology*, Vol. 24, No. 3.

READING RESPONSES

1. This is a press release from the American Psychological Association, but it highlights work done by a group of researchers. Why would the APA publish such a press release? How does it benefit the organization?
2. List all the strategies that the APA writer uses to show respect for the researchers who conducted the study. How are the researchers likely to respond to this press release?
3. The APA writer uses summary, paraphrase, and quotation to describe the study on students' resistance to flu viruses. Note an example of each in the text and note how the writer demonstrates respect for the researchers in the example.

MORE WRITING IN PSYCHOLOGY

Introduction

The report that follows is about the positive effects of writing on both mental and physical health. You can easily imagine that such a report would catch the attention of people composing a textbook about writing. In fact the authors cite several different benefits of writing (including findings that college students' immune systems improved after using the prescribed writing methods), but the report presents other lessons as well.

The report gives you another example of a qualitative method of social science research, using a case-study method that is a standard practice in qualitative research (other qualitative research appears in the chapters on writing in political science, sociology, and nursing). But, in their research review, the authors also refer to quantitative studies, which produce statistically measured results. So you can compare methods that are typical in the social sciences.

Reading the "FEW Case Illustration" section of the report recalls the report on Jane Doe in the first part of this chapter. Some of the same strategies (using quotations) and even some of the same language ("Mary reported") appear in both writing samples. Psychologists, whether in the clinic or the research lab, respect their sources and represent them fairly and accurately. In sum, this report of research will help you to see what common features (including the chapter's portable rhetorical lesson) bridge the worlds of clinical psychology and traditional published psychological research.

Focused Expressive Writing as Self-Help for Stress and Trauma

Joshua Smyth and Rebecca Helm

Journal of Clinical Psychology/In Session 2003, 59: 227–235

[Abstract] In the therapy process, the process of disclosing about stressful or traumatic events is often considered essential. One such manner is through focused expressive writing (FEW) about stressful or traumatic experiences. FEW is related to improvements in health and well-being, across a wide array of outcomes and participant characteristics. As FEW requires limited involvement of other individuals, is relatively low cost, and portable, it has tremendous potential as self-help. In particular, FEW may be an effective means to reach populations unwilling or unable to engage in psychotherapy. A case illustration of FEW is presented. Evidence and future directions for FEW as self-help are reviewed.

Keywords: writing; self-help; trauma; stress; narrative; coping; health

The expression of emotions has historically been an integral part of psychotherapy. Beginning with Breuer and Freud, most theoretical orientations engage the patient to identify, label, and disclose their stressful experiences (Smyth & Greenberg, 2000). Additionally, clients appear to believe disclosing is an important role of therapy as well—much of what a client says during therapy discloses personal information about the client (Stiles, 1995). Researchers and clinicians have been exploring alternative ways an individual can disclose outside of the therapeutic process, yet still receive benefits similar to disclosing in therapy.

One such avenue of expressing powerful emotions is through writing, be it biographical, a letter, poetry, and so on. The concept of writing within the context of therapy is not new; therapists have used journal writing for a variety of goals for many years. Progoff's (1977) method has been widely taught and used as an intensive journaling process designed to bring the conscious and unconscious selves together (Smyth & Greenberg, 2000). At this point, however, there is no known empirical research that has examined the effectiveness of this journaling method. Such research support is, of course, critical to provide evidence that writing can facilitate improvement beyond that attributable to control (or placebo) conditions. Within the context of self-help, we need to examine if writing can be effective outside of a therapeutic relationship.

Focused Expressive Writing

One recent line of inquiry has examined if focused expressive writing (FEW) may help individuals process negative emotions related to stressful and/or traumatic experiences. Furthermore, this line of research has examined if such FEW can improve health and well-being for individuals not in psychotherapy (Lepore & Smyth, 2002).

FEW involves asking participants to write about their deepest thoughts and feelings regarding the most stressful or traumatic event of their entire life. Typically, participants are brought into a research setting for several (typically three to five) sessions, usually on consecutive days. In these sessions, participants are asked to write about their assigned topic continuously for 20 to 30 min without regard to spelling or grammar.

In research studies, an attention and activity matched control group is used. The control group is asked to write, for the same duration and following the same protocol, about an emotionally neutral topic. By way of example, these control group instructions might focus on a "time management" exercise that entails writing about the participant's activities during the previous week, activities during the previous 24 hr, plans for the upcoming 24 hr, and plans for the upcoming week (over four consecutive sessions, one time frame each session).

In contrast to this unemotional writing, the treatment group is asked to write about the most traumatic experience of their entire life. The instructions generally are based upon:

> For the next four days, I would like for you to write about your very deepest thoughts and feelings about the most traumatic experience of your entire life. In your writing, I'd like you to really let go and explore your very deepest emotions and thoughts. You might tie your topic to your relationships with others, including parents, lovers, friends, or relatives, to your past, your present, or your future, or to who you have been, who you will be, or who you are now. You may write about the same general issues or experiences on all days of writing or on different traumas each day. All of your writing will be completely confidential.

Participants are asked to explore the issues related to the event they are describing without stopping, and to continue to do so until they feel as though they have exhausted all they could explore. Participants are instructed that, if during the 20- to 30-min writing session they feel they have no more to write, they are to continue exploring topics related to the event described in their writing or to move on to additional stressful or traumatic topics. Following FEW and the control writing task, outcome measures are typically collected three to six months postwriting and examined for reliable between-group differences. That is, does the FEW group show relatively greater improvements over time after writing than does the control group? Accumulating evidence suggests that this is, in fact, the case.

Research Review

We briefly describe some of the studies examining the benefits of FEW to give a sense of the varied outcomes and individuals. Writing about stressful or traumatic events (relative to individuals who wrote about neutral events) has resulted in decreased absentee rates in university employees (Francis & Pennebaker, 1992) and greater likelihood of engineers becoming reemployed after a layoff (Spera, Buhrfeind, & Pennebaker, 1994). The benefits of FEW have been demonstrated in maximum-security prison inmates (Richards, Beal, Seagal, & Pennebaker, 2000) and in students (Pennebaker, 1997; Pennebaker, Kiecolt-Glaser, & Glaser, 1988) as well as many other groups. . . .

Pennebaker first explored the impact of the writing task on health in college students. Visits to the health center for a group of students were monitored for three months prior to the writing task and for three months afterward. Pennebaker discovered the students who wrote about their most traumatic event significantly reduced the number of visits to the health center after writing than those who wrote about a neutral topic (Pennebaker, 1997; Pennebaker & Beall, 1986).

To evaluate why the number of medical visits decreased, a follow-up study evaluated how the immune system responded to the writing task. After completing the writing task, students had their blood drawn to evaluate the response of the immune systems to the introduction of foreign agents. The students who wrote about a traumatic event had an increased number of t-helper lymphocytes following exposure than those who wrote about a neutral topic—a result suggestive of an improved immune-system response (Pennebaker et al., 1988).

To evaluate the impact of writing, Smyth (1998) completed a meta-analysis examining the benefits of writing in healthy individuals. . . . Improvements were observed across a variety of outcomes, including reported physical health, psychological well-being, role-functioning, and biophysical measures (immune measures, liver enzyme function, etc.). A notable exception to this broad influence was health behavior: There was no evidence that writing influenced health behaviors or self-care behavior (e.g., sleep, exercise, diet, drug/alcohol use, etc.). . . .

As healthy individuals appear to benefit from FEW, an important question was if less healthy individuals would benefit. To address this question, several recent studies were conducted on patients with physical illnesses. The first study examined the impact of FEW on individuals with chronic illness (asthma or rheumatoid arthritis; Smyth, Stone, Hurewitz, & Kaell, 1999). Results indicated that individuals with a chronic illness may show clinically significant improvements in disease severity after engaging in FEW (Smyth et al., 1999). Stanton and colleagues (2002) evaluated FEW in women with breast cancer. Results indicated that women using FEW had fewer medical appointments for cancer-related morbidity and fewer somatic symptoms. These and other data provide additional support that FEW can be beneficial for individuals with medical problems.

Mechanisms of Action

So why is FEW beneficial? Researchers had originally hypothesized that its benefits were due to participants being able to circumvent the personal and social constraints preventing them from disclosing their thoughts and emotions regarding traumatic experiences. By not disclosing, participants were forced to actively inhibit their thoughts and emotions surrounding the event. Disclosing about the stressful or traumatic event was thought to reduce the negative influences of inhibition (e.g., disinhibit) and therefore reduce the risk of illness. Perhaps surprisingly, the notion that the effect of writing is due to the reduction in inhibition has received little support from research. . . .

One view is that FEW helps the individual reorganize the memories involving the traumatic event. FEW may promote alterations in memory structure, making the memory more coherent and organized (Smyth & Greenberg, 2000). Research suggests that the reorganization of the traumatic memory into a narrative may be a critical factor in expressive interventions for traumatized individuals (DeSavino et al., 1993) and for FEW more generally (Smyth, True, & Souto, 2001). Indeed, research suggests that merely writing about an event may not be sufficient to produce benefit. Rather, the writing may need to be narrative in format (Smyth et al., 2001).

FEW as Self-Help

Little research has been conducted on FEW as self-help, per se. Yet, FEW seems to have tremendous potential. Writing does not require a trained professional or expensive equipment to be administered. It has the ability to reach populations not normally served by a therapist. Additionally, there are relatively few structural requirements needed for an individual to be able to complete it. The individual must be able to write, find a location where there will be no disturbances, and be able set aside the allotted time for three or four (often consecutive) days. . . .

People can be structured or guided in using FEW through workbooks. Traditionally, workbooks are comprised of written homework assignments geared towards a specific problem (e.g., depression, anxiety, anger). They are designed to increase the user's awareness, critically evaluate beliefs, and teach coping and problem solving strategies. A meta-analysis evaluated the effectiveness of workbooks on physical and mental health (Smyth & L'Abate, 2001). Results indicated that the use of workbooks did lead to significant health improvements for both mental and physical health (effect size $d = .30$). Greater effect sizes were found for mental health (effect size $d = .44$) than for physical health (effect size $d = .25$). Overall, this study provided evidence that the use of workbooks is related to improvements, and such improvements were not limited to any single outcome domain or participant characteristic (suggesting a likelihood of treatment effects generalizing to new samples and outcomes). . . .

Participants who completed a self-help workbook including FEW showed significantly greater improvements in lung function from baseline to follow-up (7.9% increase) in comparison to the participants who completed a (placebo) workbook (2% increase). These data suggest that self-administered manuals containing FEW may be beneficial and that individuals will be willing to complete them without extensive supervision (Hockemeyer & Smyth, 2002). Such manualized, self-administered approaches thus represent one promising avenue for the use of FEW as a self-help technique.

FEW Case Illustration

Presenting Problem/Client Description

Mary was a 38-year-old single woman, high school educated, never married, with one child. Mary presented with a previous diagnosis of posttraumatic stress disorder (PTSD) resulting from child sexual abuse, for which she had tried psychotherapy over 20 years ago. She reported that she found the experience of therapy negative and was not comfortable in continuing with that treatment. Mary had intermittent depression and anxiety over the next 20 years, reported that she had made two suicide attempts, and had continued difficulties in personal relationships. By her own standard, she felt that her life was "dark and lonely." Mary had experienced physical abuse in a recent relationship that "brought back up" her past abuse experiences. Mary currently reported a number of symptoms including intrusions, hyperarousal and anxiety, depression, difficulty sleeping, and a variety of (medically unexplained) somatic symptoms. She also reported difficulty in intimate relationships and problems holding continued employment. (She was currently unemployed.) Mary reported an unwillingness to engage in psychotherapy, but had tried attending a support group for battered women in the local community. Mary did not find this approach helpful, indicating that she was unwilling to disclose her previous sexual abuse history in the group format, and had stopped attending.

Case Formulation

Mary was conceptualized as having PTSD exacerbated by recent abuse. Primary therapeutic goals were to promote cognitive and emotional processing regarding her past and current abuse, reduce intrusions and the negative affect associated with thoughts of the abuse, and reduce psychological and physical symptomatology. Private sessions of FEW were selected to achieve these goals while avoiding the interpersonal aspects of disclosure Mary was concerned about.

Course of Treatment

Mary completed three sets of 20-minute sessions of FEW over three consecutive days. Writing was framed as a private, safe method of allowing her to disclose her deepest thoughts and feelings about her past and current abuse, as well as to explore how these events related to her life currently and how she envisions her life in the future. Each session was private, and she was urged to write without regard for style, grammar, and spelling, but to write continuously for the allotted time. Mary was provided writing materials and the following instructions:

> I would like for you to write about your very deepest thoughts and feelings about the most traumatic experience of your entire life. In your writing, I'd like you to really let go and explore your very deepest emotions and thoughts. You might tie your topic to your relationships with others, including parents, lovers, friends, or relatives, to your past, your present, or your future, or to who you have been, who you will be, or who you are now. You may write about the same general issues or experiences on all days of writing or on different traumas each day.

Mary was initially concerned about how to approach writing and appeared hesitant in general. In particular, she was uncertain how she should write and if she would be able to write for the full amount of time. After the first session, Mary was surprised at how much she had to write, and was motivated to continue with subsequent writing sessions. She returned punctually each day and completed all writing sessions without complication.

Mary started her first writing session with the statement "My Life is living hell." The writing in this first session was physically (i.e., handwriting) and cognitively chaotic and unstructured. Intense negative emotion, directed primarily at her mother, was the governing theme. Excerpts from the first session include (reproduced verbatim): "My Mother has A choice us oR BOB. She pick BOB" and "All BecAUSe My MotheR who pick MAN over heR KiD." This theme continued until the end of the first session when Mary moved to evaluate her relationship with her own daughter, writing: "When My DaughteR Was A teenage I had hard with heR. But NeveR gave up oN heR like my MotheR Did on Me." Over the course of Mary's writing sessions, the writing became physically more linear and structured, and showed greater psychological coherence. In the third session, Mary wrote: "No one in the world knows, but I want the world to know" and "I tried to turn to religion and to pray to lord. But what Justice is there? It too late." Mary concluded her final writing session with: "It has taken me twenty years to deal with this, to try to get my life in order. I guess it is pretty hard what I went through. Not easy to deal with, but I will get there."

Outcome and Prognosis

Upon completion of FEW, Mary felt that the writing had been very helpful and valuable to her. She reported that she felt more "peaceful" than she had in years, and that she was optimistic about her future. When evaluated six weeks later, Mary reported improved mood, better sleep, and reductions in anxiety and physical symptoms. Although she still reported abuse-related intrusions, she found them less distressing and felt they interfered less with her daily life. Mary was interviewing for new employment. At a six-month follow-up, Mary remained optimistic and continued to report fewer symptoms. Furthermore, she had started a new job and worked successfully for approximately three months. Finally, she reported that she was interested in starting a new relationship and was viewing that prospect optimistically.

Clinical Issues and Summary

As FEW appears to have many benefits, the future of writing and workbooks needs to be explored further. Because most of the research on workbooks and the writing tasks has occurred within laboratory settings, it is still unclear how effective writing may be in a more naturalistic setting. If the effectiveness is, at least partially, due to the research setting giving the workbook a "legitimate" authority, the effectiveness of self-help writing may be decreased. Despite this concern, it is difficult to believe that such a process entirely accounts for the benefits observed from FEW. Even if the effectiveness of FEW administered in a self-help format is somewhat less than in the laboratory setting, such improvements are quite significant.

FEW is related to improvements in health and well-being. These benefits occur across a variety of outcomes including physical health, psychological well-being, role functioning, and biological parameters. Furthermore, the benefits of writing do not appear to be limited by demographic characteristics. It is still premature, however, to make strong claims for the effectiveness of FEW as a self-help approach. FEW, however, is a self-help method with relatively few requirements. As widely available, low-cost self-help, FEW has the potential to greatly improve health and well-being, particularly among individuals who lack other treatment options.

Select References/Recommended Readings

DeSavino, P., Turk, E., Massie, E., Riggs, D., Penkower, D., Molnar, C., & Foa, E. (1993, August). The content of traumatic memories: Evaluating treatment efficacy by analysis of verbatim descriptions of the rape scene. Paper presented at the 27th annual meeting of the Association for the Advancement of Behavior Therapy, Atlanta.

Dominguez, B., Valderrama, P., Meza, M., Perez, S., Silva, A., Martinez, G., Mendez, V., & Olvera, Y. (1995). The roles of emotional reversal and disclosure in clinical practice. In J.W. Pennebaker (Ed.), *Emotion, disclosure, and health* (pp. 255–270). Washington, DC: American Psychological Association.

Francis, M.E., & Pennebaker, J.W. (1992). Putting stress into words: The impact of writing on physiological, absentee, and self-reported emotional well-being measures. *American Journal of Health Promotion, 6,* 280–287.

Greenberg, M.A., & Stone, A.A. (1992). Emotional disclosure about traumas and its relation to health: Effects of previous disclosure and trauma severity. *Journal of Personality and Social Psychology, 63,* 75–84.

Hockemeyer, J., & Smyth, J.M. (2002). Evaluating the feasibility and efficacy of a self-administered manual-based stress management intervention for individuals with asthma: Results from a controlled study. *Behavioral Medicine, 27,* 161–172.

Lepore, S., & Smyth, J. (2002). *The writing cure: How expressive writing promotes health and emotional well-being.* Washington, DC: American Psychological Association.

Pennebaker, J.W. (1997). *Opening up: The healing power of expressive emotions* (Rev. ed.). New York: Guilford Press.

Pennebaker, J.W., & Beall, S.K. (1986). Confronting a traumatic event: Toward an understanding of inhibition and disease. *Journal of Abnormal Psychology, 95,* 274–281.

Pennebaker, J.W., Kiecolt-Glaser, J., & Glaser, R. (1988). Disclosure of traumas and immune function: Health implications for psychotherapy. *Journal of Consulting and Clinical Psychology, 56,* 239–245.

Petrie, K., Booth, R., Pennebaker, J., Davison, K., & Thomas, M. (1995). Disclosure of trauma and immune response to a hepatitis B vaccination program. *Journal of Consulting and Clinical Psychology*, 63(5), 787–792.

Progoff, I. (1977). *At a journal workshop: The basic text and guide for using the intensive journal process.* New York: Dialogue H.

Richards, J.M., Beal, W.E., Seagal, J., & Pennebaker, J.W. (2000, February). The effects of disclosure of traumatic events on illness behavior among psychiatric prison inmates. *Journal of Abnormal Psychology*, 109(1), 156–160.

Rime, B. (1995). Mental rumination, social sharing, and the recovery from emotional exposure. In J.W. Pennebaker (Ed.), *Emotion, disclosure, and health* (pp. 271–291).Washington, DC: American Psychological Association.

Schoutrop, M., Lange, A., Brosschot, J., & Everaerd,W. (1996, June). The effects of writing assignments on reprocessing traumatic events: Three experimental studies. Paper presented at The (Non) Expression of Emotions and Health and Disease Conference, Tilburg, The Netherlands.

Smyth, J.M. (1998). Written emotional expression: Effect sizes, outcome types, and moderating variables. *Journal of Consulting and Clinical Psychology*, 66, 174–184.

Smyth, J.M., & Greenberg, M.A. (2000). Scriptotherapy: The effects of writing about traumatic events. In J. Masling & P. Duberstein (Eds.), *Psychodynamic perspectives on sickness and health* (pp. 121–164). Washington, DC: American Psychological Association.

Smyth, J.M., & L'Abate, L. (2001). Using workbooks to promote health: Examining their efficacy. In L. L'Abate & M. Torem (Eds.), *Distance writing and computer-assisted intervention in psychiatry and mental health* (pp. 77–92). Westport, CT: Ablex.

Smyth, J.M., Stone, A., Hurewitz, A., & Kaell, A. (1999). Effects of writing about stressful experiences on symptom reduction in patients with asthma and rheumatoid arthritis: A randomized trial. *Journal of American Medical Association*, 281, 1304–1309.

Smyth, J.M., True, N., & Souto, J. (2001). Effects of writing about traumatic experiences: The necessity for narrative structuring. *Journal of Social and Clinical Psychology*, 20, 161–172.

Spera, S.P., Buhrfeind, E.D., & Pennebaker, J.W. (1994). Expressive writing and coping with job loss. *Academy of Management Journal*, 37, 722–733.

Stanton, A.L., Danoff-Burg, S., Sworowski, L.A., Collins, C.A., Branstetter, A.D., Rodriguez-Hanley, A., Kirk, S.B., & Austenfeld, J.L. (2002). Randomized, controlled trial of written emotional expression and benefit finding in breast cancer patients. *Journal of Clinical Oncology*, 20, 4160– 4168.

Stiles, W.B. (1995). Disclosure as a speech act: Is it psychotherapeutic to disclose? In J. Pennebaker (Ed.), *Emotion, disclosure, and health* (pp. 71–92).Washington, DC: American Psychological Association.

READING RESPONSES

1. Review the instructions that the researchers give to their subjects about how to complete the FEW writing. How would you respond to these instructions? Would you feel you had been respected? Why or why not?

2. Many people engage in informal expressive writing by keeping a journal or a blog. Do you find yourself writing to focus your thoughts or express deep feelings? What form does that writing most often take?

3. If you were "Mary," the case-study subject, what would be your emotional response to the researchers' description of you and your writing? What would make you feel respected? What would make you feel disrespected?

WRITING ASSIGNMENTS

ASSIGNMENT 1: APPLYING THE PORTABLE RHETORICAL LESSON

Background: In "Focused Expressive Writing as Self-Help for Stress and Trauma" Joshua Smyth and Rebecca Helm describe the benefits that many people experience from writing about traumatic events using Focused Expressive Writing (FEW) strategies. They describe other research that establishes a theoretical framework for their own research, their methodology, and their results. And they conclude with a case study of "Mary," using Mary's own words to describe her, her experience with FEW, and the effect of FEW on her outlook on life. Smyth and Helm caution that "It is still premature, however, to make strong claims for the effectiveness of FEW as a self-help approach." Nevertheless, they conclude, "As a widely available, low-cost self-help, FEW has the potential to greatly improve health and well-being, particularly among individuals who lack other treatment options."

Your task is to assess the claims that Smyth and Helm make for Focused Expressive Writing by trying it yourself and keeping notes on your experience. In your assessment, you will summarize and quote from your own notes as a clinical psychologist might from her sessions with a client.

Follow the instructions that Smyth and Helm provide on pages 449–50 for a FEW session. Add to those instructions these:

- Before you begin writing, describe your stress level, your mood, and your attitude toward others.
- After you finish writing, describe the same things, noting in particular any changes you feel.
- After you finish writing, jot notes to yourself about the writing session itself: did you dive into the writing immediately or did you need to warm up to the task? Did the intensity of the writing vary? How would you describe the variation? What emotions did you feel as you were writing? What prompted those emotions (the topic you were writing about, the task of writing, the setting you were writing in, etc.)?

After you've completed at least three sessions of FEW, reflect on your experience overall. Take careful notes on your answers to these questions and any others that your experience prompts:

- Did it make you feel better? In what ways?
- What evidence in your life might be evidence of your feeling better?
- If it did not make you feel better, do you feel about the same or worse? In what ways?
- What evidence in your life might be evidence of your feelings?
- What part of the writing experience most contributed to how you feel?

After you've completed your reflections, analyze what you wrote during the FEW sessions, looking for connections among memories and emotions and how memories and emotions develop in the writing you did in each session. Then, determine your assessment of FEW, setting for yourself a research question like the following:

- What help, if any did FEW provide you? How valuable was the help it provided?
- How long lasting was the help it provided?
- How did your experience match those of the subjects in Smyth and Helm's experiments?

As you begin drafting, consider carefully which of your words you will use as evidence for your claims about FEW and how you will present them to the reader. Remember to focus on your analysis of the FEW method; you should not feel obliged to reveal any personal information in what you submit to your instructor.

[Note: Writing about your feelings, especially if you have experienced emotional trauma, can be upsetting. If this assignment is in any way emotionally difficult for you, you may want to seek professional help, perhaps from your school's counseling center. Ask your professor to provide an alternative assignment.]

ASSIGNMENT 2: MAKING CONNECTIONS

In this chapter you learned how clinical psychologists respect their client as they listen and record the client's life experience. Key to doing this work well is to record the "telling details," those that open a window to full understanding of how a client thinks or why she acts as she does. Victor Villanueva opens the section from *Bootstraps* in the English education chapter with a vignette rich in these telling details. He begins with a description of the characters in the scene and then describes the action in the present tense—as if it's unfolding before his eyes.

Your task in this assignment is to describe a scene like Villanueva does, using telling details so that a few significant details will give the reader a thorough understanding of the people in the scene, their relationship, and their reason for being at the scene.

To begin, select a place where you can watch people without being too obvious such as a dorm lobby, a coffee shop, or a sporting venue. Place yourself where you can discreetly take notes on people and their conversations: note how people dress, what they bring with them, how they hold themselves, and their conversation patterns with others. Record actual dialogue if possible.

After you have observed for a while, free-write questions about what you've observed such as: For what purposes do people gather here? What issues shape the relationship between people? What do people want from each other? Then, as a way of answering the questions that you've posed for yourself, draw some conclusions about the people you have observed and their relationship with others.

When you are ready to begin drafting, review your notes, questions, and free-writing to determine the central idea you want your reader to take away from your writing. Describe the scene so that the reader can intuit the central idea from the details you choose to include in your description.

ASSIGNMENT 3: DOING THE RESEARCH

Background: In her introduction to her clinical writing, Dr. VanderGoot notes that a psychologist's clinical notes can become public evidence in legal cases. How that occurs and how juries interpret that evidence is more complex than you might expect, and investigating that complexity can deepen your understanding of the rhetorical lesson for this chapter.

Your task for this assignment is to research one aspect of the role that expert testimony on mental health issues plays in legal cases.

To begin, select one of your library's research databases that cover the legal issues (consider asking a reference librarian to help you), and search for articles on expert testimony in general and the testimony of psychologists in particular. As you read a few, begin to track your curiosity and then use that curiosity to frame a research question about expert testimony on mental health issues (Re-read Dr. VanderGoot's introduction to get ideas for interesting questions). Use this research question to conduct a more specific search of secondary sources for information that will help you answer your research question.

When you are ready to begin drafting, write out a version of your research question that reflects what you have learned during your research. Answer that question with a thesis, and support your thesis with logical reasoning and evidence.

14

MARKETING:
MOTIVATING ACTION

In marketing, it may seem obvious how authors create change: marketers persuade people to buy things. But the work of marketing is far from that simple. First, marketing is much broader than just advertising or sales to people outside the company. While it's true that professionals in marketing focus on customers, they also must communicate clearly with "partner" audiences: employees, stockholders, investors, suppliers, consultants. In effect, professionals in marketing use writing to persuade people to "buy into" a company's mission or business goals. The goal of the marketing division of a major company is to align all communication so that what the consumer sees in an advertisement matches what the employees of a company believe about their product. Marketers must use a wide variety of strategies to accomplish this complex task.

Writers for not-for-profit organizations (like the one that is the subject of this chapter's second reading) have slightly different audiences; they need to communicate a clear vision of mission to donors, volunteers, and the organization's staff. Even individuals market themselves: much of what happens in "Facebook" or "MySpace" is personal marketing—communicating a vision (real or playful) of a person's identity; that's the game of self-marketing.

If you begin by recognizing the complex goals of marketing and then add the different audiences for marketing, you can understand the challenge, and why marketers are compelled to use every available means of communication.

➡ A Portable Rhetorical Lesson:

Using "All Available Means"

for a "Common Purpose"

This chapter offers both a concrete portable rhetorical lesson and a summary of the habit of seeking rhetorical lessons on your own. In Chapter 1 we cited Aristotle's definition of rhetoric: the art of discovering "all available means" of persuasion. In this chapter, we read the writing of marketing specialists, who, in order to effectively persuade their various audiences, are experts at using all available means of persuasion. These means include themes, graphics, running metaphors, visual design elements such as bullet points—*everything* that works. So, for example, on the first page of *One Common Purpose*, a drawing commands attention. A street sign for the intersection of "Main St." and "Wall St." represents competition in the public arena—Main St.—and profitability in the market—Wall St. Images of intersections, coordination of parts, alignment and integration of products, environments, and people appear throughout the reading, unifying the individual parts.

In other words, it is not enough to use all available rhetorical tools. All of the tools must work together to focus the audience on a unified vision of a recognizable and attainable goal. The rhetorical lesson, then, is to harmonize your use of all available rhetorical strategies.

Chapter Topics: Whether in the context of promoting sales or social services, the topic of the chapter is how we persuade people: how we persuade members of an organization to commit to a common vision, and how we persuade people outside of the organization to align themselves with the organization—buying products, donating money, volunteering time, etc.

To Think About . . .

Check out Subway's Web site, www.subway.com, and make a list of the different groups of people that the company targets on its homepage. How could you tell which audience the webpage was targeting? What information does the webpage use to attract each of those audiences? What techniques do they use to present that information to the targeted audience?

Now take a look at some profiles on myspace.com or facebook.com. How do individuals market themselves? What kind of "friends" are they targeting, and how do they appeal to their audience? Does the "marketing" appeal to you? Why or why not?

Also look at band profiles on MySpace. Since bands are trying to gain a following for business purposes, they do more intentional, self-conscious marketing. Find a band you like and analyze the audience they are targeting and their marketing strategies.

WRITING IN MARKETING

Introduction by Robert Eames, Professor of Business

In January of 2001, three very different companies found themselves in similar situations. All three were preparing for major changes. Bissell, a family-owned company known for its floor sweepers and deep cleaning carpet scrubbers, was contemplating a major move into the vacuum cleaner market, where it was virtually unknown. Apple Computers, the computer maker known for its Macintosh and iMac computers, had just launched iTunes 1.0 and was beginning to develop its own digital music players. Steelcase, the world's leading designer and manufacturer of office furniture, was weathering an unprecedented downturn in demand in their industry, which threatened their leadership position. A few short years later, Bissell was the number one brand in the entire floor care category. The iPod not only grew to dominate sales in the digital music player category—to most consumers it *was* the category. And Steelcase had enjoyed a major sales resurgence. Other than phenomenal sales success in their respective markets, what did Bissell, Apple, and Steelcase have in common? They all knew their customers well and communicated that knowledge throughout their companies. That is, they all had effective marketing plans.

Writing effectively in marketing requires finding and filling needs. Great marketers thoroughly understand their customers. In fact, great marketers are obsessed with learning anything and everything about their customers, including their wants and needs—and aligning customers' needs with company objectives.

To write successfully for a business audience, a writer must be able to answer several questions, including:

Who is the primary audience?
What do they already know?
What do I want the audience to do?
What is necessary to get them to do what I want them to do?

The companies then respond to the answers to these questions with effective rhetorical choices.

One Common Purpose (OCP), written for Steelcase, Inc., is a good example of a marketing document that answers these questions well and thus expresses the key elements of a business plan. As the global market leader in the early stage of what would become a severe and prolonged industry downturn, Steelcase needed to improve their product offering *and* cut costs in order to improve profitability and maintain their leadership position. Written as a confidential internal company document, *OCP's* initial audience consisted of the executive management team. The document was also intended for use by management throughout the company in divisions such as finance, marketing, engineering, design, operations, and administration.

The writers of *OCP* wanted the executive team and the entire organization to understand, approve, and execute the plan. The goal was to persuade employees in each part of the company not only to accept the plan but also to act on it. Like most good plans, *OCP* does three things that help create change: it provides *context*, *direction*, and *motivation*. These three functions are the *what*, the content, of the plan.

The *how* of the plan, or the strategies the writers used to perform these functions, is also critical. *OCP*, for example, makes extensive use of graphic images that represent key ideas of the plan. Take note of the graphics; they show how well the writers knew their audience, which is very visually oriented because of the design-driven nature of the furniture industry. The plan also demonstrates the sophisticated understanding of how the audiences process information and learn. The graphics help to create metaphors (images that evoke comparisons to related ideas). While the power of metaphors has long been appreciated by English majors and writers, scientists and marketers using brain scanning technology have recently learned that 95 percent of our thoughts, emotions, and learning occur unconsciously in metaphors. Good business writers know the metaphors that will resonate with their audience.

Now let's look at ways that the *what* (context, direction, and motivation) is communicated by the *how* (the rhetorical strategies). Good marketing plans provide readers with *context*—a clear picture of the current market situation—usually in the form of a situation analysis. These analyses tend to be very direct and economically written. Sentence fragments, tables, and bullet points are commonly used to summarize a great deal of analytical work that needs to be efficiently presented for a busy executive audience. In *OCP*, "The Big Picture" and the "Three-Year Business Plan" sections provide this context, using metaphors to establish the critical importance of product development. Important metaphors include (1) the intersection of Wall Street and Main Street, (2) the progressive graphics showing the growth in Steelcase's market from office furniture to a much larger "AFT" (combined architecture, furniture, and technology), and (3) the product "platforms" (the common rules for all products so that they coordinate across divisions). These metaphors then carry into the last section of *OCP*, the specific studio plans for architecture, furniture, and technology (only the furniture studio section is included here). The metaphors also increase the sense of unity and significance among employees who actually develop and launch products by connecting their work to the broader context of organizational goals and strategies.

OCP provides *direction* for Steelcase in two ways. First, "The Big Picture" and "Three-year Business Plan" sections provide a road map of strategies and tactics built around the four P's of marketing: Product, Price, Place, and Promotion. This helps management communicate, implement, and control strategies by clarifying employee's specific roles and responsibilities. Second, detailed "studio" plans help management anticipate potential problems and opportunities before they arise. As you read through the excerpts from the "Furniture Studio" plan, notice the connections back to the "Driving Goals" laid out in the "Three-year Business Plan," further enforcing the sense of a single direction.

Plans also provide *motivation*. For new companies or new parts of existing companies, plans might motivate investors by demonstrating just how well the management team knows the market. For an established company like Steelcase, marketers create plans not only to increase organizational alignment and commitment to a new strategic direction, but also to make decisions to allocate scarce resources to the best opportunities. The graphics in *OCP* target internal audiences in order to get and keep people on the same page. When people feel both a sense of need and a sense that they are part of a coordinated team, they gain motivation.

The various pieces of *OCP* are integrated, coordinated, and directionally aligned. That's good marketing and good writing.

✓*READING TIPS*

You need active eyes to read this chapter because writers use multiple rhetorical strategies at the same time. On each page, consider how the words and images support, compliment, and clarify one another. At the same time, pay attention to where you are in structure of the document. The "Big Picture" section, the "Three-year Plan," and the "Furniture Studio" zoom in on particular aspects of the plan. In this document, though, the writers repeat and reinforce dominant themes and images. Images of various intersected and integrated parts—for example, the "Main St. Wall St." image you see on the first page and the "AFT" plan—are metaphors that control the overall message of the business plan.

One
Common Purpose

Three-year Business Plan
Marketing and Product Development

December 21, 2001

Company Confidential

The Big Picture

If we were to do a balance sheet on the assets which support the delivery of product, and hence the delivery of value to our customers… the vast majority could be linked to products and therefore product development.

Because product development touches everything the business does – both today and tomorrow – there are few processes or outputs of any corporation that possess the same strategic importance. The results of product development here at Steelcase have a direct impact on our competitiveness and future profitability.

Product development is the future of any manufacturing company. What a company develops today will determine its revenue stream tomorrow. In essence, today's product development results are the first look at the company's financial future.

The company with the most competitive product wins on Main Street.

The company with the most profitable product wins on Wall Street.

Success is winning on both.

One reason for the simplicity of image and theme on this page is that this business plan has to appeal to a wide range of professionals in the company. It also has to unify all those people around a single message.

The Big Picture

Different No Longer

Historically, architecture, furniture and technology have been considered different from each other... separate and distinct elements. They were subject to *different* development disciplines and cared for by *different* professions; they required *different* purchasing methods.

Our research and experience, however, indicate that when architecture, furniture and technology are synchronized to the business objectives of the organization, people are more productive. And workplace synergy permits people and organizations to work better.

So it's time to help our customers switch focus... from the differences among architecture, furniture and technology, to their similarities and interrelationships and the value this can mean to their organizations.

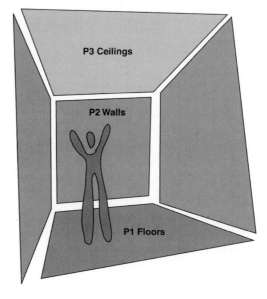

The harmonious integration of the three planes within the shell of a building.

> The plan offers the image, in the graphic, of integrated planes to counter the old "differences."

The Big Picture

AFT: Leveraging the Strengths of All Three

Architecture... the structural elements. Floors, walls, and ceilings, along with panels and post and beam, create and define the physical boundaries of the workplace – the elements of greater permanence. They determine individual and group work areas, create various levels of acoustical and visual privacy, and provide larger surface areas for information persistence.

To synchronize with furniture and technology... architectural elements require common dimensions and simple interfaces; they need to give users planning flexibility to relocate elements as needs change.

Furniture... the movable elements that exist within the three planes. Desks, tables, storage, and seating, along with panels and post and beam, set the tone for the environment, making the workplace more stimulating, more personal, and ultimately more productive. They help people work – individually and in groups – by providing the support and comfort needed to create and manage knowledge.

To synchronize with architecture and technology... furniture needs to be conveniently mobile and flexible.

Technology... is divided in two broad areas: appliances and infrastructure.

Appliances are tools: cell phones, Palm Pilots, notebooks, modems, Websigns, etc. Appliances often start out as stand-alone devices, but if they have broad appeal, they seek entree into the infrastructure.

Infrastructure is the delivery system that carries technology to every nook-and-cranny in the workplace; it crisscrosses the organization, distributing power, lighting, voice and data. Organizations depend on infrastructure to provide convenient access for communication and information sharing.

To synchronize with architecture and furniture... technology must accommodate emerging appliances and adapt to constant change.

Steelcase Inc. • December 2001 • Company Confidential

Reframing the market opportunity from furniture to the combination of architecture, furniture, and technology (AFT) was essential to gain support for the plan. The drawings portray the expanded opportunities: the top drawing shows the architecture, the second adds furniture, and the third adds technology. These graphics were also used in PowerPoint presentations.

The Big Picture

AFT Benefits

Why Customers Care

The workplace that seamlessly integrates architecture, furniture and technology enables people to focus on their work, connect with one another in meaningful ways, and share the knowledge and experience that ultimately ensures an organization's success. In addition, this integrated workplace helps "future-proof" the customer's investment.

Why Steelcase Cares

The effective implementation of AFT in the marketplace can uniquely differentiate Steelcase from our competitors. In addition, it can help us focus our investments on integrated solutions and develop new revenue opportunities for Steelcase and our dealers. It also allows us to continue building our brand.

Existing Building. *The Steelcase University Learning Center demonstrates the harmonious integration of architecture, furniture and technology within existing real estate.*

New Construction. *The Patterson Building is an excellent example of supporting users through a higher level of integration of architecture, furniture and technology in new construction.*

Steelcase Inc. • December 2001 • Company Confidential

The buildings pictured in these photos are well-known to Steelcase employees. They evoke images of expanded market opportunities, reinforcing the benefits of the plan.

The Big Picture	*Steelcase North America*

AFT: The Future and the Present

The idea of tying architecture, furniture and technology together is not unique to Steelcase. A number of our competitors, in fact, are laying claim to the same strategy. Our product development, therefore, must focus both on "catching up" to our competitors with more desirable features at lower price points, while providing innovative solutions that leap over competitive positions.

At a practical level, as well, we need to keep an eye on improving profit margins across the board to meet corporate targets.

While our current product offerings, development activities, and promotional tactics are intended to lay the foundation for establishing Steelcase as the market leader, we face critical challenges in the areas of product integration, pricing, communications, and dealer capabilities.

The volume of needed development demands that we develop products faster than we ever have before. Quicker teamwork and faster decision-making are essential.

It is also imperative that we effectively educate and energize our channel. The strength of Steelcase dealerships, aided by a well-trained Steelcase sales force can enable Steelcase to become the undeniable market leader in the AFT market.

Steelcase Inc. • December 2001 • Company Confidential

The plan recognizes challenges and risks and outlines them here. The frankness about potential trouble helps build team unity and motivation.

The Big Picture

Steelcase North America

Great Design Innovation Isn't Enough

Is it possible to have a successful business in which our products are designed separate and apart from manufacturing considerations? We don't think so.

First, design and innovation are not one in the same. Innovation is the commercial application of unique knowledge and skill that satisfies customers, thereby turning a profit.

So a truly innovative product solution is one in which both the customer and the producer are delighted with the results: the customer receives high value; and the producer receives good margins, sustains a competitive advantage, and thwarts competitive efforts to undermine investment.

In the interest of getting the most out of both design and manufacturing, we propose to have both disciplines work together under two imperatives:

> Design firms get paid to design stuff; that's how they make their money. Manufacturing firms get paid to make stuff; that's how they make their money.
>
> We need to do both.

1. Kit-of-Parts

Since we expect that customers will continue to ask for the ability to blend elements of one product line with another, we will implement a product strategy that moves away from discrete product lines to groups of product components that are systemically compatible with one another:

- To achieve greater flexibility to meet performance, visual, lifecycle-cost requirements
- To provide customers with exactly what they value
- To help migrate customers to the future, while leveraging their large installed base
- To support AFT strategy with Kit-of-Parts compatibility in the development of all architecture, furniture, and technology products

		Value	Performance	Premium
Architecture	Walls	☐	○	△
	Panels	☐	○	△
Furniture	Large Case Storage	☐	○	△
	Small Case Storage	☐	○○	△
	Desking	☐	○○	△
	Alternative Systems	☐	○	△
Seating	Primary Work Chairs	☐	○○	△△
	Support Chairs	☐	○○	△
	Alternative Postures	☐	○○	△
Wood	Systems	☐	○	△
	Seating	☐	○○	△
	Casegoods	☐	○○	△
Technology	Power	☐	○	△
	Network Connectivity	☐	○○	△
	Access Floors	☐	○○	△
	Lighting Alliance	☐	○	△

Steelcase Inc. · December 2001 · Company Confidential

> This section of the plan introduces the key initiatives: the integrated "Kit-of-Parts" and the "Product Platforms." They set the stage for the studio plans that follow.

The Big Picture

Great Design Innovation Isn't Enough *(continued)*

2. Product Platforms

Gone are the days when new Steelcase product lines are developed around their own proprietary dimensions, interfaces and aesthetics. Our new product strategy will require that all new products adhere to the guidelines of foundational Steelcase platforms that:

1. Establish a small number of "rules" that permit broad design interpretation and materials diversity
2. Adhere to manufacturing criteria established in collaboration with manufacturing norms

Conforming to platform guidelines, will allow us to:

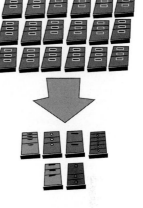

- Develop innovative product components that are systemically compatible with one another
- Employ internal tools for cost-effective manufacturing, warehousing, and distribution of our products
- Utilize common platform construction across product types, increasing flexibility and customization options
- Offer increased product compatibility across all Steelcase Inc. brands
- Simplify customer options
- Realize substantial cost savings through manufacturing efficiencies, which can be passed along to customers or result in higher profit margins for select products

Plan the Work. Work the Plan.

The studios are aligned.

As we move forward, securing alignment against this plan throughout the company will enable us all to achieve our desired goal: To maintain and grow our industry leadership position and market share with substantially improved profitability.

We look forward to you joining us on this journey.

Note the point of the last statement in "The Big Picture" section: join us on this journey.

Three-year Business Plan

Steelcase North America

Strategic Intent

Market leadership means expanding the total opportunity

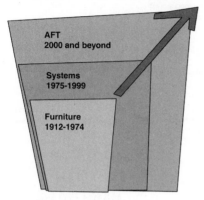

- Grow the total work environment industry by creating an AFT market and building a distinctive competency for Steelcase

- The products in this market will be differentiated by their unique, user-centered design and holistic integration of architecture, furniture and technology

- The success of these products will be the result of their design aesthetic, functional fit, and the "experience" users associate with them

- As a result of their perceived value add, these products will be able to command premium prices and result in an overall more profitable product portfolio for Steelcase

Steelcase Inc. • December 2001 • Company Confidential

As *OCP* moves from "The Big Picture" to the "Three-year Business Plan," it uses a graphic that connects expanded market opportunities to company evolution, creating employee alignment and motivation.

Three-year Business Plan

Market Trends
(As identified by ACRD Research and Steelcase North American Situation Analysis)

Recognizing and understanding market trends reveal business opportunities.

People
- Increasingly diverse workplace encompasses four generations
- Expectations of bosses and workers changed
- Hierarchies replaced by networks
- Ideas equal value, capital
- Privacy, acoustical, social, environmental needs unmet

People

Process

Technology

Space

Process
- Shift in favor of knowledge workers
- Network importance blurring corporate boundaries
- Increase in distributed team-based work, remote collaboration

Technology
- New products, markets created by technology
- Work processes, patterns impacted by technology
- Efficiency improved through alternative e-business value chain
- Old and new technology co-exist

Space
- Declining building size, office space per worker
- New construction less expensive than renovation
- Hoteling, shared spaces reduce cost per person
- People working anywhere, anytime
- Largest expenditures on sustainable architecture: lighting, HVAC, energy

Note that there is not a single complete sentence on this page. Writing effective phrases—that communicate complete thoughts—is a critical skill in business writing.

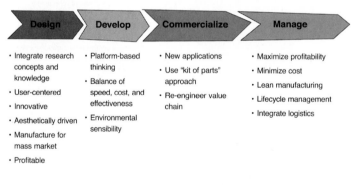

Three-year Business Plan

Driving Goals

Solidify and enhance the Steelcase position as the world's leading provider of effective work environments through:

User-Centered Design Innovation
Matching user needs with invention to develop commercially viable and innovative products

Portfolio Migration
Balancing short-term profitability while migrating customers to profitable Kit-of-Parts solutions

Profitability
Meeting and exceeding targeted corporate goals

New

Old

EVA

Overriding Strategies

Key activities of the product lifecycle process that are driven by Marketing and Product Development.

Design	Develop	Commercialize	Manage
• Integrate research concepts and knowledge	• Platform-based thinking	• New applications	• Maximize profitability
• User-centered	• Balance of speed, cost, and effectiveness	• Use "kit of parts" approach	• Minimize cost
• Innovative	• Environmental sensibility	• Re-engineer value chain	• Lean manufacturing
• Aesthetically driven			• Lifecycle management
• Manufacture for mass market			• Integrate logistics
• Profitable			

The stylized graphic of a person—"the user"—picked up on a major strategic theme of user-centered design. The image was used extensively in written communications and PowerPoint slides.

Three-year Business Plan

Critical Success Factors

We will succeed *only* if Steelcase:

Aligns on product goals at all levels of the organization

Improves the accuracy and reliability of the cost reporting system

Implements product strategies with discipline and accountability

Implements "Lean Manufacturing" to improve profitability

Educates about and aligns to the AFT market:

- Streamlines the entire value chain to maximize continuity, simplicity, cost effectiveness for AFT implementation
- Enters the sales process much earlier to effectively execute AFT
- Becomes the supplier of choice within the dealer network

Commercializes AFT with the same single-minded focus as systems in the 1980s (furniture and IOWT)

Measurements of Success

We will develop measurement targets against these criteria:

User-centered Design Innovation

- Number of icon products and product design awards
- Measured market perception
- Number of patent applications
- Recognition for environmental sensitivity
- Reaching lean manufacturing targets

Portfolio Migration

- Meeting new product sales targets
- Measured transition in applications from hierarchical/universal to community-based

Profitability

Meeting financial results targets as measured by:

- Sales
- Gross Profit
- EVA

> True performance means understanding the vision and flawlessly implementing against it. The following studio plans outline how this will be accomplished.

Furniture Studio

Steelcase North America

State-of-the-Business

The largest of the Steelcase product categories, the Furniture Studio is comprised of four main segments:

- Large Case Storage
- Small Case Storage
- Desking
- Alternative Systems

Today, these products produce over $XXX million (FY02 projected close) in N/N sales, the highest volume of Steelcase North America sales at just over XX%. The Furniture Studio is the most aligned with the company's current distribution and sales capability, and offers a pull-through opportunity for a well implemented AFT strategy.

We believe the Furniture Studio can become a greater contributor of net income for the company and provide a funding stream for growth of new horizon businesses.

This plan provides a roadmap to achieving XX% OI by FY05. This, combined with the Operations Plan, will result in XX% OI in FY05. This total view is represented in our financial summary.

Executed well, the Furniture Studio Plan represents the largest opportunity for income growth within Steelcase North America.

Steelcase Inc. • December 2001 • Company Confidential

OCP now moves into its third level—the individual studio plans for architecture, furniture, and technology. Here we give you just parts of the furniture studio plan; the other studio plans are similar in their rhetoric.

Furniture Studio

Studio Goals

To help North America reach its growth and profitability targets, the Furniture Studio has established the following measurable three-year goals:

1. User-centered Design Innovation

Design innovation in product development will be driven by user-centered opportunities; these opportunities will be guided by an understanding of:
- user needs
- user behaviors – individually, in groups and teams, in organizations
- the application of an AFT portfolio to enhance work effectiveness

The Furniture Studio has identified four areas we believe hold specific innovation opportunities:

Opportunity/User Need	Project/Product
User comfort and control, including adjustability projects supporting alternative postures	A, B
Information and object management	C, D, E
User's continual need for privacy and access to others	F
Non-cubicle standards	G/H

2. Portfolio Migration

Because of the long life cycles of systems furniture, it is not surprising that virtually all furniture sales are of older, existing products. We aim to change this situation beginning in the near term, and set a goal of achieving nearly XX% of sales from new products by FY05.

> Steelcase has focused much of its user research on areas that are ripe to convert from abstract concepts to complete product solutions including Information and Object Management.

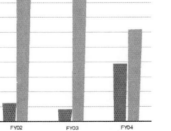

Percent

FY02   FY03   FY04
■ New Product Sales   ■ Existing Product Sales

> Implementing a user-centered Kit-of-Parts, allowing clients to choose their solution, is critical for our new product growth and meeting our financial goals.

> The textboxes and graphics in the margins serve as a running "executive summary," reminding readers of how the studio plans will help achieve the company goals.

Furniture Studio

Steelcase North America

Studio Goals

3. Sales Growth

We have established a furniture sales goal of $XXX million in FY05. This represents XX% growth over the next three years (which factors in a decline of over X% projected for FY03). To accomplish our FY05 goal, we need to grow faster than the market in Large Case Storage and Alternative Systems.

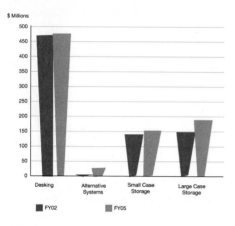

> Profits are driven by developing new products *and* rationalizing and simplifying our existing products.

4. Profitability

Starting from our current position this fiscal year, our goal is to increase profitability to XX% GP and XX% OI for the Furniture Studio by FY05. This will increase OI from $X million in FY02 to $XX million in FY05.

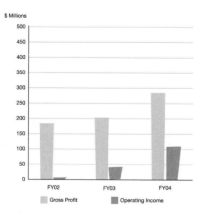

Furniture Studio

Strategies

To accomplish these goals, we have established five strategies:

1. **Innovate**
   Develop new products with innovative, user-centered features that strategically integrate with our simple, design-oriented AFT portfolio.
2. **Simplify**
   Rationalize our portfolio from products that are pulled through with "systems" projects, to a portfolio that features differentiated furniture components that are valued by users and drive profitable project sales.
3. **Discipline**
   Require that all products and projects meet or exceed corporate financial targets.
4. **Grow**
   Increase market share across component categories through exceeding customer expectations in all categories served.
5. **Inspire**
   Improve studio work effectiveness by inspiring better focus, greater collaboration, deeper understanding, and outstanding results.

Critical Success Factors

In order to achieve our goals and strategies, we must address the following critical success factors:

- Coordinate product development among all three Studios and across all Steelcase brands
  - develop products with a full price and performance spectrum
  - execute rational pricing for features offered
- Improve lifecycle management
  - rationalize current product offering
  - implement proposed culling strategy
  - migrate customers to new products
- Develop and execute platform-based products
- Successfully launch Kit-of-Parts strategy to support migration of customers to new products and customer preferences to mix-and-match across SCNA portfolio
- Develop and execute new pricing logic that aligns with Kit-of-Parts strategy and enables profitable blending

A Kit-of-Parts will require complete restructuring of our component pricing to enable profitable solutions when customers blend products or prefer a non-panel solution.

READING RESPONSES

1. Because *One Common Purpose* is a document written primarily for audiences within the company, it talks about customers in the third person. Review *One Common Purpose* and record all the references to customers. Then consider the data you collected—what do your data indicate about Steelcase's relationship with its customers?

2. In his introduction, Professor Eames notes that the authors of *One Common Purpose* paid careful attention to the metaphors they used throughout the document. Track the occurrences of the metaphor of forward movement throughout the document, paying attention to its presence in both the text and the graphics.

3. The phrase *One Common Purpose* takes on multiple meanings throughout the document. List the different meanings that *One Common Purpose* has and, for each meaning, list the rhetorical means that the authors use to communicate that meaning.

Notes on Grammar, Style, and Rhetoric:
The Language of Motivation

One Common Purpose, the Steelcase document that serves as the primary reading selection for this chapter, is a three-year business plan for marketing and product development. You might expect it to be charts, figures, diagrams, financial statements—dry business writing. You might not suspect that the piece would carry personal force. You would be wrong. *One Common Purpose* does indeed express powerful personal force and offers some significant rhetorical lessons. In fact, reading this document is like doing a case study of the essence of interpersonal motivation.

In order to motivate their co-workers, what strategies do the writers of the document use? First, they sound prominent notes of unity; they stress that they and all other Steelcase employees are part of the same team, are in this endeavor together. This strategy shows itself already in the title, *One Common Purpose*. And not too long after the title page the emphasis on being or becoming a team comes out again, this time when the writers emphasize that they "look forward to you [their co-workers] joining us on this journey" (471). Beyond this, throughout the document the writers stress that for their proposed plan to succeed, they will have to secure "alignment against this plan throughout the company. . ." (471), not just on certain levels or in particular divisions of the company. We can see the emphasis on unity perhaps most clearly through the pronouns that often appear in this piece—the plan is full of first-person plural pronouns such as *we* and *our*. Some of these, of course, stand in for referents to the writers of the document. But what is more important is that many of them stand in for referents to all Steelcase employees. We can identify both antecedents that give meaning to first-person pronouns in the following two sentences: "Is it possible to have a successful business in which our [all employees'] products are designed separate and apart from manufacturing considerations? We [the writers] don't think so" (470).

The writers' second key motivational strategy is to lay out clear and specific goals for the future of the company. They state their overarching goal as follows: "To maintain and grow our industry leadership position and market share with substantially improved profitability" (471). As the plan goes into greater detail, this overarching goal develops into additional, more specific, goals.

Interestingly, these more specific goals usually appear in one of two forms. Many goals are expressed as infinitives (the base form of the verb plus *to*, as in *to plan*). In the section dealing with product strategy, for instance, one goal is "To achieve greater flexibility to meet performance, visual, lifecycle-cost requirements" (470). Other goals appear as statements with future-tense verbs. For example, we read that "The success of these products will be the result of their design aesthetic . . ." (472). Even when the verb in a sentence is not in the future tense, it is clear that these writers are trying to get everyone in the company to focus on the future: "In essence, today's product development results are the first look at the company's financial future" (465).

However, it is also clear from this plan that it will not necessarily be easy for the company to achieve its goals for the future. We can sense this from the notes of urgency that the writers sound. To stress the urgency of the situation that the company faces, these writers use several closely related expressions such as "is critical for," "will require," "we need to," and "we must." Why this tone of urgency? To put it simply, there were some strong challenges to the company's leading position in the office-furniture business. Many of these challenges were posed by their competitors. In fact, the writers warn, "We will succeed only if. . . ." They follow the "if" with a line of action plans signaled by active verbs: "aligns," "improves," "implements," "educates." The company, it is clear, had to respond to these challenges quickly and wisely.

In Your Own Writing . . .

When you need to motivate others in a group to help you accomplish something, employ the strategies of interpersonal motivation:

- Address those you wish to motivate as if they are working with you on the same team.
- Lay out clear and specific goals.
- Use sentence fragments to offer sharply focused reminders of key concepts.
- Use appropriate linguistic markers of urgency to highlight the challenges that you face.

STUDENT WRITING IN MARKETING

Introduction by Sarah Steen, business major

The Assignment. The assignment to write a marketing plan for a real organization hit me like a slap in the face. Welcome to the real world! Invariably, all my other business writing assignments had been the typical, formulaic, often dry—and dreaded—"reflection papers." I had been expressing my thoughts and feelings about business without ever getting my hands dirty with the real thing. So I was up for a new challenge, but my first reaction was one of anxiety: "Wait a minute! No one has ever taught me how to write a marketing plan!"

The Content. But I had to start somewhere. I sat down at my computer with the assignment from my professor, a sample marketing plan from a textbook, some hot chocolate, and . . . a blank Word document. I had no idea where to begin. I frantically tried to think of important marketing concepts that might pertain to the task at hand, until I realized that it all came down to the first lesson I ever learned in marketing: it's all about the customer.

Two other students and I had been assigned to work with a non-profit organization called Safe Haven (it helps women who are suffering from abuse). It became clear, then, that their employees and their Board of Directors were our customers. The marketing plan we were creating for Safe Haven was the final piece of our group project that would tie together almost one hundred hours of our background research.

At the beginning of the project we spoke with the executive director, who shared with us her big dreams for the way our project could fit in with the larger mission of Safe Haven. She told us that they would soon be hiring a new staff member who would follow-up on our findings by creating a new church liaison program. My group members and I were excited to see how important our research would be to this organization's future, but we also hoped that we could do this project justice.

Learning to Write in Marketing. As we began the project, we thought it was important to get to know our customers by spending time at their office. After a tour and introductions, we settled into a conference room to pore over their computer files and handwritten records of the past fourteen years. After several visits we had all gained an appreciation for their work and what was before us, and each of us felt drawn to pursue different avenues of our marketing project.

Even though I now understood my customer, I still wasn't out of the woods when it came time to write the marketing plan. I fretfully reminded myself that I still didn't know how to write real business documents. My mind drifted: what *had* I learned to write? I had learned how to write informative essays: now I would show my customer that I understood their situation from an inside perspective. I had learned how to write persuasive essays: now I would persuade my customer that because I understood their situation and performed countless hours analyzing their data, I could offer the organization worthwhile suggestions. With these things in mind, I began to write. I tried to picture the executive director cocking her head and asking at certain points along the way, "How do you know that?" I rephrased things and expanded the explanations, trying to show her our line of thinking.

I finally worked out a draft and showed it to my professor. He was pleased with the content, but, as he pointed out, it was almost entirely long paragraphs, and business people apparently have no patience for such things. Those reflection papers I wrote never asked me to consider how I felt about sentence fragments, but that was my next challenge: to find lists, key words, and main ideas in my plan and make them pop with effective formatting, bullets, and sentence fragments. Unlike my initial writing struggles, this process was much more intuitive. Often I just remembered the words and phrases we used most often in our group meetings. "Geography," for example, turned out to be a key in our plan; there had been missed opportunities. For example, there were geographical locations from which a lot of Safe Haven clients came, but not many donors in those areas were giving money to Safe Haven. I figured that just as a professor will put a term on a test if he mentions it three days in a row, Safe Haven would want to understand the ideas our group kept coming back to day after day. It took some time to create a parallel structure for my lists and to make my paragraphs more concise, but I noticed that at a glance the entire document seemed a lot more accessible by the time I was finished.

Creating Change through Writing in Marketing. The most rewarding part of the entire composition process was when we finally presented the marketing plan and accompanying research to the executive director. Her face was glowing, and we were taken aback by her gratefulness and determination to take action on our plan that very day. At that moment I realized that I had accomplished what I set out to do from that first day at the computer—satisfy my customer.

Safe Haven Marketing Campaign

Sarah Steen

Executive Summary

> An "executive summary" serves its audience in ways similar to an "abstract." As you might expect from a business document, it identifies itself by its audience: executives.

The direction of this marketing plan and accompanying project is focused specifically on one of the seven goals presented in Safe Haven's Strategic Plan: "to expand and continue to cultivate consistent revenue sources." The specific focus is to find ways to increase financial support from churches.

Our team accomplished this by:

> The organizations that sought the help of my marketing class were those who need help but didn't have great financial resources. So my class worked with several not-for-profit organizations, many of which were "faith based."

- **segmenting** Kane County by geographical locations and church groups;
- **identifying** segments that have high giving potential; and
- **targeting** churches in these segments in order to initiate and strengthen relationships.

We found several trends:

1. Several zip codes in Kane County have a high average disposable income, yet churches in these areas give relatively small amounts to Safe Haven.
2. Clients come from a variety of Grand Falls suburbs in Kane County, yet Safe Haven has not made contacts with churches in all of these areas.
3. Several denominations have no contact with Safe Haven or do not currently support the organization, even though there are a significant number of Safe Haven clients that identify with that denomination.

> subgroups of major religions

Specific zip codes, denominations, computations, and other information can be found in the Recommendations section of this marketing plan and in the appendix.

Based on these findings, our team suggests the following goals:

- Make five "Raise Hope" presentations in each of the targeted denominations and zip codes within the next twelve months
- Expect an average increase in giving of $1000 by each of these churches and their members
- Establish commitments and identify a liaison with five of these churches within the next 18 months
- Expect an average increase in giving of $5000 by each of these churches

Situation Analysis

> In this largest section of the report we provide *context*, a key in marketing. By explaining the history and mission and summarizing market opportunities, we also suggest *direction* and *motivation*, the other two keys in marketing.

Safe Haven exists to provide both shelter and non-residential services for abused women and their children. They are also dedicated to raising awareness of domestic violence within the community. Safe Haven is founded on the basic principle that through charitable love they might begin to renew the human spirit and build a stronger community by ending the cycle of domestic abuse.

Safe Haven is located in Grand Falls, but their services extend to all of Kane County and beyond. It was founded in 1990 by six churches located in the heart of Grand Falls. The growth of the organization since its inception is remarkable:

Then: 1990

6 supporting churches
Yearly budget: $35,000
One shelter

Now: 2004

285 churches in contact database
Yearly budget: $447,000
Multi-faceted services

Safe Haven is able to help more than 400 women and children per year through their Harbor House and Protective Helper programs. In order to continue serving families in both these and their Lift Hope program, Safe Haven seeks volunteer, financial, and spiritual support from both individuals and church communities.

It is clear that church support has increased since Safe Haven first began:

Then: 1990

6 supporting churches
all in one denomination

Now: 2004

285 churches in contact database
25+ denominations

The preceding growth is an encouragement to Safe Haven's effort to reach a greater cross-section of its geographical location. However, there is still need to strengthen current contacts and develop new ones:

- Only 91 of the 285 churches in the database (32%) have supported Safe Haven financially
- 70% of financial support received from churches has been from within the denomination of the founding churches

Market Summary

The overarching market important to all aspects of Safe Haven is Kane County. Within Kane County, Safe Haven has three sub-markets: the client market, the awareness market, and the support market. The market most relevant to this marketing plan is the support market.

Client Market

This includes abused women and their children who need shelter, legal advocacy, counseling, and support because they presently are in an abusive relationship or as they recover from one.

Awareness Market

This includes everyone, because Safe Haven believes that every-one needs to know the realities of domestic abuse and what can be done to stop it and prevent it, including the ways that Safe Haven can help.

Support Market

Safe Haven believes that it benefits from the time, spiritual support, and financial support of people through many different outlets:

- **Individually**
- Through their **place of work**
- Through a **foundation** that they support
- Through their **church**

Of these sources, the support of churches is especially critical to the success of Safe Haven. Safe Haven has the opportunity to partner with churches in addressing the issues of domestic violence. Together they can affirm the dignity and worth of every person and offer healing and support. Over the years Safe Haven has learned that the more church members who get involved with their ministry, the more people from that same congregation who will get the help that they need.

Here's another example of how we combine direction and motivation.

This project will focus its efforts on churches, clients, and programs in Kane County, where the core of Safe Haven's activity takes place. However, Johnstown will also be included in our data because it is a geographically significant area to Safe Haven's work. It is on the border of Kane and Otswega Counties and many of the Protective Helper clients from Johnstown go to churches in Kane County. Safe Haven has reached people and churches in Grand Falls and all surrounding counties, but due to time constraints on the project it is most important to focus on clients and churches closest to the point of service.

Kane County Demographics

Within the zip codes in Kane County and Johnstown, from which Safe Haven has made church contacts with or has drawn clients, the demographic data is as follows:[*]

- The total population of the **27** zip codes is **610,077**
- The total number of households in the **27** zip codes is **237,026**
- The average house value is **$120,397.39**
- The average income per household is **$48,697.32**
- The total population based on ethnicity is:
  - White: **512,988**
  - Black: **51,530**
  - Hispanic: **40,843**

Market Needs

Within the **client** market victims of domestic abuse need to know that they are not alone and that help is available to them. They need to be aware of the services Safe Haven provides and how to access these services.

Within the **support** market churches and individuals need to know that Safe Haven provides an important service to the greater Grand Falls area and is a worthy recipient of their financial support. Because churches are a major source of funds for Safe Haven services, they need to know that Safe Haven is run by individuals who recognize the importance of faith-based service.

---

[*]Source: United States Zip Code Directory: http://www.zip-codes.com/zip_code_directory.asp

Also within the support market it is important that Safe Haven provides other ways for people to contribute to its work beyond gift-giving. Safe Haven must establish opportunities, and people in the support market must be empowered to contribute. The desire to get involved is already there, but there must be opportunities for this value exchange to take place.

Within the **awareness** market it is important for all people to understand the issues surrounding domestic violence. They also need to understand what Safe Haven has to offer any victim of domestic violence. In this way, people will be able to recognize domestic violence in their lives or the lives of their friends or family and refer them to the help that they need.

Because domestic violence is a taboo issue, it is sometimes difficult to address and discuss. Safe Haven needs to provide safe avenues for people to talk openly about domestic violence. Safe Haven has several measures already in place that may be further developed, including women's restroom flyers and other advertising campaigns, Lift Hope presentations, Domestic Violence Orientations, and the annual Faith Breakfasts.

Market Trends

Of course we could not provide direction without showing trends. Trend analysis is essential for marketing plans.

By comparing the amount of money a church gives to its involvement in Safe Haven's programs the following market trends may be inferred:

- Churches that send representatives to the annual Faith Breakfasts increase their giving by an average of 200%
- Churches that host Lift Hope presentations increase giving by an average of 90%

By reviewing the Lift Hope program evaluations and speaking with presenters the following trends are also evident:

- Response to presentations is overwhelmingly positive and appreciative
- Attendees wish to talk further about issues surrounding domestic violence with both representatives of Safe Haven and other members of their congregation
- One or more attendees approaches the presenter to share their own story of domestic abuse

By examining these trends it is clear that Safe Haven's goal should be to set up more presentations and to increase the attendance at each presentation. These presentations are meant to raise awareness, but it is clear that they are also a way for victims to begin the process of getting the help that they need.

Market Growth

Since Safe Haven began its Protective Helper program, the number of clients has increased steadily. However, the number of clients in 2002 and 2003 remained about the same, perhaps because the ministry reached its current carrying capacity.

People have become more aware of Safe Haven through the distribution of their clergy packets, through flyers in women's restrooms, and through the many presentations and orientations they host throughout Grand Falls.

However, because most of Safe Haven's contacts are within the denomination of the founding churches, this denomination's share of support has been growing while other denominations remain under-contacted and under-utilized. The six founding churches represent 54% of Safe Haven's church donations, and giving from all churches in the same denomination as the founding churches represents 70%.

Even though Safe Haven was begun by the founding churches, over the years they have received an increasing amount of support from other churches and other denominations. A great example of this is Church A which has raised more than $130,000 for Safe Haven. It would be incredibly beneficial for Safe Haven to identify a few other churches like this outside the founding denomination. Like Church A, the large congregational sizes of churches like Church B, Church C, Church D, and even Church E present great potential for giving.

It is difficult to analyze the growth of church giving because our data is limited to amount of contribution to date. However, data per year is available for Faith Breakfast attendance. From this we see that an increased number of people from multiple denominations have been attending and supporting Safe Haven through this annual event.

Not only have people from different denominations been coming to the Faith Breakfasts, overall attendance has also been on the rise. It is interesting to note, however, that after not holding a 2002 Faith Breakfast, attendance at the 2003 breakfast was down a small amount. It is important for this to remain an annual event in order to keep up the enthusiasm and momentum for supporting Safe Haven.

SWOT Analysis

A SWOT analysis is perhaps the most common feature of marketing plans—or any strategic planning.

Strengths

- 14 years of **experience** in the geographical area
- **Faith-basis** that complements the work of churches and other religious organizations
- Well-organized **methods** of raising awareness including presentations and published materials
- Basic, committed **financial support**

Weaknesses

- Small **size** of the organization with only one point of service for the entire client base
- An unspoken **taboo** that may prevent social discussion of domestic violence
- **Unfamiliarity** with denominations other than the founding denomination
- Various unorganized, missing **data**
- No history of **marketing goals**, targets, or segments

Opportunities

- Greater **awareness** due to recent publicized cases of domestic violence
- Increasingly **diverse attendance** at Faith Breakfasts
- New **staff person** to coordinate Church Liaison Program
- Large, untapped **giving potential** among Safe Haven's church contacts

Threats

- **Perception** that as Safe Haven expands it becomes too commercial and anonymity may be compromised
- **Economic downturn** that creates less disposable income
- Limit of future **growth** without increased financial support
- **Incorrect perception** that Safe Haven promotes divorce
- **Competition** between charities for donations

Alternative Providers

Safe Haven is one of the few domestic violence abuse and prevention shelter organizations in Grand Falls. The other social service agencies in the area include the YWCA and Catholic Social Services. Although these three organizations are complementary to one another, Safe Haven occupies a unique position as the only one of the three that uses a faith-based approach to all of their services.

Services Offered

Harbor House can offer short-term, emergency shelter for a maximum of 4 women and 11 children by providing a safe house and retreat. Services include: housing for victims and their children, crisis intervention, information and referrals, legal advocacy, housing and job assistance, childcare, individual counseling and support groups, a caring and professional staff, as well as a listening ear.

Protective Helper, Safe Haven's non-residential program, employs certified therapists and family advocates who offer professional, confidential services to abused women and their children. Services include: education-based support groups, therapy-based support groups, individual counseling, case management, legal advocacy, information and resources, the "I Feel Better Now" Children's Workshop Series, a resource library, and continued support for former residents of Ramoth House.

Lift Hope is the education part of Safe Haven and is organized around four specific goals:

* Raising awareness and informing
* Gaining church support
* Educating the public through presentations
* Partnering with local churches and organizations to develop and nurture relationships of time, energy, and resources

Recommendations

Here we get the focus of our plan; it's all about helping the customers see what they can do to create positive change.

In order to meet Safe Haven's second goal, "to expand and continue to cultivate consistent revenue sources," our team began by segmenting Kane County **geographically** by zip code and also **denominationally**. By studying these segments we have discovered several areas of high potential but low share:

* The following zip codes in Kane County comprise areas of high disposable income, yet the churches in these areas give relatively small amounts to Safe Haven:

59544: Wilbur	59505: NE Grand Falls
59548: Kanewood	59509: Wilsonville
59341: Rockford	59321: Comston Park

* The following suburbs of Grand Falls are home to a relatively high number of clients, yet Safe Haven has few or no contacts with churches in these areas:

    * 59544: Wilbur   8 clients   0 churches
    * 59321: Comston Park   16 clients   0 churches
    * 59341: Rockford   14 clients   5 churches

• The following denominations have a relatively high number of Safe Haven clients who identify with one of their churches yet none of the churches currently support Safe Haven financially:

Baptist, Assemblies of God, Bible, Seventh-Day Adventist, Pentecostal, Wesleyan

We suggest that Safe Haven target churches in any of the preceding areas or denominations. It is especially noteworthy that all three areas with high client and low church concentrations are also areas of high disposable income. The appendix of this marketing plan includes contact information for many churches that meet one or more of these criteria.

Potential Goals

> These possible goals put some flesh on the recommendations; they allow the customer to imagine specific actions and results.

• Make five Raise Hope presentations in each of the targeted denominations and zip codes within the next twelve months
• Expect an average increase in giving of $1000 by each of these churches and their members
• Establish covenant commitments and identify a liaison with five of these churches within the next 18 months
• Expect an average increase in giving of $5000 by each of these churches

READING RESPONSES:

1. Compare the information in the executive summary with the information contained in the rest of the marketing plan. What information would you have added to the executive summary? What information would you eliminate?

2. In her introduction, Sarah Steen notes that when she revised her first draft of the marketing plan, she shortened long paragraphs. But her marketing plan still contains many more words than the Steelcase *One Common Purpose*. Take one section of the Safe Haven report and condense it, using all the rhetorical strategies available to you.

3. If you consider the metaphors Safe Haven uses for its services, you'll quickly notice that they emphasize refuge and protection—appealing ideas to victims of domestic violence. Create a series of graphics that link the different sections to each other and that link the different sections to the central theme of Safe Haven.

PUBLIC WRITING IN MARKETING

Introduction

There are few more public kinds of writing than an advertisement. The ad reprinted here accompanies the first and last readings in this chapter, so we need not say anything more about the context of this particular product, which is part

Leap Chair Advertisement

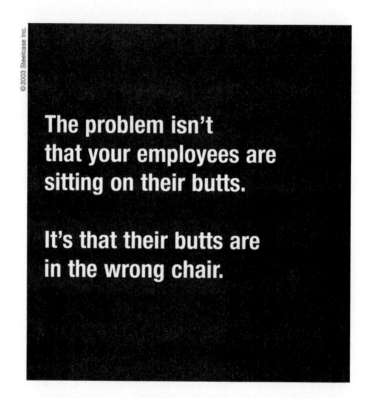

Steelcase work environments can yield real business results. In a recent study, our Leap® Chair—with ergonomic training—increased productivity by 17.8%. Details at steelcase.com/results.

  Do what you do better."

of the *One Common Purpose* business plan. Of special interest here is the strategy of gaining readers' attention with the loud, colloquial word choices and then letting readers' eyes drift down to the small-font detail that refers to the finding (as you'll see reported more fully in the last reading in the chapter) that the Leap Chair increases productivity by 17.8 percent.

READING RESPONSES

1. Analyze the different uses of language, fonts, kinds of information—all of the "means of persuasion" that the ad uses. How do various elements work individually? How do they work in harmony? Is there anything you would change about the ad? If so, explain why.
2. Using information, ideas, or graphics from the final reading in the chapter or the first reading, *One Common Purpose*, design your own advertisement for the Leap Chair.
3. This ad makes prominent use of simple black and white. List all the possible messages that this use of black and white gives to the reader.

MORE WRITING IN MARKETING

Introduction

Sometimes the best way to sell something is by letting someone else sell it for you. Think, for example, of the number of times you've heard that a health or personal care product has been recommended by a group of doctors or dentists. Third-party credibility is often a great way to position the value of a product or service in the mind of an increasingly jaded marketplace that is constantly being bombarded with claims of new and improved features and superior functionality. This was definitely the case when Steelcase launched their new Leap Chair in 2002. Why should anyone be interested in a new chair that cost more than $1,000? What would persuade purchasing agents in corporate America to buy this chair over the many other well-designed chairs on the market? The answer had to be based in cold hard facts: what could Leap do for corporate America that would make it worth the money?

Steelcase commissioned a research study (coordinated by independent agencies and conducted by independent scientists) to investigate the impact of the Leap Chair on the productivity of office workers. The report concluded that the combination of the advanced ergonomic features of the innovative chair and proper office ergonomics training resulted in a significant increase in productivity.

Steelcase knows that business people don't really enjoy reading scientific papers and dry, statistics-laden research reports. But the research was important, and Steelcase used the information to position the Leap Chair as a productivity-improving work tool in the minds of their target customers. They did this by using the statistic of greatest interest to the market—a 17.8% increase in productivity—as the headline in the report and as the basis for an advertising campaign designed to increase sales of the chair. Steelcase connected a benefit the customer cares about (worker productivity) to the features of the Leap Chair through the report, which combines elements of a research report with elements found in promotional brochures (extensive visual design and graphic content). Notice how the headlines and subheads in the report actually deal with objections commonly found in the sales process. For example, when the report calculates the payback of the cost of the chair at less than ten working days, it diminishes the price of the chair. These rhetorical devices combine to create a readable and effective claim that a high quality ergonomic office chair can increase worker productivity and improve business results. The launch of this chair proved to be one of the most successful in the company's history.

LEAP PRODUCTIVITY AND HEALTH IMPACT STUDY

In a year-long study of over 200 participants, people who received the Leap chair and office ergonomics training achieved a 17.8% increase in productivity.

Steelcase

"Employees who received the Leap chair along with training experienced a significant reduction in musculoskeletal symptoms."

Ben Amick, Ph.D.,
University of Texas,
Health Science Center at Houston

1

As the number of knowledge workers grows worldwide, so does the need to design ergonomic programs that improve the health and productivity of these workers. So what creates a healthy, inspiring office that helps people do their best work— an ergonomic chair, a keyboard support, a window view, good lighting, great tasting coffee?

It's not the coffee.

Objectives

Many studies analyze the effectiveness of ergonomic programs, but since they look at overall changes to the office, they don't readily identify which changes actually led to reduced symptoms and injuries.

Leap® seating technology was designed based on extensive research of the human body and how to support it. The Leap chair had been proven, in biomechanic laboratory tests[1], to provide exceptional fit, movement, and support. The goal of <u>this study</u> was to test the measurable effects of the Leap chair and office ergonomics training on employees' well-being and productivity in a "real world" setting.

The Study Team
Academic and research institutes in the U.S. and Canada participated in conducting the study and analyzing the results, including the University of Texas Health Science Center at Houston, W.E. Upjohn Institute for Employment Research, and other partners.

The research was coordinated by Health and Work Outcomes, an independent health research and consulting company.

The study looked at three things:

• What is the real health benefit of an ergonomic program?

• Can an ergonomic program lead to increased worker productivity?

• How quickly can an increase in productivity yield a return on investment for the company?

"This study was one of the most comprehensive scientific efforts to link an ergonomic product and training to health, employee productivity, and return on investment for a corporation," said Ben Amick, Ph.D., University of Texas, Health Science Center at Houston.

"This study was designed to assess how well a highly adjustable chair and office ergonomics training could affect ergonomic knowledge, postural behavior, health and productivity." — Ben Amick

2

1 Michigan State University, "An Evaluation of Postural Motions, Chair Motions, and Contact in Four Office Chairs" 1999

One year + over 200 participants = one in-depth study.

Study Design

Two companies participated in the study, and hundreds of employees volunteered as test subjects. The results from the first company—tracking 200 knowledge workers for one year—are complete. By the time the entire study is complete, over 450 individuals will have participated.

For the first company, over 200 volunteers were selected from a state agency that collects sales taxes. In order to qualify, each participant had to spend at least six hours a day sitting in their chair, and at least four of those hours working on a computer.

Data was collected in two areas, over a one year period:
(see side-bar for detail)

A. Health Status   B. Productivity

Volunteers were divided into three study groups:

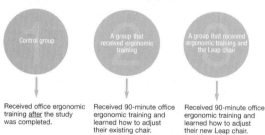

| Control group | A group that received ergonomic training | A group that received ergonomic training and the Leap chair |

Received office ergonomic training <u>after</u> the study was completed.

Received 90-minute office ergonomic training and learned how to adjust their existing chair.

Received 90-minute office ergonomic training and learned how to adjust their new Leap chair.

A. Health Status Measures

Researchers created a baseline measure (the "before" measure) by collecting data prior to the ergonomic program. After the ergonomic program began, data was collected at two, six, and twelve months. During each data collection period, participants completed short symptom surveys three times a day for one week to rate pain in different parts of the body. They also completed a longer Work Environment and Health Questionnaire to rate overall pain and discomfort.

B. Productivity Measures

One of the most significant aspects of this study was that the productivity data was objective (amount of sales tax collected per worker in the first company), rather than a subjective performance measure. The agency provided data for revenue collected and hours worked for the eleven months prior to the ergonomic program (the "before" measure), and for the twelve months following the ergonomic program.

> "The Leap chair-with-training group experienced a significant reduction in symptom growth over the course of the work day, compared to both the training-only group and the control group." — Ben Amick

3

Feeling good makes good business sense.

Study Results*

The Leap chair-with-training group showed significant improvements in both health status and productivity.

Health Status Results

The employees who received a Leap chair and ergonomic training reported significantly lower pain and discomfort in their symptom surveys and in their Work Environment and Health Questionnaires. Their overall musculoskeletal symptoms were lower than the other two groups. But that's not all. Researchers made another interesting finding.

You can normally expect people to feel more discomfort at the end of a day of sitting, compared to how they felt in the morning. For both the control group and the training-only group, the data showed this was certainly true. However, for the people receiving a Leap chair, any discomfort at the end of the day was only a slight increase compared to the morning. So not only were the people who received a Leap chair more comfortable overall, they were comfortable for longer.

Productivity Results

The study results also showed an increase in productivity. After one year, the Leap chair-with-training group achieved a 17.8% increase in productivity. This number reflects the increase in taxes collected per hour worked, which was an average increase of $6,250 collected per month, per employee. "In contrast," reported Kelly DeRango, the researcher who led the productivity portion of the study, "the training-only and the control group did not show any significant increase in productivity."

Musculoskeletal Symptom Growth Over Time

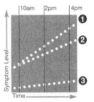

1 = Control Group
2 = Training-Only Group
3 = Leap+Training Group

> " The productivity benefits shown by the Leap chair-with-training group were quite large compared with the program's costs. In contrast, the training-only group did not show any statistically significant changes in productivity." — Kelly DeRango

4

Study Results
continued

Comparing the cost of the Leap chair to the increase in productivity, this study determined that the Leap chair paid for itself in less than ten working days.

The Leap chair's design includes several unique features that can contribute to improved well-being and productivity.

Live Back™
The Leap chair's back changes shape to support the entire spine. This can reduce the chance of lower back sag and a hunched posture, which weakens disc walls, stresses back ligaments and causes deterioration of the spine.

Upper and Lower Back Controls
Upper back force control enables users to set the amount of "push back" that they desire as they recline, regardless of their body size. Lower back firmness control enables users to set a constant amount of firmness to maintain their lower back's natural curve.

Height, Width, and Pivot Arms
Arms telescope, pivot and adjust up and down so users can find a natural position that comfortably supports the wrists, forearms, shoulders and neck.

Natural Glide System™
Seat glides forward so users can recline without leaving their Vision and Reach Zone, so they stay oriented to their work. This encourages more varied postures so there's less static load on the spine.

Seat Edge Angle Control
Enables people to ease pressure on thighs and widen the angle between legs and torso without feeling like they're sliding out of their chair. Plus, shorter people gain nearly two inches of seat height.

Adjustable Seat Depth
People don't fit neatly into three average sizes. Leg and torso lengths can vary independent of a person's overall height. Adjustable seat depth accommodates different body shapes for long-term comfort.

Leap Chair-With-Training Group's Productivity Increase

17.8%

In this study, individuals who received office ergonomic training and sat in Leap chairs increased average productivity by 17.8% after a year.

"Most importantly, the findings of this study suggest that companies may benefit by improving the seating of their office workers in conjunction with a training program in office ergonomic practices," said Kelly DeRango. "Based on the findings of this study, we believe it can make good business sense for companies to provide Leap chairs to their employees." As this study continues, the results from the second company will provide additional data to researchers on the effects of the Leap chair and office ergonomic training.

Resources

Ben Amick, Ph.D., University of Texas, Health Science Center at Houston

Dr. Amick is an internationally recognized leader in building healthy workplaces and developing new outcome-based measures of people's ability to enjoy their life and work. He received his Ph.D. from The Johns Hopkins University in 1986. From 1992 to 1999, Ben served as a research scientist at The Health Institute at Boston's New England Medical Center, world-renowned for its research on health outcomes. He was also a faculty member at both the Harvard School of Public Health and Tufts School of Medicine. Ben has also worked in the private sector as an ergonomics consultant and in management consulting with The Hay Group.

Currently, Ben is an Associate Professor at the University of Texas Health Science Center at Houston, School of Public Health.
www.benamick.com

Kelly DeRango, Ph.D., W.E. Upjohn Institute for Employment Research

Dr. DeRango is a research fellow at the W.E. Upjohn Institute for Employment Research. As an economist with the Upjohn Institute, Kelly is responsible for data analysis, instrument design, and program evaluation for projects sponsored by The Department of Labor, The Social Security Administration, and Health and Work Outcomes. He also researches urban labor markets and the effects of racial discrimination on housing and labor markets. Kelly received a Ph.D. in economics from the University of Wisconsin Madison in 2000. He earned an MBA from the University of Michigan in 1992, where he received a Ford Scholarship.

Credits

The University of Texas Health Science Center at Houston
7000 Fannin, Suite 1200
Houston, Texas 77030
Tel: 713.500.4472
www.uth.tmc.edu

W.E. Upjohn Institute for Employment Research
300 South Westnedge Avenue
Kalamazoo, Michigan 49007
Tel. 269.343.5541
Fax: 269.343.3308
www.upjohninst.org

Health and Work Outcomes
47 Rossmore Road
Brunswick, Maine 04011
Tel: 207.729.4929
www.healthandwork.com

References

Amick III, Benjamin C; Robertson, Michelle M; Bazzani, Lianna; Rooney, Ted; Moore, Anne; Harrist, Ron. "Effects of an Office Ergonomic Intervention on Musculoskeletal Symptoms." Published in the December 15, 2003 issue of SPINE Journal.

DeRango, Kelly; Amick III, Benjamin C; Robertson, Michelle M; Rooney, Ted; Moore, Anne; Bazzani, Lianna. "The Productivity Consequences of Two Ergonomic Interventions." Upjohn Institute Staff Working Paper No. WP03-95, May 2003, available at: www.upjohninst.org.

If you would like further information, please call 1.888.783.3522.

Visit www.steelcase.com

Steelcase Do what you do better.™

READING RESPONSES

1. What about the Leap Chair report was most appealing to you? Can you imagine using any of its rhetorical strategies in your own writing—even for classes that are not in business? If you think that there are useful strategies but you don't believe you could use them in your writing, explain why you believe that.

2. Compare this research report with one other scientific report in this book (there are examples in Chapters 8, 9, and 12). What features do the two have in common? Do you think that there are any features from the Leap Chair report that might improve the traditional scientific report? What might prevent traditional scientific publications from using those features?

3. What are the parts of the Leap Chair report that are most in harmony with the company business plan, *One Common Purpose*? Do you see the chair fitting into the larger vision for an integrated marketing plan? How?

WRITING ASSIGNMENTS

ASSIGNMENT 1: APPLYING THE PORTABLE RHETORICAL LESSON

Background: The fact that Americans are gaining weight at an unprecedented rate has caught the attention of most food retailers, including those who plan the menus at school cafeterias. Healthier food costs more, in general, than food laden with fat, sugar, and salt, but school dieticians are nevertheless beginning to offer more healthy eating options. Of course, a key issue for school dieticians is figuring out how to make those healthy options appeal to kids!

Your task is to write a marketing plan for improving the nutritional value of the food offered at one of the food venues on your campus. Your instructor might require you to present your plan to the appropriate university officials, and your instructor may ask you to work in a group for this assignment. First you should analyze the food options available to students on your campus and target one that seems potentially problematic. Then you should do some background research so that you understand the current and prospective customers for this food venue. What features or services do the customers value? What kinds of healthier alternatives would they accept? What factors will affect their choice to purchase and consume healthier food? Using the SWOT method (strengths, weaknesses, opportunities, and threats) that Sarah Steen and her teammates used, organize the results of your analysis, and determine a set of recommendations.

As you begin drafting, think carefully about the audience for your marketing plan—officials at your university. What are their goals? How can your marketing plan help them achieve those goals? What vital information does your marketing plan offer them? Then consider all the rhetorical strategies at your disposal. Which ones will help you communicate clearly, efficiently, and effectively?

ASSIGNMENT 2: MAKING CONNECTIONS

Background: Academic research targets important issues like the rates at which athletes receive injuries described in the biology chapter or the effect of gender on students' assessment of their abilities described in the sociology chapter. These research reports are complex and often difficult to read; readers must bring a great deal of expertise, background knowledge, and patience to the task. As a result, most people don't regularly read reports like these. But the information that these reports contain can have a positive effect on how trainers prepare their athletes or how professors teach their subject matter.

Your task is to translate the information presented in an academic research report like those mentioned above into a form that will appeal to those who can put the information to good use. You should review the ergonomic study of Steelcase's Leap Chair, paying careful attention to how the authors of that report present research findings in rhetorically effective ways.

As you begin drafting, determine the central message you want to convey to your reader—an overarching theme or metaphor that provides coherence to the recommendations that you make. Then consider what rhetorical strategies you can use to provide the three key elements of a good marketing plan that Professor Eames describes in his introduction: context, direction, and motivation.

ASSIGNMENT 3: DOING THE RESEARCH

Background: Marketing is like many other fields in that the strategies people use in day-to-day business arise from the careful research of those with impressive academic credentials. But how, exactly, do business people learn about this research? Like Sarah Steen, they learn the basics as students; throughout their careers, they keep up with new research by reading journals and magazines designed for business people.

Your task is to search these journals for new strategies for developing and presenting business plans, and to create a set of recommendations for marketing students, like Sarah Steen, who are trying to solve real-world problems with marketing solutions. You may find it easiest to consult a reference librarian to help you do the research you will need to complete for this assignment.

As you begin drafting, think carefully about the students who are the audience for your recommendations. What tasks do they face? What information do they already know? What information do they need to know? How can you present the information so that it is succinct and yet complete enough that they can use it in their work? Consider how you can use metaphors and other rhetorical strategies to convince students to trust you and to put your recommendations to use.

CREDITS

Alexander, Martin, from "Aging, Bioavailability, and Overestimation of Risk from Environmental Pollutants" by Martin Alexander. Reprinted in part with permission from *Environmental Science & Technology,* 2000, 34(20): 4259–4962, 4264–4265. Copyright © 2000 American Chemical Society.

Amercian Psychological Association, Press release, "First-year College Students Who Feel Lonely Have a Weaker Immune Response to the Flu Shot," May 1, 2005, from www.apa.org/releases/loneliness.html. Copyright © 2005 by the American Psychological Association. Reprinted with permission.

Bellah, Robert N., from "Civil Religion in America" by Robert N. Bellah from *Daedalus,* 96:1 (Winter 1967), pp. 1–21. Copyright © 1967 by the American Academy of Arts and Sciences. Reprinted by permission of MIT Press.

Bush, George W., Speech from Jackson Square, New Orleans, September 15, 2005, from Office of the federal register, National Archives and Records Administration.

Campbell, Karlyn Kohrs and Kathleen Hall Jamieson, from "Rhetoric to Forestall Impeachment," from *Deeds Done in Words: Presidential Rhetoric and the Genres of Governance* by Karlyn Kohrs Campbell and Kathleen Hall Jamieson. Copyright © 1990 University of Chicago Press. Used by permission.

Carson, Rachel, Excerpt from "Realms of the Soil", from *Silent Spring* by Rachel Carson. Copyright © 1962 by Rachel L. Carson, renewed 1990 by Roger Christie. Reprinted by permission of Houghton Mifflin Company. All rights reserved.

Clinton, William Jefferson, Speech to the Annual White House Prayer Breakfast, September 11, 1998, from Office of the federal register, National Archives and Records Administration.

Conway, George and Gary Toenniessen, "Feeding the World in the Twenty-first Century" by Gordon Conway and Gary Toenniessen from *Nature,* December 2, 1999, supplement to Vol. 402, Issue 6761, pp. C55–C58.

Coontz, Stephanie, from "Why marriage today takes more love, work—from both partners" by Stephanie Coontz from *The Christian Science Monitor,* June 28, 2005. This article first appeared in *The Christian Science Monitor* (www.csmonitor.com).

Correll, Shelley J., from "Constraints into Preferences: Gender, Status, and Emerging Career Aspirations" by Shelley J. Correll from *American Sociological Review,* Vol. 69, No. 1 (February 2003), pp. 93–113. Used by permission.

Edin, Kathryin and Maria Kefalas, from "Unmarried with Children" by Kathryn Edin and Maria Kefalas from *Contexts: Understanding People in Their Social Worlds,* 2005 4(2): 16–22. Copyright 2005 by University of California Press. Reproduced with permission of University of California Press in the format Textbook via Copyright Clearance Center.

Freire, Paulo, from "The Banking Concept of Education," Chapter 2 from *Pedagogy of the Oppressed* by Paulo Freire. Copyright © 1970, 1993 by Paulo Freire. Reprinted by permission of The Continuum International Publishing Group.

Gabbett, Tim J., from "Influence of training and match intensity on injuries in rugby league" by Tim J. Gabbett from *Journal of Sports Science,* 2004, 22: 409–17. Reprinted by permission of Taylor & Francis Ltd. (http://www.informaworld.com)

Hirsch Jr., E. D., excerpt from "The Theory Behind the Dictionary", from *The New Dictionary of Cultural Literacy,* Third Edition by E. D. Hirsch, Jr. Copyright © 2002 by Houghton Mifflin Company. Reprinted by permission of Houghton Mifflin Company. All rights reserved.

Holloway, Marguerite, Adapted from "The Female Hurt" by Marguerite Holloway from *Scientific American,* 2000, 11(3). Copyright © 2000 by Scientific American, Inc. All rights reserved. Graphic by Samuel Velasco, 5W Infographics. Participation in NCAA Sports data courtesy of The National Collegiate Athletic Association. Participation in High School Sports data courtesy of the National Federation of State High School Associations. Copyright © 2007 NFHS. All used by permission.

Landrigan, Phillip J. et al., "Health and Environmental Consequences of the World Trade Center Disaster" by Philip J. Landrigan, et. al., from *Environmental Health Perspectives,* 2004; 112(6): 731–39.

Layne, Christoper, From "Kant or Cant: The Myth of the Democratic Peace" by Christopher Layne from *International Security,* 19:2 (Fall 1994): 5–49. Copyright © 1994 by the President and Fellows of Harvard College and Massachusetts Institute of Technology. Reprinted by permission of MIT Press.

Lempert, Richard O., "Stem Cell Research" an Opinion-Editorial by Richard O. Lempert and Jack E. Dixon, August 28, 2001, from University of Michigan website, http://www.lifesciences.umich.edu/pdf/StemEdit.pdf.

Lincoln, Bruce, Letter to editor by Bruce Lincoln from *The New York Times,* November 2, 2004. Used by permission of the author.

Mason, Diane et al., "Why Isn't All Care 'Palliative Care'?: Care that's based on need rather than prognosis" from *American Journal of Nursing,* November 2004, 104(11), p. 11. Used by permission.

McKinley, Sharon et al., from "Development and testing of a Faces Scale for the assessment of anxiety in critically ill patients" by Sharon McKinley, Katherine Coote, and Jane Stein-Parbury from *Journal of Advanced Nursing,* 2003, 41(1): 73–79. Used by permission of Blackwell Publishing.

Montgomery, Lucy Maud, excerpt from *Anne of Green Gables* by Lucy Maud Montgomery, L. C. Page and Co. (190 words).

National Center for Catastrophic Sport Injury Research, Table "Head and Cervical Spine Fatalities" from National Center for Catastrophic Sport Injury Research Data Tables, Annual Survey of Football Injury Research, 1931–2003, from http://www.unc.edu/depts/nccsi/SurveyofFootballInjuries.html. Used by permission.

National Science Foundation, graph "Bachelor Degrees Earned by Women" from http://awis.org/resource/statistics/html, as submitted. (Originally from National Science Foundation.)

Owen IV, John M., reprinted by permission of *Foreign Affairs,* Vol. 84, Issue 6. Copyright © 2005 by the Council on Foreign Relations, Inc.

Paterson, Orlando and Jason Kaufman, "Bowling for Democracy" by Orlando Patterson and Jason Kaufman from *The New York Times,* May 1, 2005, p. WK15 (L). (Non-staff OP-ED)

Plomp, Michiel C., and Nadine M. Orenstein, From "Peter Breugel the Elder: Drawings and Prints" edited by Nadine M. Orenstein, Metropolitan Museum of Art, New York. Copyright © 2001The Metropolitan Museum of Art. Reprinted by permission.

Robertson, Jeanne and Craig McDaniel, from "Profile: Jane Quick-to-See Smith" from *Themes of Contemporary Art: Visual Art After 1980* by Jeanne Robertson and Craig McDaniel, 2005. By permission of Oxford University Press, Inc.

Rosin, Hanna, from "Beyond Belief" by Hanna Rosin from the *Atlantic Monthly,* January/February 2005, Vol. 295, No. 1. Used by permission of the author.

Sagar, Ambuj et. al., "The tragedy of the commoners: biotechnology and its publics" by Ambuj Sagar, Arthur Daemmrich and Mona Ashiya from *Nature Biotechnology,* January 2000,18:2–4, including globe illustration.

Schele, Linda and Mary Ellen Miller, from Chapter 4, *The Blood of Kings: Dynasty and Ritual in Maya Art* by Linda Schele and Mary Ellen Miller. Copyright © 1986 Kimbell Art Museum, Fort Worth. Used by permission.

Smyth, Joshua and Rebecca Helm, from "Focused Expressive Writing as Self-Help for Stress and Trauma" by Joshua Smyth and Rebecca Helm from *Journal of Clinical Psychology/In Session,* 2003, 59: 227–235. Copyright © 2003 Journal of Clinical Psychology. Reprinted with permission of John Wiley & Sons, Inc.

Steelcase Development Corporation, excerpts from Steelcase marketing plan, advertisement, and ergonomic study courtesy of Steelcase Development Corporation.

Thomas, Sandra P., from "A Phenomenologic Study of Chronic Pain" by Sandra P. Thomas from *Western Journal of Nursing Research,* 2000, 22(6): 683–705. Copyright 2000 by Sage Publications Inc Journals. Reproduced with permission of Sage Publications Inc Journals in the format Textbook via Copyright Clearance Center.

Villanueva, Victor, "Of Color, Classes, and Classrooms" from *Bootstraps: From an American Academic of Color* by Victor Villanueva. Copyright © 1993 by the National Council of Teachers of English. Reprinted and used with permission.

Watson, J. D., and F. H. C. Crick, "Molecular Structure of Nucleic Acids" by Watson, J. D. & Crick, F. H. C. from *Nature,* April 25, 1953, 171(4356): 737–738, with figures.

*Web*MD. from *Web*MD website. Used by permission.

Yang, Nan et. al., "Figure 1: ACTN3 Genotype Is Associated with Human Elite Athletic Performance" by Nan Yang, Daniel G. MacArthur, Jason P. Gulbin, Allan G. Hahn, Alan H. Beggs, Simon Easteal, and Kathryn North from *American Journal of Human Genetics* 73: 627–631, September 1, 2003. Used by permission.

Photo Credits

INDEX